Management Information Systems

FOR THE INFORMATION AGE

FOURTH EDITION

Stephen Haag
DANIELS COLLEGE OF BUSINESS

UNIVERSITY OF DENVER

Maeve Cummings
KELCE COLLEGE OF BUSINESS

PITTSBURG STATE UNIVERSITY

Donald J. McCubbrey
DANIELS COLLEGE OF BUSINESS

UNIVERSITY OF DENVER

 Irwin

Boston   Burr Ridge, IL   Dubuque, IA   Madison, WI   New York   San Francisco   St. Louis
Bangkok   Bogotá   Caracas   Kuala Lumpur   Lisbon   London   Madrid   Mexico City
Milan   Montreal   New Delhi   Santiago   Seoul   Singapore   Sydney   Taipei   Toronto

MANAGEMENT INFORMATION SYSTEMS FOR THE INFORMATION AGE
Published by McGraw-Hill/Irwin, a business unit of The McGraw-Hill Companies, Inc., 1221
Avenue of the Americas, New York, NY, 10020. Copyright © 2004, 2002, 2000, 1998 by
The McGraw-Hill Companies, Inc. All rights reserved. No part of this publication may be
reproduced or distributed in any form or by any means, or stored in a database or retrieval
system, without the prior written consent of The McGraw-Hill Companies, Inc., including, but
not limited to, in any network or other electronic storage or transmission, or broadcast for
distance learning.
Some ancillaries, including electronic and print components, may not be available to customers
outside the United States.

This book is printed on acid-free paper.

domestic   4 5 6 7 8 9 0 VNH/VNH 0 9 8 7 6 5 4
international   2 3 4 5 6 7 8 9 0 VNH/VNH 0 9 8 7 6 5 4

ISBN 0-07-281947-2

Publisher: *George Werthman*
Senior sponsoring editor: *Paul Ducham*
Developmental editor: *Kelly L. Delso*
Manager, Marketing and Sales: *Greta Kleinert*
Media Producer: *Greg Bates*
Senior project manager: *Kari Geltemeyer*
Lead production supervisor: *Heather D. Burbridge*
Coordinator freelance design: *Mary L. Christianson*
Photo research coordinator: *Jeremy Cheshareck*
Photo researcher: *Amy Bethea*
Senior supplement producer: *Rose M. Range*
Senior digital content specialist: *Brian Nacik*
Cover image: *© Stone/Wilhelm Scholz*
Interior freelance designer: *Kiera C. Pohl*
Typeface: *11/13 Bulmer MT*
Compositor: *ElectraGraphics, Inc.*
Printer: *Von Hoffmann Corporation*

Library of Congress Cataloging-in-Publication Data

Haag, Stephen.
    Management information systems for the information age/Stephen Haag, Maeve
Cummings, Donald J. McCubbrey.—4th ed.
        p. cm.
    Includes bibliographical references and index.
    ISBN 0-07-281947-2 (alk. paper)
    1. Management information systems. 2. Information technology. I. Cummings, Maeve.
II. McCubbrey, Donald J. III. Title
T58.6 .H18 2004
658.4'038'011—dc21

                                                              2002030943

International Edition ISBN 0-07-121466-6

www.mhhe.com

For my father, Carl. If I could achieve only one goal in life, I would want to be like him.

Stephen Haag

To Clodagh and Jerry, whose presence in my life is like warm sunshine and a gentle breeze.

Maeve Cummings

To Jani: My wife, best friend, and favorite marathon runner.

Donald J. McCubbrey

BRIEF CONTENTS

CONTENTS

FEATURES

PREFACE

The fourth edition of *Management Information Systems for the Information Age* provides you with the ultimate flexibility in tailoring content to the exact needs of your MIS or IT course. Built with nine chapters and ten Extended Learning Modules (XLMs or modules), this text allows you to decide the extent to which you want to cover technical topics and business/managerial topics.

The nine chapters form the core of material covering business and managerial topics, from strategic and competitive technology opportunities to the organization and management of information using databases and data warehouses. If you choose to cover only the chapters and none of the modules, the focus of your course will be MIS from a business and managerial point of view.

The ten Extended Learning Modules provide a technical glimpse into the world of IT, covering topics ranging from building a Web site to computer crimes and forensics to how to use Microsoft Access. If you choose to cover only the modules and none of the chapters, the focus of your course will be on the technical and hands-on aspects of technology.

Of course, we realize that you'll probably choose a course format that represents a blended mix of topics. While you may not choose to cover the technologies of networks, you may require your students to build a small database application. In that case, you would omit Module E (Network Basics) and spend more time on Module C (Designing Databases and Entity-Relationship Diagramming).

On the facing page, we've provided a table of the chapters and the modules. Notice that each module follows its corresponding chapter. For example, module H on computer crime and forensics (a new edition to the text) follows logically after Chapter 8 on protecting people and information. Of course, you can cover Chapter 8 and omit module H—that's completely up to you. As well, you can omit Chapter 8 and cover module H—you have the complete flexibility to do that as well.

As you approach putting together your course and choosing which chapters and/or modules you want to cover, we would offer the following:

- Cover any or all of the chapters as they suit your purpose
- Cover any or all of the modules as they suit your purpose
- For any given chapter, you do not have to cover its corresponding module
- For any given module, you do not have to cover its corresponding chapter
- You can cover the modules in any order you wish

As an example, consider the last item in the list above. We know that many instructors now require their students to design and implement a small database to support some sort of business and its processes. In that case, those instructors might choose to cover both modules C (Designing Databases and Entity-Relationship Diagramming) and J (Implementing a Database with Microsoft Access) at the beginning of the term. That is a powerful example of the flexibility the book's organization provides you.

We would also make one more important note here. Your students will find modules E, F, G, and J on the CD that accompanies their books. In the printed book itself, we've provided a two-page introduction to those modules. All your students have to do is go to the CD to read the full module.

The Most Flexible Presentation of Content in Any MIS Book

THE CHAPTERS	THE EXTENDED LEARNING MODULES*
CHAPTER 1 The Information Age in Which You Live	**Extended Learning Module A** Computer Hardware and Software
CHAPTER 2 Strategic and Competitive Opportunities	**Extended Learning Module B** The World Wide Web and the Internet
CHAPTER 3 Databases and Data Warehouses	**Extended Learning Module C** Designing Databases and Entity-Relationship Diagramming
CHAPTER 4 Decision Support and Artificial Intelligence	**Extended Learning Module D** Decision Analysis with Spreadsheet Software
CHAPTER 5 Electronic Commerce	**Extended Learning Module E** Network Basics
CHAPTER 6 Systems Development	**Extended Learning Module F** Building a Web Page with HTML
CHAPTER 7 IT Infrastructures	**Extended Learning Module G** Object-Oriented Technologies
CHAPTER 8 Protecting People and Information	**Extended Learning Module H** Computer Crime and Forensics
CHAPTER 9 Emerging Trends and Technologies	**Extended Learning Module I** Building an e-Portfolio
	Extended Learning Module J** Implementing a Database with Microsoft Access

*The complete text for modules E, F, G, and J are on the CD that accompanies this text.
**Extended Learning Module J is a bonus module that you would typically cover in conjunction with Chapter 3 (Databases and Data Warehouses) and/or Extended Learning Module C (Designing Databases and Entity-Relationship Diagramming).

Separation of Content between the Chapters and Extended Learning Modules

The separation of content between the chapters and Extended Learning Modules is very clear. We can sum it up by saying

- The chapters address what you want your students to know
- The modules address what you want your students to be able to do

While the chapters focus on the business and managerial applications of MIS and information technology in an organization, the modules focus on giving your students real hands-on knowledge they can apply in both their personal lives and in the workplace.

This separation gives you the complete flexibility to design your course as you see fit. You can take a very managerial approach and focus mostly on the chapters, or you can take a very technical and hands-on approach and focus mostly on the modules. Somewhere in between is where we believe you teach your course.

You should also be aware that the modules now contain full pedagogical support in the form of student learning outcomes, integrated On Your Own and Team Work projects, a summary, key terms list, short-answer questions, short-question answers, and a full page of assignments and exercises.

Chapter 3 covers databases and data warehouses from a business and managerial point of view. It focuses on what you want your students to know.

WHAT IS A DATA WAREHOUSE?

A **data warehouse** is a logical collection of information—gathered from many different operational databases—used to create business intelligence that supports business analysis activities and decision-making tasks (see Figure 3.8). Sounds simple enough on the surface, but data warehouses represent a fundamentally different way of thinking about organizing and managing information in an organization. Consider these key features of a data warehouse, detailed in the sections that follow.

DATA WAREHOUSES ARE MULTIDIMENSIONAL In the relational database model, information is represented in a series of two-dimensional tables. Not so in a data warehouse—most data warehouses are multidimensional, meaning that they contain layers of columns and rows. For this reason, most data warehouses are really *multidimensional databases*. The lay-

---

Extended Learning Module C is the corresponding module for Chapter 3 and covers how to correctly define the structure of a database. It focuses on what you want your students to be able to do.

Figure C.3
Reading an Entity-Relationship (E-R) Diagram

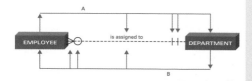

tools that you use to process information. So, your implementations of technology should match the way your business works. If you always start by defining business rules and using those rules as guides, your technology implementations will hopefully mirror how your business works. And that's the way it should be.

Once you determine that a relationship does exist, you must then determine the numerical nature of the relationship, what we refer to as minimum and maximum *cardinality*. To describe this, you use a | to denote a single relationship, a 0 to denote a zero or optional relationship, and/or a crow's foot to denote a multiple relationship. By way of illustration, let's consider the portion of your E-R diagram in Figure C.3. To help you read the symbols, we've added blue lines and arrows. Following the blue line marked A, you would read the E-R diagram as, "An *Employee* is assigned to one *Department* at a minimum and one *Department* at a maximum." So, that part of the E-R diagram states that the logical relationship between *Employee* and *Department* is that an *Employee* is assigned to one and only one *Department*. This is exactly what business rules 1 and 2 state.

Following the blue line marked B, you would read the E-R diagram as, "A *Department* is not required to have any *Employees* assigned to it but may have many *Employees*

Team Work and On Your Own Projects

There are now 69 Team Work and On Your Own projects spread throughout the text in both the chapters and Extended Learning Modules. The Team Work projects are designed for small groups of students, usually two to four. The On Your Own projects are designed to be completed by an individual student. These have been integrated into the text so that you can easily identify which projects go with which content. Many of these can be used as break-out exercises, and just as many can be assigned as homework. In the Instructor's Manual you'll find our discussion of and solutions to each of these projects.

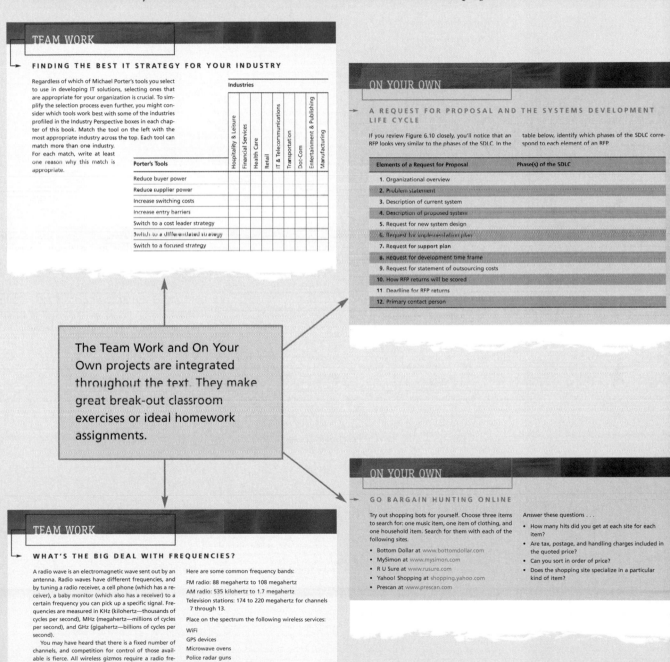

TEAM WORK

FINDING THE BEST IT STRATEGY FOR YOUR INDUSTRY

Regardless of which of Michael Porter's tools you select to use in developing IT solutions, selecting ones that are appropriate for your organization is crucial. To simplify the selection process even further, you might consider which tools work best with some of the industries profiled in the Industry Perspective boxes in each chapter of this book. Match the tool on the left with the most appropriate industry across the top. Each tool can match more than one industry.

For each match, write at least one reason why this match is appropriate.

Porter's Tools	Hospitality & Leisure	Financial Services	Health Care	Retail	IT & Telecommunications	Transportation	Dot-Com	Entertainment & Publishing	Manufacturing
Reduce buyer power									
Reduce supplier power									
Increase switching costs									
Increase entry barriers									
Switch to a cost leader strategy									
Switch to a differentiated strategy									
Switch to a focused strategy									

Industries

ON YOUR OWN

A REQUEST FOR PROPOSAL AND THE SYSTEMS DEVELOPMENT LIFE CYCLE

If you review Figure 6.10 closely, you'll notice that an RFP looks very similar to the phases of the SDLC. In the table below, identify which phases of the SDLC correspond to each element of an RFP.

Elements of a Request for Proposal	Phase(s) of the SDLC
1. Organizational overview	
2. Problem statement	
3. Description of current system	
4. Description of proposed system	
5. Request for new system design	
6. Request for implementation plan	
7. Request for support plan	
8. Request for development time frame	
9. Request for statement of outsourcing costs	
10. How RFP returns will be scored	
11. Deadline for RFP returns	
12. Primary contact person	

> The Team Work and On Your Own projects are integrated throughout the text. They make great break-out classroom exercises or ideal homework assignments.

TEAM WORK

WHAT'S THE BIG DEAL WITH FREQUENCIES?

A radio wave is an electromagnetic wave sent out by an antenna. Radio waves have different frequencies, and by tuning a radio receiver, a cell phone (which has a receiver), a baby monitor (which also has a receiver) to a certain frequency you can pick up a specific signal. Frequencies are measured in KHz (kilohertz—thousands of cycles per second), MHz (megahertz—millions of cycles per second), and GHz (gigahertz—billions of cycles per second).

You may have heard that there is a fixed number of channels, and competition for control of those available is fierce. All wireless gizmos require a radio frequency to transmit and receive, so communications companies spend billions of dollars for the rights to the part of the spectrum that's for sale. Other parts are free (like the WiFi part) and still others are set aside for government agencies like the Department of Defense.

The figure below shows the part of the spectrum in common use for wireless information delivery all day, every day.

Here are some common frequency bands:

FM radio: 88 megahertz to 108 megahertz
AM radio: 535 kilohertz to 1.7 megahertz
Television stations: 174 to 220 megahertz for channels 7 through 13.

Place on the spectrum the following wireless services:

WiFi
GPS devices
Microwave ovens
Police radar guns
TV channels 2–6
Wildlife tracking collars
CB radio
Aviation navigation
Cordless phones

ON YOUR OWN

GO BARGAIN HUNTING ONLINE

Try out shopping bots for yourself. Choose three items to search for: one music item, one item of clothing, and one household item. Search for them with each of the following sites.

- Bottom Dollar at www.bottomdollar.com
- MySimon at www.mysimon.com
- R U Sure at www.rusure.com
- Yahoo! Shopping at shopping.yahoo.com
- Prescan at www.prescan.com

Answer these questions . . .

- How many hits did you get at each site for each item?
- Are tax, postage, and handling charges included in the quoted price?
- Can you sort in order of price?
- Does the shopping site specialize in a particular kind of item?

Assignments and Exercises

Based on reviewer feedback, we've added an entire page of assignments and exercises at the end of each chapter and module. These are very similar to the Team Work and On Your Own projects in that they give your students a chance to apply their newly acquired knowledge and learn even more. As with the Team Work and On Your Own projects, you'll find our discussion of and solutions to each of these in the Instructor's Manual.

Assignments and Exercises

1. **INVESTIGATE CELL PHONE TECHNOLOGY** A wireless device that you may have used, or perhaps use all the time, is a cell phone. A cell phone is actually a radio (with a transmitter and a receiver) and uses radio waves of certain frequencies. There are different systems (called cellular access technologies) for cell phones: TDMA, GSM, CDMA. Go to the Web and find the answers to the following questions (*hint*: a good place to look is www.howstuffworks.com):
   A. What do the letters stand for?
   B. What's the difference between systems?
   C. Why are they called "cell" phones?
   D. Why was this "cellular" method used in the first place?

2. **FIND OUT ABOUT PERSONAL DIGITAL ASSISTANTS** Many people have personal digital assistants (PDAs), which are hand-held computers that allow you to perform many computer tasks wirelessly. Some of the features of PDAs are calendar management, appointment management, mini spreadsheet and word

4. **INVESTIGATE BUILDING YOUR OWN HOME NETWORK** Build your own home network on paper. Assume you have the computers already and just need to link them together. Find prices for hubs and routers on the Web. Also research Ethernet cards and cables. If you were to get a high-speed Internet connection, such as a cable modem or DSL modem, how much would it cost? Can you buy your own or would you have to rent the modems from the phone or cable company?

5. **INVESTIGATE SATELLITE RADIO** At the time of this writing there are two satellite radio stations: Sirius and XM. Do a little surfing on the Web and find out if there are any others now. Also find out what you have to buy to install each type, how much the antenna costs, how the system would work in your car, and how much the monthly subscription is.

6. **FIND OUT ABOUT FIREWALLS** Go to the Web and find out about software and hardware that protects your computer and home network

Assignments and Exercises

1. **CUSTOMIZING A COMPUTER PURCHASE.** One of the great things about the Web is the number of e-tailers that are now online offering you a variety of products and services. One such e-tailer is Dell, which allows you to customize and buy a computer. Connect to Dell's site at www.dell.com. Go to the portion of Dell's site that allows you to customize either a notebook or a desktop computer. First, choose an already prepared system and note its price and capability in terms of CPU speed, RAM size, monitor quality, and storage capacity. Now, customize that system to increase CPU speed, add more RAM, increase monitor size and quality, and add more storage capacity. What's the difference in price between the two? Which system is more in your price range? Which system has the speed and capacity you need?

2. **WEB-ENABLED CELL PHONES AND WEB COMPUTERS.** When categorizing computers by size for personal needs, we focused on PDAs, notebook computers, and desktop computers.

clunky notebooks and desktops in favor of more portable and cheaper devices such as Web-enabled cell phones and Web computers? Why or why not?

3. **OPERATING SYSTEM SOFTWARE FOR PDAS.** The personal digital assistant (PDA) market is a ferocious, dynamic, and uncertain one. One of the uncertainties is what operating system for PDAs will become the dominant one. For notebooks and desktops right now, you're pretty well limited to the Microsoft family unless you buy an Apple computer (in which case your operating system is Mac OS) or you want to venture into using Linux (which we wouldn't recommend for most people). Do some research on the more popular PDAs available today. What are the different operating systems? What different functionality do they offer? Are they compatible with each other? Take a guess—which one will come out on top?

4. **TYPES OF MONITORS AND THEIR QUALITY.** The monitor you buy will greatly affect your

Assignments and Exercises

1. **DEVELOPING M-COMMERCE SCENARIOS FOR GPS CELL PHONES** Soon, cell phones will be equipped with GPS chips that enable users to be located within a geographical location about the size of a tennis court. The primary purpose for installing GPS chips in phones is to enable emergency services to locate a cell phone user. For example, if you dial an emergency assistance number (911 in the United States) from your home now, it is possible for a computer system to use your home telephone number to access a database and obtain your address. This can be very useful in situations where you are unable to give address information to the emergency operator for some reason. The problem with trying to do the same thing with present-day cell phones is that you could be calling from anywhere.

   As you might imagine, marketers have been monitoring this development with great interest. When the new cell phones become available, they can visualize scenarios where they will

Find out what at least three e-commerce marketers are saying about personalized marketing using GPS-equipped cell phones and prepare an analysis of how they will likely be used when the technology is widely available.

2. **DEALING WITH THE GLOBAL DIGITAL DIVIDE** Dealing with the issue of the global digital divide seems to be one that is well-suited for an international body such as the United Nations.

   Find out what, if anything, the UN is doing about this issue and express an opinion on whether or not you believe their efforts will be successful. Determine if there are organizations such as private companies or foundations that have the issue high on their agendas. Do the same thing for any such organizations you find: Evaluate their efforts and express an opinion on whether or not they will be successful. Finally, search for a lesser developed country that is making significant local efforts to deal with the digital divide. If you can't find one, prepare a list of the countries you reviewed.

All of the chapters and Extended Learning Modules now contain a full page of assignments and exercises. In completing these, your students will apply their newly acquired knowledge and seek to discover more.

REAL HOT Electronic Commerce and Group Projects

The REAL HOT (**h**ands-**o**n **t**echnology) electronic commerce and group projects have always been a hallmark of the text. You'll find an electronic commerce project at the end of each chapter. These require your students to explore the Web and see what it's like to be on the "C" end of business to consumer electronic commerce and consider what it would be like to be on the "B" end of business to consumer electronic commerce. To support these projects, we've provided more than 1,000 links on the Web site for this text at www.mhhe.com/haag.

After the last module in the text, you'll find 16 REAL HOT Group projects. These projects require your students to literally roll up their sleeves and use technology to take advantage of an opportunity or solve a problem. Be careful about assigning too many of these: Some will take an entire weekend for your students to complete. You can find the data files for these projects on the Instructor's CD and on the text's Web site.

REAL HOT   Electronic Commerce

Getting Your Business on the Internet

Let's say you've decided it might be fun (and profitable) to become an e-tailer and establish an Internet-based business. You know that many e-tailers don't make it, but you'd like to be one that is successful. There are a lot of resources on the Internet that can help you with the tasks of selecting the right business in the first place, getting the site up and running, deciding who should host your site, marketing your site, understanding privacy issues, and obtaining the funds you need to pay your expenses until your business begins to show a profit. On the Web site that supports this text (www.mhhe.com/haag, select "Electronic Commerce Projects"), we've provided direct links to many useful Web sites. These are a great starting point for completing this REAL HOT section. We also encourage you to search the Internet for others.

COMPETITIVE INTELLIGENCE

The first thing you need to have is an idea for the business. What would you like to sell? A product or a service? Make sure you have expertise, or something special to offer. After you've come up with a candidate, it's time to see how much competition is out there and what they're up to. One of the things many new business owners fail to do is to see how many competitors there are before they launch their business. You may find there are too many and that they would be tough competition for you. Or, you may find that there are few competitors and the ones who are out there aren't doing a terrific job.

Seek out and look at some of the Web sites of businesses in the competitive space.

> The REAL HOT Group projects require your students to roll up their sleeves and use technology to solve a problem or take advantage of an opportunity. There are 16 of these projects in the text.

> The REAL HOT Electronic Commerce projects provide your students with a hands-on glimpse into the world of e-commerce on the Web. You'll find one of these projects at the end of each chapter.

CASE 5:
USING RELATIONAL TECHNOLOGY TO TRACK PROJECTS

PHILLIPS CONSTRUCTION

Phillips Construction Company is a Denver-based construction company that specializes in subcontracting the development of single family homes. In business since 1993, Phillips Construction Company has maintained a talented pool of certified staff and independent consultants allowing the flexibility and combined experience required to meet the needs of its nearly 300 completed projects in the Denver metropolitan area. The field of operation methods that Phillips Construction is responsible for as it relates to building include: structural development, heating and cooling, plumbing, and electricity.

The company charges its clients by billing the hours spent on each contract. The hourly billing rate is dependent on the employee's position according to the field of operations (as noted above).

Figure RHGP.1 shows a basic report that Phillips Construction managers would like to see every week concerning what projects are being assigned. Phillips Construction organizes its

Figure
RHGP.1

Phillips
Construction
Project Detail

PHILLIPS CONSTRUCTION PROJECT DETAIL						
PROJECT NAME	ASSIGN DATE	EMP LAST NAME	EMP FIRST NAME	JOB DESCRIPTION	ASSIGN HOUR	CHARGE/HOUR
Chatfield						
	Monday, June 10, 2002	Jones	Anne	Heating and Ventilation	3.4	$84.50
	Monday, June 10, 2002	Sullivan	David	Electrical	1.8	$105.00
	Tuesday, June 11, 2002	Frommer	Matt	Plumbing	4.1	$96.75
	Wednesday, June 12, 2002	Newman	John	Electrical	1.7	$105.00
	Wednesday, June 12, 2002	Bawangi	Terry	Plumbing	4.1	$96.75
Summary of Assignment Hours and Charges					15.10	$1,448.15
Evergreen						
	Monday, June 10, 2002	Smithfield	William	Structure	3.0	$35.75
	Monday, June 10, 2002	Newman	John	Electrical	2.3	$105.00
	Monday, June 10, 2002	Nenior	David	Plumbing	3.3	$96.75
	Tuesday, June 11, 2002	Marbough	Mike	Heating and Ventilation	2.6	$84.50
	Wednesday, June 12, 2002	Johnson	Peter	Electrical	2.0	$105.00
	Wednesday, June 12, 2002	Newman	John	Electrical	3.6	$105.00
	Wednesday, June 12, 2002	Olenkoski	Glenn	Structure	1.9	$35.75
Summary of Assignment Hours and Charges					18.70	$1,543.05

Opening and Closing Case Studies

To motivate your students to want to read each chapter, we've included an opening case study that deals with how an organization has successfully implemented many of the concepts in the chapter. These case studies are business vignettes with a length of one page.

To help your students apply what they've just learned, you'll find two closing case studies at the end of each chapter. In the previous edition, there was only one closing case study. Our reviewers wanted another, and we were happy to provide it. So, there are a total of 18 closing case studies in the text. Each closing case study includes approximately five to seven discussion questions for your students to answers. We've provided our thoughts regarding these questions for each chapter in the Instructor's Manual.

**OPENING CASE STUDY:
CAN TECHNOLOGY CATCH YOU HAVING AN AFFAIR?**

Well, it may seem like an odd question . . . but when you think about it, technology certainly has the capability to aid in catching you having an affair. People can use technology to test your DNA. People can use a special form of technol-

creep into your life. And, by specific design, te nology can monitor many of your actions. Uti programs on the Internet track your moveme from one Web site to the next. You probably ured this out when you first started receivi spam (unsolicited e-mail) from sites you've ited.

The simple reality is that you cannot esc technology. Of course, we all hope people

The opening case studies detail how one organization has applied the concepts presented in the chapter and are designed to motivate your students to read on.

**OPENING CASE STUDY
BUILDING THE UNBELIEVABLE—
THE HOBERMAN ARCH**

Have you ever looked at a 100-story skyscraper or a professional football stadium and wondered how in the world that enormous structure was created? Who comes up with the brilliant ideas to build these impossible structures, and how do

whose best-known invention is the plastic panding and contracting geometric ball kno as the Hoberman Sphere. The Hoberm Sphere's unique link system is based on a mat matical principle that allows a structure to pand while keeping its shape. We bet you wondering how Chuck Hoberman analyzed, signed, and built the Hoberman Arch. How he take an idea he applied to children's toys a

**OPENING CASE STUDY
DIGITAL DESTRUCTION BEYOND ALL
IMAGINATION**

While it pales in comparison to the tragic loss of life, the extensive damage to computer and communications systems in New York on September 11th, 2001, was considerable. Although the whole event was unbelievable, the fact that most

only the hardware. The most important part c computer system is not the physical equipme it's the information that's stored there. It's alm impossible to calculate the value of the pap records lost, or the value of the information hard drives, servers, tape drives, and other st age media that was lost. Given the nature of t businesses located in the World Trade Center, cluding many financial and consulting organi

HOW MUCH OF YOUR PERSONAL INFORMATION DO YOU WANT BUSINESSES TO KNOW?

The information age has brought about great debates with respect to information availability and privacy. For example, most counties in the United States provide

the historical preferences of our customers, and, for stance, see if a customer who used to buy Americ suits likes a more contemporary European look in

SPEEDPASS: THROW AWAY YOUR PLASTIC?

Speedpass is an idea that has been around since 1996, but it is now beginning to take off. Speedpass offers a short plastic cylinder, called a Key Tag, that contains an RFID (Radio Frequency Identification) transponder. The Key Tag is very lightweight, short, and can be placed on

McDonald's restaurants are testing Speedpass at locations in the Chicago metropolitan area. If it wo there, you may soon find that you will be able to bu Big Mac, fries and a Coke with your Key Tag or Car T Not only that, if it works at McDonald's, it will surely

There are two closing case studies for each chapter. They allow your students to apply what they've learned in an actual business situation.

USING NEURAL NETWORKS TO CATEGORIZE PEOPLE

Would your banker give you an A, B, or C? What about your supermarket? You know you're being graded in your classes, but did you know that you're also being graded by businesses?

Special treatment for certain customers is not new

Say you called the bank that issued you your cre card and said that you didn't want to pay the ann fee anymore. The bank could look at your credit ca activity and decide whether it's more profitable to t bank to waive your fee rather than risk your not usi

Student Learning Outcomes and Summary

At the beginning of each chapter and module, you'll find a list of student learning outcomes. These do not represent the objectives of the chapter or your teaching objectives. Rather, they focus on what your students should know or should be able to do upon completing their reading. This distinction isn't subtle. Our goal in creating the student learning outcomes was to provide your students with a road map of what they should learn and accomplish while reading a chapter or module. Teaching, after all, is all about your students and the knowledge and experiences they gain.

At the conclusion of each chapter and module, we revisit the student learning outcomes to provide a summary. These summaries are an invaluable resource for your students as they prepare to take an exam.

EXTENDED LEARNING MODULE B

THE WORLD WIDE WEB AND THE INTERNET

Student Learning Outcomes

1. DEFINE THE RELATIONSHIPS AMONG WEB SITE, WEB SITE ADDRESS, DOMAIN NAME, WEB PAGE, AND UNIFORM RESOURCE LOCATOR (URL).

2. EXPLAIN HOW TO INTERPRET THE PARTS OF AN ADDRESS ON THE WEB.

3. IDENTIFY THE MAJOR COMPONENTS AND FEATURES OF WEB BROWSER SOFTWARE.

4. DESCRIBE THE DIFFERENCES BETWEEN DIRECTORY AND TRUE SEARCH ENGINES.

5. DESCRIBE THE VARIOUS TECHNOLOGIES THAT MAKE UP THE INTERNET.

6. IDENTIFY KEY CONSIDERATIONS IN CHOOSING AN INTERNET SERVICE PROVIDER (ISP).

7. DESCRIBE THE COMMUNICATIONS SOFTWARE AND TELECOMMUNICATIONS HARDWARE YOU NEED TO CONNECT TO THE INTERNET.

Student learning outcomes drive each chapter and module. We then summarize each chapter and module by revisiting the student learning outcomes. It's the old adage . . .

1. Tell them what you're going to tell them.

2. Tell them.

3. Tell them what you told them.

Summary: Student Learning Outcomes Revisited

1. **Define the relationships among Web site, Web site address, domain name, Web page, and uniform resource locator (URL).** A *Web site* (such as www.usatoday.com for the *USA Today*) is a specific location on the Web where you visit, gather information, and perhaps even order products. A *Web site address* (www.usatoday.com) is a unique name that identifies a specific site on the Web. Technically, a Web site address is called a *domain name.* A *Web page* is a specific portion of a Web site that deals with a certain topic. Technically, the address for a specific Web page is called a *URL (uniform resource locator).*

2. **Explain how to interpret the parts of an address on the Web.** Most Web site addresses start with http://www. Beyond that, the address is

unique. The first part (using www.uts.edu.au as an example) provides the name of the organization or Web site (UTS or University of Technology in Sydney). The next part tells the type of organization and is called the *top-level domain.* For UTS, it is "edu," describing it as an educational institution. If something follows after that, it usually provides a country of origin ("au" for UTS which identifies its country of origin as Australia).

3. **Identify the major components and features of Web browser software.** The two most popular Web browsers are Internet Explorer and Netscape Communicator. Each includes a menu bar (with functions such as **File, Edit,** and **View**), a button bar (for commonly performed tasks such as printing), and an address or

Content Changes for the Fourth Edition

The content changes for the fourth edition were driven by

1. Instructor feedback on the third edition
2. Changes that have occurred in the business world
3. Advances that have occurred in the technology arena
4. Changes made by our competitors

As a group of authors and contributors working together, we carefully sifted through all the competitive scanning information we could gather to create a fourth edition that is far better than its predecessor, the third edition.

Throughout the text, you'll find new or updated opening and closing case studies, Industry Perspectives, Global Perspectives, Assignments and Exercises, REAL HOT Group projects, and Team Work and On Your Own projects, as well as new or expanded coverage of such topics as **intelligent agents, biometrics, supply chain management, customer relationship management, ebXML, application service providers (ASPs),** and **Web Services.**

We've provided all of these content updates and new pedagogical features in a visually appealing, streamlined, single-column format.

Most importantly, we're pleased to have been able to respond to reviewer suggestions and provide the following:

- New *Extended Learning Module D* on Decision Support with Spreadsheet Software
- New *Extended Learning Module F* on Building a Web Page with HTML
- Greatly enhanced *Extended Learning Module G* on Object-Oriented Technologies
- New *Extended Learning Module H* on Computer Crime and Forensics
- New *Extended Learning Module I* on Building an e-Portfolio
- Bonus *Extended Learning Module J* on Using Microsoft Access
- New Chapter 7 on IT Infrastructures
- New Chapter 9 on Emerging Trends and Technologies

Module D covers many of the advanced decision support features of Excel, including
- Lists
- Basic AutoFilter
- Custom AutoFilter
- Conditional formatting
- Pivot tables

Module F teaches your student how to build a Web site using HTML, including
- Basic text formatting
- The use of color
- Backgrounds
- Inserting and sizing images
- Creating links
- Lists (both numbered and bulleted)

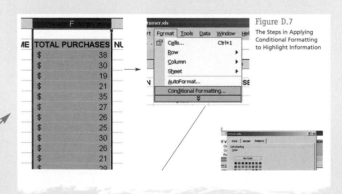

Figure D.7
The Steps in Applying Conditional Formatting to Highlight Information

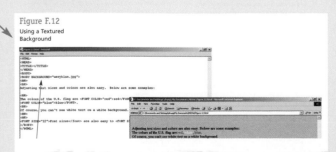

Figure F.12
Using a Textured Background

Chapter 7 is a great new chapter covering IT infrastructures, including
- ASPs
- Benchmarking
- BPR
- Collocation
- Data cleansing
- Disaster recovery
- CRM
- ERP
- Server farms
- And much, much more

Figure 7.1
The IT Infrastructure Supports the Organizational Goals

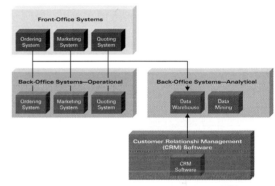

form sales lead tracking or listing potential customers for the sales team to contact. They also perform contact management, which tracks all of the times a salesperson contacts a potential customer, what they discussed, and the next steps. More sophisticated SFA systems perform detailed analysis on the market and on customers and even offer product

Figure 7.6
A Sample Customer Relationship Management (CRM) System Infrastructure

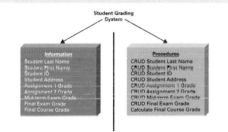

Figure G.1
Student Grading System: Separate Information and Procedure Views

Figure G.2
Student Grading System: Combined Information and Procedures

Module G is the complement to Chapter 7 and covers such object-oriented technology concepts as
- Classes
- Encapsulation
- Information Decomposition
- Inheritance
- Messages
- Polymorphism
- Scalability

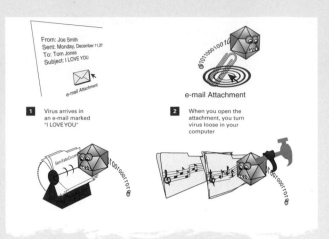

Module H is a great new module on computer crime and forensics. In it your students will learn about
- Hackers and crackers
- Denial-of-service
- Encryption
- Key loggers
- Spoofing
- Steganography
- And much, much more

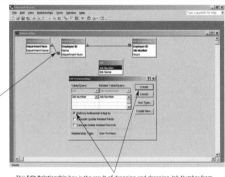

Figure H.10
Fragment of E-Mail Found in Slack Space by Encase

Unallocated disk space   Where file was on disk   File was found in slack space

Figure J.9
Defining Relationships for the *Employee* Database

By dragging and dropping *Department Num* as a primary key in the *Department* relation onto *Department Num* in the *Employee* relation as a foreign key, you create a 1:M (1-to-many) relationship between *Department* and *Employee*. The "many" is represented with the infinity symbol.

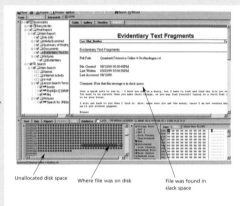

This **Edit Relationship** box is the result of dragging and dropping *Job Number* from the *Job* relation onto *Job Number* in the *Job Assignment* relation. As a general rule, always turn on **Enforce Referential Integrity**. Then, click on the **Create** button.

Module J is a bonus module that teaches your students to create a database using Microsoft Access. This is a great complement to Chapter 3 and module C.

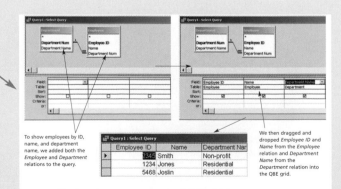

To show employees by ID, name, and department name, we added both the *Employee* and *Department* relations to the query.

We then dragged and dropped *Employee ID* and *Name* from the *Employee* relation and *Department Name* from the *Department* relation into the QBE grid.

Chapter 9 covers emerging trends and technologies. Each technology discussion is driven by a specific business or societal trend, not the other way around. This is a great way to close your discussion of MIS and IT.

Figure 9.1
Emerging Trends and Technologies

Push, Not Pull
B2C Growth
Information Supplier Convergence
C2C Explosion
Semi AI
Broadening E-government
Automatic Speech Recognition and Understanding
Digital Cash
Biometrics
3-D
Virtual Reality
Cybermediaries
CAVEs
Micro-payments
Nano Technologies
Implant Chips
Wearable Computers
Internet Phone Calls

Information Filtering
Rebirth of E-commerce
Intellectual Computing
Digital Frontier
Physiological Interaction
Portability and Mobility

Figure I.2
Sample Self-assessment Tool

Transferable Skills

Transferable skills are those that can be applied to any job or work situation. Everyone has them. Each transferable skill has keywords that can be used to describe your strengths. Select each skill below that applies to you and then write how you effectively exhibit that skill.

General Keywords			
___ critical thinking	___ self-discipline	___ general knowledge	___ self-confidence
___ research techniques	___ insight	___ cultural perspective	___ imagination
___ perseverance	___ writing	___ teaching ability	___ leadership

Research Keywords			
___ initiating	___ attaining	___ achieving	___ reviewing
___ updating	___ interpreting	___ analyzing	___ synthesizing
___ communicating	___ planning	___ designing	
___ performing	___ estimating	___ implementing	

Teaching Keywords			
___ organizing	___ assessing	___ public speaking	___ reporting
___ counseling	___ assessing	___ coordinating	___ administering
___ motivating	___ problem solving		

Personality Keywords			
___ dynamic	___ sensitive	___ responsible	___ creative
___ imaginative	___ accurate	___ easygoing	___ adept
___ innovative	___ expert	___ successful	___ efficient
___ perceptive	___ astute	___ humanistic	___ honest
___ outstanding	___ calm	___ outgoing	___ self-starting
___ reliable	___ unique	___ experienced	___ talented

Module I is very student-centric. It teaches your students how to build an e-portfolio so they can advertise themselves in the growing electronic job market.

Figure I.5
Partial Scannable Résumé

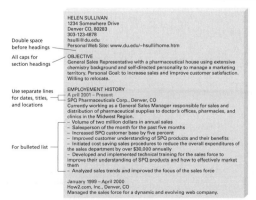

HELEN SULLIVAN
1234 Somewhere Drive
Denver CO, 80283
303-123-4878
hsulli@du.edu
Personal Web Site: www.du.edu/~hsulli/home.htm

Double space before headings

All caps for section headings

OBJECTIVE
General Sales Representative with a pharmaceutical house using extensive chemistry background and self-directed personality to manage a marketing territory. Personal Goal: to increase sales and improve customer satisfaction. Willing to relocate.

Use separate lines for dates, titles, and locations

EMPLOYEMENT HISTORY
April 2001 – Present
SPQ Pharmaceuticals Corp., Denver, CO
Currently working as a General Sales Manager responsible for sales and distribution of pharmaceutical supplies to doctor's offices, pharmacies, and clinics in the Midwest Region.

For bulleted list
– Volume of two million dollars in annual sales
– Salesperson of the month for the past five months
– Increased SPQ customer base by five percent
– Improved customer understanding of SPQ products and their benefits
– Initiated cost saving sales procedures to reduce the overall expenditures of the sales department by over $30,000 annually
– Developed and implemented technical training for the sales force to improve their understanding of SPQ products and how to effectively market them
– Analyzed sales trends and improved the focus of the sales force

January 1999 – April 2000
How2.com, Inc., Denver, CO
Managed the sales force for a dynamic and evolving web company.

The Support Package

We realize that no text is complete without a well-rounded and value-added support package. We are teachers too, and we understand that many of you face increased class sizes and perhaps limitations on the amount of support you receive. Our support package is designed to ease your teaching burden by providing you with a Web site full of valuable information, a test bank with more than 2,000 questions and easy-to-use test generating software, an Instructor's Manual that walks you through each chapter and module and provides value-added teaching notes and suggestions, and often two versions of a PowerPoint slide presentation.

THE WEB SITE AT WWW.MHHE.COM/HAAG

As in previous editions, the Web site for the fourth edition (www.mhhe.com/haag) contains a wealth of valuable information and supplements. Your students can take online quizzes in preparation for your exams, download the data files they need to complete the REAL HOT Group projects, and find more than 1,000 great links to help them complete the REAL HOT Electronic Commerce projects. They can also read reviews of some of the newest and best IT tools in speech recognition, data warehousing and data mining, and object-oriented DBMSs, just to name a few.

On the Web site, you'll find most of your instructor support, including the Instructor's Manual, the PowerPoint slide presentations, all of the in-text images, and solutions to the REAL HOT Group projects. Unfortunately, we can't place the test bank files on the Web site; cybervandals have forever changed what information we make available on the Web.

INSTRUCTOR'S MANUAL

The Instructor's Manual is provided to you in an effort to help you prepare for your class presentations. Beyond just providing an outline of the chapters and modules and answers to the various projects, exercises, and assignments, our Instructor's Manual includes some key value-added features called **Concept Reinforcement** boxes. These offer you insights concerning

- **The On Your Own projects**—when to use them, how to grade them, how long they should take, etc.
- **The Team Work projects**—the same insight as for the On Your Own projects
- **The Global Perspectives**—how to introduce them, key points to address, possible discussion questions to ask, etc.
- **The Industry Perspectives**—the same insight as for the Global Perspectives
- **Adding Value (Class Participation)**—some interesting pieces of information, perhaps a question to ask, a good Web site to visit, an article to read, a book to read, etc.
- **The REAL HOT Group Projects**—which one(s) to assign, why, etc.
- **The Extended Learning Modules**—which module could be covered, what it entails, etc.

These are the types of value-added support that we believe can help you outside the classroom as you prepare your lectures and inside the classroom as you deliver those lectures.

We've provided the Instructor's Manual files in Word format and placed them on both the Instructor's CD and the text's Web site.

TEST BANK

We must admit that building a test bank is one of the most tedious, yet important, tasks in developing a well-rounded support package for you. In past editions, we've turned this work over to an outside contractor. To be honest, it hasn't worked well.

So, in this edition, the author and contributor team has undertaken this task. It is our goal to provide you with the best possible test bank, ensuring the quality of each and every question. For each chapter and module, you'll find test bank questions in multiple-choice, true/false, and fill-in-the-blank formats. The number varies according to the length of the chapter or module but is usually in the neighborhood of 100 questions. That means you'll find approximately 2,000 questions in the test bank.

Computerized/Network Testing with Brownstone Diploma software is also available. Computest is fully networkable for LAN test administration, but tests can also be printed for standard paper delivery or posted to a Web site for student access.

POWERPOINT SLIDE PRESENTATIONS

Building PowerPoint slide presentations represents yet another challenge in providing a well-rounded support package. Some instructors want short presentations, with few slides, words, and graphics. Others want very complete presentations. And others want presentations short on words but long on graphics.

In an attempt to hit a "moving target," we've sometimes provided two PowerPoint slide presentations per chapter and module. The first is the short version with only a few graphics. The second is a very complete version with many graphics from the text.

Of course, we realize that you'll probably want to customize some of the presentations. So, we've made available to you all of the graphics in the text. You can find these on your instructor's CD as well as the Web site at www.mhhe.com/haag.

ACKNOWLEDGMENTS

As we now enter our fourth edition of this text, it has become increasingly obvious that "authors" are only a small part of the overall equation that makes a good text. Within McGraw-Hill/Irwin, there are several groups of people who have made this project successful. They include strategic management, EDP, and editorial. McGraw-Hill/Irwin's strategic management is simply second to none. We certainly acknowledge the dedicated work of Ed Stanford, J. P. Lenney, David Littlehale, and Kurt Strand. Their guidance is invaluable.

EDP includes all of those people who take our thoughts on paper and bring them to life in the form of an exciting and dynamic book. Merrily Mazza leads this wonderful group of people including Kari Geltemeyer (the book's project manager), Alyson Platt (our copy editor), Jeremy Cheshareck (photo research coordinator), and Mary Christianson (cover and interior design specialist).

Editorial includes that group of people who determine what projects to publish and have guided us every step of the way with a wealth of market intelligence. George Werthman (publisher) leads that group of people including Rick Williamson (our long-time friend), Paul Ducham (our senior sponsoring editor), and Kelly Delso, the book's developmental editor.

We would also like to acknowledge the dedicated work of a few other people at McGraw-Hill/Irwin. They include Greg Bates (media producer), Rose Range (supplement producer), and Paul Murphy (marketing manager). Without Greg and Rose, our text would be just a text, with no supplements or a great supporting Web site. Without Paul Murphy, you might never know we created this text.

We would also like to take this time to acknowledge the wonderful efforts of our contributor team: Paige Baltzan, Amy Phillips, and Merrill Wells. Each has brought to the table unique talents and knowledge, making this text truly a great success. As authors, we have come to realize that it's an impossible task to keep up with technology, not only its advancements but also how it's used in the business world. Paige, Amy, and Merrill—collectively and individually—offer special insight into the world of technology. Their contributions are invaluable.

Last, but certainly not least, we would offer our gratitude to our reviewers. They took on a thankless job that paid only a portion of its true worth. We had the best. They include

Ron Lemos
California State University, Los Angeles

Alicia Fetters
Des Moines Area Community College, Ankeny

Morris Pondfield
Towson University

David Bradbard
Winthrop University

Bennie D. Waller
Francis Marion University

Sumit Sircar
University of Texas at Arlington

Mike Raisingani
University of Dallas

Harold Wise
East Carolina University

Lawrence Andrew
Western Illinois University

Craig Tyran
Western Washington University

Ross A. Malaga
University of Maryland

Bryan Foltz
East Carolina University

Laurette Simmons
Loyola University, Maryland

Ron Berry
University of Louisiana at Monroe

Kenneth R. Lee
Delaware Valley College

Dennis Williams
Cal Poly-San Luis Obispo

Robert J. Mills
Utah State University

James Waegelein
University of Kansas, Lawrence

Brian Kovar
Kansas State University

Kent Whitman
Franklin Pierce College

Joy M. Perrine
Penn State, Shenango

Denise Nitterhouse
DePaul University

FROM STEPHEN HAAG . . . As the writing of each book comes to a close, I always enjoy drafting the front matter the most, especially the portions in which I acknowledge the support of so many people who have helped me along in my career. As always, there are people like Maeve, Don, Paige, Merrill, and Amy who make writing a true pleasure. I'm also working with several new people, Alan Rea and Jim Perry among them, who have shown me that writing textbooks is a constantly changing endeavor and never a dull one.

My colleagues in the Daniels College of Business at the University of Denver also provide unending support. I wish I could name all of you, but there isn't enough room. To Glyn Hanbery (my mentor), the ITEC faculty, Anne Logan, Jeff Englestad, and Cody Sherrod, I thank you all.

With the birth of my two sons, Darian and Trevor, my mother and father decided to move to Denver. I cannot tell you how much I've enjoyed having coffee with my father on a weekly basis and how great it is to see my sons growing up with their Nanna and Popeye as an integral part of their lives. Books offer me financial stability, but never love and companionship. My family, especially my wife Pam, offers me those.

FROM MAEVE CUMMINGS . . . My sincere thanks goes to the many people who helped directly and indirectly with this edition and the previous three. Thanks to Steve, without whom I would never have known the joys and challenges of textbook writing. Thanks to Don, who is a truly great co-author, and to the contributor team of Paige, Merrill, and Amy. Thanks to all the people at McGraw-Hill/Irwin who put in long hours and a lot of work to bring this book to completion.

Thanks to Cort Buffington who helped again with content. Thanks to Tony Veteto who always came through for me at a moment's notice. Much thanks to Jenny Cantu, my wonderful graduate assistant. Thanks to David O'Bryan and Walt Manning, who introduced me to the fascinating world of computer forensics. Thanks to Lanny Morrow and to Vicki Dennett, my special friend, who gave generously of their time and expertise. Thanks to Sumit Sircar for his helpful suggestions. Felix Dreher and Barbara Clutter were, as always, unwaveringly supportive and helpful. And thanks most of all to my students from whom I continue to learn every day.

Thanks to my great family: my parents (Dolores and Steve), sisters (Grainne, Fiona, and Clodagh), and brother (Colin). And, to my husband, Slim, the cornerstone of my life, I say "thanks—for everything."

FROM DON MCCUBBREY . . . The joy of this profession is working with students. Thanks go to them for keeping me on my toes by getting better every year. Thanks to my colleagues at the Daniels College of Business for surrounding me with an atmosphere of excellence. Thanks to my friends from the business community in Colorado, from IT consultants to EC entrepreneurs, who provide students and faculty with the seamless connectivity to the business world so essential in this field. Their appearances in the classroom as guest speakers provide assurance that the students' classroom experience is relevant and consistent with the world of practice. It also keeps me up to date.

Special thanks go to my friends from academe, industry, and government from many countries around the world. You know who you are because many of us meet each year in Bled, Slovenia. Our annual Electronic Commerce Conferences have been held there every year since 1988. Thanks to the writing team: Maeve, Paige, Amy, Merrill, and especially, the band leader, Stephen, who kept us on track and was helpful in countless ways. Thanks to the support team from McGraw-Hill, Rick, Kelly, and all the others behind the scenes. Your counsel and support added much value.

Finally, thanks to my children, Heather, Stuart, and CJ, all of whom found success in the IT field, each with their own special focus. Thanks to my 96-year-old mother, who has read all of my books. Most of all, thanks to my wife, Jani, who puts up with me and is truly one in a million.

ABOUT THE AUTHORS

STEPHEN HAAG is a professor in and Chair of the Department of Information Technology and Electronic Commerce in the Daniels College of Business at the University of Denver. Stephen holds a B.B.A. and M.B.A. from West Texas State University and a Ph.D. from the University of Texas at Arlington. Stephen has been teaching in the classroom since 1982 and publishing books since 1984. He has also written numerous articles appearing in such journals as *Communications of the ACM, Socio-Economic Planning Sciences,* and the *Australian Journal of Management.*

Stephen is the coauthor of numerous books including *Interactions: Teaching English as a Second Language* (with his mother and father), *Information Technology: Tomorrow's Advantage Today* (with Peter Keen), *Excelling in Finance,* and more than 20 books within the *I-Series.* Stephen lives with his wife, Pam, and their three sons—Indiana, Darian, and Trevor—in Highlands Ranch, Colorado.

MAEVE CUMMINGS is a professor of Information Systems at Pittsburg State University. She holds a B.S. in Mathematics and Computer Science and an M.B.A. from Pittsburg State, and a Ph.D. in Information Systems from the University of Texas at Arlington. She has published in various journals including the *Journal of Global Information Management* and the *Journal of Computer Information Systems.* She serves on various editorial boards and is a coauthor of two concepts books within the *I-Series.* Maeve has been teaching for 20 years and lives in Pittsburg, Kansas, with her husband, Slim.

DONALD J. MCCUBBREY is a professor in the Department of Information Technology and Electronic Commerce and Director of the Center for the Study of Electronic Commerce in the Daniels College of Business at the University of Denver. He holds a B.S.B.A. in accounting from Wayne State University, a Master of Business from Swinburne University of Technology in Victoria, Australia, and a Ph.D. in information systems from the University of Maribor, Slovenia.

Prior to joining the Daniels College faculty in 1984, he was a partner in a large international accounting and consulting firm. During his career as an IT consultant he participated in client engagements in the United States as well as in several other countries in the Americas and Europe. He has published articles in *Communications of the Association for Information Systems, Information Technology and People,* and *MIS Quarterly,* and coauthored the systems analysis and design text entitled *Foundations of Business Systems.* He is a cofounder and director emeritus of the Colorado Software and Internet Association and serves on the board of the EC Institute. He lives in the Colorado foothills with his wife, Janis.

PAIGE BALTZAN is a professor in the Department of Information Technology and Electronic Commerce in the Daniels College of Business at the University of Denver. Paige holds a B.S.B.A from Bowling Green State University and an M.B.A. from the University of Denver. Paige's primary concentration focuses on object-oriented technologies and systems development methodologies. Paige has been teaching Systems Analysis and Design, Telecommunications and Networking, and Software Engineering at the University of Denver for the past three years. Paige has published supplemental materials for several McGraw-Hill publications including *Using Information Technology*.

Prior to joining the University of Denver Paige spent three years working at Level(3) Communications as a technical architect and four years working at Andersen Consulting as a technology consultant specializing in the telecommunications industry. Paige lives in Lakewood, Colorado, with her husband, Tony and daughter, Hannah.

AMY PHILLIPS is a professor in the Department of Information Technology and Electronic Commerce in the Daniels College of Business at the University of Denver. Amy has a B.S. degree in Environmental Biology and a M.Ed. degree in Educational Technology. She has been teaching for more than 18 years: 5 years in public secondary education and 13 years in higher education. Amy has also been an integral part of both the academic and administrative functions within the higher education systems in Colorado and New Hampshire.

Amy's main concentration revolves around database driven Web sites focusing on dynamic Web content; specifically ASP and XML technologies. Some of the main core course selections that Amy teaches at the University of Denver include XML, Systems Analysis and Design, Database Management Systems, Using Technology to Communicate Information, and Using Technology to Manage Information. Amy has offered many workshops and seminars and has been a guest speaker at various conferences on Web development. She has just finished writing her first book, *Internet Explorer 6.0* with Stephen Haag and James Perry. This book is part of the well-received *I-Series* from McGraw Hill.

MERRILL WELLS's eighth-grade yearbook noted that she wanted to teach college and write books. Although she spent several years after completing an M.B.A. at Indiana University developing business applications, in the end teaching and writing won out. She began her career as an application software developer and then progressed to the systems analyst and finally the project manager roles gaining invaluable experience in business, database design, application design, technical writing, and programming languages.

Merrill returned to academia after her classroom experience in training users on the software that her team had developed reignited the urge to teach. For 10 years she was a computer technology faculty member at Red Rocks Community College, where she developed and taught courses in emerging technologies. She is now a professor in the Department of Information Technology and Electronic Commerce in the Daniels College of Business at the University of Denver. Other publications include *An Introduction to Computers, Introduction to Visual Basic, Programming Logic and Design, Microsoft Access 2002* (Brief, Introductory, and Complete), and *Microsoft PowerPoint 2002* (Brief and Introductory), *Microsoft Office XP, Volume I,* and *Microsoft Office XP, Volume II*.

Management Information Systems

FOR THE INFORMATION AGE

CHAPTER ONE OUTLINE

STUDENT LEARNING OUTCOMES

1. Describe the information age and the role of knowledge workers within it.

2. Define management information systems (MIS).

3. Describe key factors shaping today's economic environment.

4. Validate information as a key resource and describe both personal and organizational dimensions of information.

5. Define how people are the most important organizational resource, their information and technology literacy challenges, and their ethical responsibilities.

6. Describe the important characteristics of information technology (IT) as a key organizational resource.

7. List and describe the six roles and goals of information technology in any organization.

WEB SUPPORT

www.mhhe.com/haag

- Job databases

- Electronic résumés

- Searching newspapers for job ads

- Locating internships

- Interviewing and negotiating tips

- Organization sites and job postings

- Employment opportunities with the government

CHAPTER ONE

The Information Age in Which You Live
Changing the Face of Business

**OPENING CASE STUDY:
CAN TECHNOLOGY CATCH YOU HAVING
AN AFFAIR?**

Well, it may seem like an odd question . . . but when you think about it, technology certainly has the capability to aid in catching you having an affair. People can use technology to test your DNA. People can use a special form of technology (called a global positioning system) to track your movements. There are many ways actually. But how technology caught one man in Colorado having an affair was quite by accident.

Commerce City, Colorado, law enforcement officers installed automated photo radar systems at many intersections to catch people both speeding and running stoplights. As it turns out, a man ran a stoplight, at which time a computer took two photos—one of the back of the car to capture the license plate and one of the front of the car to capture who was in the car. Guess what? A passenger in the car with the man was a woman with whom he was having an affair.

If that wasn't bad enough already, the system automatically generated a traffic violation ticket and sent it to the man's house along with the photos. Can you imagine what would have happened had his wife opened the letter? Fortunately or unfortunately, the man got to the letter first, paid the ticket, and destroyed the evidence.

Technology is certainly pervasive today, and often invasive. Even by accident, technology can creep into your life. And, by specific design, technology can monitor many of your actions. Utility programs on the Internet track your movements from one Web site to the next. You probably figured this out when you first started receiving spam (unsolicited e-mail) from sites you've visited.

The simple reality is that you cannot escape technology. Of course, we all hope people use technology for good reasons as opposed to bad. And our focus in this first chapter and throughout the book is on both the good and the bad in two ways. First, we want to introduce you to technology and all the good ways that individuals and organizations can use it. Second, we want to turn the tables on occasion and alert you to the bad ways that technology can be used. As we do, we'll certainly tell you how to protect yourself, your information, and the technology you own.

By the way, because of the potential of photo radar systems catching people having an affair, the Colorado legislature has introduced a new bill called the adulterers amendment. It allows law enforcement agencies to continue to use automated photo radar systems (a good use of technology in the eyes of many). But it protects the privacy of citizens by requiring that the photos be kept by the law enforcement agencies and shown only to the person receiving the ticket, hopefully thwarting a potentially bad use of the technology.[1]

Introduction

It is the ***information age***—a time when knowledge is power. Today, more than ever, businesses are using information (and information technology) to gain and sustain a competitive advantage. You'll never find a business whose slogan is "What you don't know can't hurt you." Businesses understand that what they don't know can become an Achilles' heel and a source of advantage for the competition.

Think about your major. Whether it's marketing, finance, accounting, human resource management, or any of the many other specializations in a business program, you're preparing to enter the business world as a knowledge worker. Simply put, a ***knowledge worker*** works with and produces information as a product. According to *U.S. News & World Report* in 1994, knowledge workers in the United States outnumber all other workers by a four-to-one margin.[2] Unfortunately, we couldn't find a more up-to-date reference for the same statistic, but we would imagine that knowledge workers today outnumber all other types of workers by at least a five-to-one margin.

Sure, you may work with your hands to take notes or use a mouse and keyboard to produce a spreadsheet, but what you've really done is use your mind to work with, massage, and produce more information (hopefully meaningful and useful information). Accountants generate profit and loss statements, cash flow statements, statements of retained earnings, and so on, some of which appear on paper. But you wouldn't say that an accountant produces paper any more than you would say Michelangelo was a commercial painter of churches.

In the information age, management information systems is a vitally important topic. Why? Because management information systems deals with the coordination and use of three very important organizational resources—information, information technology, and people. Formally, we define MIS as follows:

> ***Management information systems (MIS)*** deals with the planning for, development, management, and use of information technology tools to help people perform all tasks related to information processing and management.

In that definition, you can find three key resources—information, information technology, and people. That is, people or knowledge workers use information technology to work with information. Indeed, if we were not in the information age, information technology would probably still be around, but it wouldn't be nearly as important as it is today.

That's what this text is all about—management information systems or MIS. What you need to remember is that the sole focus of MIS is *not* technology. Technology is a set of tools that enables you to work with information. Pragmatically speaking, people and information are the most important resources within MIS, not technology. Of course, every organization today needs all three (and many others such as capital) to compete effectively in the marketplace. So, don't think of this as a technology textbook, because it's not. You will read three very technology-focused chapters: Chapter 3 on databases and data warehouses; Chapter 4 on decision support systems and artificial intelligence; and Chapter 8 on technology infrastructures. But all the remaining six chapters, including this one, really focus on how people, information, and information technology work together to help an organization achieve a competitive advantage in the marketplace.

As we move forward in this chapter, let's first talk some more about today's exciting and dynamic market environment. Then, we'll explore information, people, and information technology as key resources. Finally, we'll address the specific roles and goals of information technology in both your life and the life of any business. These roles and goals drive our organization of this text. They also define the ways in which businesses today can and are gaining and sustaining a competitive advantage in the marketplace.

Today's Economic Environment

To be successful in business today, you have to understand and operate effectively within a dynamic, fast-paced, and changing economic environment. As you'll see later in this chapter, many businesses must undergo a sort of transformation just to stay in business and compete effectively. Other businesses remain highly competitive by continuing to innovate product and service characteristics. Whatever the case, today's economic environment is changing at a dramatic pace. As you enter today's economic environment, you must

- Know your competition, sometimes known as *competitive intelligence*
- Know your customers, through such best business practices as customer relationship management (CRM)
- Work closely with your business partners, through such best business practices as supply chain management (SCM)
- Know how each and every part of your organization works together to provide its products and services

Throughout this text, we focus on all these, including many best business practices and the technologies that support them. Right now, let's look at an overall view of today's economic environment.

THE E.CONOMY

Electronic commerce is certainly the hottest topic in business today, and we've devoted all of Chapter 5 to it, as well as significant portions of other chapters (especially the next chapter). But what exactly is electronic commerce and what does it enable a business to do? Formally defined,

> **Electronic commerce** is commerce, but it is commerce accelerated and enhanced by information technology, in particular, the Internet. It enables customers, consumers, and companies to form powerful new relationships that would not be possible without the enabling technologies.

Electronic commerce will make serious winners out of some businesses and losers out of others. Indeed, most of the early dot-com companies are out of business today because of their failure to implement electronic commerce correctly. In short, you can't simply create a Web site and expect your customers to beat a virtual path to your door. You must still follow sound business principles and guidelines. That's why most of the early dot-coms failed. They ignored sound business principles and focused solely on the technology. That's a bad road to travel, and one that will undoubtedly lead to failure. Remember: information technology is indeed a key organizational resource, but it is only one of many.

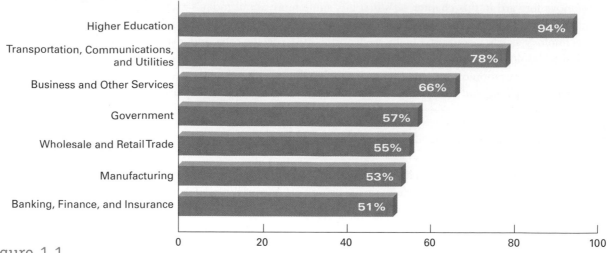

Figure 1.1

Percentage of Sites
That Plan to Add
Telecommuting[4]

Electronic commerce is giving rise to many new and innovative "best business practices," such as telecommuting and the virtual workplace (see Figure 1.1). Telecommuting and the virtual workplace go hand in hand:

Telecommuting is the use of communications technologies (such as the Internet) to work in a place other than a central location.

The **virtual workplace** is a technology-enabled workplace. No walls. No boundaries. Work anytime, anyplace, linked to other people and information you need, wherever they are.[3]

Today, more than 35 million people in the United States telecommute, and that figure is expected to grow by 20 percent over the next several years. You may be participating in a form of telecommuting if you're taking this class via *distance learning*. Distance learning essentially enables you to learn in a virtual classroom without going to campus a couple of times a week. Of course, if you are participating in distance learning, then your instructor is most probably participating in telecommuting as well. That is, he or she may be sitting at home right now sending you e-mails and leading class discussions in chat rooms.

Telecommuting is popping up in many business sectors; some make obvious sense and some may surprise you. For example, JC Penney has told its telephone service representatives who handle orders over the phone to go home and work there. In each home, JC Penney provides a computer, work space furniture, and a high-speed Internet connection. When you call the 1-800 number for JC Penney to order from its catalog, your phone call is routed to the home of a telecommuter. The telephone service representative will answer the phone and speak with you and use the high-speed Internet connection to record your order, inform you of a delivery time, and process your credit card. It makes sense when you think about it. If you're handling customer orders over the phone, all you really need is a computer with a connection to a database of product and customer information. You don't need to be sitting in a central office.

THE "NOW" ECONOMY

The "now" economy is one characterized by the immediate access customers have to the ordering of products and services. ATMs are an obvious and simple example. Using an ATM, you have access to your money any time of the day or night and just about anywhere in the world. You don't have to wait for your bank to open to cash a check or make a deposit. Business-to-consumer Web sites are also great examples. In the

I WANT IT!

Tennis shoes with lighted heels are just one of the many wants-based products that have recently surfaced. Take a walk around a mall, see how many wants-based products you can find, and then fill in the table below. Critically think about what information a business must know about its customers to identify potential buyers. Also, stay away from foods—we need very few actual food products, but our taste buds deserve variety.

Now that you've identified a few wants-based products, consider how technology could help you capture and process information relating to people who buy those products. Where would that information come from? Could you use technology to capture that information? Once you have the information, what technologies could you use to process that information?

Product	Price	Why People Want It	What Kind of People Buy It

comfort of your home, apartment, or dorm, you can buy books from Amazon.com (www.amazon.com), make airline reservations (at www.ual.com for example, United Airlines' Web site), and purchase concert tickets from such sites as Ticketmaster (www.ticketmaster.com).

The truth is we've become a very impatient society. And we've come to expect businesses to provide us with products and services (or at a minimum the ability to order them) whenever and wherever we desire. Technology is certainly an integral facilitator here. *M-commerce,* the term used to describe electronic commerce conducted over a wireless device such as a cell phone or personal digital assistant, now gives you the ability to buy and sell stocks with your cell phone while driving down the road. And, using most Web-enabled personal digital assistants, you can bid on auctions at eBay or obtain up-to-the-minute weather forecasts.

A closely related concept is that of a wants-based economy. Some 30 years ago, people mainly purchased what they needed. Not so today. Consider these two examples. First, there are tennis shoes in which the heels light up with the pressure of each footstep. Now, how many people do you think really need tennis shoes with rear lights? Very few, if any, but if that's what they want, that's what they'll buy. A second example is that of dog bakeries, some of which offer dog birthday cakes that range in price from $100 to $500. In reality, neither people nor dogs need to eat treats, but some dog owners simply want to indulge their pets.

Why is it important to understand that you're in a wants-based economy? Because you will then realize that, while you can fairly easily forecast what your customers will need, you can't always predict what they'll want. So, the better you know your customers, the better you can determine what they might want.

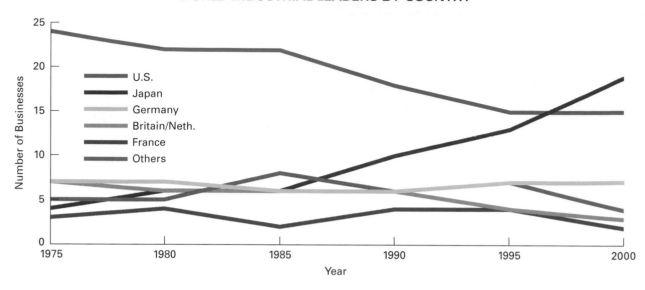

Figure 1.2

Where the Big
Companies Are[5]

THE GLOBAL ECONOMY

A *global economy* is one in which customers, businesses, suppliers, distributors, and manufacturers all operate without regard to physical and geographical boundaries. Consider the graph in Figure 1.2. It charts the world's industrial leaders from 1975 to 2000. Notice the gradual and consistent increase in the number of companies outside the United States. But don't let the numbers scare you.

Although it's true that there are many "foreign" companies competing for consumer dollars in the U.S. market, U.S.-based companies enjoy marketing their products and services throughout most of the world. So, while foreign companies are competing for the dollars in the United States of some 287 million consumers, U.S. companies are selling products and services to a market of more than 6.2 billion consumers worldwide.

You must realize that most large businesses (and even many small businesses) operate as *transnational firms*—firms that produce and sell products and services in countries all over the world. This is a substantial career opportunity for you. Think of how much better your résumé would look if you could speak a foreign language or had knowledge in subjects related to all aspects of international commerce.

THE ARRIVING DIGITAL ECONOMY

We are in the information age right now. But we are seeing a transition into the digital age. When we do arrive there, the *digital economy* will be one marked by the electronic movement of all types of information, not limited to numbers, words, graphs, and photos but including physiological information such as voice recognition and synthesization, biometrics (your retina scan and breath for example), and 3-D holograms. A hologram is a three-dimensional image projected into the air. If you've ever watched *Star Trek,* then you're familiar with the *holodeck,* a sophisticated technology-based device that allows people to experience virtual experiences without the need of today's clunky gloves, headsets, and walkers (found in current virtual reality systems).

Again, we're not there yet. But we are definitely moving in that direction. Just a few short years ago, pay-per-view movies and sporting events in your home were only a vision of the future. Today, they are a reality and a part of the upcoming digital economy. This represents another substantial career opportunity for you. Don't limit your thinking to the digital movement only of words, numbers, graphs, and photos. Think outside the box and envision moving all types of information electronically. For a rich and thought-provoking discussion of the future digital economy, you might want to flip ahead and read Chapter 9. (This isn't a work of fiction, so reading the end first won't ruin the rest of the story for you.)

Today's economic environment is indeed unique, exciting, and full of opportunities for you. Tomorrow's economic environment will be even more exciting and holds many promises for you in your career. Are you ready to help a business use technology to gain and sustain a competitive advantage?

Information as a Key Resource

Information is important for several reasons today, two of which we've already stated. First, information is one of the three key components of management information systems along with information technology and people. Second, we are in the "information" age, a time when knowledge is power. And knowledge comes from having timely access to information and knowing what to do with it.

DATA VERSUS INFORMATION

To understand the nature of information and exactly what it is, you must first understand another term—data. **Data** are raw facts that describe a particular phenomenon. For example, the current temperature, price of a movie rental, and your age are all data. **Information** then is simply data that have a particular meaning within a specific context. For example, if you're trying to decide what to wear, the current temperature is information because it's pertinent to your decision at hand (what to wear); the price of a movie rental, however, is not.

Information may be data that have been processed in some way or presented in a more meaningful fashion. In business, for instance, the price of a movie rental may be information to a checkout clerk, but it may represent only data to an accountant who is responsible for determining net revenues at the end of the month.

PERSONAL DIMENSIONS OF INFORMATION

As a knowledge worker, you work with and produce information. As you do, you can consider it from three points of view or dimensions: time, location, and form (see Figure 1.3).

THE TIME DIMENSION The time dimension of information encompasses two aspects: (1) having access to information when you need it and (2) having information that describes the time period you're considering. The first really deals with timeliness. Information can become old and obsolete. For example, if you want to make a stock trade today, you need to know the price of the stock right now. If you have to wait a day to get stock prices, you may not survive in the

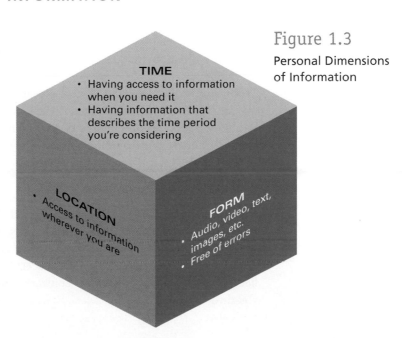

Figure 1.3

Personal Dimensions of Information

TIME
- Having access to information when you need it
- Having information that describes the time period you're considering

LOCATION
- Access to information wherever you are

FORM
- Audio, video, text, images, etc.
- Free of errors

OVERCOMING LANGUAGE BARRIERS ON THE INTERNET

The Internet is certainly a technology that has eliminated geographical and location barriers. With almost one-sixth of the world's population having access to the Internet, "location, location, location" in the physical world is becoming less and less and less important.

However, now we have new issues to deal with, notably a language barrier. What happens if you connect to a site that offers information in a language you don't understand? How can you send an e-mail to someone who doesn't speak English in Japan?

One solution is language translation software. And one company leading the way in the development of language translation software is SYSTRAN. SYSTRAN Enterprise is a suite of software tools that enables you to, among other things, translate about 3,700 words per minute, translate both e-mail and Web page content, and display Asian fonts.

Is it perfect? Not according to SYSTRAN's disclaimer, which reads, "SYSTRAN strives to achieve the highest possible accuracy, however, no automated translation is perfect nor is it intended to replace human translators. Users should note that the quality of the source text significantly affects the translation." As you might expect, automated translation software has a particularly difficult time with idioms.

Indeed, when Kentucky Fried Chicken wanted to translate its slogan "finger-lickin' good" into Chinese, it came out as "eat your fingers off." Now, KFC wasn't using SYSTRAN's software, but this example does illustrate the difficulty of translating idiomatic phrases from one language to another. Product names are another example. When General Motors (GM) tried to sell the Chevy Nova in South America, people didn't buy it. As is turns out, *No va* means "it won't go" in Spanish. GM subsequently changed the name to *Caribe* for its Spanish markets.

By the way, you should connect to SYSTRAN's Web site at www.systransoft.com. There, you can type in a phrase or sentence and choose the language into which you would like it translated.[6]

turbulent securities market. It's no wonder that over one-third of all stock transactions today occur over the Internet.

The second time aspect deals with having information that describes the appropriate time period. For example, most utility companies provide you with a bill that not only tells you of your current usage and the average temperature but also compares that information to the previous month and perhaps the same month last year. This type of information can help you better manage your utilities or simply understand that this month's high utility bill was caused by inclement weather.

THE LOCATION DIMENSION   The location dimension of information deals with having access to information no matter where you are. This simply means that you should be able to access needed information from an airplane, in a hotel room, at home, in the student center of your campus, at work, or even when driving down the road. Of course, because of the Internet you can be almost anywhere in the world and access almost any information you need.

To keep certain information private and secure while providing remote access for employees, many businesses are creating intranets. An ***intranet*** is an internal organizational Internet that is guarded against outside access by a special security feature called a firewall (which can be software, hardware, or a combination of the two). So, if your organization has an intranet and you want to access information on it while away from the office, all you need is Web browser software, a modem, and the password that will allow you through the firewall.

US West, for example, has created an intranet called the *Global Village*.[7] Employees can connect to the *Global Village* and meet in online chat rooms, exchange documents, and discuss ongoing projects, even with employees located in remote geographical areas. While doing this, the firewall ensures that no one outside of US West can gain access to the intranet-based information.

THE FORM DIMENSION   The form dimension of information deals with two primary aspects. The first is simply having information in a form that is most usable and understandable by you—audio, text, video, animation, graphical, and others. The second deals with accuracy. That is, you need information that is free of errors. Think of information as you would think of a physical product. If you buy a product and it's defective, you become an unsatisfied customer. Likewise, if you receive information that is incorrect, you're very unhappy as well.

For all these various information dimensions, you also should be mindful that you provide your customers with information. Information you provide to your customers should be timely, should describe the appropriate time dimension, should be accessible from anywhere, in the most usable form, and free of errors. Information is a valuable resource and also a commodity you provide to customers. Make sure they get it the way they want it.

ORGANIZATIONAL DIMENSIONS OF INFORMATION

Even if your choice in life is to be an entrepreneur and to run your own business, you also need to consider various organizational dimensions of information. These include information flows, what information describes, information granularity, and how information is used (for either mainly transaction processing or analytical processing, which we'll discuss in an upcoming section).

INFORMATION FLOWS   Information in an organization flows in four basic directions: up, down, horizontally, and outward. To consider these flows, let's first briefly look at the structure of an organization. Most people view a traditional organization as a pyramid with four levels and many sides (see Figure 1.4). At the top is *strategic*

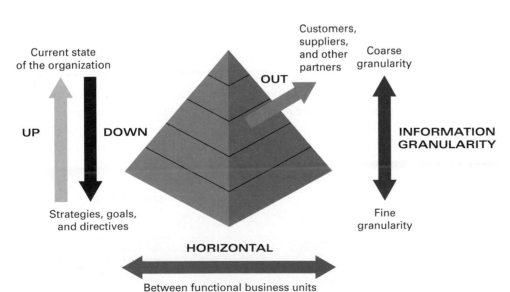

Figure 1.4

An Organization, Its Information Flows, and Information Granularity

management, which provides an organization with overall direction and guidance. The second level is often called *tactical management,* which develops the goals and strategies outlined by strategic management. The third level is *operational management,* which manages and directs the day-to-day operations and implementations of the goals and strategies. Finally, the fourth level of the organization comprises nonmanagement employees who actually perform daily activities, such as order processing, developing and producing goods and services, and serving customers. If you consider your school as an example, strategic management would include the chancellor, president, and various vice presidents. Tactical management would include the deans. Operational management would include the department chairs and directors of academic programs. The final level would include instructors who are responsible for teaching the classes.

Information that flows upward, or the *upward flow of information,* describes the current state of the organization based on its daily transactions. When a sale occurs, for example, that information originates at the lowest level of the organization that then is passed up through the various levels of management. Information that is gathered as a part of everyday operations is consolidated by information technology and passed upward to decision makers who monitor and respond to problems and opportunities.

The *downward flow of information* consists of the strategies, goals, and directives that originate at one level and are passed to lower levels. Information that flows horizontally, or the *horizontal flow of information,* is between functional business units and work teams. For example, at your school various departments are responsible for scheduling courses. That information is passed horizontally to the registrar's office, which creates a course schedule for your entire campus (which may be online—timely and accessible from anywhere by you).

Finally, the *outward flow of information* consists of information that is communicated to customers, suppliers, distributors, and other partners for the purpose of doing business. This outward flow of information (and its corresponding inward flow of information) is really what electronic commerce is all about. Today, no organization is an island, and you must ensure that your organization has the right information technology tools to communicate outwardly with all types of business partners. In a later section and in more detail in Chapter 2, we'll discuss this outward flow of information within the context of creating business partnerships and alliances.

INFORMATION GRANULARITY   Figure 1.4 also illustrates another dimension of information—granularity. *Information granularity* refers to the extent of detail within the information. On one end of this spectrum is coarse granularity, or highly summarized information. At the other end is fine granularity, or information that contains a great amount of detail. As you might guess, people in the highest levels of the organization deal mainly with a coarse granularity of information, with sales by year being an example. People in the lowest levels of the organization, on the other hand, need information with fine granularity. If you consider sales again, nonmanagement employees need information in great detail that describes each transaction—when it occurred, whether by credit or cash, who made the sale, to whom the sale was made, and so on.

So, when transaction information originates at the lowest level of an organization (with fine granularity), it is consolidated to a more coarse granularity as it moves up through the organization (the upward flow of information).

WHAT INFORMATION DESCRIBES   Another organizational dimension of information is what the information describes. Information can be internal, external, objective, subjective, or some combination of the four.

MICHAEL DELL PREACHES IMMEDIATE INFORMATION ACCESS

We can all learn a lot from Michael Dell, CEO and founder of Dell Computer. In the mid-1980s, Michael couldn't even wait to get out of college (the University of Texas) to start his own direct-sales computer business. In the 18 years since he started that small operation in his dorm room, Dell Computer has definitely become the market leader, with over $30 billion in revenues in 2001.

While speaking to a group of entrepreneurs recently, Michael had this to say about the importance of timely information:

> One of the great things about our business is that we have immediate information; we don't have to wait a week or a month. We get information every day, so that I know that yesterday we sold 77,850 computers. I know it by customer type, by product type, by geography, and what the mix was. So that immediacy of information is incredibly valuable to everything in our business, because it's changing very, very rapidly. We just continue to shrink the time and space and distance between our customers and our suppliers and make that as efficient as we can. We're down to about three to four days of inventory now. We get deliveries every two hours based on what we just sold. You take out the guessing.

That's a powerful statement. Look closely at it again. By having access to timely information, Dell Computer is able to carry only three to four days of inventory. That's remarkable when you compare it to the industry standard of about 45 days. Businesses in the technology sector cannot afford to carry 45 days' worth of inventory when you consider the rapid speed at which technology is changing.

Notice also that timely information takes out the "guess work" for Dell. If your business is guessing to determine its next move, you won't be in business very long. Perhaps it's time to get timely information.[8]

---

1. *Internal information* describes specific operational aspects of the organization.
2. *External information* describes the environment surrounding the organization.
3. *Objective information* quantifiably describes something that is known.
4. *Subjective information* attempts to describe something that is unknown.

Consider a bank that faces the decision of what interest rate to offer on a CD. That bank will use internal information (how many customers it has who can afford to buy a CD), external information (what other banks are offering), objective information (what is today's prime interest rate), and subjective information (what prime interest is expected to be several months down the road). As well, what other banks are offering is not only an example of external information (it describes the surrounding environment) but also objective information (it is quantifiably known).

As a general rule, people in the lowest levels of the organization deal mainly with internal and objective information (the price of a movie rental is an example). People in the highest levels of the organization, on the other hand, deal with all types of information.

People as a Key Resource

The single most important resource in any organization is its people. People (knowledge workers) set goals, carry out tasks, make decisions, serve customers, and, in the case of IT specialists, provide a stable and reliable technology environment so the organization can run smoothly and gain a competitive advantage in the marketplace. This discussion is all about you. You're preparing to be a knowledge worker.

INFORMATION AND TECHNOLOGY LITERACY

In business, your most valuable asset is *not* technology but rather your *mind*. IT is simply a set of tools that helps you work with and process information, but it's really just a *mind support* tool set. Technology such as spreadsheet software can help you quickly create a high-quality and revealing graph. But it can't tell you whether you should build a bar or a pie graph, and it can't help you determine whether you should show sales by territory or sales by salesperson. Those are your tasks, and that's why your business curriculum includes classes in human resource management, accounting, finance, marketing, and perhaps production and operations management.

Nonetheless, technology is an important set of tools for you. Technology can help you be more efficient and can help you dissect and better understand problems and opportunities. So, it's important for you to learn how to use your technology set. And it's equally important that you understand the information to which you're applying your technology tools.

A ***technology-literate knowledge worker*** is a person who knows how and when to apply technology. The "how" aspect includes knowing what technology to buy, how to exploit the many benefits of application software, and what technology infrastructure is required to get businesses connected to each other, just to name a few. If you've had a class that deals with learning personal productivity software, then you already know the benefits of application software: Use them all. In this text, we want to help you decide what technology (if any) an organization needs and how best to use it to support organizational goals and achieve a competitive advantage. If you can do that, then you'll truly be a technology-literate knowledge worker.

In many unfortunate cases, people and organizations have blindly decided to use technology to help solve some sort of business problem. What you need to understand is that technology is not a *panacea*. You can't simply apply technology to any given process and expect that process instantly to become more efficient and effective. Look at it this way—if you apply technology to a process that doesn't work correctly, then you'll only be doing things wrong millions of times faster. There are cases when technology is not the solution. Being a technology-literate knowledge worker will help you determine when and when not to apply technology.

Information-literate knowledge workers

- Can define what information they need
- Know how and where to obtain that information
- Understand the information once they receive it
- Can act appropriately based on the information to help the organization achieve the greatest advantage

Consider a unique, real-life example of an information-literate knowledge worker.

Several years ago, a manager of a retail store on the East Coast received some interesting information: diaper sales on Friday evening accounted for a large percentage of total sales for the week. Most people in this situation would immediately jump to the decision to ensure that diapers are always well stocked on Friday evenings or to run a special on diapers during that time to increase sales further, but not our information-literate knowledge worker. She first looked at the information and decided it was not complete. That is, she needed more information before she could act.

She decided the information she needed was why a rash of diaper sales (pardon the pun) occurred during that time and who was buying them. That information was not stored within the computer system, so she stationed an employee in the diaper aisle on

POLAROID IS POLAR-PEOPLE

People really are the most important resource in any organization, no matter how big or small and no matter in what industry. People possess *intellectual capital,* and intellectual capital is what enables an organization to innovate.

At Polaroid, film isn't the most important asset—it's simply the product produced. The most important asset is the group of scientists who know everything about the chemistry of film. So Polaroid has created a very sophisticated model for its hiring requirements.

The model first combines employee-turnover information with forecasts and known trends of its current workforce. For example, Polaroid forecasts probable retirement dates of each scientist and estimates how many people in each given skill area will leave within the next decade.

That information is then used extensively in the interviewing and hiring processes. Where Polaroid sees an intellectual capital vacancy upcoming in the next several years, it focuses its hiring efforts.

How many businesses do you believe have such an elaborate system for hiring new employees?[9]

Friday evening to record any information pertinent to the situation (i.e., she knew how and where to obtain information). The store manager learned that young businessmen purchased the most diapers on Friday evening. Apparently, they had been instructed to buy the weekend supply of diapers on their way home from work. Her response was to stock premium domestic and imported beer near the diapers. Since then, Friday evening is not only a big sale time for diapers but also for premium domestic and imported beer.

This is a true story of an information-literate knowledge worker. Her ability to define what information she needed, know how and where to obtain that information, and understand the meaning of the information once she received it enabled her to determine that diapers and premium beer were complementary products for most young businessmen. Would you have made that connection? By the way, this is an example of a wants-based economic environment. Although diapers are a very necessary product (just ask any parent), premium beer is a wants-based product.

YOUR ETHICAL RESPONSIBILITIES

Your roles as a technology-literate and information-literate knowledge worker extend far beyond using technology and information to gain an advantage in the marketplace for your organization. You must also consider your social responsibilities: This is where ethics become important. *Ethics* are the principles and standards that guide our behavior toward other people. Ethics are different from laws. Laws either require or prohibit some sort of action on your part. Ethics are more of a matter of personal interpretation, and thus have a right and wrong outcome according to different people. Consider the following examples:

1. Copying software you purchased, making copies for your friends, and charging them for the copies
2. Making an extra backup of your software just in case both the copy you are using and the primary backup fail for some reason
3. Giving out the phone numbers of your friends and family, without their permission, to a telecom provider of some sort of calling plan so you can receive a discount

E-MAIL: ELECTRONIC MAIL OR EXPENSIVE MAIL?

In February 1995, an employee at Chevron came across what he thought was an interesting and funny list—"25 Reasons Why Beer Is Better Than Women." He quickly logged into his e-mail and distributed the list to many people. The only problem was that one of the people who received the e-mail was a woman, and she was offended by it. What followed was a lot of legal mumbo jumbo and an eventual out-of-court settlement worth $2 million that Chevron had to pay to the offended employee—definitely an example of when e-mail becomes expensive mail.

Most people agree that the original sender should not have distributed the list. It was mail that was potentially embarrassing and offensive to some people and, therefore, should not have been distributed as a matter of ethics. What people don't agree on, however, is whether or not the company was at fault for not monitoring and stopping the potentially offensive mail. What are your thoughts? Before you decide, follow the accompanying diagram and consider the consequences of your answers.[10]

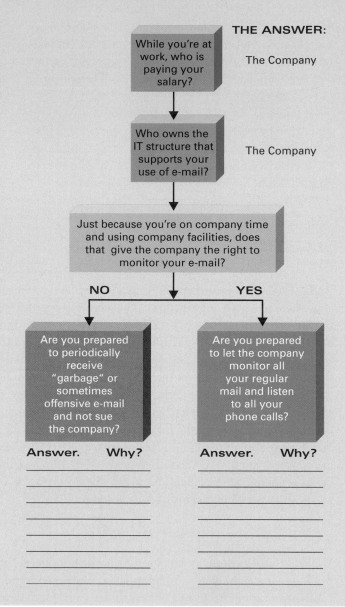

Each of these is either ethically or legally incorrect. In the second example, you may have been ethically correct in making an extra backup copy (because you didn't share it with anyone), but according to most software licenses you're prohibited by law from making more than one backup copy.

To help you better understand the relationship between ethical and legal acts (or the opposite), consider Figure 1.5. The graph is composed of four quadrants, and you always want your actions to remain in quadrant I. If all your actions fall in that quadrant, you'll always be acting legally and ethically, and thus in a socially responsible way.

In business, the question of ethics is an overriding concern because of the widespread use of IT to capture information. For example, if a business invests money to capture information about you as you make a purchase, does that information then belong to the business or do you still have privacy rights regarding its distribution?

Being socially and ethically responsible not only includes the actions you undertake yourself but also deals with the actions of others, which may involve protecting yourself against cyber crimes. Hackers are one group of people who commit cyber crimes. A *hacker* is a very knowledgeable computer user who uses his or her knowledge to invade other people's computers. There are actually many types of hackers today—white-hat hackers, black-hat hackers, crackers, hacktivists, and script bunnies. Each has different motives for hacking, and each is largely a different group of people. To protect yourself and your organization from their hacking, you need to understand who they are and what they do. We explore hackers in more detail in *Extended Learning Module H.*

People, again, are the most valuable resource in any organization. People, like you as a knowledge worker, use IT to work with and massage information. The most successful people understand their information and information-processing needs, and they understand the benefits of technology and know how to use technology to facilitate their working with information.

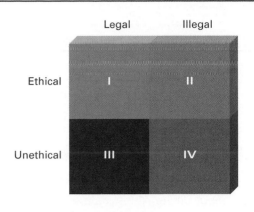

Figure 1.5
Acting Ethically and Legally[11]

Information Technology as a Key Resource

Within management information systems (MIS), the third key resource is information technology. Formally defined, *information technology (IT)* is any computer-based tool that people use to work with information and support the information and information-processing needs of an organization. So, IT includes a cell phone or PDA that you might use to obtain stock quotes, your home computer that you use to write term papers, large networks that businesses use to connect to other businesses, and the Internet that almost one in every six people in the world currently use.

KEY TECHNOLOGY CATEGORIES

There are two basic categories of technology: hardware and software (see Figure 1.6 on the following page). *Hardware* is the physical devices that make up a computer (often referred to as a computer system). *Software* is the set of instructions that your hardware executes to carry out a specific task for you. So, if you have a Nintendo Gamecube, the Gamecube box itself and the controller are hardware devices, while the games you play are software. Let's briefly look at hardware and software; for a more thorough discussion, read "Extended Learning Module A: Computer Hardware and Software," which follows this chapter.

TECHNOLOGY HARDWARE   All hardware falls into one of six categories: input devices, output devices, storage devices, CPU and RAM, telecommunications devices, and connecting devices. Here's a quick summary.

- An *input device* is a tool you use to capture information and commands; input devices include such tools as a keyboard, mouse, touch screen, game controller, bar code reader, and skimmer (used for swiping credit cards and the like).

- An *output device* is a tool you use to see, hear, or otherwise accept the results of your information-processing requests. Output devices include such tools as a printer, monitor, and set of speakers.
- A *storage device* is a tool you use to store information for use at a later time. Output devices include such tools as a floppy disk, hard disk, CD, and DVD.

Figure 1.6

Information Technology
Hardware and Software

Description	Examples
Hardware—The physical devices that make up a computer	
Input device—Tool you use to capture information and commands	• Keyboard, mouse • Touch screen, game controller • Bar code reader, skimmer
Output device—Tool you use to see, hear, or otherwise accept the results of your information-processing requests	• Printer • Monitor • Set of speakers
Storage device—Tool you use to store information for use at a later time	• Floppy disk • Hard disk • CD, DVD
Central processing unit (CPU)—The actual hardware that interprets the software instructions and coordinates how all the other hardware devices work together	• Pentium 4 • AMD Athlon XP Thunderbird
RAM (random access memory)—Temporary memory that holds information, application software, and operating system software	• Many manufacturers make RAM that will fit in a variety of computers
Telecommunications device—Tool you use to send information to and receive it from another person or location	• Telephone modem • DSL modem • Cable modem • Microwave • Satellite
Connecting devices—Tools that connect devices to each other	• Printer cord • Parallel and serial ports
Software—The set of instructions that your hardware executes to carry out a specific task for you	
Application software—Software that enables you to solve specific problems or perform specific tasks	• Word processing software • Payroll software • Spreadsheet software • Inventory management software
Operating system software—System software that controls your application software and manages how your hardware devices work together	• Windows XP • Windows 2000 Me • Mac OS • Linux • UNIX
Utility software—Software that provides additional functionality to your operating system	• Anti-virus software • Screen saver • Disk optimization software • Uninstaller software

IDENTIFYING HARDWARE AND SOFTWARE

Pick up a recent copy of your local newspaper or perhaps a computer magazine such as *PC Magazine* or *Wired* and find an ad for a personal computer system. What is the price of the complete system? What hardware devices does it include and in which of the six hardware categories does each belong? What software does it include? Which software, if any, is application software? Which software, if any, is operating system software? Which software, if any, is utility software?

Now compare that system to a similar one that you can find on the Internet (you might want to start at Dell at www.dell.com). Which is cheaper? Does this surprise you? Why or why not?

- The ***central processing unit (CPU)*** is the actual hardware that interprets and executes the software instructions and coordinates how all the other hardware devices work together. Popular personal CPUs include the Pentium 4 and AMD Athlon XP Thunderbird. ***RAM,*** or ***random access memory,*** is temporary storage that holds the information you're working with, the application software you're using, and the operating system software you're using. Together, the CPU and RAM make up the brains of your computer.

- A ***telecommunications device*** is a tool you use to send information to and receive it from another person or location. For example, if you connect to the Internet using a modem, the modem (which could be a telephone, DSL, cable, wireless, or satellite modem) is a telecommunications device.

- Connecting devices include such things as parallel ports into which you would connect a printer, connector cords to connect your printer to the parallel port, and internal connecting devices that mainly include buses over which information travels from one device such as the CPU to RAM.

That may be the shortest and most concise overview of hardware you've ever read. If you need more detail, please read the extended learning module on hardware and software that follows this chapter.

TECHNOLOGY SOFTWARE   There are two main types of software: application and system. *Application software* is the software that enables you to solve specific problems or perform specific tasks. Microsoft Word, for example, can help you write term papers, so it's application software. From an organizational perspective, payroll software, collaborative software such as videoconferencing, and inventory management software are all examples of application software.

System software handles tasks specific to technology management and coordinates the interaction of all technology devices. Within system software, you'll find operating system software and utility software. *Operating system software* is system software that controls your application software and manages how your hardware devices work together. Popular personal operating system software includes Microsoft Windows XP, Microsoft Windows 2000 Me, Mac OS (for Apple computers), and Linux (an open source operating system).

Utility software is software that provides additional functionality to your operating system. Utility software includes anti-virus software, screen savers, disk optimization software, uninstaller software (for properly removing unwanted software), and a host of others. Again, in the extended learning module that follows this chapter, we discuss software in greater detail.

DECENTRALIZED COMPUTING AND SHARED INFORMATION

All organizations use hardware and software to connect people to each other; to reach out to customers, distributors, suppliers, and business partners; and to provide a reliable and stable computing environment for smooth operations. Because so many people perform so many different tasks within a business environment, the concepts of decentralized computing and shared information are very important (see Figure 1.7).

Decentralized computing is an environment in which an organization splits computing power and locates it in functional business areas as well as on the desktops of knowledge workers. This is possible because of the proliferation of less expensive, more powerful, and smaller systems including notebooks, desktops, minicomputers, and servers. The Internet is a great example of a decentralized computing environment. You use your computer or perhaps cell phone or PDA to access the information and services of host computers on the Internet. In this case, your computer is called a *client computer*, while the host computers are referred to as *server computers*.

Shared information is an environment in which an organization's information is organized in one central location, allowing anyone to access and use it as he or she needs to. Shared information enables people in the sales department, for example, to access work-in-progress manufacturing information to determine when products will be available to ship. At your school, the registrar's office can access the information within the financial aid office to determine how much of your tuition bill is covered by a scholarship or loan. To support shared information, most businesses organize information in the form of a database. In fact, databases have become the standard by which businesses organize their information and provide everyone access to it. We've devoted all of Chapter 3 to databases as well as data warehouses, tools for organizing information to support decision-making tasks.

Now that we've provided you with a brief overview of information technology, let's look specifically at the roles and goals of information technology in any business. IT is an essential enabler of business operations. In the information age, all businesses need technology as tools for working with information.

Figure 1.7

Decentralized Computing
and Shared Information

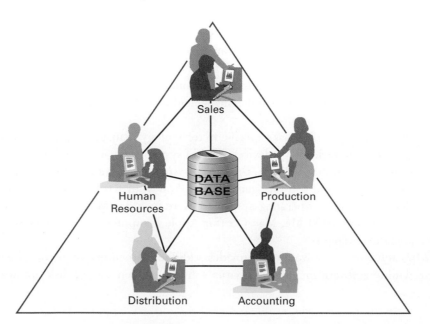

Roles and Goals of Information Technology

The roles and goals of information technology are many and varied. Here we introduce you to six important roles and goals. And we will constantly refer back to these throughout the chapter. They're not only important to learn so you can do well on an exam, they will also help you better organize your view of technology within an organization. The six major roles and goals of information technology (see Figure 1.8) include

1. Increase employee productivity
2. Enhance decision making
3. Improve team collaboration
4. Create business partnerships and alliances
5. Enable global reach
6. Facilitate organizational transformation

INCREASE EMPLOYEE PRODUCTIVITY

The original and still most fundamental role of information technology is to increase productivity. In short, because of its great speed and ability to store and process massive amounts of information accurately, IT can greatly reduce the time, errors, and costs associated with processing information in a variety of ways.

Figure 1.8

The Roles and Goals of Information Technology

Role/Goal	IT Tools Examples	Business Benefits Examples
1. Increase employee productivity	• OLTP • TPS • CIS	• Reduce time • Reduce errors • Reduce costs • Enable customers to process their own transactions
2. Enhance decision making	• OLAP • DSS • GIS • EIS • AI • Data warehouses	• Generate alternatives • Recommend solutions • Drill down through information
3. Improve team collaboration	• Collaboration System • Groupware	• Manage knowledge within the organization • Support geographically dispersed teams • Facilitate communications • Develop applications quickly
4. Create business partnerships and alliances	• IOS • EDI	• Manage supply chains • Share expertise and intellect • Enable B2B e-commerce
5. Enable global reach	• Internet • Translation phones	• Take advantage of a cheaper/larger workforce • Advertise locally made • Tap into global intellectual expertise
6. Facilitate organizational transformation	• Just about any technology you can name, depending on its use	• Stay competitive • Offer new customer interfaces • Enter new markets

For example, if you have an automated payroll system, it can process payroll sheets and generate checks more quickly than if you were doing it by hand. If your employees can submit time cards and expense reimbursement sheets electronically as opposed to submitting handwritten documents, then the likelihood of an error occurring is reduced. And when you decrease processing times and errors, you decrease costs. When you use technology to process transaction information, it's called ***online transaction processing (OLTP)***—the gathering of input information, processing that information, and updating existing information to reflect the gathered and processed information.

IT systems, such as our payroll example, are called transaction processing systems. A ***transaction processing system (TPS)*** processes transactions that occur within an organization. Today, we pretty well accept these as rather dull and mundane. But your customers see them differently. If your TPSs don't process information correctly or don't work at all because of a computer outage, your customers may choose to do business with one of your competitors. Indeed, if you call an airline to make a reservation and you're informed that the computers don't work and your reservation cannot be processed, you may call another airline.

A vitally important hybrid of a TPS is a customer-integrated system. *A **customer-integrated system (CIS)*** is an extension of a TPS that places technology in the hands of an organization's customers and allows them to process their own transactions (see Figure 1.9). ATMs are a good example of a CIS. ATMs provide you with the ability to do your own banking anywhere at anytime. What's really interesting is that ATMs actually do nothing new, but they give you greater flexibility in accessing and using your money. CISs further decentralize computing power in an organization by placing that power in the hands of customers.

Figure 1.9

Transaction Processing and Customer-Integrated Systems

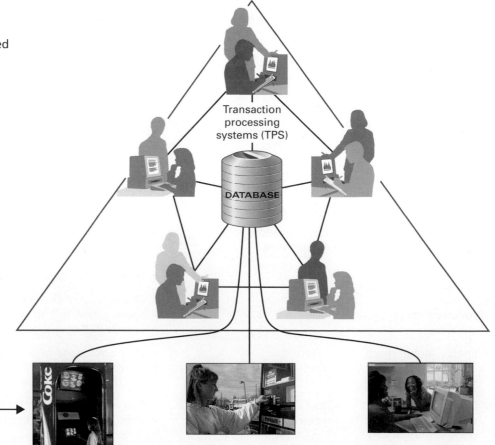

Transaction processing systems (TPS)

DATABASE

Customer-integrated systems (CIS)

The Web is full of examples of customer-integrated systems. When you use any Web site that allows you to order and pay for products and services, you're using a CIS. Customer-integrated systems are the new popular IT system today. You can use a CIS to scan your groceries, pay for fuel at the pump instead of going inside, and perhaps even register for classes online. When you enter the business world, first make sure your transaction processing systems work correctly and all the time. Then, try to convert them to customer-integrated systems. It's a win-win situation for your organizations and your customers.

ENHANCE DECISION MAKING

The counterpart to online transaction processing is ***online analytical processing (OLAP)***—the manipulation of information to support decision making. And IT can definitely play a significant role here. Some decisions are easy to make. If you're deciding what to wear to school, you'll look at today's weather forecast and decide whether to wear shorts and a T-shirt or perhaps a sweatshirt and pants. However, deciding what to major in or which job to accept upon graduation is much more difficult. Likewise, in business, deciding how many inventory units to reorder is relatively simple, while deciding where to build a new distribution center is not.

Technology to support decision making falls into one of two general categories: (1) those that help you analyze a situation and then leave the decision entirely up to you and (2) those that actually make some sort of recommendation concerning what to do. The first category includes such IT tools as decision support systems, executive information systems, and geographic information systems. For example, an ***executive information system (EIS)*** is a highly interactive IT system that allows you to first view highly summarized information and then choose how you would like to see greater detail, which may alert you to potential problems or opportunities. In Figure 1.10, you can see three graphs that might appear in an EIS. The first one at the left shows sales by year. By clicking on a particular year, you can view sales by territory for that year. Then, by clicking on a particular territory, you can view sales by product line for that territory within a given year. These types of IT systems offer you great speed in massaging information, developing alternatives, and viewing information from various perspectives. However, they do not make recommendations concerning what you should do.

Figure 1.10

Drilling Down with an Executive Information System

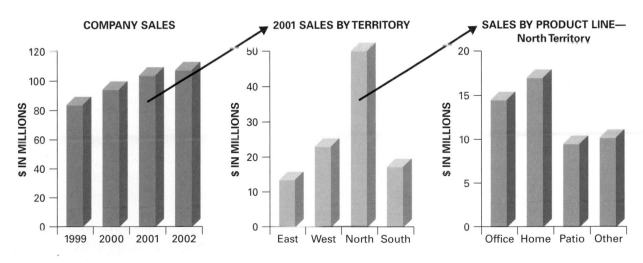

The second category includes technologies in the area of artificial intelligence. *Artificial intelligence (AI)* is the science of making machines imitate human thinking and behavior. For example, a *neural network* is an artificial intelligence that is capable of finding and differentiating patterns. Your credit card company probably uses a neural network to monitor your card use and identify potential fraud if someone else happens to steal your card and attempt to use it. In this instance, the neural network has been fed every single credit card transaction you've performed, and it has developed a pattern of how, when, and why you use your card. Then, when a transaction occurs that doesn't fit the pattern of your profile, the neural networks alert someone that your credit card may have been stolen.

We explore technology support for decision making throughout this text and specifically in Chapter 4.

IMPROVE TEAM COLLABORATION

Teams would certainly be characterized as a best business practice today. The old adage "two heads are better than one" does hold true. Of course, teams in the business world are often composed of more than two people with many being spread all over the globe, and that's why information technology plays such an important role in team collaboration. Collaborative-enabling technologies such as chat rooms and the Internet in general are all fundamental to the success of a team.

A *collaboration system* is a system that is designed specifically to improve the performance of teams by supporting the sharing and flow of information. The foundation of any collaboration system is *groupware*, the popular term for the software component that supports the collaborative efforts of a team. Popular groupware suites include Lotus/Notes Domino, Microsoft Exchange, Novell Groupwise, and NetSys WebWare.

Groupware contains software components for supporting the following three team functions:

1. **Team dynamics**—Communications among team members and the facilitation and execution of meetings. Specific technologies that support team dynamics include group scheduling software, electronic meeting software, video-conferencing software, and whiteboard software.

2. **Document management**—A *group document database* that acts as a powerful storage facility for organizing and managing all documents related to specific teams. Most group document databases employ multiple levels of security, allowing some teams to access the information of other teams. In these databases, you can store and search information of all kinds: text, graphs, images, audio clips, and even videos.

3. **Applications development**—Facilities that allow a team to develop unique applications quickly, so the teams can literally "get to work."

All of these technology-based tools and many more enable teams to work effectively, even when team members are geographically dispersed. Teams, as you'll learn in later chapters, are vitally important to the success of any organization. But concepts such as the virtual workplace and telecommuting are almost contradictory to the success of teams. If you consider even further that today's economy is a global one, any given team may be composed of people all over the world. In this case, technology, and specifically groupware, is an essential enabler of team innovation.

We'll talk more about the technologies that support team collaboration throughout this text and especially in Chapter 4. Your career opportunity lies in learning how to

TEAMS GROOVE WITH GROOVE ON THE INTERNET

Ray Ozzie—have you ever heard of him? Probably not, but you may have heard of one of his software inventions, Lotus Notes. In 1995, IBM bought Lotus (the corporation) for $3.5 billion just so it could own Lotus Notes. To date, more than 68 million licenses of Lotus Notes have been sold.

Lotus Notes is the typical groupware suite from a technical point of view. It contains a powerful group document database that organizes and manages all documents related to teams and their work. Ray's newest software invention, Groove, isn't. Groove works on the same basis as Napster. That is, Groove doesn't require a central server on which the group document database would reside.

Instead, Groove allows any member of a team to access the information on the computers of other team members. So, team members can easily work via the Internet in remote locations and easily share all types of digital information. As Bill Gates describes it, Groove is "a deep and innovative software product that is a great indicator of where the Internet is going." It never hurts to have the endorsement of Bill Gates.

Companies across all business sectors are lining up to use Groove. Some of those include:

- Alliance Consulting—For intercompany transactions in the business supply chain
- Componentry Solutions—To help companies manage insurance claims
- GE—In its aircraft division supply chain
- Glaxo Smith Kline—For collaboration on R&D projects
- SAP—To allow knowledge workers to access corporate information[12]

work effectively in a team environment. Many of your classes in school will probably require that you work in teams. And the reason is because teams are such an important part of the business world.

CREATE BUSINESS PARTNERSHIPS AND ALLIANCES

Each and every business contains unique and strategically sensitive expertise and intellect. Wal-Mart, for example, is a premier retailer of home and family products such as clothing. Vanity Fair, on the other hand, is a premier manufacturer of clothing including Lee and Wrangler jeans. So these two organizations have created a strong and highly successful business partnership.

When a customer buys a pair of Wrangler jeans at a Wal-Mart store on a Wednesday, for example, that information is sent that night to Vanity Fair, via computer, of course. If Vanity Fair has a replacement pair in stock, it's immediately sent out on Thursday and arrives at Wal-Mart on Saturday. Three days for inventory replenishment is an outstanding feat and would not be possible without the use of technology.

But speed isn't the only advantage. Vanity Fair's market-response system also takes the guesswork out of reordering and provides retailers with only the best-selling styles and lines. Vanity Fair's extended market-response system will even analyze the sales databases of retailers and determine groups of products—for instance, matching jeans, shirts, and jackets—to help retailers forecast ideal inventory supply levels. As you can see, business partnerships and alliances enable each participating organization to tap into the intellectual capital of the other participating organizations.

This type of business partnership is enabled by interorganizational systems and is a form of Business to Business (B2B) e-commerce. An *interorganizational system (IOS)*

FINDING BUSINESS PARTNERS AND ALLIANCES ON THE WEB

Like any other type of business, no dot-com on the Web can be an island. Indeed, dot-coms have determined that they must develop business partners on the Web. These Web-based partnerships manifest themselves in many different ways. One such way is through a banner ad. A *banner ad* is a small ad on one Web site that advertises the products and services of another business, usually another dot-com business. Visit the Web and go exploring. Find five Web sites on which banner ads appear. Which Web sites did you find with banner ads? What business was each banner ad for? Did you find any Web sites with more than one banner ad? If so, which site(s)? Now, wait a day and visit the same five sites. Did any of the banner ads change? If so, why do you think they changed?

automates the flow of information between organizations to support the planning, design, development, production, and delivery of products and services. A typical IOS includes *electronic data interchange (EDI)*—the direct computer-to-computer transfer of transaction information contained in standard business documents, such as invoices and purchase orders, in a standard format. In short, EDI replaces paper documents with digital records exchanged between business partnerships' computers. R. J. Reynolds uses EDI to order materials from its suppliers. In doing so, R. J. Reynolds has been able to cut order processing costs from $75 per order (using paper) to only $0.93 using EDI.

EDI is becoming so important that most large businesses won't do business with your company if it doesn't support EDI. For example, General Motors will only order raw materials and parts from suppliers that support EDI capabilities. The federal government plans to have everyone in the United States filing income tax returns electronically by the year 2010. EDI will enable this. So, as an individual, you'll soon become a business partner with the federal government.

Another important and related concept to EDI is electronic funds transfer (EFT). EFT allows organizations to complete the full transaction without physically sending anything, including the payment. So, EDI supports the electronic transfer of information such as sales invoice, and EFT supports the electronic transfer of the monies to pay the sales invoice amount. Just as EDI is becoming a common business practice, so is EFT. Think about filing your income tax returns electronically. It doesn't make much sense to file the paperwork and then still have to send a personal check or receive a refund check from the federal government.

ENABLE GLOBAL REACH

As we've already stated, you can characterize today's operating environment as one of a global economy. Because of technology, you now have the ability to market your products and services in countries all over the world and develop partnerships and alliances (which we just discussed) with other businesses throughout the globe. Not only can you do this, you *must* to be successful in the long run. Think about Honda cars for a moment, considered by most people to be manufactured in Japan, its home country headquarters. Honda actually produces more cars outside than inside Japan. Not only that, Honda exports more cars from the United States than does General Motors, Ford, or Chrysler.

A business can gain significant advantages by enabling global reach through technology. It can take advantage of a cheaper and larger workforce; many businesses in the

SAMSUNG OUT-PATENTS ITS JAPANESE COMPETITORS

In 1970, Samsung Electronics, a Korean-based company, began making inexpensive 12-inch black-and-white televisions under the label of Sanyo. Today, Samsung is considered to be one of the top companies in the technology sector, as evidenced by its recent $16 billion deal with Dell Computer to provide components.

And last year, Samsung ranked fifth worldwide in patents, behind only IBM, NEC, Canon, and Micron Technology. To put it in another way, Samsung filed for more patents in that year than Matsushita, Sony, Hitachi, Mitsubishi Electric, and Fujitsu. All of those are Japanese-based companies.

But Samsung isn't content with filing for more patents than its well-known Japanese competitors. Samsung wants to be seen worldwide as a provider of quality products. So it spent $400 million in 2002 on stylish worldwide marketing campaigns. Even more so, Samsung is removing its products from discount chains such as Wal-Mart and Kmart and instead selling them in more upscale stores.

Samsung is already among the elite in countries such as China and Russia. But it knows it must move west to the United States if it wants to be a true global competitor. Samsung wants to become Korea's first well-known and well-respected global company. To do that, it will have to beat its Japanese-based competitors, but it will also have to prove itself to the American public. By creating partnerships with U.S. companies such as Dell, Hewlett-Packard, and IBM, Samsung seems to be well on its way.[13]

United States locate their back-end office functions (accounting and the like) in Ireland for this reason. It can advertise products as being "American made," in the instance of Honda although it is a Japan-based company. It can also tap into the intellectual expertise of a workforce in another country. Many "U.S." software publishers actually write and produce much of their software in such countries as India and Pakistan.

To operate effectively using global reach, businesses must use technology to overcome the barriers of time and location. One simple example is that of translation phones. AT&T is currently perfecting a translation phone that will allow you to call anywhere in the world and use your native language for speaking while the person on the other end hears your speech in his or her native tongue. In between is a powerful automatic speech recognition system that captures your speech, converts it into another language digitally, and then synthesizes the speech in that language to the person on the other end of the line. There are also utilities on the Web that translate Web pages from one language to another.

To also operate effectively using global reach, you must consider the culture of other countries. *Culture* is the collective personality of a nation or society, encompassing language, traditions, currency, religion, history, music, and acceptable behavior, among other things. For example, in many countries around the world workers take extended breaks at lunch well into the afternoon hours. So, you shouldn't schedule a virtual team meeting during those particular hours. It's a simple example, but it does illustrate the fact that you have to consider the culture, in this case the work hours, of your various team members.

FACILITATE ORGANIZATIONAL TRANSFORMATION

And last, but certainly not least, information technology plays a critical role in facilitating organizational transformation. Organizational transformation is very necessary to respond to the ever-changing needs (and wants) of today's marketplace. But organizational

NOKIA—FROM PAPER, TO RUBBER, TO CELL PHONES AND TELECOMMUNICATIONS

The Nokia Company began a long time ago (over 150 years) as a producer of paper. In 1967, the Nokia Corporation was formed through a merger of the Nokia Company (paper), Finnish Rubber Works (rubber), and Finnish Cable Works (telecommunications cables).

As Nokia moved through the remainder of the 1960s, all of the 1970s, and into the 1980s, it saw huge possibilities in the wire-free telephone market. By transforming itself and focusing its energies in that area, Nokia produced the original and first hand-portable telephone in 1987.

You probably know the rest of the story. Today, Nokia is regarded as the premier innovator and manufacturer of cell phones. And it hasn't forgotten its past. For example, while producing rubber as a primary product, Nokia was the first to manufacture and sell brightly colored rubber boots (you might as well be in fashion while at work). So, it's no surprise that Nokia innovated the multicolored, clip-on facias that literally made cell phones an overnight fashion sensation.

Businesses don't have to go out of business just because the products they manufacture are no longer needed in our society. If your business finds itself in a shrinking market, be bold and innovative. Undertake some sort of dramatic organizational transformation. Nokia went from a premier manufacturer of rubber boots to the world's leading provider of cell phones in less than 15 years. That's a rather dramatic organizational transformation, wouldn't you say?[14]

transformation doesn't have to be like going from a cocoon to a beautiful butterfly (one of nature's most dramatic and wonderful transformations). Businesses today can undergo a transformation by simply changing the way they deliver their products and services.

Consider Blockbuster Video. It has recently undergone one transformation (renting video games as opposed to just movies) and is in the middle of another. Blockbuster has created a business partnership with many cable TV services. Through a cable TV service, Blockbuster is now offering pay-per-view movies. So you don't have to go to a Blockbuster store to rent a video, you can order it from the comfort of your own home for about the same price. Not only that, once you order a movie, you can typically watch it several times within 24 hours.

This transformation for Blockbuster lies in changing how it delivers its products to you. Even more important, Blockbuster realizes that pay-per-view movies is the wave of the future, not going to a store to rent a video. Don't be surprised if in 10 years you can't find a local video rental store. Of course, technology plays a key role in Blockbuster's transformation. Without enabling network technologies and large servers that digitally store videos, Blockbuster would have no way of offering you pay-per-view movies.

Every business today must be willing to change, sometimes in minor ways but often in dramatic and "knee-breaking" ways. Just ask the folks at Kmart. At one point in time, Kmart was considered to be a premier discount retailer. But it failed to transform itself to meet the changing desires of the market, and Kmart filed for Chapter 11 in 2002.

As we study business transformations in this text, you'll learn about some information technologies including enterprise software and object-oriented technologies. As you learn about them, don't focus too much on the technology itself. Instead, focus on how businesses can use those technologies to enable organizational transformation.

Summary: Student Learning Outcomes Revisited

1. **Describe the information age and the role of knowledge workers within it.** The *information age* is a time when knowledge is power. That is to say, what you don't know can in fact hurt you and put you out of business. A *knowledge worker,* in the information age, works with and produces information as a product.

2. **Define management information systems (MIS).** *Management information systems (MIS)* deals with the planning for, development, management, and use of information technology tools to help people perform all tasks related to information processing and management. MIS includes three key resources: information, information technology, and people.

3. **Describe key factors shaping today's economic environment.** Key factors shaping today's economic environment include:
   - *The E.conomy*—Characterized by *electronic commerce,* which is commerce accelerated and enhanced by information technology, in particular, the Internet.
   - *The "Now" economy*—Immediate access customers have to the ordering of products and services.
   - *Global economy* In which customers, businesses, suppliers, distributors, and manufacturers all operate without regard to physical and geographical boundaries.
   - *The arriving digital economy*—The electronic movement of all types of information, not limited to numbers, words, graphs, and photos but including physiological information such as voice recognition and synthesization.

4. **Validate information as a key resource and describe both personal and organizational dimensions of information.** Information is not only one of the three key components of management information systems (MIS), but we are also in the "information age," a time when knowledge is power. The personal and organizational dimensions of information include

   - Personal
     - Time—Access to information when you need it and information that describes the time period you're considering
     - Location—Access to information no matter where you are
     - Form—Information in a form that is most usable and understandable (audio, text, video, animation, graphical, and others) and information that is free of errors
   - Organizational
     - Information flows—Up, down, horizontal, and outward with respect to an organization
     - *Granularity*—The extent of detail within information
     - What information describes—*Internal* (specific operational aspects of the organization), *external* (the environment surrounding the organization), *objective* (quantifiably describing something that is known), and *subjective* (attempting to describe something that is unknown)

5. **Define how people are the most important organizational resource, their information and technology literacy challenges, and their ethical responsibilities.** People are the single most important resource in any organization, setting goals, carrying out tasks, and making decisions.
   - *Technology-literate knowledge workers* are people who know how and when to apply technology.
   - *Information-literate knowledge workers* (1) can define what information they need; (2) know how and where to obtain that information; (3) understand the information once they receive it; and (4) can act appropriately based on the information.
   - Most importantly, knowledge workers must be ethical. *Ethics* are the principles and standards that guide our behavior toward other people.

6. **Describe the important characteristics of information technology (IT) as a key organizational resource.** *Information technology (IT)* is any computer-based tool that people use to work with information and support the information and information-processing needs of an organization. All technology is either *hardware* (the physical devices that make up a computer) or *software* (the set of instructions that your hardware executes).

7. **List and describe the six roles and goals of information technology in any organization.** The roles and goals of information technology include

   - Increase employee productivity—Reducing the time, errors, and costs associated with processing information.

   - Enhance decision making—Helping you analyze a situation and then leaving the

decision entirely up to you or actually making some sort of recommendation concerning what to do.

- Improve team collaboration—Improving the performance of teams by supporting the sharing and flow of information.

- Create business partnerships and alliances—Helping organizations work together to provide better and more timely products and services.

- Enable global reach—Marketing your products and services in countries all over the world and developing partnerships and alliances with other businesses throughout the globe.

- Facilitate organizational transformation—Responding to the ever-changing needs (and wants) of today's marketplace.

CLOSING CASE STUDY ONE

YOU AND YOUR INFORMATION

In the opening case study, you read about how pervasive and invasive technology is in your life today. And many people simply accept this fact and think little beyond it. No matter what you do or where you go, your information travels with you and is eventually captured and stored by a number of organizations (a law enforcement agency in the case of the opening case study). In this all-encompassing information and IT environment, let's consider two issues: trust and accuracy. As you'll see, both are related.

First, answer the questions below (with a simple *yes* or *no*), which pertain to your everyday life.

1. Do you keep a paper record of all your long-distance phone calls—when you placed them by date and time, to whom, and the length—and then compare that list to your monthly phone bill?

   Yes ☐ No ☐

2. Do you meet with the meter reader to verify the correct reading of your water, gas, or electricity usage?

   Yes ☐ No ☐

3. As you shop, do you keep a record of the prices of your groceries and then compare that record to the register receipt?

   Yes ☐ No ☐

4. Do you frequently ask to see your doctor's medical record on you to ensure that it's accurate?

   Yes ☐ No ☐

5. When you receive a tuition bill, do you pull out your calculator, add up the amounts, and verify that the total is correct?

   Yes ☐ No ☐

6. Have you ever purchased a credit report on yourself to make sure your credit information is accurate?

   Yes ☐ No ☐

7. Have you ever called the police department to verify that no outstanding traffic violations have been inadvertently assigned to you?

   Yes ☐ No ☐

8. Do you count your coin change when you receive it from a store clerk?

   Yes ☐ No ☐

9. Do you verify your credit card balance by keeping all your credit card receipts and then matching them to charges on your statement?

   Yes ☐ No ☐

10. Do you keep all your paycheck stubs to verify that the amounts on your W-2 form at the end of the year are accurate?

   Yes ☐ No ☐

How many of these questions did you answer *yes*? How many did you answer *no*? More than likely, you probably answered *no* to almost all the questions (if not all of them). What does that have to say about your trust that organizations are maintaining accurate information about you? Well, it basically says that you trust organizations to keep accurate information about you. The real question is, Is that necessarily the case?

Now answer the set of questions below, which relate to the level of confidence organizations have in the accuracy of information you give them.

1. When interviewing with potential employers, do they take your word that you have a college degree?

   Yes ☐ No ☐

2. If you deposit several checks into your checking account at once, does the bank trust you to correctly add the amounts?

   Yes ☐ No ☐

3. When you register for a class that has a prerequisite, does your school assume that you have actually taken the prerequisite class?

   Yes ☐ No ☐

4. When you make a deposit at an ATM and enter the amount, does the bank assume that you entered the correct amount?

   Yes ☐ No ☐

5. When you're buying a house and negotiating a loan, does the bank assume that the price you're paying for the house is correct and not inflated?

   Yes ☐ No ☐

6. When insuring your car, does the insurance company assume that you have a good driving record?

   Yes ☐ No ☐

7. When you apply for a parking permit at your school, does it assume that the car belongs to you?

   Yes ☐ No ☐

8. When you file your taxes, does the IRS assume that you've correctly reported all your income over the past year?

   Yes ☐ No ☐

The answer to each of these questions is probably *no*. And what does that say about the extent to which organizations trust you to provide accurate information? In this instance, it may not be strictly a matter of trust. Organizations today can't afford to have dirty information—information that's not accurate. Because organizations base so many of their decisions on information, inaccurate information creates a real problem that may equate to inefficient processes and lost revenue.

So, on the one side, you're probably very trusting in your assumptions that organizations are maintaining accurate information about you. On the other side, organizations don't really depend on you to provide accurate information.

Questions

1. Should you really trust organizations to maintain accurate information about you? In many instances, is it even worth your time and energy to verify the accuracy of that information?

2. What other examples can you think of in which you simply trust that your information is accurate? What other examples can you think of in which specific organizations don't assume that you're providing accurate information?

3. What sort of impact will cyberspace business have on the issues of trust and accuracy? Will it become easier or more difficult for cyberspace business to assume that you're providing accurate information? Will you trust cyberspace business to maintain your information more accurately than traditional organizations?

4. What are the ethical issues involved in organizations sharing information about you? In some instances it may be okay and in your best interest. But what if the shared information about you is inaccurate? What damage could it cause? What recourse do you have, if any?

5. It's a real dilemma: Most people think that

credit card offerers charge extremely high interest rates. But how many people do you know who actually go through the process of calculating their average daily balances, applying the interest rates, and then verifying that the interest charged on their accounts is correct? Why do people complain that they are being charged excessive interest rates and then fail to check the accuracy of the interest calculations?

6. What about the future? As more organizations maintain even more information about you, should you become more concerned about accuracy? Why or why not?

CLOSING CASE STUDY TWO

HOW MUCH OF YOUR PERSONAL INFORMATION DO YOU WANT BUSINESSES TO KNOW?

The information age has brought about great debates with respect to information availability and privacy. For example, most counties in the United States provide searchable Internet-based databases with real estate information. You can type in an address and see what a family paid for a home, when they bought it, and often even how it's financed. You can also type in a person's name and find the same information. Is that good or bad? It probably depends on your perspective. You can also use special search engine utilities such as Yahoo! People Search (http://people.yahoo.com/) to find the phone numbers and addresses of people all over the United States. You might want to see if you can find yourself.

From an organizational perspective, businesses need information about you to provide the best possible products and services. The more a business knows about you, the more it can tailor its offerings to you. In many ways, this is good. We all want personalized service. But, in a way, it could also be bad. Just how much of your personal information do you want businesses to know? Consider these examples.

MITCHELLS OF WESTPORT

Mitchells is an upscale old-fashioned clothing retailer that's exploiting technology and information to create one-to-one customer service. With a database of more than 50,000 customers and 10 years of transaction data, Mitchells can sift through information to better serve its customers. As CEO Jack Mitchell explains, "What that means in real terms is that we can look at the historical preferences of our customers, and, for instance, see if a customer who used to buy American suits likes a more contemporary European look in his clothing."

Mitchells even tracks information on its high-revenue customers such as the company they work for, their position, birthdays, anniversaries, and kids' name and ages. Mitchells uses this type of information to constantly communicate with its customers and create a very real one-to-one relationship.

ACXIOM CORP.

Most people have never heard of Acxiom Corp., but it is most certainly aware that you exist, even to the extent that it may know your height and weight. Acxiom specializes in providing information to organizations that want to market products and services. Since the mid-1980s, Acxiom has been gathering information and building a special file called InfoBase. InfoBase contains some or all of the following facts on more than 200 million Americans: home ownership, age, estimated income, cars owned, occupation, buying habits, types of credit cards used, children, and even height and weight.

For a fee, you can buy any or all of this information from Acxiom on any customer demographic (perhaps just the people who live in your neighborhood). And Acxiom does sell this information to other organizations. For example, Allstate Corp. buys information concerning insurance applicants' credit reports, driving records, claims histories, and family relationships (just in case you have a relative who likes to speed) from Acxiom.

In today's world, information is big business, and the use of it is definitely enabled by information technology. Perhaps the real question isn't, How much information is too much? but rather, Who has access to that information and for what purposes are they using it?

These are the sorts of questions you'll face throughout the rest of your life. And you'll do so from two perspectives. The first is a personal one. How much of your information do you want others to be able to access? If you fill out sweepstakes entries on the Internet or even a warranty card for a new product you've recently purchased, you are giving up a great deal of privacy.

The second perspective deals with how you'll use information in the business world. Will you check on your potential customers by using the Internet to see if and when they've purchased a home? Is that legal? Certainly. Is it ethical? That depends on you; ethics, after all, are a matter of personal interpretation.[15,16]

Questions

1. What is the role of information technology at Acxiom? Could it still maintain and provide such a wealth of information without using IT? Acxiom's InfoBase holds 350 terabytes of information. How much information is that? How many double-spaced pages of text would it take to hold all that information?

2. How has Mitchells used information and information technology to enable organizational transformation? Consider how Mitchells operated before it gathered and kept such a wealth of information and how it operates now in the information age.

3. Acxiom and Mitchells have two entirely different sets of business goals: Acxiom uses information to sell as a product (or commodity if you wish) to other businesses, while Mitchells uses information to better serve individual consumers. For each, discuss the flows of information relative to upward, downward, horizontal, and outward directions.

4. What are the ethical and legal issues relating to the fact that Acxiom may know your height and weight and is certainly willing to sell that information to the highest bidder? Can Acxiom legally own that information and sell it to any and every organization?

5. From where do you think Acxiom gathers its information? Could it establish a partnership with other organizations such as Mitchells and buy personal information? How do you feel about this?

6. Many people dream of having a close personal relationship with a clothing retailer such as Mitchells. You simply walk in and the salesperson seems to know everything about you (and remembers you well). However, Mitchells communicates extensively with its customers by e-mail. Do you ever get tired of receiving e-mails that solicit your business? How many of those e-mails do you receive now on a weekly basis? What steps can you take to avoid them?

7. Overall, what's your view of the information age in which we live? Are we better off because we have access to a wealth of information, including personal information? Should organizations such as Acxiom and Mitchells exploit their information for all its worth? Should they consider your feelings?

Key Terms and Concepts

Application software, 19
Artificial intelligence (AI), 24
Banner ad, 26
Central processing unit (CPU), 19
Collaboration system, 24
Culture, 27
Customer-integrated system (CIS), 22
Data, 9
Decentralized computing, 20

Digital economy, 8
Electronic commerce, 5
Electronic data interchange (EDI), 26
Ethics, 15
Executive information system (EIS), 23
External information, 13
Global economy, 8
Group document database, 24
Groupware, 24

Short-Answer Questions

1. How does a knowledge worker differ from other types of workers?
2. What is management information systems (MIS)?
3. What is electronic commerce?
4. How are telecommuting and the virtual workplace related?
5. How is today's economy wants-based?
6. What is a transnational firm?
7. What is the relationship between data and information?
8. What are the personal dimensions of information?
9. What are the three levels of management in an organization?
10. What is information granularity? How does it differ according to the levels of an organization?
11. What is the difference between internal and external information?
12. What are the six categories of information technology (IT) hardware?
13. How are decentralized computing and shared information related to each other?
14. What are the six roles and goals of information technology?

Short-Question Answers

For each of the following answers, provide an appropriate question.

1. The information age.
2. Information, information technology, and people.
3. M-commerce.
4. Global economy.
5. Data.
6. An internal organizational Internet.
7. The downward flow of information.
8. Subjective information.
9. A person who knows how and when to apply technology.
10. Your behavior toward other people.
11. CPU and RAM.
12. Decentralized computing.
13. An extension of a transaction processing system.
14. The manipulation of information to support decision making.

Assignments and Exercises

1. **SURVEYING THE GLOBAL ECONOMY** Visit a local store in your area that sells clothing and perform a small survey. Pick up 10 different pieces of clothing (shoes, shirts, pants, belts, etc.) and note the country in which they were made. Based on just those 10 pieces of clothing, what percentage was made outside the United States? What percentage was made in the United States? Do you think your results are typical of the distribution of clothes made within and outside the United States? Do your results support or contradict our assertion that we now live in a global economy? Why?

2. **FINDING TRUST IN TRUSTe** TRUSTe (www.truste.org) is an organization on the Web that has created specific guidelines for the use of your private information by Web sites to whom you offer it. If a Web site adheres to all of TRUSTe's guidelines, that Web site can then display the TRUSTe logo on its site. That way, you know your private information is protected. TRUSTe has four main guidelines or principles that Web sites displaying its logo must follow. Connect to TRUSTe. What are the four guidelines? Are any or all of these guidelines important to you as an individual? If so, which one or ones and why? Should the government require that all Web sites follow these guidelines or a similar set? Why or why not?

3. **REPORTING ON INTERNET STATISTICS BY BUSINESS SECTOR** NUA (www.nua.ie) claims to be the world's leading resource for Internet statistics and trends. Connect to NUA and choose one of the business sectors located along the left side of the page. Pick a specific article discussing that particular business sector and prepare a short report for your class. Which business sector did you choose? What was the focus of the article you chose? Did some of the statistics surprise you? Considering that you might be interested in working in a business sector on which NUA tracks Internet statistics, would you find NUA's site useful in preparing to go into that business sector? Why or why not?

4. **LEARNING ABOUT AN MIS MAJOR** Using your school's catalog of majors and courses (or the catalog of another school), briefly outline what classes you would have to take to major in management information systems (MIS). Do any of the courses mention specific technology tools such as Java or Oracle? If so, which technology tools are listed? Now, do some searching on the Internet for salaries in the MIS field. What did you find? Does this particular major appeal to you? Why or why not?

5. **REVIEWING THE 100 BEST COMPANIES TO WORK FOR** Each year *Fortune* magazine devotes an issue to the top 100 best companies to work for. Find the most recent issue of *Fortune* that does this. First, develop a numerical summary that describes the 100 companies in terms of their respective industries. Which industries are the most dominant? Pick one of the more dominant industries (preferably one in which you would like to work) and choose a specific highlighted company. Prepare a short class presentation on why that company is among the 100 best to work for.

6. **REDEFINING BUSINESS OPERATIONS THROUGH IT INNOVATION** Many businesses are building customer-integrated systems (CISs) as a way of redefining their operations through the use of information technology. We discussed several in this chapter, with the most notable and obvious example probably being that of banks offering ATMs. For the eight types of businesses below, identify how they are using technology to offer customer-integrated systems. As you describe a CIS for each business type, be sure to include what advantages you receive as a customer. Also, describe how you would have to interface with each type of business if it did not offer a CIS.
   - Airlines
   - Grocery stores
   - Phone companies
   - Hotels
   - Fuel stations
   - Utility companies
   - Cable TV providers
   - Universities and colleges

Discussion Questions

1. Knowledge workers dominate today's business environment. However, many industries still need workers who do not fall into the category of knowledge workers. What industries still need skilled workers? Can you see a time when these jobs will be replaced by knowledge workers? Can you envision circumstances that would actually cause an economy to do an "about face" and begin needing more skilled workers than knowledge workers?

2. The three key resources in management information systems (MIS) are information, information technology, and people. Which of these three resources is the most important? Why? The least important? Why?

3. Telecommuting is like all things: it has a good side and it has a bad side. What are some of the disadvantages or pitfalls of telecommuting? How can these be avoided?

4. As an information-literate knowledge worker for a local distributor of imported foods and spices, you've been asked to prepare a customer mailing list that will be sold to international cuisine restaurants in your area. If you do, would you be acting ethically? If you don't consider the proposal ethical, what if your boss threatened to fire you if you didn't prepare the list? Do you believe you would have any legal recourse if you didn't prepare the list and were subsequently fired?

5. How is your school helping you prepare to take advantage of information technology? What courses have you taken that included teaching you how to use technology? What software packages were taught? To best prepare to enter the job market, how can you determine what software you need to learn?

6. Consider the ATM system that is now worldwide. How does it address your personal dimensions of time, location, and form? Besides just tracking what transactions you've completed using an ATM, what other information might your bank want to know and use concerning your use of the ATM system?

7. Information granularity changes according to the level of an organization. Consider your school, the classes it offers, and the number of students who register in those classes. What sort of information exhibiting coarse granularity would people at the highest levels of your school want to know? What sort of information exhibiting fine granularity would people at the lower levels of your school want to know? As a consumer (student), do you need fine or coarse information? Or perhaps both?

8. In addition to using neural networks to monitor credit card fraud, the same companies also use neural networks to determine whether or not you are a creditworthy risk. By feeding in thousands of credit card applications, the neural network develops a pattern of who is and what isn't a creditworthy risk. Basically, the neural network compares your credit application to those of past ones and recommends an action. What do you think about that? Should you be given or denied a credit card based on what others have done (or failed to do)? Why or why not?

9. Many schools use groupware to offer distance learning classes. Instead of going to class, you communicate with your instructors and classmates via technology. Would you like to take distance learning classes? What are the advantages? Can you learn as much without going to class and personally interacting with your instructor and classmates? What might be some of the disadvantages of distance learning? Is there a happy medium—how about going to school for only one class session per week and then attending the other virtually via technology? Is this a good or bad idea?

10. We often say that hardware is the *physical* interface to a technology system while software is the *intellectual* interface. How is your hardware your physical interface to your computer? How is your software your intellectual interface to your computer? Do you see technology progressing to the point that we may no longer distinguish between hardware and software and thus no longer perceive differing physical and intellectual interfaces?

Using the Internet as a Tool to Find a Job

Electronic commerce is a great new business horizon. And it's not "just around the corner" any more. Electronic commerce is already here, and businesses all over the world are taking advantage of it. Today, information technology can help you land a job. You can use your knowledge of IT and IT itself to help you find potential employers, place your résumé in their hands, locate summer internships, and learn the art of selling yourself during the interview and negotiation process. How? By simply cruising the Internet and using online job databases and service providers as well as accessing information about how to prepare for an interview (among other things).

Are you taking advantage of the Internet to find a job? If you're not, we'd like to help you by introducing you to just a few of the thousands of Web sites that can help you find a job. In this section, we've included a number of Web sites related to finding a job through the Internet. On the Web site that supports this text (www.mhhe.com/haag, select "Electronic Commerce Projects"), we've provided direct links to all these Web sites as well as many, many more. These are a great starting point for completing this REAL HOT section. We would also encourage you to search the Internet for others.

JOB DATABASES

There are, quite literally, thousands of sites that provide you with databases of job postings. Some are better than others. Some focus on specific industries; others offer postings only for executive managers. For the best review of job Web sites, connect to two different places. The first is the 100 Top Network (www.100.com, choose Career). The second is the Career Resources Homepage at www.careerresource.net. This site provides the most comprehensive list of the available job Web sites. There, you'll find a list of more than 1,000 job Web sites.

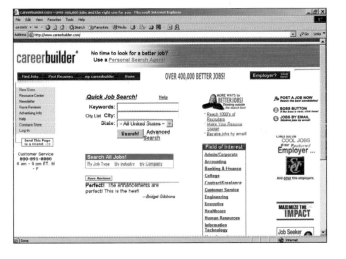

Think for a moment about the job you want. What would be its title? In which industry do you want to work? In what part of the country do you want to live? What special skills do you possess? (For example, if you're looking for an accounting job, you may be specializing in auditing.) Is there a specific organization for which you would like to work?

Connect to a couple of different databases, search for your job, and answer the following questions for each database.

- **A.** What is the date of the last update?
- **B.** Are career opportunities abroad listed as a separate category or are they integrated with domestic jobs?
- **C.** Can you search for a specific organization?
- **D.** Can you search by geographic location? If so, how? By state? By city? By ZIP code?
- **E.** Does the site provide direct links to e-mail addresses for those organizations posting jobs?

F. Can you apply for a position online? If so, how do you send your résumé?

G. Can you search by a specific industry?

CREATING AND POSTING AN ELECTRONIC RÉSUMÉ

Most, if not all, job databases focus on two groups: employers and employees. As a potential employee, you search to find jobs that meet your qualifications and desires. Likewise, employers search job databases that contain résumés so they can find people (like you) who meet their qualifications and desires. In this instance, you need to build an electronic résumé (e-résumé or e-portfolio which we discuss in "Extended Learning Module I") and leave it at the various job database sites as you perform your searches. That way, organizations performing searches can find you.

Almost all the job database sites we've listed give you the ability to create and post an electronic résumé. Visit two new job database sites (different from those you visited to find a job). In each, go through the process of creating an e-résumé, posting it, and making some sort of modification to it. As you do, answer the following questions for each of the sites.

A. Do you have to register as a user to build an e-résumé?

B. Once a potential employer performs a search that matches your e-résumé, how can that employer contact you?

C. What valuable tips for building a good e-résumé are available?

D. Once you build your e-résumé, can you use it to perform a job search?

E. When you modify your e-résumé, can you update your existing e-résumé or must you delete the old one and create a new one?

F. How many key terms concerning your qualifications can you include in your e-résumé?

G. For what time frame does your e-résumé stay active?

SEARCHING NEWSPAPERS THE NEW-FASHIONED WAY

One of today's most popular ways to find a job is to search the classified sections of newspapers. Each Sunday (if your library is open) and Monday you can visit your local library and find a gathering of people searching through the classified sections of the *Los Angeles Times, Boston Herald,* and *Dallas Morning News* in the hope of finding a job. Most of these people are attempting to find a job in a specific geographic location. For example, a person looking in the *Dallas Morning News* is probably most interested in finding a job in the Dallas/Ft. Worth area. And as you might well guess, newspapers are not to be left off the Internet bandwagon. Today you can find hundreds of online editions of daily newspapers. And the majority of these provide their classified sections in some sort of searchable electronic format. Pick several newspapers, perform an online search for a job that interests you at each newspaper, and answer the following questions.

A. Can you search by location/city?

B. Can you search back issues or only the most recent issue?

C. Does the newspaper provide direct links to Web sites or provide some other profile information for those organizations posting jobs?

D. Does the newspaper provide direct links to e-mail addresses for those organizations posting jobs?

E. Is the newspaper affiliated with any of the major job database providers? If so, which one(s)?

LOCATING THAT "ALL IMPORTANT" INTERNSHIP

Have you ever noticed that a large number of jobs require experience? That being the case, how does someone gain relevant experience through a job when experience is required to get the job? As it turns out, that has always been a perplexing dilemma for many college students, and one way to solve it is by obtaining an internship. Internships provide you with valuable knowledge about your field, pay you for your work, and offer you that valuable experience you need to move up in your career.

At the end of this section, we've provided you with a number of Web sites that offer internship possibilities—visit a few of them. Did you find any internships in line with your career? What about pay? Did you find both paying and nonpaying internships? How did these internship sites compare to the more traditional job database sites you looked at earlier? Why do you think this is true?

INTERVIEWING AND NEGOTIATING

The Internet is a vast repository of information—no doubt more information than you'll ever need in your entire life. During the job search process, however, the Internet can offer you very valuable specific information. In the area of interviewing and negotiating, for example, the Internet contains more than 5,000 sites devoted to interviewing skills, negotiating tips, and the like.

Interviewing and negotiating are just as important as searching for a job. Once you line up that first important interview, you can still not land the job if you're not properly prepared. If you do receive a job offer, you may be surprised to know that you can negotiate such things as moving expenses, signing bonuses, and allowances for technology in your home.

We've provided Web sites for you that address the interviewing and negotiating skills you need in today's marketplace. Review some of these sites (and any others that you may find). Then, develop a list of do's and don'ts for the interviewing process. Finally, develop a list of tips that seem helpful to you that will increase your effectiveness during the negotiation process. Once you've developed these two lists, prepare a short class presentation.

GOING RIGHT TO THE SOURCE: THE ORGANIZATION YOU WANT

Today, many organizations are posting positions they have open on their own Web sites. Their idea is simple. If you like an organization enough to visit its Web site, you might just want to work there. For example, if you connect to the *Gap* at www.gap.com and buy clothes online, you might consider working there if the opportunity is right.

Choose several organizations that you'd be interested in working for. For each organization, connect to its Web site, look for job opportunities, and answer the following questions:

A. Are you able to find job opportunities?
B. How difficult is it to find the job opportunities?
C. Are positions grouped or categorized by type?
D. Is a discussion of career paths included?
E. How do you obtain an application form?
F. Are international opportunities available? Do the job descriptions include a list of qualifications?
G. Are there direct links to e-mail addresses for further questions?

EXTENDED LEARNING MODULE A

COMPUTER HARDWARE AND SOFTWARE

Student Learning Outcomes

1. DEFINE INFORMATION TECHNOLOGY (IT) AND ITS TWO BASIC CATEGORIES: HARDWARE AND SOFTWARE.

2. DESCRIBE CATEGORIES OF COMPUTERS BY SIZE.

3. COMPARE THE ROLES OF PERSONAL PRODUCTIVITY, VERTICAL MARKET, AND HORIZONTAL MARKET SOFTWARE.

4. DESCRIBE THE ROLES OF OPERATING SYSTEM AND UTILITY SOFTWARE AS COMPONENTS OF SYSTEM SOFTWARE.

5. DEFINE THE PURPOSES OF THE SIX MAJOR CATEGORIES OF HARDWARE.

Introduction

In this extended learning module, we cover the basics of computer hardware and software, including terminology, characteristics of various devices, and how everything works together to create a complete and usable computer system. If you've had a previous computing concepts course, this material will be a quick, solid review for you. If this is your first real exposure to hardware and software technologies, you'll definitely learn a great deal from this module.

Information technology (IT) is any computer-based tool that people use to work with information and support the information and information-processing needs of an organization. So information technology (IT) is composed of the Internet, a personal computer, a cell phone that can access the Web, a personal digital assistant you use for note taking and appointment scheduling, presentation software you use to create a slide show, a printer, a joystick or gamepad for playing video games . . . the list is almost endless (see Figure A.1).

All of these technologies help you perform specific information-processing tasks. For example, a printer allows you to create a paper version of a document, the Internet connects you to people all over the world, a floppy disk allows you to store information for use at a later time, and word processing software helps you create letters, memos, and term papers.

So, do you need all of these various technologies? Yes and no. As you'll read throughout this module, there are categories of both hardware and software. More than likely, you'll need some sort of technology within each category. But you certainly won't need every single piece of available technology.

Figure A.1
Information Technology (IT) Includes Many Tools

A Quick Tour of Technology

There are two basic categories of technology: hardware and software. **Hardware** is the physical devices that make up a computer (often referred to as a *computer system*). **Software** is the set of instructions that your hardware executes to carry out a specific task for you. If you create a graph, you would use various hardware devices such as a keyboard to enter information and a monitor to see the graph, and you would use software such as Microsoft Excel, the most popular spreadsheet software.

All hardware falls into one of six categories. Here's a quick summary (see Figure A.2).

1. An **input device** is a tool you use to capture information and commands.

2. An **output device** is a tool you use to see, hear, or otherwise accept the results of your information-processing requests.

Figure A.2

Six Categories of
Computer Hardware

Mice and keyboards are the most
popular input devices.

DSL modems are
telecommunications devices.

Monitors are the most
common output devices.

The Intel Pentium 4 is a CPU.

Video cards connect a monitor to the
rest of the hardware.

Floppy disks are common storage devices.

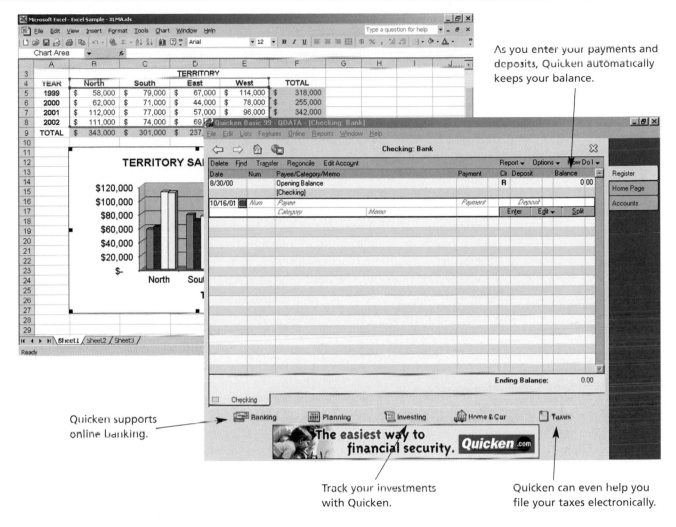

As you enter your payments and deposits, Quicken automatically keeps your balance.

Quicken supports online banking.

Track your investments with Quicken.

Quicken can even help you file your taxes electronically.

Figure A.3

Quicken and Excel Are Application Software Tools

3. A *storage device* is a tool you use to store information for use at a later time.

4. The *central processing unit (CPU)* is the actual hardware that interprets and executes the software instructions and coordinates how all the other hardware devices work together. *RAM,* or *random access memory,* is temporary storage that holds the information you're working with, the application software you're using, and the operating system software you're using.

5. A *telecommunications device* is a tool you use to send information to and receive it from another person or location.

6. Connecting devices include such things as parallel ports into which you would connect a printer and connector cords to connect your printer to the parallel port.

There are two main types of software: application and system. *Application software* is the software that enables you to solve specific problems or perform specific tasks (see Figure A.3). Microsoft PowerPoint, for example, can help you create slides for a presentation, so it's application software. So is Microsoft FrontPage because it helps you create and publish a Web page or Web site. From an organizational perspective, payroll software, collaborative software such as videoconferencing (within groupware), and inventory management software are all examples of application software.

System software handles tasks specific to technology management and coordinates the interaction of all technology devices. System software includes both operating system software and utility software. *Operating system software* is system software that controls your application software and manages how your hardware devices work together. Popular personal operating system software includes Microsoft Windows XP, Microsoft Windows 2000 Me, Mac OS (for Apple computers), and Linux (an open source operating system). There are also operating systems for networks (Microsoft Windows NT is an example), operating systems for personal digital assistants (Windows CE is an example), and operating systems for just about every other type of technology configuration.

Utility software is software that provides additional functionality to your operating system. Utility software includes anti-virus software, screen savers, disk optimization software, uninstaller software (for properly removing unwanted software), and a host of others. Just because utility software provides "additional" functionality doesn't mean that this type of software is optional. For example, anti-virus software protects you from computer viruses that can be deadly for your computer. You definitely need anti-virus software.

So ends our quick tour of technology. In the remainder of this module we'll explore categories of computers by size, software in more detail, hardware in more detail, and finally how all technology components work together to perform a specific task for you.

Categories of Computers by Size

Computers come in different shapes, sizes, and colors. Some are small enough that you can carry them around with you, while others are the size of a telephone booth. Size in some way equates to power and speed, and thus price.

PERSONAL DIGITAL ASSISTANTS (PDAS)

A *personal digital assistant (PDA)* is a small hand-held computer that helps you surf the Web and perform simple tasks such as note taking, calendaring, appointment scheduling, and maintaining an address book. The PDA screen is touch sensitive, allowing you to write directly on the screen with the screen capturing what you're writing. PDAs today cost between $200 and $500.

NOTEBOOK COMPUTERS

A *notebook computer* is a fully functional computer designed for you to carry around and run on battery power. Notebooks come equipped with all of the technology you need to meet your personal needs and weigh as little as 4 pounds. If you need a fully functional computer in a variety of places—home, work, school, and/or on the road—then a notebook computer may be just the answer. Notebook computers range in price from about $800 to several thousand dollars.

DESKTOP COMPUTERS

A *desktop computer* is the most popular choice for personal computing needs. You can choose a desktop computer with a horizontal system box (the box is where the CPU, RAM, and storage devices are held) and place a monitor on top of it or choose a desk-

Some desktops have vertical system boxes called "towers."

PDAs are small hand-held computers.

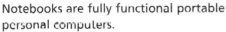

Notebooks are fully functional portable personal computers.

Figure A.4

PDAs, Notebooks, and Desktops

top computer with a vertical system box (called a tower) that you usually place on the floor near your work area. Desktop computers range in price from a little less than $500 to several thousand dollars. Dollar for dollar with comparable characteristics, a desktop computer is faster and more powerful than a notebook computer.

Which you need—PDA, notebook, or desktop computer—is a function of your unique individual needs. PDAs offer great portability and allow you to keep a calendar, send and receive e-mail, take short notes, and even access the Web. But they certainly can't help you write a term paper, build a Web site, or create a complex graph with statistical software. For any of those tasks, you would need either a notebook or a desktop computer.

So, there's another question. You need a computer that supports full word processing, spreadsheet, presentation, Web site development, and some other capabilities. Should you buy a notebook or a desktop computer? In short, you need to decide *where* you'll need your computer. If you need to use your computer at home and at school (or perhaps at work), then you should buy a notebook computer because it is, in fact, portable. But, if you think you might want a notebook because it would be nice to take it with you on vacation, think again. Do you really want to sit in your hotel room and work on your computer instead of having fun on the beach? Probably not.

In the future, we believe the capabilities of PDAs will improve so that you can in fact perform "complex" tasks such as creating an elaborate spreadsheet or graph and even integrating speech recognition. To learn more about some of today's best PDAs, connect to the Web site that supports this text at www.mhhe.com/haag.

MINICOMPUTERS, MAINFRAME COMPUTERS, AND SUPERCOMPUTERS

PDAs, notebooks, and desktop computers are designed to meet your personal information-processing needs. In business, however, many people often need to access and use the same computer simultaneously. In this case, businesses need computing technologies that multiple people can access and use at the same time. Computers of this type include minicomputers, mainframe computers, and supercomputers (see Figure A.5).

A ***minicomputer*** (sometimes called a ***mid-range computer***) is designed to meet the computing needs of several people simultaneously in a small to medium-size business environment. Minicomputers are more powerful than desktop computers but also cost more, ranging in price from $5,000 to several hundred thousand dollars. Businesses often use minicomputers as servers, either for creating a Web presence or as an internal computer on which shared information and software is placed. For this reason, mini-

Figure A.5

Minicomputers, Mainframes, and Supercomputers

Mainframe computers support the information-processing tasks of large businesses.

Supercomputers are very expensive and fast "number crunchers."

Minicomputers are well suited for small to medium size businesses.

computers are well suited for business environments in which people need to share common information, processing power, and/or certain peripheral devices such as high-quality, fast laser printers.

A *mainframe computer* (sometimes just called a *mainframe*) is a computer designed to meet the computing needs of hundreds of people in a large business environment. So mainframe computers are a step up in size, power, capability, and cost from minicomputers. Mainframes can easily cost in excess of $1 million. With processing speeds greater than 1 trillion instructions per second (compared to a typical desktop that can process about 2.5 billion instructions per second), mainframes can easily handle the processing requests of hundreds of people simultaneously.

Supercomputers are the fastest, most powerful, and most expensive type of computer. Organizations such as NASA that are heavily involved in research and "number crunching" employ supercomputers because of the speed with which they can process information. Other large, customer-oriented businesses such as General Motors and AT&T employ supercomputers just to handle customer information and transaction processing.

How much do you really need to know about the technical specifics (CPU speed, storage disk capacity, and so on), prices, and capabilities of minicomputers, mainframe computers, and supercomputers? Not much, unless you plan to major in information technology. As a typical and well-informed knowledge worker you really only need to know what we've stated above. What you should definitely concentrate on, though, is the technical specifics, prices, and capabilities of PDAs, notebooks, and desktop computers. These will be your companions for your entire business career. Learn and know them well.

Software: Your Intellectual Interface

The most important tool in your technology tool set is software. Software contains the instructions that your hardware executes to perform an information-processing task for you. So, software is really your *intellectual interface*, designed to automate processing tasks that you would undertake with your mind. Without software, your computer is a very expensive and useless doorstop. As we've stated before, there are two categories of software: application and system.

APPLICATION SOFTWARE

Application software is the software you use to meet your specific information-processing needs, including payroll, customer relationship management, project management, training, word processing, and many, many others.

PERSONAL PRODUCTIVITY SOFTWARE

Personal productivity software helps you perform personal tasks—such as writing a memo, creating a graph, and creating a slide presentation—that you can usually do even if you don't own a computer. You're probably already familiar with some personal productivity software tools including Microsoft Word and Excel, Netscape Communicator or Internet Explorer, and Quicken (personal finance software).

Category	Examples*
Word processing—Helps you create papers, letters, memos, and other basic documents	• Microsoft Word • Corel WordPerfect
Spreadsheet—Helps you work primarily with numbers, including performing calculations and creating graphs	• Microsoft Excel • LotusIBM Lotus 1-2-3
Presentation—Helps you create and edit information that will appear in electronic slides	• Corel Presentations • LotusIBM Freelance Graphics
Desktop publishing—Extends word processing software by including design and formatting techniques to enhance the layout and appearance of a document	• Microsoft Publisher • Quark QuarkXPress
Personal information management (PIM)—Helps you create and maintain (1) to-do lists, (2) appointments and calendars, and (3) points of contact	• Corel Central • LotusIBM Organizer
Personal finance—Helps you maintain your checkbook, prepare a budget, track investments, monitor your credit card balances, and pay bills electronically	• Quicken Quicken • Microsoft Money
Web authoring—Helps you design and develop Web sites and pages that you publish on the Web	• Microsoft FrontPage • LotusIBM FastSite
Graphics—Helps you create and edit photos and art	• Microsoft PhotoDraw • Kodak Imaging for Windows
Communications—Helps you communicate with other people	• Microsoft Outlook • Internet Explorer
Database management system (DBMS)—Helps you specify the logical organization for a database and access and use the information within a database	• Microsoft Access • FileMaker FileMaker Pro

* Publisher name given first.

Figure A.6

Categories of Personal Productivity Software

In fact, two modules in this text help you learn how to use two of these tools—*Extended Learning Module D* (for Microsoft Excel, spreadsheet software) and *Extended Learning Module J* (for Microsoft Access, database management system software). Figure A.6 lists and describes the 10 major categories of personal productivity software and includes some of the more popular packages within each.

VERTICAL AND HORIZONTAL MARKET SOFTWARE

While performing organizational processes in your career, you'll also frequently use two other categories of application software: vertical market software and horizontal market software.

Vertical market software is application software that is unique to a particular industry. For example, the health care industry has a variety of application software that is unique to it, including radiology software, patient-scheduling software, nursing allocation software, and pharmaceutical software. This type of software is written with a specific industry in mind. So, health care industry patient-scheduling software wouldn't work for scheduling hair and manicure appointments in a beauty salon.

Horizontal market software is application software that is general enough to be suitable for use in a variety of industries. Examples of horizontal market software include

BUYING PERSONAL PRODUCTIVITY SOFTWARE SUITES

When you buy personal productivity software, we recommend that you do so in the form of a suite. A *software suite (suite)* is bundled software that comes from the same publisher and costs less than buying all the software pieces individually.

In this project, your team has two tasks. First, research the most popular personal productivity software suites. These include Microsoft Office, Corel WordPerfect Office, and LotusIBM SmartSuite. For each, identify which specific software pieces fall into the 10 categories of personal productivity software listed on page 48. Then, try to find some information that describes the market share of each personal productivity software suite.

Second, choose one specific personal productivity software suite. Determine the individual price for each piece of software included in it. Now, perform a price comparison. How much cheaper is the entire suite? Can you think of a situation in which someone would buy the individual pieces as opposed to the entire suite? If so, please describe it.

- Inventory management
- Payroll
- Accounts receivable
- Billing
- Invoice processing
- Human resource management

The preceding functions (and many others) are very similar, if not identical, in many different industries. So, software publishers have developed one particular piece of software (e.g., accounts receivable) that can be used by many different industries.

If you think about it, personal productivity software is actually a type of horizontal market software in that it is general enough to be suitable for use in a variety of industries. No matter in which industry you work, you need basic word processing software for creating memos, business plans, and other basic documents.

There are, however, some key differences between personal productivity software and horizontal and vertical market software. One difference is the issue of price. You can buy a full suite of personal productivity software for less than $400. In contrast, some individual horizontal and vertical market software packages may cost as much as $500,000 or more. Second is the issue of customizability. When you purchase personal productivity software, you cannot change the way it works. That is, you're buying the right to use it but not to change how it operates. With horizontal and vertical market software you may in fact also be able to purchase the right to change the way the software works. So, if you find a payroll software package that fits most of your organizational needs, you can buy the software and the right to change the operation of the software so that it meets 100 percent of your needs. This is a very common business practice when purchasing and using horizontal and vertical market software.

In Chapter 6 (Systems Development), we discuss how organizations go about the process of developing software unique to their particular needs, including how organizations can and do purchase vertical and horizontal market software and then customize that software.

SYSTEM SOFTWARE

System software is that category of software that controls how your various technology tools work together as you use your application software to perform specific information-processing tasks. System software includes two basic categories: operating system and utility.

OPERATING SYSTEM SOFTWARE

Operating system software is system software that controls your application software and manages how your hardware devices work together. For example, while using Excel to create a graph, if you choose to print the graph, your operating system software would take over, ensure that you have a printer attached, ensure that the printer has paper (and notify you if it doesn't), and send your graph to the printer along with instructions on how to print it.

Your operating system software also supports a variety of useful features, one of which is multitasking. *Multitasking* allows you to work with more than one piece of software at a time. Suppose you wanted to create a graph in Excel and insert it into a word processing document (see Figure A.7). With multitasking, you can have both pieces of application software open at the same time, and even see both on the screen. So, when you complete the creation of your graph, you can easily copy and paste it into your word processing document without having to go through a series of steps to exit out of the spreadsheet software and then start your word processing software.

Within operating system software, there are different types for personal environments and for organizational environments that support many users simultaneously (these are called *network operating systems* or *NOSs,* and we explore some of these in greater detail in *Extended Learning Module E: Network Basics*). Popular personal operating systems include

- *Microsoft Windows 2000 Professional (Windows 2000 Pro)*—For people who have a personal computer connected to a network of other computers at work or at school.
- *Microsoft Windows 2000 Millennium (Windows 2000 Me)*—For a home computer user with utilities for setting up a home network and performing video, photo, and music editing and cataloging.
- *Microsoft Windows XP Home*—Microsoft's latest upgrade to Windows 2000 Me, with enhanced features for allowing multiple people to use the same computer.
- *Microsoft Windows XP Professional (Windows XP Pro)*—Microsoft's latest upgrade to Windows 2000 Pro.
- *Mac OS*—The operating system for today's Apple computers.
- *Linux*—An open-source operating system that provides a rich operating environment for high-end workstations and network servers.

If you're considering purchasing a notebook computer that you'll use extensively at school connected to a network there, we recommend that you contact your school's technology support department to determine which operating system is best for you.

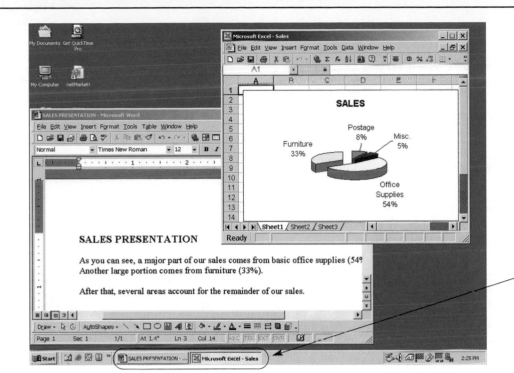

Figure A.7

Most Operating Systems
Support Multitasking

The task bar area tells
you what software
you're currently working
with.

UTILITY SOFTWARE

Utility software is software that adds additional functionality to your operating system. A simple example is that of screen saver software (which is probably also a part of your operating system). Most importantly, utility software includes anti-virus software. *Anti-virus software* is utility software that scans for and often eliminates viruses in your RAM and on your storage devices. Viruses are everywhere today, with 200 to 300 new ones surfacing each month. Some viruses are benign: they cause your screen to blank (or something like that) but do not corrupt your information. Other viruses are deadly, often reformatting your hard disk or altering the contents of your files. You definitely need anti-virus software to combat them. We talk much more about this vitally important topic, including denial-of-service attacks, in Chapter 8.

Other types of utility software include

- *Crash-proof software*—Utility software that helps you save information if your system crashes and you're forced to turn it off and then back on again.
- *Uninstaller software*—Utility software that you can use to remove software from your hard disk that you no longer want.
- *Disk optimization software*—Utility software that organizes your information on your hard disk in the most efficient way.

We would once again state that utility software is not optional software just because it adds additional functionality to your computer. You definitely need utility software. The four specific pieces we described above are just a few of the many you'll find in a utility software suite.

EVALUATING UTILITY SOFTWARE SUITES

Just as you can purchase personal productivity software suites that contain many pieces of software, you can also purchase utility software suites. In the table below, we've included the three most popular utility software suites: McAfee Office Pro, Norton SystemWorks, and Ontrack SystemSuite.

As a team, do some research and determine what major pieces of software are included in each. As you do, fill in the table.

Now, pick a particular utility suite and visit its Web site. What is the process for updating your software? Is it free? How often does the site recommend that you update your utility software?

Utility software piece	McAfee Office Pro	Norton SystemWorks	Ontrack SystemSuite

Hardware: Your Physical Interface

To properly understand the significant role of your hardware (the physical components of your computer), it helps to know something about how your computer works differently from you. You work with information in the form of characters (A–Z, a–z, and special ones such as an asterisk) and numbers (0–9). Computers, on the other hand, work in terms of bits and bytes. Basically, computers use electricity to function, and electrical pulses have two states: on and off.

A *binary digit (bit)* is the smallest unit of information that your computer can process. A bit can either be a 1 (on) or a 0 (off). The challenge from a technological point of view is to be able to represent all our characters, special symbols, and numbers in binary form. Using ASCII is one way to do this. *ASCII (American Standard Code for Information Interchange)* is the coding system that most personal computers use to represent, process, and store information. In ASCII, a group of eight bits represents one natural language character and is called a *byte.*

For example, if you were to type the word *cool* on the keyboard, your keyboard (a hardware device) would change it into four bytes—one for each character—that would look like the following used by other parts of your computer (see Figure A.8):

01100011	01001111	01001111	01001100
c	o	o	l

This grouping of 1s and 0s is then used throughout the rest of your computer, as it travels from one device to another, is stored on a storage device, and is processed by your CPU.

There are three important conclusions that you should draw from the previous discussion. First, your hardware works with information in a different form (although with the same meaning) than you do. You work with characters, special symbols, and the numbers 0–9. Your computer, on the other hand, represents all these in a binary form, a collection of unique 1s and 0s. Second, the term *byte* is the bridge between people and a computer. A computer can store one character, special symbol, or number in the form of a byte. One byte is essentially one character. So, a floppy disk with a storage capacity of 1.44 megabytes can hold approximately 1.44 million characters of information.

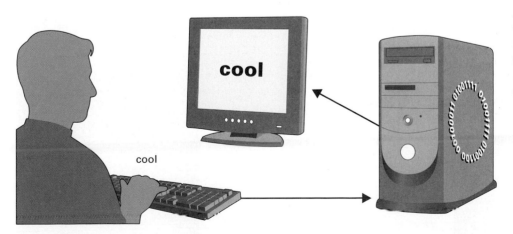

Figure A.8

Information Representations as It Moves throughout Your Computer

Finally, a primary role of your input and output devices (such as a keyboard and monitor) is to convert information from one form to another, either from how you understand information to bits and bytes (the role of input devices) or from computer-stored bits and bytes to a form you understand (the role of output devices). All other hardware internally works with information in the form of bits and bytes.

COMMON INPUT DEVICES

An *input device* is a tool you use to capture information and commands. You can, for example, use a keyboard to type in information and use a mouse to point and click on buttons and icons. And, as we just stated, input devices are responsible for converting your representation of information (the letter *c* for example) into a form that the rest of your computer can work with (01100011).

Within almost any complete technology environment, you'll find numerous input devices, some of which have more suitable applications in a business setting than in a personal setting. Some common input devices (see Figure A.9) include

- *Keyboard*—Today's most popular input technology.
- *Point-of-sale (POS)*—For capturing information at the point of a transaction, typically in a retail environment.

Figure A.9

Popular Input Devices

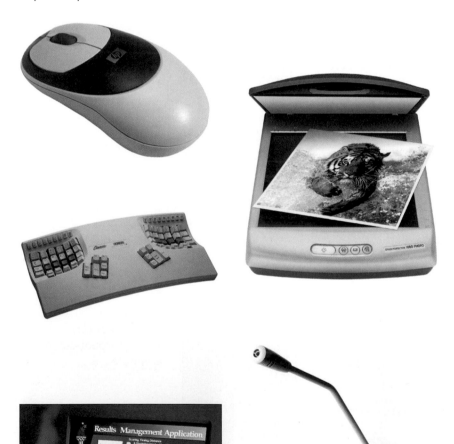

- *Microphone*—For capturing live sounds such as a dog barking or your voice (for automatic speech recognition).
- *Mouse*—Today's most popular "pointing" input device.
- *Trackball*—An upside-down, stationary mouse in which you use the ball instead of the device (mainly for notebooks).
- *Pointing stick*—Small rubberlike pointing device that causes the pointer to move on the screen as you apply directional pressure (popular on notebooks).
- *Touch pad*—Another form of a stationary mouse on which you move your finger to cause the pointer on the screen to move (popular also on notebooks).
- *Touch screen*—Special screen that lets you use your finger to point at and touch a particular function you want to perform.
- *Bar code reader*—Captures information that exists in the form of vertical bars whose width and distance apart determine a number.
- *Optical mark recognition (OMR)*—Detects the presence or absence of a mark in a predetermined place (popular for multiple choice exams).
- *Scanner*—Captures images, photos, and artwork that already exist on paper.

COMMON OUTPUT DEVICES

An *output device* is a tool you use to see, hear, or otherwise accept the results of your information-processing requests. Among output devices, printers and monitors are the most common, but you'll also usually find speakers and even plotters (special printers that draw output on a page) being used. And output devices are responsible for converting computer-stored information into a form that you can understand.

MONITORS

Monitors come in two varieties: CRT or flat-panel display (see Figure A.10). *CRTs* are monitors that look like television sets, while *flat-panel displays* are thin, lightweight monitors that take up much less space than CRTs. When considering monitors as an output device, you need to think about monitor size, viewable screen size, resolution, monitor type, and dot pitch.

Monitor size determines how large your entire monitor is, measured diagonally from corner to corner. Monitor size, especially for CRTs, gives you some idea of the amount of space your monitor will require. However, the size that really is of interest to you is

Figure A.10

Monitors Are Common Output Devices

viewable screen size, often expressed as *VIS* or *viewable inch screen*. Viewable screen size tells you the size of your screen, which is measured diagonally from corner to corner and is always smaller than monitor size. Viewable screen size tells you the size of the screen on which you will see things. So, a monitor with a 17-inch VIS has a screen on which you will see things that measures 17 inches diagonally.

The ***resolution of a screen*** is the number of pixels it has. Pixels (picture elements) are the dots that make up an image on your screen. For example, a monitor with a resolution given as 1,024 × 768 has 1,024 pixels horizontally and 768 pixels vertically. The number of dots varies with the type of monitor you have, but larger numbers (of pixels) provide clearer and crisper screen images than smaller ones. Monitor types range from basic VGA (with a resolution of 640 × 480) to QXGA (with a resolution of 2,048 × 1,536). QXGA monitors obviously cost the most and provide the clearest images.

Dot pitch is the distance between the centers of a pair of like-colored pixels. So, a monitor with .24 mm dot pitch (.24 millimeters between pair of like-colored pixels) is better than one with .28 mm dot pitch because the dots are smaller and closer together, giving you a better quality image.

PRINTERS

Printers are another common type of output device, creating output on paper. A printer's sharpness and clarity depend on its resolution. The ***resolution of a printer*** is the number of dots per inch (dpi) it produces, which is the same principle as the resolution in monitors. So, the more dots per inch, the better the image, and usually, the more costly the printer.

Most high-end personal printers have a resolution of 1,200 × 1,200 dpi or better. Multiplying these numbers together gives you 1,440,000 dots per square inch. Also, printers that have the same number of dots per inch both vertically and horizontally give you a better quality image.

Common types of printers (see Figure A.11) include

- ***Inkjet printers***—Make images by forcing ink droplets through nozzles. Standard inkjet printers use four colors: black, cyan (blue), magenta (purplish pink), and yellow. Some inkjet printers produce high-quality images and are often advertised as photo printers. These have six colors (offering a second shade of magenta and cyan).

Figure A.11

Printers Are Also
Common Output Devices

FINDING A PRINTER TO MEET YOUR NEEDS

A printer for a personal environment is definitely a personal choice. Some people care only about print quality for words and numbers. Others may want a personal printer that creates high-quality color images. Whatever the case, you need to choose a printer carefully.

As you think about buying a printer, do so first in terms of quality and speed. Once you've considered those two aspects, find one inkjet, one laser, and one multifunction printer that will meet your needs. Compare them based on price and capability. Which would you choose and why?

Finally, check out some complete computer systems that you can buy at a local computer store. Do they include a printer for free? If so, would getting this printer for free encourage you to purchase the system? Why or why not?

- *Laser printers*—Form images using an electrostatic process, the same way a photocopier works. Laser printers are more expensive than inkjet printers but do provide higher quality images. Most common personal laser printers print only in black and white. You can buy high-end color laser printers, but be ready to spend a lot more money.
- *Multifunction printers*—Scan, copy, and fax, as well as print. These are becoming quite popular in the personal technology arena, mainly because they cost less than if you bought separate tools (printer, scanner, copier, and fax machine). Multifunction printers can be either inkjet or laser, with the latter being more expensive and providing better quality.

CHARACTERISTICS OF CPUS AND RAM

Together, your CPU and RAM make up the real brains of your computer. Your CPU will largely determine the price of your computer system. The *central processing unit (CPU)* is the actual hardware that interprets and executes the software instructions and coordinates how all the other hardware devices work together. *RAM*, or *random access memory*, is temporary storage that holds the information you're working with, the application software you're using, and the operating system software you're using.

The CPU is often referred to as a microprocessor or a CPU chip. The dominant manufacturers of CPUs today include Intel (with its Celeron and Pentium lines for personal computers) and AMD (with its Athlon series). The most helpful information when comparing CPUs is their relative speeds.

CPU speed is usually quoted in megahertz and gigahertz. *Megahertz (MHz)* is the number of millions of CPU cycles per second. *Gigahertz (GHz)* is the number of billions of CPU cycles per second. The number of CPU cycles per second determines how fast a CPU carries out the software instructions; more cycles per second means faster processing. And, as you might expect, faster CPUs cost more than their slower counterparts.

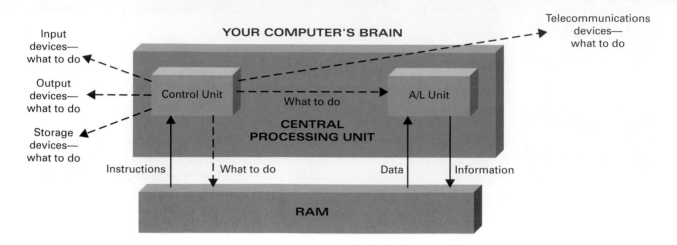

Figure A.12

Your CPU and RAM at Work

A CPU contains two primary parts: control unit and arithmetic/logic unit (see Figure A.12). The ***control unit*** interprets software instructions and literally tells the other hardware devices what to do, based on the software instructions. The ***arithmetic/logic unit (A/L unit)*** performs all arithmetic operations (for example, addition and subtraction) and all logic operations (such as sorting and comparing numbers).

These two units perform very different functions. The control unit actually gets another instruction from RAM, which contains your software (this is called a *retrieve*). It then interprets the instruction, decides what each other device must do, and finally tells each device what to do (this is called *decoding*). The A/L unit, on the other hand, responds to the control unit and does whatever it dictates, either performing an arithmetic or a logic operation (this is called an *execution*). At the end of this module, we'll take you through a small program that demonstrates all these steps at work.

RAM is a sort of chalkboard that your CPU uses while it processes information and software instructions. That is why we refer to RAM as "temporary." When you turn off your computer, everything in RAM is literally wiped clean. That's also why people (and your operating system) will always tell you to save your work before shutting down your computer. So, while you type in a term paper using word processing software, the contents of your term paper (that appear on your screen) are actually stored in RAM. When you perform a save function, the contents are copied from RAM to your designated storage device.

RAM capacity is expressed in bytes, with megabytes being the most common. A ***megabyte (MB or M or Meg)*** is roughly 1 million bytes. So, if your computer has 256MB of RAM, your RAM can hold roughly 256 million characters of information and software instructions. RAM is cheap compared to most other parts of your computer, so don't hesitate to buy as much as you need.

COMMON STORAGE DEVICES

As opposed to RAM, which is temporary, storage devices don't lose their contents when you turn off your computer. Although we use the term *permanent* for storage devices, most do give you the ability to change your information or erase it altogether. When considering which storage device(s) are best, you should look at two questions: (1) Do you need to be able to update the information on the storage device? and (2) How much information do you have to store?

Some storage devices, such as a hard disk, offer you easy update capabilities and a large storage capacity. Others, such as floppy disks, offer you easy update capabilities but with limited storage capacities. Still others, such as CD-ROM, offer no update capabilities but do possess large storage capacities. When we talk about storage device capacities, we still measure it in terms of bytes including megabytes, gigabytes, and terabytes. A *gigabyte (GB* or *Gig)* is roughly 1 billion characters. A *terabyte (TB)* is roughly 1 trillion bytes. Most standard desktops today have a hard disk with storage capacity in excess of 20GB. And hard disks (sometimes called hard disk packs) for large organizational computer systems can hold in excess of 100TB of information. To give you some idea of capacity, consider that a typical double-spaced page of pure text is roughly 2,000 characters. So, a 20GB (20 gigabyte or 20 billion character) hard disk can hold approximately 10 million pages of text.

Common storage devices (see Figure A.13) include

- *Floppy disk*—Great for portability of information and ease of updating but hold only 1.44MB of information.
- *High-capacity floppy disk*—Great for portability and ease of updating and hold between 100MB and 250MB of information. Superdisks and Zip disks are examples.
- *Hard disk*—Rests within your system box and offers both ease of updating and great storage capacity.
- *CD-ROM*   Optical or laser disc that offers no updating capabilities with about 800MB of storage capacity. Most software today comes on CD-ROM.
- *CD-R (compact disc-recordable)*—Optical or laser disc that offers one-time writing capability with about 800MB of storage capacity.
- *CD-RW (compact disc-rewritable)*—Offers unlimited writing and updating capabilities on the CD.
- *DVD-ROM*—Optical or laser disc that offers no updating capabilities with upward of 17GB of storage capacity. The trend is now for movie rentals to be on DVD.
- *DVD-R*—Optical or laser disc that offers one-time writing capability with upward of 17GB of storage capacity.
- *DVD-RW, DVD-RAM,* or *DVD+RW* (all different names by different manufacturers)—Optical or laser disc that offers unlimited writing and updating capabilities on the DVD.

Figure A.13
Common Storage Devices

TELECOMMUNICATIONS DEVICES

Telecommunications is the most dynamic, changing, exciting, and technically complicated aspect of MIS and IT today. Telecommunications basically describes our ability to be *connected,* to almost anyone, anywhere, and at anytime. Because this topic is so vast, we've devoted all of *Extended Learning Module E* to it. Here, we want to just introduce you to the basics of telecommunications and its associated technologies, by focusing on your personal needs while at home.

Telecommunications enables the concept of a network. A computer ***network*** (which we simply refer to as a network) is two or more computers connected so that they can communicate with each other and share information, software, peripheral devices, and/or processing power. A simple example of a network is two computers connected to the same printer. The most well-known (and complicated) example of a network is the millions of computers connected all over the world that make up the Internet.

Let's talk about how you would connect to the Internet from home. First, you need some sort of modem that will serve as a connection from your home computer to another network, that is, the Internet. There are many types of modems, including

- telephone modems
- Digital Subscriber Line (DSL) modems
- cable modems
- satellite modems

In *Extended Learning Module E,* we cover DSL, cable, and satellite modems in more detail; here, let's focus on a telephone modem.

A ***telephone modem*** is a device that connects your computer to your phone line so that you can access another computer or network (see Figure A.14). If you use your standard telephone line for connecting to a network, a telephone modem is necessary because it acts as a converter of sorts. Your computer (and the network you're connecting to) work in terms of digital signals, while a standard telephone line works in terms of analog signals. Digital signals are discrete with each signal representing a bit (either 0 or 1). Think of analog signals as being wavy. Your modem must convert the digital signals of your computer into analog signals so they can be sent across the telephone line (this conversion process is called *modulation*). At the other end, another modem (similar to yours) translates the analog signals into digital signals, which can then be used by the

Figure A.14

The Role of a Telephone Modem

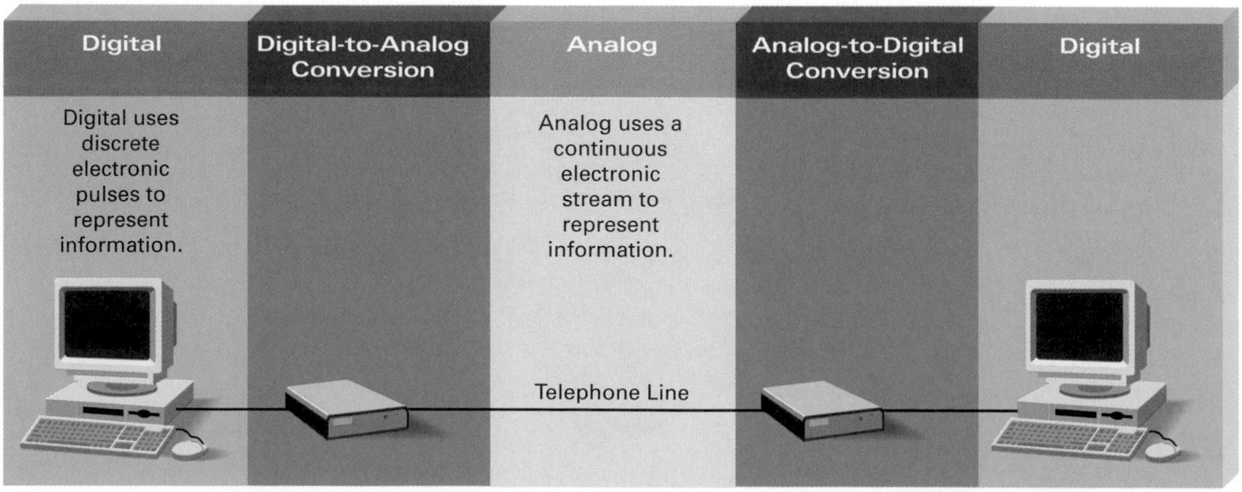

Digital	Digital-to-Analog Conversion	Analog	Analog-to-Digital Conversion	Digital
Digital uses discrete electronic pulses to represent information.		Analog uses a continuous electronic stream to represent information.		

Telephone Line

other computer or network (this conversion process is called *demodulation*). So, modems **mo**dulate and **dem**odulate signals, which is where we derive the term *modem*.

When you type information on a Web form to order a product, that information starts in digital form within your computer. When you hit the submit button, your modem converts that information to an analog form and sends it on its way through your telephone line. At the other end, another modem converts it back to a digital form, which allows a server computer to process your request. Then the server computer prepares its response in digital form and sends it through a modem that converts it to analog form. When the information reaches you, your modem first converts it to digital form so your computer can display it to you.

As you may recall, whenever you use your computer for any task, you need both hardware and software. For telecommunications, your hardware—in our example of connecting to the Internet—is a modem. You also need communications software, specifically,

Figure A.15

Connecting with Connectivity Software

- *Connectivity software*   Enables you to use your computer to "dial up" or connect to another computer
- *Web browser software*—Enables you to surf the Web
- Probably *e-mail software* (short for *electronic mail software*) Enables you to electronically communicate with other people by sending and receiving e-mail.

For example, if you want to connect to your school so that you could surf the Web and send and receive e-mail, you would first use connectivity software to dial up your school's computer (see Figure A.15). Once you are connected to your school's computer, you can then use Web browser software to surf the Web or e-mail software (such as Microsoft Outlook in Figure A.16) to send and receive e-mail.

Again, this is a very brief introduction to telecommunications and focuses only on using your home computer and a telephone modem to connect to your school so you can get to the Internet. We encourage you to read *Extended Learning Module E* for a more complete discussion of networks and telecommunications devices.

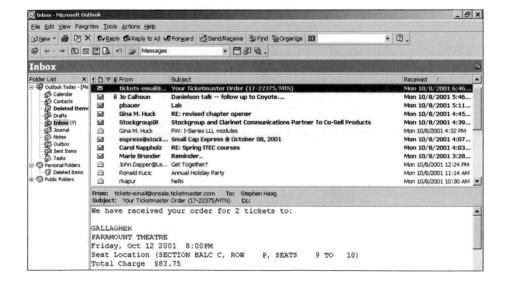

Figure A.16

Microsoft Outlook Is E-Mail Software

CONNECTING DEVICES

Connecting devices enable all your hardware components to communicate with each other. For example, you use a connector, called a *parallel connector,* to plug your printer into your system box. When you do, you're plugging it into a parallel port that is connected to an expansion card. That card is connected to the expansion bus (via an expansion slot), which moves information between various devices and RAM. The expansion bus is a part of the larger system bus, which moves information between the RAM and CPU and to and from various other devices. That may seem like an awful lot of technical jargon, so let's break it down a bit.

BUSES, EXPANSION SLOTS, AND EXPANSION CARDS

The ***system bus*** consists of the electronic pathways which move information between basic components on the motherboard, including between your CPU and RAM (see Figure A.17). A part of the system bus is called the ***expansion bus,*** which moves information from your CPU and RAM to all of your other hardware devices such as your microphone and printer. So, there's actually only one common "highway" that connects all of your hardware.

Along the expansion bus, you'll find expansion slots. An ***expansion slot*** is a long skinny socket on the motherboard into which you insert an expansion card. An ***expansion card*** is a circuit board that you insert into an expansion slot. Expansion cards include such things as video cards (for your monitor), sound cards (for your speakers and microphone), and modem cards (obviously for your modem). Each expansion card contains one or more ports (which we'll discuss further in the next section) into which you plug a connector (which we'll also discuss further in the next section) that is connected to some other hardware device such as a printer.

When you buy a complete computer system, it will come already equipped with the expansion cards inserted into the expansion slots. All you have to do is plug the appropriate connectors into the right ports. If, however, you decide to buy a new monitor and want increased video capacity, you may have to remove your old expansion card and insert a new one.

Figure A.17

Buses, Expansion Slots, and Expansion Cards

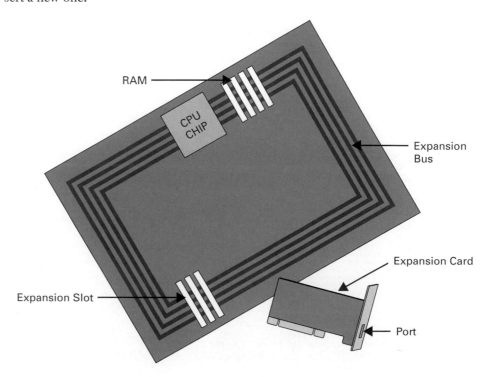

PORTS AND CONNECTORS

Different hardware devices require different kinds of ports and connectors. **Ports** are simply the plug-ins found on the outside of your system box (usually in the back) into which you plug a connector (see Figure A.18). Popular connectors include

- *USB (universal serial bus)*—These are becoming the most popular means of connecting devices to a computer. Most standard desktops today have at least two USB ports, and most standard notebooks have at least one.
- *Serial connector*—Usually has nine holes but may have 25, which fit into the corresponding number of pins in the port. Serial connectors are often most used for monitors and certain types of modems.
- *Parallel connector*—Has 25 pins, which fit into the corresponding holes in the port. Most printers use parallel connectors.

You can also have a special type of port called an *IrDA*, which has no physical corresponding connector. *IrDA (infrared data association) ports* are for wireless devices that work in essentially the same way as the remote control on your TV. To use IrDA, both your computer and the wireless device (such as a mouse) must have an IrDA port, which is why we say that IrDA ports have no physical corresponding connectors. We discuss the technical specifics of wireless communication in *Extended Learning Module E.*

Now that you've seen what's under the hood and what it takes to connect everything together, let's see how your computer processes a piece of application software.

Figure A.18
Ports and Connectors

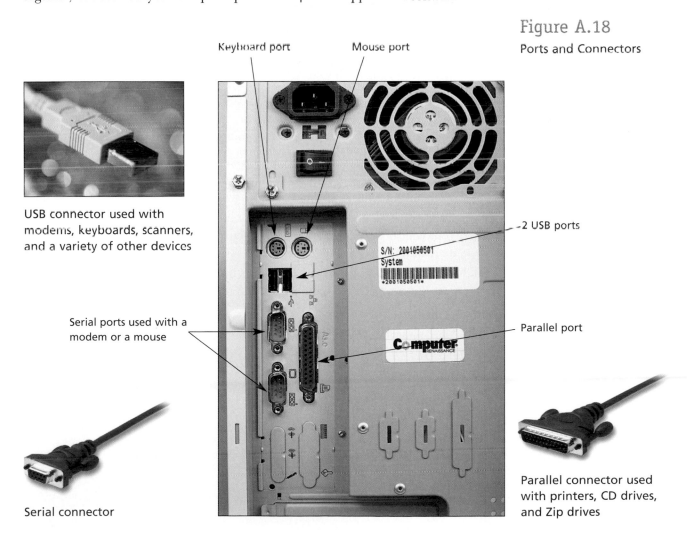

Keyboard port   Mouse port

USB connector used with modems, keyboards, scanners, and a variety of other devices

2 USB ports

S/N: 2001050501
System

Serial ports used with a modem or a mouse

Parallel port

Serial connector

Parallel connector used with printers, CD drives, and Zip drives

The Complete Computer at Work

As we explore a simple example of how your computer processes a piece of application software, remember first, that no matter what you want to do with your computer, you need both hardware and software. For our example, let's suppose that you have an icon on your Windows desktop for a special program that you use frequently. That program allows you to enter two numbers and then it displays the result of adding the two numbers together. Of course, we realize that you would never use such a piece of software, but it suits our illustration just fine.

When you double-click on that icon, your mouse sends that command to your CPU. Using the operating system instructions which reside in your internal memory (RAM), your control unit (inside your CPU) determines that you want to launch and use a program. So your control unit determines the path to that program and sends a message to your hard disk. That message includes where the program is located on your hard disk and instructions that tell your hard disk to get it and transfer it to your RAM. Then, your control unit tells your RAM to hold the program for processing.

With that stage set, let's look at the software as well as what happens on your screen. The software is shown in Figure A.19 and what appears on your screen is shown in Figure A.20. Looking at Figure A.19, you can see the program contains six lines of code. The first line of code is line 10, with the last being line 60. Below, we list each line of code and the corresponding series of internal instructions that your computer must perform.

10 CLS

  10.1 Your control unit must first send a message to your RAM telling it to pass the first line of code (fetch).

  10.2 Your control unit interprets the line of code and determines what each hardware device needs to do (decode).

  10.3 Your control unit sends a message to your screen, telling your screen to build a small window with no contents (execution).

20 PRINT "Please enter two numbers"

  20.1 Your control unit sends a message to your RAM telling it to pass the next line of code (fetch).

  20.2 Your control unit interprets the line of code (which is a display function) and determines what each hardware device needs to do (decode).

  20.3 Your control unit takes what is between quotes (Please enter two numbers), passes it to your screen, and tells your screen to display it (execute).

30 INPUT A, B

  30.1 Your control unit sends a message to your RAM telling it to pass the next line of code (fetch).

Figure A.19

Software Program for Adding Two Numbers

```
10    CLS
20    PRINT "Please enter two numbers"
30    INPUT A, B
40    C = A + B
50    PRINT "The result is:"; C
60    STOP
```

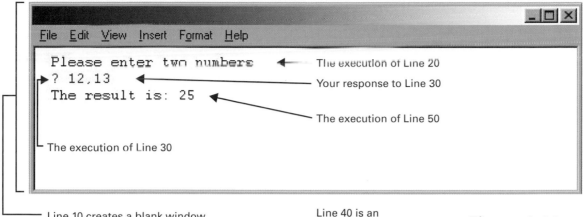

Line 10 creates a blank window.

Line 40 is an arithmetic instruction. Nothing is displayed on your screen as this instruction is executed.

30.2 Your control unit interprets the line of code (which is a data entry function) and determines what each hardware device needs to do (decode).

30.3 Your control unit sends a message to your screen telling it to display a question mark (execute).

30.4 Your control unit sends a message to your keyboard telling it to accept two numbers and pass those to RAM (another execute).

30.5 Your control unit sends a message to your RAM telling it to accept two numbers from your keyboard and store them in memory positions A and B (another execute—beginning to get the idea?).

40 C = A + B

40.1 Your control unit sends a message to your RAM telling it to pass the next line of code (fetch).

40.2 Your control unit interprets the line of code (which is an arithmetic function) and determines what each hardware device needs to do (decode).

40.3 Your control unit sends a message to RAM telling it to pass the contents of A and B to your A/L unit (execute).

40.4 Your control unit sends a message to your A/L unit telling it to accept the two numbers from RAM, add the two numbers together, and pass the result back to RAM (another execute).

40.5 Your control unit sends a message to your RAM to accept the result from the A/L unit, and store the result in memory position C.

50 PRINT "The result is:" ; C

50.1 Your control unit sends a message to your RAM telling it to pass the next line of code (fetch).

50.2 Your control unit interprets the line of code (which is another display function) and determines what each hardware device needs to do (decode).

50.3 Your control unit sends a message to your RAM telling it to pass the contents of memory position C to your screen.

50.4 Your control unit sends a message to your screen telling it to display the text between the quotes (the answer is:) and the content of memory position C that was passed to it by RAM (execute).

60 STOP

60.1 Your control unit sends a message to your RAM telling it to pass the next line of code (fetch).

60.2 Your control unit interprets the line of code (which is a termination function) and determines what each hardware device needs to do (decode).

60.3 Your control unit sends out a broadcast message telling each hardware device to "stand down" and await further instructions (execute).

This is a very realistic example of what goes on inside your computer while you use software. What is amazing is that most software packages include millions of lines of code and require that buttons, images, and icons appear on the screen.

Summary: Student Learning Outcomes Revisited

1. **Define information technology (IT) and its two basic categories: hardware and software.** *Information technology (IT)* is any computer-based tool that people use to work with information and support the information and information-processing needs of an organization. IT includes cell phones, PDAs, software such as spreadsheet software, and a printer. *Hardware* is the physical devices that make up a computer (often referred to as a computer system). *Software* is the set of instructions that your hardware executes to carry out a specific task for you.

2. **Describe categories of computers by size.** Categories of computers by size include personal digital assistants, notebook computers, desktop computers, minicomputers, mainframe computers, and supercomputers. A *personal digital assistant (PDA)* is a small hand-held computer that helps you surf the Web and perform simple tasks such as note taking, calendaring, appointment scheduling, and maintaining an address book. A notebook computer is a fully functional computer designed for you to carry around and run on battery power. A *desktop computer* is the most popular choice for personal computing needs. These three are all computers designed for use by one person. A *minicomputer (mid-range computer)* is designed to meet the computing needs of several people simultaneously in a small to medium-size business environment. A

mainframe computer (mainframe) is a computer designed to meet the computing needs of hundreds of people in a large business environment. A *supercomputer* is the fastest, most powerful, and most expensive type of computer. In the order given, PDAs are the smallest, least powerful, and least expensive while supercomputers are the largest, most powerful, and most expensive.

3. **Compare the roles of personal productivity, vertical market, and horizontal market software.** *Personal productivity software* helps you perform personal tasks—such as writing a memo, creating a graph, and creating a slide presentation—that you can usually do even if you don't own a computer. *Vertical market software* is application software that is unique to a particular industry. *Horizontal market software* is application software that is general enough to be suitable for use in a variety of industries. Personal productivity software is very inexpensive when compared to both vertical market and horizontal market software. With personal productivity software, you do not obtain the right to change the way the software works. If you buy vertical market or horizontal market software, you can often buy the right to change the way the software works.

4. **Describe the roles of operating system and utility software as components of system software.** *System software* handles tasks specific to technology management and coordinates the

interaction of all technology devices. Within system software, you will find operating system software and utility software. ***Operating system software*** is system software that controls your application software and manages how your hardware devices work together. So, operating system software really enables you to use your computer to run application software. ***Utility software*** is software that adds additional functionality to your operating system. It includes such utilities as anti-virus software, screen savers, crash-proof software, uninstaller software, and disk optimization. Although these would be considered to add "additional" functionality, you need utility software, especially anti-virus software.

5. **Define the purposes of the six major categories of hardware.** The six major categories of hardware include

- ***Input devices***—Help you capture information and commands and convert information in a

form that you understand into a form your computer can understand.
- ***Output devices***—Help you see, hear, or otherwise accept the results of your information-processing requests and convert information in a form that your computer understands into a form that you can understand.
- ***CPU and RAM***—The real brains of your computer that execute software instructions (CPU) and hold the information, application software, and operating system software you're working with (RAM).
- ***Storage devices***—Help you store information for use at a later time.
- ***Telecommunications devices***—Help you send information to and receive it from another person or location.
- Connecting devices—Help you connect all your hardware devices to each other.

Key Terms and Concepts

Anti-virus software, 51
Application software, 43
Arithmetic/logic unit (A/L unit), 58
ASCII (American Standard Code for Information Interchange), 53
Bar code reader, 55
Binary digit (bit), 53
Byte, 53
CD-R (compact disc-recordable), 59
CD-ROM, 59
CD-RW (compact disc-rewritable), 59
Central processing unit (CPU), 43
Communications software, 48
Connectivity software, 61
Control unit, 58
Crash-proof software, 51
CRT, 55
Database management system (DBMS) software, 48
Desktop computer, 44
Desktop publishing software, 48
Disk optimization software, 51
Dot pitch, 56
DVD-R, 59
DVD-ROM, 59
DVD-RW, DVD-RAM, DVD+RW, 59
E-mail (electronic mail) software, 61

Expansion bus, 62
Expansion card, 62
Expansion slot, 62
Flat-panel display, 55
Floppy disk, 59
Gigabyte (GB or Gig), 59
Gigahertz (GHz), 57
Graphics software, 48
Hard disk, 59
Hardware, 42
High-capacity floppy disk, 59
Horizontal market software, 48
Information technology (IT), 41
Inkjet printer, 56
Input device, 42
IrDA (infrared data association) port, 63
Keyboard, 54
Laser printer, 57
Linux, 50
Mac OS, 50
Mainframe computer (mainframe), 47
Megabyte (MB or M or Meg), 58
Megahertz (MHz), 57
Microphone, 55
Microsoft Windows 2000 Millennium (Windows 2000 Me), 50

Short-Answer Questions

1. What are the two categories of information technology (IT)?
2. What are the six categories of hardware?
3. What is the difference between application and system software?
4. What are the four categories of computers by size? Which is the least expensive? Which is the most powerful?
5. Dollar for dollar with comparable characteristics, which is faster and more powerful—a desktop computer or notebook computer?
6. What are the major categories of personal productivity software?
7. What is the difference between vertical market and horizontal market software?
8. Why is anti-virus software important today?
9. What do the terms *bits* and *bytes* mean?
10. What are some popular pointing input devices for notebook computers?
11. How are resolution of a screen and resolution of a printer different and how are they similar?
12. What are the major types of storage devices? How do they compare in terms of updating capabilities and amount of storage?
13. What is the role of expansion slots, expansion cards, ports, and connectors?

Short-Question Answers

For each of the following answers, provide an appropriate question.

1. Cell phones, PDAs, software such as word processing, and a printer are all examples.
2. Helps you capture information and commands.
3. Operating system software and utility software.
4. Surfing the Web, note taking, calendaring, appointment scheduling, and maintaining an address book.
5. Very expensive "number crunchers."
6. For creating slides for a presentation.
7. It includes enhanced design and formatting techniques.
8. Using more than one piece of software at a time.
9. A collection of bits.
10. QXGA
11. Megahertz and gigahertz.
12. CD-RW.
13. Modem.

Assignments and Exercises

1. **CUSTOMIZING A COMPUTER PURCHASE.** One of the great things about the Web is the number of e-tailers that are now online offering you a variety of products and services. One such e-tailer is Dell, which allows you to customize and buy a computer. Connect to Dell's site at www.dell.com. Go to the portion of Dell's site that allows you to customize either a notebook or a desktop computer. First, choose an already prepared system and note its price and capability in terms of CPU speed, RAM size, monitor quality, and storage capacity. Now, customize that system to increase CPU speed, add more RAM, increase monitor size and quality, and add more storage capacity. What's the difference in price between the two? Which system is more in your price range? Which system has the speed and capacity you need?

2. **WEB-ENABLED CELL PHONES AND WEB COMPUTERS.** When categorizing computers by size for personal needs, we focused on PDAs, notebook computers, and desktop computers. There are several other variations including Web-enabled cell phones that include instant text messaging and Web computers. For this project, you'll need a group of four people, which you will then split into two groups of two. Have the first group research Web-enabled cell phones, their capabilities, and their costs. Have that group make a purchase recommendation based on price and capability. Have the second group do the same for Web computers. What's your vision of the future? Will we ever get rid of clunky notebooks and desktops in favor of more portable and cheaper devices such as Web-enabled cell phones and Web computers? Why or why not?

3. **OPERATING SYSTEM SOFTWARE FOR PDAS.** The personal digital assistant (PDA) market is a ferocious, dynamic, and uncertain one. One of the uncertainties is what operating system for PDAs will become the dominant one. For notebooks and desktops right now, you're pretty well limited to the Microsoft family unless you buy an Apple computer (in which case your operating system is Mac OS) or you want to venture into using Linux (which we wouldn't recommend for most people). Do some research on the more popular PDAs available today. What are the different operating systems? What different functionality do they offer? Are they compatible with each other? Take a guess— which one will come out on top?

4. **TYPES OF MONITORS AND THEIR QUALITY.** The monitor you buy will greatly affect your productivity. If you get a high-resolution, large-screen monitor, you'll see the screen content better than if you get a low-resolution, small-screen monitor. One factor in this is the monitor type. There are seven major monitor types available today: HDTV, QXGA, SVGA, SXGA, UXGA, VGA, and XGA. Do a little research on these monitor types. Rank them from best to worst in terms of resolution. Also, determine a price for each.

CHAPTER TWO OUTLINE

STUDENT LEARNING OUTCOMES

1. Illustrate how the creative use of information technology can give an organization a competitive advantage.

2. Describe how to develop business strategies for the Internet Age and use tools that can help.

3. Describe how e-commerce technologies up the stakes and give organizations even more opportunities.

4. Summarize how one specific industry has consistently used information technology for competitive advantage.

5. Summarize how to use information technology for competitive advantage in an organization.

WEB SUPPORT

www.mhhe.com/haag

- Auction houses
- Books and music
- Clothing and accessories
- Computers
- Automobiles
- Information Partnerships

CHAPTER TWO

Strategic and Competitive Opportunities
Using IT for Competitive Advantage

OPENING CASE STUDY:
ZARA: FASHION FAST FORWARD

At Zara's flagship apparel store in downtown Madrid, the store manager scans the racks holding the latest fashions. Quickly, she notes which items are selling well and which are not. Currently, leather items—particularly the short skirts—are selling briskly; so are the tailored jeans, the black sequined shirts, and the red and blue gabardine blazers.

Making her bet on which items will be next week's hot sellers, she pulls out her hand-held computer and enters an order that is transmitted over the Internet to Zara headquarters in the northwestern Spanish town of La Coruña.

There, Zara's designers and product managers are deciding what to create. Every day they gather suggestions from the flagship store in Madrid and from 518 other store managers worldwide. Importantly, however, they don't just want specific orders. They ask for and get ideas for cuts, fabrics, or even a new line.

After evaluating the store managers' input, the team in La Coruña decides what to make. Designers draw up the latest ideas on their computers and send them over Zara's intranet to one of its nearby factories. Within days, the cutting, dyeing, stitching, and pressing begin. And in just three weeks, the clothes will hang in stores from Barcelona to Berlin to Beirut. Zara isn't just a bit faster than rivals such as Gap, whose lead time is nine months. It's 12 times faster!

What sets Zara apart from its competitors is a computerized network that ties the stores to the design shops and company-owned factories in real time. The Zara model may be unique, but at its heart is a perfectly simple principle: In fashion, nothing is as important as time to market.

For years, apparel companies have manufactured their garments in lesser-developed countries in pursuit of lower costs. Zara decided against that. The company believed that the ability to respond quickly to shifts in consumer tastes would create far greater efficiencies than outsourcing to low-cost countries could. "The fashion world is in constant flux and is driven not by supply but by customer demand," says one of the company's executives. "We need to give consumers what they want, and if I go to South America or Asia to make clothes, I simply can't move fast enough."

Once the company decided it would have the world's most responsive supply chain, the pieces of its operating model fell logically into place. Zara has a twice-a-week delivery schedule that not only restocks old styles but brings in entirely new designs; rival chains tend to receive new designs only once or twice a season. "It's like you walk into a new store every two weeks," noted one prominent retail industry executive. The advantages of world-beating time to market, according to Zara, more than offset manufacturing costs that run 15 percent to 20 percent higher than those of its rivals. For example, Zara almost never needs to absorb inventory write-offs to correct merchandising blunders. And the company maintains steady profit margins of 10 percent—in line with the best in the industry.[1]

Introduction

There are many examples of ways that organizations have used and are using information technology in creative ways to give themselves a competitive advantage. A company gains a ***competitive advantage*** by providing a product or service in a way that customers value more than what the competition is able to do. We'll give you some examples in a moment. First, it's important for you to get the right perspective about it. It's not the technology that gives a company a competitive advantage; it's the way that people *use* the technology that makes the difference. For example, let's assume that there is a Porsche Boxster S parked outside and there are two people available to drive it: a trained professional race car driver and a senior citizen who usually drives a six-year-old Buick, as shown in Figure 2.1. Although both people would have access to the same technology, there's probably no question in your mind that the professional race car driver would do a better job of utilizing the technology embodied in the Boxster.

In a way, it's the same with information technology. With the widespread availability and ever-decreasing cost of computers, telecommunications, and the Internet, the same technology is available to just about everyone. The real difference comes in the way that different people use the technology. Those that are well trained, proficient, and creative in its use are going to be able to get the most out of it and give their organizations a competitive advantage. These people are the knowledge workers we discussed in Chapter 1.

Designing an information system that gives a competitive advantage requires at least two things. First, it requires an understanding of the business problem you're trying to solve or the business situation in which you're trying to get a competitive advantage. Second, it requires an understanding of available technologies to know which ones to use in designing a creative solution for the business situation. This is why studying management information systems (MIS) is so important. MIS emphasizes both business processes and technical solutions.

If you're building a house, it's important to design it before you start to build it. Otherwise, there's no telling what you might end up with. Most people hire an architect for the job. It's similar with information systems. As we discuss in Chapters 6 and 7, it's important to design a system before you build it. As a matter of fact, ***application architects*** are what we call information technology professionals who can design creative technology-based business solutions, working hand-in-hand with their business management counterparts from marketing, manufacturing, accounting, and human resources, for example. Skilled application architects are in short supply. They are among the most sought-after of knowledge workers.

Figure 2.1

Who Can Get the Most Out of the Boxster S?

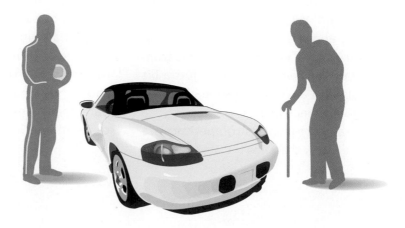

Competitive Advantage Examples

Seeing competitive advantage in action is perhaps the best way for you to learn how to implement it in your organization. As we look at the following examples, we'll introduce you to some "best business practices" as well.

FEDERAL EXPRESS

It used to be that if you wanted to track a package you'd shipped somewhere via FedEx you had to call an 800 number and listen to some music for awhile until a customer service representative came on the line. Then you had to give him or her the tracking number from the receipt you got when you shipped the package. The customer service representative would enter the tracking number into a computer system that would access a database containing up-to-date information on the location of your package. You could find out whether or not it had been delivered and, if so, when it had been delivered and who signed for it.

Someone at FedEx got the idea that with today's technology, life could be much easier for the customer. So, FedEx designed a system that lets you access that same database through your Internet connection and Web browser. Now, all you have to do is go to the FedEx Web site, find your way to the tracking screen, and key in your tracking number. The system will respond by giving you the same information you used to get from a customer service representative (see Figure 2.2).

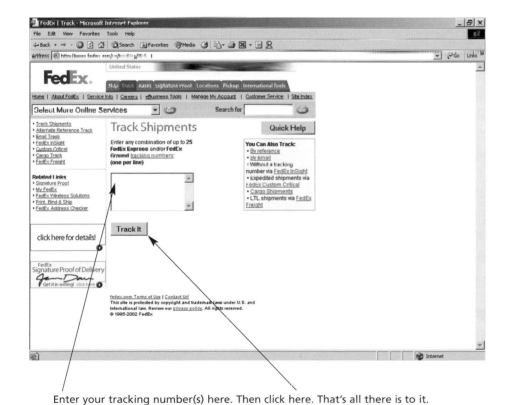

Figure 2.2

FedEx Package Tracking Screen

Enter your tracking number(s) here. Then click here. That's all there is to it.

The FedEx tracking system, and similar systems that benefit both the customers and the company, are often called win-win systems. The FedEx tracking system is better for the customer because it's easier and faster. Customers no longer have to spend time waiting in "voice mail jail." It's better for FedEx because it's cheaper. FedEx doesn't need nearly as many customer service representatives to handle the incoming calls. Plus, it gets a competitive advantage by delivering superior customer service, at least until the competition develops a similar system of its own, as UPS and FedEx's other competitors soon concluded they had to do.

This illustrates an important point about using information technology for competitive advantage. A competitive advantage you achieve for your company usually turns out to be temporary because the competition soon figures out that they have to offer a similar system to their customers or risk losing them to you. Even a temporary advantage can make a difference, however, because the first mover usually makes some gains at the expense of the competition. A *temporary advantage* simply means that whatever you do, sooner or later the competition duplicates what you've done, or even leap-frogs you with an even better system. Despite this, the *first mover,* the company who is first to market with a new IT-based product or service, may well capture new customers it never gives up, and it often gains additional benefits by being viewed as an innovative market leader.

CHARLES SCHWAB

Charles Schwab was a pioneer in the discount brokerage business. The company began operations more than 25 years ago serving investors who were comfortable in making their own trades and did not need the advice and counsel provided by full service brokers who charged a higher commission. Over the years, the company evolved into one that offers services to independent investors as well as investors who prefer to have more in the way of professional guidance. Schwab was a first mover in offering stock trades over the Internet, along with other online brokers such as E*Trade. Using the latest in Internet and telephone technologies, Schwab offers its customers around-the-clock personal services. Its 3 million online customers manage more than $250 billion in assets and trade more than $11 billion in securities over www.schwab.com each week. Schwab is not only the largest, it's perceived as being the best. Gomez (www.gomez.com) is a highly regarded company in the Internet Quality Measurement (IQM) business, and Schwab appears at the top of their list of 29 discount brokers.[2] The willingness of Schwab's management to embrace the Internet early on as a way of serving the company's customers more efficiently and effectively has made Schwab the largest online broker, and one of world's most successful e-businesses.

DELL COMPUTER

Dell computer has a direct sell model that gives the company a huge advantage over any competitor still using a traditional model of selling through retailers. The traditional way that PC manufacturers get their product to customers is to build a bunch of PCs and ship them to wholesalers, distributors, or maybe directly to retailers. The PCs sit on the

You don't have to be a part of a traditional for-profit organization in order to get into the habit of looking for ways to use IT for competitive advantage. Not-for-profits and governmental agencies can get benefits from IT as well. For example, most universities are considered to be not for profit. See if you can come up with ways that your college or university could get a competitive advantage from the way it uses IT. You might try by taking the customer's perspective (yours) as a point of departure. Other candidates could be your state or local government. How complicated is it to get your driver's license renewed? How difficult is it to get information on various governmental services? How could information access be improved with the creative use of IT systems?

retailers' shelves or in a warehouse until you come in and buy one. If you looked at a typical distribution chain you would see that there are a lot of PCs in inventory. (A *distribution chain* is simply the path followed from the originator of a product or service to the end consumer.) In a typical distribution chain you'd find inventory at the manufacturer's warehouse, at the wholesalers, at the distributors, and at the retailers. Holding on to all of this inventory costs money, because whoever owns the inventory has to pay for it as well as pay for the operation of the warehouses or stores while waiting for someone to buy it.

Dell's model is different.[3] It sells computers directly from its Web site. The company makes it easy for you to log on and configure a computer just the way you want it. Once you've done that and given Dell your credit card number, you click to order, and your computer arrives in a few days. Shortly after you click to order, Dell has your money! Then it gets busy sending electronic orders to other companies—their alliance partners—who assemble and ship your computer. An *alliance partner* is a company you do business with on a regular business in a cooperative fashion, usually facilitated by IT systems. Dell pays its alliance partners for their efforts a bit later. Arrangements such as this are also called information partnerships. An *information partnership* (supported by interorganizational systems, which we introduced in Chapter 1) lets two or more companies cooperate by integrating their IT systems, thereby providing customers with the best of what each can offer.

To learn more about information partnerships, visit the Web site that supports this text at www.mhhe.com/haag.

This is a win-win-win situation. You win because you get a computer made expressly for you, which arrives in good shape in a couple of days. Dell wins because all this occurred without the sale having to tie up a lot of money in inventory in the distribution chain. Dell's alliance partners win because they get a lot of business from Dell. The differences between Dell's "sell, source, and ship" model and the traditional "buy, hold, and sell" model are illustrated in Figure 2.3 on the following page.

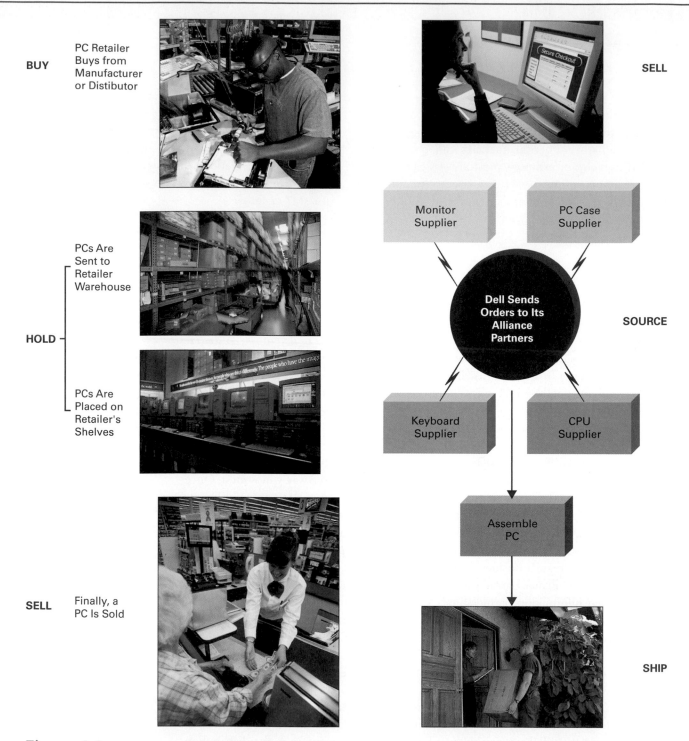

BUY — PC Retailer Buys from Manufacturer or Distibutor

SELL

HOLD —
PCs Are Sent to Retailer Warehouse

PCs Are Placed on Retailer's Shelves

Monitor Supplier

PC Case Supplier

Dell Sends Orders to Its Alliance Partners

SOURCE

Keyboard Supplier

CPU Supplier

Assemble PC

SELL — Finally, a PC Is Sold

SHIP

Figure 2.3
Buy-Hold-Sell versus Sell-Source-Ship

GE LEADERSHIP LEADS THE WAY IN COMPETITIVE IT

Jack Welch, the former chairman and CEO of General Electric (GE), earned wide recognition as an outstanding corporate manager. During his 20 years at the helm of GE, he raised the corporation's profits from $1.6 billion to more than $10 billion on revenues of $110 billion. Under his leadership, GE created a business culture that is widely regarded as the best in the world. GE became the envy of many for its ability to run a global company efficiently and profitably.

While a lot of executives and traditional businesses have been slow to react to the competitive advantages made possible by the Internet, Jack Welch and GE were not among them. He recognized early on that the potential of the Internet would bring new threats and opportunities that GE could not afford to ignore.

He urged managers of GE's business units to examine their competitive positions and think "destroyyourbusiness.com." In other words, he asked them to try to visualize how a competitor could use the Internet to make inroads into their markets or gain a competitive advantage over them. Thinking that way, GE managers would be able to innovate and change their businesses before a new competitor arrived on the scene.

He was also known for leading by example, unlike many of his peers at other companies. One of the ways he did this was to assign young mentors to himself and 3,000 other top GE executives to teach them how to use the Web.

Welch was serious about changing the culture at GE from a traditional one to one that was Internet-driven, and it worked. He saw the potential for using the Web to eliminate unnecessary layers of middle management, promote teamwork, improve customer service, and make GE more competitive.

Jack Welch remains a great example of the kind of vision, leadership, and understanding that winning corporations need from their CEOs if they are going to be able to thrive in the information economy.[4]

CISCO SYSTEMS

Dell Computer is in both the B2B and B2C space. This is shorthand for "Business to Business" and "Business to Consumer." *Business to Business (B2B)* refers to companies whose customers are primarily other businesses while *Business to Consumer (B2C)* is the term used for companies whose customers are primarily individuals. (Some companies, such as Dell Computer, have both B2B and B2C lines of business.)

Cisco Systems sells switches and routers, machines that manage information flowing through telecommunications networks in the B2B space. Cisco has been a leader in utilizing the direct sell model over the Internet. It currently sells over $15 billion a year this way. Customers like the direct sell system because it lets them log on to a home page that they can customize to reflect the particular way that they deal with Cisco. Then, they can order Cisco products and configure them to their exact specifications. Cisco likes the system because it puts the management of the customer order process in the hands of the customer, thus freeing up Cisco employees for other tasks.

Recently, Cisco announced a partnership with Ariba, one of the leading suppliers of Web-based purchasing tools.[5] Ariba's software, which manages buying, selling, and e-commerce processes, will be combined with Cisco Web-based ordering tools, which provide pricing and configuration capabilities. Cisco says that its newly streamlined order entry process will increase customer productivity by as much as 20 percent. So, you see, Cisco has found a couple of ways to get a competitive advantage through the creative use of information technology.

First, Cisco made it easy to turn the management of the customer ordering process over to the customers themselves, and then it formed a software alliance with Ariba to increase the productivity of the customer ordering process even more. As you might expect, both Cisco and its customers are pleased with the results.

Developing a Strategy for the Internet Age

Professor Michael Porter's frameworks have long been accepted as useful tools for business people to use when thinking about business strategy. Several of his colleagues, Professor Warren McFarland among them, showed how they also could be used in coming up with ideas of how information technology could be used to create a competitive advantage. Acknowledging the power of the Internet, in a recent article Professor Porter observed that the Internet provides better opportunities for companies to establish distinctive business strategies than previous generations of information technology.[6]

Porter's three frameworks are

1. The five forces model
2. The three generic strategies
3. The value chain

THE FIVE FORCES MODEL

The *five forces model* was developed to determine the relative attractiveness of an industry. Porter's intention was that it be used as a tool for business managers to use when they were trying to decide if they should enter a particular industry or expand their operations if they were already in it. As illustrated in Figure 2.4, the five forces are buyer power, supplier buyer, threat of substitute products or services, threat of new entrants, and rivalry among existing competitors.

BUYER POWER   *Buyer power* is high when buyers have many choices of whom to buy from, and low when the choices are few. If the buyers in a particular industry hold a lot of the power, the industry is less attractive to enter.

SUPPLIER POWER   *Supplier power* is high when buyers have few choices of whom to buy from, and low when there are many choices. If the suppliers in a particular industry hold a lot of the power, the industry is also less attractive to enter.

Figure 2.4

The Five Forces Model

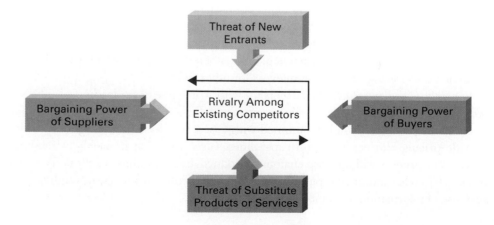

THREAT OF SUBSTITUTE PRODUCTS OR SERVICES   If there are very few alternatives to using the product or service the ***threat of substitute products or services*** is low, and it is an advantage to the supplier. Or, if there are switching costs associated with the product or service, it is an advantage to the supplier as well. ***Switching costs*** are costs that can make customers reluctant to switch to another product or service. For example, you may decide to keep your virus protection software even if a slightly better one becomes available because you don't want to invest the time and money to install and learn the new package.

THREAT OF NEW ENTRANTS   The ***threat of new entrants*** is high when it is easy for competitors to enter the market. If it's easy, that's not good, for pretty soon you'll have a ton of competitors going after your customers. If it's difficult for others to enter the market, that's good news for those who are already there.

RIVALRY AMONG EXISTING COMPETITORS   An industry is less attractive when the ***rivalry among existing competitors*** is high and more attractive when it is low. Competition is more intense in some industries than in others. The intensity of competition in the industry is another factor that you should consider before entering an industry.

THE THREE GENERIC STRATEGIES

Porter says that a business should adopt only one of ***three generic strategies:*** cost leadership, differentiation, or a focused strategy. As illustrated in Figure 2.5, a focused strategy can focus on either cost leadership or differentiation. According to Porter, trying to follow more than one of these strategies at the same time is almost always unsuccessful.

Taking examples from U.S. retailers, Wal-Mart follows a broadly targeted cost leadership strategy. Nordstrom with its emphasis on superior customer service and in-store experience follows a broadly targeted differentiation strategy. Walgreen's pursues a cost leadership strategy, but is focused on drugstore items.

USING THE FIVE FORCES MODEL

Warren McFarlan had the idea that a company could use information technology to alter one or more of the five forces in their favor, or to reinforce one of the three generic strategies. When he shared this idea with business people, they quickly found that it worked. Some good examples of where it worked are provided next.

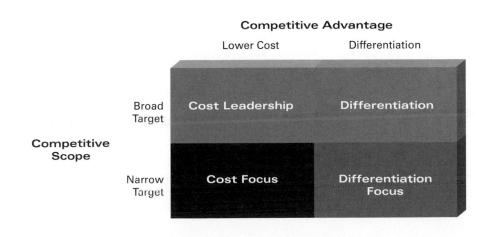

Figure 2.5

The Three Generic Strategies[7]

BUYER POWER   Because there are many hotels competing for the business traveler's business, buyers have many choices, and therefore hold power over the suppliers of hotel rooms. To counteract this, most hotel chains have created loyalty programs that give points for each stay which can be cashed in for free hotel stays at one of their resort hotels, for example, or for other rewards. Such programs, supported by state-of-the-art information systems, have the effect of increasing the likelihood that a traveler will stay at a single chain.

SUPPLIER POWER   One of the best ways to decrease supplier power is to locate alternative sources of supply. The B2B marketplaces on the Internet can have the effect of doing this. A *B2B marketplace* is an Internet-based service which brings together many buyers and sellers. One example is the cooperative Internet purchasing venture established by the automotive industry, Covisint. It uses Internet technology to "speed the flow of material through the supply chain, increase response to consumer demand, and deliver new products to market faster than ever before."[8]

Another way of reducing supplier power is to find a way to put more information in the hands of the buyer. The Internet has played a huge role in this in many industries. Probably the best example is the retail automobile industry. It used to be that when you wanted to buy a new car you really put yourself at the mercy of the dealer. The new car salesperson knew what the car cost the dealer, knew how much your trade-in was really worth, and knew how much money the dealership could make on optional equipment, extended warranties, and financing. Now, all of the information that only the dealer had is freely available on the Internet. The new car buyer can thus begin negotiations having roughly the same amount of information the dealer has. Supplier power is effectively reduced.

THREAT OF SUBSTITUTE PRODUCTS OR SERVICES   Many professionals find that their normal way of making a living is threatened by the introduction of new information technology–enabled products or services. One example is that of a local Certified Public Accountant who made a good portion of her living by doing tax returns for individuals. Her income from tax return preparation was reduced substantially after inexpensive and easy-to-use tax return software packages such as TurboTax hit the market. One of the challenges for professionals is to find a way to counter IT-based threats to their livelihoods. Can you think of other professionals who might be threatened by information technology–based alternatives?

THREAT OF NEW ENTRANTS   It is not a good thing to try to survive in an industry that is very easy for others to enter. All that does is make it more crowded with competitors. Successful companies try to use information technology to erect what is called barriers to entry or entry barriers. An *entry barrier* is a product or service feature that customers have come to expect from companies in a particular industry. Entry barriers make it more difficult for competitors to enter a particular market. A good example of an entry barrier is what we have come to expect from banks. We want to be sure our bank can offer us an ATM card that works at lots of locations locally and even around the world. We'd also like to be able to view our account and pay bills on the Internet. When one bank in a region first introduced such IT services, they gained a competitive advantage. Other banks saw that they had to introduce similar services or face the loss of some of their customers to the bank that was more advanced. Now such services are entry barriers to anyone who thinks of starting a new bank.

RIVALRY AMONG EXISTING COMPETITORS   There are many ways that information technology can make one company better prepared than its rivals in an intensely competitive setting. For example, many retailers compete on the basis of price, particularly with products that are commoditylike in nature. It probably doesn't matter where you buy a six-pack of Diet Pepsi, at a convenience store or at a discount chain. The Pepsi will taste the same. What will likely be different is the price you paid for that six-pack. Probably it will be quite a bit cheaper at the discount chain store than at the convenience store. The reason it's cheaper at the discount chain store is because of the way that the chain store uses information systems to make itself more efficient. Having information systems that let a retailer be more efficient and lower its costs so that it can offer lower prices to its customers is a definite competitive advantage.

BRIDGING THE GAP BETWEEN BUSINESS PEOPLE AND TECHNICAL PEOPLE

Think of a company where the technical people are all computer science majors and the business people all have degrees in marketing or accounting, with little training in MIS. Then, let's say that the biggest business problem for the company is to increase the number of repeat buyers on its B2C Web site. If we turned this problem over to a computer scientist, he might not know (or care) enough about buyer behavior to be able to come up with a solution that works.

If we turned the problem over to the marketing manager, she might know a lot about buyer behavior but not have a clue about how to make the company's Web site "sticky." Usually this problem is solved by forming a project team to come up with a solution that draws the best knowledge of the business problem from the business people and the best technical solution from the technical people. A *project team* is a team designed to accomplish specific one-time goals, which is disbanded once the project is complete. When this process works well, the project team comes up with a great solution. When it doesn't work, companies find that the business people and the technical people simply can't communicate with each other well enough to focus their respective strengths on solving the problem.

If you want a better appreciation of what we're talking about, just think about the last time you asked one of your favorite geeks a technical question and he tried to snow you with his answer. See what we mean?

REMOTE SURGERY: A NEW EXPORT INDUSTRY?

Recently, two doctors removed the gall bladder of a 69-year-old patient lying on an operating table in Strasbourg, France. The most unusual aspect of this otherwise routine operation was that the surgeons were in New York.

They used joysticks and voice commands to direct three robotic arms in the operating room and watched their work on monitors. France Telecom provided a secure fiber-optic line to connect the control console to the robotic arms and instruments, while surgeons and nurses in France monitored the patient and switched the instruments as needed.

Such technology could eventually save the lives of patients who need a surgeon but can't reach one. Even sooner, remote robotic surgery systems will offer surgeons the chance to collaborate and teach new techniques without having to travel.[10]

VIEWING THE BUSINESS PROBLEM FROM ANOTHER PERSPECTIVE

Too often, when project teams try to come up with the design of an information system, they view the business problem from their own internal perspective rather than from the perspective of the people the system is designed to serve. It's often more effective to put yourself in the place of the primary user of the system and try to come up with ways in which the user would not only be served, but be *delighted* by the system. Take the perspective of a customer of the company. How could the information system be designed so that it enhances the customer's experience?

The Federal Express online tracking system we discussed previously in this chapter is a pretty good example.

USING THE THREE GENERIC STRATEGIES

Companies use the three generic strategies and information technology to change the basis of competition in ways that are favorable to them. For example, if they find that they are embroiled in a fierce competitive marketplace where all of the players are competing on the basis of price, they could use information technology to develop and support a strategy based on differentiation. Amazon.com deals with many commoditylike products where competition (as we saw with the Diet Pepsi example) is usually based on who can sell a product for the lowest price. New books, CDs, and videos are all commodity-like products. It doesn't really matter where you buy them, they will all be the same.

You may have noticed, however, that although Amazon.com has good prices, its price is often not the lowest. What Amazon.com has done well, however, is to make our buying experience a pleasurable one by making its site informative and easy to navigate and by using sophisticated software to personalize the site for each individual customer. The company has used information technology to pursue a differentiated strategy in what would otherwise be a low-cost marketplace.

DEMANDING A CREATIVE DESIGN

One of the biggest mistakes people make when designing new information systems is to come up with a design that is ordinary, something very similar to what other companies are doing. If you want a competitive advantage, you need a creative design. A *creative*

FINDING THE BEST IT STRATEGY FOR YOUR INDUSTRY

Regardless of which of Michael Porter's tools you select to use in developing IT solutions, selecting ones that are appropriate for your organization is crucial. To simplify the selection process even further, you might consider which tools work best with some of the industries profiled in the Industry Perspective boxes in each chapter of this book. Match the tool on the left with the most appropriate industry across the top. Each tool can match more than one industry.
For each match, write at least one reason why this match is appropriate.

Industries

Porter's Tools	Hospitality & Leisure	Financial Services	Health Care	Retail	IT & Telecommunications	Transportation	Dot-Com	Entertainment & Publishing	Manufacturing
Reduce buyer power									
Reduce supplier power									
Increase switching costs									
Increase entry barriers									
Switch to a cost leader strategy									
Switch to a differentiated strategy									
Switch to a focused strategy									
Enhance value-added activities									
Lower value-reducing activities									

design of an IT system is one that solves the business problem in a new and highly effective way rather than the same way others have done it.

Let's say you won the lottery, and you decided to spend $3 million on that dream house you always wanted. One way to do it would be to look at existing houses that are on the market, buy one that you liked, and then make any necessary modifications to tailor it to your needs. Another way to do it would be to hire a talented architect to design your house from scratch.

If you hired an architect, one of the first things she would do is interview you to discover what sort of house you want. How many bedrooms, how many bathrooms, what does the kitchen and family room need to have? What sort of entertaining space do you need, and what sort of space do you want for work and for quiet times? How about decks, a home theater, an indoor squash court, or an outdoor swimming pool? To finish up, she would want to see the lot you had selected in the foothills of Colorado, with a snow-capped mountain view.

With this information, she would go away and design a home to meet your needs. She would make sure that your requirements were met, but would also strive to meet them creatively, with a pleasing design. (For $3 million, you don't want a house that looks like every other house!) She probably would build a model of the house or use computer-aided design tools to help give you an appreciation of what your house would look like after it was built. If you don't like the model, you should reject the design, and ask the architect to make changes until you're absolutely satisfied. Then, you can give her your approval to begin the construction phase.

We said that this was similar to the process of designing and building information systems. If you bought an existing house, it would be like buying a precoded application software package, like one of Siebel Systems' eBusiness applications, for example. If you decided that you didn't like any of the available precoded package applications, you would appoint a project team to design a custom system for you, similar to the way you would hire an architect to design your house. If the project team came to you with an ordinary design, you can be almost certain that it would not give you a competitive advantage. Worse yet, the system could be obsolete by the time it was put into operation because in all likelihood the competition was not standing still. So, in order to get your money's worth from your investment, you have every right to send your design team back to the drawing board until they come up with a design that delights you. That's the one that is likely to give you a competitive advantage.

THE VALUE CHAIN

Once you have an understanding of how IT can help you develop a business strategy, it's important that you reinforce this view by ensuring IT support for all important business processes. A *business process* is a standardized set of activities that accomplishes a specific task, such as processing a customer's order. One important graphic tool that helps you identify those important processes is Michael Porter's value chain. The *value chain* views the organization as a chain—or series—of processes, each of which adds value to the product or service for the customer. Customers patronize your organization because of the value that it adds to its products and services. If you view your organization as a value chain, you can identify the important processes in adding value for customers and, thus, identify IT systems that support those processes.

Figure 2.6 depicts the components of a value chain. The chain of primary value processes along the bottom half takes the raw materials and makes, delivers, markets and sells, and services your organization's products or services. Processes along the top half of the chain, such as management, accounting, finance, legal, human resources, research and development, and purchasing, support the primary value processes. Your organization requires these support value processes to ensure the smooth operation of the primary value processes.

Figure 2.6

The Components of a Value Chain

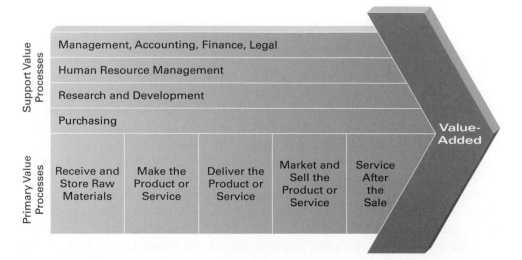

All value processes process an individual value. However, these processes combined have a total value greater than the sum of their individual values. We call this additional value value-added, and it's depicted on the far right of the value chain. The larger the value added, the more value customers place on an organization's product or service. To the organization, this can mean a competitive advantage and often greater profits. Let's look at how a firm might use the value chain to identify both value-added and value-reducing processes.

If you've ever purchased a necktie, you may have heard of the Robert Talbott company of Carmel Valley, California.[11] Talbott is the premier necktie manufacturer in the United States. Talbott has always shunned technology; all of its tie orders, historically, were written on paper forms.

That used to work fine, because Talbott has always ensured added value by utilizing high-quality workmanship, unique designs, and fabrics. However, customer "wants" drive their demands, and those demands are always changing. Today customers want constantly updated styles and more of them. In fact, Talbott now creates four neckwear lines for Nordstrom each year with up to 300 designs per line. Given this situation, how could the value chain help Talbott plan for a better way of meeting customer demands? Well, it would begin by identifying both value-added and value-reducing processes. Let's look at the identification of value-added processes first.

IDENTIFYING PROCESSES THAT ADD VALUE   Talbott should begin by looking at the firm's business processes and identifying, with help from customers, those processes that add the most value. These include manufacturing high-quality ties and purchasing quality materials. Then Talbott should graphically depict the customer responses on a value chain. Figure 2.7 is one possible result. Notice how the processes are sized to depict the value that customers attribute to those processes. The largest value-added source is the high-quality manufacturing process. Still, a close second is the purchasing process that provides access to high-quality silks and other fabrics. As these processes are the ones that are most visible to the customers, they will quickly add even more value when supported by new IT systems. Therefore, Talbott created a computer-aided design system to reduce the time it takes to create and manufacture new ties.

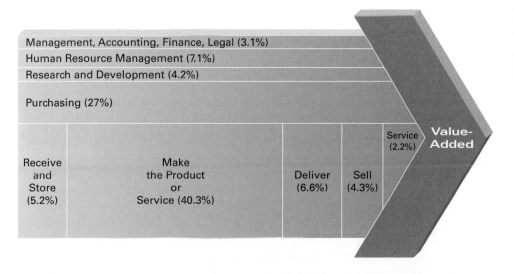

Figure 2.7

The Value-Added View of a Necktie Manufacturer

Figure 2.8

The Value-Reduced View of a Necktie Manufacturer

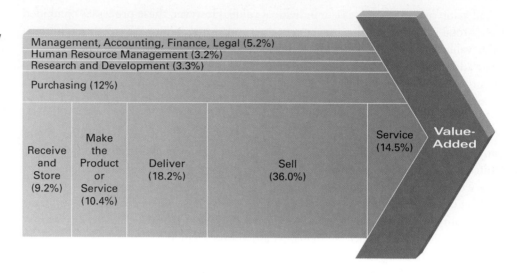

IDENTIFYING PROCESSES THAT REDUCE VALUE   In addition to identifying value-added processes, it's important to identify those processes that reduce value for the customer. Using the same technique to gather this information from the customers, Talbott should create a value-reducing value chain. Talbott identified the sales process as the process that reduced value the most, as shown in Figure 2.8. It found sales were lost because salespeople were promising neckties that were out of stock. Customers were beginning to lose faith in Talbott's ability to deliver high-quality ties. They saw this process failure as one that reduced Talbott's value to them as customers.

To correct its sales process deficiencies, Talbott implemented a new IT system to get timely product information to the sales force. Using laptop computers, the sales force now carries product-line custom CD-ROMs on the road with them. They place orders over their computers from their hotel rooms and receive inventory updates at the same time. As a result, customers have new faith in an old friend who now adds more value than ever.

LOOKING BEYOND THE FOUR WALLS OF THE COMPANY

We talked about information partnerships (which are supported by interorganizational systems) a little earlier in this chapter. If you want to do business with Wal-Mart, for example, the company expects you to be able to connect your information systems with its systems and do business electronically. Instead of Wal-Mart sending you a paper purchase order through the mail, it will send you an electronic purchase order over a telecommunications network. If you can't handle this, you'll have to sell your stuff to someone else because Wal-Mart won't buy from you. Its written policy is shown in Figure 2.9.

As you can see, it uses a technology called *electronic data interchange* (EDI) to support inter-organizational communications. We introduced EDI in Chapter 1 and we'll discuss it in more detail in Chapter 5. EDI is one of the earliest examples of e-commerce and is still widely used today to support such applications as just-in-time (JIT) manufacturing inventory control systems.

Just-in-time is an approach that produces or delivers a product or service just at the time the customer wants it. Automobile assembly plants, for example, rely on their suppliers to deliver the right quantities of needed parts to the assembly line just shortly be-

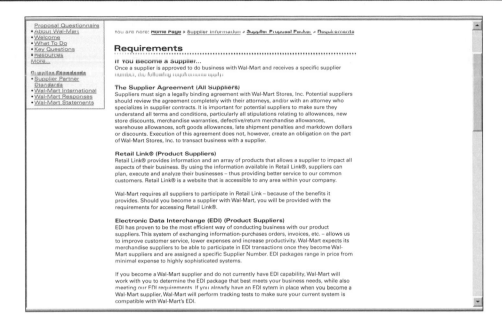

Figure 2.9
Wal-Mart Wants All of Its
Suppliers to Use EDI

fore they are needed. JIT can greatly reduce the amount of money that manufacturers need to spend to maintain inventories at their factory sites.

Wal-Mart is known for its "Always Low Prices." One of the most important strategies for achieving this is managing its supply chain processes. A *supply chain* consists of the paths reaching out to all of a company's suppliers of parts and services. It consists not only of a company's suppliers, but of its suppliers' suppliers as well. Wal-Mart buys at the lowest possible prices, and then, working with members of its supply chain, makes sure that the steps undertaken by either company from that point on are accomplished as efficiently as possible. Think of the process Wal-Mart is following as one in which it is linking its value chain with those of its suppliers.

Manufacturers of consumer goods and retailers are now working together on a process known as collaborative planning, forecasting, and replenishment.[12] *Collaborative planning, forecasting, and replenishment (CPFR)* is a concept that encourages and facilitates collaborative processes between members of a supply chain. In the past, retailers would track their sales and place orders from time to time, perhaps once a week, when their stock levels reached a certain level. One of the techniques used in CPFR is to have retailers share sales information that manufacturers obtained from store check-out scanners with the manufacturers on a daily basis. This provides manufacturers much more current and accurate information with which to schedule their production. Excess inventories are eliminated from manufacturers' warehouses, retail distribution centers, and store shelves. Stock-outs are reduced, as are total costs in the supply chain.

Key E-Commerce Strategies

There are many examples where companies have created competitive advantage through the creative use of IT, and we've already discussed some of them. In recent years, however, the advent of the Internet and, in particular, the World Wide Web gave rise to a new burst of creative entrepreneurship. New ways were found to reach out to customers and suppliers. New businesses have been created using business models never seen before. It has been a time of experimentation with some spectacular successes and failures.

The big difference between the new economy and the old economy is the Internet. The Internet is global in scope, can now be found everywhere, and is either free or quite inexpensive in many countries. Three capabilities made possible by the Internet that companies should keep in mind when searching for ways to use new economy technologies for competitive advantage are

1. Mass customization and personalization
2. Disintermediation
3. Global reach

Let's examine how each of these works.

MASS CUSTOMIZATION AND PERSONALIZATION

Mass customization and personalization are two different concepts that are sometimes confused. With *mass customization,* a business gives its customers the opportunity to tailor its product or service to the customer's specifications. For example, if you order an automobile from the factory, you can have it made with exactly the list of options and colors you wish. The way Dell sells computers, as we discussed previously in this chapter, is an example of mass customization in an Internet business. Another example is the customized CDs you can order through www.Hamaracd.com, a company based in India. Usually when you buy a CD there are about 12 tracks on it and you're lucky if you like three of them. So, you end up playing the tracks you like and skipping past the ones you don't. Hamaracd and others now let you create your own CD containing only tracks you like, as illustrated in Figure 2.10. You pick them and the CD is created for you. (Of course, in this example, it helps if you like music that is popular in India.)

Personalization takes a different twist. The idea of *personalization* is that a Web site can know enough about your likes and dislikes that it can fashion offers that are more likely to appeal to you. Think about personalization this way. What if you could open up

Figure 2.10

Create Your Own Custom
CD at Hamaracd

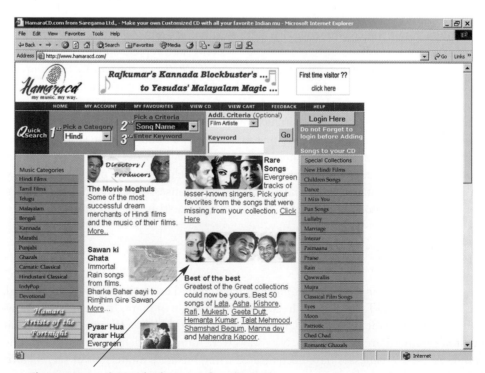

Choose your artists and select your favorite tracks.

the daily newspaper and the only ads you saw were ads for products or services that you were really interested in. No more ads for mattresses, wireless phones, or mortgages. Personalization techniques try to do the same thing: get offers in front of you that you are much more likely to find interesting.

One of the best examples is the books that Amazon.com will suggest to you when you log onto its site. Using a technique called collaborative filtering, Amazon.com keeps track of your taste in books. *Collaborative filtering* is a method of placing you in an affinity group of people with the same characteristics. Based on buying patterns you establish over time, the Web site places you in an affinity group of people who like the same sort of topics. Then, it tracks the buying patterns of the affinity group as well as yours, and makes suggestions to you for books the affinity group is buying that you have not yet bought. With the creative use of IT, it can give you the personal service you might expect from a small, owner-managed bookstore in your hometown where the owner knew your tastes and could suggest books you would be interested in reading.

DISINTERMEDIATION

Disintermediation simply means that with the Internet as a delivery vehicle, intermediate players in a distribution channel can be bypassed, as illustrated in Figure 2.11. For example, if you buy a book from Amazon.com, the bookstore on Main Street is bypassed. Many Internet business models took advantage of the ability to bypass intermediaries such as wholesalers and retailers to reach the consumer directly. Good advice for anyone who occupies an intermediary position in a distribution channel is to think

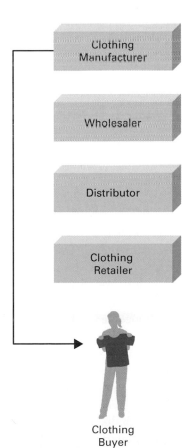

TRADITIONAL SUPPLY CHAIN   **DISINTERMEDIATED SUPPLY CHAIN**

Figure 2.11
Disintermediation at Work

HOW DO YOU SAY "COOL" IN JAPANESE? *TSUTAYA.*

Tsutaya is Japan's largest purveyor of movies, recorded music, and game software. Its 1,100 shops reflect the fashion and culture that appeal to Japanese youth. The most popular outlets offer movie theaters and Starbucks coffee and symbolize all that's cool today in Japan. Founder Muneaki Masuda says he owes much of his success to an early bet on information technology. Tsutaya has systems that can analyze trends hourly at each store. They also track demographics, consumer tastes, and other data in every major urban district—information that helps managers decide what software to stock or where to open a new outlet.

Tsutaya's online site is the most popular destination on the mobile Internet service i-mode, run by NTT DoCoMo. Some 2.4 million users regularly log on to conduct searches and order movie and music titles.[13]

through how an e-business might enter the market and take customers away from them. There are scores of examples of this happening, to people such as stockbrokers, insurance agents, real estate agents, mortgage brokers, as well as merchants selling commoditylike items such as books, videos, and CDs.

One interesting example is Egghead Software. Egghead Software used to have stores in strip malls in many cities. It soon found that it was being disintermediated by the Internet. Customers who might normally come into an Egghead store and buy a shrink-wrapped software package off the shelf were finding that it was more convenient to buy software from a Web site and have it downloaded immediately. What did Egghead do? It closed its brick-and-mortar stores and set up shop in cyberspace. Unfortunately, its refocusing strategy came too late. It filed for bankruptcy on August 15, 2001. In late November 2001, Amazon.com bought the rights to the Egghead.com domain name and intellectual property. Now, if you type www.egghead.com into your browser, you'll be directed to an Amazon.com Web page on which the Egghead.com logo still survives.[14]

GLOBAL REACH

Sausage Software (www.sausagetools.com) is a software developer located outside of Melbourne, Australia. It makes a pretty good Web editor called Hot Dog. If you want to try it out, you can log on to its Web site and download a trial copy that you can use free for 30 days.

At the end of the 30-day trial period, if you want to continue to use Hot Dog, you'll have to log back on to the Web site and give your credit card number. Sausage will send you a code by return e-mail. The code opens up the software for you to use forever, just as if you had bought it at a store. Think about what just happened. You bought a piece of software, had it delivered and paid for, all over the Internet. Without the Internet, if Sausage wanted to reach you, it would have had to put salespeople on an airplane for Los Angeles, the salespeople would have to find a software retailer like CompUSA, and convince them to add copies of Hot Dog to their stores' shelves. Since shelf space is limited and Hot Dog is not well known, Sausage probably would have to pay the retailer $20,000 or so as a "stocking fee" just to get Hot Dog on the shelves of a few stores. The Internet gives even small companies like Sausage Software *global reach,* the ability to extend reach to customers anywhere there is an Internet connection, and at a much lower cost. So much the better if the product is digital, for then it can be both sold and delivered over the Internet.

HERE COMES ELECTRONIC INK

E Ink (www.eink.com) is a proprietary material that can be processed into a lightweight, flexible film, not unlike paper, that can be used for electronic displays. Ultimately, it could be used for highly portable devices (a book that could be folded like a pocket handkerchief, for example).

For now, E Ink offers changeable signage to the retail store market. Signs on display shelves that describe products or post prices, or larger advertising signs, contain information retailers want customers to see. Using E Ink's technology, signs can be instantly changed from a centrally controlled computer. Prices and other information can be changed to accommodate local conditions. A shop could raise the price for umbrellas on a rainy day, or a grocer could reduce the price for bananas that are getting a bit overripe.[15]

The U.S. Airline Industry: A Great Example

To give you a feel for how much of what we have been discussing in this chapter can come together in a single industry, it's hard to think of a better example than the U.S. air travel industry. The large U.S. airlines, in particular, have given ample evidence over a number of years that they know how to use information technology for competitive advantage. Let's show you how.

AIRLINE RESERVATION SYSTEMS

The airlines really got started using IT in a significant way when American Airlines and United Airlines introduced the first airline reservations systems, SABRE and APOLLO. At the time they pretty much divided up the market between them. They marketed the reservation systems to travel agents who got a special computer terminal from either SABRE or APOLLO when they signed up. Typically, a travel agent signed up for one or the other system, but not both. Airline companies who did not have their own reservation systems, Frontier Airlines for example, paid for the privilege of being a "cohost" on SABRE or APOLLO, which permitted their flights to be listed on the systems, and available to travel agents. American and United got a tremendous competitive advantage from being the owners of the reservation systems. First, the systems were very profitable. Second, American and United had access to information on the sales volumes of such competitors as Frontier because it was all available in the reservation systems' databases. If Frontier wanted to have special competitive analyses prepared, they could request special reports, but they had to pay for them and wait for them to be prepared. Also, SABRE and APOLLO were accused by their cohosts of "screen bias."[16] This meant that when a travel agent keyed in a request for available flights between Chicago and San Francisco, for example, the first flights shown were those of the airline who owned the reservation system. Flights of cohosts like Frontier were listed further down.

FREQUENT FLYER PROGRAMS

When the airlines introduced frequent flyer programs (the airline industry's form of a loyalty program), it was to increase the likelihood that their most valued customers, their frequent business travelers, would fly them instead of the competition. Until frequent flyer programs were introduced, business people had no particular incentive to fly the same airline all the time.

After frequent flyer programs came into being, with their mileage and other perks, air travelers saw that it made sense to concentrate their travel with a single airline as much as possible in order to get free trips and upgrades to first and business class. Frequent flyer programs became very popular and now almost every airline in the world has some sort of program. Frequent flyer programs require complex IT systems to handle all of the record keeping and reporting. They are a good example of using IT to alter Porter's five forces in the airlines' favor. They reduced buyer power by making it less likely a traveler would choose another airline; they reduced the threat of substitute products or services by increasing switching costs; and they erected entry barriers by making a frequent flyer program a practical necessity for any airline to compete effectively.

YIELD MANAGEMENT SYSTEMS

Yield management systems are designed to maximize the amount of revenue that an airline generates on each flight. Basically, what they do is alter the price of available seats on a flight minute by minute as the date of the flight approaches, depending on the number of seats that have been sold compared to an estimate of what was expected. So, if fewer seats have been sold, more low-cost seats are made available for sale. If more seats have been sold than what was estimated, fewer low-cost seats will be made available for sale. The objective is to have the airplane take off full at the highest possible average cost per seat, as illustrated in Figure 2.12. (Airlines would rather make something on a low cost seat than make nothing on an empty seat.)

Yield management systems are the reason that an airfare you're quoted over the phone can be $100 higher when you call back an hour later. Yield management systems are also why you should never ask your seatmate what she paid for her ticket unless you're prepared to be disappointed. They're a good example of how the *value chain concept* used IT to add value to the sales and marketing process.

DISINTERMEDIATING THE TRAVEL AGENT

Travel agents in the United States used to get a commission from the airlines on every ticket they sold. Airlines, realizing that agents' commissions were their third highest cost after payroll and fuel, decided to first reduce and, finally, eliminate, travel agents' commissions. At the same time, they made it easier for air travelers to make reservations di-

Figure 2.12

The Payoff from Yield Management

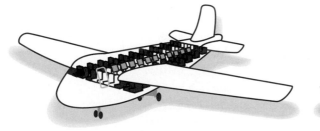

Average seat = $420
Yield = $50,400

120 seats occupied at average price of $420 per seat = $50,400 total yield for the flight.

Average seat = $325
Yield = $65,000

200 seats occupied at average price of $325 per seat = $65,000 total yield for the flight.

HELPING THE LITTLE GUY COMPETE

Assume that a friend of your family owns a small travel agency located in a neighborhood shopping center. The business has provided a comfortable living for him and his family for over 20 years. With the recent changes in the air travel distribution industry, however, he is becoming concerned about whether or not he can survive in the new competitive environment. Airline companies have reduced commissions paid to travel agents, and at the same time have encouraged members of their frequent flyer programs (the best cus-

tomers) to bypass travel agents and deal with airlines directly. In addition, new competition has arisen from Internet-based travel sites. Using IT-enabled techniques such as e-tickets seems to be part of a never-ending process to squeeze travel agents. With new technologies being introduced all the time, your friend is concerned that there is no way he can survive.

See if you can come up with some suggestions for how he could use IT to improve his ability to compete.

rectly with the airlines either through a Web site or by using a toll-free 800 number. They encouraged their frequent flyers to bypass travel agents by doing three additional things:

1. They offered up to 1,000 frequent flyer miles to travelers who made their reservations on the Web.

2. They gave out restricted toll-free 800 numbers to members of frequent flyer "elite" groups, with shorter waiting times and specially trained reservationists.

3. They introduced "e-tickets," which eliminated the need for a paper ticket. One of the travel agent's most valued functions was to see that the traveler had his or her ticket well in advance of the flight. With the introduction of e-tickets, the paper ticket disappeared, replaced by a digital record in the airlines' computer systems.

Travel agents had to start charging fees for their services to make up for the lost airline commission payments. Many travelers were not willing to pay a fee to a travel agent since they could make reservations themselves at no cost. As a result, travel agents' revenues have declined. Expert surveys have estimated that the number of travel agents in the United States will be sharply reduced as a result of these and other moves by the airline companies.

One of the more interesting aspects of this trend (unless, of course, you happened to be a travel agent) is that the airlines made no secret about the fact that they were trying to eliminate travel agents from the distribution chain. Usually, the originators of a product or service are more subtle about disintermediation strategies. For example, when Levi Strauss announced that it was going to sell 501 jeans over its Web site, retailers told Levi Strauss they were going quit selling Levi's jeans altogether. Levi Strauss quickly backed off that particular disintermediation strategy.[17]

UTILIZING EMERGING TECHNOLOGIES

Note, however, that the competitive landscape in the air travel industry continues to change as tech-savvy entrepreneurs come up with new business ideas. Internet-based travel services such as Expedia, Travelocity, and Trip.com have entered the market, as has Priceline.com, where customers can name their own price. Last-minute deals to be sure all those seats are filled are sent out by personalized e-mails on Wednesday of each week. You've told the airline's Web site that you want to know when there are last-minute

RIVALWATCH: KEEPING AN EYE ON THE COMPETITION

In the physical world, monitoring the competition down the street or across town is a relative snap, but keeping track of a global base of online competitors is all but impossible. The problem is that there can be so many competitors and so much information on each of them. Adding to the problem is that information on their prices and products can change several times a day. Keeping tab on what they are doing can be very useful to your company, however, and might even give you some valuable insight into one of your competitors' next moves.

Trying to keep track of them without some expert help, using IT, would be next to impossible. This is where a company called RivalWatch (www.rivalwatch.com) comes to the rescue. By using its proprietary software, RivalWatch will keep a close eye on as many competitors as a company can identify. It keeps its clients up to date on the competition's pricing, product assortment, availability, and even promotional activities. Rivalwatch has software that downloads information for its customers from competitors' Web sites and then uses it to produce reports, accessible securely over the Web. RivalWatch focuses on adding some analysis and presenting information in a useful form. It specializes in surveying digital commerce sites so customers can be sure they're pricing their merchandise competitively.

"We present the data in a form [that lets you] make a business decision," says Ann Hsu, vice president for business development and a cofounder of RivalWatch. "Just giving you a spreadsheet with the prices of 10,000 products is not helpful. Only 5,000 are a direct overlap with your site, and out of these, we summarize the price differences. So you can see [that one group of] products is competitive, but these [others] are 25 percent higher."

As you might imagine, the growing availability of software like RivalWatch has generated interest in developing software products that block electronic snooping. It will be interesting to see the way intelligence-gathering and intelligence-blocking products evolve.[18]

bargain fares to New York, and given the airline permission to send you those e-mails. *Permission marketing* is when you have given a merchant your permission to send you special offers. Auction sites such as bid4vacations.com are another approach. Wireless applications are on the way. You can sign up to have your airline call your cell phone and give you current updates on the status of your flight. Mechanics will soon be able to locate spare parts quickly using wireless devices. Airlines are experimenting with smart card solutions that will speed up the check-in process and improve security at the same time. Iris scan devices and facial recognition devices offer alternative solutions.

You can see how the airlines have employed (and continue to employ) Michael Porter's frameworks as well as some of the other approaches discussed in this chapter: taking the customers' perspective, demanding creativity, personalization, disintermediation, and coming up with new ways to relate to customers and suppliers.

Summing It Up

We've talked about ideas for using IT for competitive advantage, discussed tools companies use to generate such ideas, and given several examples of IT systems that have given their organizations a competitive advantage. Now, we'll summarize some of the most important considerations you should keep in mind as you work to bring an IT competitive advantage to your organization. These include

1. Be efficient and effective.
2. Competition is all around you.

BUILDING ON THE STATE OF THE ART

It's good to get into the habit of noticing the ways that companies are using or not using IT effectively. You can start to build up your own catalog of ideas for your own organization. It's always good to use a state-of-the-art application and see if you can build on it to come up with something even better. Pick a company that you think is getting a competitive advantage from IT and try to suggest ways that it could be improved. This is the time to let your imagination run free and to consider using some of the new emerging technologies.

3. Push the state of the art.

4. IT competitive advantages are only temporary.

First, remember that what you are trying to do is to make your organization more efficient and more effective. That means that you should be applying IT to solving important business problems. It's the difference between doing something right and doing the right thing. IT resources are limited in most organizations so it's important that they be applied to solving the most important business problems or exploiting the opportunities with the highest potential payoff.

Second, remember that your organization is in a competitive environment. The reason we emphasize competitive advantage is that you and your competitors are both trying to attract and retain the same customers. You are all competing for that customer's business. We all tend to buy from the company that gives us the best product or service at the price we want to pay, and the customers of your organization are no different. Companies should strive to "delight the customer," by giving them more value than what they were expecting to receive. Keep that in mind when you're reviewing proposals for new IT systems. Will they help you to delight your customers? Also, it's always smart to try to anticipate how your competitor might use IT for competitive advantage. Why let them get a first mover advantage?

Third, in addition to the other suggestions we made in this chapter, if an IT system is going to give you a competitive advantage it must push the state of the art. In order to push the state of the art, you must find out what a state-of-the-art IT system is for the business problem you're trying to solve. Do a little research to find out which company has the best solution and then try to surpass it. And don't restrict your search to just your industry. A state-of-the-art system for a hospital, for example, might find some ideas in a manufacturing control system. Don't let your imagination be limited by just considering technologies that are currently available, or discard currently available technologies because they're too expensive. If you place artificial boundaries like these on candidate solutions, you may inhibit creativity unnecessarily. You can always bring an overly ambitious solution back to reality, but if you don't evaluate it, the opportunity will be lost.

Finally, it's worth reemphasizing that using IT for competitive advantage usually provides only a temporary advantage. This is because your competitors are forced to duplicate (or to better) what you have. This means that your organization must be continually looking for ways to use IT for competitive advantage so you stay ahead of, or don't fall behind, the competition.

That may sound like a lot of work, and a never-ending cycle, but the reassuring reality is that there will be continuing opportunities for you to come up with creative IT solutions to business problems.

Summary: Student Learning Outcomes Revisited

1. **Illustrate how the creative use of information technology can give an organization a competitive advantage.** Smart companies like Federal Express, Charles Schwab, Dell Computer and Cisco Systems spend a lot of time, money, and effort in designing and installing IT systems because they realize a competitive advantage when IT systems deliver creative solutions to business problems. A *competitive advantage* can be gained by providing a product or service in a way that customers value more than the competition's. Some concepts related to IT systems are the following:

   - *Temporary advantage*—whatever you do, sooner or later the competition duplicates what you've done, but a temporary advantage can linger in customers' minds and have lasting effects.

   - *First mover*—first to market with a new IT-based product or service can gain competitive advantage.

   - *Information partnership*—two or more companies acting in cooperation by integrating their IT systems to provide customers with the best of what each can offer.

   - *Alliance partner*—companies that you do business with on a regular basis in a cooperative fashion.

   - *Business to Business (B2B)*—IT-enabled business with other businesses.

   - *Business to Consumer (B2C)*—IT-enabled business with individual customers.

2. **Describe how to develop business strategies for the Internet Age and use tools that can help.** Michael Porter's frameworks have long been accepted as useful tools for developing business strategy. They continue to be valuable tools in the Internet Age. They include

   a. *The five forces model*
      - *Buyer power*
      - *Supplier power*
      - *Threat of substitute products or service*
      - *Threat of new entrants*
      - *Rivalry among existing competitors*

   b. *Three generic strategies*
      - *Cost leadership*
      - *Differentiation*
      - *Focused strategy*

   c. *The value chain*—a view of the organization as a chain—or series—of processes, each of which adds value to the product or service for the customer.

   Other important considerations in developing IT systems that give an organization a competitive advantage include:

   - Bridging the gap between business people and technical people
   - Viewing the business problem from another perspective
   - Demanding a creative design
   - Looking beyond the four walls of the company

3. **Describe how e-commerce technologies up the stakes and give organizations even more opportunities.** E-commerce makes it even more important for you to focus on competitive advantage. The main reason for this is that the Internet and related technologies provide new capabilities to establish more effective information partnerships along the supply and distribution chains and to forge closer relationships with customers. Key e-commerce strategies include:

   - *Mass customization*—when a business gives its customers the opportunity to have its product or service tailored to the customer's specifications

   - *Personalization*—when an Internet site can know enough about your likes and dislikes that it can fashion offers that are more likely to appeal to you (supported by techniques such as *collaborative filtering*)

   - *Disintermediation*—with the Internet as a delivery vehicle, intermediate players in a distribution channel can be bypassed

   - *Global reach*—the ability to extend reach to customers anywhere there is an Internet connection, and at a much lower cost

4. **Summarize how one specific industry has consistently used information technology for competitive advantage.** The U.S. air travel industry is a good industry for you to study to see how companies can consistently use IT for competitive advantage over a period of many years to both reduce costs and create differentiation. For example, the airlines' frequent flyer programs increase customer loyalty by encouraging frequent flyers to take most or all of their flights on a single airline. Using Porter's five forces framework, frequent flyer programs reduce buyer power and increase switching costs. And frequent flyers like them! Because they do, frequent flyer programs also are an example of an entry barrier. If you want to be in the airline business you pretty much have to have a frequent flyer program. Frequent flyer programs also illustrate how a competitive advantage is often only temporary as competitors race to duplicate innovative IT systems. Other examples of the use of IT for competitive advantage include the airline reservation systems, yield management systems, and the airline companies' e-commerce initiatives.

5. **Summarize how to use information technology for competitive advantage in an organization.** Try to get into the habit of looking for ways that IT could be used to solve a business problem in your organization. Work with IT professionals to get their ideas and look around to see what the state of the art is, not only in your industry, but in others as well. Keep in mind that you are operating in a competitive environment and that it will be useful for you to try to anticipate what your competition's next move in the IT arena might be. Remember that the nature of a competitive environment is that there are winners and losers. IT *can* give you a competitive advantage, but "if you snooze, you'll lose"!

CLOSING CASE STUDY ONE

GM TRIES TO LURE CUSTOMERS WITH ONSTAR

General Motors Corporation has suffered a loss in market share in the United States in the past few years. Partly this is because many of its cars are viewed as boring by consumers. GM recently added an in-car cellular service to many of its cars in an attempt to update its image and increase sales.

The service is called OnStar and was originally offered in Cadillacs as an emergency concierge and road service. It uses a global positioning system (GPS) combined with a cellular telephone and a 24-hour call center where highly trained "virtual advisors" are on duty. Drivers can access a virtual advisor whenever they wish and get specialized services such as the latest news, sports information, and stock quotes. The virtual advisor can also help you plan trips, make restaurant reservations, tell you what's playing at the movies, and give you driving directions to reach your destination. Of course, you can also make a hands-free cellular telephone call using OnStar.

Have you ever been stuck in a traffic jam and wondered what in the world was going on up ahead? Or, have you ever been late for an appointment and wondered if there was a traffic problem on your normal route? Well, with OnStar, drivers in 70 U.S. metropolitan areas can also get information on traffic conditions such as accidents, delays, and construction within a 5-mile radius of their vehicle.

OnStar subscribers can also get emergency roadside assistance if they have car trouble on the road. The integrated GPS combined with the cellular connection to the call center provides assurance that a vehicle can be located no matter what. OnStar can even run a diagnostic check of your car's engine while you drive. And, if you ever have the bad luck to have your car stolen (or forget where you left it in a huge shopping center parking lot), the OnStar virtual advisor can track it and guide the police (or you) to its location.

Fees for the OnStar service start at $199 for an annual subscription. You may have seen ads on television for OnStar, showing a driver who is calling the OnStar call center because he has locked his keys in his car. The OnStar call center operator tells him not to worry and unlocks his car doors with a remote signal from the center. Problem solved. As one more example, emergency assistance is automatically dispatched if the OnStar system detects that the car's airbags have been deployed.

Industry analysts have commented that adding services like OnStar is something GM had to do in order to improve its brands' images in the minds of consumers. GM is betting that being the leader with an on-board technology like OnStar will show that it is once again a technology leader rather than a follower.

OnStar is one of the many ways that GM president Rick Wagoner wants to keep the company innovative. As another example, former Chrysler executive, Bob Lutz, was recently hired to revitalize GM's product lines. Known in the industry as a "car guy," Lutz is sharpening GM's focus on design and finding ways to get new products to market faster. Under the new business process for designing and manufacturing cars that Lutz is overseeing, design moves to the forefront. For every vehicle idea, three teams will compete to create what will eventually make it to market. Lutz held just such a contest to develop the Pontiac Solstice concept car—a two-seat roadster that has been lauded for its looks at auto shows. Lutz views OnStar as a technology that can only add value to the innovative car designs he intends to develop and introduce.

OnStar is now installed in about 1.7 million vehicles. It is available in 36 GM models and is also licensed to Acura, Audi, and Lexus. Although some automobile manufacturers are already talking about offering similar products in their cars, others may find it more economical to license OnStar from GM than develop an offering of their own like Acura, Audi, and Lexus did. Still, some industry analysts remain skeptical about the OnStar initiative. They agree that OnStar offers some interesting features that will be valued by consumers. On the other hand, they point out that GM must continue to focus on its fundamental problem, the style of its cars. Perhaps the combination of OnStar and Bob Lutz will go a long way to solving some of GM's problems.[19]

Questions

1. The chapter discussed several examples of companies that have used IT for competitive advantage. Is there anything about the OnStar system that makes it a good example as well? Is OnStar a feature that is likely to give GM a competitive advantage for an extended period of time or is it likely to give, if anything, a temporary advantage?

2. Evaluate the OnStar system from the perspectives of the five forces model and the three generic strategies. Explain how OnStar might alter the five forces in GM's favor. Where would you place the OnStar system in the three generic strategies grid illustrated in Figure 2.5?

3. Is OnStar a good example of a company incorporating emerging technologies into its product strategies? Why or why not? What features do you think a system such as OnStar might offer five years from now? Is GM taking any risks by placing such a large bet on OnStar's being accepted by the marketplace? What are those risks, if any?

4. If you were a product designer for Ford Motor Company, what would your reaction be to GM's rollout of OnStar? Do you think that systems such as OnStar will become an entry barrier? Log on to the Internet and see if you can find out what the other major automobile manufacturers, both U.S. and non-U.S., are doing in response to the OnStar system. Draw a conclusion as to which responses you think will be most effective.

5. What would your reaction to OnStar be if you were a marketing strategist for a cell phone, Internet portal, or GPS service provider? Would you consider OnStar to be a competitive threat to your company? If so, why, and what would your response be? If you would not consider OnStar to be a threat, why not?

CLOSING CASE STUDY TWO

SPEEDPASS: THROW AWAY YOUR PLASTIC?

Speedpass is an idea that has been around since 1996, but it is now beginning to take off. Speedpass offers a short plastic cylinder, called a Key Tag, that contains an RFID (Radio Frequency Identification) transponder. The Key Tag is very lightweight, short, and can be placed on your key ring. It communicates wirelessly with receiving devices over short distances. It was developed by Mobil Oil Corporation (now part of ExxonMobil) as a substitute for using a credit card at the gasoline pump. Instead of waiting for a credit card authorization, Speedpass users simply wave their Key Tag at the gasoline pump and their billing information is transmitted and recorded for subsequent billing. Speedpass is not available in all areas yet, but if it's available in your area, you can get a Speedpass transponder for free.

In the US state of New Jersey, you can get a Speedpass Car Tag as well as a Key Tag. The Car Tag is a device placed inside the rear window of your car. In the same way as the Key Tag, the Car Tag activates Speedpass technology. So far it is accepted at Mobil fuel and Exxon fuel pumps, but only in New Jersey. You can sign up and also learn more about Speedpass and the way the technology works at www.speedpass.com.

The advantage of the Car Tag version is that you don't have to wave it at anything. When you get close enough to the gasoline pump, the Car Tag transmits your billing information to the pump. You still have to get out of your car and pump the gasoline, however. But wait; there is another technology on the horizon that will make your life even easier. One of the other big oil companies has been developing a "smart" gasoline pump. It can recognize the make and model of the automobile you are driving, and, based on that, know where the fuel door is located and what grade of gasoline you should use. Just think of the day, not that far away, when we will be able to pull up to a gasoline station, "fill 'er up," and pay without getting out of the driver's seat by using Speedpass combined with smart pumps. Great for late nights or rainy days!

Speedpass can also be used at properly equipped cash registers as well. With cash register purchases, not only is there no waiting for authorization, there is also no need for customers to sign a paper receipt.

McDonald's restaurants are testing Speedpass at 400 locations in the Chicago metropolitan area. If it works there, you may soon find that you will be able to buy a Big Mac, fries and a Coke with your Key Tag or Car Tag. Not only that, if it works at McDonald's, it will surely be adopted by other retailers who would like to take advantage of the technology.

There are currently some 5 million users of Speedpass in the United States, with more being added every day. Customers are signing up because they like its convenience. This will encourage more retailers to offer the technology because they can see that customers will be more likely to shop at their stores if they can offer Speedpass in addition to cash, credit, and debit cards.

Another interesting variation is the new Speedpass-enabled Timex Watch, which is also undergoing market testing in Chicago. Whereas the traditional Key Tag is attached to a user's key ring, the Speedpass-enabled Timex Watch looks and functions just like a regular watch. Inside the watch, however, is a Speedpass transponder that works just like the Key Tag. The new Speedpass-enabled Timex Watch will give customers a hands-free option that enables them to pay for purchases by simply positioning their watch in front of an electronic reader located at a gasoline pump, the checkout counter, or the drive-through window. The Timex version of Speedpass is not available yet, but should be soon if the testing goes as well as expected.

Speedpass earns its revenues by taking a small portion of each transaction as a fee, similar to the way a credit card company does. In some ways, Speedpass acts like a loyalty program because it encourages customers to return to shop at retailers who offer the Speedpass technology. However, it differs from traditional loyalty programs because it does not offer free tickets or other incentives. The incentive to Speedpass's customers is the sheer convenience of it, and maybe that's enough to make Speedpass a market success.[20]

Questions

1. With 5 million users signed up already, Speedpass has a pretty good first-mover advantage. In addition, they seem to be

embarked on a strategy of continuous innovation that will keep them in the lead. What sort of companies can you imagine would be likely competitors to Speedpass and what sort of strategies might they use to overcome the lead that Speedpass has established?

2. Speedpass has some critics who claim that its technology has some serious security problems in comparison to credit cards. For example, with a credit card, there is a signature on the back that a merchant can use to compare with the purchaser's signature if the sale is made at a cash register. If you were promoting Speedpass's solution, how would you respond to this issue?

3. Evaluate Speedpass by using as many elements of Porter's five forces model as you think are appropriate. For example, consider the threat of substitute products. What are the substitute products (or services) for Speedpass? Are they serious threats? If so, how could they be overcome? Can you think of other technologies that might be threats?

4. The case stated that Speedpass had no plans at the moment to incorporate elements of a loyalty program into its strategy. Do you agree with this decision on their part? If so, why? If not, can you come up with an approach that would let Speedpass merchants incorporate features of a loyalty program for Speedpass users?

5. Pick another country that you have visited or perhaps one that you have lived in for awhile. (It could be your country of origin.) Using the Internet, see if you can find out if Speedpass is being used in that country. If not, try to determine why it is not. Is it just that the technology is not known there yet? Is there a competing technology that is well accepted, or in the process of becoming well accepted? Are there some elements of the culture in the country you have chosen that makes Speedpass a bad bet for that country? Is the level of technology development such that it is too soon to try to introduce Speedpass?

Key Terms and Concepts

Alliance partner, 75
Application architect, 72
Business to Business (B2B), 77
B2B marketplace, 80
Business to Consumer (B2C), 77
Business process, 84
Buyer power, 78
Collaborative filtering, 89
Collaborative planning, forecasting, and
    replenishment (CPFR), 87
Competitive advantage, 72
Creative design, 82
Disintermediation, 89
Distribution chain, 75
Entry barrier, 80
First mover, 74
Five forces model, 78

Global reach, 90
Information partnership, 75
Just-in-time, 86
Mass customization, 88
Permission marketing, 94
Personalization, 88
Project team, 81
Rivalry among existing competitors, 79
Supplier power, 78
Supply chain, 87
Switching costs, 79
Temporary advantage, 74
Threat of new entrants, 79
Threat of substitute products or services, 79
Three generic strategies, 79
Value chain, 84

Short-Answer Questions

1. What are the two things you need, as a minimum, in order to design an information system that gives an organization a competitive advantage?

2. What do application architects do?

3. Why are competitive advantages achieved through IT usually only temporary?

4. What do we call a company that is the first to market with a product or service?

5. What are interorganizational systems?

6. What is meant by B2B and B2C?
7. When is buyer power high?
8. What is a B2B marketplace?
9. What is CPFR? How do companies who use it get a competitive advantage?
10. What is the *value chain?* How is it used?
11. What is an example of a value-added process not discussed in the chapter?
12. What do we call an approach that produces or delivers a product or service just at the time the customer wants it?
13. What is the difference between mass customization and personalization? Give some examples not included in the chapter.
14. What is meant by *global reach?* Why might it be important for an importer in Lincoln, Nebraska, to be concerned about it?

Short-Question Answers

For each of the following answers, provide an appropriate question.

1. No. It's the way that people use the technology in creative ways to solve a business problem.
2. A distribution chain.
3. It's a way to bridge the communications gap between the business people and the technical people.
4. Send them back to the drawing board.
5. Buyer power, supplier power, barriers to entry, threat of substitute products or services, rivalry among existing competitors.
6. Cost leadership, differentiation of a focused strategy.
7. New books, CDs, and videos.
8. Amazon.com.
9. A standardized set of activities that accomplishes a specific task.
10. Supply chain.
11. Mass customization and personalization, disintermediation, and global reach.
12. Collaborative filtering.
13. Frequent flyer programs.
14. E-tickets.

Assignments and Exercises

1. **EVALUATING TELEMEDICINE** The Industry Perspective on page 82 mentioned that perhaps health care could someday become an export industry. The example that was cited as a possibility was remote surgery. Assume that you work for a university-based medical center and have been given the assignment to evaluate whether or not remote medicine, in general, is likely to be more common in the coming years and, if so, how your medical center and its health care professionals should respond to such a trend. To get you started on this assignment, you might try to find out what is being written about telemedicine.

   Telemedicine is the term that describes the remote delivery of health care services enabled, of course, by computer and telecommunications technologies. For example, a small town in a remote part of the country typically does not have access to skilled medical specialists such as radiologists. If someone is injured and requires an Xray for diagnosis, it is possible to take an Xray locally and then transmit the results to your medical center where it would be reviewed and evaluated by a radiologist. Of course, if the Xray can be transmitted to your medical center, it could be transmitted to a medical center anywhere in the world. Prepare a brief analysis on the possibilities for telemedicine and recommend whether or not your medical center should begin to evaluate its competitive opportunities and threats.

2. **COMPARING PARCEL DELIVERY SERVICES** The chapter mentioned that, almost always, competitive advantages gained through the creative use of information technology are temporary. The need for continuous innovation is always present. If companies stand still, time and

time again we have seen their competitors leapfrog them with new innovations. In the Federal Express example discussed in the chapter, we described their package tracking system as a good example of using IT for competitive advantage. Recently, Federal Express introduced additional features to its package tracking system that make it more useful and convenient to its customers. Called FedEx Insight, you can see what they have done by going to the FedEx Web site. Go to the FedEx Web site at www.fedex.com and navigate your way to the page where FedEx Insight is described. Make a note of the features that it offers customers compared to the basic package tracking service described in the chapter. Now go to one of the competitor's sites, UPS, at www.ups.com. Note what it is offering its customers in the way of tracking services and compare them with those of Federal Express. Prepare a short comparison of the features of each and pick the company you would prefer to use if your selection were being made strictly on the basis of tracking services.

3. **DISINTERMEDIATION IN THE TRAVEL AGENT INDUSTRY** We discussed the concept of

disintermediation in the chapter and gave several examples. One of the examples discussed at some length was the air travel distribution industry and how it has affected smaller travel agents, in particular. There is probably a small travel agency located either on or near your campus. It would be interesting for you to hear from the owner or manager of that travel agency just exactly how the use of IT by the airlines and by Internet travel services has affected them personally, and how business has changed as a result. Find and visit a small local travel agency with an agent who would be willing to spend a little time with you telling his or her impressions of how their business has changed, and what he or she had to do to react to the new competitive pressures. This is an assignment you may want to undertake in groups of two or three, and do a little preplanning so that not everyone is imposing on the time of the same travel agency. If there are only one or two travel agents nearby, see if you can arrange a telephone interview, or perhaps choose one of the other professions mentioned in the chapter.

Discussion Questions

1. What is meant by the term *competitive advantage?* Why is it important? Give some examples of companies you deal with which you think have achieved competitive advantage and explain the technique(s) they used to achieve it. Next, give some examples of companies you deal with, or know of, that have used IT in creative ways to get a competitive advantage. Come up with at least three examples that are not discussed in the chapter.

2. How does Dell get a competitive advantage from its "sell, source, and ship" model? Why do you suppose other manufacturers of personal computers let Dell get and maintain a first mover advantage with its business model and not simply do business the same way as Dell as soon as they saw how effective it was?

3. The chapter states that it is important to view the business problem from another perspective if you are to develop an IT system that gives your organization a competitive advantage. Why is

this important? What are some of the other perspectives that you could use in order to generate fresh ideas for solving a business problem?

4. In the chapter, we gave examples of some common entry barriers in the banking industry such as ATMs and Internet banking. Pick an industry you are familiar with and give an example of an entry barrier that was created using IT. Identify other examples of companies who have used IT to alter Porter's five forces model in their favor.

5. In the Industry Perspective on page 77 we discussed how Jack Welch urged GE managers to come up with new ideas for using the Internet to improve the efficiency and effectiveness of their business units. He urged them to think "destroyyourbusiness.com," or, in other words, to drop old ways of doing business in favor of new ways before the competition did. How important do you suppose it is for presidents and

CEOs to act in similar ways if an organization is going to be able to use IT for competitive advantage? For example, do you think it will be likely that a company's managers will make the effort to find ways to use IT for competitive advantage if IT seems to be about number 23 on the CEO's priority list?

6. Identify a make and model of automobile that would be properly placed in each quadrant of Michael Porter's three generic strategies model as illustrated in Figure 2.5 on page 79. For example, where would you place the Honda Civic? How about a Ferrari?

7. Assume you are in business as a real estate agent. Should you feel threatened by the possibility of being disintermediated? Right now, you get a handsome commission for every house that you sell, perhaps as much as 6 percent or 7 percent. You know that some tech-savvy entrepreneurs are placing listings of homes for sale on the Internet. Many of their Web sites have search engines that let prospective buyers look for the kinds of homes they want in neighborhoods where they want to live. Some of the sites offer virtual home tours as well. You realize that the technology is only going to get better, and that buyers may feel they can get along without at least some of the services you offer and either bypass you completely or negotiate a reduced commission for fewer services. Is it time to start looking for another career?

8. Think of other good examples of industries in which companies have used IT for competitive advantage the way the U.S. airline industry has. Which industries seem to be ahead of others in the way they use IT? Come up with examples of others in the way they use IT. Then, come up with examples of industries that are behind the curve. Why do you suppose some industries lag behind others in the way they use IT?

Ordering Products and Services on the Internet

For most people, electronic commerce is all about business-to-consumer (B2C). On the Internet, you (as an individual consumer) can purchase groceries, clothes, computers, automobiles, music, antiques, books, and much more. If you want to buy it, there's probably an Internet site selling it. Even more, there are probably hundreds of Internet sites selling what it is you want, giving you the opportunity to shop for the best buy.

You can indeed find almost anything you want to buy on the Internet. However, you should carefully consider the person or organization from whom you're making the purchase. You want to be sure you are doing business with someone you can trust. This is especially true if you have to provide a credit card number to make the purchase.

BOOKS AND MUSIC

Books and music make up one category of products you can readily find to purchase on the Internet. One of the most widely known and acclaimed Internet sites performing electronic commerce is Amazon.com at www.amazon.com. Amazon offers several million book and music titles for sale.

Of course, as with all products you buy on the Internet, you need to consider price and the amount you'll save on the Internet compared to purchasing books and music from local stores. Sometimes prices are higher on the Internet, and you can certainly expect to pay some sort of shipping and handling charges.

Make a list of books, music CDs, or cassettes that you're interested in purchasing. Find their prices at a local store. Next, visit three Web sites selling books and music and answer the following questions.

    A. What are the books, CDs, or cassettes or you're interested in?

    B. What are their prices at a local store?

    C. Can you find them at each Internet site?

    D. Are the local prices higher or lower than the Internet prices?

    E. How do you order and pay for your products?

    F. How long is the shipping delay?

    G. What is the shipping charge?

    H. Overall, how would you rate your Internet shopping experience compared to your local store shopping experience?

CLOTHING AND ACCESSORIES

It might seem odd, but many people purchase all types of clothing on the Internet—from shoes to pants to all kinds of accessories (including perfume). The disadvantage in shopping for clothes on the Internet is that you can't actually try them on and stand in front of the mirror. But if you know exactly what you want (by size and color), you can probably find and buy it on the Internet.

Connect to several clothing and accessory sites and experience cyber-clothing shopping. As you do, consider the following.

A. How do you order and pay for merchandise?

B. What sort of description is provided about the clothing—text, photos, perhaps 3D views?

C. What is the return policy for merchandise that you don't like or doesn't fit?

D. Finally, is shopping for clothes on the Internet as much fun as going to the mall? Why or why not?

INTERNET AUCTION HOUSES

Auction houses act as clearing stations on which you can sell your products or purchase products from other people in an auction format (essentially, Consumer to Consumer or C2C electronic commerce). EBay, one of the more popular auction houses, boasts millions of items for sale.

It works quite simply. First, you register as a user at a particular auction house. Once you do, you'll have a unique user ID and password that allow you to post products for sale or bid on other products. When the auction is complete for a particular product (auction houses set time limits that last typically from one to 10 days), the auction house will notify the seller and the winning bidder. Then, it's up to you and the other person to exchange money and merchandise.

So, think of a product you'd like to buy or sell—perhaps a rare coin, a computer, a hard-to-find Beanie Baby, or a car. Connect to a couple of different Internet auction houses and answer the following questions for each.

A. What is the registration process to become a user?

B. Do you have to pay a fee to become a user?

C. Is your product of interest listed?

D. How do you bid on a product?

E. What does the auction house charge you to sell a product?

F. What is the duration of a typical auction?

G. Can you set a minimum acceptable bid for a product you want to sell?

H. How does the auction house help you evaluate the credibility of other people buying and selling products?

AUTOMOBILES

Another product category that you may not expect to find on the Internet is automobiles. That's right—on the Internet you can find literally any automobile you'd be interested in purchasing. Muscle cars, Jaguars, Rolls Royces, Hondas, and thousands more are for sale on the Internet.

Try connecting to a few of these sites and browse for an automobile you'd like to own. As you do, think about these issues. What variety can you find (color, engine size, interior, etc.)? Are financing options available? How do you "test drive" a car for sale on the Internet? What happens if you buy a car and then don't like it? What about used cars? Can you trust people selling a used car on the Internet? How do you pay for a car, typically a relatively large purchase?

You can find a variety of sites that provide competitive pricing information concerning cars. Many of these sites are for all cars in general, not just those for sale on the Internet. One of the best sites is AutoSite at www.autosite.com. If you're ever shopping for a new or used car, you should definitely check out that site.

EXTENDED LEARNING MODULE B

THE WORLD WIDE WEB AND THE INTERNET

Student Learning Outcomes

1. DEFINE THE RELATIONSHIPS AMONG WEB SITE, WEB SITE ADDRESS, DOMAIN NAME, WEB PAGE, AND UNIFORM RESOURCE LOCATOR (URL).

2. EXPLAIN HOW TO INTERPRET THE PARTS OF AN ADDRESS ON THE WEB.

3. IDENTIFY THE MAJOR COMPONENTS AND FEATURES OF WEB BROWSER SOFTWARE.

4. DESCRIBE THE DIFFERENCES BETWEEN DIRECTORY AND TRUE SEARCH ENGINES.

5. DESCRIBE THE VARIOUS TECHNOLOGIES THAT MAKE UP THE INTERNET.

6. IDENTIFY KEY CONSIDERATIONS IN CHOOSING AN INTERNET SERVICE PROVIDER (ISP).

7. DESCRIBE THE COMMUNICATIONS SOFTWARE AND TELECOMMUNICATIONS HARDWARE YOU NEED TO CONNECT TO THE INTERNET.

Introduction

Perhaps the most visible and explosive information technology tool is the Internet, and subsequently the World Wide Web (Web). No matter where you look or what you read, someone always seems to be referring to one of the two. On television commercials, you find Web site addresses displayed (such as www.ibm.com for an IBM commercial or www.toyota.com for a Toyota commercial). In almost every magazine these days, you'll find articles about the Internet because of its growing significance in our society. Most major business publications, such as *Fortune, Forbes,* and *Business Week,* devote entire issues each year to the Internet and how to use it for electronic commerce. Of course, many such publications have been carrying articles detailing how and why so many dot-coms failed in recent years (now affectionately referred to as *dot-bombs*).

The Internet really is everywhere—and it's here to stay. What's really great about the Internet is that it takes only a couple of hours to learn. Once you've read the text for this module, you should try your hand at the Internet scavenger hunts. You'll be surprised to learn how easy it is to find information on the Internet.

World Wide Web

The **World Wide Web,** or **Web** as you probably know it, is a multimedia-based collection of information, services, and Web sites supported by the Internet. The **Internet** is a vast network of computers that connects millions of people all over the world. Schools, businesses, government agencies, and many others have all connected their internal networks to the Internet, making it truly a large network of networked computers. So the Internet and all its technological infrastructure is really what makes the Web possible. Most people consider the Web and the Internet to be the same. Although there are both subtle and distinct differences between the two, we'll not delve into those differences here.

WEB SITES, ADDRESSES, AND PAGES

As you use the Web, you'll most often be accessing Web sites. A **Web site** is a specific location on the Web where you visit, gather information, and perhaps even order products. Each Web site has a specific Web site address. A **Web site address** is a unique name that identifies a specific site on the Web. Technically, this address is called a domain name. A **domain name** identifies a specific computer on the Web and the main page of the entire site. Most people use the term *Web site address* instead of the technical term *domain name.* For example, the Web site address for *USA Today* is www.usatoday.com (see Figure B.1).

Most Web sites include several and perhaps hundreds of Web pages. A **Web page** is a specific portion of a Web site that deals with a certain topic. The address for a specific Web page is called a URL. A **URL (uniform resource locator)** is an address for a specific Web page or document within a Web site. Most people opt for the common term of *Web page address* when referring to a URL. As you can see in Figure B.1, you can click on the link for **Sports** on the main page for the *USA Today.* By clicking on that link, you will then be taken to a specific Web page within the *USA Today* Web site. The URL or Web page address for that page is www.usatoday.com/sports/sfront.htm. Links are important on the Web. A **link** (the technical name is **hyperlink**) is clickable text or an image that takes you to another site or page on the Web.

Web site address or domain name

Figure B.1

The *USA Today* Web Site and Sports Web Page

Links

UNDERSTANDING ADDRESSES

When you access a certain Web site or page, you do so with its unique address, such as www.usatoday.com (for our *USA Today* example). Addresses, because they are unique, tell you some important information about the site or page. Let's consider two different examples (see Figure B.2): Priceline (www.priceline.com) and the University of Technology in Sydney, Australia (www.uts.edu.au).

Most addresses start with http://www, which stands for *hypertext transfer protocol* (http) and *World Wide Web* (www). The http:// part is so common now that you don't even have to use it in most cases. The remaining portion of the address is unique for each site or page. If you consider www.priceline.com, you know that it's the address for Priceline. You can also tell it's a commercial organization by the last three letters: com. This three-letter extension can take on many forms and is referred to as the ***top-level domain.*** Top-level domains include

- **com**—Commercial or for-profit business
- **coop**—Cooperatives
- **edu**—Educational institution
- **gov**—U.S. government agency
- **mil**—U.S. military organization
- **net**—Internet administrative organization
- **org**—Professional or nonprofit organization
- **int**—International treaties organization
- **info**—General information
- **biz**—Business
- **museum**—Accredited museums
- **name**—Personal
- **pro**—Accountants, doctors, and lawyers, to start

The top-level domain ".com" identifies Priceline as a commercial or for-profit organization.

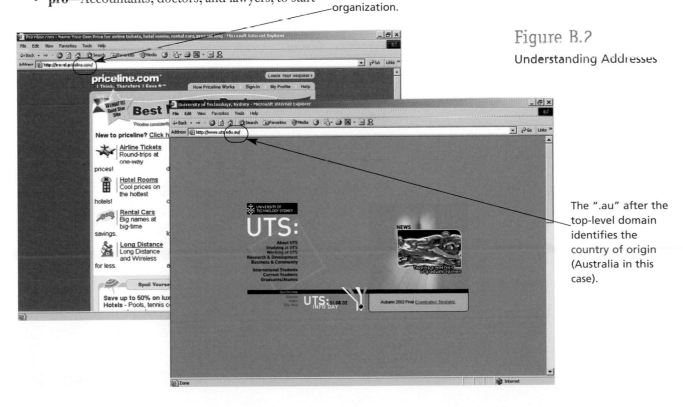

Figure B.2
Understanding Addresses

The ".au" after the top-level domain identifies the country of origin (Australia in this case).

Some addresses have a two-character extension that follows the top-level domain. In this case, it's to identify the country location of the site. For example, the site address for the University of Technology in Sydney, Australia, is www.uts.edu.au. From that address, you can tell it's for an educational institution (edu) located in Australia (au).

USING WEB BROWSER SOFTWARE

Web browser software enables you to surf the Web. It is, in fact, the software we used to view sites for the *USA Today*, Priceline, and University of Technology in Sydney, Australia. The most popular Web browsers today are Internet Explorer and Netscape Communicator. They are free for you to use; Internet Explorer is standard on most computers today.

To demonstrate how you use Web browser software, let's take a quick tour of Internet Explorer and Netscape Communicator. In Figures B.3 (on this page) and B.4 (on the opposite page), you can see we are using Internet Explorer and Netscape Communicator, respectively, to view the Web site for eBay (www.ebay.com). In Figure B.3, you can see the menu bar for Internet Explorer that includes the functions for **File, Edit, View, Favorites, Tools,** and **Help.** In Figure B.4, you can see the menu bar for Netscape Communicator that includes the functions of **File, Edit, View, Go, Communicator,** and **Help.** Both menu bars are very similar and support the same basic functions. For example, if you click on **File** in either Internet Explorer or Netscape Communicator, you'll see a pull-down menu that allows you to initiate other actions such as printing the Web site and sending the Web site via e-mail to someone else.

Below the menu bar, you'll find a button bar on both Web browsers that supports more functions. We won't go into any of these in detail here; you can play with them at your leisure. Below the button bar is the **Address** field for Internet Explorer and the **Location** field for Netscape Communicator. Both are the same. If you know the address for where you want to go, click in either of these two fields, type in the address, and then hit **Enter.**

Figure B.3
Internet Explorer

Menu bar

Button bar

Address field

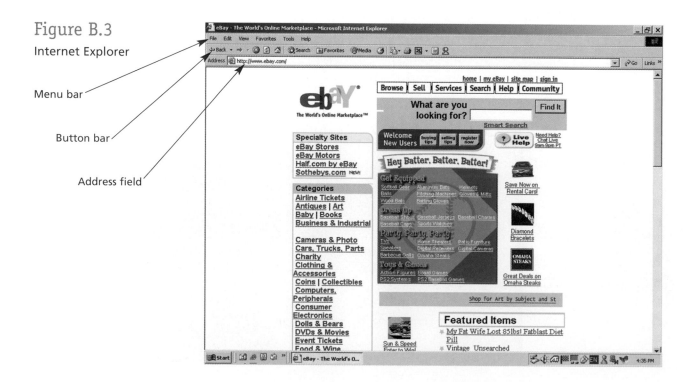

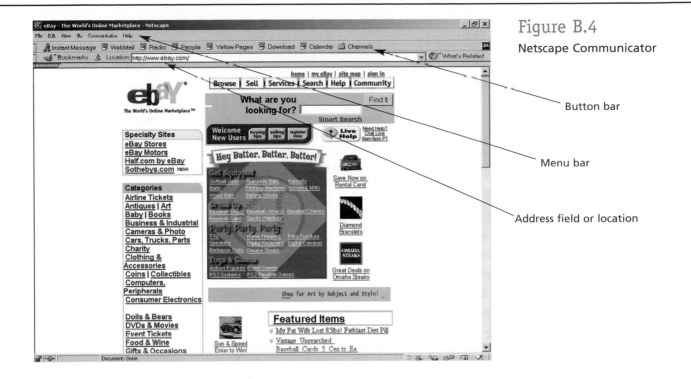

Figure B.4

Netscape Communicator

One of the most important features of any Web browser is that you can create and edit a list of your most commonly visited places on the Web. In Internet Explorer, it's called a **Favorites list,** and in Netscape Communicator it's called a **Bookmarks list.** So, if you frequently visit eBay, you can save the address in one of these lists while you're viewing it. In Internet Explorer, click on the **Favorites** button and then **Add.** In Netscape Communicator, click on the **Bookmarks** button and then **Add Bookmark.** Later, when you want to visit eBay, click on the appropriate button (**Favorites** for Internet Explorer or **Bookmarks** for Netscape Communicator) and then click on the eBay link. That's all there is to it.

Web browser software is the easiest personal productivity software to learn. Most people find that they need very little instruction and seldom need a book. Just connect to the Web, start the Web browser of your choice, play around for an hour or so, and you'll soon be a Web surfing expert.

It really is quite simple. When you start your Web browser software, you'll first see what is called a *home page*—the Web site that your Web browser automatically connects to and displays when you first start surfing. Once you're there, you can click on any of the links that interest you, or you can type in a new address and go to any other site.

If you're not sure of the exact Web site address, you begin to search for it in one of two ways. The first is to use a search engine, which we'll discuss in the next section. The second is to type in a logical name in the **Address** field (using Internet Explorer) or the **Location** field (using Netscape Communicator). For example, if you want to download tax forms from the IRS Web site but don't know the address of the IRS, you can simply type in "IRS" or "internal revenue service" in the **Address** or **Location** field. Your Web browser will automatically begin a search for Web sites related to those terms and hopefully will find the right site for you. (In the instance of searching for the IRS, both Internet Explorer and Netscape Communicator do take you to the site you need.)

Search Engines

There will be occasions when you want to find information and services on the Web, but you don't know exactly which site to visit. In this case, you can type in a logical name as we just demonstrated, or you can use a search engine. A *search engine* is a facility on the Web that helps you find sites with the information and/or services you want. There are many types of search engines on the Web, the two most common being directory search engines and true search engines.

A *directory search engine* organizes listings of Web sites into hierarchical lists. Yahoo! is the most popular and well known of these. If you want to find information using a directory search engine, start by selecting a specific category and continually choose subcategories until you arrive at a list of Web sites with the information you want. Because you continually narrow down your selection by choosing subcategories, directory search engines are hierarchical.

A *true search engine* uses software agent technologies to search the Internet for key words and then places them into indexes. In doing so, true search engines allow you to ask questions as opposed to continually choosing subcategories to arrive at a list of Web sites. *Ask Jeeves* is the most popular and well-known true search engine.

Let's now consider the task of finding who won the Academy Awards in 2002 to see how directory and true search engines differ.

USING A DIRECTORY SEARCH ENGINE

As we stated, Yahoo! is the most popular and well-known directory search engine. Figure B.5 shows the sequence of pages (categories) through which you would traverse using Yahoo! to determine who won the Academy Awards in 2002. The sequence of categories includes

- **Arts & Humanities**
- **Awards**
- **Movies and Film@**
- **Academy Awards**
- **74th Annual Academy Awards**

In the final screen you can see a list of Web sites from which you can choose.

There are some definite advantages to performing a search in this way. If you look at the next-to-last screen, for example **(Academy Awards),** it also includes subcategories for the Academy Awards in each of the last six years (1996–2001). So, you can easily find related information using a directory search engine.

You can also use directory search engines in a different fashion. For example, in the first screen, we could have entered **academy +awards +2002** in the field immediately to the left of the **Search** button and then clicked on the **Search** button. This particular search would yield a list of Web sites that is very similar to the list we received by choosing subcategories.

You might notice that we included the plus sign (+) in a couple of different places in our key terms list. By doing so, we limited the search to finding just sites that included all three words. Likewise, if you want to limit a search so that it won't show Web sites that contain certain key words, you would use a minus sign (–). For example, if you wanted to find Web sites that contain information about the Miami Dolphins NFL team, you could enter **Miami +Dolphins.** That would probably yield a list of suitable sites, but

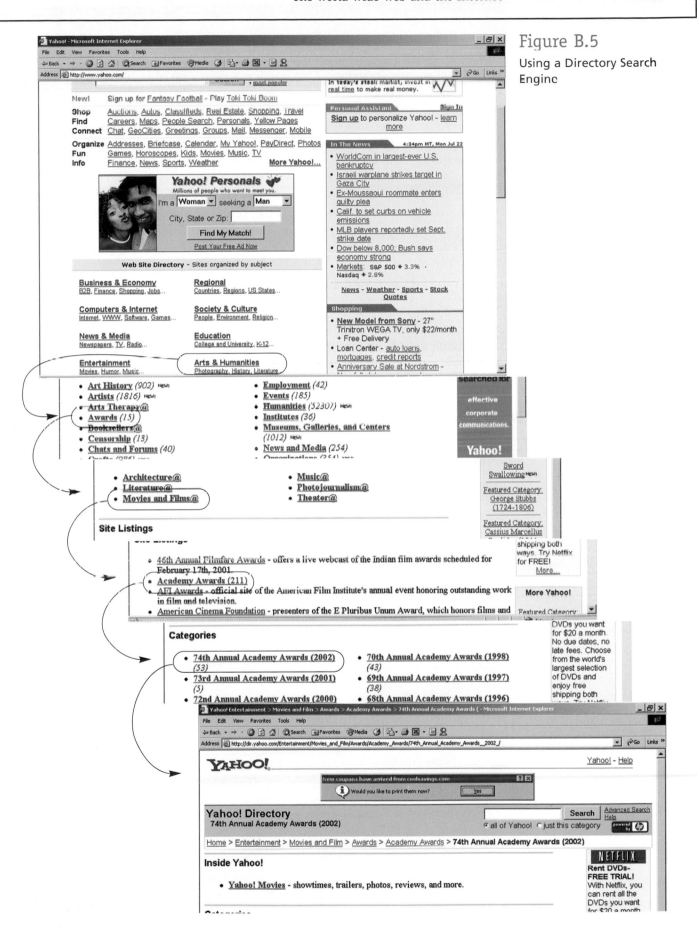

Figure B.5

Using a Directory Search Engine

it might also include sites that include information about watching dolphins (the aquatic version) in Miami. You can further refine your search by entering something like **Miami +Dolphins –aquatic –mammal.** That search will yield a list of Web sites that have the terms *Miami* and *Dolphins* but will eliminate any sites that have the term *aquatic* or *mammal.*

When you use a directory search engine and type in specific terms instead of traversing through subcategories, we definitely recommend that you make use of the plus sign and/or minus sign. For example, if you want to find sites about wind tunnels, using **wind tunnel** will return a list of sites related to wind tunnels but also the wind (weather sites) and tunnels in general. On the other hand, **wind +tunnel** will yield a more refined list of sites. We recommend that you complete the Team Work project (Finding and Using Search Engines) on page 000. As you do, you'll find that some search engines support advanced and unique capabilities that can help you further refine your search criteria.

USING A TRUE SEARCH ENGINE

Ask Jeeves is the most popular and well-known true search engine. Using Ask Jeeves, you simply ask a question. For finding out who won the Academy Awards in 2002, we would simply enter **Who won the Academy Awards in 2002?** and hit the **Ask** button. As you can see in Figure B.6, Ask Jeeves returned not only a list of possible Web sites but also some related questions to which you might like answers.

Both types of search engines are very easy to use. Which you choose is really a function of how you think. Some people think in terms of hierarchical lists while others think in terms of questions. What you'll undoubtedly find is that directory search engines are better in some cases while true search engines are better in others.

Figure B.6

Using a True Search Engine

FINDING AND USING SEARCH ENGINES

Search engines are easy to find on the Web and even easier to use. In fact, there are about 100 search engines that you can use to find almost any information you need.

Your group's tasks include (1) creating a list of the 10 most popular search engines on the Web and (2) per-

forming a search on each for the same information. As you complete the second task, evaluate how easy or difficult it was to use each search engine. Also, evaluate the quality of the Web site list you received from each search engine.

Internet Technologies

To best take advantage of everything the Web has to offer, it often helps to understand what's going on behind the Web, that is, the Internet. The Internet is really the enabling structure that makes the Web possible. Without the Web, the Internet still exists and you can still use it. But the reverse is not true. The Internet is the set of underlying technologies that makes the Web possible. The Web is somewhat of a graphical user interface (GUI) that sets on top of the Internet. The Web allows you to click on links to go to other sites, and it allows you to view information in multiple forms of media.

THE INTERNET BACKBONE

The *Internet backbone* is the major set of connections for computers on the Internet (see Figure B.7). A *network access point (NAP)* is a point on the Internet where several connections converge. At each NAP is at least one computer that simply routes Internet traffic from one place to another (much like an airport which allows you to switch planes in an attempt to get to your final destination). These NAPs are owned and maintained by network service providers. A *network service provider (NSP)*, such as MCI or AT&T, owns and maintains routing computers at NAPs and even the lines that connect the NAPs to each other. In Figure B.7, you can see that Dallas is a NAP, with lines converging from Atlanta, Phoenix, Kansas City, and Austin.

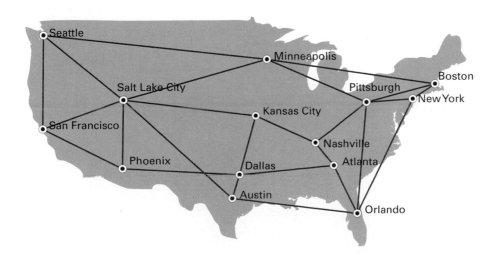

Figure B.7

The Internet Backbone in the United States

At any given NAP, an Internet service provider may connect its computer or computers to the Internet. An ***Internet service provider (ISP)*** is a company that provides individuals, organizations, and businesses access to the Internet. ISPs include AOL, Juno (which is free), and perhaps even your school. In turn, you "dial up" and connect your computer to an ISP computer. So, your ISP provides you access to the Internet (and thus the Web) by allowing you to connect your computer to its computer (which is already connected to the Internet).

If you live in the San Francisco area and send an e-mail to someone living near Boston, your e-mail message might travel from San Francisco to Salt Lake City, then to Minneapolis, and finally to Boston. Of course, your e-mail message may very well travel the route of San Francisco, Phoenix, Dallas, Atlanta, Nashville, Pittsburgh, Orlando, New York, and then Boston. But, no matter—your message will get there. Can you imagine the route that your e-mail message would travel if you were in San Francisco sending it to someone in Venice, Italy? One time, it might go west around the world through Australia. The next time, it might go east around the world through New York and then on to London.

INTERNET SERVERS

There are many types of computers on the Internet, namely, router (which we've already discussed), client, and server computers (see Figure B.8). The computer that you use to

Figure B.8

Servers on the Internet

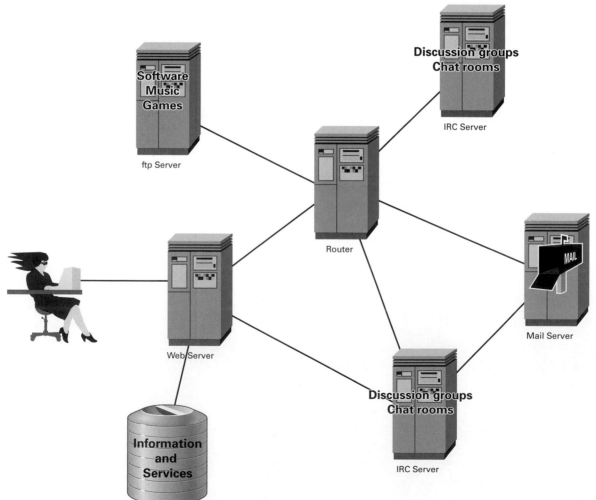

USING A WEB PORTAL

Most Web browser software is already configured to take you to a certain Web site when you start surfing. For example, Internet Explorer usually starts at the Microsoft Network site (MSN at www.msn.com). Sites such as MSN, Yahoo!, and The Go Network (www.go.com) are often referred to as Web portals. A **Web portal** is a site that provides a wide range of services, including search engines, free e-mail, chat rooms, discussion boards, and links to hundreds of different sites.

The nice thing about Web portals is that they often let you customize the first page you see. So, you can request a ticker of your favorite stocks, the weather forecast for your area over the next three days, and a list of sites you commonly visit.

In this project, you are to create a customized and personal Web portal at two different places on the Web. We recommend that you do so at one of these sites (although there are many others):

- www.msn.com
- www.go.com
- www.excite.com
- www.yahoo.com

As you build each personalized Web portal, answer the following questions.

1. What is the registration process required to build a Web portal?
2. Can you receive a free e-mail account? If so, must you establish it?
3. Can you create categories of your most commonly visited sites?
4. Can you request customized local information for your area? If so, what type of information?
5. How do you adjust your Web browser settings so that it automatically takes you to your Web portal page?

access the Internet and surf the Web is called a *client computer*. Your client computer can be a traditional desktop or notebook computer, a Web or Internet appliance, a PDA, or perhaps even a cell phone.

Internet server computers are computers that provide information and services on the Internet. There are four main types of server computers on the Internet: Web, mail, ftp, and IRC servers. A **Web server** provides information and services to Web surfers. So, when you access www.ebay.com, you're accessing a Web server (for eBay) with your client computer. Most often, you'll be accessing and using the services of a Web server.

A **mail server** provides e-mail services and accounts. Many times, mail servers are presented to you as a part of a Web server. For example, Hotmail is a free e-mail server and service provided by MSN. An **ftp (file transfer protocol) server** maintains a collection of files that you can download. These files can include software, screen savers, music files (many in MP3 format), and games. An **IRC (Internet Relay Chat) server** supports your use of discussion groups and chat rooms. IRC servers are popular hosting computers for sites such as www.epinions.com. There, you can share your opinions about various products and services, and the site will even pay you (in the form of *e-royalties*) if people read the reviews you write.

COMMUNICATIONS PROTOCOLS

As information moves around the Internet, bouncing among network access points until it finally reaches you, it does so according to various communications protocols. A **communications protocol (protocol)** is a set of rules that every computer follows to transfer information. The most widely used protocols on the Internet include TCP/IP, http, and ftp.

TCP/IP, or *transport control protocol/Internet protocol,* is the primary protocol for transmitting information over the Internet. Whenever any type of information moves over the Internet, it does so according to TCP/IP. *Hypertext transfer protocol (http)* is the communications protocol that supports the movement of information over the Web, essentially from a Web server to you. That's why Web site addresses start with "http://." Most Web browser software today assumes that you want to access a Web site on the Internet. So you don't even have to type in the "http://" if you don't want to.

File transfer protocol (ftp) is the communications protocol that allows you to transfer files of information from one computer to another. When you download a file from an ftp server (using ftp), you're using both TCP/IP (the primary protocol for the Internet) and ftp (the protocol that allows you to download the file). Likewise, when you access a Web site, you're using both TCP/IP and http (because the information you want is Web based).

Connecting to the Internet

To access the Web (via the Internet), you need an Internet service provider (ISP), as we discussed earlier. ISPs can include your school, your place of work, commercial ISPs such as AOL, and free ISPs such as Juno. Which you choose is a function of many things.

One of the nice benefits of going to school or being employed is that you often get free Web access through school or your work. All you have to do is connect your home computer to your school's or work's computer (we'll talk about this process in a moment) and you're ready to surf. However, some schools and places of business may restrict where you can go on the Web. And they may even monitor your surfing.

Commercial ISPs charge you a monthly fee, just as your telephone company charges you a monthly fee for phone service. This fee usually ranges from a few dollars a month to about $20. Popular worldwide commercial ISPs include Microsoft (MSN), AOL, CompuServe, and AT&T WorldNet, just to name a few.

Free ISPs are absolutely free, as their names suggest—you don't pay a setup fee, you don't pay a monthly fee, and you usually have unlimited access to the Web. But there are some catches. Many free ISPs do not offer you Web space, as opposed to most commercial ISPs which do. *Web space* is a storage area where you keep your Web site. So, if you want to create and maintain a Web site, you may have to choose a commercial ISP over a free ISP (your school probably also offers you Web space). Also when using a free ISP, you will often see banner ads that you can't get rid of (see Figure B.9). You can move them around and from side to side, but you can't remove them completely from your screen. Technical support is often limited with a free ISP. Some offer only e-mail support, while others do offer phone support but no toll-free number.

In spite of those drawbacks, many people do choose free ISPs over commercial ISPs, mainly because of cost (remember, $20 per month equals $240 per year). Popular free ISPs include FreeLane (www.freelane.excite.com), FreeInternet.com (www.freei.com), Juno (www.juno.com, see Figure B.9), and NetZero (www.netzero.com). To decide which type of ISP is best for you, ask these questions:

- *Do you need Web space?* If yes, a free ISP may not be the right choice.
- *Is great technical support important?* If yes, then a commercial ISP may be the right choice.

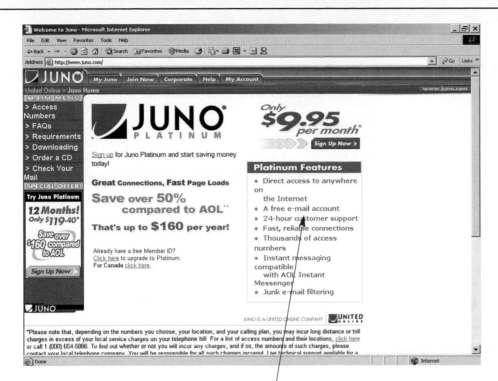

Juno's free ISP service will require that you see a lot of banner ads. If you want, you can subscribe to Juno's Platinum service (at a cost of $9.95) per month which has fewer advertisements.

- *Is money a serious consideration?* If yes, then a commercial ISP may not be the right choice.
- *Is privacy important to you?* If yes, then your school or work may not be the right choice.

COMMUNICATIONS SOFTWARE

To access and use the Web, you need communications software, namely,

- ***Connectivity software***—Enables you to use your computer to dial up or connect to another computer
- ***Web browser software***—Enables you to surf the Web
- ***E-mail software***—(Short for ***electronic mail software***) enables you to electronically communicate with other people by sending and receiving e-mail

Connectivity software is the first and most important. With connectivity software, you essentially use your computer (and a phone line) to call up and connect to the server computer of your ISP. Connectivity software is standard on most personal computers today. To use connectivity software, you really only need to know the number to call. Then it's a relatively easy process: within Microsoft Windows, click on **Start, Programs, Accessories, Communications, Network and Dial-up Connections,** and then select **Make New Connection** (your exact sequence may vary slightly according to which version of Windows you're using).

Web browser software and e-mail software are also standard software today. If your school or work is your ISP, then you'll most often be using commercially available Web browser software such as Internet Explorer or Netscape Communicator, and the e-mail software you use will vary according to your school's or work's preference. If you're using a commercial or free ISP, then your choice of Web browser software and e-mail software will depend on that particular organization.

EVALUATING ISP OPTIONS

Choosing an Internet service provider (ISP) is an important, but not too terribly complicated, task. In this project, your group is to evaluate three different ISPs: a well-recognized commercial ISP such as AOL or AT&T WorldNet, a free ISP such as Juno (there are many others), and a local or regional ISP in your area (you may need to look in your phone book to find one of these).

As you evaluate these three different ISPs, do so in terms of (1) price per month, (2) amount of Web space provided, (3) monthly limit of hours you can be connected without paying an additional fee, (4) customer support, and (5) the ability to have e-mail.

Of the three, which would you choose and why?

Regardless of your choice of ISP, the unique Web browser software and e-mail software provided work in similar fashion. So, if you're used to using Internet Explorer and then choose AOL as your ISP, you will see that AOL has its own Web browser software. It will look different on the screen, but it supports the same functionality (favorites list, moving forward and backward through your list of visited Web sites, and so on). All you have to do is get used to a new interface. Different e-mail software will also look different but support the same functionality.

TELECOMMUNICATIONS HARDWARE

In addition to communications software, you also need some telecommunications hardware to access the Web (again, via the Internet). If you're at school or work, you'll probably be able to connect your computer directly to a network that is then connected to the Internet. This often amounts to simply plugging a network line into your computer and starting your preferred Web browser or e-mail software. We discuss this type of connection to the Internet in more detail in *Extended Learning Module E*.

If you're connecting from home, you'll need some sort of modem. There are many types of modems, including

- A *telephone modem*—A device that connects your computer to your phone line so that you can access another computer or network
- *Digital Subscriber Line (DSL) modem*—A high-speed Internet connection using phone lines, which allows you to use your phone line for voice communication at the same time
- A *cable modem*—A device that uses your TV cable to deliver an Internet connection
- A *satellite modem*—A modem that allows you to get Internet access from your satellite dish

DSL, cable, and satellite modems are among the newest, most expensive, and fastest. They also don't tie up your phone line. If, for example, you're using a basic telephone modem, you can't use your telephone line for voice communications at the same time. A DSL modem on the other hand, for example, basically splits your telephone line so that you can use it simultaneously for voice communications and for connecting to the Internet (see Figure B.10). Even more so, DSL, cable, and satellite modems offer you an "always-on" Internet connection.

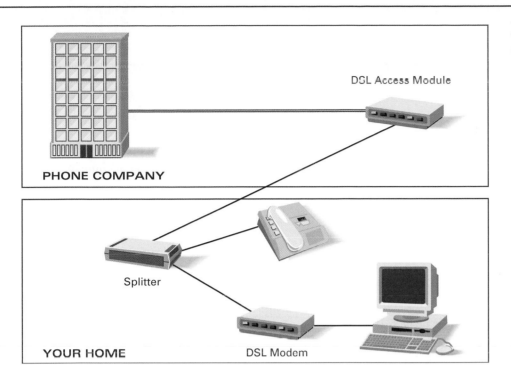

Figure B.10
DSL Modem Connection

The biggest factor in determining your choice of telecommunications hardware (beyond price) may be that of availability. In many areas of the country, phone companies and cable TV service providers do not yet support the use of DSL, cable, and satellite modems. So, you may limited to just using a basic telephone modem. If some of the other options are available to you, we definitely recommend that you research them.

Summary: Student Learning Outcomes Revisited

1. **Define the relationships among Web site, Web site address, domain name, Web page, and uniform resource locator (URL).** A *Web site* (such as www.usatoday.com for the *USA Today*) is a specific location on the Web where you visit, gather information, and perhaps even order products. A *Web site address* (www.usatoday.com) is a unique name that identifies a specific site on the Web. Technically, a Web site address is called a *domain name*. A *Web page* is a specific portion of a Web site that deals with a certain topic. Technically, the address for a specific Web page is called a *URL (uniform resource locator).*

2. **Explain how to interpret the parts of an address on the Web.** Most Web site addresses start with http://www. Beyond that, the address is unique. The first part (using www.uts.edu.au as an example) provides the name of the organization or Web site (UTS or University of Technology in Sydney). The next part tells the type of organization and is called the *top-level domain.* For UTS, it is "edu," describing it as an educational institution. If something follows after that, it usually provides a country of origin ("au" for UTS which identifies its country of origin as Australia).

3. **Identify the major components and features of Web browser software.** The two most popular Web browsers are Internet Explorer and Netscape Communicator. Each includes a menu bar (with functions such as **File, Edit,** and **View**), a button bar (for commonly performed tasks such as printing), and an address or

location field into which you can type a Web site address. Web browsers also include capabilities for maintaining a list of commonly visited sites. In Internet Explorer, these are called a **Favorites list,** while Netscape Communicator refers to them as a **Bookmarks list.**

4. **Describe the differences between directory and true search engines.** *Search engines* are facilities on the Web that help you find sites with the information and/or services you want. A *directory search engine* organizes listings of Web sites into hierarchical lists. Using a directory search engine, you start by selecting a specific category and continually refine your search by choosing subsequent subcategories. A *true search engine* uses software agent technologies to search the Internet for key words and then places them into indexes. You use a true search engine by asking a question.

5. **Describe the various technologies that make up the Internet.** At the heart of the Internet is the *Internet backbone,* the major set of connections for computers on the Internet. A *network access point (NAP)* is a point on the Internet where several connections converge. *Network service providers (NSPs),* such as MCI or AT&T, own and maintain routing computers at NAPs and even the lines that connect the NAPs to each other. Besides your computer (called a client computer) which you use to access the Internet, there are also four types of *Internet server computers* that provide information and services on the Internet. These include *Web servers* (providing information and services to Web surfers), *mail servers* (providing e-mail services and accounts), *ftp servers* (maintaining a collection of files that you can download), and *IRC servers* (supporting your use of discussion groups and chat rooms). As information travels from these servers to you, it

follows a set of *communications protocols*—sets of rules that every computer follows to transfer information. The most common protocols include *TCP/IP* (the primary protocol for transmitting information), *http* (for supporting the movement of information over the Web), and *ftp* (for allowing you to transfer files of information from one computer to another).

6. **Identify key considerations in choosing an Internet service provider (ISP).** When choosing an ISP—whether it is a commercial ISP, a free ISP, your school, or your work—you need to consider the following:

   - Web space—If you want to publish a Web site, then your ISP must provide you with Web space

   - Technical support—Which can be in the form of e-mail, 24-hour toll-free assistance, or perhaps none at all

   - Money—Commercial ISPs are the most expensive, while free ISPs, your school, and your work are free

   - Privacy—Your school or work may monitor your surfing activities

7. **Describe the communications software and telecommunications hardware you need to connect to the Internet.** Communications software for connecting to the Internet includes *connectivity software* (for dialing up another computer), *Web browser software* (for actually surfing the Web), and *e-mail software* (for electronically communicating with other people). Telecommunications hardware includes the device that you use to physically connect your computer to a network, which may connect through a phone line or cable line. These devices are called modems and include a *telephone modem, DSL modem, cable modem,* and *satellite modem.*

Key Terms and Concepts

Short-Answer Questions

1. How do the Web and Internet differ?
2. What is the relationship between a Web site and a Web page?
3. Why are links important on the Web?
4. What is the difference between a directory search engine and a true search engine?
5. How can you use plus signs (+) and minus signs (–) to refine a search?
6. What is the relationship between the Internet backbone, a network access point, and a network service provider?
7. What is the role of an ISP?
8. What are the four major types of servers on the Internet?
9. What are the advantages and disadvantages of choosing a commercial ISP?
10. What communications software do you need to use the Web?
11. What are the four main types of modems you can use to access the Internet while at home?
12. Why is it important to consider the availability of Web space when choosing an ISP?

Short-Question Answers

For each of the following answers, provide an appropriate question.

1. Web site.
2. It the technical representation of a Web page address.
3. com and edu are examples.
4. It allows me to surf the Web.
5. It's called a bookmark in Netscape Communicator.
6. True search engine.
7. Yahoo!
8. They are owned and maintained by NSPs.
9. For transferring files from one computer to another.
10. Web space.
11. Cable modem.
12. Web portal.

Assignments and Exercises

For each of the following questions, find the answer on the Web. When you do, write down the answer as well as the address where you found it. One restriction: You are not allowed to use encyclopedia sites such as *Encyclopedia Britannica*.

1. What is the weight of the moon?

    Answer: _____

    Address: _____

2. Who was the first U.S billionaire?

    Answer: _____

    Address: _____

3. Who is Olive Oyl's brother?

    Answer: _____

    Address: _____

4. Who wrote "It was the worst of times . . ."?

    Answer: _____

    Address: _____

5. What does the Seine River empty into?

    Answer: _____

    Address: _____

6. What is a lacrosse ball made of?

    Answer: _____

    Address: _____

7. Who lives at 39 Stone Canyon Drive?

    Answer: _____

    Address: _____

8. What is the color of Mr. Spock's blood?

    Answer: _____

    Address: _____

9. At what did the Nasdaq stock market close yesterday?

    Answer: _____

    Address: _____

10. What is the most frequently broken bone in the human body?

    Answer: _____

    Address: _____

11. What is a pregnant goldfish called?

    Answer: _____

    Address: _____

12. Who was the first pope to visit Africa?

    Answer: _____

    Address: _____

13. How many tusks does an Indian rhinoceros have?

    Answer: _____

    Address: _____

14. What does a pluviometer measure?

    Answer: _____

    Address: _____

15. What is the fear of the number 13 called?

    Answer: _____

    Address: _____

16. Which ear can most people hear best with?

    Answer: _____

    Address: _____

17. Who is the patron saint of England?

    Answer: _____

    Address: _____

18. What boxer's life story was titled *Raging Bull*?

    Answer: _____

    Address: _____

19. What was the first domesticated bird?

    Answer: _____

    Address: _____

20. What is the population of the United States right now?

    Answer: _____

    Address: _____

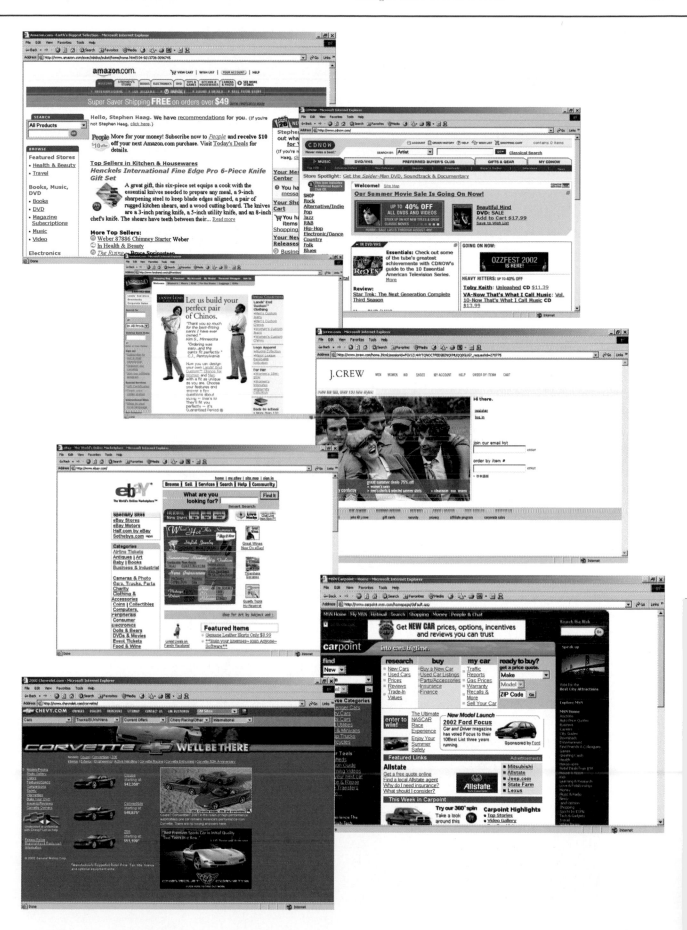

CHAPTER THREE OUTLINE

STUDENT LEARNING OUTCOMES

1. Describe business intelligence and its role in an organization.

2. Differentiate between databases and data warehouses with respect to their focus on online transaction processing and online analytical processing.

3. List and describe the key characteristics of a relational database.

4. Define the five software components of a database management system.

5. List and describe the key characteristics of a data warehouse.

6. Define the four major types of data mining tools in a data warehouse environment.

7. List key considerations in managing the information resource in an organization.

CHAPTER THREE

Databases and Data Warehouses
Building Business Intelligence

OPENING CASE STUDY:
HIGH TECH BATTLES HIGH
SCHOOL TRUANCY

The Boston public school system is charged with monitoring the daily attendance of more than 63,000 students throughout its district. And whereas daily average attendance sits at a comfortable 92.7 percent, tracking information on the remaining 7.3 percent of the students is a daunting task.

Currently, attendance officers working in the field must carry a printout of student records that is about as thick as a 3-inch phone book. The printout contains information including student names, school ID numbers for each student, contact information, names of their schools, and homeroom teachers. Lugging around a printout that's 3 inches thick doesn't make much sense in the information age.

The field attendance officers are then given a list of students not in attendance on a particular day. Each attendance officer must correlate that list with the information in the printout. Then the attendance officer must perform his or her duties in following up on the student and the reason the student is not in attendance. It's a time-consuming, but very necessary and important, task. Unfortunately, working with paper-based information only leads to more time spent.

So, the Boston public school system is teaming up with AirClic, Inc., to create a wireless truancy system. The system will allow attendance officers in the field to use either cell phones or PDAs to access student attendance information. By simply typing in a student's name or ID number, an attendance officer can view all of the student's information and even make updates to a central database. The central database tracks hundreds of pieces of information per student, including a daily attendance record.

The estimated cost of the system is very minimal, as both AirClic and Nextel have agreed to donate their time, services, and technology.

The real "information age" aspect of this system isn't necessarily the wireless accessing abilities of cell phones and PDAs, however. The heart of this system is the central database. Databases are fundamental technologies that help organizations of all kinds today organize and manage information. When information in a database is organized in the most effective way, anyone can easily access it, even with a cell phone or PDA.

But as organizations begin to organize their information in the form of a database, we have new and bigger issues to consider. For example, if all attendance records are located in one electronic database, what's to stop anyone (including other students) from accessing them? As you might well guess, security then is a key issue. Although it's true someone could steal the 3-inch printout of student information, it's actually much easier to steal information in electronic form. Not only that, but when someone does steal electronic information, he or she really only takes an electronic copy of it, often leaving no trace that the information has been stolen.

As you'll read in this chapter, organizations do need databases (and data warehouses) for organizing and managing information. But as we've stated all along, the technology itself is often easy to implement. It's the implementation of security and privacy measures that's difficult.[1]

Introduction

Imagine that you're the inventory manager for a multimillion-dollar firm and that you can accurately predict selling trends by the week, territory, salesperson, and product line. Imagine that you own an accounting firm and can accurately predict which and how many of your clients will file for tax extensions. Imagine that you're an accounts manager and can accurately determine creditworthy risks. Sound impossible? Not really; it's quite possible that you could make these predictions with a 95 percent accuracy rate, or even higher.

How? Obviously your education has a lot to do with it. But so does access to and the ability to work with two resources that every organization owns today: information and business intelligence. *Access to* information and business intelligence implies that they are organized in such a way that you can easily and quickly get to them. *Working with* information and business intelligence implies that you have the right information-processing tools. That's what this chapter is all about—organizing information and business intelligence and having the right tools to work with them.

Throughout this chapter, we focus on (1) databases and data warehouses as methods for organizing and managing information and business intelligence and (2) database management systems and data mining tools as IT tools you use to work with information and business intelligence.

Business Intelligence

Business intelligence sounds like a great term. But what exactly is it? ***Business intelligence*** is knowledge—knowledge about your customers, your competitors, your partners, your competitive environment, and your own internal operations. Business intelligence comes from information. It enables your organization to extrapolate the true meaning of information to take creative and powerful steps to ensure a competitive advantage. So, business intelligence is much more than just a list of the products you sell. It would combine your product information perhaps with your advertising strategy information and customer demographics to help you determine the effectiveness of various advertising media on demographic groups segmented by location (see Figure 3.1).

Of course, business intelligence doesn't just magically appear. You must first gather and organize all your information. Then, you must have the right IT tools to define and analyze various relationships within the information. In short, knowledge workers such as you use IT tools to create business intelligence from information. The technology won't simply do it for you. However, technology such as databases, database management systems, data warehouses, and data mining tools can definitely help you build and use business intelligence.

As you begin working with these IT tools (which we'll discuss in great detail throughout this chapter), you'll be performing the two types of information processing we alluded to in Chapter 1: online transaction processing and online analytical processing. ***Online transaction processing (OLTP)*** is the gathering of input information, processing that information, and updating existing information to reflect the gathered and processed information. Databases and DBMSs are the technology tools that directly support OLTP. Databases that support OLTP are most often referred to as ***operational databases.*** Inside these operational databases is valuable information that forms the basis for business intelligence.

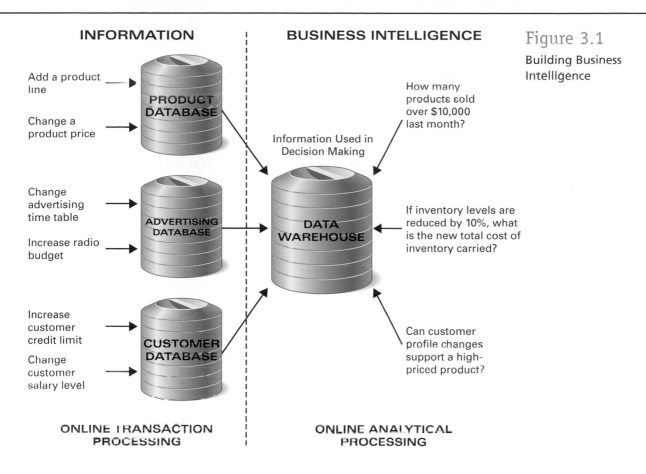

Figure 3.1

Building Business
Intelligence

Online analytical processing (OLAP) is the manipulation of information to support decision making. At Mervyn's, a subdivision of Dayton Hudson Corp., OLAP is a must and a definite improvement over the way things used to work.[2,3] According to Sid Banjeree, "Mervyn's had people who spent hours poring over shopping carts full of paper reports" to gather product information by units, by dollars, by a single store, by season, by region, and by ad zone. Now, those same people spend just a few seconds to perform the same tasks with OLAP and a data warehouse. As Sue Little, Mervyn's manager of merchandise planning and logistics systems, points out, "We're finally comparing apples to apples, and now we're spending only 10 percent of our time gathering data and 90 percent acting upon it, instead of the other way around."

A data warehouse is, in fact, a special form of a database that contains information gathered from many operational databases for the purpose of supporting decision-making tasks. When you build a data warehouse and use data mining tools to manipulate the data warehouse's information, your single goal is to create *business intelligence*. So, data warehouses support only OLAP; they do not at all support OLTP.

As this chapter unfolds, we'll look specifically at (1) databases and database management systems and (2) data warehouses and data mining tools. Databases today are the foundation for organizing and managing information, and database management systems provide the tools you use to work with a database. Data warehouses are relatively new and explosive technologies that help you organize and manage business intelligence, and data mining tools help you extract that vitally important business intelligence.

The Relational Database Model

For organizing and storing basic and transaction-oriented information (that is eventually used to create business intelligence), businesses today use databases. There are actually four primary models for creating a database. The object-oriented database model is the newest and holds great promise; we'll talk more about the entire object-oriented genre in Chapter 7 and in *Extended Learning Module G*. Right now, let's focus on the most popular database model: the relational database model.

As a generic definition, we would say that any *database* is a collection of information that you organize and access according to the logical structure of that information. In reference to the *relational database model,* we say that it uses a series of logically related two-dimensional tables or files to store information in the form of a database. The term *relation* often describes each two-dimensional table or file in the relational model (hence its name *relational* database model). A relational database is actually composed of two distinct parts: (1) the information itself, stored in a series of two-dimensional tables, files, or relations (people use these three terms interchangeably) and (2) the logical structure of that information. Let's look at a portion of an *Inventory* database to further explore the characteristics of the relational database model.

COLLECTIONS OF INFORMATION

In Figure 3.2 (on the facing page) we've created a view of a portion of an *Inventory* database. Notice that the *Inventory* database contains two files: *Part* and *Facility*. (In reality, it would contain many more files including *Orders, Distributors,* and so on.) A facility is simply a storage place for parts (similar to a warehouse). The *Part* and *Facility* files are related for two reasons. First, parts are stored in various facilities, so each file contains a common field: *Facility Number*. Second, you would use both files to manage your inventory, a common function in almost any business.

Within each file, you can see specific pieces of information (what we often call *attributes*). For example, the *Part* file contains *Part Number, Part Name, Cost, Percentage Markup, Distributor ID, Facility Number,* and *Bin Number. Bin Number,* in this case, describes the physical location of a given part in a facility. In the *Facility* file, you can see specific information including *Facility Number, Facility Name, Phone Number, Street Location,* and *Manager Number.* These are all important pieces of information that an inventory database would need to maintain. Moreover, you would need all this information (and probably much more) to effectively manage your inventory.

CREATED WITH LOGICAL STRUCTURES

Using the relational database model, you organize and access information according to its logical structure, not its physical position. So, you don't really care in which row of the *Part* file 50' tape measures appear. You really need to know only that the *Part Number* is 1003 or, for that matter, that the name of the part is 50' tape measure. In the relational database model, a *data dictionary* contains the logical structure for the information. When you create a database, you first create the data dictionary. The data dictionary contains important information or logical properties about your information. The screen in Figure 3.2 shows how you can build the data dictionary for the *Part* file using Microsoft Access (a popular personal database package). Notice that the data dictionary identifies all field names, types (Currency for *Cost,* for example), sizes, formats, default values, and so on.

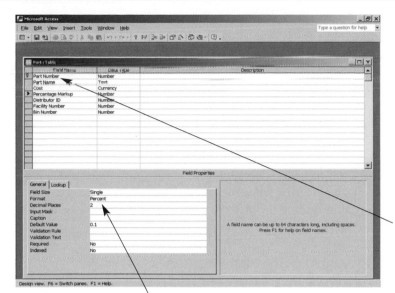

Figure 3.2

A Portion of an Inventory
Database and Data
Dictionary

Part Number is the
primary key because of
the key icon beside it.

For *Percentage Markup,* we defined its Format as "Percent" and its
number of decimal places as 2.

. . . is composed of

PART FILE

Part Number	Part Name	Cost	Percentage Markup	Distributor ID	Facility Number	Bin Number
1003	50' Tape Measure	$11.90	40.00%	10	291	2988
1005	25' Tape Measure	$9.95	40.00%	10	291	3101
1083	10 Amp Fuse	$0.07	50.00%	14	378	3984
1109	15 Amp Fuse	$0.07	50.00%	14	378	3983
2487	25 Amp Fuse	$0.08	50.00%	14	378	3982
2897	U.S. Socket Set	$29.75	25.00%	12	411	8723
3789	Crimping Tool	$14.50	30.00%	13	411	3298
3982	Claw Hammer	$9.90	30.00%	10	291	2987
4101	Metric Socket Set	$23.75	25.00%	12	411	4123
5908	6" Pliers	$7.45	25.00%	11	411	4567
6743	8" Pliers	$7.90	25.00%	11	411	4385

FACILITY FILE

Facility Number	Facility Name	Phone Number	Street Location	Manager Name
291	Pegasus	378-4921	3578 W. 12th St.	Greg Nelson
378	Medusa	379-2981	4314 48th Ave.	Sara Wood
411	Orion	298-8763	198 Red Ln.	James Riley

This is quite different from other ways of organizing information. For example, if you want to access information in a certain cell in most spreadsheet applications, you must know its physical position—row number and column character. With a relational database, however, you need only know the field name of the column of information (for example, *Percentage Markup*) and its logical row, not its physical row. As a result, in our *Inventory* database example, you could easily change the percentage markup for part number 1003, without knowing where that information is physically stored (by row or column).

And with spreadsheet software, you can immediately begin typing in information, creating column headings, and providing formatting. You can't do that with a database. Using a database, you must first clearly define the characteristics of each field by creating a data dictionary. So you must carefully plan the design of your database before you can start adding information.

WITH LOGICAL TIES AMONG THE INFORMATION

In a relational database, you must create ties or relationships in the information that show how the files relate to each other. Before you can create these relationships among files, you must first specify the primary key for each file. A **primary key** is a field (or group of fields in some cases) that uniquely describes each record. In our *Inventory* database, *Part Number* is the primary key for the *Part* file and *Facility Number* is the primary key for the *Facility* file. That is to say, every part in the *Part* file must have a unique *Part Number* and every facility in the *Facility* file must have a unique *Facility Number*.

As well, when you define that a specific field in a file is the primary key, you're also stating that the field cannot be blank. That is, you cannot enter the information for a new part in the *Part* file and leave the *Part Number* field blank. If that were possible, you could potentially do it for more than one part. Then you would have two parts with identical primary keys (blank), which is not possible in a database environment.

Again, this is quite different from working with spreadsheets. Using a spreadsheet, it would be almost impossible to ensure that each field in a given column (for example, *Part Number* in the *Part* file) is unique. This reinforces the notion that, while spreadsheets work with information according to physical location, databases work with information logically.

Figure 3.3

Creating Logical Ties with Primary and Foreign Keys

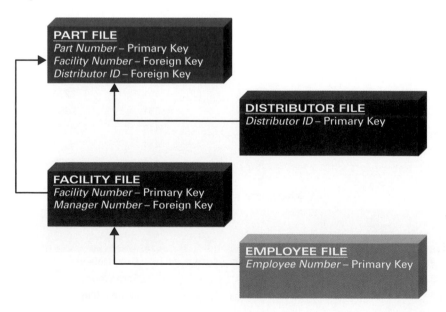

If you look back at Figure 3.2, you can see that *Facility Number* also appears in the *Part* file. This creates the logical relationship between the two files and is an example of a foreign key. A **foreign key** is a primary key of one file that appears in another file. Now look at Figure 3.3. In it, we've added the *Distributor* file and the *Employee* file in the *Inventory* database. In doing so, we can illustrate two more examples of foreign keys.

Notice *Distributor ID* in the *Distributor* file: It is the primary key for that file. It also appears in the *Part* file; this enables us to track from whom we get our parts. So, *Distributor ID* is the primary key in the *Dis-*

PRIMARY KEYS, FOREIGN KEYS, AND INTEGRITY CONSTRAINTS

Let's consider the information that your school tracks for a class. In this instance, a class is a scheduled course. For example, your school may have FINA 2100—Introduction to International Financial Markets as a course. If the school offers it in the fall, then it becomes a class. Below, we've provided many pieces of information that your school probably tracks about the class. First, which is the primary key (place an X in the second column)? Second, for each piece of information, identify if it's a foreign key (a primary key of another file). If it is, write down the filename in the third column. Finally, in the fourth column for each piece of information, write down any integrity constraints you can think of. For example, can it be blank or must it contain something? Can it be duplicated across multiple records (classes)? If it's a number, does it have a specific range in which it must fall? There are many others.

Information	Primary Key?	Foreign Key?	Integrity Constraints
Department designation (e.g., FINA)			
Course number (e.g., 2100)			
Course name			
Course description			
Prerequisite			
Number of credit hours			
Lab fee			
Instructor name			
Room number			
Time of day			
Day of week			

tributor file and is also a foreign key that appears in the *Part* file. Now, take a look at *Employee Number* in the *Employee* file: It is the primary key for that file. It also appears in the *Facility* file as *Manager Number*. This enables us to track the manager for each facility. So, *Employee Number* is the primary key in the *Employee* file and is also a foreign key that appears in the *Facility* file.

Foreign keys are essential in the relational database model. Without them, you have no way of creating logical ties among the various files. As you might guess, we use these relationships extensively to create business intelligence because they enable us to track the logical relationships among many types of information.

WITH BUILT-IN INTEGRITY CONSTRAINTS

By defining the logical structure of information in a relational database, you're also developing *integrity constraints*—rules that help ensure the quality of the information. For example, by stating that *Facility Number* is the primary key of the *Facility* file and a foreign key in the *Part* file, you're saying (1) that no two facilities can have the same

Facility Number and (2) that a part in the *Part* file cannot be assigned to a facility number that does not exist in the *Facility* file. So, as you add a new part to the inventory, you must specify a facility in which it will be located that already exists in the *Facility* file. Likewise, you can't choose to eliminate a facility if parts are still assigned to it. This makes perfect sense. If you want to close a certain facility, you must first move all of the parts in it to a different facility.

Consumer Reports magazine has rated the Ritz-Carlton first among luxury hotels.[4] Why? It's simple: Ritz-Carlton has created a powerful guest preference database to provide customized, personal, and high-level service to guests of any of its hotels. For example, if you leave a message at a Ritz-Carlton front desk that you want the bed turned down at 9 P.M., prefer no chocolate mints on your pillow, and want to participate in the 7 A.M. aerobics class, that information is passed along to the floor maid (and others) and is also stored in the guest preference database. By assigning to you a unique customer ID that creates logical ties to your various preferences, the Ritz-Carlton transfers your information to all of its other hotels. The next time you stay in a Ritz-Carlton hotel, in Palm Beach for example, your information is already there, and the hotel staff immediately knows of your preferences.

For the management at Ritz-Carlton, achieving customer loyalty starts first with knowing each customer individually. That includes your exercise habits, what you most commonly order from the snack bar in your room, how many towels you use daily, and whether you like a chocolate on your pillow. To store and organize all this information, Ritz-Carlton uses a relational database, and employees use it to meet your needs (or whims).

Database Management System Tools

When working with word processing software, you create and edit a document. When working with spreadsheet software, you create and edit a workbook. The same is true in a database environment. A database is equivalent to a document or a workbook because they all contain information. And, while word processing and spreadsheet are the software tools you use to work with documents and workbooks, you use database management system software to work with databases. A *database management system (DBMS)* helps you specify the logical organization for a database and access and use the information within a database. A DBMS contain five important software components (see Figure 3.4 on the facing page):

1. DBMS engine
2. Data definition subsystem
3. Data manipulation subsystem
4. Application generation subsystem
5. Data administration subsystem

The DBMS engine is perhaps the most important, yet seldom recognized, component of a DBMS. The *DBMS engine* accepts logical requests from the various other DBMS subsystems, converts them into their physical equivalent, and actually accesses the database and data dictionary as they exist on a storage device. Again, the distinction between logical and physical is important in a database environment. The *physical view* of information deals with how information is physically arranged, stored, and accessed on some type of storage device such as a hard disk. The *logical view* of information, on the other hand, focuses on how you as a knowledge worker need to arrange and access information to meet your particular business needs.

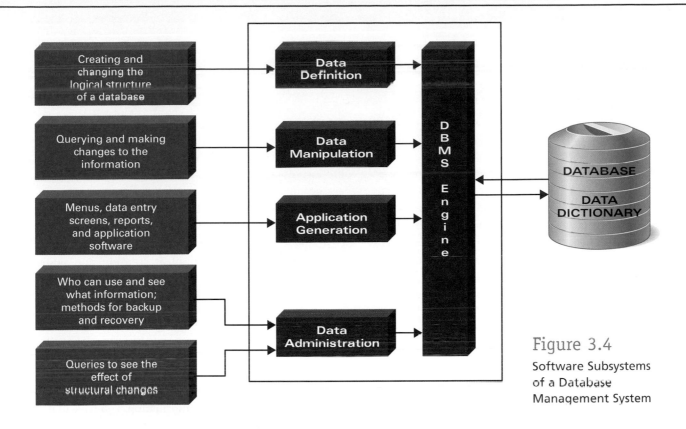

Figure 3.4

Software Subsystems
of a Database
Management System

Databases and DBMSs provide two really great advantages in separating the logical from the physical view of information. First, the DBMS handles the physical tasks. So you, as a database user, can concentrate solely on your logical information needs. Second, although there is only one physical view of information, there may be numerous knowledge workers who have different logical views of the information in a database. That is, according to what business tasks they need to perform, different knowledge workers logically view information in different ways. The DBMS engine can process virtually any logical information view or request into its physical equivalent.

DATA DEFINITION SUBSYSTEM

The *data definition subsystem* of a DBMS helps you create and maintain the data dictionary and define the structure of the files in a database. In Figure 3.2 on page 131, we provided a screen capture of the data definition subsystem using Microsoft Access. In that screen, we created the data dictionary and defined the structure of the *Part* file of our *Inventory* database.

When you create a database, you must first use the data definition subsystem to create the data dictionary and define the structure of the files. This is very different from using something like spreadsheet software. When you create a workbook, you can immediately begin typing in information and creating formulas and functions. You can't do that with a database. You must define its logical structure before you can begin typing in any information. Typing in the information is the easy part: Defining the logical structure is more difficult. In the *Extended Learning Module C* that follows this chapter, we take you through the process of defining the logical structure for a database. We definitely recommend that you read that module—knowing how to define the correct structure of a database can be a substantial career opportunity for you.

USING A DATABASE TO BUILD A SINGLE VIEW FOR THE CUSTOMER

According to George Foulke, vice president of Information Technology for MetLife, ". . . if we could get a customer's entire portfolio online, the customer would view us as a savvy company, the customer's satisfaction goes up when they see results, and the customer doesn't have to have human interaction, so our costs are reduced." As George then goes on to explain, it does, in fact, cost just a few pennies to serve a customer via the Internet, while it costs several dollars when customers speak with a person on the phone.

George is talking about MetLife's new initiative to create a database environment that will be accessible by customers through the Internet. MetLife sells a variety of products, including banking, investment services, life insurance, and financial planning. Currently, these are not all contained in a single database.

That makes it difficult to get one single view of the customer internally. And it makes it impossible for the customer to obtain one single view from the Internet. How successful is your school at creating one single view for you of all your information?[5]

If you ever find that a certain file needs another piece of information, you have to use the data definition subsystem to add a new field in the data dictionary. Likewise, if you want to delete a given field for all the records in a file, you must use the data definition subsystem to do so.

As you create the data dictionary, you're essentially defining the logical properties of the information that the database will contain. Logical structures of information include the following:

Logical Properties	Examples
Field name	*Part Number, Bin Number*
Type	Alphabetic, numeric, date, time, etc.
Form	Is an area code required for a phone number?
Default value	If no percentage markup is entered, the default is 10%.
Validation rule	Can percentage markups exceed 100%?
Is an entry required?	Must you enter a *Facility Number* for a part or can it be blank?
Can there be duplicates?	Primary keys cannot be duplicates; but what about percentage markups?

These are all important logical properties to a lesser or greater extent depending on the type of information you're describing. For example, a typical address might have a field name of *Customer Address* and a type of alphanumeric (allowing for both numbers and letters). Beyond those, the logical properties are not quite as important, with the possible exception of requiring that the field cannot be blank.

However, if you're describing something like *Percentage Markup* in our *Inventory* database, you'll want to define such logical properties as a default value and perhaps some sort of validation rule.

DATA MANIPULATION SUBSYSTEM

The ***data manipulation subsystem*** of a DBMS helps you add, change, and delete information in a database and mine it for valuable information. Software tools within the data manipulation subsystem are most often the primary interface between you as a user and the information contained in a database. So, while the DBMS engine handles your information requests from a physical point of view, it is the data manipulation tools within a DBMS that allow you to specify your logical information requirements. Those logical information requirements are then used by the DBMS engine to access the information you need from a physical point of view.

In most DBMSs, you'll find a variety of data manipulation tools, including views, report generators, query-by-example tools, and structured query language.

VIEWS   A ***view*** allows you to see the contents of a database file, make whatever changes you want, perform simple sorting, and query to find the location of specific information. Views essentially provide each file in the form of a spreadsheet workbook. The screen in Figure 3.5 shows a view in Microsoft Access for the *Part* file of our *Inventory* database. At this point, you can click on any specific field and change its contents. You could also point at an entire record and click on the Cut icon (the scissors) to remove a record. If you want to add a record, simply click in the *Part Number* field of the first blank record and begin typing.

Note: we've sorted the file in ascending order by *Part Number.* You can easily achieve this by clicking on the A→Z Sort button in the view window. If you want to sort in descending order by *Percentage Markup,* simply point to any *Percentage Markup* field and click on the Z→A Sort button. You can also perform searches within views. For example, if you wanted to find all parts that have the term *pliers* in the *Part Name* field, simply point anywhere in that column, click on the Find Text button (the binoculars) and enter *pliers.* Access will respond by highlighting each *Part Name* field where the word *pliers* appears.

As with most other types of personal productivity software, DBMSs support such functions and tasks as cutting and pasting, formatting (for example, bolding a field), spell checking, hiding columns (just as you would do using spreadsheet software), filtering, and even adding links to Web sites.

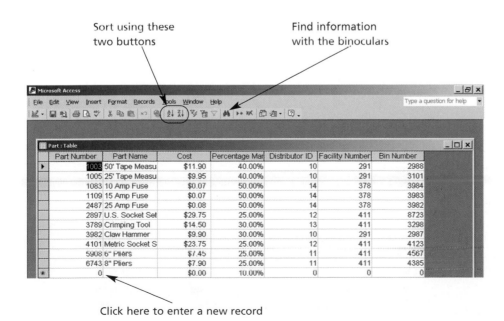

Sort using these two buttons

Find information with the binoculars

Click here to enter a new record

Figure 3.5

A View in Microsoft Access

REPORT GENERATORS *Report generators* help you quickly define formats of reports and what information you want to see in a report. Once you define a report, you can view it on the screen or print it. Figure 3.6 shows two intermediate screens in Microsoft Access. The first allows you to specify which fields of information are to appear in a report. We have chosen to include *Part Number, Part Name, Cost,* and *Percentage Markup.* The second allows you to choose from a set of predefined report formats. Following a simple and easy-to-use set of screens (including the two in Figure 3.6), we went on to specify that sorting should take place by *Part Name* and that the name of the report should be "Part Report." The completed report is also shown in Figure 3.6. Notice that it only displays those fields we requested, that it's sorted by *Part Name,* and that the title is "Part Report."

A nice feature about report generators is that you can save a report format that you use frequently. For example, if you think you'll use the report in Figure 3.6 often, you can save it by giving it a unique name. Later, you can request that report and your DBMS will generate it, using the most up-to-date information in the database. You can also choose from a variety of report formats (we chose a simple one for our illustration). And you can choose report formats that create intermediate subtotals and grand totals, which can include counts, sums, averages, and the like.

Figure 3.6

Using a Report
Generator

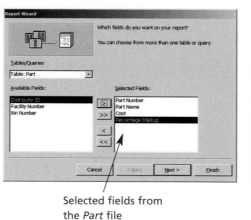
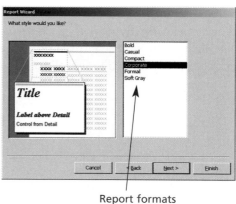

Selected fields from
the *Part* file

Report formats

PART REPORT

Part Number	Part Name	Cost	Percentage Markup
1003	50' Tape Measure	$11.90	40.00%
1005	25' Tape Measure	$9.95	40.00%
1083	10 Amp Fuse	$0.07	50.00%
1109	15 Amp Fuse	$0.07	50.00%
2487	25 Amp Fuse	$0.08	50.00%
2897	U.S. Socket Set	$29.75	25.00%
3789	Crimping Tool	$14.50	30.00%
3982	Claw Hammer	$9.90	30.00%
4101	Metric Socket Set	$23.75	25.00%
5908	6" Pliers	$7.45	25.00%
6743	8" Pliers	$7.90	25.00%

QUERY-BY-EXAMPLE TOOLS   *Query-by-example (QBE) tools* help you graphically design the answer to a question. In our *Inventory* database, for example, is the question, What are the names and phone numbers of the facility managers who are in charge of parts that have a cost greater than $10? The question may seem simple considering that we have very few parts and even fewer facilities and managers in our database. However, can you imagine trying to answer that question if 100 facilities and 70,000 parts were involved? It would not be fun.

Fortunately, QBE tools can help you answer this question and perform many other queries in a matter of seconds. In Figure 3.7, you can see a QBE screen that formulates the answer to our question. When you perform a QBE, you (1) identify the files in which the information is located, (2) drag any necessary fields from the identified files to the QBE grid, and (3) specify selection criteria.

For names and phone numbers of facility managers in charge of parts with costs over $10, we first identified two files: *Part* and *Employee*. Second, we dragged *Part Number, Facility Number,* and *Cost* from the *Part* file to the QBE grid and dragged *Employee Name* and *Employee Phone Number* from the *Employee* file to the QBE grid. Finally, we specified in the Criteria box that we wanted to view only those parts with costs exceeding $10. Access did the rest and provided the information in Figure 3.7.

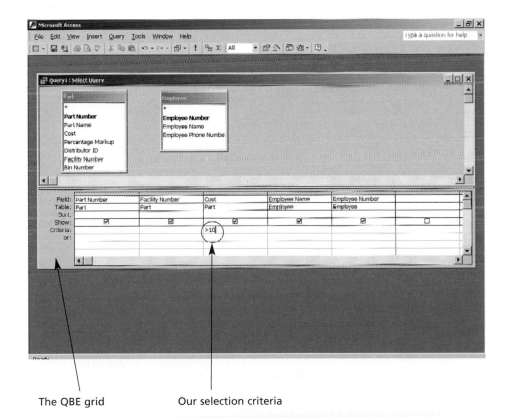

Figure 3.7

Using a Query-by-Example to Find Information

The QBE grid   Our selection criteria

Part Number	Cost	Employee Name	Employee Phone Number
4101	$23.75	James Riley	376-2900
3789	$14.50	James Riley	376-2900
1003	$11.90	Greg Nelson	376-2455
2897	$29.75	James Riley	376-2900

QBEs rely heavily on the logical relationships within a database to find information. For example, part 4101 has a cost exceeding $10. So, the QBE tool took the *Facility Number* from the *Part* file and found a match in the *Facility* file. It then used the *Manager Number* in that matching record and performed another search of the *Employee* file to find another match. When it found a match, it then gathered the *Employee Name* and *Employee Phone Number*. Without the logical relationships correctly defined, this QBE query would never have worked.

STRUCTURED QUERY LANGUAGE   *Structured query language (SQL)* is a standardized fourth-generation query language found in most DBMSs. SQL performs the same function as QBE, except that you perform the query by creating a statement instead of pointing, clicking, and dragging. The basic form of an SQL statement is

SELECT . . . FROM . . . WHERE . . .

After the SELECT, you list the fields of information you want; after the FROM, you specify what logical relationships to use; and after the WHERE, you specify any selection criteria. If you consider our QBE above of What are the names and phone numbers of the facility managers who are in charge of parts that have a cost greater than $10? the SQL statement would look like the following:

SELECT Part.[Part Number], Part.Cost, Employee.[Employee Name],
         Employee.[Employee Number]
FROM   Part, Employee
WHERE (((Part.Cost)>10));

Thoroughly introducing you to the syntax of building SQL statements is outside the scope of this text and would easily require almost 100 pages of material. But you should be aware that SQL does exist. If you're majoring in IT or MIS, you'll undoubtedly take a course in SQL.

APPLICATION GENERATION SUBSYSTEM

The *application generation subsystem* of a DBMS contains facilities to help you develop transaction-intensive applications. These types of applications usually require that you perform a detailed series of tasks to process a transaction. Application generation subsystem facilities include tools for creating visually appealing and easy-to-use data entry screens, programming languages specific to a particular DBMS, and interfaces to commonly used programming languages that are independent of any DBMS.

As with SQL, application generation facilities are most often used by IT specialists. As a knowledge worker, we recommend that you leave application generation to IT specialists as much as you can. You need to focus on views, report generators, and QBE tools. These will help you find information in a database and perform queries so you can start to build and use business intelligence.

DATA ADMINISTRATION SUBSYSTEM

The *data administration subsystem* of a DBMS helps you manage the overall database environment by providing facilities for backup and recovery, security management, query optimization, concurrency control, and change management. The data administration subsystem is most often used by a data administrator or database administrator—someone responsible for assuring that the database (and data warehouse) environment meets the entire information needs of an organization.

Backup and recovery facilities provide a way for you to (1) periodically back up in-

FLOATING DATABASES ABOARD ROYAL CARIBBEAN CRUISE SHIPS

Databases are not a "land-locked" technology, as anyone at Royal Caribbean Cruises will tell you. With floating hotellike structures that include restaurants, casinos, duty-free shops, and Internet cafés, Royal Caribbean has sophisticated database technologies aboard each ship. According to Thomas Murphy, Royal Caribbean CIO, "The technology is becoming so much more important in running a cruise ship. Customer satisfaction depends on it, but so does the basic operation of the ship."

Aboard a cruise ship, databases track everything including general customer information, customer complaints and inquiries, on-demand movie requests, Internet café use, shopping purchases, meal purchases, and even pay-for-use services such as massages and hair cuts. The system even tracks male customers according to what size of tuxedo they reserve. That information can be used again if the same passenger takes another cruise on a Royal ship.

Royal Caribbean is also planning to build a centralized land-based data warehouse. Each ship, as it records information in its database, will use wireless telecommunications technologies to upload information into the data warehouse. Service planners will then be able to better predict what types of services will be needed on future cruises. For example, by time of year and cruise destination, service planners will know what sizes of tuxedos to stock and approximately how many massages will be performed. What fields of information would you have in a "massage" record?

If you're on land and want to take a virtual tour of a Royal Caribbean cruise ship, you can do that. Just visit the Internet and connect to Royal Caribbean's Web site (www.royalcaribbean.com) and you can view estate rooms, eating facilities, spa facilities, and general entertainment areas. Of course, Royal Caribbean ultimately wants you to enjoy your virtual experience so much that you book a cruise. But if you're not quite ready yet, Royal Caribbean would like for you to leave some contact information at its Web site.

It will then store that information in its database and, from time to time, send you some cruise information.[6,7]

---

formation contained in a database and to (2) restart or recover a database and its information in case of a failure. These are important functions you cannot ignore in today's information-based environment. Organizations that understand the importance of their information take precautions to preserve it, often by running backup databases, a DBMS, and storage facilities parallel to the primary database environment. In Chapters 7 and 8, we talk specifically about how to develop plans and strategies in the event of some sort of failure: We call this contingency planning.

Security management facilities allow you to control who has access to what information and what type of access those people have. In many database environments, for example, some people may need only view access to database information, but not change privileges. Still others may need the ability to add, change, and/or delete information in a database. Through a system of user-specification and password levels, the data administration subsystem allows you to define which users can perform which tasks and what information they can see. At car dealership JM Family Enterprises (JMFE), security management facilities are an absolute must because its technology is highly decentralized and includes users of mobile technologies.[8] JMFE's system supports encryption and passwords to protect databases, files, and many hardware resources. The system even supports automatic log-offs after a certain amount of time if users accidentally leave their systems running.

DBMS SUPPORT FOR OLTP, OLAP, AND INFORMATION MANAGEMENT

In the table below, we've listed the various DBMS subsystems or tools. For each of these, identify whether it supports online transaction processing, online analytical processing, both online transaction and analytical processing, or the management of a database.

DBMS Tool	OLTP	OLAP	Both	Management
DBMS engine				
View				
Report generator				
QBE				
SQL				
Data entry screen				
DBMS programming language				
Common programming language				
Data administration subsystem				

Query optimization facilities often take queries from users (in the form of SQL statements or QBEs) and restructure them to minimize response times. In SQL, for example, you can build a query statement that might involve working with as many as 10 different files. As you might well guess, when working with 10 different files, there may be several different solutions for combining them to get the information you need. Fortunately, you don't have to worry about structuring the SQL statement in the most optimized fashion. The query optimization facilities will do that for you and provide you with the information you need in the fastest possible way.

Reorganization facilities continually maintain statistics concerning how the DBMS engine physically accesses information. In maintaining those statistics, reorganization facilities can optimize the physical structure of a database to further increase speed and performance. For example, if you frequently access a certain file by a specific order, the reorganization facilities may maintain the file in that presorted order to create an index that maintains the sorted order in that file. What's really nice is that you don't have to be aware of the changes to your database with respect to physical locations—the DBMS engine will take care of it for you.

Concurrency control facilities ensure the validity of database updates when multiple users attempt to access and change the same information. This is crucial in today's networked business environment. Consider your school's online registration system. What if you and another student try to register for a class with only one seat remaining at the exact same time? Who gets enrolled in the class? What happens to the person that does

> ## TRUCKLOADS OF INFORMATION IN TRUCKING AREN'T NECESSARILY VALUABLE

Today, organizations aren't necessarily starving for data; they're starving for meaningful information they can quickly extract from their data. Consider Schneider National. Schneider is the largest transportation and logistics company in North America, transporting goods of all kinds by truck, rail, and sea all over the world. A significant portion of its $2.4 billion in annual revenue comes from logistical support it provides to big companies such as Wal-Mart, BASF, General Motors, and Ford. But, as Bill Braddy of Schneider explained it, "We were drowning in data but starving for information."

Here's an example Bill provided. Suppose an analyst wanted to know why it cost 20 cents per pound to make deliveries to a Ford dealership in Texas but only 17 cents to most other locations. Although the reasons could be numerous, the analyst was forced—because of how Schneider's information was organized—to choose only one at a time to investigate.

The analyst then had to write an information request and submit it to a department data engineer.

That data engineer then had to write a custom program to extract the information and yet another custom program to format the information into a report, which was eventually e-mailed back to the analyst. The entire process usually took an entire week. And, even if the information wasn't any good, the analyst tried to use it anyway instead of going through the weeklong process of requesting new information.

Two problems were very evident at Schneider. First, its information was so disorganized that it literally took a rocket scientist to write the custom programs to extract precise information. Second, businesses shouldn't need data extraction experts. Businesses should empower all employees and knowledge and technology tools so that they can find whatever information they need.

By the way, that's just what Schneider did by acquiring Cognos, a leading business intelligence software suite. You should check it out at www.cognos.com.[4]

not get his or her desired class schedule? These are important questions that must be answered, and, once answered, defined in the database environment using concurrency control facilities.

Change management facilities allow you to assess the impact of proposed structural changes to a database environment. For example, if you decide to add a character identifier to a numeric part number, you can use the change management facilities to see how many files will be affected. Recall that *Part Number* would be the primary key for a *Part* file and that it would also be a foreign key in many other files. Sometimes, structural changes may not have much effect on the database (adding a four-digit Zip code extension), but others can cause widespread changes that you must assess carefully before implementing.

All of these—backup and recovery, security management, query optimization, reorganization, concurrency control, and change management—are vitally important facilities in any DBMS and thus any database environment. As a user and knowledge worker, you probably won't deal with these facilities specifically as far as setting them up and maintaining them is concerned. But how they're set up and maintained will affect what you can do. So knowing that they do exist and understanding their purposes are important.

Data Warehouses and Data Mining

Suppose as a manager at Victoria's Secret, you wanted to know the total revenues generated from the sale of shoes last month. That's a simple query, which you could easily implement using either SQL or a QBE tool. But what if you wanted to know, "By actual versus budgeted, how many size 8 shoes in black did we sell last month in the southeast and southwest regions, compared with the same month over the last 5 years?" That task seems almost impossible, even with the aid of technology. If you were actually able to build a QBE query for it, you would probably bring the organization's operational database environment to its knees.

This example illustrates the two primary reasons so many organizations are opting to build data warehouses. First, while operational databases may have the needed information, the information is not organized in such a way that lends itself to building business intelligence within the database or using various data manipulation tools. Second, if you could build such a query, your operational databases, which are probably already supporting the processing of hundreds of transactions per second, would seriously suffer in performance when you hit the Start button to perform the query.

To support such intriguing, necessary, and complex queries to create business intelligence, many organizations are building data warehouses and providing data mining tools. A data warehouse is simply the next step (beyond databases) in the progression of building business intelligence. And data mining tools are the tools you use to mine a data warehouse and extrapolate the business intelligence you need to make a decision, solve a problem, or capitalize on an opportunity to create a competitive advantage.

Figure 3.8

A Multidimensional Data Warehouse with Information from Multiple Operational Databases

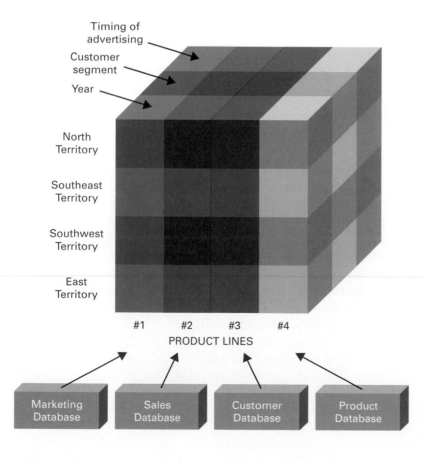

WHAT IS A DATA WAREHOUSE?

A **data warehouse** is a logical collection of information—gathered from many different operational databases—used to create business intelligence that supports business analysis activities and decision-making tasks (see Figure 3.8). Sounds simple enough on the surface, but data warehouses represent a fundamentally different way of thinking about organizing and managing information in an organization. Consider these key features of a data warehouse, detailed in the sections that follow.

DATA WAREHOUSES ARE MULTIDIMENSIONAL   In the relational database model, information is represented in a series of two-dimensional tables. Not so in a data warehouse—most data warehouses are multidimensional, meaning that they contain layers of columns and rows. For this reason, most data warehouses are really *multidimensional databases*. The layers in a data warehouse represent information according to different dimensions. This multidimensional representation of information is referred to as a *hypercube*.

In Figure 3.8, you can see a hypercube that represents product information by product line and region (columns and rows), by year (the first layer), by customer segment (the second layer), and by the timing of advertising media (the third layer). Using this hypercube, you can easily ask, According to customer segment A, what percentage of total sales for product line 1 in the southwest territory occurred immediately after a radio advertising blitz? The information you would receive from that query constitutes business intelligence.

Any specific subcube within the larger hypercube can contain a variety of summarized information gathered from the various operational databases. For example, the forward-most and top-left subcube contains information for the North territory, by year, for product line 1. So, it could contain totals, average, counts, and distributions summarizing in some way that information. Of course, what it contains is really up to you and your needs.

DATA WAREHOUSES SUPPORT DECISION MAKING, NOT TRANSACTION PROCESSING In an organization, most databases are transaction-oriented. That is, most databases support online transaction processing (OLTP) and, therefore, are operational databases. Data warehouses are not transaction-oriented: They exist to support decision-making tasks in your organization. Therefore, data warehouses support only online analytical processing (OLAP).

As we just stated, the subcubes within a data warehouse contain summarized information. So, while a data warehouse may contain the total sales for a year by product line, it does not contain a list of each individual sale to each individual customer for a given product line. Therefore, you simply cannot process transactions with a data warehouse. Instead, you process transactions with your operational databases and then use the information contained within the operational databases to build the summary information in a data warehouse.

WHAT ARE DATA MINING TOOLS?

Data mining tools are the software tools you use to query information in a data warehouse. These data mining tools support the concept of OLAP—the manipulation of information to support decision-making tasks. Data mining tools include query-and-reporting tools, intelligent agents, multidimensional analysis tools, and statistical tools (see Figure 3.9). Essentially, data mining tools are to data warehouse users what data manipulation subsystem tools are to database users.

Figure 3.9

The Data Miner's Tool Set

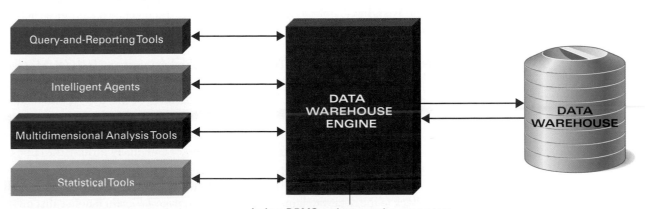

As in a DBMS, a data warehouse system
has an engine responsible for converting your
logical requests into their physical equivalent.

CROSS-SELLING INSURANCE PRODUCTS IN AUSTRALIA

Selling insurance products is competitive all over the world, mainly because of the push by financial services companies into the insurance businesses. Of course, insurance companies can respond by providing more and better products, but that's only part of the solution.

So, many insurance companies, like Australian P&C Direct, are developing strategies based on customer relationship management, data warehouses, and cross-selling. To achieve those strategies, P&C is creating a customer information data warehouse that includes the typical customer information coupled with census data and lifestyle codes. In doing so, the company can better cross-sell to its customers (e.g., selling a life insurance policy to a customer who has also purchased a health insurance policy from P&C).

P&C is also incorporating its marketing campaign information into the data warehouse. That way, P&C agents can view all of the products a given customer has purchased and more accurately determine what marketing campaigns the customer is likely to respond to.[10]

QUERY-AND-REPORTING TOOLS *Query-and-reporting tools* are similar to QBE tools, SQL, and report generators in the typical database environment. In fact, most data warehousing environments support simple and easy-to-use data manipulation subsystem tools such as QBE, SQL, and report generators. Most often, data warehouse users use these types of tools to generate simple queries and reports.

INTELLIGENT AGENTS Intelligent agents utilize various artificial intelligence tools such as neural networks and fuzzy logic to form the basis of "information discovery" and building business intelligence in OLAP. For example, Wall Street analyst Murray Riggiero uses OLAP software called Data/Logic, which incorporates neural networks to generate rules for his highly successful stock and bond trading system.[11] Other OLAP tools, such as Data Engine, incorporate fuzzy logic to analyze real-time technical processes.

Intelligent agents represent the growing convergence of various IT tools for working with information. Previously, intelligent agents were considered only within the context of artificial intelligence and were seldom thought to be a part of the data organizing and managing functions in an organization. Today, you can find intelligent agents not only being used for OLAP in a data warehouse environment but also for searching for information on the Web. In Chapter 4, we'll explore artificial intelligence techniques such as intelligent agents.

MULTIDIMENSIONAL ANALYSIS TOOLS *Multidimensional analysis (MDA) tools* are slice-and-dice techniques that allow you to view multidimensional information from different perspectives. For example, if you completed either of the two recommended Real HOT group projects for Chapter 1, you were using spreadsheet software to literally slice and dice the provided information. Within the context of a data warehouse, we refer to this process as "turning the cube." That is, you're essentially turning the cube to view information from different perspectives.

This turning of the cube allows you to quickly see information in different subcubes. If you refer to back to the data warehouse in Figure 3.8 on page 144, you'll notice that information by customer segment and timing of advertising are actually hidden. Using MDA tools, you can easily bring those to the front of the data warehouse for viewing. What you've essentially done is to slice the cube vertically by layer and bring some of the background layers to the front. As you do this, the values of the information are not affected.

STATISTICAL TOOLS   Statistical tools help you apply various mathematical models to the information stored in a data warehouse to discover new information. For example, you can perform a time-series analysis to project future trends. You can also perform a regression analysis to determine the effect of one variable on another.

Sega of America, one of the largest publishers of video games, uses a data warehouse and statistical tools to effectively distribute its advertising budget of more than $50 million a year.[12,13] With its data warehouse, product line specialists and marketing strategists "drill" into trends of each retail store chain. Their goal is to find buying trends that will help them better determine which advertising strategies are working best (and at what time of the year) and how to reallocate advertising resources by media, territory, and time. Sega definitely benefits from its data warehouse, and so do retailers such as Toys "R" Us, Wal-Mart, and Sears—all good examples of customer relationship management through technology.

To learn more about today's best data warehousing and data mining tools, visit the Web site that supports this text at www.mhhe.com/haag.

DATA MARTS: SMALLER DATA WAREHOUSES

Data warehouses are often perceived as organizationwide, containing summaries of all the information that an organization tracks. However, some people need access to only a portion of that data warehouse information as opposed to all of it. In this case, an organization can create one or more data marts. A ***data mart*** is a subset of a data warehouse in which only a focused portion of the data warehouse information is kept (see Figure 3.10).

Lands' End first created an organizationwide data warehouse for everyone to use, but soon found out that there can be "too much of a good thing."[14] In fact, many Lands' End employees wouldn't use the data warehouse because it was simply too big, too complicated, and included information they didn't need access to. So, Lands' End created several smaller data marts. For example, Lands' End created a data mart just for the merchandising department. That data mart contains only merchandising-specific information and not any information, for instance, that would be unique to the finance department.

Figure 3.10

Data Marts Are Subsets of Data Warehouses

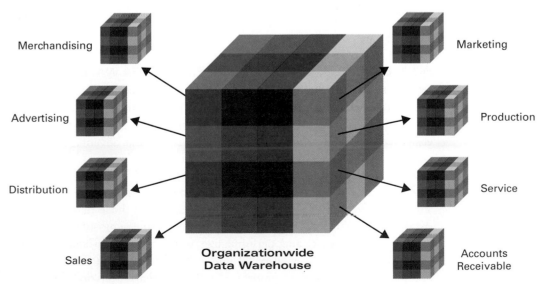

Merchandising

Advertising

Distribution

Sales

Organizationwide Data Warehouse

Marketing

Production

Service

Accounts Receivable

Because of the smaller, more manageable data marts, knowledge workers at Lands' End are making better use of information. If some of your employees don't need access to organizationwide data warehouse information, consider building a smaller data mart for their particular needs.

If you do choose to build smaller data marts for your employees, the data mining tools are the same. That is, data marts support the use of query-and-reporting tools, intelligent agents, multidimensional analysis tools, and statistical tools. This yields efficiency in an organization with respect to training. Once you've trained your employees to use any or all data mining tools, they can apply them to an organizationwide data warehouse or smaller data marts.

IMPORTANT CONSIDERATIONS IN USING A DATA WAREHOUSE

As with all types of technology, you can't simply implement a data warehouse and use data mining tools just because they're a "hot" set of technologies. Let your business needs drive your technology decisions. With respect to data warehouses and data mining tools, following are some questions to consider.

DO YOU NEED A DATA WAREHOUSE?   If you ask most people in the business world if they need a data warehouse, they'll immediately say yes. But they may be wrong. Although data warehouses are a great way to bring together information from many different databases, and data mining tools are a great way to manipulate that information, they're not necessarily the best technologies for all businesses. Why? There are three reasons.

1. Data warehouses and data mining tools are expensive. These are among the most expensive of all technologies, and your organization will devote considerable time to create a data warehouse. Training in the use of data mining tools is also expensive.

2. Some organizations simply don't need a data warehouse. You may find that you can easily extract necessary information to support decision making from operational databases. If so, don't use a data warehouse.

3. Many IT departments suffer from supporting too many applications and application tools. As David Tanaka, a DSS manager at Hospital Health Plan Management Corp., points out, "Right now, we are support-strapped. If we introduce something like OLAP, we will have to give it a lot of support."[15] Technology and its use requires constant support. If you can't support it, don't implement it.

DO ALL YOUR EMPLOYEES NEED AN ENTIRE DATA WAREHOUSE?   As we've already discussed, some of your employees may not need access to an organizationwide data warehouse. If this is the case, definitely consider building data marts. Data marts are smaller than data warehouses, and therefore more manageable and easier to access. The easier technology is to use, the more your users will take advantage of it.

HOW UP-TO-DATE MUST THE INFORMATION BE?   Data warehouses contain information from other databases. From an operational perspective, it's important to consider how often you should extract information from those databases and update the data warehouse. Instantaneously is usually not feasible in most organizations because of communications costs and performance considerations. So some organizations take "snapshots" of databases every 30 minutes and update the data warehouse, whereas other organizations perform updates nightly or perhaps even on a weekly basis.

HOW UP-TO DATE SHOULD DATA WAREHOUSE INFORMATION BE?

Information timeliness is a must in a data warehouse—old and obsolete information leads to poor decision making. Below is a list of decision-making processes that people go through for different business environments. For each, specify whether the information in the data warehouse should be updated monthly, weekly, daily, or by the minute. Be prepared to justify your decision.

1. To adjust class sizes in a university registration environment
2. To alert people to changes in weather conditions
3. To predict scores for professional football games
4. To adjust radio advertisements in light of demographic changes
5. To monitor the success of a new product line in the clothing retail industry
6. To adjust production levels of foods in a cafeteria
7. To switch jobs to various printers in a network
8. To adjust CD rates in a bank
9. To adjust forecasted demands of tires in an auto parts store

WHAT DATA MINING TOOLS DO YOU NEED? User needs should always drive what data mining tools are necessary: query-and-reporting tools, intelligent agents, multidimensional analysis tools, statistical tools, or some combination of the four. Whatever you choose, training is key. It's important for your organization to first make users aware of the capabilities of the entire data mining tool set. Then, once they decide on which tools are best, you'll need to provide training. If your users can fully exploit all the features of their chosen data mining tools, your entire organization will reap the benefits.

Managing the Information Resource in an Organization

As you prepare to enter today's fast-paced, exciting, and information-based business world, you must be prepared to help your organization manage and organize its information. After all, you will be a knowledge worker—a person who works primarily with information. Your organization will be successful, in part, because of your ability to organize and manage information in a way that best moves the organization toward its goals. Following is a list of questions to keep in mind. The answers to some of them are definitely moving targets. As business and technology change, your answers may have to change as well.

WHO SHOULD OVERSEE THE ORGANIZATION'S INFORMATION?

Organizations today can have chief executive officers (CEOs), chief operating officers (COOs), and chief financial officers (CFOs), among others. You can also find another title—chief information officer. The *chief information officer (CIO)* is responsible for overseeing an organization's information resource. A CIO's responsibilities may range from approving new development activities for data warehouses and data marts to monitoring the quality and use of information within those data warehouses and data marts.

DO YOU WANT TO BE A CIO?

Regardless of your industry or business sector, one of the highest paid IT jobs is that of chief information officer. According to *InformationWeek Research*'s 2002 National IT Salary Survey, managers in IT earn a median base salary of $83,000, while staffers earn a median base salary of $61,000. Those numbers sound pretty good. But compared to the median salary of CIOs ($119,000), they fall well short.

So, what does it take to be a CIO? We know of two things for sure. The first is an intimate knowledge of how a business environment works. And the second is an intimate understanding of how information technology can help a business work more efficiently and effectively. Those are givens.

If we were to offer you a third, we would say that the new generation of CIOs will come out of the data warehousing arena. Why? Because data warehousing specialists must understand the entire business in great detail, and they must know how to use information technology.[16]

Two important functions associated with overseeing an organization's information resource are data and database administration. **Data administration** is the function in an organization that plans for, oversees the development of, and monitors the information resource. It must be completely in tune with the strategic direction of the organization to assure that all information requirements can and are being met.

Database administration is the function in an organization that is responsible for the more technical and operational aspects of managing the information contained in organizational databases (which can include data warehouses and data marts). Database administration functions include defining and organizing database structures and contents, developing security procedures, developing database and DBMS documentation, and approving and monitoring the development of databases and database applications.

In organizations of any great size, both functions are usually handled by a steering committee rather than a single individual. These steering committees are responsible for their respective functions and reporting to the CIO. It's definitely a team effort to manage most organizational resources—information is no different in that it needs careful oversight and management.

However, information is different from many "typical" organizational resources. For example, information is intangible, so it becomes extremely difficult to measure its worth or value. What dollar value would you attach to a customer record? Can a business realistically do that? The answer to the latter question is no. So, if you can't place a value on information, how can you know how much you should spend on information technology tools? It is a difficult question to answer.

Since information is intangible, it can also be shared by numerous people and not actually be "consumed." Money is different. If you have money in your department budget and spend it on travel, you can't very well use that same money for employee education expenses. In a way, then, the intangibility of information is good because many people can use it. But as we've alluded to many times, you now have to make special and unique considerations for the security of information that you do not have to make for other organizational resources, such as money.

CRUD: DEFINING INFORMATION OWNERSHIP

One easy way to determine information ownership is to think in terms of **CRUD**—**c**reate, **r**ead, **u**pdate, and **d**elete. If you can create, update, and/or delete information, then in some way you own that information because you are responsible for its quality.

Here again, let's consider your school as an example and focus on your personal and transcript information. That information includes your student ID, name, address, phone number, GPA, declared major, declared minor (if you have one), and courses completed (this is your transcript).

For each of those pieces, first identify who has create, update, and delete privileges. There may be many individuals or departments that have these sorts of information privileges. If so, who is ultimately responsible for your personal and transcript information? Second, identify all the groups of people at your school who can only view your information.

HOW WILL CHANGES IN TECHNOLOGY AFFECT ORGANIZING AND MANAGING INFORMATION?

If there has ever been a moving target that businesses are trying to hit, it's probably information technology. It seems that businesses are faced with new technologies every day that are faster, better, and provide more capabilities than the technologies of yesterday. Chasing technology in a business environment can be very expensive and is not what we would consider to be a best business practice.

What you have to remember is that technology is simply a set of tools for helping you work with information, including organizing and managing it. As new technologies become available, you should ask yourself whether those technologies will help you organize and manage your information *better*. You can't simply say, "A new technology is available that will allow us to organize and manage our information in a different way, so we should use it." The real question is whether that different way of organizing and managing information is better than what you're currently doing. If the answer is yes, you should seriously consider the new technology in light of the strategic goals of the organization. If the answer is no, stay with what you've got until a tool comes along that allows you to do a *better* job.

One of the greatest technological changes that will occur over the coming years is a convergence of different tools that will help you better organize and manage information. Environment Canada's Ice Services, for example, is providing a combination of a data warehouse and Internet-based information resources that seafarers can use.[17] This new system gathers ice charts stored in the Internet and logically organizes them in the form of a data warehouse. Using this new system, seafarers can obtain updated maps and charts that reflect changing ice conditions every 4 hours instead of every 12 hours. Who knows—the *Titanic* might still be here today if this system had been available in 1912.

IS INFORMATION OWNERSHIP A CONSIDERATION?

Information sharing in your organization means that anyone—regardless of title or department—can access and use whatever information he or she needs. But information sharing brings to light an important question: Does anyone in your organization own any information? In other words, if everyone shares information, who is ultimately responsible for providing that information and assuring the quality of the information?

DO MOVIES AFFECT YOUR VIEW OF ETHICS?

Many movies today deal with ethical issues. It's not that movie producers make movies just so you'll think about your own ethics. But if a movie does have within it an ethical dilemma, you'll want to discuss it with your friends. That, in turn, makes your friends want to pay to see the movie. It's a simple matter of providing the viewing public with a story that raises significant questions and encourages more people to see the movie.

Consider *Gattaca,* a movie about the future. In its version of the future, a person's DNA determined his or her entire future. DNA was used to determine the type of job and whether or not the person would go to school. Everyone's DNA was stored in a large central database that organizations and the government accessed often.

In one particular scene, a young woman met a young man at a nightclub. She was quite taken by him.

So, she stole a small strand of his hair and went to a nearby booth. The person working the booth analyzed the hair, accessed the young man's DNA, and provided the young woman with his complete biological profile. She used that information, of course, to determine whether or not to pursue a relationship with him.

Although it may seem like a rather outlandish view of the future, it does raise some important questions. Should we, as a society, be tracking that kind of information? If so, who should have access to it and for what reasons? Should you be able to pay to access someone else's medical information (as the young woman did)?

These are important questions that you cannot ignore. You may not have to deal with them right now, but you certainly will in the future. How will you respond?

Information ownership is a key consideration in today's information-based business environment. Someone must accept full responsibility for providing specific pieces of information and ensuring the quality of that information. If you find that the wrong information is stored in the organization's data warehouse, you must be able to determine the source of the problem and whose responsibility it is.

This issue of information ownership is similar to other management functions. If you manage a department, you're responsible for the work in the department as well as expenses and people. The same is true for information. If information originates in your department, you essentially own that information because you're providing it to those who need it and ensuring its quality.

WHAT ARE THE ETHICS INVOLVED IN MANAGING AND ORGANIZING INFORMATION?

Throughout this text, we address many ethical issues associated with information and information technology. Many of our discussions focus on your organization's societal obligations with respect to customers. Within the organization, those same issues are a concern. By bringing together vast amounts of information into a single place (a database or data warehouse) and providing software (a DBMS or data mining tools) that anyone can use to access that information, ethics and privacy become key concerns.

For example, as a manager of marketing research, should you be able to access the salaries of people in distribution and logistics? Should you be able to access medical profiles of those in accounting? Should you be able to access counseling records of those in manufacturing? The answer to some of these questions is obviously no. But how does an organization safeguard against the unethical use of information within the organization?

While most DBMSs provide good security facilities, it's far easier for someone within your organization to obtain information than it is for someone outside the organization. So what's the key? Unfortunately, we don't know the answer and neither does anyone else. But it all starts with each person always acting in the most ethical way with respect to information. Ethics, security, and privacy will always be great concerns. You can do your part by always acting ethically. Remember, being sensitive to the ethics of other people is an important challenge that you must meet.

Summary: Student Learning Outcomes Revisited

1. **Describe business intelligence and its role in an organization.** *Business intelligence* is knowledge—knowledge about your customers, your competitors, your partners, your competitive environment, and your own internal operations. Business intelligence is much more than just a list of your products or to whom you've sold them. It would combine your product information perhaps with your advertising strategy information and customer demographics to help you determine the effectiveness of various advertising media on demographic groups segmented by location.

2. **Differentiate between databases and data warehouses with respect to their focus on online transaction processing and online analytical processing.** A *database* is a collection of information that you organize and access according to the logical structure of that information. Databases support both online transaction processing (OLTP) and online analytical processing (OLAP). Databases that support OLTP are often referred to as *operational databases.* These databases contain detailed information about transactions that have taken place. And using various data manipulation tools, you can query a database to extract meaningful information. A *data warehouse* is a collection of information—gathered from many different operational databases—used to create business intelligence that supports business analysis activities and decision-making tasks. So, data warehouses support only OLAP, not OLTP.

3. **List and describe the key characteristics of a relational database.** The *relational database model* uses a series of logically related two-dimensional tables or files to store information in the form of a database. Key characteristics include

   - A collection of information—Composed of many files or tables of information that are related to each other
   - Contain logical structures—You care only about the logical information and not about how it's physically stored or where it's physically located
   - Have logical ties among the information—All the files in a database are related in that some primary keys of certain files appear as foreign keys in others
   - Possess built-in integrity constraints—When creating the data dictionary for a database, you can specify rules by which the information must be entered (e.g., not blank, etc.)

4. **Define the five software components of a database management system.** The five software components of a database management system include

   - *DBMS engine*—Accepts logical requests from the various other DBMS subsystems, converts them into their physical equivalent, and actually accesses the database and data dictionary as they exist on a storage device
   - *Data definition subsystem*—Helps you create and maintain the data dictionary and define the structure of the files in a database
   - *Data manipulation subsystem*—Helps you add, change, and delete information in a database and mine it for valuable information
   - *Application generation subsystem*—Contains facilities to help you develop transaction-intensive applications

- *Data administration subsystem*—Helps you manage the overall database environment by providing facilities for backup and recovery, security management, query optimization, concurrency control, and change management

5. **List and describe the key characteristics of a data warehouse.** The key characteristics of a data warehouse include

   - Multidimensional—While databases store information in two-dimensional tables, data warehouses include layers to represent information according to different dimensions

   - Support decision making—Data warehouses, because they contain summarized information, support business activities and decision-making tasks, not transaction processing

6. **Define the four major types of data mining tools in a data warehouse environment.** The four major types of data mining tools in a data warehouse environment include

   - *Query-and-reporting tools*—Similar to QBE tools, SQL, and report generators in the typical database environment

   - *Intelligent agents*—Utilize various artificial intelligence tools such as neural networks and

fuzzy logic to form the basis of "information discovery" and building business intelligence in OLAP

   - *Multidimensional analysis (MDA) tools*— Slice-and-dice techniques that allow you to view multidimensional information from different perspectives

   - *Statistical tools*—Help you apply various mathematical models to the information stored in a data warehouse to discover new information

7. **List key considerations in managing the information resource in an organization.** Key considerations in managing the information resource in an organization include these questions:

   - Who should oversee the organization's information?

   - How will changes in technology affect organizing and managing information?

   - Is information ownership a consideration?

   - What are the ethics involved in managing and organizing information?

CLOSING CASE STUDY ONE

WE'VE GOT OLTP COVERED; LET'S GO ON TO OLAP

In business environments today, you'll find rich, technically correct, and very supportive databases that meet transaction processing needs (OLTP or online transaction processing). But many of those same organizations have failed to implement the necessary technologies that support business analysis and decision-making needs (OLAP or online analytical processing). And this situation makes sense. It's far easier to implement a database for processing something like sales transactions than it is to provide the necessary technology tools and information that would support someone, for example, in determining where to build a new distribution center.

So, we've pretty well got OLTP covered. We need now to focus on OLAP. Consider these three companies

and the pains they took to support OLAP. They are not unique situations, nor are they bad ones. In fact, we would say that these are leading-edge companies because they are willing to acknowledge their problems, face them, and strive to do something about them.

EASTMAN CHEMICAL COMPANY

As Jerry Hale, CIO at Eastman explains it, managers don't have easy access to the information they need to make effective decisions. He further explains that there is a variety of reasons for this problem: too much information is available, much of the information is in incompatible formats, and most of the decision support software is too difficult for managers to use. According to Jerry, "A high percentage of the data is there. The challenge is in extracting it and presenting it in a way that's useful for managers to make decisions."

To combat such problems, Eastman is currently considering several alternatives. The first is to create a simple menu of reports from which managers can choose. And, upon choosing a specific report, managers will also have the ability to request to see the aggregated information in more detail. Eastman is also planning to incorporate external information into its data warehouse. This will allow managers to compare external information such as economic and chemical-industry leading-indicator information to internal information such as production and forecasted demand. The goal, according to Jerry, is "to bring this to another level of access and ease of use." Sounds good.

TEXAS INSTRUMENTS

Texas Instruments (TI) faces equally difficult challenges. For example, it has a semiconductor fabrication plant in Kilby, Texas. That plant tests and manufactures new semiconductor products and streamlines the production and yield processes before manufacturing the chips at high volume. The plant tracks huge amounts of performance information from production equipment and prototype semiconductors. Ideally, that information is then used to make design and production decisions for the chips.

But as Joe Lebowitz, TI's yield and product engineering director at the plant, explains it, the information needed to make those decisions must be pulled from multiple databases. One database contains semiconductor defect data, another database tracks and maintains process equipment history, and yet another database tracks and maintains electrical test data. As Joe describes it, "One of the big tasks at hand is tying those databases together and extracting the data we need."

Currently, several IT specialists do nothing all day except build data-extraction programs and reports to provide managers with the information they need. And that time could be better spent making decisions instead of just extracting the information.

CIGNA CORPORATION

Cigna Corporation, an employee benefits company with $85 billion in revenues, is actually half-pleased with its efforts to provide information that supports OLAP. According to Marc Bloom, Cigna's insurance division business technology and information services di-

rector, "I think they get more than half of what they need." The challenge now is to get the other half.

Within the insurance division, managers make daily decisions on managing based on financial and operational information. This information primarily shows fluctuations in financial and operating metrics such as an increase or decrease in claims processing. Managers can receive this information in a variety of ways: through ad hoc facilities that allow them to build their own reports, report templates already prepared by the IT staff, and complete reports delivered to their desktop and notebook computers.

It really all depends on the skill set of the manager. As Marc explains it, "Everybody's got a different skill set. It's a question of having the right people and the right tools to access it, turning that data into useful information, and being able to do it quickly enough to make a timely decision."[18]

QUESTIONS

1. In your view, what is the single most important factor that hinders all organizations in general from providing good online analytical processing (OLAP) support? Why is it so much easier for organizations to provide good online transaction processing support (OLTP)?

2. Consider Eastman. According to Jerry, most of the decision support software is too difficult for managers to use. One identified solution is to provide a menu of predefined reports. Will that completely solve the problem? What other steps should Eastman take so that managers don't find the decision support software too difficult to use?

3. Now consider Texas Instruments. Its managers need information for decision making that resides in several different databases. One potential solution here is to build a data warehouse and extract the necessary information from the various databases. Will this solve the problem? Why or why not? If TI does indeed build a data warehouse, what sort of training will its managers need? How can TI convince its managers that learning how to use yet another technology tool will be beneficial?

4. Finally, consider Cigna. According to Marc, Cigna is halfway home in providing OLAP support. If you have only half the information you need to make a decision, how effective do you think you'll be? Can you expect to make the right

decision 50 percent of the time if you have only 50 percent of the information you need? What if you have 90 percent of the information you need? Will you be 90 percent correct in making your decisions? Why or why not?

5. Neil Hastie, CIO at TruServe Corporation, describes most decision making in all types of businesses as "a lot of by-guess and by-golly, a lot of by-gut, and a whole lot of paper reports."

That statement is not kind to managers in general nor to IT specialists charged with providing the right people with the right technology to make the right decisions. What's the key to turning Neil's statement into a positive one? Is it training? Is it providing timely information access? Is it providing easy-to-use tools? Other solutions? Perhaps it's a combination of several answers.

MINING DINING DATA

Restaurants, fast-food chains, casinos, and others use data warehouses to determine customer purchasing habits and to determine what products and promotions to offer and when to offer them. Some of the leading data warehouse users include AFC Enterprises (operator and franchiser of more than 3,300 Church's Chicken, Popeyes' Chicken and Biscuits, Seattle Coffee Company, Cinnabon, and Torrefazione outlets worldwide); Red Robin International (a 135-unit casual-dining chain); Harrah's Entertainment (owner of 26 U.S. casinos); Pizzeria Uno; and Einstein/Noah Bagel (operator of 428 Einstein's and 111 Noah's New York Bagel stores).

AFC ENTERPRISES

AFC Enterprises cultivates a loyal clientele by slicing and dicing its data warehouse to strategically configure promotions and tailor menus to suit local preferences. AFC's data warehouse helps it better understand its core customers and maximize its overall profitability. AFC tracks customer-specific information from name and address to order history and frequency of visits. This enables AFC to determine exactly which customers are likely to respond to a given promotion on a given day of the week.

AFC also uses its data warehouse to anticipate and manipulate customer behavior. For example, AFC can use its data warehouse to determine that coffee is added to the tab 65 percent of the time when a particular dessert is ordered and 85 percent of the time when that dessert is offered as a promotional item. Knowing that, AFC can run more promotions for certain desserts

figuring that customers will respond by ordering more desserts and especially more coffee (coffee is a high-margin item in the restaurant business).

RED ROBIN INTERNATIONAL

Red Robin's terabyte-size data warehouse tracks hundreds of thousands of point-of-sale (POS) transactions, involving millions of menu items and more than 1.5 million invoices. As Howard Jenkins, Red Robin's vice president of information systems, explains it, "With data mining in place, we can ask ourselves, 'If we put the items with high margins in the middle of the menu, do we sell more versus putting it at the top or bottom, [and if so], to whom and where?' We can also tell if something cannibalizes the sale of other items and can give the marketing department an almost instant picture of how promotions are being sold and used."

The placement of items on a menu is strategic business, just as the placement of promotional items in a grocery store can mean increased sales for one item and reduced sales for another. The job of finding the right mix is definitely suited to mining a data warehouse.

HARRAH'S ENTERTAINMENT

Harrah's Entertainment uses its data warehouse to make decisions for its highly successful Total Gold customer recognition program. Depending on their spending records, Total Gold members can receive free vouchers for dining, entertainment, and sleeping accommodations. Knowing which rewards to give to which customers is key.

John Boushy, senior vice president of entertainment and technology for Harrah's, says, "We can determine what adds value to each customer and provide that value at the right time." Dining vouchers or free tickets for shows are awarded to day visitors, not sleeping accommodations. Customers who consistently visit a particular restaurant and order higher-end foods receive free dinners and cocktails, not vouchers for free (and cheaper) breakfasts.

PIZZERIA UNO

Pizzeria Uno uses its data warehouse to apply the 80/20 rule. That is, it can determine which 20 percent of its customers contribute to 80 percent of its sales and adjust menus and promotions to suit top patron preferences. These changes can often lead to converting some of the other 80 percent of Pizzeria Uno's customers to the more profitable 20 percent.

EINSTEIN/NOAH BAGEL

Einstein/Noah Bagel uses its data warehouse in real time to maximize cross-selling opportunities. For example, if data warehouse information reveals that a manager in a given store might be missing a cross-selling opportunity on a particular day, an e-mail is automatically sent out to alert managers to the opportunity. Salespeople can then respond by offering the cross-selling opportunity ("How about a cup of hot chocolate with that bagel since it's so cold outside?") to the next customer.[19, 20]

QUESTIONS

1. Consider the issue of timely information with respect to the businesses discussed in the case. Which of the businesses must have the most up-to-date information in its data warehouse? Which business can have the most out-of-date information in its data warehouse and still be effective? Rank the five businesses discussed with a 1 for the one that needs the most up-to-date information and a 5 for the one that is least sensitive to timeliness of information. Be prepared to justify your rankings.

2. Harrah's Entertainment tracks a wealth of information concerning customer spending habits. If you were to design Harrah's Entertainment's data warehouse, what dimensions of information would you include? As you develop your list of dimensions, consider every facet of Harrah's business operations, including hotels, restaurants, and gaming casinos.

3. AFC Enterprises includes information in its data warehouse such as customer name and address. Where does it (or could it) gather such information? Think carefully about this, because customers seldom provide their names and addresses when ordering fast food at a Church's or Popeyes. Is AFC gathering information in an ethical fashion? Why or why not?

4. Visit a local grocery store and walk down the breakfast cereal aisle. You should notice something very specific about the positioning of the various breakfast cereals. What is it? On the basis of what information do you think grocery stores determine cereal placement? Could they have determined that information from a data warehouse or from some other source? If another source, what might that source be?

5. Suppose you're opening a pizza parlor in the town where you live. It will be a "take and bake" pizza parlor in which you make pizzas for customers but do not cook them. Customers buy the pizzas uncooked and take them home for baking. You will have no predefined pizza types but will make each pizza to the customer's specifications. What sort of data warehouse would you need to predict the use of toppings by time of day and by day of the week? What would your dimensions of information be? If you wanted to increase the requests for a new topping (such as mandarin oranges), what information would you hope to find in your data warehouse that would enable you to do so?

Key Terms and Concepts

Application generation subsystem, 140
Business intelligence, 128

Chief information officer (CIO), 149
Data administration, 150

Short-Answer Questions

1. What is business intelligence? Why is it more than just information?
2. What is online transaction processing (OLTP)?
3. What are databases called that support OLTP?
4. What is online analytical processing (OLAP)? How is it different from OLTP?
5. What is the most popular database model?
6. What is the role of a data dictionary in a database environment?
7. How are primary and foreign keys different? How are they the same?
8. What are the five important software components of a database management system?
9. How are QBE tools and SQL similar? How are they different?
10. What part of a DBMS helps you manage the overall database environment?
11. What is a data warehouse? How does it differ from a database?
12. What are the four major types of data mining tools?
13. What database tools are similar to data mining query-and-reporting tools?
14. What is a data mart? How is it similar to a data warehouse?
15. How often should you update information in a data warehouse?
16. What is the role of a chief information officer (CIO)?
17. How do the functions of data administration and database administration differ?

Short-Question Answers

For each of the following answers, provide an appropriate question.

1. It's more than just information.
2. Operational databases.
3. Relation.
4. Database.
5. A primary key of one file that appears in another file.
6. Rules that help ensure the quality of information.
7. Handles the physical view in a database environment.
8. Data dictionary.
9. Tools including views, report generators, QBE, and SQL.
10. The graphical equivalent of SQL.
11. Security management is an example.
12. It is multidimensional and supports only OLAP.
13. Slice-and-dice techniques.
14. A smaller version of a data warehouse.
15. CIO.
16. The function that plans for, oversees the development of, and monitors the information resource.

Assignments and Exercises

1. **FINDING "HACKED" DATABASES** *The Happy Hacker* (www.happyhacker.org/news/index.shtml) is a Web site devoted to "hacking"—breaking into computer systems. When people hack into a system, they often go after information in databases. There, they can find credit card information and other private and sensitive information. Sometimes, they can even find designs of yet-to-be-released products and other strategic information about a company. Connect to *The Happy Hacker* Web site and find an article that discusses a database that was hacked. Prepare a short report for your class detailing the incident.

2. **DEFINING QUERIES FOR A VIDEO RENTAL STORE** Consider your local video rental store. It certainly has an operational database to support its online transaction processing (OLTP). The operational database supports such things as the adding of new customers, the renting of videos (obviously), the ordering of videos, and a host of other activities. Now, assume that the video rental store also uses that same database for online analytical processing (OLAP) in the form of creating queries to extract meaningful information. If you were the manager of the video rental store, what kinds of queries would you build? What answers are you hoping to find?

3. **CREATING A QUERY** On the Web site that supports this text (www.mhhe.com/haag, choose Chapter 3 and then Inventory database), we've provided the Inventory database (in Microsoft Access) we illustrated in this chapter. Connect to the text's Web site and download that database. Now, create three queries using the QBE tool. The first one should extract information from only one file (your choice). The second one should extract information found in at least two files. The third should include some sort of selection criteria. How easy or difficult was it to perform these three queries? Would you say that a DBMS is just as easy to use as something like word processing or spreadsheet software? Why or why not? (By the way, *Extended Learning Module J* takes you through the step-by-step process of creating a query in Access.)

4. **CAREER OPPORTUNITIES IN YOUR MAJOR** Knowledge workers throughout the business world are building their own desktop databases (often called end-user databases or knowledge worker databases). To do so, they must understand both how to design a database and how to use a desktop DBMS such as Microsoft Access of FileMaker (made by FileMaker). The ability to design a database and use a desktop DBMS offers you a great career advantage. Research your chosen major by looking at job postings (the Web is the best place to start). How many of those jobs want you to have some database knowledge? Do they list a specific DBMS package? What's your take—should you expand your education and learn more about databases and DBMSs? Why or why not?

5. **SALARIES FOR DATABASE ADMINISTRATORS** Database administrators (DBAs) are among the highest paid professionals in the information technology field. Many people work for 10 to 20 years to get a promotion to DBA. Connect to Monster.com (www.monster.com) or another job database of your choice and search for DBA job openings. As you do, select all locations and job categories and then use "dba" as the keyword search criteria. How many DBA job postings did you find? In what industries were some of the DBA job openings? Read through a couple of the job postings. What was the listed salary range (if any)? What sort of qualifications were listed?

Discussion Questions

1. Databases and data warehouses clearly make it easier for people to access all kinds of information. This will lead to great debates in the area of privacy. Should organizations be left to police themselves with respect to providing access to information or should the government impose privacy legislation? Answer this question with respect to (1) customer information shared by organizations, (2) employee information shared within a specific organization, and (3) business information available to customers.

2. Business intelligence sounds like a fancy term with a lot of competitive advantage potentially rolled into it. What sort of business intelligence does your school need? Specifically, what business intelligence would it need to predict enrollments in the coming years? What business intelligence would it need to determine what curriculums to offer? Do you think your school gathers and uses this kind of business intelligence? Why or why not?

3. Consider your school's registration database that enforces the following integrity constraint: to enroll in a given class, the student must have completed or currently be enrolled in the listed prerequisite (if any). Your school, in fact, probably does have that integrity constraint in place. How can you get around that integrity constraint and enroll in a class for which you are not taking nor have completed the prerequisite? Is this an instance of when you should be able to override an integrity constraint? What are the downsides to being able to do so?

4. In this chapter, we listed the five important software components of a DBMS: the DBMS engine, the data definition, data manipulation, application generation, and data administration subsystems. Which of those are most and least important to users of a database? Which of those are most and least

important to technology specialists who develop data applications? Which of those are most and least important to the chief information officer (CIO)? For each of your responses, provide justification.

5. Some people used to believe that data warehouses would quickly replace databases for both online transaction processing (OLTP) and online analytical processing (OLAP). Of course, they were wrong. Why can data warehouses not replace databases and become "operational data warehouses"? How radically would data warehouses (and their data mining tools) have to change to become a viable replacement for databases? Would they then essentially become databases that simply supported OLAP? Why or why not?

6. Consider that you work in the human resources management department of a local business and that many of your friends work there. Although you don't personally generate payroll checks, you still have the ability to look up anyone's pay. Would you check on your friends to see if they're earning more money than you? For that matter, would you look up their pay just out of simple curiosity, knowing that you would never do anything with the information or share it with anyone else? Why or why not? People working at the Internal Revenue Service (IRS) were caught just curiously looking up the reported incomes of movie stars and other high-profile public figures. Is this acceptable? Why or why not?

7. As we discussed in the Industry Perspective on page 152, movies such as *Gattaca* do play a role in our view of ethics. Make a list of the movies you've recently seen that raise ethical questions. What are the movies? What ethical questions do they raise? Did any of them, by chance, change your ethical view? Why or why not?

Searching Online Databases and Information Repositories

As you find sites on the Internet that provide information, many of them will do so in the form of a database—a searchable grouping of information that allows you to find specific information by entering key words and key phrases. These words and phrases are, in fact, some sort of key (similar to primary and foreign keys we discussed in this chapter) that are used as matching criteria in a field of the database.

In this section, you'll explore a variety of information topics that you can find on the Internet. To help you, we've included a number of Web sites related to searching online database and information repositories. On the Web site that supports this text (www.mhhe.com/haag), we've provided direct links to all these Web sites as well as many, many more. These are a great starting point for completing this *REAL HOT* Electronic Commerce section.

FINANCIAL AID RESOURCES

On the Internet, you can find valuable databases that give you access to financial aid resources as you attend school. These resources can be in the form of scholarships—money you don't have to pay back—and standard student loans. And there are a variety of financial aid lenders, ranging from traditional banks, the government, and private parties wanting to give something back to society. Find at least three Web sites that provide a financial aid database and answer the following questions for each.

   A. Do you have to register as a user to access information?

   B. Do you have to pay a fee to access information?

   C. Can you build a profile of yourself and use it as you search?

   D. Can you apply for aid while at the site or must you request paper applications that you need to complete and return?

   E. By what sort of categories of aid can you search?

LIBRARIES

LEXIS-NEXIS is now completely on the Internet. Many libraries and other such sites even offer full books online for you to read. You may never have to go to a physical library again. Think for a moment about a term paper you're currently writing or may have to write soon. What is the major topic? Now connect to a couple of different library sites and try to find some of the information you'll need. As you do, answer the following questions for each site.

   A. What organization supports the site? Is the organization reputable?

   B. Do you have to pay a subscription fee to access the information provided?

   C. How good are the search capabilities?

   D. How can you obtain printed versions of information you find?

   E. Is finding information in libraries on the Internet easier or more difficult than finding information in a traditional library?

CONSUMER INFORMATION

Many consumer organizations also provide databases of information on the Internet. At those sites you can read about the latest product reviews, search for new pharmaceuticals that cure diseases (or alleviate symptoms of them), and access safety information for products such as automobiles and children's toys.

Connect to several consumer organization sites and do some digging around. As you do, think about a product you're considering buying or perhaps have just bought. Is the information helpful? Is the information opinion only, completely factual, or a combination of the two? How important will this type of consumer information become as electronic commerce becomes more widespread on the Internet?

DEMOGRAPHICS

Recall from Chapter 1 that we characterized our economy today as wants-driven. That is, a large portion of purchases are made based on what people *want* and not necessarily what they *need*. This presents a real marketing and product development challenge.

For organizations focusing on meeting those wants or desires, the demographic makeup of the target audience is key. It's simple: The more you know about your target audience, the better equipped you are to develop and market products based on wants.

And you can find all sorts of demographic information on the Internet. Connect to a couple of different demographic-related Web sites and see what they have to offer. As you do, answer the following questions for each.

A. Who is the target audience of the site?

B. Who is the provider of the site?

C. Is the provider a private (for-profit) organization or a not-for-profit organization?

D. How often is the demographic information updated?

E. Does the site require that you pay a subscription fee to access its demographic information?

F. How helpful would the information be if you wanted to start a new business or sell various types of products?

REAL ESTATE

You can't actually live on the Internet, although some people may seem as though they want to try. But you can find real estate for sale and rent. You can find sites that take you through a step-by-step process for buying your first home, that provide mortgage and interest rate calculators, that offer financing for your home, and that even offer crime reports by neighborhood. Connect to several real estate–related sites and see what they have to offer. As you do, answer the following questions for each.

A. What is the focus of the site (residential, commercial, rental, and so forth)?

B. Does the site require you to register as a user to access its services?

C. Can you request that e-mail be sent to you when properties in which you are interested become available?

D. How can you search for information (by state, by Zip code, by price range, by feature such as swimming pool)?

E. Does the site offer related information such as loans and mortgage calculators?

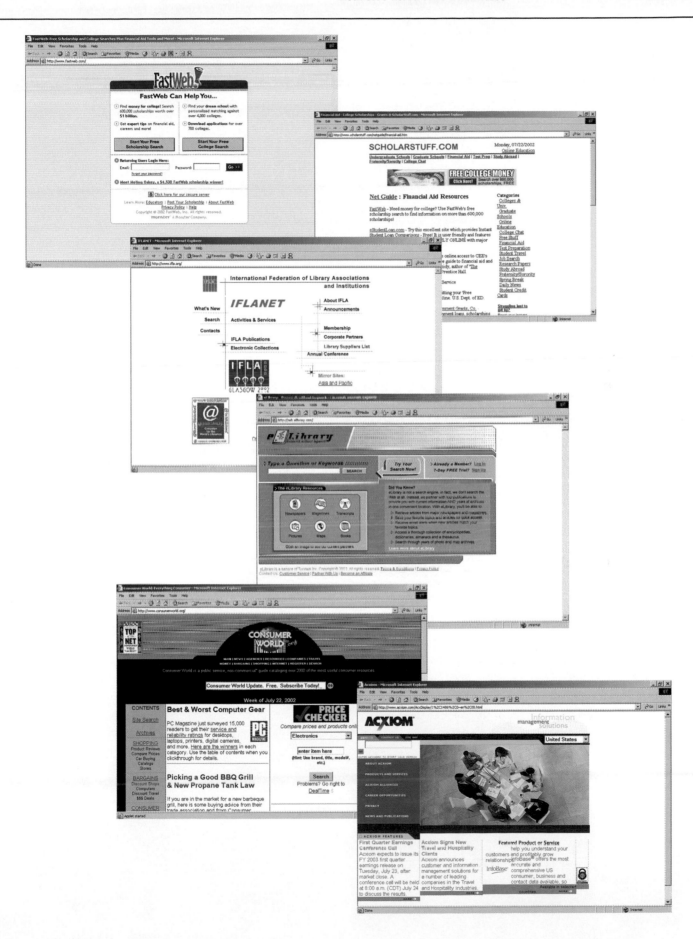

EXTENDED LEARNING MODULE C

DESIGNING DATABASES AND ENTITY-RELATIONSHIP DIAGRAMMING

Student Learning Outcomes

1. IDENTIFY HOW DATABASES AND SPREADSHEETS ARE BOTH SIMILAR AND DIFFERENT.

2. LIST AND DESCRIBE THE FOUR STEPS IN DESIGNING AND BUILDING A RELATIONAL DATABASE.

3. DEFINE THE CONCEPTS OF ENTITY CLASS, INSTANCE, PRIMARY KEY, AND FOREIGN KEY.

4. GIVEN A SMALL OPERATING ENVIRONMENT, BUILD AN ENTITY-RELATIONSHIP (E-R) DIAGRAM.

5. LIST AND DESCRIBE THE STEPS IN NORMALIZATION.

6. DESCRIBE THE PROCESS OF CREATING AN INTERSECTION RELATION TO REMOVE A MANY-TO-MANY RELATIONSHIP.

Introduction

As you learned in Chapter 3, databases are quite powerful and can aid your organization in both transaction and analytical processing. But you must carefully design and build a database for it to be effective. Relational databases are similar to spreadsheets in that you maintain information in two-dimensional files. In a spreadsheet, you place information in a cell (the intersection of a row and column). To use the information in a cell, you must know its row number and column character. For example, cell C4 is in column C and row 4.

Databases are similar and different. You still create rows and columns of information. However, you don't need to know the physical location of the information you want to see or use. For example, if cell C4 in your spreadsheet contained sales for Able Electronics (one of your customers), to use that information in a formula or function, you would reference its physical location (C4). In a database, you simply need to know you want *sales* for *Able Electronics*. Its physical location is irrelevant. That's why we say that a ***database*** is a collection of information that you organize and access according to the logical structure of that information.

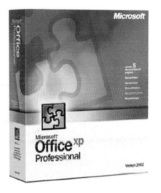

So, you do need to design your databases carefully for effective utilization. In this module, we'll take you through the process of designing and building a relational database, the most popular of all database types. A ***relational database*** uses a series of logically related two-dimensional tables or files to store information in the form of a database. There are well-defined rules to follow, and you need to be aware of them.

As far as implementation is concerned, you then just choose the DBMS package of your choice, define the tables or files, determine the relationships among them, and start entering information. We won't deal with the actual implementation in this module. However, we do show you how to implement a database using Microsoft Access in *Extended Learning Module J*.

Once you've implemented your database, you can then change the information as you wish, add rows of information (and delete others), add new tables, and use simple but powerful reporting and querying tools to extract the exact information you need.

Designing and Building a Relational Database

Using a database amounts to more than just using various DBMS tools. You must also know *how* to actually design and build a database. So, let's take a look at how you would go about designing a database. The four primary steps include

1. Defining entity classes and primary keys
2. Defining relationships among entity classes
3. Defining information (fields) for each relation (the term *relation* is often used to refer to a file while designing a database)
4. Using a data definition language to create your database

Let's assume you own a small business and are interested in tracking employees by the department in which they work, the job assignments, and the number of hours assigned to each job. Below is a list of important business rules that you follow:

1. Each employee must be assigned to one and only one department.
2. A department may have many employees or may not have any.
3. Each employee must be assigned to at least one job and can be assigned to many jobs.
4. A job can have many different employees assigned to it, but a given job does not have to have any employees assigned to it.

Employee ID	Name	Department Num	Department Name	Num of Employees	Job Number	Job Name	Hours
1234	Jones	43	Residential	3	14	Acct	4
					23	Sales	4
2345	Smith	15	Commercial	1	14	Acct	8
6548	Joslin	43	Residential	3	23	Sales	6
					46	Admin	2
9087	Mills	43	Residential	3	23	Sales	5
					14	Acct	3
8797	Jones	69	Non-profit	1	39	Maint	8

Figure C.1

A Sample Report for
Your Employee Database

Figure C.1 contains a sample employee report you would like to generate. Let's look at it briefly and review some of the business rules in action.

First, notice that each employee is assigned to only one department. For example, Mills is assigned to only department—number 43. Second, notice that several employees are assigned to department number 43—these employees include Jones, Joslin, and Mills. Third, notice that each employee is assigned to at least one job and that several employees have more than one job. Finally, notice that more than one employee is assigned to the same job. For example, both Jones and Smith are assigned to the job "Acct" (its job number is 14).

Even before you begin the process of designing a database, it's important that you first understand the business rules. These business rules will help you define the correct structure of your database.

STEP 1: DEFINING ENTITY CLASSES AND PRIMARY KEYS

The first step in designing a relational database is to define the various entity classes and the primary keys that uniquely define each record or instance within each entity class. An *entity class* is a concept—typically people, places, or things—about which you wish to store information and that you can identify with a unique key (called the primary key). A *primary key* is a field (or group of fields in some cases) that uniquely describes each record. Within the context of database design, we often refer to a record as an instance. An *instance* is an occurrence of an entity class that can be uniquely described.

From the employee report you want to generate, you can easily identify the entity classes *Employee*, *Job*, and *Department*. Now, you have to identify their primary keys. For most entity classes, you cannot use names as primary keys because duplicate names may exist. For example, you have two employees with the last name *Jones*. However, our sample report does show that each employee has a unique *Employee ID*. So, *Employee ID* should be the primary key for the *Employee* entity class.

If you consider *Department* as an entity class, you'll find three pieces of information describing it in the report: *Department Num*, *Department Name*, and *Num of Employees*. The logical choice for a primary key here is *Department Num*. Although each *Department Name* is unique, we would still suggest that you not use names.

Likewise, if you consider *Job* as an entity class, you'll find two pieces of information describing it: *Job Number* and *Job Name*. Again, we recommend that you use *Job Number* as the primary key.

For each of these entity classes, you can also easily identify instances. Smith is an instance of the *Employee* entity class, Residential is an instance of the *Department* entity class, and Sales is an instance of the *Job* entity class.

DEFINING ENTITY CLASSES AND PRIMARY KEYS

Learning how to design a relational database really requires that you roll up your sleeves and practice, practice, practice. It's not actually that difficult to design a relational database, and practice will make you proficient. To help with this, you'll be designing a relational database that might be used at your school while we go carefully through the process of designing the relational database for your employee information. Below is a description of a hypothetical relational database that might be used at your school.

In conjunction with taking an introductory computer concepts course, your school has decided to test the idea of offering weekend seminars to cover the basics of the Internet and the Web. Initially, your school will offer two such seminars: Web101—The Basics of the Web and Internet and Web205—Building a Web Site. Web101 will have five different sections, and Web205 will have four different sections.

Although they are not required to, students can enroll in one or both seminars. The seminars are held for eight hours on a single day. There is no cost associated with taking the seminars. One teacher, from a pool of qualified teachers, will be assigned to each section of each seminar. Some teachers will obviously not be assigned to teach any sections, and some teachers may be assigned to several different sections.

Finally, the system should track the final grade assigned to each student. One more thing. Your school is simply testing this idea in this particular term. So don't worry about the term (e.g., Fall, Winter, Spring, or Summer) or the year.

In the table to follow, list all of the entity classes you can find in the preceding description. Next to each, identify a potential primary key. Finally, below the table, record as many business rules as you can find provided in the description.

Entity Class	Primary Key

Business Rules

STEP 2: DEFINING RELATIONSHIPS AMONG THE ENTITY CLASSES

The next step in designing a relational database is to define the relationships among the entity classes. To help you do this, we'll use an entity-relationship diagram. An ***entity-relationship (E-R) diagram*** is a graphic method of representing entity classes and their relationships. An E-R diagram includes five basic symbols:

1. A rectangle to denote an entity class
2. A dotted line connecting entity classes to denote a relationship
3. A | to denote a single relationship
4. A 0 to denote a zero or optional relationship
5. A crow's foot (shown as ⋖) to denote a multiple relationship

To use these symbols, you must first decide among which entity classes relationships exist. If you determine that two particular entity classes have a relationship, you simply draw a dotted line to connect them and then write some sort of verb that describes the relationship.

In Figure C.2, you can see the E-R diagram for your employee database. Let's take some time to explore it. To determine where the relationships exist, simply ask some questions and review your business rules. For example, is there a relationship between employees and departments? The answer is yes because employees are assigned to departments. Likewise, employees are assigned jobs (another relationship). However, there is no logical relationship between departments and jobs. So, we drew dotted lines between *Employee* and *Department* and between *Employee* and *Job*. We then added some verbs to describe the relationships. For example, an *Employee* is assigned to a *Department,* and an *Employee* performs a *Job*.

It should also make sense (both business and logical) when you read the relationships in reverse. To do this, simply flip the location of the nouns in the sentence and change the verb accordingly. For example,

- *Employee-Department:* An *Employee* is assigned to a *Department*.
- *Department-Employee:* A *Department* has an *Employee* assigned to it.
- *Employee-Job:* An *Employee* undertakes a *Job*.
- *Job-Employee:* A *Job* is performed by an *Employee*.

Each of the preceding statements makes logical sense, follows the relationships we identify in Figure C.2, and reflects the business rules listed on page 165. Again, we stress the importance of using business rules. Technology (databases, in this instance) is a set of

Figure C.2

An Entity-Relationship Diagram

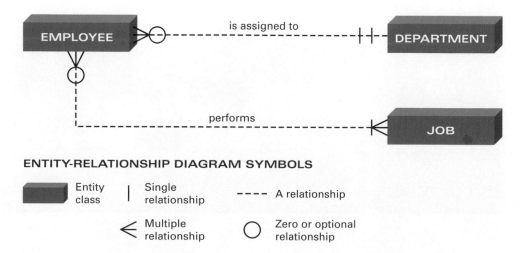

ENTITY-RELATIONSHIP DIAGRAM SYMBOLS

| | Entity class | | Single relationship | ---- A relationship |
| | Multiple relationship | | | Zero or optional relationship |

DEFINING RELATIONSHIPS AMONG ENTITY CLASSES

Let's continue exploring how to design a relational database for your school and its offering of weekend seminars. If your group correctly completed the tasks in the Team Work on page 167, you know that there are four entity classes. They include (along with their primary keys):

Now your task is to define among which of those entity classes relationships exist and then write some verbs that describe each relationship just as we did in Figure C.2. We've drawn rectangles for each of the four entity classes. Connect the rectangles with dotted lines where relationships exist and write the appropriate verbs to describe the relationships.

Entity Class	Primary Key
Seminar	Seminar 3-character identifier and number (e.g., Web101 and Web205)
Seminar Section	Seminar 3-character identifier, number, and section number (e.g., Web101-1 through Web101-5 and Web205-1 through Web205-4)
Student	Student ID (whatever your school happens to use)
Qualified Teacher	Teacher ID (your school may use social security number)

```
+------------------+
|     Seminar      |
+------------------+




                                              +--------------------+
                                              |  Seminar Section   |
                                              +--------------------+

+------------------+
| Qualified Teacher|
+------------------+




+------------------+
|     Student      |
+------------------+
```

Figure C.3

Reading an Entity-Relationship (E-R) Diagram

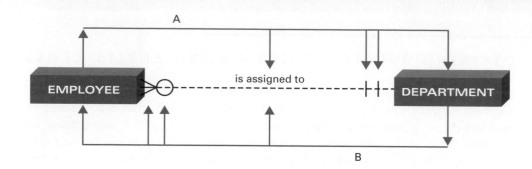

tools that you use to process information. So, your implementations of technology should match the way your business works. If you always start by defining business rules and using those rules as guides, your technology implementations will hopefully mirror how your business works. And that's the way it should be.

Once you determine that a relationship does exist, you must then determine the numerical nature of the relationship, what we refer to as minimum and maximum *cardinality*. To describe this, you use a | to denote a single relationship, a 0 to denote a zero or optional relationship, and/or a crow's foot to denote a multiple relationship. By way of illustration, let's consider the portion of your E-R diagram in Figure C.3. To help you read the symbols, we've added blue lines and arrows. Following the blue line marked A, you would read the E-R diagram as, "An *Employee* is assigned to one *Department* at a minimum and one *Department* at a maximum." So, that part of the E-R diagram states that the logical relationship between *Employee* and *Department* is that an *Employee* is assigned to one and only one *Department*. This is exactly what business rules 1 and 2 state.

Following the blue line marked B, you would read the E-R diagram as, "A *Department* is not required to have any *Employees* assigned to it but may have many *Employees* assigned to it." That statement again reinforces business rules 1 and 2, which are given on page 165.

Similarly, you can also develop statements that describe the numerical relationships between *Employee* and *Job* based on that part of the E-R diagram in Figure C.2. Those numerical relationships would be as follows:

- An *Employee* must be assigned to one *Job* at a minimum and can be assigned to many *Jobs* (maximum).
- A *Job* may not have any *Employees* assigned to it but may have many *Employees* assigned to it.

Again, these statements reinforce business rules 3 and 4, which are given on page 165.

To properly develop the numerical relationships (cardinality) among entity classes, you must clearly understand the business situation at hand. That's why it's so important to write down all the business rules.

DEFINING THE CARDINALITY AMONG ENTITY CLASSES

As we continue with the design of the relational database at your school, it's time to define the cardinality among the entity classes. If you correctly completed the Team Work project on page 169, the relationships among the entity classes are as follows.

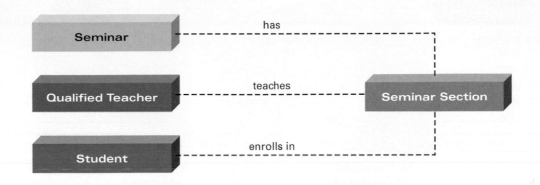

Your task is to create the numerical relationships by adding the symbols of I, O, and crow's foot in the appropriate places. Once you do, complete the table that follows by providing a narrative description of each numerical relationship.

Relationship	Narrative Description
Seminar-Seminar Section	
Seminar Section-Seminar	
Qualified Teacher-Seminar Section	
Seminar Section-Qualified Teacher	
Student-Seminar Section	
Seminar Section-Student	

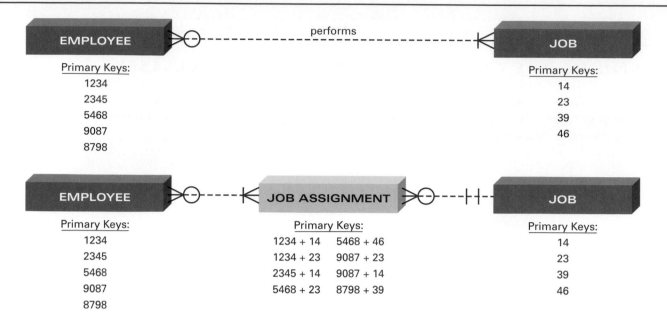

Figure C.4

Creating an Intersection Relation to Remove a Many-to-Many Relationship

After developing the initial E-R diagram, it's time to begin the process of normalization. ***Normalization*** is a process of assuring that a relational database structure can be implemented as a series of two-dimensional relations (remember: *relations* are the same as files or tables). The complete normalization process is extensive and quite necessary for developing organizationwide databases. For our purposes, we will focus on the following three rules of normalization:

1. Eliminate repeating groups or many-to-many relationships
2. Assure that each field in a relation depends only on the primary key for that relation
3. Remove all derived fields from the relations

The first rule of normalization states that no repeating groups or many-to-many relationships can exist among the entity classes. You can find these many-to-many relationships by simply looking at your E-R diagram and noting any relationships that have a crow's foot on each end. If you look back at Figure C.2, you'll see that a crow's foot is on each end of the relationship between *Employee* and *Job.* Let's look at how to eliminate it.

In Figure C.4, we've developed the appropriate relationships between *Employee* and *Job* by removing the many-to-many relationship. Notice that we started with the original portion of the E-R diagram and created a new relation between *Employee* and *Job* called *Job Assignment,* which is an intersection relation. An ***intersection relation*** (sometimes called a ***composite relation***) is a relation you create to eliminate a many-to-many relationship. It's called an intersection relation because it represents an intersection of primary keys between the first two relations. That is, an intersection relation will have a ***composite primary key*** that consists of the primary key fields from the two intersecting relations. The primary key fields from the two original relations now become foreign keys in the intersection relation. A ***foreign key*** is a primary key of one file (relation) that appears in another file (relation). When combined, these two foreign keys make up the composite primary key for the intersection relation.

For your employee database, the intersection relation *Job Assignment* represents which employees are assigned to each job. Listed on the next page is how you would read the relationships between *Employee* and *Job Assignment* and *Job* and *Job Assignment* (see Figure C.5).

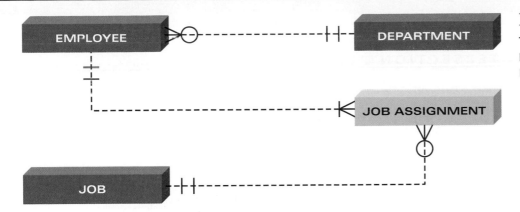

Figure C.5

The Completed E-R
Diagram for Your
Employee Database

- *Employee-Job Assignment*
  - From left to right: An *Employee* can have many *Job Assignments* and must have at least one *Job Assignment*.
  - From right to left: An *Employee* found in *Job Assignment* must be found and can be found only one time in *Employee*.
- *Job-Job Assignment*
  - From left to right: A *Job* can be found in many *Job Assignments* but may not be found in any *Job Assignments*.
  - From right to left: A *Job* found in *Job Assignment* must be found and can be found only one time in *Job*.

If you compare the E-R diagram in Figure C.5 to the E-R diagram in Figure C.2, you'll notice that they are very similar. The only difference is that the E-R diagram in Figure C.5 contains an intersection relation to eliminate the many-to-many relationship between *Employee* and *Job*.

And removing many-to-many relationships is the most difficult aspect when designing the appropriate structure of a relational database. If you do find a many-to-many relationship, here are some guidelines for creating an intersection relation:

1. Just as we did in Figure C.5, start by drawing the part of the E-R diagram that contains a many-to-many relationship at the top of a piece of paper.
2. Underneath each relation for which the many-to-many relationship exists, write down some of the primary keys.
3. Create a new E-R diagram (showing no cardinality) with the original two relations on each end and a new one (the intersection relation) in the middle.
4. Underneath the intersection relation, write down some composite primary keys (these will be composed of the primary keys from the other two relations).
5. Create a meaningful name (e.g., Job Assignment) for the intersection relation.
6. Move the minimum cardinality appearing next to the left relation just to the right of the intersection relation.
7. Move the minimum cardinality appearing next to the right relation just to the left of the intersection relation.
8. The maximum cardinality on both sides of the intersection relation will always be "many" (the crow's foot).
9. As a general rule, the new minimum and maximum cardinalities for the two original relations will be one and one.

CREATING AN INTERSECTION RELATION

Back to work on the project for your school. If you completed the Team Work project on page 171, you are now able to identify a many-to-many relationship between *Student* and *Seminar Section.* That is, a given

Seminar Section may have many *Students,* and a given *Student* can enroll in many different *Seminar Sections* (two, to be exact). So, that portion of your E-R diagram looks like what follows.

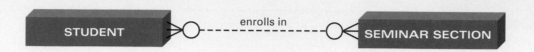

Your task is to eliminate the above many-to-many relationship by creating an intersection relation. As you do, we would encourage you to follow the guidelines

given on page 173. What did you name the intersection relation? What does the completed E-R diagram look like?

STEP 3: DEFINING INFORMATION (FIELDS) FOR EACH RELATION

Once you've completed steps 1 and 2, you must define the various pieces of information that each relation will contain. Your goal in this step is to make sure that the information in each relation is indeed in the correct relation and that the information cannot be derived from other information—the second and third rules of normalization.

In Figure C.6 (on the facing page), we've developed a view of the relations based on the new E-R diagram with the intersection relation. To make sure that each piece of information is in the correct relation, look at each and ask, "Does this piece of information depend only on the primary key for this relation?" If the answer is yes, the information is in the correct relation. If the answer is no, the information is in the wrong relation.

Let's consider the *Employee* relation. The primary key is *Employee ID,* so each piece of information must depend only on *Employee ID.* Does *Name* depend on *Employee ID?* Yes, so that information is in the correct relation. Does *Department Num* depend on *Employee ID?* Yes, because each employee's department designation depends on the particular employee you're describing. In this case, *Department Num* in the *Employee* relation is an example of a foreign key. What about *Department Name?* The answer here is no. The name for a particular department doesn't depend on which employee is in that department.

So the question becomes, "In which relation should *Department Name* appear?" The answer is in the *Department* relation, because *Department Name* depends on the primary key *(Department Num)* that uniquely describes each department. Therefore, *Department Name* should not be in the *Employee* relation, but, rather, in the *Department* relation.

Now, take a look at the intersection relation *Job Assignment.* Notice that it includes the field called *Hours. Hours* is located in this relation because it depends on two things: the employee you're describing and the job to which he or she is assigned. So, *Hours* does depend completely on the composite primary key *Employee ID + Job Number* in the *Job Assignment* relation.

If you follow this line of questioning for each relation, you'll find that all other fields are in their correct relation. Now you have to look at each field to see whether you can derive it from other information. If you can, the derived information should not be stored in your

EMPLOYEE RELATION

Employee ID	Name	Department Num	Department Name
1234	Jones	43	Residential
2345	Smith	15	Commercial
5468	Joslin	43	Residential
9087	Mills	43	Residential
8798	Jones	69	Non-profit

JOB RELATION

Job Number	Job Name
14	Acct
23	Sales
39	Maint
46	Admin

DEPARTMENT RELATION

Department Num	Department Name	Num of Employees
15	Commercial	1
43	Residential	3
69	Non-profit	1

JOB ASSIGNMENT RELATION

Employee ID	Job Number	Hours
1234	14	4
1234	23	4
2345	14	8
5468	23	6
5468	46	2
9087	23	5
9087	14	3
8798	39	8

Hours belongs in this relation because it depends on a combination of who *(Employee ID)* is assigned to which job *(Job Number).*

Figure C.6

A First Look at the Relations in Your Employee Database

database. When we speak of "derived" in this instance, we're referring to information that you can mathematically derive: counts, totals, averages, and the like. Currently, you are storing the number of employees *(Num of Employees)* in the *Department* relation. Can you derive that information from other information? The answer is yes—all you have to do is count the number of occurrences of each department number in the *Employee* relation. So you should not store *Num of Employees* in your database (anywhere).

Once you've completed step 3, you've completely and correctly defined the structure of your database and identified the information each relation should contain. Figure C.7 shows your database and the information in each relation. Notice that we have removed *Department Name* from the *Employee* relation (following the second rule of normalization) and that we have removed *Num of Employees* from the *Department* relation (following the third rule of normalization).

EMPLOYEE RELATION

Employee ID	Name	Department Num
1234	Jones	43
2345	Smith	15
5468	Joslin	43
9087	Mills	43
8798	Jones	69

JOB RELATION

Job Number	Job Name
14	Acct
23	Sales
39	Maint
46	Admin

DEPARTMENT RELATION

Department Num	Department Name
15	Commercial
43	Residential
69	Non-profit

JOB ASSIGNMENT RELATION

Employee ID	Job Number	Hours
1234	14	4
1234	23	4
2345	14	8
5468	23	6
5468	46	2
9087	23	5
9087	14	3
8798	39	8

Figure C.7

The Correct Structure of
Your Employee Database

STEP 4: USING A DATA DEFINITION LANGUAGE TO CREATE YOUR DATABASE

The final step in developing a relational database is to take the structure you created in steps 1 to 3 and use a data definition language to actually create the relation. Data definition languages are found within a database management system. A **database management system (DBMS)** helps you specify the logical organization for a database and access and use the information within the database. This is the point at which we'll end this extended learning module. But you shouldn't stop learning. We've written *Extended Learning Module J* to take you through the process of using the data definition language in Access to create the database we just designed. Keep learning.

CREATING THE FINAL STRUCTURE FOR YOUR SCHOOL

Now it's time for you to fly solo and try a task by yourself. If your group successfully completed the Team Work project on page 174, you should have a relational database model with five relations: *Seminar, Seminar Section, Student, Qualified Teacher,* and *Seminar Section Class Roll.* The first four you identified early on. The last one is the result of eliminating the many-to-many relationship between *Seminar Section* and *Student.* We named this intersection relation *Seminar Section Class Roll.* We did so because it represents a list of students enrolling in all of the sections. If you group those students by section, then you get class rolls.

Your task is to complete a table for each relation. We've provided a sample table below. That is, you must first fill in the column headings by identifying what information belongs in each relation. Be sure to follow steps 2 and 3 of normalization. Then, we encourage you to add in some actual data entries.

A word of caution. You could easily identify hundreds of pieces of information that need to be present in this database. For *Qualified Teacher,* for example, you could include birth date, rank, office hours, phone number, e-mail address, office location, employment starting date, and many more. Here, simply identify no more than five key pieces of information for each relation. And, by all means, identify the primary and foreign keys for each relation.

Seminar Relation

Summary: Student Learning Outcomes Revisited

1. **Identify how databases and spreadsheets are both similar and different.** Databases and spreadsheets are similar in that they both store information in two-dimensional files. They are different in one key aspect: physical versus logical. Spreadsheets require that you know the physical location of information, by row number and column character. Databases, on the other hand, require that you know logically what information you want. For example, in a database environment you could easily request total sales for Able Electronics, and you would receive that information. In a spreadsheet, you would have to know the physical location—by row number and column character—of that information.

2. **List and describe the four steps in designing and building a relational database.** The four

steps in designing and building a relational database include

1. Defining entity classes and primary keys
2. Defining relationships among entity classes
3. Defining information (fields) for each relation
4. Using a data definition language to create your database

3. **Define the concepts of entity class, instance, primary key, and foreign key.** An *entity class* is a concept—typically people, places, or things—about which you wish to store information and that you can identify with a unique key (called a primary key). A *primary key* is a field (or group of fields in some cases) that uniquely describes each record. Within the context of database design, we often refer to a record as an instance.

An *instance* is an occurrence of an entity class that can be uniquely described. To provide logical relationships among various entity classes, you use *foreign keys*—primary keys of one file (relation) that also appear in another file (relation).

4. **Given a small operating environment, build an entity-relationship (E-R) diagram.** Building an entity-relationship (E-R) diagram starts with knowing and understanding the business rules that govern the situation. These rules will help you identify entity classes, primary keys, and relationships. You then follow the process of normalization, eliminating many-to-many relationships, assuring that each field is in the correct relation, and removing any derived fields.

5. **List and describe the steps in normalization.** *Normalization* is the process of assuring that a relational database structure can be implemented as a series of two-dimensional tables. The normalization steps include

   1. Eliminate repeating groups or many-to-many relationships

   2. Assure that each field in a relation depends only on the primary key for that relation

3. Remove all derived fields from the relations

6. **Describe the process of creating an intersection relation to remove a many-to-many relationship.** To create an intersection relation to remove a many-to-many relationship, follow these steps:

   1. Draw the part of the E-R diagram that contains a many-to-many relationship

   2. Create a new E-R diagram with the original two relations on each end and a new one (the intersection relation) in the middle

   3. Create a meaningful name for the intersection relation

   4. Move the minimum cardinality appearing next to the left relation just to the right of the intersection relation

   5. Move the minimum cardinality appearing next to the right relation just to the left of the intersection relation

   6. The maximum cardinality on both sides of the intersection relation will always be "many"

   7. As a general rule, the new minimum and maximum cardinalities for the two original relations will be one and one

Key Terms and Concepts

Composite primary key, 172
Database, 165
Database management system (DBMS), 176
Entity class, 166
Entity-relationship (E-R) diagram, 168
Foreign key, 172

Instance, 166
Intersection relation (composite relation), 172
Normalization, 172
Primary key, 166
Relational database, 165

Short-Answer Questions

1. How are relational databases and spreadsheets both similar and different?
2. What is a database?
3. What are the four steps in designing and building a relational database?
4. What are some examples of entity classes at your school?
5. What is the role of a primary key?
6. What is an entity-relationship (E-R) diagram?
7. How do business rules help you define minimum and maximum cardinality?

8. What is normalization?
9. What are the three major rules of normalization?
10. What is an intersection relation? Why is it important in designing a relational database?
11. Why must you remove derived information from a database?
12. What is a database management system (DBMS)?

Short-Question Answers

For each of the following answers, provide an appropriate question:

1. Logical access to and use of information.
2. Entity class.
3. Primary key.
4. E-R diagram.
5. It denotes a zero or optional relationship.
6. It denotes a multiple relationship.
7. It denotes a relationship.
8. Normalization.
9. Intersection relation.
10. Foreign key.
11. Composite primary key.
12. DBMS.

Assignments and Exercises

1. **DEFINING ENTITY CLASSES FOR THE MUSIC INDUSTRY** The music industry tracks and uses all sorts of information related to numerous entity classes. Find a music CD and carefully review the entire contents of the jacket. Now, list as many entity classes as you can find (for just that CD). Now, go to a music store and pick out a CD for a completely different music genre and read its jacket. Did you find any new entity classes? If so, what are they?

2. **DEFINING BUSINESS RULES FOR A VIDEO RENTAL STORE** Think about how your local video rental store works. There are many customers, renting many videos, and many videos sit on the shelves unrented. Customers can rent many videos at one time. And some videos are so popular that the video rental store keeps many copies. Write down all the various business rules that define how a video rental store works with respect to entity classes and their relationships.

3. **CREATING AN E-R DIAGRAM FOR A VIDEO RENTAL STORE** After completing assignment 2 above, draw the initial E-R diagram based on the rules you defined. Don't worry about going through the process of normalization at this point. Simply identify the appropriate relationships among the entity classes and define the minimum and maximum cardinality of each relationship. By the way, how many many-to-many relationships did you define?

4. **ELIMINATING A MANY-TO-MANY RELATIONSHIP** Consider the following situation. At a small auto parts store, customers can buy many parts. And the same part can be bought by many different customers. That's an example of a many-to-many relationship. How would you eliminate it? What would you call the intersection relation? This one

is particularly tough: You'll have to actually create two intersection relations to model this correctly.

5. **DEFINING THE CARDINALITY AMONG TWO ENTITY CLASSES** Consider the two entity classes of *Student* and *Advisor* at your school. How would you build an E-R diagram to show the relationship between these two entity classes? What is the minimum and maximum cardinality of the relationship?

6. **MAKING SOME CHANGES TO YOUR SCHOOL'S OFFERING OF WEEKEND SEMINARS** Throughout this module, you've been creating the correct structure for a database that will support your school's offering of weekend seminars on the Internet and Web. Now, you need to make a few changes. Implement the following business rules: (1) Each student must take at least one seminar; (2) each seminar section must be assigned to a building and a room (some rooms won't have any seminar sections scheduled in them); and (3) each qualified teacher is assigned to only one academic department (and each academic department must have at least one qualified teacher in it). What does the new E-R diagram look like?

7. **MAKING SOME CHANGES TO YOUR EMPLOYEE DATABASE** Throughout this module, you followed along with us as we created the correct structure for a database that will help you manage your employees, their departments, and their job assignments. Implement the following business rules: (1) Each department must have one manager who is also an employee (some employees may not be managers) and (2) each employee has at least one of the following skills—team building, project management, and/or follow-up. What does the new E-R diagram look like?

CHAPTER FOUR OUTLINE

STUDENT LEARNING OUTCOMES

1. Define decision support system, list its components, and identify the type of applications it's suited to.

2. Define collaboration systems along with their features and uses.

3. Define geographic information systems and state how they differ from other decision support tools.

4. Define artificial intelligence and list the different types that are used in business.

5. Define expert systems and describe the type of problems to which they are applicable.

6. Define neural networks, their uses, and a major strength and weakness of these AI systems.

7. Define genetic algorithms and list the concepts on which they are based, and the types of problems they solve.

8. Define intelligent agents, list the four types, and identify the types of problems they solve.

WEB SUPPORT

www.mhhe.com/haag

- Learning about investing
- Researching the company behind the stock
- Finding other sources of company financials
- Making trades online
- Retrieving stock quotes
- Computer-aided decision support

CHAPTER FOUR

Decision Support and Artificial Intelligence
Brainpower for Your Business

OPENING CASE STUDY:
CONTINENTAL AIRLINES FLIES HIGH
WITH DECISION SUPPORT

In 1992, things looked bleak for the major airlines. The weather was very bad and they lost $4.8 billion. In 1999, the weather was bad again AND labor costs were higher AND jet fuel prices were higher. However, that year, the airlines had *earnings* of $4.8 billion. The problems were greater in 1999, but the business decisions were better—largely because of decision support systems.

Continental Airlines is a case in point. In 1993, Continental Airlines didn't even have e-mail. In 1994, a new team of executives took control after bankruptcy reorganization and hired IT specialists to develop decision support software. For years Continental executives had made decisions based on the information that employees dutifully compiled, by hand, from paper tickets—information that was weeks old. While they were copying numbers from one bit of paper to another, market conditions (fares, demand for tickets, competition) were changing all around them.

Then information technology came to the rescue. Continental's new decision support systems provide up-to-the-minute information on each flight. Continental can now analyze that information together with other variables such as the daily cost of jet fuel. Continental discovered lots of new information, such as the fact that 18 percent of its flights operated at a loss. Continental was under the impression that its hub in Greensboro, North Carolina, had made a profit in 1993, but with more detailed information and decision support analysis, they found out that the hub was actually losing money—to the tune of $60 million per year.

Continental has about 2,200 flights a day with 30,000 possible routings. Its decision support system can analyze whether a seat on a particular flight should be sold for $100 or should be held back in case a last-minute business traveler wants the seat and will pay $1,000 for it. Sometimes it may actually make more sense to sell to the low-paying customer if there's a high likelihood of even higher-paying passengers showing up at a stop-over location. The part of the system that figures this out raised Continental's revenue by about $50 million.

Another decision support system calculates the cost of cancelled or delayed flights. Yet another shows the amount of revenue "aboard" each flight, even before it takes off, and makes suggestions such as holding a flight for high-paying customers whose connections are late.

No detail is too small for decision support. The system can flag planes full of cheap-ticket vacationing passengers and assign snack sacks, while planes that show a significant proportion of business travelers get hot meals.

A test of Continental's efficiency came in the first quarter of 2001, when almost all major airlines posted large losses. The exceptions were Continental and Southwest Airlines, both of which actually made a profit. Later in 2001, when airlines were hit hard by the events of September 11th, Continental had the IT infrastructure in place to make things easier for customers, staff members, and rerouted flight crews.[1,2]

Introduction

In the opening case study, Continental Airlines turned what industry analysts had forecast as a very bleak future into a very profitable one with decision support systems. The role of IT was to help Continental's management make decisions that would decrease costs, take full advantage of opportunities, and thereby increase revenues. In the frantic world of air travel, time is of the essence. A great analysis delivered today pointing to what management should have done yesterday is worse than useless.

People in business everywhere regularly make decisions as complex as those that Continental faces. Information technology can help in the decision-making process, regardless of whether you're running an airline or a doggie grooming business. The big winners in tomorrow's business race will be those organizations, according to *Management Review,* that are "big of brain and small of mass."[3] For example, with only 35 people, the Adtrack company is able to track 10 million records (in a data warehouse) of information pertaining to newspaper and magazine ads. These 35 people perform complex tasks to provide newspapers and ad agencies with information on their relative position against competitors.[4,5]

For many years, computers have been crunching numbers faster and more accurately than people can. A computer can unerringly calculate a payroll for 1,000 people in the time it takes a pencil to fall from your desk to the floor. Because of IT, knowledge workers have been freed of much of the drudgery of manually handling day-to-day transactions. And now, IT power is augmenting brainpower and thought processes in ways previously seen only in science fiction. In some cases, IT power is actually *replacing* human brainpower to a limited degree.

Businesses, like individuals, use brainpower to make decisions, some big, some small, some relatively simple, and some very complex. As an effective knowledge worker, you'll have to make decisions on issues such as whether to expand the workforce, extend business hours, use different raw materials, or start a new product line. IT can help you in most, if not all, of these decisions. The extended brainpower that IT offers you as a decision maker comes in the form of decision support systems and artificial intelligence.

Whether to use a decision support system (there are several variations) or some form of artificial intelligence depends on the type of decision you have to make and how you plan to go about making it. So let's first look at different types of decisions and the process you go through to make a decision. Then we'll discuss decision support systems and artificial intelligence—IT brainpower (see Figure 4.1). To learn even more about decision support systems and artificial intelligence, visit the Web site that supports this text at www.mhhe.com/haag.

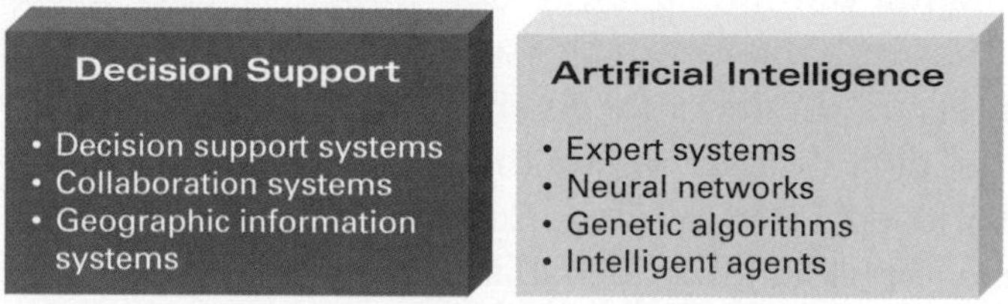

Figure 4.1

The Two Categories of Computer-Aided Decision Support

Decision Support

- Decision support systems
- Collaboration systems
- Geographic information systems

Artificial Intelligence

- Expert systems
- Neural networks
- Genetic algorithms
- Intelligent agents

Decisions, Decisions, Decisions

You make many decisions every day from the simplest to the very complex. For example, you may want to made a decision on what mozzarella cheese to buy based on cost. Contrast that decision with the one where you try to decide which job offer to take. Choosing the right job is definitely a more complex decision because it has multiple decision criteria, not all of which are quantifiable. Therefore, it's much more difficult to select the "best" of the alternatives.

Decision making is one of the most significant and important activities in business. Organizations devote vast resources of time and money to the process. In this section, we'll consider the phases of decision making and different decision types to help you better understand how IT can benefit that process.

HOW YOU MAKE A DECISION

In business, decision making has four distinct phases (see Figure 4.2).[6] These four phases are as follows:

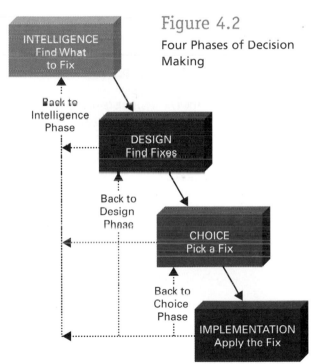

Figure 4.2

Four Phases of Decision Making

1. *Intelligence* (find what to fix): Find or recognize a problem, need, or opportunity (also called the diagnostic phase of decision making). The intelligence phase involves detecting and interpreting signs that indicate a situation which needs your attention. These "signs" come in many forms: consistent customer requests for new-product features, the threat of new competition, declining sales, rising costs, an offer from a company to handle your distribution needs, and so on.

2. *Design* (find fixes): Consider possible ways of solving the problem, filling the need, or taking advantage of the opportunity. In this phase, you develop all the possible solutions you can.

3. *Choice* (pick a fix): Examine and weigh the merits of each solution, estimate the consequences of each, and choose the best one (which may be to do nothing at all). The "best" solution may depend on such factors as cost, ease of implementation, staffing requirements, and timing. This is the prescriptive phase of decision making—it's the stage at which a course of action is prescribed.

4. *Implementation* (apply the fix): Carry out the chosen solution, monitor the results, and make adjustments as necessary. Simply implementing a solution is seldom enough. Your chosen solution will always need fine-tuning, especially for complex problems or changing environments.

This four-phase process is not necessarily linear: You'll often find it useful or necessary to cycle back to an earlier phase. When choosing an alternative in the choice phase, for example, you might become aware of another possible solution. Then you would go back to the design phase, include the newly found solution, return to the choice phase, and compare the new solution to the others you generated.

TYPES OF DECISIONS YOU FACE

It's pretty clear that deciding which cheese to buy when you want the cheapest is a decision with a simple comparison that leads to a correct answer. Thus, it is an example of a structured decision, whereas choosing the right job is an example of a decision with nonstructured and structured elements. That is, some parts are quantifiable and some are not.

A *structured decision* involves processing a certain kind of information in a specified way so that you will always get the right answer. No "feel" or intuition is necessary. These are the kinds of decisions that you can program—if you use a certain set of inputs and process them in a precise way, you'll arrive at the correct result. Calculating gross pay for hourly workers is an example. If hours worked is less than or equal to 40, then gross pay is equal to hours times rate of pay. If hours worked is greater than 40, then gross pay is equal to 40 times rate of pay plus time and a half for every hour over 40. You can easily automate these types of structured decisions with IT.

A *nonstructured decision* is one for which there may be several "right" answers, and there is no precise way to get a right answer. No rules or criteria exist that guarantee you a good solution. Deciding whether to introduce a new product line, employ a new marketing campaign, or change the corporate image are all examples of decisions with nonstructured elements.

In reality, most decisions fall somewhere between structured and nonstructured. The job choice decision is an example (see Figure 4.3). In choosing the right job, the salary part of the decision is structured, whereas the other criteria involve nonstructured aspects (for example, your perception of which job has the best advancement opportunity). Stock market investment analysis is another example of "somewhere in between" because you can calculate financial ratios and use past performance indicators. However, you still have to consider nonstructured aspects of the companies, such as projected prime interest rate, unemployment rates, and competition.

Another way to view decisions is by the frequency with which the decision has to be made. The decision of which job to take is the sort of decision you don't make on a regular basis; this is a nonrecurring, or ad hoc, decision. On the other hand, determining pay for hourly employees is a routine decision that businesses face periodically. Therefore, determining gross pay for hourly employees is a recurring decision.

A *recurring decision* is one that happens repeatedly, and often periodically, whether weekly, monthly, quarterly, or yearly. You'll usually use the same set of rules each time. When you calculate pay for hourly employees, the calculation is always the same regardless of the employee or time period. A *nonrecurring,* or *ad hoc, decision* is one that you make infrequently (perhaps only once), and you may even have different criteria for determining the best solution each time. A company merger is an example. These don't happen often, although they are becoming more frequent. And if the managers of a company need to make the merger decision more than once, they will most likely have to

Figure 4.3

Viewing Structured
versus Nonstructured
Decision Making as a
Continuum

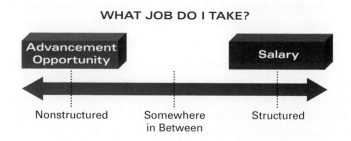

evaluate a different set of criteria each time. The criteria depend on the needs of the companies considering the merger, the comparability of their products and services, their debt structure, and so on.

Decision Support Systems

In Chapter 3, you saw how data mining can help you make business decisions by giving you the ability to slice and dice your way through massive amounts of information. Actually, a data warehouse with data mining tools is a form of decision support. The term *decision support system,* used broadly, means any computerized system that helps you make decisions. However, there's also a more restrictive definition. It's rather like the term *medicine.* Medicine can mean the whole health care industry or it can mean cough syrup, depending on the context.

Narrowly defined, a ***decision support system (DSS)*** is a highly flexible and interactive IT system that is designed to support decision making when the problem is not structured. A DSS is an alliance between you, the decision maker, and specialized support provided by IT (see Figure 4.4). IT brings speed, vast amounts of information, and sophisticated processing capabilities to help you create information useful in making a decision. You bring know-how in the form of your experience, intuition, judgment, and knowledge of the relevant factors. IT provides great power, but you—as the decision maker—must know what kinds of questions to ask of the information and how to process the information to get those questions answered. In fact, the primary objective of a DSS is to improve your effectiveness as a decision maker by providing you with assistance that will complement your insights. This union of your know-how and IT power makes you better able to respond to changes in the marketplace and to manage resources in the most effective and efficient ways possible. Following are some examples of the varied applications of DSSs:

- A national insurance company uses a DSS to analyze its risk exposure when insuring drivers with histories of driving under the influence. The DSS revealed that married male homeowners in their forties with one DUI conviction were rarely repeat offenders. By lowering its rates to this group the company increased it market share without increasing its risk exposure.[7]
- Burlington Northern and Santa Fe (BNSF) railroad regularly tests the rails its trains ride on to prevent accidents. Worn out or defective rails result in hundreds

What You Bring	Advantages of a DSS	What IT Brings
Experience	Increased productivity	Speed
Intuition	Increased understanding	Information
Judgment	Increased speed	Processing capabilities
Knowledge	Increased flexibility	
	Reduced problem complexity	
	Reduced cost	

Figure 4.4

The Alliance between You and a Decision Support System

of derailments every year, so it's important to address the problem. Using a decision support system to schedule rail testing, BNSF decreased its rail-caused derailments by 33 percent in 2000, while the other three large railroad companies had a 16 percent rise in such accidents.[8]

- Customer relationship management (CRM) is an important part of any successful company's strategy. Decision support is an important part of CRM. On Wall Street, retail brokerage companies analyze customers' behaviors and goals with decision support, which highlights opportunities and alerts brokers to beginning problems.[9]

COMPONENTS OF A DECISION SUPPORT SYSTEM

DSSs vary greatly in application and complexity, but they all share specific features. A typical DSS has three components (see Figure 4.5): data management, model management, and user interface management.

Before we look at these three components individually, let's get a quick overview of how they work together. When you begin your analysis, you tell the DSS, using the user interface management component, which model (in the model management component) to use on what information (in the data management component). The model requests the information from the data management component, analyzes that information, and sends the result to the user interface management component, which in turn passes the results back to you (see Figure 4.5 on the facing page). Here's an example of a decision support system at Lands' End clothing business.

- *Model management:* The DSS at Lands' End has to have models to analyze information. The models create new information that decision makers need to plan product lines and inventory levels. For example, Lands' End uses a statistical model called regression analysis to determine trends in customer buying patterns and forecasting models to predict sales levels.
- *Data management:* The DSS's data management component stores Lands' End's customer and product information. In addition to this organizational information, the company also needs external information, such as demographic information and industry and style trend information.
- *User interface management:* A user interface enables Lands' End decision makers to access information and specify the models they want to use to create the information they need.

Now we'll examine the three DSS components in more general terms.

MODEL MANAGEMENT COMPONENT   The *model management* component consists of both the DSS models and the DSS model management system. A model is a representation of some event, fact, or situation. Businesses use models to represent variables and their relationships. For example, you would use a statistical model called analysis of variance to determine whether newspaper, television, and billboard advertising are equally effective in increasing sales. DSSs help in various decision-making situations by utilizing models that allow you to analyze information in many different ways. The models you use in a DSS depend on the decision you're making and, consequently, the kind of analysis you require. For example, you would use what-if analysis to see what effect the change of one or more variables will have on other variables, or optimization to find the most profitable solution given operating restrictions and limited resources. You can use spreadsheet software such as Excel to create a simple DSS for what-if analysis. Figure 4.5 has an example of a spreadsheet DSS you might build to compare how much you'd pay for a house at different interest rates and payback periods.

Figure 4.5

Components of a Decision Support System

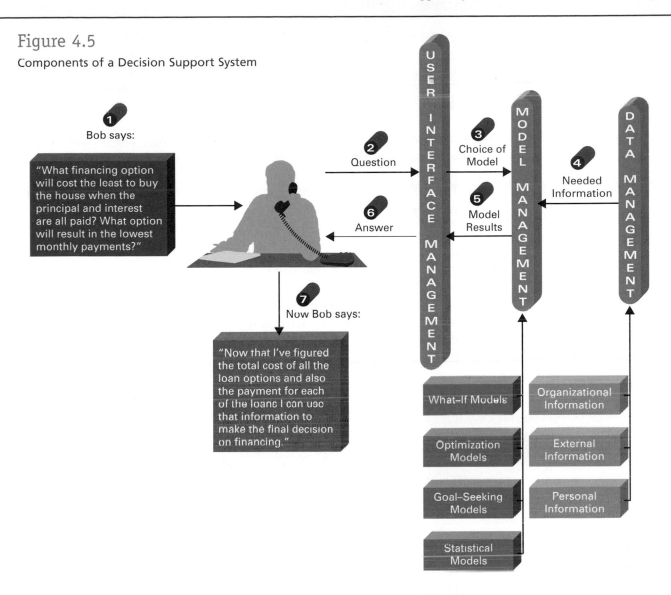

1 Bob says:

"What financing option will cost the least to buy the house when the principal and interest are all paid? What option will result in the lowest monthly payments?"

2 Question

3 Choice of Model

4 Needed Information

5 Model Results

6 Answer

7 Now Bob says:

"Now that I've figured the total cost of all the loan options and also the payment for each of the loans I can use that information to make the final decision on financing."

USER INTERFACE MANAGEMENT

MODEL MANAGEMENT

DATA MANAGEMENT

What–If Models

Optimization Models

Goal–Seeking Models

Statistical Models

Organizational Information

External Information

Personal Information

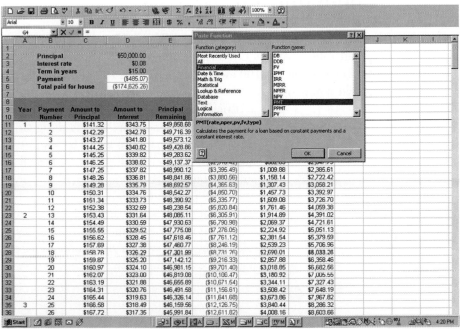

The model management system stores and maintains the DSS's models. Its function of managing models is similar to that of a database management system. The model management component can't select the best model for you to use for a particular problem—that requires your expertise—but it can help you create and manipulate models quickly and easily.

DATA MANAGEMENT COMPONENT   The *data management* component performs the function of storing and maintaining the information that you want your DSS to use. The data management component, therefore, consists of both the DSS information and the DSS database management system. The information you use in your DSS comes from one or more of three sources:

1. *Organizational information:* You may want to use virtually any information available in the organization for your DSS. You can design your DSS to access this information directly from your company's databases and data warehouses.
2. *External information:* Some decisions require input from external sources of information. Various branches of the federal government, Dow Jones, and the Internet, to mention just a few, can provide additional information for use with a DSS.
3. *Personal information:* You can incorporate your own insights and experience—your personal information—into your DSS.

USER INTERFACE MANAGEMENT COMPONENT   The *user interface management* component allows you to communicate with the DSS. It consists of the user interface and the user interface management system. This is the component that allows you to combine your know-how with the storage and processing capabilities of the computer. The user interface is the part of the system you see; through it you enter information, commands, and models. If you have a DSS with a poorly designed user interface—if it's too rigid or too cumbersome to use—you simply won't use it no matter what its capabilities. The best user interface uses your terminology and methods and is flexible, consistent, simple, and adaptable.

Collaboration Systems

Toronto Hydro of Toronto, Canada, has 650,000 customers, 1,700 employees, and five corporate offices. As you can imagine, the company gets and sends a lot of e-mail messages. The volume was 100 megabytes per day in 1999 and had increased to more than a gigabyte a day by 2002.

E-mail is a simple form of a collaboration system. A *collaboration system* is software that is designed specifically to improve the performance of teams by supporting the sharing and flow of information (see Figure 4.6). E-mail is, of course, vital to survival, but for many companies, it's no longer enough. In fact, almost 60 percent of companies surveyed by *InformationWeek* in February 2002 said that they intended to increase their collaboration initiatives in the near future. Collaboration software takes many forms with many combinations of features and varying degrees of complexity.

Figure 4.6

Collaboration Software Connects People

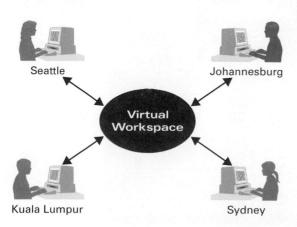

Seattle

Johannesburg

Virtual Workspace

Kuala Lumpur

Sydney

ENTERPRISEWIDE COLLABORATION

Toronto Hydro, for example, found it needed employees also to have access to each other's calendars, group scheduling, imaging, automated workflow, task and document management, message management, as well as e-mail. We touched on several of these in Chapter 1. For these tasks the company now uses groupware called Lotus Notes.[10] Microsoft has a comparable product called Exchange, which allows integration with Access, Excel, Word, and even Visual Basic.

Like the Toronto utility company, many companies first use e-mail and then move on to integrated collaboration systems such as Lotus Notes or Exchange. After that, they may need to migrate to more sophisticated collaboration systems that incorporate tele-, video-, and Web conferencing in real time, and may even include project management and work flow automation. For example, Ford Motor Company gets parts for vehicles from places as far apart as France and Singapore, so coordinating ordering, shipping, and delivery with production is very complex, particularly in a just-in-time environment. Electronic collaboration and information sharing are important for any business. But, the task becomes particularly critical the more geographically scattered employees, customers, and suppliers are.

SUPPLY-CHAIN COLLABORATION

As you already saw in Chapter 2, a supply chain includes the paths reaching out to all of the suppliers of parts and services to a company. It consists not only of a company's suppliers, but of its suppliers' suppliers as well. Supply chain management means working with your suppliers and distributors in all phases of planning, production, and distribution. This involves the routine sharing of information to reduce inventories and improve cash flow.

You might want your suppliers to be able to add or change information. Boeing is a case in point. The company conducts the whole design process for its 777 jets online. All plans, schedules, orders, confirmations, and so on, are online and are available to engineers, customers, maintenance staff, project managers, and suppliers all over the world. Changing from physical models and paper blueprints with fax, phone, and travel has cut the time for delivery of a plane from three years to less than 12 months. So, Boeing reaps the twin benefits of happier customers and a tripling in its production rate.[11]

You might want to share information with clients, too. You could set up a collaboration system whereby your customers can access information but can't change or delete it. Ogilvy & Mather, the company that handles advertising for IBM, Ford, and American Express, among others, does this. Ogilvy & Mather has a collaboration system that lets clients view images, text, and multimedia files.[12]

WEB-BASED COLLABORATION

One of the major application areas of collaboration systems is in e-commerce. As you'll see in Chapter 5, e-commerce is simply traditional business in a new form. It's conducted in cyberspace but is still based on relationships, which means people working together. Web-based collaboration tools use the power of the Internet to enable people to work together effectively and efficiently.

Web-based collaboration software can support a wide-open sharing of information on the Internet where anyone can access it, such as Lands' End Live, where anyone with Web access can interact with representatives of the company. Or, it can support a special virtual workspace with access restricted to a select few. For example, CareGroup Health-Care System, a network of doctors and six Boston-area hospitals, uses a collaboration

COLLABORATION TO FIND CURES

Projects that require collaboration between different departments in a company use collaboration software that goes beyond e-mail, instant messaging, and calendar management. Such software would include workflow management, project management, and other tools that improve the efficiency of work processes.

GlaxoSmithKline, a British pharmaceutical company, is a case in point. The company spends $4 billion a year on research and has 4,000 researchers whose work is stored in more than a dozen databases in various for-

mats. There are separate databases for chemical and biological information as well as another for the specimen inventory. In 2001, the company set up an intranet collaboration system that searches all the company databases and even goes out onto the Web to find any and all research done on a given molecule. By reducing the cost of finding information, the company can spend more time and money developing new medicines.[13]

system available to parents of newborn babies and the doctors who tend to them. While the baby stays in the hospital, a private Web page, accessible only to the neonatal center at the hospital and to the parents, is set up so that the parents can find out about the baby at any time. The hospital staff puts information onto the Web site about feeding, weight, and medical care along with digital photos of the baby. When the new baby goes home, the parents can hold videoconferences with hospital staff so that they can keep a close watch on the baby's progress.[14,15]

Another example of a by-invitation-only virtual workspace exists at Intel, the maker of the Pentium chip. More than half of Intel's direct material suppliers are in Asia, so the Internet is a great way for the company to speed up communication and information access. But Intel doesn't necessarily want everyone in the world to be able to snoop into company information. So, Intel's suppliers can use passwords to access Intel's demand forecasts, engineering plans, orders, and invoices. Suppliers can get demand, inventory, and receipt information automatically from the factory without human intervention. Intel plans to eventually make the entire company completely electronic.[16]

PEER-TO-PEER COLLABORATION Groove and NextPage are both examples of a special kind of information-sharing software called peer-to-peer collaboration software. It's based on the same principle as Napster, that is, the ability to communicate in real time and share documents between peers without going through a central server. The peer-to-peer file-sharing feature in the collaboration software is combined with the ability to create and edit documents collaboratively, and to send and receive text and voice messages.

Here's an example of how it might work. Let's say you're a representative working at FastTrucks, a company that ships perishable goods all over the country. One of your customers is LettuceSupply, a Florida-based company that grows and distributes lettuce. You're both using the Groove collaboration system. One day a truck filled to the brim with lettuce and other perishables is headed through Buffalo, New York, but so is a major winter storm. To avert disaster in the form of rotting lettuce and a stranded truck, you could go online and bring up the virtual workspace that you share with your LettuceSupply counterpart. From there you could check on the lettuce company's current and past shipments and also access records on routing plans and other pertinent information. This is the file sharing part of the operation. You could then contact your counterpart in LettuceSupply and negotiate a new route, thereby saving the lettuce and the day.[17]

Geographic Information Systems

Suppose you've decided to go on a two-week vacation that will include camping, sight-seeing, and mall touring in Minnesota (after all, Minneapolis boasts the largest shopping mall in the United States—the Mall of America). What maps should you buy? Some will show roads for traveling from one place to another; others will show campgrounds in the state that boasts 10,000 lakes. Others will pinpoint historic landmarks; and still others will detail hotels around the Mall of America as well as the locations of the hundreds of stores in the mall.

To get a truly comprehensive picture of your proposed vacation, you'd consolidate the information by redrawing all the maps into a single map. But what about a business that needs to analyze different maps with geographic, demographic, highway, and other information?

Fortunately there's a special type of DSS for just this kind of problem—it's called a geographic information system. A *geographic information system (GIS)* is a decision support system designed specifically to work with spatial information. Spatial information is any information that can be shown in map form, such as roads, the distribution of bald eagle populations, sewer systems, and the layout of electrical lines.

Today GISs are helping businesses perform such tasks as

- Identifying the best site to locate a branch office based on number of households in a neighborhood
- Targeting pockets of potential customers in a particular market area
- Repositioning promotions and advertising based on sales
- Determining the optimal location of a new distribution outlet

When businesses combine textual information and spatial information, they are creating a new type of information called *business geography*. GISs are well-suited to storing, retrieving, and analyzing business geography to support the decision-making process. To obtain information you can go to the U.S. Census Bureau for demographic information, the Bureau of Labor Statistics for employment information, and polling companies such as Scarborough Research Corporation for consumer habit information.

A GIS is actually a combination of sophisticated graphics and database technology. Using a GIS, you can logically link textual and spatial information. For example, you could gather geographic information about the distribution of customers who buy yachts (spatial information). You could also gather information about their color preferences (textual information) and link it to the spatial information. Then, using queries similar to those illustrated in Chapter 3, you could analyze both the spatial and textual information, generating output in the form of maps, graphs, or numeric tables.

A GIS database represents information thematically. That means that a GIS map is composed of many separate, overlapping information layers, each of which has its own theme. For example, the first layer might be roads, the next might be utilities (water, electricity, etc.), the third layer might be school-age children, and the fourth might be homes

Figure 4.7
Geographic Information
Systems

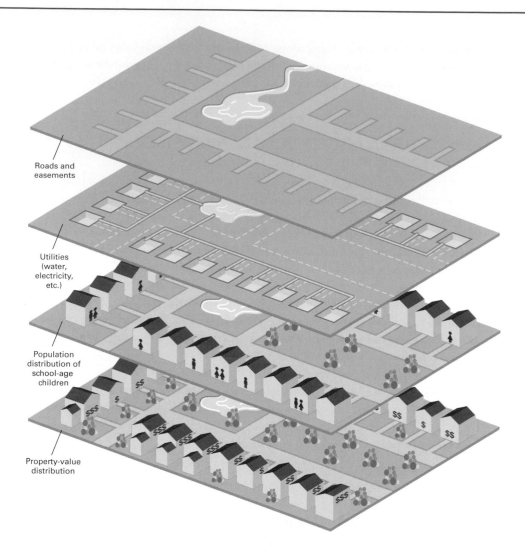

Roads and
easements

Utilities
(water,
electricity,
etc.)

Population
distribution of
school-age
children

Property-value
distribution

The information on the
radiation levels is shown
graphically in map form.

within a certain price range (see Figure 4.7). This feature of a GIS, to show map information and attribute information as layers, distinguishes a GIS from another type of decision support system. Studies show that how information is presented significantly impacts the effectiveness and efficiency of the decision-making process.[18]

Here are other examples of GISs in use:

- Clean Harbor is the company that hauled away potentially anthrax-tainted debris from the offices of the NCB during the anthrax scare of 2001. Since hazardous waste removal is such a dangerous job, the company had to keep track of the shipment every minute. Clean Harbor used software that incorporated a GIS map and GPS information to monitor the trucks along their journey.[19]

- Branson, Missouri, is a small town in the Ozark Mountains that boasts more than two dozen theaters offering 75 performances per day to the 5 to 7 million visitors the town hosts every year. The town's motto is "the show must go on." But the show can't go on without electricity. The White River Valley Electric Cooperative (WRVEC) that supplies power to the area has a Web-based GIS where employees can access all the information they need, such as the precise location of poles, meters, transformers, capacitors, and underground facilities.[20]

Artificial Intelligence

DSSs, collaboration systems, and GISs are IT systems that augment business brainpower. IT can further expand business brainpower by means of artificial intelligence—the techniques and software that enable computers to mimic human behavior in various ways. Financial analysts use a variety of artificial intelligence systems to manage assets, invest in the stock market, and perform other financial operations.[21] Hospitals use artificial intelligence in many capacities, from scheduling staff, to assigning beds to patients, to diagnosing and treating illness. Many government agencies use artificial intelligence, including the IRS and the armed forces. Credit card companies use artificial intelligence to detect credit card fraud, and insurance companies use artificial intelligence to spot fraudulent claims.[22] Artificial intelligence lends itself to tasks as diverse as airline ticket pricing, food preparation, oil exploration, and child protection. It is widely used in the insurance, meteorology, engineering and aerospace industries and by the military. It was artificial intelligence that guided cruise missiles during the Gulf War in 1991.[23]

Artificial intelligence (AI) is the science of making machines imitate human thinking and behavior. For example, an expert system is an artificial intelligence system that makes computers capable of reasoning through a problem to reach a conclusion. We use the process of reasoning to find out, from what we already know, something that we don't know.

Today computers can see, hear, smell, and, important for business, think (in a manner of speaking). Robots are a well-known form of AI. A *robot* is a mechanical device equipped with simulated human senses and the capability of taking action on its own (in contrast to a mechanical device such as an automobile, which requires direction from the driver for its every action). Robots are in use in many industries. For example, Piedmont Hospital's Pharmacy Dosage Dispenser is a robotic prescription-filling system. Using bar code technology, this pharmaceutical robot receives medication orders online, retrieves prepackaged doses of drugs, and sends them to hospital patients.[24] One of the most exciting new areas of research in robotics is the development of microrobots that can be introduced into human veins and arteries to perform surgery.

ROBOTS TO THE RESCUE: BIG ONES AND BABY ONES

Along with the police, fire fighters, and volunteers who converged on the World Trade Center to help look for victims and clear the rubble, there were robots. They came from Waltham and Somerville, Mississippi; San Diego, California; Tampa, Florida; Nanaimo, British Columbia; and Arlington, Virginia, to work under the direction of the Center for Robot Assisted Search and Rescue based in Littleton, Colorado.

The larger robots, carrying their own batteries, moved around on tracks carrying video and infrared cameras. Smaller robots, tethered to larger ones, crawled into the tightest spaces to look for victims. The University of South Florida supplied "marsupial" robots that were the size of shoe boxes. They were carried by the larger robots and then released in the locations where they were needed.

In the future, the baby robots will have artificial intelligence software to enable them to find their own way around rubble or difficult terrain without cords.

Search and rescue are not the only applications of robots. You've probably seen Friendly Robotics' Robo-Mower, Sony's Abo, and Honda's competing Asimo, which are consumer robots. Here are some others.

- The Pentagon has a robot that delivers mail in an automated truck which follows a wire in the floor to move from office to office. As it enters each office, the robot calls the occupants to come and pick up their mail.

- For many years the food service industry has used robots to prepare pizzas, tacos, and other tasty morsels. Robots also pour drinks and transport food to conveyer belts ready for delivery to customers. Some in the food service industry are predicting that, in the not-too-distant future, when better and more sophisticated software that includes wireless and video capabilities are incorporated into robots, a single employee can remotely control multiple service robots.

- In London is a restaurant with a robot waiter that delivers drinks to customers. The robot software enables the robot to know the location of different tables.[25,26,27]

A recent U.S. Commerce Department survey reported that 70 percent of the top 500 companies use artificial intelligence as part of decision support, and the sale of artificial intelligence software is rapidly approaching the $1 billion mark. The AI systems that businesses use most can be classified into the following major categories:

- *Expert systems,* which reason through problems and offer advice in the form of a conclusion or recommendation
- *Neural networks,* which can be "trained" to recognize patterns
- *Genetic algorithms,* which can generate increasingly better solutions to problems by generating many, many solutions, choosing the best ones, and using those to generate even better solutions
- *Intelligent agents,* which are adaptive systems that work independently, carrying out specific, repetitive, or predictable tasks

Expert Systems

Suppose you own a real estate business, and you generate more than 40 percent of your revenue from appraising commercial real estate. Consider further that only one person in your firm is capable of performing these appraisals. What if that person were to quit?

PLEASE SEND ALL APPLICATIONS TO THE EXPERT SYSTEM

Companies that hire many hourly workers sometimes use an expert system or some other form of artificial intelligence to sort through the list of candidates and help managers identify the employees who are the best qualified and will stay the longest. Bennigans, Target, Blockbuster, and Universal Studios use a system called Unicru, which was developed by psychologists (who served as domain experts) to identify the best applicants.

Applicants sit at a computer and spend a half hour answering questions after which time a report is sent to the hiring manager with a recommendation of no, maybe, or yes. Yes usually results in an interview; maybe is accompanied by suggestions on what follow-up questions to ask; and no usually results in the application being sent to the recycle bin.

The system has helped Blockbuster cut the time it takes to hire someone from two weeks to 72 hours. The system has also resulted in a reduction in the turnover rate for its users by up to 30 percent, which is very important since the turnover rate in this kind of job can be up to 150 percent per year.

Here's a sample of the type of questions the system asks:

True or false: I was meant to work at Target

True or false: Slow people irritate me

True or false: A lot of people do annoying things

True or false: I like a job that's quiet and predictable

True or false: I can smile and chat with anyone

True or false: I am good at taking charge

True or false: I'd rather do things my way than follow the rules

When a vice president of Macy's West was testing the Unicru system, it told him he wasn't qualified to be a clerk in his own store. He was outraged until a Unicru executive explained that with his drive, ambition, and salary requirements, he'd be frustrated and bored to death and would soon quit. The VP had forgotten the difference between being able to do a job and being a good match for the position.[28]

How do you replace that expertise? How fast can you find someone else? How much business would you lose if it took you a month to find a suitable replacement?

In business, people are valuable because they perform important business tasks. Many of these business tasks require expertise, and people often carry expertise in their heads—and often that's the only place it can be found in the organization. AI can provide you with an expert system that can capture expertise, thus making it available to those who are not experts so that they can use it, either to solve a problem or to learn how to solve a problem.

An *expert system,* also called a *knowledge-based system,* is an artificial intelligence system that applies reasoning capabilities to reach a conclusion. Expert systems are excellent for diagnostic and prescriptive problems. Diagnostic problems are those requiring an answer to the question, "What's wrong?" and correspond to the intelligence phase of decision making. Prescriptive problems are those that require an answer to the question, "What to do?" and correspond to the choice phase of decision making.

An expert system is usually built for a specific application area called a *domain.* You can find expert systems in the following domains:

- *Accounting*—for auditing, tax planning, management consulting, and training
- *Medicine*—to prescribe antibiotics where many considerations must be taken into account (such as the patient's medical history, the source of the infection, and the price of available drugs)
- *Process control*—to control offset lithographic printing, for example

- *Human resource management*—to help personnel managers determine whether they are in compliance with an array of federal employment laws
- *Financial management*—to identify delinquency-prone accounts in the loan departments of banks
- *Production*—to guide the manufacture of all sorts of products, such as aircraft parts
- *Forestry management*—to help with harvesting timber on forest lands

A DSS sometimes incorporates expert systems, but an expert system is fundamentally different from a DSS. To use a DSS, you must have considerable knowledge or expertise about the situation with which you're dealing. As you saw earlier in this chapter, a DSS *assists* you in making decisions. That means that you must know how to reason through the problem. You must know which questions to ask, how to get the answers, and how to proceed to the next step. However, when you use an expert system, the know-how is in the system—you need only provide the expert system with the facts and symptoms of the problem for which you need an answer. The know-how, or expertise, that actually solves the problem came from someone else—an expert in the field. What does it mean to have expertise? When someone has expertise in a given subject, that person not only knows a lot of facts about the topic but also can apply that knowledge to analyze and make judgments about related topics. It's this human expertise that an expert system captures.

Let's look at a very simple expert system that would tell a driver what to do when approaching a traffic light. Dealing with traffic lights is the type of problem to which an expert system is well-suited. It is a recurring problem, and to solve it you follow a well-defined set of steps. You've probably gone through the following mental question-and-answer session hundreds of times without even realizing it (see Figure 4.8 on the facing page).

When you approach a green traffic light, you proceed on through. If the light is red, you try to stop. If you're unable to stop, and if traffic is approaching from either side, you'll probably be in trouble. Similarly, if the light is yellow, you may be able to make it through the intersection before the light turns red. If not, you will again be faced with the problem of approaching traffic.

Let's say that you know very little about what to do when you come to a traffic light, but you know that there are experts in the field. You want to capture their expertise in an expert system so that you can refer to it whenever the traffic light situation arises. To gain an understanding of what's involved in the creation and use of an expert system, let's now consider the components of an expert system individually with the traffic light example in mind.

COMPONENTS OF AN EXPERT SYSTEM

An expert system, like any IT system, combines information, people, and IT components.

Information types	People	IT components
Domain expertise	Domain expert	Knowledge base
"Why?" information	Knowledge engineer	Knowledge acquisition
Problem facts	Knowledge worker	Inference engine
		User interface
		Explanation module

These components and their relationships are shown in Figure 4.9 on page 198.

Rule	Symptom or Fact	Yes	No	Explanation
1	Is the light green?	Go through the intersection.	Go to Rule 2.	Should be safe if light is green. If not, need more information.
2	Is the light red?	Go to Rule 4.	Go to Rule 3.	Should stop, may not be able to.
3	Is the light likely to change to red before you get through the intersection?	Go to Rule 4.	Go through the intersection.	Will only reach this point if light is yellow, then you'll have two choices.
4	Can you stop before entering the intersection?	Stop.	Go to Rule 5.	Should stop, but there may be a problem if you can't.
5	Is traffic approaching from either side?	Prepare to crash.	Go through the intersection.	Unless the intersection is clear of traffic, you're likely to crash.

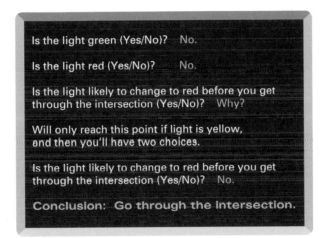

Figure 4.8

Traffic Light Expert System Rules

INFORMATION TYPES   The traffic light *domain expertise* is the core of the expert system, because it's the set of problem-solving steps—the reasoning process that will solve the problem. You'll also want to ask the expert system how it reached its conclusion, or why it asked you a question. The "Why" information included in the expert system allows it to give you the answers. It's information that's provided by the expert—the traffic expert in our example. With the domain expertise and the "Why" information, the expert system is now ready to solve traffic light problems. So now you need to enter the *problem facts,* which are the specifics of your traffic light situation. Problem facts are the symptoms of and assertions about your problem. You'll enter these problem facts as answers to the expert system's questions during your consultation.

PEOPLE   Three separate roles must be filled in the development and use of an expert system. The first role is that of the domain expert, who knows how to solve the problem. The *domain expert* provides the domain expertise in the form of problem-solving strategies. In our traffic light expert system, the domain expert could be an official from the department of motor vehicles. This official, turned domain expert, would also be able to indicate where to gather further domain expertise, and might direct you to the local police station or give you a booklet with the rules of the road. Eventually, the combination of these sources will produce the five steps shown in Figure 4.8.

Figure 4.9

Developing and Using an Expert System

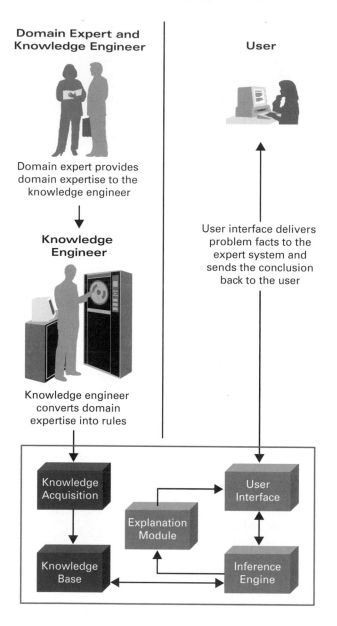

Domain Expert and Knowledge Engineer

Domain expert provides domain expertise to the knowledge engineer

Knowledge Engineer

Knowledge engineer converts domain expertise into rules

User

User interface delivers problem facts to the expert system and sends the conclusion back to the user

Knowledge Acquisition

Explanation Module

Knowledge Base

User Interface

Inference Engine

The domain expert usually works with an IT specialist, a ***knowledge engineer,*** who formulates the domain expertise into an expert system. In this case, the knowledge engineer might consider it best to represent the five steps in the form of rules, making a ***rule-based expert system.*** The knowledge engineer will see to it that the rules are in the correct order and that the system works properly.

The knowledge worker or user—that's you—will then apply the expert system to the problem of what to do when approaching a traffic light. When you face the traffic light problem, you would run a *consultation* (see Figure 4.8) and provide the expert system with the problem facts. You would answer the questions as they appear on the screen, with the expert system applying the appropriate rules and asking you more questions. This process continues until the expert system presents you with a conclusion (telling you what to do) or indicates that it can't reach a conclusion (telling you that it doesn't know what you should do).

IT COMPONENTS   When the knowledge engineer has converted the domain expertise into rules, the ***knowledge base*** stores the rules of the expert system (see Figure 4.9). All the rules must be in place before a consultation, because the expert system won't be able to offer a conclusion in a situation for which it has no rules. For example, if the traffic light is broken and has been replaced by a four-way stop sign, the expert system, as it stands, would not be able to reach a conclusion. The knowledge engineer could, of course, go back to the domain expert and enter rules about four-way stops. The knowledge engineer uses the ***knowledge acquisition*** component of the expert system to enter the traffic light rules. The domain expertise for the rules can come from many sources, including human experts, books, organizational databases, data warehouses, internal reports, diagrams, and so on.

The ***inference engine*** is the part of the expert system that takes your problem facts and searches the knowledge base for rules that fit. This process is called *inferencing.* The inference engine organizes and controls the rules; it "reasons" through your problem to reach a conclusion. It delivers its conclusion or recommendation based on (1) the problem facts of your specific traffic light situation and (2) the rules that came from the domain expert about traffic light procedures in general. The user interface is the part of the expert system that you use to run a consultation. Through the user interface, the expert system asks you questions, and you enter problem facts by answering the questions. In the traffic light expert system, you would enter yes or no. These answers are used by the inference engine to solve the problem.

The domain expert supplies the "Why" information, which is entered by the knowledge engineer into the ***explanation module,*** where it is stored. During a consultation, you—as the knowledge worker or user—can ask why a question was posed and how the

TRAFFIC LIGHTS REVISITED

Create a table similar to Figure 4.8 to extend the traffic light expert system. Include the following situations in the table:

1. There is a wreck in the middle of the intersection.
2. You are turning left at the intersection.
3. You are turning right at the intersection.
4. A pedestrian is crossing in front of you.
5. A dog has wandered into the intersection.
6. A ball belonging to children playing near the intersection has rolled into the street.
7. The car in front of you has stalled.

expert system reached its conclusion. If you're using the expert system as a training tool, then you'll be very interested in how it solved the problem.

In Figure 4.9 you can clearly see the distinction between the development and use of an expert system. The domain expert and the knowledge engineer develop the expert system, then the knowledge worker can apply the expert system to a particular set of circumstances.

WHAT EXPERT SYSTEMS CAN AND CAN'T DO

An expert system uses IT to capture and apply human expertise. For problems with clear rules and procedures, expert systems work very well and can provide your company with great advantages. An expert system can

- Handle massive amounts of information
- Reduce errors
- Aggregate information from various sources
- Improve customer service
- Provide consistency in decision making
- Provide new information
- Decrease personnel time spent on tasks
- Reduce cost

You can, however, run into trouble in building and using an expert system. Difficulties can include the following:

1. Transferring domain expertise to the expert system is sometimes difficult because domain experts cannot always explain how they know what they know. Often experts are not aware of their complete reasoning processes. Experience has given them a feel for the problem, and they just "know."

2. Even if the domain expert can explain the whole reasoning process, automating that process may be impossible. The process may be too complex, requiring an excessive number of rules, or it may be too vague or imprecise. In using an expert system, keep in mind that it can solve only the problems for which it was designed. It cannot deal with inconsistency or a newly encountered problem situation. An expert system can't learn from previous experience and can't apply previously acquired expertise to new problems the way humans can.

199

3. An expert system has no common sense or judgment. One of the early expert systems built into an F-16 fighter plane allowed the pilot to retract the landing gear while the plane was still on the ground and to jettison bombs while the plane was flying upside down, both highly dangerous actions.

Neural Networks

Suppose you see a breed of dog you've never encountered before. Would you know it's a dog? For that matter, would you know it's an animal? Probably so. You know, because you've learned by example. You've seen lots of living things, have learned to classify them, and so can recognize a dog when you see one. A neural network simulates this human ability to classify things without taking prescribed steps leading to the solution. A *neural network* (often called an *artificial neural network* or *ANN*) is an artificial intelligence system that is capable of finding and differentiating patterns. Your brain has learned to consider many factors in combination to recognize and differentiate objects. This is also the case with a neural network. A neural network can learn by example and can adapt to new concepts and knowledge. Neural networks are widely used for visual pattern and speech recognition systems. If you've used a PDA that deciphered your handwriting, it was probably a neural network that analyzed the characters you wrote.[29]

Neural networks are useful to a variety of other situations, too. For example, bomb detection systems in U.S. airports use neural networks that sense trace elements in the air that may indicate the presence of explosives. The Chicago Police Department uses neural networks to identify corruption within its ranks.[30] In medicine, neural networks check 50 million electrocardiograms per year, check for drug interactions, and detect anomalies in tissue samples that may signify the onset of cancer and other diseases. Neural networks can detect heart attacks and even differentiate between the subtly different symptoms of heart attacks in men and women.[31,32,33] In business, neural networks are very popular for securities trading, fraud detection, real estate appraisal, evaluating loan applications, and target marketing, to mention a few. Neural networks are even used to control machinery, adjust temperature settings, and identify malfunctioning machinery.

Neural networks are most useful for identification, classification, and prediction when a vast amount of information is available. By examining hundreds, or even thousands of examples, a neural network detects important relationships and patterns in the information. For example, if you provide a neural network with the details of numerous credit card transactions and tell it which ones are fraudulent, eventually it will learn to identify suspicious transaction patterns.

Here are some examples of the uses of neural networks:

- Many banks and financial institutions use neural networks. For example, Citibank uses neural networks to find opportunities in financial markets.[34] By carefully examining historical stock market data with neural network software, Citibank financial managers learn of interesting coincidences or small anomalies (called market inefficiencies). For example, it could be that whenever IBM stock goes up, so does Unisys stock. Or it might be that a U.S. Treasury note is selling for 1 cent less in Japan than it is in the United States. These snippets of information can make a big difference to Citibank's bottom line in a very competitive financial market.

- In Westminster, California, a community of 87,000 people, police use neural network software to fight crime. With crime reports as input, the system detects

CAUTION! THE NEURAL NETWORK IS WATCHING YOU

Neural networks are used in all sorts of situations where a pattern of conditions or behavior signals an event, either past or future. For example, there's a neural network that predicts what play a football team is likely to run under a particular set of circumstances.

Mostly, when financial institutions use neural networks for fraud detection, they're looking for certain signals, things that are outside the usual usage pattern of the customer. Sometimes, it's the characteristics of the use of the financial instrument itself that trips the alarm.

For example, many credit card companies send their customers convenience checks. They encourage cardholders to transfer balances from other accounts, and allow you to pay for purchases when the merchant won't accept that credit card. However, convenience checks are ripe for theft. First, they're easier to steal or counterfeit than credit cards. Second, they're often available in trash cans (tear or shred your convenience checks if you don't want to use them!). Third, they're easy to order under a false name. Fourth, it's simple for thieves to open a checking account with a convenience check. Fifth, people heading into bankruptcy sometimes use convenience checks to try and cover their financial problems.

Neural networks use certain flags to spot possible convenience check fraud. For example, if the check is written for an unusually large sum, or if multiple checks are written out of sequence, there might be a problem. If a cardholder hasn't used convenience checks before or if a particular check doesn't fit the cardholder's spending pattern, there might be a problem. Another red flag is a higher-than-normal use of automated inquiries to check balances followed by several convenience checks being submitted for payment.[35,36]

and maps local crime patterns. Police say that with this system they can better predict crime trends, improve patrol assignments, and develop better crime-prevention programs.[37]

- Fingerhut, the mail order company based in Minnesota, has 6 million people on its customer list. To determine which customers were and were not likely to order from its catalog, Fingerhut recently switched to neural network software. The company finds that the new software is more effective and expects to generate millions of dollars by fine-tuning its mailing lists.[38]

- Fraud detection is one of the areas in which neural networks are used the most. Visa, MasterCard, and many other credit card companies use a neural network to spot peculiarities in individual accounts. MasterCard estimates neural networks save them $50 million annually.[39]

- Many insurance companies (Cigna, AIG, Travelers, Liberty Mutual, Hartford) along with state compensation funds and other carriers use neural network software to identify fraud. The system searches for patterns in billing charges, laboratory tests, and frequency of office visits. A claim for which the diagnosis was a sprained ankle and which included an electrocardiogram would be flagged for the account manager.[40]

- FleetBoston Financial Corporation uses a neural network to watch transactions with customers. The neural network can detect patterns that may indicate a customer's growing dissatisfaction with the company. The neural network looks for signs like a decrease in the number of transactions or in the account balance of one of Fleet's high-value customers.[41]

HOW WOULD YOU CLASSIFY PEOPLE?

Some people have suggested that neural networks could be applied to people to indicate how likely they are to develop disease or even become criminals. The idea is to input a child's personal characteristics, demographics, and genealogy into a neural network, and the neural network will classify that youngster as being at risk for a disease or for aberrant behavior.

Choose either susceptibility to disease or to criminal behavior, discuss it with your group, and make the following lists, explaining why you chose each one.

1. What personal characteristics would be useful?
2. What demographic factors would strongly influence a person's future?
3. What, if any, inherited characteristics can predict a child's future?

Would such classification on a large scale be legal? Would it be ethical? Would it be effective? Why? Why not? (to all three questions).

All of the above situations have pattern recognition in common. They all require identification and/or classification, which may then be used to predict a finding or outcome. Neural networks are often called predictive systems since they can see patterns in huge volumes of information.

TYPES OF NEURAL NETWORKS

There are two basic types of neural networks, and the one you use depends on the problem you're facing. The first is a self-organizing neural network and the second is a back-propagation neural network. The difference between them is how the "learning" is done.

The **self-organizing neural network** finds patterns and relationships in vast amounts of data by itself. If you have a lot of experimental data, and you're looking for commonalties, you'd use this type. Self-organizing neural networks often form part of data-mining tools for data warehouses (see Chapter 3 for more information on data warehouses and data mining).

A **back-propagation neural network,** on the other hand, is a neural network trained by someone. You'd "teach" the neural network the same way you would teach a child. That is, you'd show the neural network multiple examples of a dog, a cat, a donkey, and so forth until the neural network could correctly identify the animal by itself.

INSIDE A NEURAL NETWORK

Neural networks are so called because they attempt to mimic the structure and functioning of the human brain. Conceptually, neural networks consist of three layers of virtual nerve cells, or neurons. There's an input layer and an output layer and between them is a hidden layer, although there may be more than one hidden layer. The input and output layers are connected to the middle layer(s) by connections called weights of various strengths (see Figure 4.10). If you were to train a neural network to recognize a "good" stock portfolio, you would input many, many examples of good and bad portfolios, telling the neural network which was which. As the neural network is learning to differentiate between good and bad, the weights change. The flow of information to the output layer also changes. After you have fed the system enough examples, the weights stabilize, and the neural network then consistently classifies portfolios correctly.

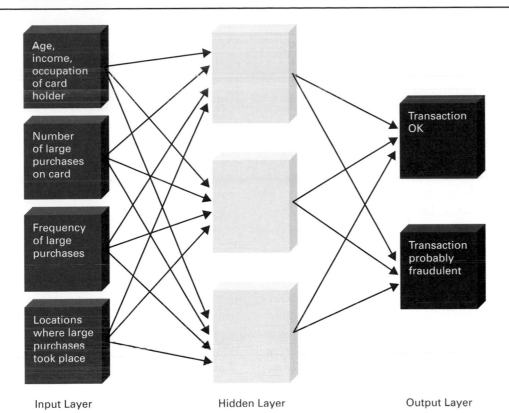

Figure 4.10
The Layers of a Neural
Network

Input Layer   Hidden Layer   Output Layer

So, you may be asking, how is a neural network different from an expert system, since both can take input and produce an answer as to which group the input belongs? An expert system, as we saw, can also classify; that is, it asks questions and, based on the answers, can diagnose or prescribe. The difference is that an expert system does not adjust by itself and is rigid in its application of the rules. For example, if a credit card fraud detection expert system had a rule that said to flag a purchase over a certain amount on certain types of accounts, the expert system would flag a transaction that was even one penny over. A neural network, on the other hand, would learn the spending behavior of cardholders and would be better able to evaluate whether deviations were large enough to be queried or not. A neural network can even adjust to situations not explicitly used in training. For example, if when the neural network was learning, mortgage rates were between 6 percent and 10 percent, the system could interpolate if the rate were to drop to 5 percent.

Neural networks have many advantages. For example, neural networks can

- Learn and adjust to new circumstances on their own
- Lend themselves to massive parallel processing
- Function without complete or well-structured information
- Cope with huge volumes of information with many dependent variables
- Analyze nonlinear relationships in information and have been called fancy regression analysis systems

The biggest problem with neural networks to date has been the fact that the hidden layers are "hidden." That is, you can't see how the neural network is learning and how the neurons are interacting. Newer neural networks no longer hide the middle layers. With these systems you can manually adjust the weights or connections giving you more flexibility and control.

Genetic Algorithms

Have you ever wondered how chefs around the world create recipes for great-tasting foods? For example, how did the Chinese discover that cashew nuts and chicken taste good when combined? How did Mexican chefs arrive at combining tomatoes, onions, cilantro, and other spices to create pica de gallo? All those great recipes came about through *evolutionary processes*. Someone decided to put together a few ingredients and taste the result. Undoubtedly, many of those combinations resulted in unpalatable concoctions that were quickly discarded. Others were tasty enough to warrant further experimentation of combinations.

Today significant research in AI is devoted to creating software capable of following a similar trial-and-error process, leading to the evolution of a good result. Such a software system is called a genetic algorithm. A *genetic algorithm* is an artificial intelligence system that mimics the evolutionary, survival-of-the-fittest process to generate increasingly better solutions to a problem. In other words, a genetic algorithm is an optimizing system: It finds the combination of inputs that give the best outputs.

Here's an example. Suppose you were trying to decide what to put into your stock portfolio. You have countless stocks to choose from but a limited amount of money to invest. You might decide that you'd like to start with 20 stocks and you want a portfolio growth rate of 7.5 percent.

Probably you'd start by examining historic information on the stocks. You would take some number of stocks and combine them, 20 at a time, to see what happens with each grouping. If you wanted to choose from a pool of 30 stocks, you would have to examine 30,045,015 different combinations. For a 40-stock pool, the number of combinations rises to 137,846,500,000. It would be an impossibly time-consuming, not to mention numbingly tedious, task to look at this many combinations and evaluate your overall return for each one. However, this is just the sort of repetitive number-crunching task at which computers excel.

So, instead of a pencil, paper, and calculator, you might use a genetic algorithm. You could input the appropriate information on the stocks, including the number of years the company has been in business, the performance of the stock over the last five years, price to earnings ratios, and other information.

You would also have to tell the genetic algorithm your exact "success" criteria. For example, you might use a growth rate in the company over the last year of at least 10 percent, a presence in the marketplace going back at least three years, a connection to the computer industry, and so forth. The genetic algorithm would simply combine and recombine stocks eliminating any combinations that don't fit your criteria and continuing to the next iteration with the acceptable combinations—those that give an aggregate growth rate of at least 7.5 percent while aiming for as high a growth rate as possible.

Genetic algorithms use three concepts of evolution:

1. *Selection*—or survival of the fittest. The key to selection is to give preference to better outcomes.

2. *Crossover*—or combining portions of good outcomes in the hope of creating an even better outcome.

3. *Mutation*—or randomly trying combinations and evaluating the success (or failure) of the outcome.

Genetic algorithms are best suited to decision-making environments in which thousands, or perhaps millions, of solutions are possible. Genetic algorithms can find and evaluate solutions intelligently and can get through many more possibilities more thor-

THE EVOLUTION OF FARMING EQUIPMENT

There is an almost infinite number of combinations possible for features on a car. This is true for many products, as Deere, a company that makes agricultural equipment, knows all too well. Deere's customers demand all sorts of variations in planters. These different combinations of features make creating a good manufacturing schedule by hand all but impossible. Deere found that genetic algorithm software not only makes the task manageable but can compute the best schedule that offers the easiest and fastest way to utilize the production line to optimize production.

The initial stages of the huge project were very expensive, but the software gave the company a way to meet customer demand quickly and to gain competitive advantage. It worked so well for Deere that the company's supplier, Auburn Consolidated Industries, is also using it and Deere is reaping the benefits of improved supply chain management.

As always, technology alone is not the answer. To benefit significantly from technology, the production and business processes have to be efficient and effective.[42]

oughly and faster than a human can. As you might imagine, businesses face decision-making environments for all sorts of problems like engineering design, computer graphics, strategies for game playing, anything, in fact, that requires optimization techniques. Here are some other examples.

- Genetic algorithms are used by business executives to help them decide which combination of projects a firm should invest in, taking complicated tax considerations into account.[43]

- They're used by investment companies to help in trading choices and decisions.[44]

- In any garment that you buy, the fabric alone accounts for between 35 percent and 40 percent of the selling price. So, when cutting out the fabric to make the garment, it's important that there be as little waste as possible. Genetic algorithms are used to solve this problem of laying out the pieces of the garment and cutting fabric in a way that leaves as little waste as possible.[45]

- US West uses a genetic algorithm to determine the optimal configuration of fiber-optic cable in a network that may include as many as 100,000 connection points. By using selection, crossover, and mutation, the genetic algorithm can generate and evaluate millions of cable configurations and select the one that uses the least amount of cable. At US West, this process used to take an experienced design engineer almost two months. US West's genetic algorithm can solve the problem in two days and saves the company $1 million to $10 million each time it's used.[46]

Genetic algorithms are good for these types of problems because they use selection, crossover, and mutation as methods of exploring countless solutions and the respective worth of each.

You have to tell the genetic algorithm what constitutes a "good" solution. That could be low cost, high return, among other factors, since many potential solutions are useless or absurd. If you created a genetic algorithm to make bread, for example, it might try to boil flour to create moistness. That obviously won't work, so the genetic algorithm would simply throw away that solution and try something else. Other solutions would eventually be good, and some of them would even be wonderful. According to David Goldbert, a genetic algorithm pioneer at the University of Illinois at Urbana-Champaign,

BE A GENETIC ALGORITHM AND PUT NAILS IN BOXES

This project involves packaging nails so that you make the most profit possible (this is a profit maximizing problem). Say you have five types of nails and can make as many as you need of each. These are 4-inch, 3.5-inch, 3-inch, 2.5-inch, 2-inch, and 1.5-inch nails. The cost of making each type of nail depends on how big a nail it is. Those cost and selling prices are listed in the table below along with the weights. The nails will be sold in boxes of up to 30 nails. There must be no more than 10, but no less than 5, of each of three types of nails in each box. The nails in each box should weigh no more than 20 ounces. You're looking for the combination with the highest profit using a trial-and-error method.

A spreadsheet would be helpful for completing this project. You'll most likely find that you identify some promising paths to follow right away and will concentrate on those to reach the best one.

Nail	Weight	Cost	Selling price
4 inch	1 oz	4 cents	8 cents
3.5 inch	0.85 oz	3.5 cents	6 cents
3 inch	0.7 oz	3 cents	5 cents
2.5 inch	0.5 oz	2.5 cents	4 cents
2 inch	0.25 oz	2 cents	3 cents
1.5 inch	0.1 oz	1.5 cents	2 cents

evolution is the oldest and most powerful algorithm there is, and "three billion years of evolution can't be wrong!"[47]

Intelligent Agents

Do you have a favorite restaurant? Is there someone there who knows you and remembers that you like Italian dressing, but not croutons, on your salad; and ice cream and a slice of cheddar cheese on your apple pie? Does this person familiar with your tastes put a glass of diet cola on your favorite table when you come in the door? If so, he or she has the qualities that artificial intelligence scientists are working on incorporating into intelligent agents. An ***intelligent agent*** is software that assists you, or acts on your behalf, in performing repetitive computer-related tasks. Future intelligent agents will most likely be autonomous, acting independently, and will learn and adapt to changing circumstances.

You may not realize it, but you're probably already familiar with a primitive type of intelligent agent—the shifty-eyed paper clip that pops up in some versions of Word. For example, if your document looks as if it is going to be a business letter—that is, you type in a date, name, and address—the animated paper clip will offer helpful suggestions on how to proceed.

You can find hundreds of intelligent agents, or bots, for a wide variety of tasks. The BotSpot and SmartBot Web sites at www.botspot.com and www.smartbots.com are good places to look for the different types of agents available.

Essentially there are four types of intelligent agents:

1. Buyer agents or shopping bot
2. User or personal agents
3. Monitoring-and-surveillance agents
4. Data-mining agents

BUYER AGENTS

Buyer agents travel around a network (very likely the Internet) finding information and bringing it back to you. Buyer agents are also called shopping bots. These agents search the Internet for goods and services that you need and bring you back the information.

A **buyer agent** or **shopping bot** is an intelligent agent on a Web site that helps you, the customer, find products and services you want. Shopping bots work very efficiently for commodity products such as CDs, books, electronic components, and other one-size-fits-all products.

Shopping bots make money by selling advertising space, conducting special promotions in cooperation with merchants, or charging click-through fees, which are payments to the site that provided the link to the merchant site. Some shopping bots give preference to certain sites for a financial consideration. The people who run shopping bot sites have two competing objectives. They want to present as many listings as possible to the consumer in the most useful way, but they also want to make money doing it.

MySimon.com (see Figure 4.11) is the most successful shopping bot to date with more than a million visitors a month according to Nielsen/NetRatings. MySimon searches for millions of products on thousands of Web sites.[48]

Government sites have search-and-retrieve agents you can use to get the information you need. FERRET (Federal Electronic Research and Review Extraction Tool) was developed jointly by the Census Bureau and the Bureau of Labor Statistics. With FERRET

Figure 4.11
MySimon Shopping Bot Site

You can tell the shopping bot what you're looking for and it will find lots of sources for you.

you can find information on employment, health care, education, race and ethnicity, health insurance, housing, income and poverty, aging, and marriage and family.

You may have encountered a shopping bot without having specifically requested its services. For example, Amazon.com will offer you a list of books that you might like to buy based on what you're buying now and what you have bought in the past. The Amazon site uses an intelligent agent—a shopping bot—to provide this service. As you saw in Chapter 2, Amazon's agent uses collaborative filtering, which consists of matching each customer with a group of users who have similar tastes and presenting choices common in that group.

Collaborative filtering is one of many techniques that predict your preferences. Following are four that are currently being used or considered for use at online shopping sites.

- *Collaborative filtering* is a method of placing you in an affinity group of people with the same characteristics. Then, likes and dislikes are associated with all members of that group.
- *Profile filtering* requires that you choose terms or enter keywords. This provides a more personal picture of you and your preferences.
- *Psychographic filtering* anticipates your preferences based on the answers you give to a questionnaire. This method is also more personal than collaborative filtering.
- *Adaptive filtering* asks you to rate products or situations and also monitors your actions over time to find out what you like and dislike.[49]

Collaborative filtering, although it can be quite effective, has two big disadvantages. First, since this method bases your future choices on past purchases of the group to which it deems you to belong, it usually won't offer new or obscure products that might be just what you want. Second, the Web site needs vast amounts of information to be able to use collaborative filtering in the first place. This puts the method out of reach for smaller businesses.

Given these drawbacks, shopping bot designers are experimenting with incorporating the other three methods into shopping agents. The last three, profile filtering, psychographic filtering, and adaptive filtering, tend to discover more personal traits of individuals and, therefore, if applied well, can better anticipate what you'd like to buy.

USER AGENTS

User agents (sometimes called *personal agents*) are intelligent agents that take action on your behalf. In this category belong those intelligent agents that already perform, or will shortly perform, the following tasks:

- Check your e-mail, sort it according to priority (your priority), and alert you when good stuff comes through—like college acceptance letters.
- Play computer games as your opponent or patrol game areas for you.
- Assemble customized news reports for you. There are several versions of these. A CNN Custom News bot will gather news from CNN on the topics you want to read about—and only those topics.
- Find information for you on the subject of your choice.
- Fill out forms on the Web automatically for you. They even store your information for future reference.
- Scan Web pages looking for and highlighting the text that constitutes the "important" part of the information there.
- "Discuss" topics with you from your deepest fears to sports.

One expanding application of intelligent agent technology is in automating business functions. For example, Mission Hockey, a company that manufacturers and distributes in-line and ice hockey skates and other gear, uses software from Sweden called Movex that has a user agent component. Movex will search the Internet or a company intranet or extranet to negotiate and make deals with suppliers and distributors. An *intranet* is an internal organizational Internet that is guarded against outside access by a special security feature called a firewall. An *extranet* is an intranet that is restricted to an organization and certain outsiders, such as customers and suppliers. You can read more on intranets and extranets in Chapters 5 and 7. In the Movex case, the intelligent agent is incorporated into an enterprise resource planning system. *Enterprise resource planning (ERP)* is a very important concept in today's business world. The term refers to a method of getting and keeping an overview of every part of the business (a bird's eye view, so to speak), so that production, development, selling, and servicing of goods and services will all be coordinated to contribute to the company's goals and objectives. You'll learn more about the concept of ERP in Chapter 7.

In the future, user agents for personal use will be available for both your wired and your wireless computer devices. Sprint has recently announced an e-assistant that will carry out verbal requests.[50] In the future, we'll see personal agents that

- Interact with the personal agents of colleagues to set up a meeting time
- Incorporate shopping bots that can take your preferences for features on a new car (or anything else) along with a price range and then haggle with car dealers (or their personal agents) to find you the best deal

MONITORING-AND-SURVEILLANCE AGENTS

Monitoring-and-surveillance agents (also called *predictive agents*) are intelligent agents that observe and report on equipment. For example, NASA's Jet Propulsion Laboratory has an agent that monitors inventory, planning, and scheduling equipment ordering to keep costs down.[51] Other monitoring agents work on the manufacturing shop floor, finding equipment problems and locating other machinery that will do the same job.

DATA MINING IN THE BODY SHOP

Have you ever taken a catalog out of your mailbox and thrown it straight into trash, perhaps even before you brought it into your home? If you're like most people, you probably have. The Body Shop International, like most businesses, knows that. This U.K.-based company would much prefer to send their catalogs only to those who will place orders for products and so it uses predictive analysis, which is one type of data mining. Data mining involves using technology to find trends and patterns in a vast quantity of information. Predictive analysis consists of forecasting and propensity analysis. Forecasting finds trends and then predicts the future based on those trends. Propensity analysis uses statistical methods like regression analysis and clustering in combination with neural networks to determine the likelihood that a particular consumer will respond to an offer, or buy a product or service. Propensity analysis is also used to predict what customers are most likely to default on a loan or payment plan.

Using data mining, the Body Shop was able to cut in half the number of catalogs it sent out in 2001 after identifying a new 120,000 customers from its Web, store, and customer database. And, not only that, revenue per catalog increased 20 percent.

A few years ago, if you wanted to conduct a complex predictive analysis with lots of variables, you'd need access to a supercomputer. Today, your desktop computer can do the job.[52]

Monitoring-and-surveillance agents are often used to monitor complex computer networks. Allstate Insurance has a network with 2,000 computers. The company uses a network monitoring agent from Computer Associates International called Neugent that watches its huge networks 24 hours a day. Every 5 seconds, the agent measures 1,200 data points and can predict a system crash 45 minutes before it happens. Neugent combines intelligent agent technology with neural network technology to look for patterns of activity or problems. The neural network part can learn what conditions predict a downturn in network efficiency or a slowing in network traffic. Neugent also watches for electronic attacks from hackers, detecting them early so that they can be stopped.

Another type of monitoring-and-surveillance agent that works on computer networks keeps track of the configuration of each computer connected to the network. It tracks and updates the central configuration database when anything on any computer changes, like the number or type of disk drive changes. An important task in managing networks is in prioritizing traffic and shaping bandwidth. That means sending enough network capacity or bandwidth to the most important tasks over those tasks that are of secondary importance. At a university, for example, processing end-of-semester grades might take precedence over net surfing.

Some further types of monitoring-and-surveillance agents include agents that

- Watch your competition and bring back price changes and special offer information
- Monitor Internet sites, discussion groups, mailing lists, and so on, for stock manipulation, insider training, and rumors that might affect stock prices
- Monitor sites for updated information on the topic of your choice
- Watch particular products and bring back price or term changes
- Monitor auction sites for products or prices that you want

DATA-MINING AGENTS

A ***data-mining agent*** operates in a data warehouse discovering information. A data warehouse brings together information from lots of different sources. Data mining is the process of looking through the data warehouse to find information that you can use to take action, like ways to increase sales or retain customers who are considering defecting to the competition. Data mining is so called because you have to sift through a lot of information for the gold nuggets that will affect the bottom line. This sort of nugget spotting is similar to what the FBI and CIA do when they bring together little bits of information from diverse sources and use the overall pattern to spot trouble brewing.

As you learned in Chapter 3, database queries answer questions such as, How much did we spend on transportation in March of this year? Multidimensional analysis is the next step in complexity and answers questions such as, How much did we spend on transportation in the Southeast during March of the last five years? Data mining goes deeper and finds answers to questions you may not even have asked such as, What else do young men buy on Friday afternoons when they come in to buy diapers? The answer, culled by data mining tools, is beer.[53]

One of the most common types of data mining is classification, which finds patterns in information and categorizes items into those classes. You may remember that this is just what neural networks do best. So, not surprisingly, neural networks are part of many data-mining tools. And data-mining agents are another integral part, since data-mining agents search for information in a data warehouse.

A data-mining agent may detect a major shift in a trend or a key indicator. It can also detect the presence of new information and alert you. Volkswagen uses an intelligent agent system that acts as an early-warning system about market conditions. If conditions become such that the assumptions underlying the company's strategy are no longer true, the intelligent agent alerts managers.[54] For example, the intelligent agent might see a problem in some part of the country that is or will shortly cause payments to slow down. Having that information early on lets managers formulate a plan to protect themselves.

COMPONENTS OF AN INTELLIGENT AGENT

To be truly "intelligent" systems, intelligent agents must have three qualities: autonomy, adaptivity, and sociability.[55]

- ***Autonomy*** means that they act without your telling them every step to take. Many of the intelligent agents in use today have this quality. They check networks, index Web pages, retrieve football scores from any information source, tell you when a competitor has an offer you should be aware of, and so on.

- ***Adaptivity*** is discovering, learning, and taking action independently. This means that the intelligent agent learns about your preferences and makes judgments by itself. If you were to fly to Chicago to visit your mother the last weekend of every month, the intelligent agent would discover that it needed to start looking for cheap fares to Chicago at least three weeks ahead of time. It would then do this without your intervention.

- ***Sociability*** is conferring with other agents. For example, a buyer agent, or shopping bot, might go out looking for a product or service. At various branches of a retail store there might be a store agent that knows the merchandise and prices in its own store. The store agents would communicate with each other and the buyer agent to produce results for you. These agents communicate with each other using the Knowledge Query and Manipulation Language (KQML), which has become the de facto standard for interagent communications.

At the moment no intelligent agent software has all these qualities. Various agents are autonomous, and some are adaptive with a reasonable amount of success. Sociability is a very hot research area at the moment and more a goal than a reality. Some artificial intelligence scientists believe that many of one-purpose agents working together are the way to create a very sophisticated artificial intelligence system.

Summary: Student Learning Outcomes Revisited

1. **Define decision support system, list its components, and identify the type of applications it's suited to.** A *decision support system (DSS)* is a highly flexible and interactive IT system that is designed to support decision making when the problem is not structured. A DSS has three components: data management, model management, and user interface management. It's primarily an analysis tool to support your decision making, but you make the final decision.

2. **Define collaboration systems along with their features and uses.** *Collaboration systems* are designed specifically to improve the performance of teams by supporting the sharing and flow of information. Features of collaboration software are instant messaging, calendar management, group scheduling, conferencing of various kinds, workflow, and task and document management. You would use collaboration software whenever members of a team are separated, whether on different floors of a building or on the other side of the globe.

3. **Define geographic information systems and state how they differ from other decision support tools.** A *geographic information system (GIS)* is a decision support system designed specifically to work with spatial information. It's used for the analysis of information in map form. Information is stored in layers which can be overlaid as appropriate. It's the layering and presentation that separates a GIS from other decision support tools.

4. **Define artificial intelligence and list the different types that are used in business.** *Artificial intelligence* is the science of making machines imitate human thinking and behavior. The types used in business include expert

systems, neural networks, genetic algorithms, and intelligent agents.

5. **Define expert systems and describe the types of problems to which they are applicable.** An *expert system* (or *knowledge-based system*) is an artificial intelligence system that applies reasoning capabilities to reach a conclusion. A rule-based expert system asks the user questions and, based on the answers, asks other questions until it has enough information to make a decision or a recommendation. Expert systems are good for diagnostic (what's wrong) and prescriptive problems (what to do). For example, you could use an expert system to diagnose illness or to figure out why a machine is malfunctioning. And, you could use an expert system to determine what to do about the problem.

6. **Define neural networks, their uses, and a major strength and weakness of these AI systems.** A *neural network* (also called an *artificial neural network* or *ANN*) is an artificial intelligence system that is capable of finding and differentiating patterns. Neural networks are good for finding commonalties in situations that have many variables. The major strength of a neural network is that it can learn and adapt. Its major weakness is that it's not usually clear how the system reached its result and it's hard, therefore, to verify its solutions.

7. **Define genetic algorithms and list the concepts on which they are based, and the types of problems they solve.** A *genetic algorithm* is an artificial intelligence system that mimics the evolutionary, survival-of-the-fittest process to generate increasingly better solutions to a problem. Genetic algorithms use the principles of *selection, crossover,* and *mutation* from

evolution theory. These systems are best suited to problems where hundreds or thousands of solutions are possible and you need an optimum solution.

8. **Define intelligent agents, list the four types, and identify the types of problems they solve.** An *intelligent agent* is software that assists you, or acts on your behalf, in performing repetitive computer-related tasks. The four types are

   - *Buyer agents* (or *shopping bots*) search the Web for products and services

- *User agents* (or *personal agents*) take action for you, particularly in repetitive tasks like sorting e-mail
- *Monitoring-and-surveillance agents* (or *predictive agents*) track conditions, perhaps on a network, and signal changes or troublesome conditions
- *Data-mining agents* search data warehouses to discover information

CLOSING CASE STUDY ONE

USING NEURAL NETWORKS TO CATEGORIZE PEOPLE

Would your banker give you an A, B, or C? What about your supermarket? You know you're being graded in your classes, but did you know that you're also being graded by businesses?

Special treatment for certain customers is not new. Airline customers who fly first class have always received preferential treatment, even when flights were cancelled or delayed. You won't find them napping on a stone floor with their backpacks as pillows. This makes business sense to the airlines, since these are the customers who are most profitable.

Although companies have always offered preferential treatment to their more profitable customers, the speed and capacity of computers today is making the segmenting of customers possible to a degree unheard of just a few years ago. Part of the reason for this is neural networks. Using neural network software, businesses now have the ability to look for patterns in their customer information and classify customers according to how they affect the company's bottom line and thus to gauge whether it's worth the trouble of making them happy.

BANKS

The First Union Bank uses software that categorizes people into red, green, and yellow depending on the customer's history and value to the bank. Customers who are green might get better credit card rates than customers who are red and are judged to add less to the bank's bottom line.

Say you called the bank that issued you your credit card and said that you didn't want to pay the annual fee anymore. The bank could look at your credit card activity and decide whether it's more profitable to the bank to waive your fee rather than risk your not using the credit card anymore.

CREDIT CARD COMPANIES

Visa has saved millions of dollars using neural network software to spot fraud and to determine which of their customers might default or go bankrupt. Neural networks are good at spotting patterns, and if your profile looks like that of people who have defaulted, you'll be tossed into that category.

SUPPLIERS

Neural network classifying software can be applied to finding the best suppliers, too. Weyerhaeuser Corporation's door factory executives have software to rank suppliers and distributors based on price, speed of delivery, and innovation. Using this information, Weyerhaeuser doubled its sales and increased its return on net assets from 2 percent to 24 percent.

SUPERMARKETS

Catalina Supermarkets keeps track of what customers buy which products, how frequently, and what price they pay. Using neural network software, the supermarket chain can identify high-value customers and work at retaining them with offers of services such as free home delivery.

MOVIES

Even the movie business is getting in on the act. Twentieth Century Fox slices and dices its information in its databases to determine the most popular movies, actors, and plots in certain theaters, cities, and areas of the country. The aim is to show movies in those areas that will add the most to the bottom line. The result may be that people in certain areas will not get the chance to see certain movies.

There was a time when certain neighborhoods or geographic regions were redlined. That meant that banks and other businesses wouldn't deal with anyone who lived there. Some people think that this sort of market segmentation is a new form of redlining. Do you? Following are some questions for you to answer regarding this practice.[56]

Questions

1. A neural network learns to recognize patterns based on past information. Is this fair or reliable when applied to people? How accurate is it for a business to predict the future behavior of customers on the basis of historic information? Don't people change? Have you ever changed your behavior in the course of your life?

2. Customers are not likely ever to see the information that companies are using to pigeonhole them. Even the company executives may not know what criteria the neural network uses. How important are the assumptions underlying the software (i.e., the facts that the neural network is given about customers)? Even the IT specialists who design neural networks can't always vouch for their accuracy or specify exactly how the neural network reaches its conclusions. Is this safe for businesses? What are the possible business consequences of using

neural networks without assurances of their reliability?

3. Businesses can use segmenting to suggest products and services to you, or if you request it, prevent your getting junk mail you don't want. Is that good? Would receiving wanted information or avoiding junk mail be worth the price of being categorized?

4. Say you run a business that supplies medical equipment (not prescription drugs)—wheelchairs, hospital beds, heating packs. You're trying to determine which customers you should give preferential treatment to. What assumptions or variables would you use (for example, age, income, and so on) to segment your customer population?

5. Do you think that this segmentation practice is fair? First, consider the business stockholders, then consider the customers. Does it matter whether it's fair or not? Why or why not? Should there be laws against it, or laws controlling it, or none at all? Explain and justify your answer.

6. Does this differentiating practice make business sense? If you owned stock in a company, how would you feel about this practice? Do you think you should get better treatment if you're a better customer? Do you think people who are not such good customers should get the same deal that you get? Would it make any difference whether the company collected the information and did the neural network analysis itself, or bought the information or the whole package from a third party?

7. Is this practice of classifying the same as redlining, or is it okay because it looks at behavior and classifies people rather than assuming characteristics based on membership in a particular group?

DECISION SUPPORT AND ARTIFICIAL INTELLIGENCE IN HEALTH CARE

Good health care is based largely on good information. Information technology helps with diagnosing illness and treating it. It also aids research in identifying and finding cures for illness. Following are two examples of the use of information technology in health care.

MENTAL HEALTH IN OHIO

In 1996, the Ohio Department of Mental Health wanted a consistent, statewide approach to evaluating and reporting results of treatment performed by the state's publicly funded community mental health system. So the Ohio Mental Health Outcomes Task Forces was set up to find a way to achieve this objective.

The Ohio mental health system serves 250,000 patients with its 500 local service agencies run by 50 community health boards. The state wanted to make sure that those who provide services are accountable and that services continue to improve.

The task force was made up of members of community mental health boards and agencies, health care providers, and patients and their families who met for 16 months to decide on strategies, outcomes, methods of measurement, goals, and problems.

The task forces agreed on four basic measurements:

1. Clinical status, which included the severity of symptoms
2. The patient's ability to handle everyday tasks
3. Quality of life, as perceived by the patient
4. Safety and health of the patient and those around him or her.

The patient population was divided into three groups: adults with severe disabilities, other adults, and children and adolescents.

The group outsourced the system they required to Nova Behavioral Health and solved the problem of having to develop and/or run the system locally.

Nova first collects information on patients electronically using a hand-held device. When the questionnaire is complete, the unit is connected to its docking station, and the information is sent to the central repository. Then all collected information is available

for analysis. The Ohio mental health group has found great benefit in the new system. The annual survey administration costs are 75 percent lower with the electronic survey system than with pencil and paper. The hand-held devices, far from being intimidating, have proven to be very easy to use and take only 10 minutes as opposed to the 30 minutes the survey used to take. Errors in information collection and analysis have been reduced dramatically. All in all, the group is very pleased with the new system.

PHYSICAL HEALTH IN CONNECTICUT

Health Connecticut is a consortium of 22 hospitals that wanted to give hospitals a decision support system to help manage their health care and billing. After an 18-month-long study, the group finally had a plan to create a comprehensive data warehouse of information that would enhance the hospitals' quality assurance and aid in financial planning.

The problem is the same one encountered by countless enterprises—how to bring together all the information needed for tracking and serving customers and how to get that information into a form that would enable better financial analysis. For example, it was taking six weeks to get information from the pharmacy on pneumonia cases. Tracking heart attack patients wasn't possible at all. The hospitals had all the information on the patients' stay at the hospital but couldn't link that to follow-up exams in the doctor's office or see a report on the drugs that were used to treat the patient. That was no way to track whether the patient had home care services or needed special equipment during the recovery period.

The group decided on a health care software package called W3Health and has seen annual savings of $300,000 in salaries for computer personnel and computer equipment over what it was costing to run the previous system. But, even more importantly, the hospitals can view the whole patient population and spot trends in health or sickness and quickly estimate the potential cost of the trends. Health care workers can view data from the pharmacy and, with just a few clicks, find out about any type of drug along with a profile of the patients it was prescribed for and link that to other patient information. Hospital staff can perform their own analysis using the sophisticated user interface and no longer have to wait for computer programmers to write code to perform the necessary operations to get a report.[57,58]

QUESTIONS

1. Both health groups had essentially the same goals—to track symptoms, treatment, and outcomes—that require the collection and maintenance of a huge amount of qualitative and quantitative information. What type of software would you recommend for storing this information so that it can be easily accessed and analyzed? What sort of software query tools would you suggest?

2. Would there be a role for a geographic information system in either of these examples? How could it be useful? Are there extreme cases, perhaps natural disasters, where a GIS would be useful?

3. How could a neural network help the Ohio Department of Mental Health task force to generate the information it needs? Would it be advisable to automate the medication process for routine illnesses by connecting the pattern recognition abilities of a neural network to a robot that dispenses pills thereby letting medical staff deal with more complicated cases? Why? Why not?

4. An expert system is designed to ask questions, and then ask more questions based on the answers to the previous questions. Isn't that what medical specialists do when they're diagnosing your illness? Would you, therefore, like to dispense with visiting a doctor and just buy a medical expert system that you could install on your home computer and consult when you don't feel well? Why or why not?

5. What sort of collaboration might be helpful for the Ohio Department of Mental Health and the Health Connecticut groups? What situations can you envisage where a video or a Web conference would be helpful?

6. For both cases, describe tasks that the various types of artificial intelligence software would lend themselves to and state specifically what tasks each AI system is suited to.

7. Part of quality assurance in any organization is the identification of things that went wrong and ways in which processes can be improved. It's no different in health care—errors are inevitable. However, it's part of the mission of health care workers to keep these errors as small and as infrequent as possible. How could a decision support system help in the implementation of safer procedures? What part could expert systems, neural networks, and intelligent agents play?

Key Terms and Concepts

Adaptive filtering, 208
Adaptivity, 211
Artificial intelligence (AI), 193
Autonomy, 211
Back-propagation neural network, 202
Buyer agent (shopping bot), 207
Choice, 183
Collaboration system, 188
Collaborative filtering, 208
Crossover, 204
Data management, 188
Data-mining agent, 211
Decision support system (DSS), 185
Design, 183

Domain expert, 197
Domain expertise, 197
Expert system (knowledge-based system), 195
Explanation module, 198
Extranet, 209
Genetic algorithm, 204
Geographic information system (GIS), 191
Implementation, 183
Inference engine, 198
Intelligence, 183
Intelligent agent, 206
Intranet, 209
Knowledge acquisition, 198
Knowledge base, 198

Short-Answer Questions

1. What are the four types of decisions discussed in this chapter? Give an example of each.
2. What are the four steps in making a decision?
3. What is a DSS? Describe its components.
4. What sort of a system would you use if you wanted to work with your suppliers electronically?
5. What are three of the features that collaboration systems might have?
6. What is a geographic information system used for?
7. How is information represented in a geographic information system?
8. What is artificial intelligence? Name the artificial intelligence systems used widely in business.
9. What are the components of an expert system?
10. What does the domain expert do?
11. How does a neural network work?
12. What three concepts of evolution are used by the genetic algorithm?
13. What are intelligent agents? What tasks can they perform?
14. What do shopping bots do?
15. What do monitoring-and-surveillance agents do?

Short-Question Answers

For each of the following answers, provide an appropriate question.

1. A decision that you face every day.
2. The part of a DSS where the models are stored.
3. Any system that simulates human senses and can act on its own.
4. A domain expert must provide the rules for this AI system.
5. The person who enters the rules into the expert system.
6. Classification is the strong suit of this AI system.
7. This AI system takes its cue from evolution.
8. It recognizes patterns and classifies input.
9. This type of software usually has e-mail, instant messaging, and calendar management.
10. It can find the best price for a product on the Internet.
11. Adaptivity and sociability are two of its qualities.
12. It shows information in map form.
13. Crossover and mutation are features of how this software works.
14. It's the second stage of decision making.
15. It's the name for the process that slices and dices the information in a data warehouse.

Assignments and Exercises

1. **MAKE A GIS** Make a GIS-type map using transparencies. Draw a map of your campus on one plastic transparency sheet. You can use software or felt-tip pens to do the actual drawing of the map. Next, use a second sheet as an overlay and mark on it what classes you have taken in what buildings. Take a third sheet and enter the type of classroom you had the course in (i.e., auditorium, lab, small, medium, large room). Make a fourth layer with special facilities, like a computer lab or a biology lab, and so on. What problems did you encounter while designing your GIS? What other information would you like to see in a real GIS of this type? Would this handmade GIS be helpful for new students? What layers would you keep for general use? What layers would you keep for sentimental value when your college days are over?

2. **COLLABORATION WORK** In a group of two or more students, collaborate on a project to make a list of 100 videos or music CDs. Classify the videos or CDs into groups. For example, if you choose movies, your categories might be adventure, comedy, classic, horror, musicals, among others. All communication about the project must be electronically communicated (but not by phone). You could use e-mail, set up a Web site, use a chat room, or use a collaboration e-room, if your university has that facility. Print out a copy of all correspondence on the project and put the correspondence together in a folder in chronological order. Was this task very different from collaborating face-to-face with your partners? In what ways was it better,

in what ways worse? What additional problems or advantages would you expect if the person or people you're working with were in a different hemisphere?

3. **CHOOSE A FINANCING OPTION** Using a spreadsheet (like Excel, for example) evaluate your options for a $12,000 car. Compare the payments (use the =pmt function in Excel), the total amount of interest, and the total you'll pay for the car under the following four options:
   a. 3 years at 0 percent interest
   b. 2 years at 1.99 percent annual percent rate (APR)
   c. 4 years at 5 percent APR
   d. 6 years at 6 percent APR
   What other considerations would you take into account if you were going to buy a new car? Are there considerations other than the interest rate and the other parts that can be calculated? What are they? How is a car different from other purchases, such as CDs or TV sets or computers?

4. **WHICH SOFTWARE WOULD YOU USE?** Which type or types of computer-aided decision support software would you use for each of the situations in the following table? Note why you think each of your choices is appropriate. The decision support alternatives are

   - Decision support system
   - Collaboration system
   - Geographic information system
   - Expert system
   - Genetic algorithm
   - Intelligent agent

Problem	Type of Decision Support
You and another marketing executive on a different continent want to develop a new pricing structure for products	
You want to predict when customers are about to take their business elsewhere	
You want to fill out a short tax form	
You want to determine the fastest route for package delivery to 23 different addresses in a city	
You want to decide where to spend advertising dollars (TV, radio, newspaper, direct mail, e-mail)	
You want to keep track of competitors' prices for comparable goods and services	

5. **WHAT SHOULD THE MUSIC STORE OWNER DO?**
A music store owner wants to have enough of the hottest CDs in stock so that people who come in to buy a particular CD won't be disappointed   and the store won't lose the profit. CDs that are not sold within a certain length of time go onto the sale table where they may have to be sold at cost, if they sell at all.

She wants to design a decision support system to try and predict how many copies she should purchase and what information she will need. List some of the considerations that would go into such a system. Here is a couple to start you off: (1) the population of the target market; (2) sales for particular types of music in similar markets.

Discussion Questions

1. Some experts claim that if a business gets 52 percent of its decisions right, it will be successful. Would using a decision support system guarantee better results? Why or why not? What does the quality of any decision depend on? Do you think it matters what type of decisions are included in this 52 percent? For example, would getting the right type of paper clips be as influential a decision as deciding where to locate the business? Can you think of a situation where the type of paper clip matters a great deal?

2. Consider the topic of data warehouses in Chapter 3. In the future, AI systems will be increasingly applied to data warehouse processing. Which AI systems do you think might be helpful? For which tasks, or situations, might they best be applied? Do you think that AI systems will someday play a greater role in the design of databases and data warehouses? Why or why not?

3. Consider the differences and similarities among the four AI techniques discussed in this chapter. Name some problems that might be amenable to more than one type of AI system. Say you sell baseballs from your Web site. What types of AI systems could you use to generate information that would be useful to you in deciding what direction to take your company in the future? If you were pretty successful at selling baseballs, would you expect to have the amount of information on customers that, say Wal-Mart, has? Why or why not?

4. AI systems are relatively new approaches to solving business problems. What are the difficulties with new IT approaches in general? For each of the systems we discussed, identify some advantages and disadvantages of AI systems over traditional business processes. Say you were selling specialty teas and had both brick and click stores. Would you use the same type of AI systems for each part of your business? In what way would you use them or why would you not? Is there a place for decision support and artificial intelligence techniques in small specialty businesses? In what way would decision support add value? Can you think of how a DSS or an AI system would be value reducing (in terms of Porter's value chain theory)? What do you see as the major differences between running a mammoth concern and a small specialty business?

5. Neural networks recognize and categorize patterns. If someone were to have a neural network that could scan information on all aspects of your life, where would that neural network potentially be able to find information about you? Consider confidential (doctor's office) as well as publicly available (department of motor vehicles) information.

6. What type of AI systems could your school use to help with registration? Intelligent agents find vast amounts of information very quickly. Neural networks can classify patterns instantaneously. What sort of information might your school administration be able to generate using these (or other AI systems) with all of its student information?

Finding Investment Opportunities on the Internet

When you buy stock in a company, you're betting on the success of that firm. Sometimes that bet is a good one, and sometimes it's not. Finding a company that's a good bet involves lots of research. To further complicate matters, some people prefer investing in large, safe companies, whereas others prefer the higher return of a small, more risky firm. So how do you make sense of all the options? Well, now you have access to financial information that professional investors use to evaluate stocks. The Internet brings together information-hungry investors with companies that have been anxiously looking to reach out to investors online. More than 900 companies now offer investment information on the World Wide Web, and the number is increasing rapidly. Remember, though, you must proceed with caution. Do your best to verify the source of any information.

You'll find many links on the Web site that supports this textbook (www/mhhe.com/haag, and select "Electronic Commerce Projects").

LEARNING ABOUT INVESTING

Investing can be as simple as finding a company that performs well financially and buying some of their stock. Or, if you want to spread your investment over a number of stocks and you don't want to select each stock personally, you can invest in a mutual fund. Of course, there are thousands of mutual funds with all types of investment objectives. So, any way you go you must pick your investment wisely. To help you get up to speed quickly, you'll find many helpful Web sites on the Internet.

For starters, you might explore the National Association of Securities Dealers (NASD) at www.nasdr.com. Check out their Investor Resources with its Education and Tools. You might also want to retrieve more general information from the online versions of traditional print media such as the *Wall Street Journal* or *Money* magazine.

Find three investment reference sites and explore what information is available. Then answer the following questions.

A. Is the site designed for first-time investors or those that are more experienced?

B. Can you search for a specific topic?

C. Are specific stocks or mutual funds reviewed or evaluated?

D. Does the site provide direct links to brokerage or stock quoting sites?

E. Is a forum for submitting questions available? If so, are frequently asked questions (FAQs) posted?

F. Who sponsors the site? Does it seem as if the sponsor is using the site to advertise its own products or services?

G. Can you download reference documents to read later?

RESEARCHING THE COMPANY BEHIND THE STOCK

One excellent way to pick a stock investment is to research the company behind that stock. Focusing on items such as sales revenues and profits to pick a stock is called *fundamental research.* So you might choose to invest in Hughes stock because you've discovered their sales revenues have been climbing steadily for the last three years. Or you might initially consider buying some Disney stock but change your mind when you find that EuroDisney revenues have been below expectations.

Now that you're ready to research a stock investment, connect to four different company sites. You can find your own or go to the Web site that supports this text where you will find a list of many other company sites. As you connect to the four sites, look up each company's financials and answer the questions that follow. You'll probably want to include at least two companies with which you are familiar and two that are new to you. In addition to reviewing company financials, look around each company site and see to what degree the site is investor oriented.

A. Do all the company sites offer financial information?

B. Is the information targeted at investors? How can you tell?

C. Can you download financial information to your computer and use it in a spreadsheet?

D. Can you download the company's annual report? Is it a full-color version?

E. Does the site provide direct links to e-mail addresses for requesting additional information?

F. Do the companies provide comparisons to others in their industry?

G. Does the site provide stock quotes as well as financials?

H. Can you search the site for financial-related information such as press releases?

I. Was there a charge for retrieving the financial information?

FINDING OTHER SOURCES OF COMPANY FINANCIALS

Searching for a company's financials may be a bit more difficult than you may have first imagined. First, you must determine the Internet address for the company either by guessing the address and typing it in or using one of the many search engines available. Both of these methods are fraught with error. For example, if you guessed that www.amex.com was the address for American Express you'd be wrong. And even if you did guess a company's address, many companies don't provide their financials on their company-sponsored Web site. Take Adidas Corporation, for example, at www.adidas. com. No financials are available at this site. You'll find that many company Web sites lack information for investors.

The reason many companies don't provide financials on their Web sites is that they view the primary purpose of their Web sites as reaching consumers not investors. So, many companies elect to post their financials on a financial provider site or simply to let investors view the company's submissions to the Securities and Exchange Commission at the SEC's Web site.

Pick three providers of financial information, access their Web sites, and answer the following questions.

A. Is there a charge for retrieving the information?

B. Do you have a choice about the information's format?

C. Are companies listed alphabetically?

D. Does the site offer more than just annual reports?

E. Are there direct links from the site to the desired company's page?

F. How many companies are available on each Web site?

G. Are the represented companies mostly large and established or small and relatively unknown?

MAKING TRADES ONLINE

If you want to invest in securities, you might do what a lot of people do, go to a stockbroker. However, many of the same services offered by stockbrokers are now available on the Internet.

Virtually all of the stockbrokers with offices you can visit have Web sites that support online investing and more. These services include account information, financial planning, and online investing services. Before you go online to look at some of these stockbrokers you should be sure you understand the difference between a full-service brokerage house and a discount brokerage house. As the names imply, the full-service brokerage offers many more services than does the discount brokerage. And it's important to understand that the price for many of these services is built into the fees to buy and sell stocks and mutual funds. So you pay for having these services available even if you don't use them at a full-service brokerage. So, let's venture online and see what the various brokerages have to offer us.

Find three brokerages on the Web, examine what it takes to conduct an online investment transaction, and answer the following questions.

- **A.** Must you already have an investment account with the brokerage to purchase stocks or mutual funds?
- **B.** Which sites are full-service brokerages and which are discount brokerages? How can you tell?
- **C.** Is online research available? Is it free?
- **D.** Can you retrieve stock price quotes for free?
- **E.** If you already have an account with the brokerage, do they offer special services for these customers? What kinds of services are offered?
- **F.** Is the site aimed at experienced investors or new investors?
- **G.** If you are investing for the first time, would you feel comfortable using online investing? Why or why not?

RETRIEVING STOCK QUOTES

Once you find the right stock to buy, you'll then be asking yourself, How much will this stock cost me? Stocks and mutual funds are both offered by the share and so you can easily buy as much or as little of the stock or mutual fund as you like. Still, some individual shares are priced in the hundreds or thousands of dollars, and that alone might make the purchase undesirable to you.

In addition to pricing individual shares to assess the affordability of an investment, you'll probably want to see how the price has varied over time. Even though most financial advisors will tell you that historical price variations provide no indication of future performance, most everyone uses price history to get a feel for whether the investment is trading at all-time highs or lows. So finding a chart of a stock price online might be helpful when deciding to make your purchase.

And even after you've made your purchase, you'll probably want to follow how your investment is doing. The thrill of realizing a "paper profit" is enough to keep many investors checking their investments daily. Of course, realizing a "paper loss" can be equally disappointing. And even if daily tracking isn't for you, you'll certainly want to check on your investments regularly, and doing so online can be quick and painless.

Pick three stock quoting services, examine what it takes to retrieve a stock or mutual fund quote, and answer the following questions.

A. Are the quotes provided free of charge or for a fee?

B. Does the site require a ticker symbol (the abbreviation used by experienced investors) or can you type in a company name?

C. Are the quotes in real time or are they delayed (15 to 20 minutes old)?

D. Does the site require registration?

E. Are historical prices available?

F. Are price charts available? Can you customize the chart display?

G. Can you create and save a personal portfolio of stocks?

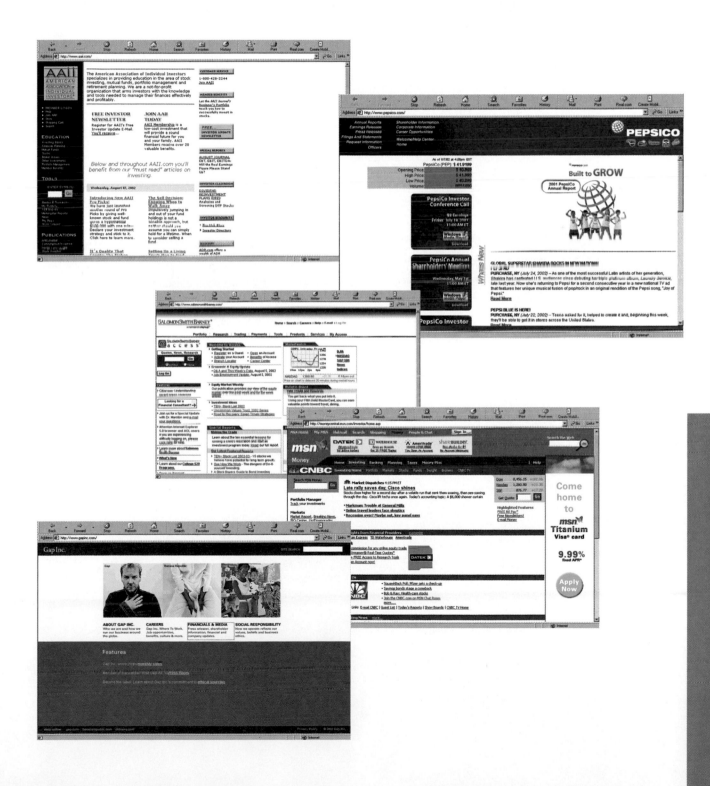

EXTENDED LEARNING MODULE D

DECISION ANALYSIS WITH SPREADSHEET SOFTWARE

Student Learning Outcomes

1. DEFINE A LIST AND LIST DEFINITION TABLE WITHIN THE CONTEXT OF SPREADSHEET SOFTWARE AND DESCRIBE THE IMPORTANCE OF EACH.

2. COMPARE AND CONTRAST THE AUTOFILTER FUNCTION AND CUSTOM AUTOFILTER FUNCTION IN SPREADSHEET SOFTWARE.

3. DESCRIBE THE PURPOSE OF USING CONDITIONAL FORMATTING.

4. DEFINE A PIVOT TABLE AND DESCRIBE HOW YOU CAN USE IT TO VIEW SUMMARIZED INFORMATION BY DIMENSION.

Introduction

As you just read in Chapter 4, technology can and does play a vitally important role in both supporting decision making and, in some instances, actually making decisions or recommendations. In this module, we'll focus on decision-making support, by exploring many of the advanced and productive features of Microsoft Excel.

Microsoft Excel is spreadsheet software that allows you to work with any kind of information, with each individual piece of information located in a cell. A cell is the intersection of a row and column and is uniquely identified by its column character and row number. In Figure D.1 you can see a simple workbook (the terms *workbook* and *spreadsheet* are used interchangeably). It shows the number of customers by region (North, South, East, and West) and by rent versus own.

There are a total of 487 customers (cell D9), of which 262 own a home (cell B9) and 225 rent (cell C9). Within this workbook, you can easily see some interesting information. For example, there are 148 customers in the East region while only 98 live in the South region. By region and ownership status, 82 own a home in the East region while only 47 rent in the South region.

Of course, now the question becomes, How is that information helpful? Well, it depends on the nature of your decision-making task. If you believe that home owners spend more money than those who rent and want to target advertising to the largest region, the information in Figure D.1 might be helpful. Then again, it might not be. It could very well be that home owners actually spend less than customers who rent. And, perhaps you generate more sales in regions with a lower number of customers.

Let's see how spreadsheet software can help you make better decisions. As we do, we'll introduce you to some spreadsheet features including AutoFilter, conditional formatting, and pivot tables. Our goal here is not to provide in great detail how each of these

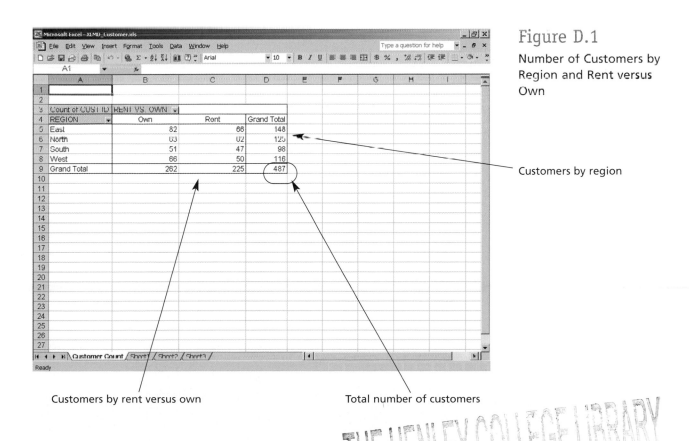

Figure D.1

Number of Customers by Region and Rent versus Own

Customers by region

Customers by rent versus own

Total number of customers

work, but rather what's most important about each one of them in supporting your decision-making tasks. After completing this module, you'll definitely be able to use all features in their basic forms. We recommend that you continue to explore them in detail.

Lists

What we showed in Figure D.1 was a pivot table. A pivot table is a spreadsheet function that summarizes information by category. In our case, it summarized information by region and rent versus own. To create a pivot table (and use many of the other features we'll discuss in this module), you have to first build a list. You should work along with us on this. Connect to the Web site that supports this text (www.mhhe.com/haag and select XLM/D). There, you can download the file called XLMD_Customer.xls.

A *list* is a collection of information arranged in columns and rows in which each column displays one particular type of information. In spreadsheet software, a list possesses the following characteristics:

1. Each column has only one type of information
2. The first row in the list contains the labels or column headings
3. The list does not contain any blank rows
4. The list is bordered on all four sides by blank rows and blank columns (it may not have a blank line above it, if it starts in the first row)

Take a look at the workbook in Figure D.2. It contains detailed information about our customers. In fact, we used this very list to generate the pivot table in Figure D.1.

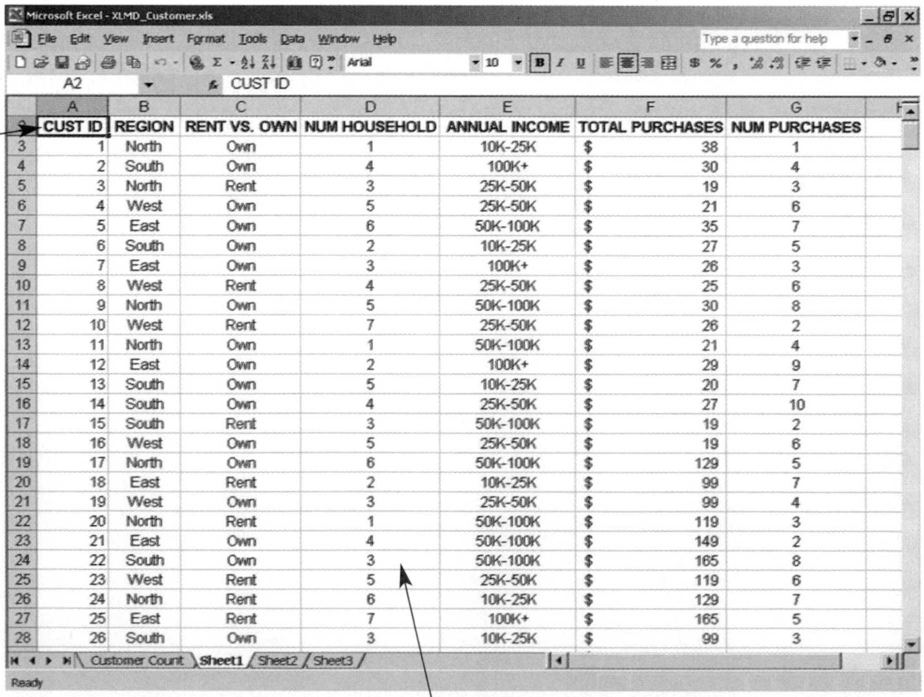

Figure D.2

The Complete List of Customers

Labels or column headings

Each column has only one type of information

First, notice that each column contains only one type of information: column A contains *CUST ID*, column B contains *REGION*, and so on. Second, notice that the first row (row 1) contains the labels or column headings. Third, if you scroll down completely through the list, you'll notice that there are 487 customers and there are no blank rows. Finally, notice that the list is bordered on all sides (except the top) by blank rows and columns. So, this is a list according to the four characteristics we listed.

We're going to be working extensively with this list throughout this module, so let's take a little time to explore the information in it. The columns of information include

A. *CUST ID*—A unique ID for each customer
B. *REGION*—The region in which the customer lives (North, South, East, or West)
C. *RENT VS. OWN*—Whether the customer rents or owns a home
D. *NUM HOUSEHOLD*—Number of family members in the household
E. *ANNUAL INCOME*—Total combined annual income of all family members
F. *TOTAL PURCHASES*—Dollar total of all purchases made by the customer within the last six months
G. *NUM PURCHASES*—Count of all purchases made by the customer within the last six months.

What we listed above is a called a **list definition table,** a description of a list by column. List definition tables are important. If you can create one just as we did, then you can create a list in a workbook with the appropriate characteristics. If you can't, then you may not be able to use many of the features we're about to show you.

Basic AutoFilter

Working with small lists that can be displayed in their entirety on a screen is seldom a problem. With a small list you can see the entire domain of information without scrolling up or down. But our list is much larger, containing 487 customers. So, you have to scroll through it to see all the information. If you were looking for specific information, such as all the customers in the North region, you could sort using the *REGION* column but you still get all the information (not to mention that customers in the North would come after the customers in the East region, alphabetically).

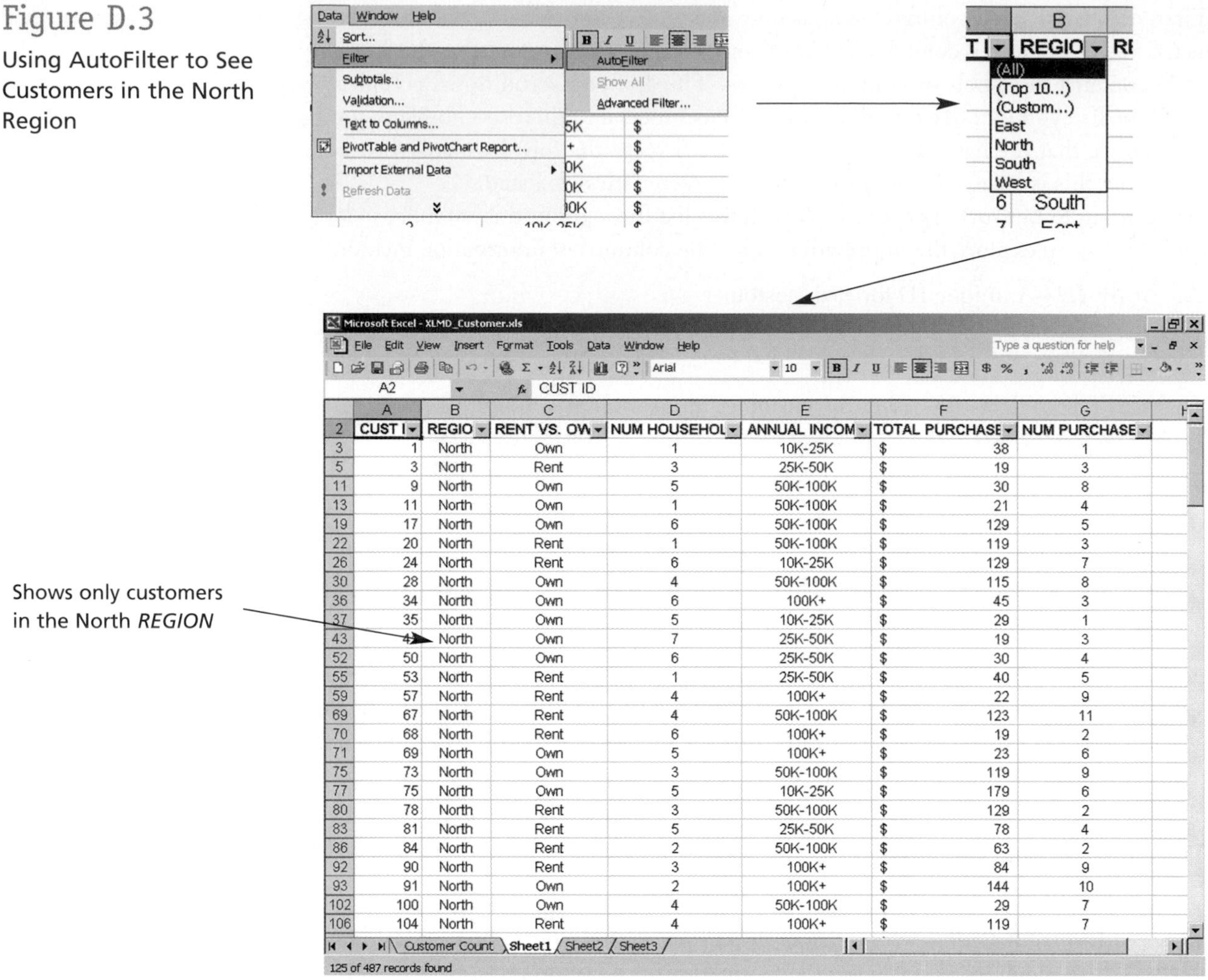

Figure D.3

Using AutoFilter to See Customers in the North Region

Shows only customers in the North *REGION*

To quickly create smaller lists out of a much larger list, you can use the AutoFilter function. The ***AutoFilter function*** filters a list and allows you to hide all the rows in a list except those that match criteria you specify. To filter a list with the AutoFilter function, perform the following steps (see Figure D.3):

1. Click in any cell within the list

2. From the menu bar, click on **Data,** point at **Filter,** and click on **AutoFilter**

Once you complete those two steps, Excel will place list box arrows next to each label or column heading. Now, all you have to do is click on the appropriate list box arrow and select the type of filtering you want. In Figure D.3, you can see that we clicked on the *REGION* list arrow box and chose North. Excel then presented us with a filtered list of only those customers in the North region. Our list is still quite long, but it does show only customers in the North.

To turn off the AutoFilter function, from the menu bar, click on **Data,** point at **Filter,** and click on **AutoFilter.**

When using the AutoFilter function, you're not limited to working with just one column. In Figure D.3, we filtered using the *REGION* column. Now, what if you want a filtered list of those customers in the North who own a home and have only one household member? That's easy. Click in the *RENT VS. OWN* list arrow box and choose **Own.**

LISTS, LIST DEFINITION TABLES, AND USING AUTOFILTER

Now it's your turn to practice using the basic AutoFilter function on a list. Go to the Web site that supports this text (www.mhhe.com/haag), select XLM/D, and download the file called XLMD_Customer2.xls. Take a moment and review the information in that workbook.

First, in the table below, create the list definition for it just as we did on page 227.

Now perform the following AutoFilter exercises:

1. Show only those customers in the state of California.

2. Show only those customers whose type of business is nonprofit.

3. Show only those customers in the retail business sector.

4. Show only those customers in Texas whose type of business is government.

5. Show only those customers in the manufacturing business sector.

Column Name	Description

Then, click in the *NUM HOUSEHOLD* list arrow box and choose **1.** That will show you the complete list (4 to be exact) of customers in the North who own a home and have only one household family member (see Figure D.4).

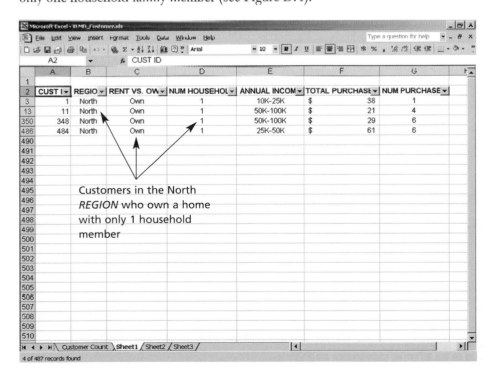

Customers in the North *REGION* who own a home with only 1 household member

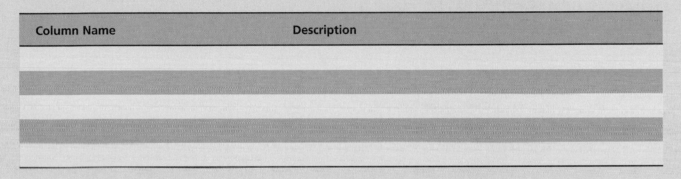

Figure D.4

A List Generated with Three Filters

Custom AutoFilter

The basic AutoFilter function allows you to create sublists using exact match criteria: *REGION* must be North, *NUM HOUSEHOLD* must be 1, and so forth. But what if you want to know all those customers who have at least four people in their households? In that case, you can't use the basic AutoFilter function—you need to use the Custom AutoFilter function. The *Custom AutoFilter function* allows you to hide all the rows in a list except those that match criteria, besides "is equal to," you specify. Let's see how to use the Custom AutoFilter function.

Figure D.5

Using a Custom AutoFilter

Only customers with more than four people in their households

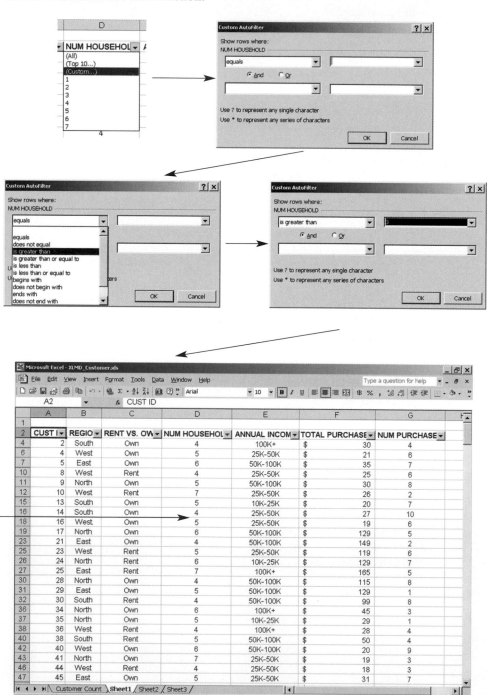

Given that you want to see a list of all customers who have at least four people in their households, perform the following steps:

1. Make sure you can see the entire list with the AutoFilter function turned on
2. Click on the *NUM HOUSEHOLD* list arrow box
3. Select **(Custom . . .)**

What you'll then see is a Custom AutoFilter box (the top right box in Figure D.5). For the top-left entry field, click on its pull-down arrow and select **is greater than.** For the top-right entry box, click on its pull down arrow and select **3** (or type the number **3** directly into the box). Then, all you have to do is click on **OK.** Excel does the rest and shows you the appropriate list of customers with at least four people in their households.

You should notice in Figure D.5 that the Custom AutoFilter box allows you to enter two criteria for creating a filtered list. So, you can easily create a Custom AutoFilter that answers the following question: What customers have spent less than $20 or more than $100 in the past six months? In Figure D.6, we've shown you how to do that along with the result.

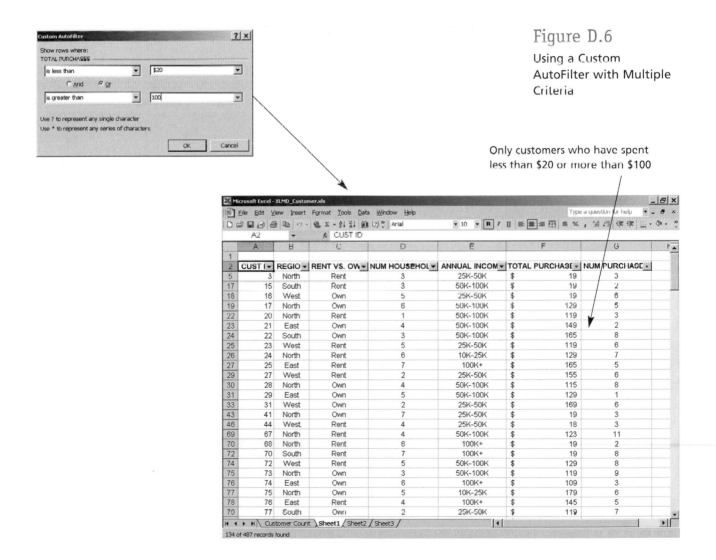

Figure D.6

Using a Custom AutoFilter with Multiple Criteria

Only customers who have spent less than $20 or more than $100

USING CUSTOM AUTOFILTERS

Now it's your turn to practice using the Custom Auto-Filter function on a list. Go to the Web site that supports this text (www.mhhe.com/haag), select XLM/D, and download the file called XLMD_Customer2.xls (the same one you used previously for the On Your Own project). Now perform the following Custom AutoFilter exercises:

1. Show only those customers who have more than 100 employees.

2. Show only those customers who have fewer than 100 employees.

3. Show only those customers who have at least 50 employees but no more than 100 employees.

4. Show only those customers in Tennessee who have fewer than 10 employees.

Conditional Formatting

When you use AutoFilter (either basic or custom), in a way you're highlighting information you want to see by basically hiding the other information you don't. As an alternative, you might want to highlight certain information while still being able to see the other information. If so, you can use conditional formatting. *Conditional formatting* highlights the information in a cell that meets some criteria you specify.

For example, what if you still wanted to be able to scroll through the entire list of customers but also wanted to have all *TOTAL PURCHASES* greater than $100 highlighted. This is a simple process in Excel. To do that, perform the following steps (see Figure D.7 on the facing page):

1. Select the entire *TOTAL PURCHASES* column (move the pointer over the F column identifier and click once)

2. From the menu bar, click on **Format** and then click on **Conditional Formatting**

You will then see a Conditional Formatting box as shown in the middle-left of Figure D.7.

Now, click on the pull down arrow for the field second from the left and click on **greater than.** In the field on the right, enter **100.** Finally, you need to select the conditional formatting for the information. To do so, click on the **Format** button. You will then see a Format Cells box. Across the top, you'll see tabs for Font, Border, and Patterns.

In our example, we clicked on the Patterns tab, chose the color red, and clicked on **OK.** Excel returned us to the Conditional Formatting box at which time we clicked on the **OK** button. As you can see in Figure D.8, Excel left the list intact and highlighted all cells in the *TOTAL PURCHASES* column in which the value exceeded $100.

To remove conditional formatting, first highlight the entire column again. Second, from the menu bar, click on **Format** and click on **Conditional Formatting.** Third, click on the **Delete** button in the Conditional Formatting box. Fourth, select **Condition 1** in the Delete Conditional Format box. Finally, click on **OK** in the Delete Conditional Format box, and click on **OK** in the Conditional Format box.

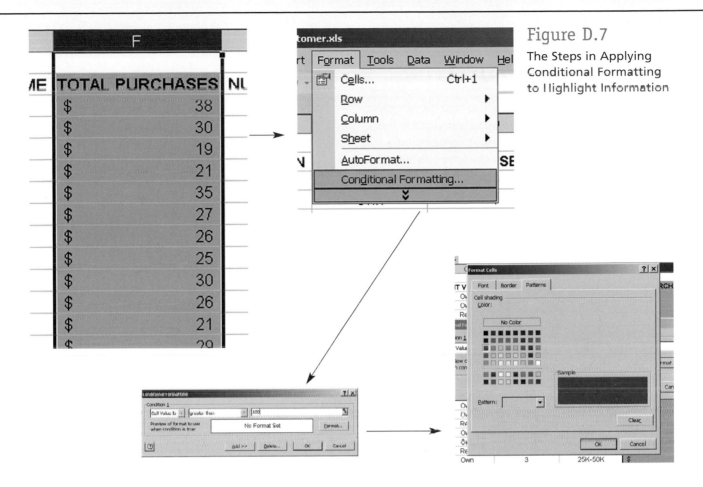

Figure D.7

The Steps in Applying
Conditional Formatting
to Highlight Information

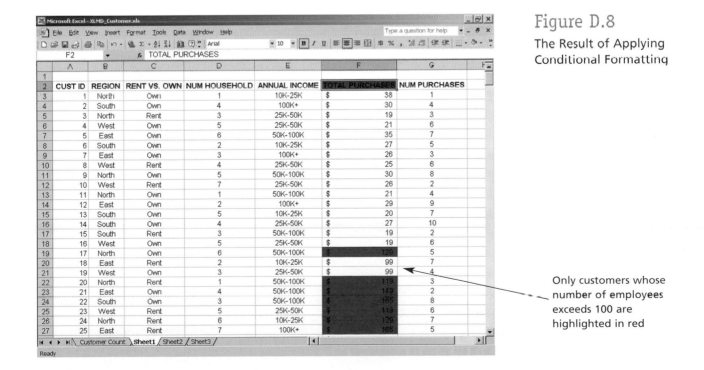

Figure D.8

The Result of Applying
Conditional Formatting

Only customers whose
number of employees
exceeds 100 are
highlighted in red

CONDITIONAL FORMATTING

On the Web site that supports this text (www.mhhe.com/haag and select XLMD), we've provided a workbook titled XLMD_Production.xls. It contains information concerning batches of products produced. Each batch is produced using only one machine by one employee. For each batch, a batch size is provided as well as the number of defective products produced in the batch.

Highlight the following by applying conditional formatting:

1. All batches made by Employee 1111.
2. All batches for which the number of defective products is greater than 10.
3. All batches for which the batch size is greater than 1,000.
4. All batches for Product 10.

Pivot Tables

Now, let's return to our original pivot table in Figure D.1 on page 225. Formally defined, a ***pivot table*** enables you to group and summarize information. That's just what we did in Figure D.1. We created a pivot table that displayed a count of customers by *REGION* and by *RENT VS. OWN.* Of all the Excel decision-support features we demonstrate in this module, pivot tables take the most steps to create, but they also tend to yield highly valuable information.

To create a pivot table, first ensure that your list has no conditional formatting and that you do not have the AutoFilter function turned on. To create any pivot table, follow the four steps at the top of the next page (see Figure D.9).

Figure D.9

The First Steps in Creating a Pivot Table

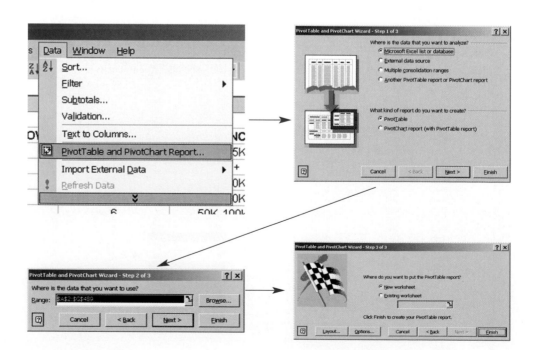

1. From the menu bar, click on **Data** and **PivotTable and PivotChart Report**
2. In the Step 1 of 3 box, click on **Next**
3. In the Step 2 of 3 box, click on **Next**
4. In the Step 3 of 3 box, click on **Finish**

What you will then see is the skeletal structure of a pivot table as shown in Figure D.10 below.

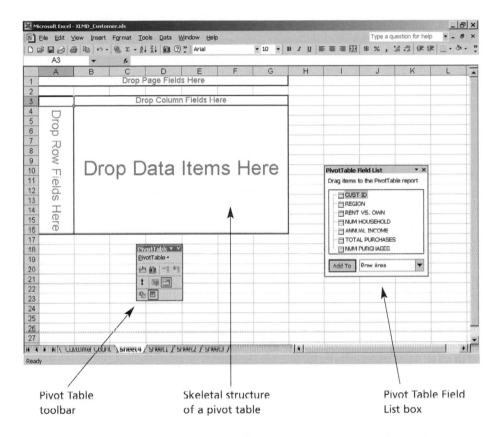

Pivot Table toolbar   Skeletal structure of a pivot table   Pivot Table Field List box

Figure D.10

The Skeletal Structure of a Pivot Table and the Pivot Table Toolbar

BUTTON NAME	PURPOSE
PivotTable	Drop-down that displays shortcut menu of pivot table commands
Format Report	Displays a list of pivot table report styles
Chart Wizard	Creates a chart sheet from a pivot table
MapPoint	Creates map from PivotTable data
Hide Detail	Hides detail lines of a pivot table field
Show Detail	Reveals detail lines of a pivot table field
Refresh Data	Updates a pivot table
Include Hidden Items in Total	Items you have hidden are still counted in the PivotTable totals
Always Display Items	Controls when Excel goes to an external data source to determine a pivot table value
Field Settings	Opens the PivotTable field dialog box containing options you can apply to the selected pivot table field
Hide/Show Field Test	Toggles between hiding and displaying the field list

To provide a brief explanation of what we've done so far, let's examine the three dialog boxes in Figure D.9 on page 234. The first box allows you to choose the location of the information from which you want to build a pivot table. We wanted to use an Excel list so we accepted the default. The first box also gives you the ability to choose between creating a pivot table or a pivot table chart. We wanted a pivot table so we accepted the default.

The second box allows you to choose a range of information from which to build a pivot table. The default is the entire list, which we accepted. Finally, the third box allows you to specify a location for the pivot table. The default is a new worksheet, which we accepted. At some point in time, you should explore the various other options.

What you see in Figure D.10 on page 235 takes some more explaining. In the upper left portion is the skeletal structure of the pivot table. To the right, you can see the Pivot Table Field List box. It includes a list of all the labels or column headings we have in the list.

Near the bottom left, you can see the Pivot Table toolbar. It includes numerous buttons for different functions. The primary one of interest to us now is the **Field Settings** button, the lowest and leftmost button in the toolbar. Figure D.10 lists and explains all the buttons in the Pivot Table toolbar.

What you do now is to drag and drop the appropriate labels or columns headings from the Pivot Table Field List box into the appropriate areas of the pivot table itself.

Recall that we are attempting to build a pivot table that looks like the one in Figure D.1 on page 225. So, you know that the row information is by *REGION*. To achieve this, drag the *REGION* label from the Pivot Table Field List box to the pivot table and drop it into the area marked "Drop Row Fields Here" (see Figure D.11). You also know that the column information is by *RENT VS. OWN*. So, drag that label from the Pivot Table Field List box and drop it into the area marked "Drop Column Fields Here."

Figure D.11

Creating a Pivot Table by Dragging and Dropping Information

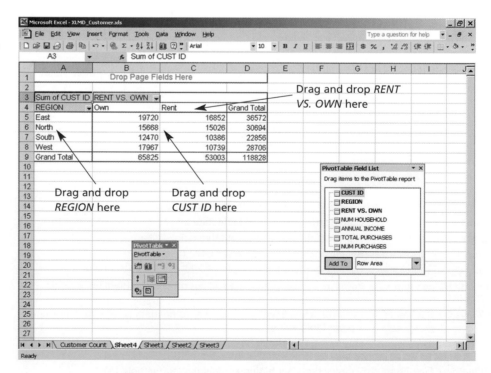

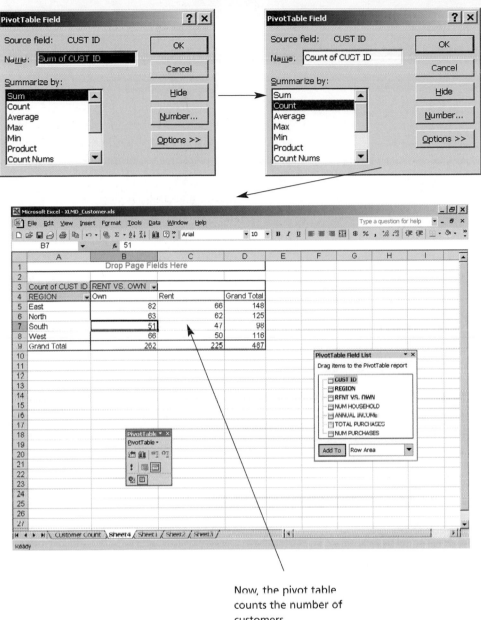

Now, the pivot table
counts the number of
customers

Finally, you need to place something in the main area of the pivot table that will enable you to count customers by region and rent versus own. The simplest way to achieve this is to drag *CUST ID* from the Pivot Table Field List box and drop it into the area marked "Drop Data Items Here." What you will then have is a pivot table that looks like the final screen in Figure D.11 on page 236, which is not at all what we want. Why?

When you drop information into the main area of a pivot table, the default aggregation or summarization is by summation. You don't want to sum customer IDs—that doesn't make any sense. What you want to do is count them. To change this, perform the following steps (see Figure D.12):

1. Click on the **Field Settings** button in the Pivot Table toolbar
2. In the PivotTable Field box, click on **Count** in the **Summarize by** list
3. Click on **OK**

The final screen in Figure D.12 shows the correct information.

ON YOUR OWN

CREATING A PIVOT TABLE

Let's return to our workbook containing production information (XLMD_Production.xls). Using it, create separate pivot tables that show

- The number of different machines used to produce each product
- The number of defective products produced by employee by product
- The total number of products produced by each employee
- The total number of products produced by each employee as well as the total number of defective products produced by each employee

We now have a pivot table that shows a count of customers by *REGION* and *RENT VS. OWN*. But depending on what decision you're trying to make, that may not be enough information. What else might be helpful? Again, depending on the decision, it might be helpful to also know the total of all purchases by *REGION* and *RENT VS. OWN*. If so, you don't need to create another pivot table. You can simply add the field *TOTAL PURCHASES* to the main area of the pivot table. To do so, drag that label from the Pivot Table Field List box and drop it into the main area of the pivot table. Figure D.13 shows the result.

Is the information helpful? Again, it depends on the decision you're trying to make. But adding another piece of information to the main area of a pivot table is easy, and it does illustrate the true productivity of spreadsheet software.

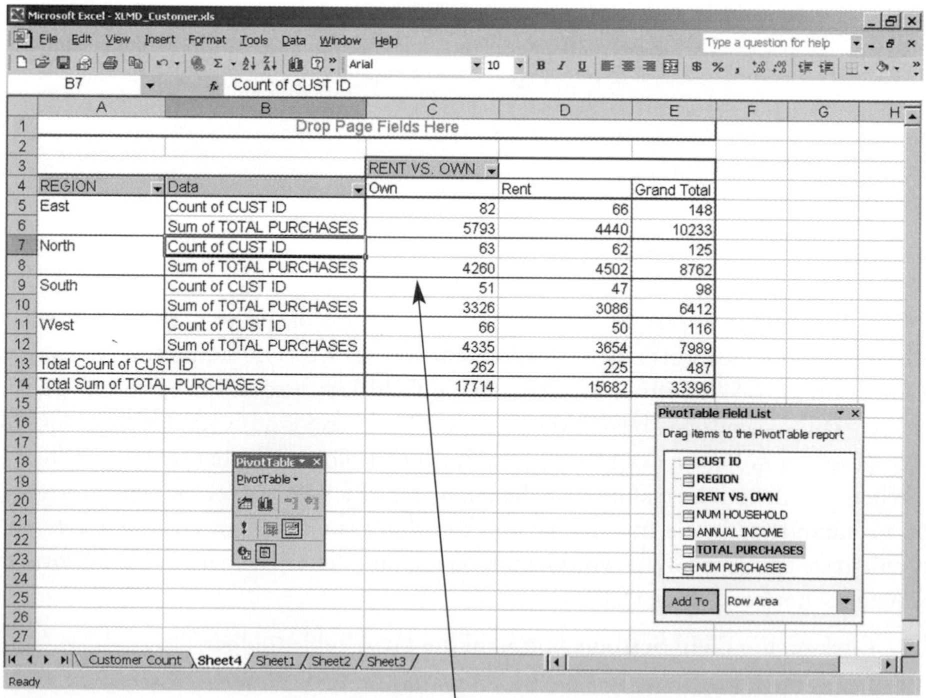

REGION	Data	RENT VS. OWN: Own	Rent	Grand Total
East	Count of CUST ID	82	66	148
	Sum of TOTAL PURCHASES	5793	4440	10233
North	Count of CUST ID	63	62	125
	Sum of TOTAL PURCHASES	4260	4502	8762
South	Count of CUST ID	51	47	98
	Sum of TOTAL PURCHASES	3326	3086	6412
West	Count of CUST ID	66	50	116
	Sum of TOTAL PURCHASES	4335	3654	7989
Total Count of CUST ID		262	225	487
Total Sum of TOTAL PURCHASES		17714	15682	33396

Drag and drop *TOTAL PURCHASES* here to obtain a summary of another dimension of information

Figure D.13

An Added Field of Information to a Pivot Table

Back to Decision Support

Let's take a break from the computer for a moment and discuss what we've just demonstrated within the context of decision support. After all, you don't need to learn the various tools of spreadsheet software just because "they are there." You should learn them because they will be beneficial to you.

In general, the spreadsheet features we've just shown you give you the ability to look at vast amounts of information quickly. Indeed, our customer workbook contained information on 487 customers. Can you imagine trying to summarize or aggregate information on 48,700 customers without the use of spreadsheet software? Even creating simple totals and subtotals would be a daunting task.

AUTOFILTER

The AutoFilter function (either basic or custom) helps you quickly create a view of a partial list of information. The basic AutoFilter function creates a partial list based on exact match criteria, while the custom AutoFilter function allows you to specify ranges (e.g., greater than, less than, and so on).

The purpose of the AutoFilter function is really to help you quickly focus on only the information that's important to you by "hiding" the information that isn't. It's rather like having a very good search engine that only gives you a list of useful articles to help you write a term paper.

CONDITIONAL FORMATTING

Conditional formatting maintains the view of the entire list of information but highlights key pieces of information that you may be looking for. This gives you the ability to see the entire list of information but quickly draws your attention to specific information.

PIVOT TABLE

A pivot table helps you quickly aggregate or summarize information by *dimension*. This gives you a nice overview of the information without bogging you down in any of the details.

Further, a pivot table can help you see relationships among the information. If you look back at the pivot table in Figure D.13 on page 238, you can see the relationship between the number of customers and their total purchases within *REGION* and *RENT VS. OWN*. These types of relationships can certainly be insightful.

Can any of these tools or functions make a decision for you? Definitely not. But they can help you make that decision. That's why spreadsheet software is often called *decision support* software.

Summary: Student Learning Outcomes Revisited

1. **Define a list and list definition table within the context of spreadsheet software and describe the importance of each.** A *list* is a collection of information arranged in columns and rows in which each column displays one particular type of information. A *list definition table* is a description of a list by column. Lists are important within the context of spreadsheet software because they enable you to use such spreadsheet features as AutoFilter, conditional formatting, and pivot tables. Creating a list definition table is important because it requires you to adhere to the necessary rules for creating a list.

2. **Compare and contrast the AutoFilter function and Custom AutoFilter function in spreadsheet software.** The *AutoFilter function* filters a list and allows you to hide all the rows in a list except those that match specific criteria you specify. The *Custom AutoFilter function* allows you to hide all the rows in a list except those that match criteria, besides "is equal to," you specify.

So, the basic AutoFilter function makes use of "is equal to" as the criteria, while the Custom AutoFilter function allows you to use other criteria such as greater than, less than, and so on.

3. **Describe the purpose of using conditional formatting.** *Conditional formatting* highlights the information in a cell that meets some criteria you specify. So, conditional formatting allows you to view the entire list while having certain information called to your attention.

4. **Define a pivot table and describe how you can use it to view summarized information by dimension.** A *pivot table* enables you to group and summarize information. When creating a pivot table, you create dimensions of information by specifying how information is to be summarized by dimension. You define the dimensions by dragging and dropping information labels or column headings into the row and column areas of a pivot table.

Key Terms and Concepts

AutoFilter function, 228
Conditional formatting, 232
Custom AutoFilter function, 230

List, 226
List definition table, 227
Pivot table, 234

Assignments and Exercises

1. **WHAT PRODUCTION PROBLEMS DO YOU HAVE?** Throughout this module, you've been practicing some spreadsheet features using XLMD_Production.xls. Its list definition table is as follows:

   A. *BATCH*—A unique number that identifies each batch or group of products produced

   B. *PRODUCT*—A unique number that identifies each product

   C. *MACHINE*—A unique number that identifies each machine on which products are produced

   D. *EMPLOYEE*—A unique number that identifies each employee producing products

   E. *BATCH SIZE*—The number of products produced in a given batch

   F. *NUM DEFECTIVE*—The number of defective products produced in a given batch

   It seems you have some real problems. There are an unacceptable number of defective products being produced. Your task is to use some combination of AutoFilter, conditional formatting, and pivot tables to illustrate where the problems seem to be concentrated, perhaps by product, by employee, by machine, or even by batch size. Based on your analysis, recommend how to correct the problems.

2. **EVALUATING TOTAL PURCHASES AND ANNUAL INCOME** Using XLMD_Customer.xls, create a pivot table that illustrates the relationship between *TOTAL PURCHASES* and *ANNUAL INCOME*. What trends do you see in the information? Suppose your task is to concentrate marketing efforts and resources. On which annual income level would you concentrate? Why? If you were the marketing manager, what additional information would be helpful as you make your decision? Where would you be able to obtain such information?

3. **FINDING OUT INFORMATION ABOUT YOUR EMPLOYEES** Suppose you own a small business and have a workbook with the following list:
   A. *ID*—Unique employee's identification number
   B. *First Name*—Employee's first name
   C. *Last Name*—Employee's last name
   D. *Department*—Employee's department
   E. *Title*—Employee's job title
   F. *Salary*—Employee's annual salary
   G. *Hire Date*—Date employee was hired
   H. *Birth Date*—Employee's birthday
   I. *Gender*—Female (F) or male (M)
   J. *Clearance*—N (none), C (confidential), S (secret), or TS (top secret)

   You can obtain this workbook from the Web site that supports this text (www.mhhe.com/haag and select XLM/D). Its filename is XLMD_Employee.xls. Perform the following tasks:
   a. Create a pivot table that shows average salary by gender within department.
   b. Create a pivot table that shows the number of employees by clearance.
   c. Use conditional formatting to highlight those employees in the Engineering department.
   d. Use conditional formatting to highlight those employees who have no clearance (none).
   e. Use basic AutoFilter to show only those employees who have top secret clearance (TS).
   f. Use Custom AutoFilter to show only those employees who earn more than $50,000.

4. **EXPLORING INFORMATION AT B&B TRAVEL** Benjamin Travis and Brady Austin are co-owners of B&B Travel Consultants, a medium-size business in Seattle with several branch offices. B&B specializes in selling cruise packages. Ben and Brady maintain a workbook that contains the following list for each cruise package sale:
   A. *LOCATION #*—A unique number that identifies which office location recorded the sale
   B. *TRAVEL AGENT #*—A unique number that identifies which travel consultant recorded the sale
   C. *CRUISE LINE*—The name of the cruise line for which the package was sold
   D. *TOTAL PACKAGE PRICE*—The price charged to the customer for the package
   E. *COMMISSION*—The amount of money B&B made from the sale of the package

   Ben and Brady have decided to scale back their operations. So, they're looking to you for help. The workbook name is XLMD_Travel.xls and you can find it on the Web site that supports this text at www.mhhe.com/haag (select XLM/D). Using AutoFilter, conditional formatting, and pivot tables, prepare a short report that answers each of the following questions and illustrates the justification for your answers.
   a. Which, if any, location should be closed?
   b. Which, if any, travel consultants should be downsized?
   c. On which cruise lines should B&B focus its sales efforts?

5. **CREATE A LIST FOR A BOOKSTORE** Suppose that you're the manager for your school's bookstore. Your task is to create a list in a workbook that contains information about the textbooks it sells. In addition to tracking price, first author name, and publisher, identify five other pieces of information for each textbook. For this list, first provide a list definition table. Second, enter some information for 20 textbooks. Third, illustrate the use of the basic AutoFilter function, the Custom AutoFilter function, conditional formatting, and pivot tables. Finally, address how your bookstore might be able to use this information to support its decision-making tasks.

CHAPTER FIVE OUTLINE

STUDENT LEARNING OUTCOMES

1 Describe the four main perspectives of e-commerce, its current status, and the global growth expected in the next few years.

2 Identify the advantages of business to consumer (B2C) e-commerce.

3 Describe the techniques that lead to success in B2C e-commerce ventures.

4 Describe the variety of ways that business to business (B2B) e-commerce technologies are being used, and describe next-generation models which may widen the adoption of global B2B e-commerce.

5 Identify the unique aspects of e-government applications.

6 Describe the status and options for e-commerce payment systems.

WEB SUPPORT

www.mhhe.com/haag

- Competitive intelligence
- Storefront software
- Hosting services
- Marketing the site
- B2B marketplaces

CHAPTER FIVE

Electronic Commerce
Strategies for the New Economy

OPENING CASE STUDY:
SODAS AND SNACK FOOD ON THE WEB

Cans of soda are probably one of the last things we would think of buying online. They're available on nearly every street corner.

Despite this, Pepsi-Cola Company (PepsiCo) has a number of Internet initiatives under way, from music sites to banner ads to Internet sweepstakes. And more are on the drawing board. Even though it is currently spending only 3 percent of its $400 million ad budget on the Internet, Pepsi is placing a lot of emphasis on the medium as an effective way of reaching the most desirable customers. For example, in a deal put together with Yahoo!, Pepsi agreed to put the Yahoo! logo on 1.5 billion cans of Pepsi. In return, Yahoo! encouraged its visitors to visit the "Pepsi Stuff" site.

Three million consumers logged on to Pepsi Stuff and provided Pepsi with detailed demographic information about themselves. Pepsi's sales volume was up by 5 percent as a result of the promotion at a cost of about one-fifth of a traditional mail-in project.

Pepsi intends to keep using the Web as its medium of choice because it is also the medium of choice for its target market—those under 25. They simply decided that it makes sense to flash the Pepsi logo where their target customers hang out.

As it moves forward, Pepsi will expand its Web-centric marketing efforts. While banner ads and other more traditional methods have had some success, it's the creation of engaging Pepsi Web sites that has given the brand the best results online. As the technology expands, Pepsi expects the creative potential of what can be done on the Web to explode.

Well, you can't just have a Pepsi without having some snack foods to go with it, and Frito-Lay makes a bunch of them. As a matter of fact, if you go to their Web site (www.frito-lay.com), you'll be able to find their mission statement: "To be the world's favorite snack and always within arm's reach." (Not a bad mission statement when you think about it. After all, they'll sure sell more snack food if they're within arm's reach!) And Frito-Lay has a ton of snack food brands to sell you: Lays and Ruffles potato chips, Doritos tortilla chips, Tostitos, Cracker Jack, and Grandma's cookies among them.

Frito-Lay is a unit of PepsiCo and, as you might expect, also uses the Web as a way to reach out to its customers. They attract customers to their Web site by offering dietary information (to make you feel less guilty about snacking) as well as recipes that may never have occurred to you (such as Lays potato chip cookies). They are also reaching out to a younger audience by operating ePloids (www.eploids.com), the "World's 1st On-Line Auction for Kids." Ploids can be obtained from specially marked snack food packages and used as digital currency for the auction.[1]

Introduction

You've probably heard the ancient Chinese curse, "May you live in interesting times." It's a curse because it is often easier to live in times that are not so interesting, when things move along pretty much as expected, as they always have. The past few years of the new economy introduced by the World Wide Web have certainly been interesting. There has been an entrepreneurial frenzy unlike anything the world has ever seen. Fortunes have been made and lost. Dot-com millionaires and billionaires were created. Some have seen their fortunes increase while others have watched their dot-com business wonders turn into "dot-bombs." Despite all the turmoil, most observers of the e-commerce scene believe that the revolution in business promised by the Internet has just begun. One has said it's "like we're in the first minute of the first period of a hockey game." We have some hint of how e-commerce is going to unfold. We are learning what works and what doesn't work. But there is a lot of uncharted territory ahead. There will be new winners and new losers. That is why it is so important that you learn ways to help your organization develop a winning strategy for the new economy.

The Growth of E-Commerce

Maybe we ought to start with a definition, because there are many definitions of e-commerce. We like this one. **_E-commerce_** is commerce, but it is commerce accelerated and enhanced by IT, in particular the Internet. It enables customers, consumers, and companies to form powerful new relationships that would not be possible without the enabling technologies.

But let's not forget that, fundamentally, it's all still about _commerce,_ people buying and selling products and services from and to each other. The Internet facilitates commerce by its awesome ability to move digital information at low cost.

As illustrated in Figure 5.1, there are four main perspectives for e-commerce: Business to Business (B2B), Business to Consumer (B2C), Consumer to Business (C2B), and Consumer to Consumer (C2C). We'll focus on B2C and B2B in this chapter, but we have also included a short discussion on the roles that governments can play as well.

B2C is what you read about the most in the popular press. These are the e-commerce sites that sell products and services, or provide information services directly to consumers. They include such well-known companies as Yahoo!, Amazon.com, and LandsEnd.com.

Figure 5.1

Four Categories of E-Commerce[2]

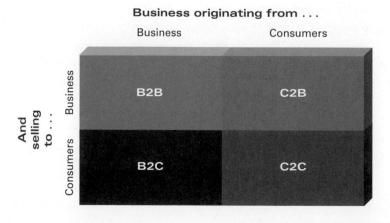

Even though most of the media's attention is focused on B2C, the dollar volume of e-commerce has always been widely expected to be concentrated in the B2B segment, where businesses buy and sell from and to each other. This is because the B2B segment is so much larger, regardless of whether we're talking about e-commerce or traditional commerce.

The C2C sector is where consumers deal with each other. Probably the best examples of C2C e-commerce are the online auction sites. EBay is the most well-known such site and is one of the real success stories of e-commerce.

Finally, the C2B sector is the one in which the Internet makes it possible for many consumers who want to buy the same or similar products to band together in order to obtain volume discounts from a business. This process is known as demand aggregation. **Demand aggregation** combines purchase requests from multiple buyers into a single large order, which justifies a discount from the business. While it's possible to aggregate consumer demand on the Internet, the best-known company to try it, Mercata, was unsuccessful and went out of business. If you'd like to see an example of a company that aggregates demand of consumers interested in high speed Internet access, go to www.sugarloaf.net, a company that brags that it brings "Bandwidth to the Boonies." Demand aggregation is also possible and much more widespread, of course, in the B2B sector (see www.unistarllc.com/ for an example).

GLOBAL E-COMMERCE GROWTH PROJECTIONS

As shown in Figure 5.2, NUA estimated that there were 544 million Internet users worldwide in February 2002. The *Computer Industry Almanac* estimates that this will rise to 945 million by the year 2004.[3] While growth cannot continue at such a pace for very long, the ultimate number of Internet users worldwide will clearly be an impressive figure.

In a survey released in September 2001, Jupiter Media Matrix estimated that 36 percent of all U.S. B2B spending, or $5.4 trillion, would be done online by the year 2006.[4] Later, in May of 2002, ElectricNews.Net reported that European business-to-business

Figure 5.2

How Many Online?

Based in Dublin, Ireland, NUA is an Internet thought leader and consultancy that is perhaps best known for its Internet surveys. Its Web site, (www.nua.com) is a good source of information on Internet demographics and activity. Here is NUA's "educated guess" as to the number of users online worldwide in February 2002.[5]

	Millions Online
Africa	4.15
Asia/Pacific	157.49
Europe	171.35
Middle East	4.65
Canada & USA	181.23
Latin America	25.33
World total	**544.20**

e-commerce sales are expected to grow from $500 billion in 2002 to $2.3 trillion by 2005.[6] In April 2002, eMarketer estimated worldwide e-commerce sales of $557 billion, about 86 percent of it in the B2B space.[7]

You must use growth projections such as the ones cited here with caution, because they are, in fact, estimates. Nevertheless, the consensus of knowledgeable observers of the e-commerce scene is consistent in their expectations that it has nowhere to go but up (and up).

THE DIGITAL DIVIDE

You will notice from Figure 5.2 that the number of Internet users varies from region to region in the world. Less-developed regions have fewer users than more-developed regions. This phenomenon is called the "digital divide." The phrase the *digital divide* expresses the fact that different peoples, cultures, and areas of the world or within a nation do not have the same access to information and telecommunications technologies. For example, Finland and the other Scandinavian countries have a high population online. These small countries are affluent, with a tradition of good telecommunications systems. Just the opposite is true in Africa and Latin America, as another example. Many of these areas have large populations, are poor, and do not have state-of-the-art computer and telecommunications infrastructures, thus creating a global digital divide. The *global digital divide* specifically describes the differences in IT access and capabilities between different countries or regions of the world. Many e-commerce policy experts are concerned that the global digital divide threatens to restrict the benefits of global e-commerce to just the wealthy nations.

The Advantages of Business to Consumer E-Commerce

We noted previously in this chapter that B2C e-commerce was relatively small compared to B2B e-commerce. It is also small compared to the other forms of retail commerce, principally catalogs and retail stores. As we discuss in this section, although retailers based solely on the Internet will continue to exist, the overall trend in the B2C space seems to be one in which retailers increasingly view the Internet as simply another channel by which to reach their customers. As we shall see, however, it is a channel that possesses some unique and powerful advantages over traditional channels when it is used effectively. Knowing when to use it, how to use it effectively, and when to use it in combination with other channels, is key.

In addition to the opportunity to employ the techniques of mass customization and personalization we discussed in Chapter 2, the Internet has several current and potential advantages over the traditional retailing channels of brick-and-mortar stores and catalog sales. The Internet's most prominent advantages are

1. Shopping can be faster and more convenient.
2. Offerings and prices can change instantaneously.
3. Call centers can be integrated with the Web site.
4. Broadband telecommunications will enhance the buying experience.

THE RIGHT TOOL FOR ACE HARDWARE

In most small hardware stores, there's a gray-haired guy wearing a red shop apron who can answer any question you might have. For example, if you say you want to put a bird feeder on a pole, the wise old guy says, "You need a flange fastener." Or, if you want to hang shutters he'll tell you, "You need pintles." He knows all the doohickeys: T-joints, pan head screws, toggle bolts, rheostats, turnbuckles, and ball valves. Even more importantly, he also knows where they are in the store.

That's great for the customers, but where do the Ace Hardware dealers themselves turn when they need some advice on how to run their businesses better; how to find and serve business customers better, for example?

Up to now, Ace's dealers were out of luck. They met to compare notes at conventions only a couple of times a year. Many had little further contact with each other, or even with Ace headquarters, because dealers operate as independents. They sell some Ace products but don't work for Ace and are free to offer goods made by other suppliers.

Recently, Ace began deploying a Web site that illustrates the power of a Web-based community by demonstrating that "Nobody is as smart as everybody." They began with an electronic meeting-place—a sort of virtual gray-haired guy for the 300 or so dealers that peddle Ace products to businesses. The move was so successful it was expanded to serve all 5,000 Ace dealers. While some information and advice is available on the site, the main attraction for Ace's dealers is that they can discuss do's, don'ts, and doohickeys with each other.

Ace and its dealers are delighted with the site. Although Ace won't get too specific, it does say that the exchange of ideas and information by the online community has increased sales so much that it achieved a 500 percent return on its investment in the first six months.[8]

SHOPPING CAN BE FASTER AND MORE CONVENIENT

Some brick-and-mortar stores are open 24 hours a day, seven days a week, but most are not. Internet sites are open all the time. You've probably experienced the frustration of going from one store to another, from one shopping mall to another, fighting traffic, trying to find a place to park, looking for that one certain item.

Catalog shopping avoids some of the irritations of brick-and-mortar shopping by letting you pick out the item you want from a catalog, dial a toll-free telephone number, and order the item. Many catalog retailers such as Lands' End and Eddie Bauer are open 24 hours a day, seven days a week, but others are not. Although the service of some catalog retailers is very good, others put you on hold and make you listen to music you don't like until the customer service rep comes on the line. In order to comparison shop, you must have all the right catalogs and then page through them in a cumbersome fashion.

Shopping on the Internet, however, can be faster and more convenient. If you don't find what you want at the right price on one e-tailer's Web site, a click of the mouse will take you to a competitor's site. The term *e-tailer* describes an Internet retail site. E-tailers are further divided into pure plays and clicks-and-mortar sites. *Pure plays* are Internet retailers such as Amazon.com that have no physical stores. *Clicks-and-mortar* retailers, (also called *bricks-and-clicks*), are like Nordstrom, which has both an Internet presence and one or more physical stores. They often have catalogs as well. As far as we

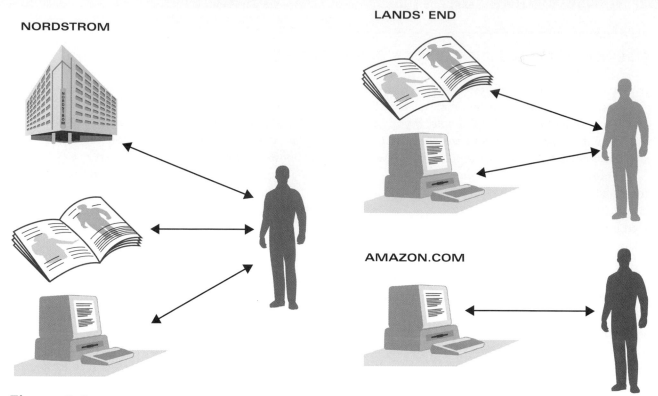

Figure 5.3

Alternative Channels for Selling to Consumers

know, no one has invented a term to describe catalog retailers such as Lands' End that have an Internet presence but no physical stores. Figure 5.3 illustrates these alternative sales channels.

Compare the convenience of shopping on the Internet to driving from one store to another or flipping from catalog to catalog. On the Internet, not only can you go from site to site with the click of a mouse, but you can access sites that offer product and price comparisons as well (e.g., www.mysimon.com). One of the applications suggested for m-commerce relates to price comparisons. *M-commerce* describes e-commerce conducted over a wireless device such as a cell phone or personal digital assistant (PDA). As one example, let's say you're in an electronics store and you notice a DVD player at what seems to be a good price. With m-commerce, you'll be able to find the price at other merchants for the same item simply by using your wireless device. Internet-based services will search the Web and tell you whether the price you see for the item in front of you is a good deal or not. It will be similar to what you can do now sitting in front of your PC.

The emergence of m-commerce has the potential to create what some call a "freedom economy" wherein commerce is not constrained by location. Buying and selling can be done anywhere, at any time. Access to information in corporate databases will also be easily available from anywhere to employees of corporations as well as to customers and suppliers. As with any emerging technology, there are problems to be worked out, but in the opinion of experts, the future for m-commerce is bright enough that it cannot be ignored.[9]

If the product you want to buy is digital, such as software, music, and books, it can be delivered *immediately* over the Internet. This, of course, represents a tremendous advantage over both stores and catalog retailers.

IF I WANT YOUR ADVICE I'LL ASK FOR IT

PK-35 is an amateur soccer team in a suburb of Helsinki, Finland. Like most sports teams, PK-35 has players and a coach. What makes PK-35 different is that their coach, Janne Viljamaa, asks for suggestions from 300 fans via cell phone text messages. Each week, Viljamaa provides between 3 and 10 questions to answer about training, team selection, and game tactics. Fans get three minutes to enter responses, and they get the re-sults back three minutes later. (Fan-driven decisions can produce dramatic results, like the decision to use a sub-stitute who scored a last-minute goal in a critical end-of-season game.)

Noting that the concept works for him, Viljamaa went on to say that "because of our high rate of cell-phone use, Finnish soccer can serve as a test bed before taking the concept to the rest of the world."[10]

OFFERINGS AND PRICES CAN CHANGE INSTANTANEOUSLY

Another advantage e-tailers have is that product offerings and prices can be changed in-stantaneously in response to changes in customer demand. One of the most difficult as-pects of managing a retail operation, particularly with high-fashion goods, is to know how much to order at the beginning of the selling season. You also need to have enough information to reorder early if sales are better than expected, and to reduce prices early if sales are not up to your expectations. Children's toys, for example, also fall into this category because toys can be "hot" during the critical holiday selling season. One year it's Pokemon and the next year it's the PlayStation.

In March or April of each year, retail merchandisers try to estimate the quantity of each item they will sell in November and December, because that's when orders must be placed with manufacturers. When the selling season arrives, actual sales are measured against estimated sales. If sales are taking off, an early order to the manufacturer will make it more likely that more of the hot product can be shipped. If the retailer waits too long, none will be available because everyone else has ordered more, and the manufac-turer either cannot keep up with the incoming orders or they've moved on to produce products for sale after the holiday season. If sales are slower than expected, the retailer must react quickly to reduce the product's price, or there will be piles of unsold products on the shelves. As you know, sometimes an unpopular item is hard even to give away.

Think about the advantage e-tailers have in managing this process. They can obtain real-time information on how sales are going against expectations. More important, they can adjust prices immediately if sales are not going as well as expected. In a way, it's sim-ilar to the yield management systems of the airlines we discussed in Chapter 2, but it is a tremendous advantage for the e-tailer. Many e-tailers have clearance areas on their sites to alert their customers to last minute bargains.

If a catalog retailer wants to reduce its price what does it have to do? Produce moun-tains of catalogs to mail to its customers. If a traditional retailer wants to advertise a sale, usually it must incur the expense and delay of newspaper advertising. E-tailers not only can change prices across the board instantly, but, if they wish, can offer special pric-ing to their best customers by using the personalization techniques we discussed in Chapter 2.

B2C SERVICES

Just about any product you can imagine is offered for sale to consumers over the Internet: books, videos, CDs, automobiles, clothes, groceries. Not only can you buy products over the Internet, you can buy services. There are sites where you can get financial advice, medical advice, weather reports, and more. Find at least 10 sites offering *services* (not products) on the Internet. Many of the sites offering services are free. Make 5 of the 10 sites on your list sites where the consumer must pay for the service.

CALL CENTERS CAN BE INTEGRATED WITH THE WEB SITE

One of the more innovative adaptations in e-tailing has been Web sites that give customers the ability to contact a customer service representative using interactive chat. *Interactive chat* lets you engage in real-time typed exchange of information between you and one or more other individuals over the Internet. LandsEndLive, on the Lands' End site (www.landsend.com) goes even further and gives you the option of communicating with a customer service representative using your choice of interactive chat or the telephone. If you choose to use the telephone, you'll need a second line on which the customer service representative can call you back or you'll need a direct Internet connection. Soon, you'll be able to connect directly to the customer service representative using Internet telephony as long as your computer has a microphone and speakers. *Internet telephony* is a combination of hardware and software that uses the Internet as the medium for transmission of telephone calls in place of traditional telephone networks.

Before long, speech recognition software will reach the point where the need for call center representatives will be reduced, particularly for routine inquiries. Speech recognition helps computers identify spoken words (discussed in more detail in the Chapter 9). If you'd like to see how a speech recognition service works in providing information services to consumers, just dial 800-555-tell in the United States. You'll be connected with "Tell Me," a service that can respond to your spoken commands and provide information on a variety of topics: weather, stock quotes, movie guides, and even driving directions.

BROADBAND TELECOMMUNICATIONS WILL ENHANCE THE BUYING EXPERIENCE

We've already discussed some of the ways that wireless technologies will enhance e-commerce. When broadband telecommunications become widely available the buying experience will also be greatly enhanced. You'll be able to purchase a full-length feature film, for example, and download it in minutes. In addition, the inventory of available films will not be limited to what a video store is able to stock on its shelves. You'll be able to choose any film that has ever been made and it will always be available.

Travel sites will offer full-motion video tours of vacation destinations that will let you get a better appreciation of what that beachfront resort in Costa Rica will really be like before you book it. Automobile buying sites will be able to offer virtual test drives to let you narrow down your choices before you take the time to visit an auto dealership. Think of what will be possible with virtual reality (basically, a 3-D simulation in which you physically participate; this is discussed in more detail in Chapter 9). You will indeed be able to experience Costa Rica without spending the time and money as to actually go there. (Unfortunately—or not—it's unlikely that the relatively inexpensive virtual experience will ever completely match an actual experience.) Can you think of other ways that broadband technologies will enhance the retail e-commerce buying experience?

BROADBAND SERVICES: WHERE DO YOU PLACE YOUR BETS?

Assume that your Aunt Millie has just died and left you $10 million in her will. Because you're young, adventurous, and technologically astute, you decide to invest the entire $10 million in stocks of companies in sectors that will be sure to benefit from the coming surge in broadband telecommunications supporting B2C e-commerce applications.

Because there is intense competition in the industry, and several competing technologies, you decide to consult some of your classmates to decide how to allocate the $10 million. You have the option of keeping all or a portion of the $10 million in T-bills while you wait to see how things unfold.

Allocate the $10 million among the following broadband technologies (or T-bills). Which technol-ogies do you feel will be most successful for B2C e-commerce applications in the United States? Pick one other country and do the same. Be prepared to justify your decisions, and feel free to add other technologies:

ISDN

DSL

Cable

Satellite

Fixed wireless

Fiberless optics

Other

T-bills

Keys to Success in Business to Consumer E-Commerce

It is important to reflect on what lessons have been learned thus far so that new B2C entrepreneurs (perhaps you and a group of classmates) can increase their chances of being successful. Some of the most important lessons are:

1. Commoditylike items work best.
2. Digital products are the best of all.
3. Attracting and retaining customers.
4. Remember the importance of merchandising.
5. You must execute well.
6. Watch the competition.

COMMODITYLIKE ITEMS WORK BEST

People tend to be more comfortable buying items on the Internet that are commodity-like, that is, uniform. You're comfortable buying a book on the Internet because you know it will be just like the one you'd get if you bought it from your local bookstore. You might be less comfortable buying "high touch" products such as furniture. When you buy a chair, you probably want to sit in it to be sure it feels the way you want it to feel. PCs are commoditylike. When you log on to Dell Computer's Web site and configure a computer the way you want it, you can count on its being identical to one configured in the same way by another buyer miles away.

GREEN E-COMMERCE

There are some 4 billion people in the world whose per capita income is less than a tenth that of the United States and other developed countries. One of the challenges facing the world is how to formulate plans for sustainable economic development in lesser-developed countries; that is, development that does not increase global warming, water supply shortages, fisheries depletion, deforestation, and the like. Many think it is possible to use new technologies and new business models to help close the income gap between rich and poor populations in ways that are consistent with the principles of sustainable development. Internet-enabled e-services may prove to be one of the most useful tools to employ in this challenging effort, in the opinion of experts who study this issue.[11]

Two industries that will be interesting to watch in this context are automobiles and groceries. In the case of automobiles, it really doesn't matter where you buy a new car. Whether you buy it from a local dealer or you buy it from a dealer hundreds of miles away at a lower price, you can still get exactly the same car. In theory, you could also log on to the manufacturer's Web site, configure your car just the way you want it, and have it built to your specifications, as if it were a Dell computer. If they could, automobile manufacturers would like to have a process where you do just that because it would help them avoid building cars that sell slowly and sit in dealers' lots. The manufacturers typically subsidize dealers' inventory carrying costs and on top of that, often have to offer rebates to buyers to get rid of surplus cars. The biggest reason the manufacturers have not gone to a direct sell model is the resistance they got from the National Automobile Dealers Association when they floated the idea. The dealers concluded they had no intention of getting disintermediated like the travel agents and had enough clout to force the manufacturers to back down. Don't be surprised if the manufacturers keep trying, though.

The reason grocery sales over the Internet will be interesting to watch is that the things we buy in grocery stores are a mixture of commodity and noncommodity items. Examples of commodity items are laundry detergents or breakfast cereals. Examples of noncommodity items are produce and fish. You might not mind having someone else pick a box of breakfast cereal off the shelf for you, but you might prefer to choose your own tomatoes or salmon. One of the most spectacular of the dot-com failures was Webvan, an online grocer. Still others, like Peapod (www.peapod.com), are still in business. Groceries may well settle in as an industry where a bricks-and-clicks model ultimately makes the most sense.

DIGITAL PRODUCTS ARE THE BEST OF ALL

The reasons we say that digital products are best suited for B2C e-commerce are the following:

1. They are commoditylike products.
2. They can be mass-customized and personalized.
3. They can be delivered at the time of purchase.
4. They foster disintermediation.
5. They have global reach.

We first introduced some of these ideas in Chapter 2 when we gave customized CDs and downloaded software as examples. There are, of course, many other examples: videos (when the necessary bandwidth becomes available) and any text product such as books, newspapers, articles, or manuscripts.

Now, much of the information available on the Internet is free. You can go to the Web sites of many newspapers and magazines and get current information and search the on-line archives of back issues. At the present time, most such sites are either losing money or attempting to support themselves with advertising. Some, such as the online version of the *Wall Street Journal* charge an annual subscription fee. Others, such as *Business Week,* make some information free and restrict access to other stories to their print subscribers.

Many observers forecast that, in time, you'll be asked to pay for much of the information you now get for free. One technology that will hasten this is called micro-payments. *Micro-payments* are techniques to facilitate the exchange of small amounts of money for an Internet transaction. Most B2C transactions today are paid for by credit card. It is not practical to process small payments on credit cards because of credit card transaction processing costs. With micro-payments, however, an online newspaper in London could charge you 5 cents for a theater timetable. If you were on your way to London and wondering which play to see, you might find that 5 cents was a bargain. And for the newspaper, 5 cents here and 5 cents there could soon add up to some real money. We'll talk more about micro-payments later in this chapter when we discuss smart cards.

ATTRACTING AND RETAINING CUSTOMERS

Designing an attractive Web site that is easy to use is one of the key factors in the success of a B2C venture. As previously mentioned, and as you well know, it's very easy for potential customers to leave your site for your competitor's site with a click of the mouse. So, once they've found your site, it's important to keep them there until they purchase something, and once they've purchased something, you need to give them an incentive to return. You must not turn them off with an unattractive or customer-unfriendly Web site. Some tips from a professional Web site designer are listed in Figure 5.4.

Figure 5.4

Do's and Don'ts of Web Site Design[12]

Toni Will-Harris has 10 do's and don'ts for Web site design. A condensed version appears here. The complete version can be found on her Web site: http://www.efuse.com/Design/top_10_do_s_and_don_ts.html.

1. Keep graphic files small. The longer a graphic file takes to load, the higher the probability the user will leave before it's done.
2. Keep text files small for the same reason.
3. Design text and backgrounds for easy reading.
4. Design for 256 colors and 640 × 480 resolution. It's the lowest common denominator for older computers.
5. Use "ALT" tags on graphics. ALT text appears before the graphic does, or in place of the graphic for users who have turned graphics off for speed.
6. Include your company name, address, e-mail address, and your phone and fax numbers on every page.
7. Keep your site fresh. It's important to change content frequently so people have something to come back for.
8. Be generous. The more detail you offer, the more reason you give people to visit your site.
9. Be backward compatible. Using cutting-edge technology may shut out some readers.
10. Test your site as visitors will see it, using all versions of the popular browsers.

SHOULD YOU OUTSOURCE YOUR COMPANY'S LOGISTICS TO UPS?

UPS (www.ups.com) established a new business unit, UPS Supply Chain Solutions, in February 2002. The new organization makes it easier for customers to access UPS's expanding range of logistics, freight, financial, and consulting services in order to improve the performance of their global supply chains.

UPS Supply Chain Solutions offers customers the combined services of UPS Logistics Group, UPS Freight Services, UPS Capital, UPS Consulting, and UPS Mail Innovations. Together, these companies provide supply chain design and management, freight forwarding, customs brokerage, mail services, multimodal transportation, consulting, and financial services.

The company's supply chain services also leverage UPS's expertise in building and operating global IT and physical infrastructures and managing complex networks. Companies who do not possess world-class competence in supply chain management systems could let UPS run their systems for them (for a fee, of course).[13]

Because entry barriers can be lower on the Internet than in traditional retailing, there can be many Web sites competing for the same customers. Successful B2C businesses have learned that attracting and retaining customers is vitally important.

Of course, with a B2C Web site, it's not enough to simply "build it and they will come." You have to find a way to let potential customers know that you are there and that, among the many choices they have, your Web site is the one they should choose to visit. Your Web site needs to be marketed.

When marketing professionals consider how to market and promote a business, they talk about the marketing mix. *Marketing mix* is the set of marketing tools that the firm uses to pursue its marketing objectives in the target market.[14] Bricks-and-mortar retailers have traditionally used a combination of techniques such as newspaper advertising, direct mail, radio, and television to attract customers to their stores. Traditional marketing techniques such as those just mentioned are also used by dot-com companies. For example, you've probably seen magazine ads with a company's Web site address prominently displayed, or seen television ads for a dot-com company.

In the B2C e-commerce space, there are additional techniques for attracting customers using the Internet itself. Some of these include:

1. Registering with search engines
2. Online ads
3. Viral marketing
4. Affiliate programs
5. Selling to existing customers

REGISTERING WITH SEARCH ENGINES Many Web surfers use search engines to find what they need. So, one of the first things you should do is to register with the various search engines.

You can register your site with some search engines by filling out some forms on their Web sites. There are services that will do this for you for a fee. For some search engines, it is important to put the keywords people will be using in their search arguments in the Web site text or meta tags. *Meta tags* are part of a Web site text not displayed to users but accessible to browsers and search engines for finding and categorizing Web sites.

ONLINE ADS   Many Web sites use banner ads, a small ad on one Web site that advertises the products and services of another business, usually another dot-com business. You've probably seen them on many Web sites that you've visited. According to a recent study published by the Interactive Advertising Bureau,[15] marketers view online advertising as a good way to induce consumers to visit a Web site. Although observers expect the banner ad to be around for awhile, you may have noticed that larger ads are becoming more popular. In addition, new technologies such as Flash and DHTML are being employed more frequently and are thought to hold great promise. More interactive advertising is also in the works for the future. Just as with TV now, some of the most entertaining content we will see on the Internet may well be the ads.

E-MAIL AND VIRAL MARKETING   E-mail marketing has proven to be especially effective for B2C e-commerce. In 2001, for example, e-mail generated 15 percent of online sales in the United States, up from only 3 percent in the year 2000.[16] Sites have various ways of asking for your e-mail address. Most commonly, you supply it when you order something so the site can send you a confirmation of your order. Most sites, at the same time, will ask your permission to send you occasional e-mails announcing special sales or information that may be of interest to you about specials from other B2C companies. The more the company knows about you, the more e-mail offers can be personalized to appeal to you. Much of what makes B2C e-commerce potentially so effective is the ability of companies to build customer databases and then use sophisticated data mining software to help in crafting personal appeals.

Most people don't like to receive spam and immediately delete it from their e-mail inboxes without taking the time to read it. ***Spam*** is unsolicited e-mail. Viral marketing is a technique that gets around spam. ***Viral marketing*** encourages users of a product or service supplied by a B2C company to ask friends to join in as well. A good example is a technique that Blue Mountain Arts (www.bluemountain.com), the e-greeting card company, uses. Whereas its service used to be free, now it charges for it. When your friend sends you an e-birthday card, for example, you receive an e-mail from Blue Mountain containing a Web site address on the Blue Mountain Web site where you can view your card (see Figure 5.5). After reading your card, you'll be invited to send your friend a card

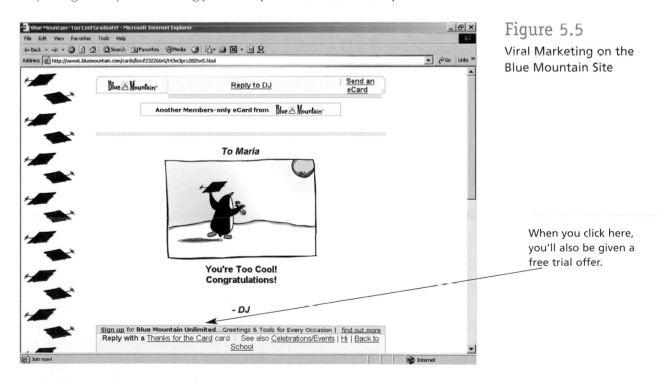

Figure 5.5

Viral Marketing on the Blue Mountain Site

When you click here, you'll also be given a free trial offer.

Figure 5.6

How to Become an
Amazon.com Associate

Here's how it works.

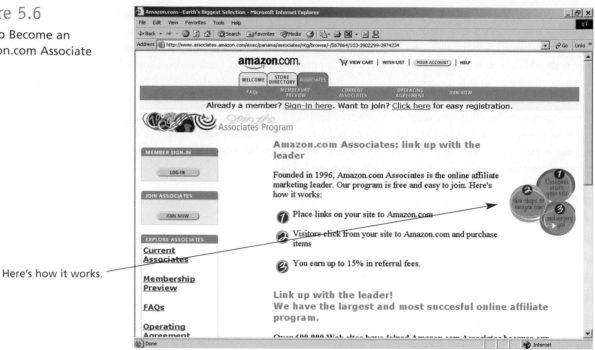

in reply, and if you do, you'll be offered a free one-month trial of the Blue Mountain service. The principle behind viral marketing is that people are more likely to respond to an invitation that was initiated by a friend than one that comes from a company they are not familiar with.

AFFILIATE PROGRAMS   *Affiliate programs* are arrangements made between e-commerce sites that direct users from one site to the other. If a sale is made as a result, the originating site receives a commission. Usually this is done using an online ad in combination with click-throughs or some other measure of effectiveness. ***Click-throughs*** are a count of the number of people who visit one site, click on an ad, and are taken to the site of the advertiser. Software is able to determine the source of visitors to the destination site and give an accurate count of the number who clicked through from the source site so that it can be compensated. For example, Amazon.com has more than 500,000 associates, Web sites with ads directing customer traffic to the Amazon.com site. Every time a customer clicking on the Amazon.com ad on an associate's Web site buys something at Amazon.com, the associate receives a commission of up to 15 percent of the amount of the sale. Information on Amazon.com's associate program is available on its Web site (see Figure 5.6).

SELLING TO EXISTING CUSTOMERS   One of the keys to success in the B2C space is to encourage customers to continue buying from you. As in traditional businesses, B2C entrepreneurs call this "repeat business." It doesn't do you much good to spend a lot of money on marketing programs if customers buy from you only once. One of the most effective ways of generating repeat business is to build a customer database and use it for e-mail permission marketing. As you may recall, unlike spam, permission marketing is when you give a merchant permission to send you offers.

Now we'll show you how one prominent B2C retailer, eBags (www.ebags.com), is using a combination of techniques on its path to profitability. It attracts customers to its Web site using online ads, affiliate programs, and ads in traditional media. Its Web site is well designed and easy to use, content-rich, with multiview photos of products, detailed product descriptions, and customer ratings. It is building a database of customers and asks for permission to e-mail them information on special offerings at reduced prices. It uses a frequent flyer mileage sweepstakes and viral marketing to help build the database.

As customers return to the site, eBags analyzes their usage patterns and learns which products they're most interested in. It adds this information to its database and uses powerful data mining tools to help personalize offers to its customers.

It keeps track of the conversion rate and the amount of the average sale. ***Conversion rate*** is the percentage of customers who visit the site who actually buy something. Knowing the number of visits it receives each day, as well as the conversion rate and average sale amount, eBags can easily project sales revenue per day. Knowing its costs, it is able to determine where its breakeven point lies. It can also quickly forecast the effect on profits if it's able to increase the number of visitors to the site, increase the conversion rate, or increase the average sale amount.

REMEMBER THE IMPORTANCE OF MERCHANDISING

A B2C business must do an effective job of merchandising. That means it must understand its customer base well enough to be able to select products that will appeal to them and that are attractively displayed. An example of a company that does this well is RedEnvelope (www.redenvelope.com). RedEnvelope is a site that specializes in gifts (see Figure 5.7). It takes its name from the Asian tradition of presenting gifts in a red envelope to signify good fortune, love, and appreciation. It is a site worth visiting to see how an e-tailer has combined attractive design, ease of use, and skillful product selection. It offers a wide variety of products for the gift-giver. One of its most creative features is a category called "Express Gifts," designed to serve procrastinators. If you order a gift from this category before midnight, RedEnvelope guarantees that it will be delivered the next day.

Figure 5.7

Red Envelope's Home Page: A Very Well-Designed Site

Clicking here will take you to the Express Gifts page. Great when you're late!

EVALUATING COMPETING WEB SITES

Team up with two or three classmates to select and compare the Web sites of two local retailers that are in the same business. For example, you might choose two bicycle shops, two musical instrument stores, or two pet shops, but the choice is yours. Use the list of "do's and don'ts" from Figure 5.4 to compare the two sites, along with other criteria you might like to add. Look at the range of information resources and services used in the sites and the ways in which they are organized, designed, and presented.

The basic question your group should attempt to answer is how well the sites support the conduct of e-commerce. After analyzing the sites, prepare a set of PowerPoint slides comparing the strengths and weaknesses of the two sites. Draw a conclusion as to which one you think does the best job of attracting customers to the Web site and retaining them once they get

there. Also, comment on how well you think each site

- Offers a fast and convenient shopping experience
- Provides access to help or additional information
- Selects desirable products and displays them and describes them in an attractive and easy-to-understand manner
- Describes its method for getting your purchase to you promptly
- Uses online ads, affiliate programs, viral marketing, and e-mail marketing

In your presentation, be sure to highlight important similarities and differences between the two sites. In the conclusion, explain which one your team liked the best, and why, as well as what you learned from this analysis.

YOU MUST EXECUTE WELL

Executing well simply means that when a customer places an order on your Web site, you have to follow through and execute the necessary business processes to get the right item to the customer in a timely fashion. A good B2C site immediately sends an e-mail acknowledgement of the order, containing all of the order details and an estimated ship date. Thus, the customer is reassured the order is received and is being processed. An order number and instructions for follow-up with customer service is also included. When the order is shipped, the customer receives another e-mail giving details on the shipment such as a carrier tracking number and expected delivery date.

Making it easy to return unwanted items is also important. Some B2C companies include easy cost-free instructions for returning items along with each shipment. Clicks-and-mortar companies have an advantage in this respect if they permit online customers to return items to the local store. Part of the shakeout among online toy retailers began during the holiday selling season in 1999, when toys were not delivered in time for Christmas morning. The reputations of some retailers suffered so much by their failure to execute well that they never recovered.

WATCH THE COMPETITION

Watching the competition is good advice for any business, but it's especially important for B2C businesses. The reason for this is that, as we have previously discussed, retaining customers is one of the keys to e-commerce success. Because it is so easy to lose a customer to a competitor who comes up with a better idea, it's important to be alert to what the competition is up to. You should try to "get inside the heads" of your competitors as a way of anticipating what their next move might be. Put yourself in their place. What would you do next if you were them?

There are a number of ways you can do this. For example, if you walk into the conference room of a supermarket's corporate office, you'll likely find the walls plastered with their newspaper ads side by side with those of their competitors. Since the Web has global reach, you could have thousands of competitors offering the same products as you. Trying to keep track of what thousands of competitors are doing is next to impossible.

You could spend time on the Web surfing around seeing what's going on in your competitive space by looking at the Web sites of known competitors. Or, you could use one of the Web-based shopping comparison services to compare your prices and delivery options to the competition. You could also use the services of a company like Rival-Watch (www.rivalwatch.com). For a price, it will monitor the activities of as many Web-based competitors as your company can identify. It will inform you on the competition's pricing, product assortment, availability, and even promotional activities. RivalWatch is careful to point out that all of the information they gather on behalf of their clients is publicly available. It's just that most clients don't have the software power to gather and analyze the information for themselves.

Business to Business E-Commerce

B2B e-commerce defines e-commerce that takes place between organizations. Trade is global; companies do business with other companies in countries all over the world. You probably have an idea how common this is if you look at the tag inside your blouse or shirt and see that it was made in Malaysia, Sri Lanka, Peru, or Mongolia.

If you look at the total amount of money that is spent on buying and selling products and services, you'll find that most of it is spent by businesses selling to each other or governments buying from businesses. For example, in order to run an airline, you have to spend a lot of money buying aircraft, fuel, spare parts, and the like. Most such purchases are made from other companies rather than from individuals. To turn it around, by far, most of the sales that Boeing Company makes are to airline companies such as United Airlines rather than to individual consumers. (Occasionally, a rock star will purchase a Boeing 737.) Common estimates are that somewhere between 85 and 90 percent of commerce expenditures are in the B2B space, and that 85 to 90 percent of *e-commerce* dollars will also be spent in the B2B space. Clearly, B2B e-commerce is worth learning more about.

One of the most important ways that B2B e-commerce contrasts with B2C e-commerce is in the importance of relationships. In B2C e-commerce, establishing a relationship with your customer is important because you want customers to return to your Web site to buy from you again, rather than lose them to a competitor. In the B2B space, relationships are even more important. Businesses tend to form longer term relationships with some of their most trusted trading partners. Suppose you're the manager of production in a manufacturing firm when you suddenly get an unexpectedly large rush order from one of your best customers. It will be much easier for you to order the necessary materials you need to build and fill that order if your suppliers are people you've done business with over a period of years. They know you, you know them, and just like a friend, you can count on them to step in and help you out when you need it. Think of how difficult obtaining those needed materials would be if you tried to obtain them quickly from companies you had never done business with before.

Figure 5.8

The Value Network

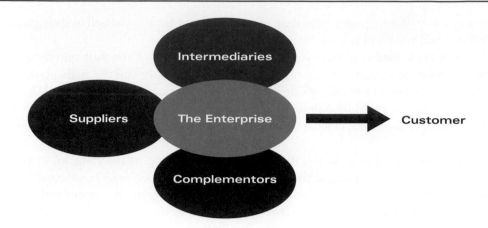

VALUE NETWORKS

Relationships are taking on new forms in the e-commerce environment. Peter Keen and Mark McDonald note that e-commerce "more and more involves a complex network of relationships to operate between the enterprise, its customers, intermediaries, complementors and suppliers."[17] (See Figure 5.8.) *Intermediaries* are specialist companies that provide services better than their client companies can themselves. Examples include such categories as call centers and UPS deliveries. *Complementors* provide products and services that complement the offerings of the enterprise and thereby extend its value-adding capabilities to its customers. Yahoo!, for example, has 10,000 complementors providing services such as weather information, financial news, general news, and so forth that add value to the Yahoo! site. Keen and McDonald go on to emphasize the importance of trading partner relationships in forming a company's value network. A *value network* is all of the resources behind the click on a Web page that the customer doesn't see, but that together create the customer relationship—service, order fulfillment, shipping, financing, information brokering, and access to other products and offers. Some of these resources are provided by software, some are outsourced to trusted trading partners, some are provided by electronic links to alliance partners, and others are handled by more efficient and effective business processes. Managers now have many more choices in how to deliver products and services to you when, where, and how you want them. If a trusted trading partner can perform an essential function better than your company can internally, you have the potential for a winning combination for yourself, your trading partner, and your customer.

CORPORATE PURCHASING SEGMENTS

In the B2B space, most attention has traditionally been given to the ways that e-commerce could streamline the purchasing of materials. This does not mean that e-commerce applications in functions such as sales, transportation, and payments are not important and growing areas; it simply means that attention has been devoted to purchasing because this is where the most money is spent. Purchasing applications are usually divided into three segments:

1. Purchasing of direct materials
2. Purchasing of indirect materials (MRO)
3. Purchasing of services

CORPORATE EXPRESS UPGRADES ITS ONLINE CUSTOMER SERVICE

Corporate Express (www.corporateexpress.com) sells office products, office furniture, and computer supplies both online and through a direct sales force. Their online ordering system, E-Way, has more than 400,000 active users who are expected to purchase more than $1 billion in 2002. Corporate Express plans to introduce a context-sensitive help solution provided by Motive (www.motive.com) as part of an upgrade of E-Way. With the upgrade, when customers have a question or problem, they can simply click on a button available on every page and be presented with a list of questions and answers specifically tailored to that particular page or process.

Overall, Corporate Express believes that Motive's system will improve the online ordering process for its customers, increase customer satisfaction, reduce demand on the service center, and extend its competitive advantage.[18]

Direct materials are materials that are used in production in a manufacturing company or are placed on the shelf for sale in a retail environment. They are called direct because they have a direct relation to the company's primary business.

Indirect materials (commonly called MRO materials) are materials that are necessary for running a modern corporation, but do not relate to the company's primary business activities. MRO is the acronym for **m**aintenance, **r**epair, and **o**perations materials. Examples of MRO materials include everything from ballpoint pens to three-ring binders, repair parts, and lubricating oil.

Examples of purchased services include corporate travel, consulting services, hiring of part-time workers, and the like. Although there are B2B solutions for the purchase of services, most activity in the B2B space is focused on either direct materials or MRO, so this is where we'll focus our discussion.

PURCHASING OF DIRECT MATERIALS   One of the most important contributions to a company's effectiveness made by its purchasing department is in the purchase of direct materials; searching out reliable sources of supply, negotiating price, quality, and delivery performance expectations, and monitoring supplier performance. In the typical setting, a purchasing department reaches an agreement with a supplier based on an estimate of the quantity required over the course of a year. Then, as goods are needed to satisfy production requirements, the supplier is asked to ship a certain amount to one or more factory or store locations. The requested quantity is determined by the purchasing company's current needs, often by a just-in-time (JIT) or collaborative planning, forecasting, and replenishment (CPFR) system.

The foundation of B2B e-commerce and the most important form of B2B e-commerce today, in dollar volume, is electronic data interchange, which we introduced in Chapter 2. *Electronic data interchange (EDI)* is the direct computer-to-computer transfer of transaction information contained in standard business documents such as invoices and purchase orders, in a standard format. EDI replaces paper documents with digital records exchanged between trading partners' computers. Although EDI can be and is used to support MRO purchasing, it is most commonly used to support the purchase of direct materials.

Figure 5.9

An EDI Hub and Spoke
Arrangement

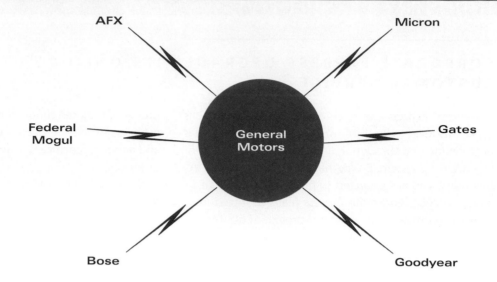

EDI spread in what is called a "hub and spoke" manner, as shown in Figure 5.9. For example, suppose a large company such as General Motors (GM)—the hub—decides to use EDI to support a JIT manufacturing process at its assembly plants. The purchasing department at GM notifies its parts suppliers (such as Gates Rubber Company—the spoke) that it expects Gates to be able to use EDI from now on.

Although there are other ways to exchange digital information between businesses, EDI practitioners say that if it doesn't meet the three criteria in the definition it is not EDI.

1. *Computer-to-computer exchange* means just that. It must travel from one company's computer system to another's over a telecommunications network of some sort, be it a private network, a VAN, or the Internet. (For more discussion on network options, see *Extended Learning Module E.*)

2. *Standard business documents* means that EDI is restricted to standard business forms such as purchase orders, purchase releases, advance shipping notices, invoices, and the like, and not free-form business correspondence such as business letters.

3. *Standard format* means that trading partners have agreed that the digital information exchanged will be in a standard format so that the computer systems at either company can interpret what is being transmitted and use it for further processing without human intervention. Companies using EDI developed national and international EDI standards so that the same data formats are widely used. The most commonly used standards in the United States and Europe are ASC X12 and UN/EDIFACT, respectively.

Value-added networks (VANs) make it easier for trading partners to establish telecommunications links with each other. Rather than sending EDI transactions directly from a hub company to a spoke company, or vice versa, companies usually send a stream of orders to many trading partners directly to a VAN. The VAN places them in an electronic mailbox for each trading partner. Other trading partners do the same thing. Then, once or twice a day, for example, Gates's computer connects with the VAN and downloads all EDI transactions from all of its trading partners at one time, as illustrated

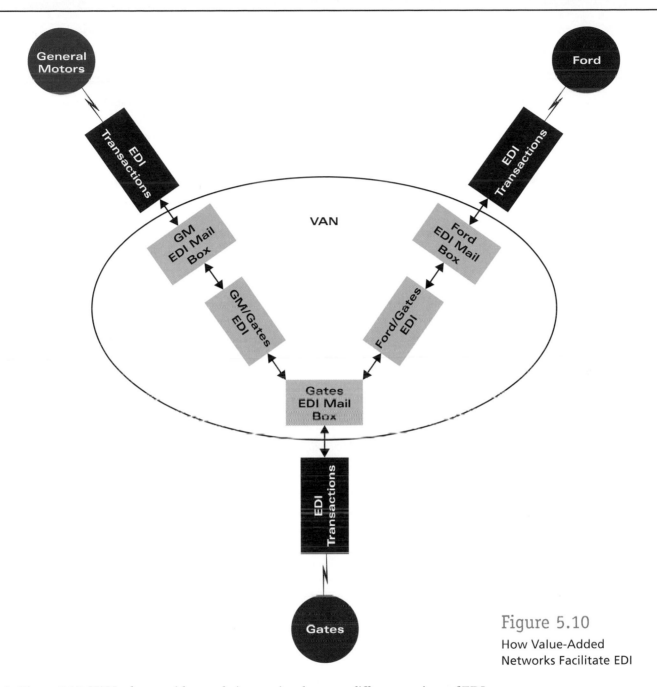

Figure 5.10

How Value-Added
Networks Facilitate EDI

in Figure 5.10. VANs also provide translation services between different versions of EDI standards, audit services, and control services, and will even translate EDI messages from hubs to fax messages for smaller spokes who are not prepared to conduct true EDI. Virtual private networks (VPNs) are an increasingly popular and less costly alternative to VANs. A *virtual private network* uses software to establish a secure channel on the Internet for transmitting data.

PURCHASING OF INDIRECT MATERIALS (MRO)   Most corporate purchasing departments do not want to be bothered with the paperwork required to process purchase orders for MRO materials, but at the same time, they do not want to let MRO purchases go completely uncontrolled. Although the amounts on individual MRO purchase orders are small, collectively they can add up. To deal with this problem, many purchasing departments negotiate with MRO providers for discounted prices on a range of items. Then, the MRO supplier prints a custom catalog for the company showing the items that can be ordered together with a price sheet. If an administrative assistant needs to order supplies, he or she finds the item in the catalog, calls the MRO supplier, and the item is delivered the next day. E-commerce solutions for MRO do about what you would expect them to do. The supplier replaces the paper catalog with an electronic catalog accessible through a Web browser. Powerful search engines locate the items needed. The administrative assistant orders the MRO item over the Internet in a manner similar to the way he or she orders a B2C item, and it is delivered the next day.

NEXT-GENERATION SOLUTIONS: XML AND WEB SERVICES

Several efforts are now under way to create a new generation of EDI for B2B transactions that will be easier to set up and use, and thereby be more attractive to smaller companies. The vision for the next generation of EDI is one in which a company could create a purchase order on a PC Web form and send it out over the Internet to a company it has never done business with before. The transaction would contain within itself access to the information a computer at the receiving company needs to interpret it and begin to process it, much the same as if it were a purchase order received in the mail and opened by a human. Most of the next-generation EDI efforts involve the Internet as a substitute for private networks or VANs because the Internet is cheaper. Also, most of them are built around an emerging technology for creating Web documents called XML. ***XML (eXtensible Markup Language)*** is a coding language for the Web that lets computers interpret the *meaning* of information in Web documents.

Most Web documents now are developed using the HTML coding language. HTML uses tags to tell a browser what a Web page should look like. For example, HTML can tell your browser that a line of text should be capitalized or in color. XML also uses tags, but the advantage of XML is that its tags define what the text actually means. Compare the two Web documents in Figure 5.11. The one on the left is a few lines from a document coded in HTML and the one on the right is a few lines from an XML document. The important thing to notice is that in the XML document, the tags inserted before and after Charles and Cadwell, for example, let you or a computer know that Charles is the person's first name and Cadwell is his last name.

XML is more useful than HTML in many ways. As just one example, search engines will find relevant information much more easily because they will know the meaning of the text between XML tags. For B2B e-commerce, however, the value of XML is that business documents created for the Web can be easily created and understood by trad-

Figure 5.11

A Person's Name Coded in HTML and in XML

Mr. Charles Johnson Cadwell IV in HTML:	Mr. Charles Johnson Cadwell IV in XML:

`<B>Mr. Charles Johnson Cadwell IV</B>`	`<PersonName>`
	    `<PersonNameTitle>Mr.</PersonNameTitle>`
	    `<PersonFirstName>Charles</PersonFirstName>`
	    `<PersonMiddleName>Johnson</PersonMiddleName>`
	    `<PersonSurname>Cadwell</PersonSurname>`
	    `<PersonNameSuffix>IV</PersonNameSuffix>`
	`</PersonName>`

Note how the XML tags convey the meaning of the information between the tags. HTML simply presents the information and provides formatting instructions (which XML can also do).

A RANGE OF POSSIBILITIES FOR NEXT-GENERATION EDI

Below are links to Web sites of some of the companies or groups that are working on alternatives to traditional EDI where XML plays a role. Take a look at each of them and find one that, in your opinion, holds the most promise for the future. Feel free to see if you can find articles on the Web that compare and contrast the alternative approaches to support your conclusions.

- Electronic Business XML (ebXML): www.ebxml.org
- Web Services: www.w3.org/2002/ws/
- .Net (Microsoft): www.microsoft.com/net/
- WebSphere (IBM): www-3.ibm.com/software/info1/websphere/
- Sun ONE (Sun Microsystems): www.sun.com/sunone/

ing partners' computers. This makes B2B e-commerce more accessible and affordable to small and medium-sized businesses and will hasten the spread of B2B e-commerce. Two of several possibilities for B2B e-commerce currently in the spotlight are ebXML and Web Services.

The first, *ebXML,* is a set of technical specifications for business documents built around XML designed to permit enterprises of any size and in any geographical location to conduct business over the Internet.[19,20] Think of ebXML as a replacement for current EDI standards such as ASC X12 or UN/EDIFACT. Small companies tend to avoid using EDI unless an important customer insists on it because they find the current standards complex and expensive to use.

The second approach that is getting a lot of attention is Web Services. While the Internet makes it easy for anyone with a Web browser to obtain information from Web sites no matter what sort of computer it resides on, it can still be difficult for computer systems to get information from other computer systems that have not been designed to share information widely. This is a problem for many corporations that have separate computer applications for different business units. For example, your college or university may have separate computer systems for registration, student academic records, student financial records, and campus residence information. It can be very difficult to compile a complete profile on you because the individual computer systems do not talk to each other easily. Naturally, separate companies have different computer systems so it is also difficult for trading partners to easily share information for B2B e-commerce applications. Web services are designed to address this issue.

Web Services are software applications that talk to other software applications over the Internet using XML as a key enabling technology.[21] Initial applications of Web Services are focused on internal applications so a company's computer systems work together more easily. This is because companies want to get some experience with it before extending it to their supply chain partners. The ultimate vision for Web Services, though, is to make it easier for separate companies to do business together electronically.

The next generation of EDI, whatever form(s) it eventually takes, should truly make the benefits of electronic exchange of standard business documents available to companies of all sizes, all over the world. The On Your Own project in this section asks you to compare some of the current ideas for next-generation EDI that are currently in the works.

A B2B EXCHANGE FOR THE DAIRY INDUSTRY

If buyers and sellers of dairy products can't find each other quickly enough, the products could spoil. That presented an opportunity for a B2B exchange called Dairy.com (www.dairy.com), owned and operated by MomentX Corporation in Dallas. Dairy.com operates a B2B exchange that lets dairy product producers and processors buy and sell raw dairy products using a spot market model.

Currently, spot market transactions for liquid dairy products such as skim milk and cream are made through phone calls and faxes. This is a risky and inefficient process since dairy products have to be delivered and used while they're fresh. In contrast, Dairy.com's business model matches buyers and sellers online and lets them complete a transaction in a matter of minutes.[22]

B2B MARKETPLACES

B2B marketplaces seem to be a natural for the Web. **B2B marketplaces** are Internet-based services that bring together buyers and sellers. They have the potential to bring together large numbers of buyers and sellers, thereby giving buyers more choices and aggregating demand for the sellers. Transaction costs can be reduced, resulting in potential savings for both buyers and sellers. The company operating a marketplace often has software that facilitates matching buyers and sellers and helps them with the transaction. One commonly used technique is to have the marketplace conduct a reverse auction. **Reverse auction** is the process in which a buyer posts its interest in buying a certain quantity of items, and sellers compete for the business by submitting successively lower bids until there is only one seller left. Marketplaces usually make their money by charging a transaction fee for their services. For example, FreeMarkets (www.freemarkets.com) is a company that holds auctions so corporations can buy industrial parts, materials, and services from suppliers via the Internet. Recently, one of its customers, Cooper Industries, used FreeMarkets to get bids for its air-freight service. It attracted 11 bidders, and the increased competition for its business saved them $1.2 million. More than 19,000 suppliers from more than 70 countries have bid through FreeMarkets since 1995. Of course, companies don't have to use a company like FreeMarkets to conduct an auction. They can arrange one of their own or join together in an industry group as the automobile companies have done with Covisint (www.covisint.com).

B2B marketplaces are still evolving, and as we have come to see with other e-commerce ventures, not all of them will succeed. They seem to hold the most promise in the MRO space inasmuch as relationships are often not as important there, because the risks of doing business with a new supplier are lower. Working with a new direct materials supplier presents the risk of shutting down an assembly line because of late delivery or quality problems. In addition, you have to remember that the legacy EDI systems of many large companies are the way that the supply chain is managed, and these systems, while complicated to set up, are working well. Finally, many suppliers will try to avoid letting anyone get between them and their customers. (Remember in Chapter 2 how we described all the tactics the airlines are using to recapture their best customers from travel agents.)

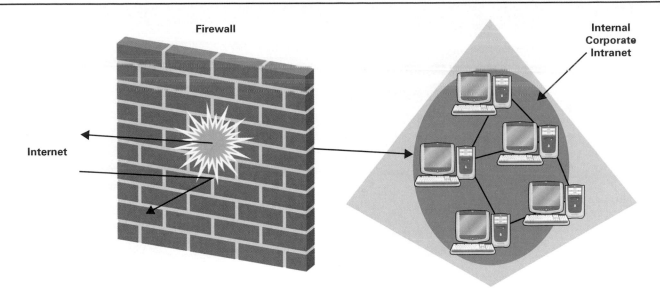

Figure 5.12
Intranet Structure

INTRANETS AND EXTRANETS

An *intranet* is an internal organizational Internet that is guarded against outside access by a special security feature called a firewall (which can be software, hardware, or a combination of the two) (see Figure 5.12). An *extranet* is an intranet that is restricted to an organization and certain outsiders, such as customers and suppliers. In contrast to intranets and extranets, the Internet can be accessed by anyone, although, of course, many Web sites require user names and passwords for access.

THE WAY INTRANETS ARE USED   Intranets are used to facilitate communication within an organization and to manage many internal business processes. It would be hard for you to go into a modern office today and not see a PC on almost every desk. Giving employees access via their Web browsers to information that used to be available only on paper can result in tremendous cost savings as well as provide assurance that the information on the corporate intranet is the most current information available. For example, just about every organization of any size has an employee handbook in which the human resources department documents policies regarding fringe benefits, vacations, sick leave, and the like. Putting the handbook on the corporate intranet makes it readily accessible to most employees, and when changes are made, a broadcast e-mail can be sent out asking employees to take notice. Intranet applications can range from simple ones, such as these, to putting expense reports and other forms online, as well as newsletters, employee feedback, and sophisticated knowledge management systems.

THE WAY EXTRANETS ARE USED   Extranet applications expand the audience to include persons external to the organization, most often customers and suppliers. Extranets are used to share product and inventory information, news and information, and as a collaboration platform for joint projects. Extranets can be a vehicle for implementing more advanced supply chain management and customer relationship management systems.

Customer relationship management (CRM) systems use information about customers to gain insights into their needs, wants, and behaviors in order to serve them better. CRM systems can enable a company to obtain a complete picture of all of its relationships with a customer and identify areas where better services are needed. For example, if someone has a mortgage, an auto loan, an IRA, and a large personal checking account with one bank, it makes sense for the bank to treat this person well each time

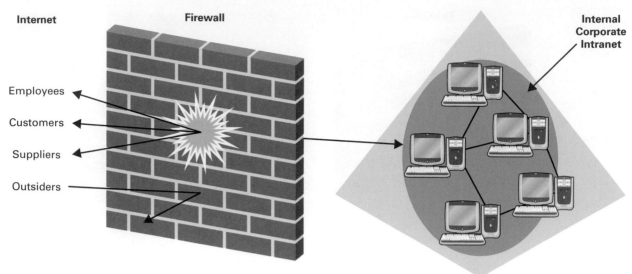

Figure 5.13
Extranet Structure

it has any contact with him or her. Treating the customer well may include giving personalized access to information on all of the customer accounts on an extranet.[23] See Figure 5.13 for a schematic of an extranet.

The Role of E-Government

E-Government describes the application of e-commerce technologies in governmental agencies. It is a great place to use e-commerce technologies now and could be an employment opportunity for you.

Many government agencies have long been active in using e-commerce technologies in the purchase of direct and indirect materials. Previously, we talked about how hub companies encourage small and medium-sized companies to adopt e-commerce technologies such as EDI. Well, in most countries, the federal government is by far the largest hub of all. In the United States, for example, the federal government encourages its suppliers to deal with it electronically, and it would prefer to pay its suppliers electronically as well. Many small and medium sized companies have become e-commerce enabled in this way.

In most cases, governments have lagged behind the private sector in the application of e-commerce technologies. In some areas, however, the government is actually leading the private sector. One example is in the adoption of biometrics for access to secured areas and in the use of face recognition technology for detecting persons who might present security threats at airports.

Currently, there is a lot of activity in the e-government space in using the Internet to provide better services and information to citizens. In a way, you're a customer of your government, but all too often you are not treated as a valued customer. This is changing with e-government initiatives. Governments are asking themselves how they could serve you better and coming up with ways to do so. Ask yourself how well your government agencies are treating you as a customer. (If they were a company, would you buy their stock?)

For example, state governments are usually where you have to go in the United States if you need a copy of a "vital record" such as a birth certificate or marriage license. In some states, copies can be ordered online. Many U.S. states permit you to order a fish-

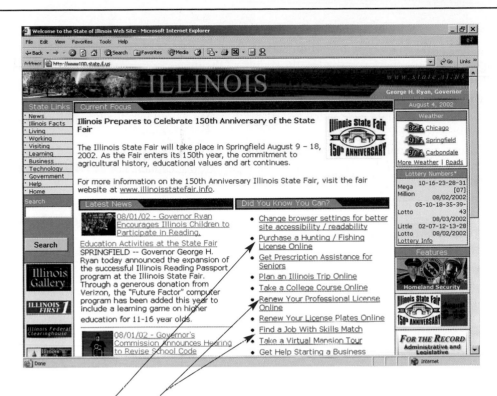

Figure 5.14
Some of the Things
Citizens Can Do on
Illinois's Web Site

Get a fishing license, renew your license plates, find a job.
You can get lots of services online in the State of Illinois!

ing license or register for a campground site online. Previously, these were the sorts of things you would have requested in writing (and waited for a reply), or have driven to an office somewhere to stand in line.

In the United States, you can pay your federal and state taxes online (in most states). In some states, you can buy coffee mugs and T-shirts with your state's logo on it online and even file an online complaint if you don't like the service you receive. States are creating customer-oriented portals to make it easy for you to log on and easily find the service or information you are looking for. The portal for the State of Illinois illustrated in Figure 5.14 is a good example.

One issue that e-government must deal with is the digital divide, discussed earlier in this chapter. Since access to Internet technologies is tilted in favor of citizens at the higher ends of the income scale, governments must devise solutions to be sure that all citizens have access to e-government services. Although governments are not likely to give PCs and free Internet access to those who can't afford it anytime soon, they can try to devise solutions that can serve lower income groups. One example is the use of ATMs to distribute welfare payments instead of sending checks through the mail or using electronic direct deposits to checking accounts. (Many welfare recipients do not have bank accounts.)

E-Commerce Payment Systems

Just as there are traditional EDI transactions for purchase orders and other standard business documents, there are EDI transactions for payments. The use of EDI for payments is called *financial EDI (FEDI)*. Financial EDI has not gained the same acceptance as EDI for one simple reason. Corporate treasurers, who are responsible for managing corporate cash, have not seen it to be advantageous to speed up payments to suppliers. When a payment is dropped into the mail, the payer can earn interest on the money until the check is cashed by the supplier. Oftentimes, corporate treasurers will see that a payment is mailed in time to reach the supplier by the due date, but the check will be drawn on a bank in another part of the country that will take days to clear. An electronic payment would clear much faster, and the payer would lose the use of the money for those extra few days.

Next-generation EDI approaches include FEDI transactions as a part of their proposed solutions. Still, the obstacle to more widespread acceptance of FEDI is not technical, but the reluctance of people to change their business processes. The U.S. federal government is moving forward aggressively with electronic payments, encouraging them for businesses and for direct deposits to the bank accounts of social security recipients whenever possible.

CREDIT CARDS AND SMART CARDS

In many countries, credit cards are the most common method of payment for e-commerce transactions, particularly in the B2C space. In the early years of B2C, consumers were reluctant to enter their credit card numbers on a Web site for fear that they would be stolen. Then it was pointed out that you were much more likely to have your credit card number stolen by a waiter or waitress in a restaurant than by a thief lurking on the Internet. Still, the lack of widespread use of credit cards by consumers in some countries, such as China and India, creates hurdles that B2C companies in such countries will have to overcome.

Smart cards are one option that has been experimented with for some time. ***Smart cards*** are plastic cards the size of a credit card that contain an embedded chip on which digital information can be stored. When the stored digital information is monetary, the

Figure 5.15
The PayPal Web Site

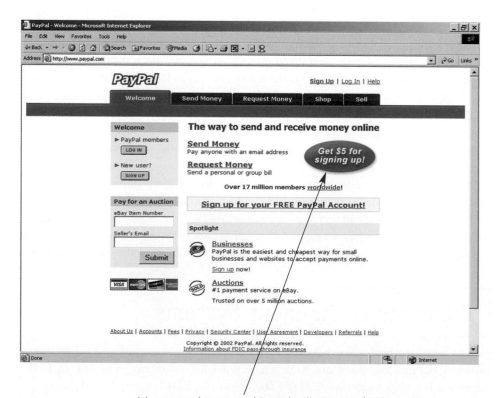

It's easy to sign up, and PayPal will give you $5 if you do.

smart card is called a stored value card. One of the best-known smart card initiatives is Mondex (see www.mondex.com). The Mondex chip contains an "electronic purse" that is loaded with electronic cash and then spent at retailers that have a Mondex card reader. Electronic cash is transferred from the buyer's Mondex card to the seller's device. Electronic cash is added to a Mondex card using a telephone connection to your bank.

The Mondex solution is one possible answer to the micro-payments issue we discussed earlier in this chapter, making it possible to purchase low-value items on the Internet. We discuss more about Internet digital cash and smart cards in Chapter 9.

FINANCIAL CYBERMEDIARIES

Financial cybermediaries are Internet-based companies that make it easy for one person to pay another person over the Internet. One of the best known and another e-commerce success story is PayPal (www.paypal.com) which was recently acquired by eBay. PayPal makes it easy for individuals to exchange money for goods or services purchased over the Internet. It is particularly useful in C2C space electronic auctions, but you can use it anytime you want to send money to another person over the Internet. You create a PayPal account by logging on to the PayPal Web site and providing it with personal data and credit card information. When you want to send money, you simply go to the PayPal site and enter the person's name, e-mail address, and the amount you want to send. The payee receives an e-mail notification that the cash has been deposited in his or her PayPal account. The payee can then transfer the cash to a checking account, request a check, send the funds to someone else, or just leave it there for awhile.

ELECTRONIC BILL PRESENTMENT AND PAYMENT

We all get bills in the mail every month, from the gas and electric company, the telephone company, the cable TV provider, department stores, and credit card companies. It costs money for the companies to print and mail the bills, and it costs us money to put a check in the mail. A technique called Electronic Bill Presentment and Payment is just beginning to take hold to reduce the time and paper in this process (and save us some trees in the process). *Electronic Bill Presentment and Payment (EBPP)* systems send us our bills over the Internet and give us an easy way to pay them if the amount looks correct. Electronic bill payment systems available through our local banks or such services as Checkfree and Quicken have been around for a while. What is different with EBPP systems is that our bills appear on a Web site or arrive in our e-mail in-boxes instead of our home mail boxes.

Summary: Student Learning Outcomes Revisited

1. **Describe the four main perspectives of e-commerce, its current status, and the global growth expected in the next few years.** There are four main perspectives for e-commerce: Business to Business (B2B), Business to Consumer (B2C), Consumer to Business (C2B), and Consumer to Consumer (C2C). Experts who are in the business of forecasting the growth of global e-commerce may differ in their estimates, but all agree that we can expect to see tremendous growth in the next few years. Jupiter Media Matrix estimates that 36 percent of all U.S. B2B spending, or $5.4 trillion, will be done online by the year 2006. ElectricNews.Net reported that European business-to-business e-commerce sales are expected to grow from

$500 billion in 2002 to $2.3 trillion by 2005. Most experts agree that 85 to 90 percent of e-commerce sales will be in the B2B space.

Countries in the developed world are more likely to reap the benefits of e-commerce than countries in the lesser developed world. This phenomenon is known as the *digital divide.* Policy experts are searching for ways to close the gap.

2. **Identify the advantages of business to consumer (B2C) e-commerce.** B2C e-commerce has several advantages over other methods of retailing, including:

    - Shopping can be faster and more convenient
    - Offerings and prices can be changed instantaneously
    - Call centers can be integrated with the Web site
    - Broadband telecommunications will enhance the buying experience

    Many traditional retailers are finding that adding the Internet as another channel to their existing channels is a profitable strategy. M-commerce and broadband technologies, when they become more widely available, will offer powerful new ways for retailers to reach their customers.

3. **Describe the techniques that lead to success in B2C e-commerce ventures.** Internet retailers (e-tailers) find that commoditylike products sell best, and that digital products work the best of all, because they can be bought, paid for, and—most of all—delivered immediately. Successful e-tailers have learned the importance of good Web site design and marketing to attract and retain consumers, the importance of merchandising, the importance of executing well, and the need to continuously monitor the competition. E-tailing has become more difficult to succeed in now that the easy-money early days of the Internet are behind us.

4. **Describe the variety of ways that business to business (B2B) e-commerce technologies are being used, and describe next-generation models which may widen the adoption of global B2B e-commerce.** Although relationships can be important in the B2C space, they tend to be more important in the B2B space because of the interdependencies that exist among trading partners, particularly for direct materials. More complex relationships known as *"value networks"* are made possible by e-commerce technologies. Relationships tend to be more important in the purchasing of direct materials than in the purchase of indirect materials. *Electronic Data Interchange (EDI)* has facilitated the smooth operation of B2B e-commerce, which is driving paper out of many interorganizational business processes. EDI has not spread beyond large "hub" companies and their smaller "spoke" trading partners because it can be difficult to set up and administer. Next-generation EDI techniques such as *ebXML* and *Web Services* hope to address this problem. Internet-based *B2B marketplaces* using techniques such as reverse auctions hold out the promise of cost savings by making it easier for buyers and sellers to find each other and for buyers to obtain better prices. Their future, however, is as yet unclear. *Intranets* and *extranets* are important ways to extend the benefits of Internet technologies to restricted participants such as employees, customers, and suppliers.

5. **Identify the unique aspects of e-government applications.** Many government agencies have fostered the spread of e-commerce by using e-commerce technologies for purchasing and payments. There are tremendous opportunities for governmental bodies to serve citizens better if the potential of the Internet is creatively applied to the provision of governmental services and information.

6. **Describe the status and options for e-commerce payment systems.** Although financial EDI has been available for B2B payments for some time, it has not attained wide acceptance, partly because of corporate treasurers' reluctance to employ it. In the U.S. B2C space, most e-commerce transactions are paid for with credit cards. Credit card payments have limitations for e-commerce because they are not suitable for small amounts and because there are many countries where the use of credit cards is not as well accepted as in the United States. *Smart cards* have been proposed as alternatives, but they have not yet achieved widespread acceptance. *Financial cybermediaries* such as PayPal, have made significant inroads for making

payments over the Internet, particularly in the C2C space. Electronic Bill Presentment and Payment (EBPP) is an emerging technique that holds the promise of driving paper out of the

B2C billing process for companies such as utilities, department stores, and credit card companies.

CLOSING CASE STUDY ONE

EBAGS: AN E-COMMERCE SUCCESS STORY

For a real e-commerce success story you don't have to go any further than eBags (www.ebags.com). While many pure play e-commerce sites have fallen by the wayside, eBags is not only surviving, it is thriving. They are the world's leading online provider of bags and accessories for all lifestyles. With 150 brands and more than 6,000 items, eBags has sold more than 1.5 million bags since their launch in March 1999. They carry a complete line of premium and popular brands, including Samsonite, JanSport, North Face, Eagle Creek, and Liz Claiborne. You can buy anything from backpacks and carry-ons to computer cases and handbags at extremely competitive prices from their Web site. You can even do a search, by airline, for bags that meet the airline's carry-on requirements.

They have received several awards for excellence in online retailing, among them the Bizrate.com Circle of Excellence Platinum Award, the Web site of the Year honors at Catalog Age's 16th Annual Catalog/I.Merchant Awards, and the Best Email Marketer Award from ClickZ/Message Media.

A good part of the reason for their success is their commitment to providing each of their customers with superior service, 24 hours a day, 365 days a year. They provide their customers with the ability to contact customer service representatives for personal assistance by telephone or e-mail and also provide convenient, real-time UPS order tracking.

Although you would never know it, this superior customer service is not provided by eBags employees. For the last two years, eBags has outsourced both the handling of phone orders and customer service calls to Finali Corporation (www.finali.com). "The call center is often the only human contact customers have with our brand," says eBags CEO Jon Nordmark. "By maintaining a call center staff that can think on its feet, Finali

delivers real value to our customers and a measurable return on our call center investment."

Typically, the conversion rate of inbound customer calls to sales at the call center has been about 25 percent. But during the 2001 holiday season, special training and incentives for Finali call center reps servicing the eBags Web site helped raise that number to 44 percent. In addition, the average size of orders placed through the call center hit $100, topping the average Web order of just over $75. The increased conversion rates and order size meant that for every dollar eBags spent with Finali, Finali generated $3.79 in sales!

eBags announced profits for the first time in December 2001, posting 5.4 percent earnings before interest, taxes, depreciation, and amortization. "Part of that achievement was due to smart outsourcing like the call center," says eBags CFO Eliot Cobb.

In February of 2002, eBags announced a partnership with custom-bag manufacturer Timbuk2 which permits eBags customers to order customized Timbuk2 bags. Timbuk2 (www.timbuk2.com), which launched its e-commerce Web site in 2000, saw its sales over the Internet jump to 50 percent of its total sales. They expect to see their Internet sales climb higher very quickly with the eBags partnership. An option for eBags would have been simply to establish an affiliate relationship with Timbuk2 whereby eBags shoppers would click on a Tibbuk2 ad on the eBags site and be taken to the Timbuk2 Web site to place their orders. Instead, eBags chose to integrate Timbuk2's software into its own system and create a feature called Build a Bag, which allows eBags shoppers to design their own Timbuk2 messenger bags online without leaving the eBags site.

Timbuk2 had already developed the software that let its customers order customized messenger bags, laptop sleeves, and commuter bags. On the messenger bag, for example, customers can specify any one of several sizes, colors, fabrics, and special features such as a center divider or bottom boot. (A left-handed option is free.)

Before the partnership was established, eBags was already selling Timbuk2's ready-made bags on its site. Now, using the Build a Bag option, you can design a Timbuk2 bag to your own specifications from the eBags Web site. If you want to see how it works, just go to www.ebags.com/BagBuilder.

And the partnership is working. Timbuk2 is getting more orders for its customized bags, and eBags customers have even more choices on the eBags site.

Compared to this arrangement, the disadvantage of an affiliate agreement for a retailer the size of eBags is obvious. Why have a setup where a customer must leave your Web site in order to get what she wants? If she stays on your Web site, she might put a few more items into her shopping cart before she leaves.[24]

QUESTIONS

1. Pick any two of the advantages of B2C e-commerce discussed in the chapter and describe how eBags has used them to gain a competitive advantage over traditional bricks-and-mortar retailers of bags and accessories.

2. Do you think that m-commerce or broadband are technologies that could provide an enhanced buying experience for eBags customers when such services become more widely available? Do you see a way that eBags

could gain a competitive advantage from being one of the first e-tailers to use one or both of these technologies? Why or why not?

3. The case describes how eBags has chosen to engage a call center specialist firm, Finali Corporation, to handle its call center operations for them. Refer to the discussion of value networks on page 260 and to Figure 5.8. Would you describe Finali Corporation's relationship with eBags in this venture as being a supplier, an intermediary, or a complementor? Explain the reasons for your choice.

4. Refer to the discussion of value networks on page 260 and to Figure 5.8. Would you describe Timbuk2's relationship with eBags as described in the case as being a supplier, an intermediary, or a complementor? Explain the reasons for your choice. The case describes the advantages of the eBags/Timbuk2 relationship over a simple affiliate relationship. What disadvantages are there to the existing relationship?

5. In the chapter, we said that successful B2C e-commerce companies must execute well. Visit the eBags Web site at www.ebags.com. What assurances do they give their customers that they will receive the item they ordered when promised? Would you have confidence in ordering from eBags based on what you conclude from examining their Web site? Why or why not?

CLOSING CASE STUDY TWO

MAKING TOYOTA'S VISION A REALITY

Toyota Motor Corporation has plans to build an IT system that will let it fabricate digitally designed cars and build them in digitally designed factories. When installed, the system will enable Toyota to cut years out of the time it takes to turn concepts into cars. Toyota will use the system to model the entire process of car production, from original design to the development of component parts, to the sequence in which components are assembled, and even to the design of the factory that builds them.

The system is not inexpensive. In order to move forward with the system, Toyota signed a contract worth an estimated $800 million to $1.2 billion for software, hardware, and services. The software is Dassault Systèmes S.A.'s 3D Product Lifecycle Management suite, an integrated set of software that includes design collaboration, product-life-cycle management (PLM), and production-support applications. Implementation will include hardware, software, and services from IBM. Development is expected to take three to five years and will ultimately link Toyota's 56 plants in 25 countries and more than 1,000 suppliers. The system will replace Toyota's proprietary CAD platform, Togo, and its homegrown product data management system.

Toyota is revered for quality and efficiency. The fact that it chose third-party software to replace its much-praised, much-studied, proprietary production system indicates an acceptance of a core competence strategy and willingness to outsource combined with a strong desire to stay ahead of the car-market curve.

In a somewhat unusual series of steps, Toyota visited one of its competitors, DaimlerChrysler, which was already using some of the software they were evaluating and willing to share their experience with Toyota. Karenann Terrell, director of E-connect, the business-to-business infrastructure group for DaimlerChrysler, said that Toyota was "particularly interested in how DaimlerChrysler was pulling suppliers into the design process using our PLM tools." Dassault's design-collaboration software, called Catia, and its product-life-cycle management tool, Enovia, cut 60 percent to 90 percent off the time DaimlerChrysler needed to communicate design changes to suppliers and get back required changes, Terrell said.

The new system will let Toyota's designers collaborate with each other as well as with those 1,000 suppliers that will eventually build component parts. Designers from both Toyota and its suppliers will use Catia tools, which will permit them to test component designs developed on computers for "manufacturability," i.e. how easily they will be able to be manufactured in the first place and, later, installed on cars on the assembly line. To aid in achieving this objective, Toyota intends to start by setting goals for manufacturing efficiency and then working backward toward a car's concept and design.

The Catia deployment also will let Toyota reuse designs for component parts, such as a hood, in a process known as "morphing." For example, Toyota engineers will be able to search a repository of existing hoods, use Catia's tools to make changes to the design, and automatically test the morphed design for manufacturability.

As engineers work on the design of a new-car model, production-support software, called Delmia, will let engineering teams use design and manufacturability data to specify the order in which parts should be installed in a car as it moves down the production line. Ultimately, engineers will be able to model the entire factory environment digitally, specifying what's done at each stop in the production process;

which tools, supplies, and parts will be used; how many people will be stationed at each assembly stop; and exactly what they will do.

Only after all the pieces fit together—the design, the production plan, and the factory floor strategy—will Toyota roll the specs for the new-car model into its production and supply-chain management systems. The integration of digital design and digital manufacturing will let Toyota speed new models to market in months, rather than years. That's increasingly important because cars have become fashion statements as much as transportation, especially with young people, who buy cars such as the Chrysler PT Cruiser, the Pontiac Vibe, or the Volkswagen Beetle, relying on many of the same impulses that guide them when they buy clothes or electronics.

The new system could give Toyota an edge in realizing the ultimate prize for automakers: the ability to build a car to customer specifications and deliver it within days, much like Dell does with computer systems. A marketing model for automobiles that would permit that amount of mass customization is one that would have broad appeal to many buyers. Perhaps someday soon, you'll be able to log on to the Internet, spec out your new car just the way you like it, and have it delivered to your front door.[25]

QUESTIONS

1. Refer to the discussion of value networks on page 260 and to Figure 5.8. Would you describe IBM's relationship with Toyota in this venture as being a supplier, an intermediary, or a complementor? Explain the reasons for your choice.

2. When the new system is implemented, Toyota will get their suppliers involved in the design process earlier than what might normally be the case. In addition, there will be a considerable amount of collaboration all along the way. What are the advantages to the suppliers and to Toyota in doing so?

3. The new system, when operational, will require the use of e-commerce technologies to support the purchase, delivery, and payment for direct materials shipped from Toyota's suppliers to its new plants. Should Toyota plan to use EDI for these purposes, or would it be better for them to plan to use one of the next-generation technologies such as ebXML or Web Services? Why or why not?

4. The case mentions that perhaps someday you will be able to mass-customize and order an automobile the way you can mass-customize and order a computer today. Do you think this is a realistic possibility? Is a car really a commoditylike product? What are the obstacles that would need to be overcome to make this idea a reality?

5. Experts have estimated that between 12 percent and 20 percent of the cost of an automobile is incurred after it is shipped from the factory. Most of this cost is tied up in automobile dealers' inventories. If you could save this amount of money by ordering a new car directly from the factory and bypassing your local dealer, would you do it? Why or why not?

Key Terms and Concepts

Affiliate program, 256
B2B marketplace, 266
Clicks-and-mortar, 247
Click-throughs, 256
Complementor, 260
Conversion rate, 257
Customer relationship management (CRM) system, 267
Demand aggregation, 245
Digital divide, 246
Direct material, 261
EbXML, 265
Electronic Commerce, 244
E-government, 268
Electronic Bill Presentment and Payment (EBPP), 271
Electronic data interchange (EDI), 261
E-tailer, 247
Extranet, 267
Financial cybermediary, 271
Financial EDI (FEDI), 269

Global digital divide, 246
Indirect material, 261
Interactive chat, 250
Intermediary, 260
Internet telephony, 250
Intranet, 267
Marketing mix, 254
M-commerce, 248
Meta tag, 254
Micro-payment, 253
Pure play, 247
Reverse auction, 266
Smart card, 270
Spam, 255
Value network, 260
Viral marketing, 255
Virtual private network (VPN), 263
Web Services, 265
XML (eXtensible Markup Language), 264

Short-Answer Questions

1. What is the digital divide? What is the global digital divide?
2. In which sector of e-commerce is the greatest dollar volume concentrated?
3. What are four advantages of B2C e-commerce over traditional retailing?
4. Why are digital products the best ones to sell over the Internet?
5. What is the attraction of affiliate programs to e-tailers?
6. What are three techniques used to attract customers to B2C Web sites?
7. What are value networks?
8. What do the letters *EDI* stand for?
9. What is a large EDI buyer company called?
10. What is a supplier to a large EDI buyer company called?
11. What are Internet-based services that bring buyers and sellers together called?
12. What is XML?
13. What is the name for an internal organizational intranet also open to customers and suppliers?
14. In which areas is the government leading the private sector in the use of e-technology?
15. Why has financial EDI been slow to gain acceptance?

Short-Question Answers

For each of the following answers, provide an appropriate question.

1. Business to Business (B2B), Business to Consumer (B2C), Consumer to Business (C2B), and Consumer to Consumer (C2C).
2. 544 million.
3. Demand aggregation.
4. M-commerce.
5. Commoditylike.
6. Pure plays.
7. Interactive chat.
8. Micro-payments.
9. Meta tags.
10. MRO.
11. ASC X12 and EDIFACT.
12. Reverse auctions.
13. ebXML and Web Services.
14. E-government.
15. Mondex.

Assignments and Exercises

1. **DEVELOPING M-COMMERCE SCENARIOS FOR GPS CELL PHONES** Soon, cell phones will be equipped with GPS chips that enable users to be located within a geographical location about the size of a tennis court. The primary purpose for installing GPS chips in phones is to enable emergency services to locate a cell phone user. For example, if you dial an emergency assistance number (911 in the United States) from your home now, it is possible for a computer system to use your home telephone number to access a database and obtain your address. This can be very useful in situations where you are unable to give address information to the emergency operator for some reason. The problem with trying to do the same thing with present-day cell phones is that you could be calling from anywhere.

   As you might imagine, marketers have been monitoring this development with great interest. When the new cell phones become available, they can visualize scenarios where they will know who you are (by your telephone number) and where you are (by the GPS chip). One possible way they could use this information, for example, is to give you a call when you are walking past their shop in the mall and let you know of a special sale on items they know you would be interested in buying. Of course, retailers would have to possess IT systems that would permit them to craft such personalized offers, and you would have had to give them permission to call you.

   Find out what at least three e-commerce marketers are saying about personalized marketing using GPS-equipped cell phones and prepare an analysis of how they will likely be used when the technology is widely available.

2. **DEALING WITH THE GLOBAL DIGITAL DIVIDE** Dealing with the issue of the global digital divide seems to be one that is well-suited for an international body such as the United Nations.

   Find out what, if anything, the UN is doing about this issue and express an opinion on whether or not you believe their efforts will be successful. Determine if there are organizations such as private companies or foundations that have the issue high on their agendas. Do the same thing for any such organizations you find: Evaluate their efforts and express an opinion on whether or not they will be successful. Finally, search for a lesser developed country that is making significant local efforts to deal with the digital divide. If you can't find one, prepare a list of the countries you reviewed.

3. **ALTERNATIVES FOR PERSONALIZED DIGITAL MUSIC** Sony Music Entertainment and Universal Music Group recently formed a joint venture called PressPlay (www.pressplay.com) that gives subscribers new ways to listen to or buy recorded music. If you visit their Web site, you'll see that you have three options. You can listen to samples online, you can download tracks to your hard drive, or you can burn tracks onto a CD. PressPlay is a subscription service. You sign up for a plan and pay a monthly fee by credit card.

Your activity is limited depending on the plan you choose. It offers visitors a free 14-day trial with up to 200 streams or 20 downloads.

Evaluate PressPlay's business idea in comparison with a company that offers to create a custom CD and mail it to you. Prepare an assessment of the two approaches for presentation in class.

Discussion Questions _____

1. In what ways can shopping over the Internet be more convenient for consumers? In what ways can it be less convenient? List at least five products you would have no hesitation in buying over the Internet, five products you may want to think about a bit before you do it, and five products you would never consider buying over the Internet. Justify your reasons in each case.

2. Why is the ability to change prices instantaneously considered an advantage for e-tailers? When might the use of personalized pricing be a disadvantage for an e-tailer?

3. There have been a string of e-tailers running out of cash, not being able to attract more money from investors, and going out of business as a result. What are some of the main reasons this happened?

4. Under what circumstances would it be appropriate to consider using viral marketing? See if you can think of an organization with an online presence that could benefit from viral marketing but is not currently using it. It could be your school, for example, or it could be an organization you are involved with. How would you suggest the organization go about using viral marketing in order for it to achieve the desired results? What are some of the other marketing techniques available for an e-tailer to use? Why is it important to consider a mix of techniques rather than just relying on a single one?

5. Some Internet retailers that started as pure plays are now sending catalogs to their customers, opening up another channel. Some are well-known companies, Amazon.com and Red Envelope are only two of many possible examples. Do you think companies such as Amazon.com or Red Envelope should consider opening up a third channel by opening stores in your local shopping mall? Why or why not? What factors should they consider in evaluating such a decision? If they decided to do so, how would you suggest they go about it? What factors do you think it would be important for them to consider in order for them to be successful?

6. Why has traditional EDI been so slow to gain acceptance with small and medium-sized companies? Do you think that traditional EDI will ever gain enough acceptance with small and medium sized companies to make widespread B2B e-commerce a global reality? Why or why not? How do some of the ideas for next-generation EDI intend to address this issue? What will it take for some of the new approaches like ebXML and Web Services to be successful? What are some of the things you can think of that would cause them to fail in reaching their objectives?

7. Describe the services provided by value-added networks that make it easier for companies to exchange EDI transactions with each other. What are the pros and cons of using value-added networks for B2B e-commerce instead of the Internet? Why don't more companies use the Internet for EDI since it is much cheaper than using a value-added network? Assume that you work for a telecommunications company that operates a value-added network (AT&T or GE Information Services). What sort of strategies would you encourage your company to explore to deal with the possibility of losing considerable amounts of revenues as your customers leave you in favor of using the Internet?

8. What are the advantages and disadvantages of B2B marketplaces for buyers? For sellers? How could a supplier company play on the relationships that it has with a long-standing customer to avoid getting pulled in to a reverse auction in an open B2B marketplace? Why do some observers say that B2B marketplaces can be risky ventures?

REAL HOT   Electronic Commerce

Getting Your Business on the Internet

Let's say you've decided it might be fun (and profitable) to become an e-tailer and establish an Internet-based business. You know that many e-tailers don't make it, but you'd like to be one that is successful. There are a lot of resources on the Internet that can help you with the tasks of selecting the right business in the first place, getting the site up and running, deciding who should host your site, marketing your site, understanding privacy issues, and obtaining the funds you need to pay your expenses until your business begins to show a profit. On the Web site that supports this text (www.mhhe.com/haag, select "Electronic Commerce Projects"), we've provided direct links to many useful Web sites. These are a great starting point for completing this REAL HOT section. We also encourage you to search the Internet for others.

COMPETITIVE INTELLIGENCE

The first thing you need to have is an idea for the business. What would you like to sell? A product or a service? Make sure you have expertise, or something special to offer. After you've come up with a candidate, it's time to see how much competition is out there and what they're up to. One of the things many new business owners fail to do is to see how many competitors there are before they launch their business. You may find there are too many and that they would be tough competition for you. Or, you may find that there are few competitors and the ones who are out there aren't doing a terrific job.

Seek out and look at some of the Web sites of businesses in the competitive space you're thinking of entering. As you do, answer the following questions.

A. How many sites did you find that are offering the same product or service you're planning to offer?

B. How many are in your country and how many are in other countries?

C. Did you come across a site from another country that has a unique approach that you did not see on any of the sites within your own country?

E. Evaluate the competitor sites based on some of the criteria listed in Figure 5.4 (page 253).

STOREFRONT SOFTWARE

If you decide to sell products, there is software that you can use to make it easy to create a Web site. There are many products to choose from. Some will cost you a lot of money, but others are free. FreeMerchant.com, for example, has a Basic Store for $9.95 per month, a Bronze Package for $24.95 per month, a Silver Package for $49.95 per month, and a Gold Package for $99.95 per month. What you get in each of these packages is listed in detail on the FreeMerchant.com Web site (www.freemerchant.com). Since there are many options to choose from, it would be worth your while to do a little research to see if you can find an article that compares current versions of storefront software. A site like ZDNet.com (www.zdnet.com)

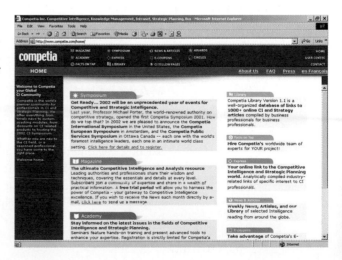

would be a good place to start your search. Build up a list of features that you will need for your e-tailing site, and then compare your needs with the features offered by the various software packages. They all sound good when you read about them on the vendors' Web sites so be sure you take a "test drive" of the software before you sign up.

Another possibility would be to sign up for a shopping mall. Find your way to Amazon.com's zShops or Yahoo!Store and see what you think of these alternatives. Finally, you'll need a way for your customers to pay you for what they buy. This involves getting a merchant account which permits you to accept credit cards. Most of the storefront sites will explain how merchant accounts work and will help you get a merchant account (see www.bigstep.com, for example).

- **A.** What features have you decided your storefront software must provide?
- **B.** How have you evaluated the pros and cons of using a storefront software package versus the options offered by Amazon.com and Yahoo!?
- **C.** See if you can track down users of software options you are considering. Send them an e-mail and ask them what they like and dislike about it. You may be surprised at their answers.

HOSTING SERVICES

You've got some options here. You can decide to acquire the necessary computer and communications hardware and software to manage your own technical infrastructure, or you can let a specialist firm do it for you. Unless you're really into the technical side of things, it's probably better to work with a firm that specializes in it. They are called *Web hosting services* and there are plenty of them around. Cost, reliability, security, and customer service are some of the criteria you might use in selecting a hosting service. If you're planning to have your business located in a country with poor telecommunications services, don't forget that you can choose a hosting service located in a country with a more reliable telecommunications infrastructure, anywhere in the world. Some companies provide directories that make it easy for you to find and compare prices and features of Web hosting companies, sort of like shopping malls for Web hosting services. An example of such a company is FindYourHosting.com (www.findyourhosting.com). Take a look at its site to see some of the options available. As you consider Web hosting services, answer the following questions.

- **A.** Compare the costs of the various hosting services. Were you able to find one that seems to be within your budget?
- **B.** How can you evaluate the reliability of the various Web hosting services?
- **C.** How can you evaluate the quality of a Web hosting company's customer service? What do you have a right to expect in the way of customer service and security, for example?

MARKETING THE SITE

In this chapter, we discussed several options for marketing a Web site: registering with search engines, online ads, viral marketing, affiliate programs, and marketing to existing customers, as well as using traditional media. Deciding on the marketing mix that will be most effective and still permit you to stay within a reasonable budget will be critical to the success of your venture. You may want to consider employing an Internet marketing consultant to help you lay out a marketing plan. One, AdDesigner.com (www.addesigner.com), even offers some free services. Also, you may want to see what markcting services your storefront software or Web hosting service may offer. As you consider how to market your site, answer the following questions.

A. How have you defined your target market? Who are the people that will be most interested in your product or service?

B. Which of the available marketing techniques have you selected as being most appropriate to market your site? Why have you selected this particular marketing mix?

C. What have you decided about using the services of a marketing consultant? How did you justify your decision?

EXTENDED LEARNING MODULE E
NETWORK BASICS

Student Learning Outcomes

1. IDENTIFY AND DESCRIBE THE FOUR BASIC CONCEPTS ON WHICH NETWORKS ARE BUILT.

2. LIST THE COMPONENTS YOU NEED TO SET UP A SMALL PEER-TO-PEER NETWORK AT HOME.

3. COMPARE AND CONTRAST THE VARIOUS INTERNET CONNECTION POSSIBILITIES.

4. DESCRIBE CLIENT/SERVER BUSINESS NETWORKS FROM A BUSINESS AND PHYSICAL POINT OF VIEW.

5. DEFINE LOCAL AREA NETWORKS (LANS), MUNICIPAL AREA NETWORKS (MANS), AND WIDE AREA NETWORKS (WANS).

6. COMPARE AND CONTRAST THE TYPES OF COMMUNICATIONS MEDIA.

Taking Advantage of the CD

When surfing the Web, accessing software on your school's server, sending e-mail, or letting your roommate use his/her computer to access the files on your computer, your computer is part of a network. A ***computer network*** (which we simply refer to as a network) is two or more computers connected so that they can communicate with each other and share information, software, peripheral devices, and/or processing power. Many networks have dozens, hundreds, or even thousands of computers.

Networks come in all sizes from two computers connected to share a printer, to the Internet, which is the largest network on the planet, joining millions of computers of all kinds all over the world. In between are business networks, which vary in size from a dozen or fewer computers to many thousands.

Some networks are extremely complex with perhaps thousands of computers connected together. These networks require highly skilled professionals to keep them up and running. However, regardless of their size, some basic principles apply to all networks.

1. Each computer on a network must have a network card (either as an expansion card or integrated into the motherboard) that provides the entrance or doorway for information traffic to and from other computers.

2. A network usually has at least one connecting device (like a hub or a router) that ties the computers on the network together and acts as a switchboard for passing information.

3. There must be communications media like cables or radio waves connecting network hardware devices. The communications media transport information around the network between computers and the connecting device(s).

4. Each computer must have software that supports the movement of information in and out of it. This could be modem software and/or a network operating system.

We definitely believe that it's worth your time and energy to pop in the CD and read this module. This module is the same as the modules in your text—it includes Team Work and On Your Own projects and great end-of-module Assignments and Exercises. In it, you'll learn many things including

- Two ways to build a peer-to-peer network at home or in your dorm
  - With network cards, cabling and a network connecting device
  - With existing phone wiring
- Five ways of connecting to the Internet
  - Phone line and dial-up modem
  - Phone line and Digital Subscriber Line (DSL) modem
  - Cable TV line and cable modem
  - Satellite dish and satellite modem
  - Wireless access points
- How to add wireless access to a network
- Client/server networks from a business point of view
- Client/server networks from a physical point of view
- What differentiates LANs, MANs, and WANs
- The types of telecommunications media that networks use

CHAPTER SIX OUTLINE

STUDENT LEARNING OUTCOMES

1. List the seven steps in the systems development life cycle and an associated activity for each step.

2. List four reasons why your participation during the systems development life cycle is critical.

3. Describe three of the five reasons why projects fail.

4. Define the three different ways you can staff a system development project.

5. List two of the three advantages of selfsourcing.

6. Describe prototyping and profile an example of a prototype.

7. Describe two of the five advantages of prototyping.

WEB SUPPORT

www.mhhe.com/haag

- Using your computer for more than work

- Animating your computer screen

- Protecting your computer investment

- Searching for freeware and shareware

- Project planning and management

CHAPTER SIX

Systems Development
Steps, Tools, and Techniques

OPENING CASE STUDY:
BUILDING THE UNBELIEVABLE—
THE HOBERMAN ARCH

Have you ever looked at a 100-story skyscraper or a professional football stadium and wondered how in the world that enormous structure was created? Who comes up with the brilliant ideas to build these impossible structures, and how do they actually go about building them? Think about the Eiffel Tower and the Statue of Liberty. Imagine how the concepts probably began on a piece of paper and were transformed into larger-than-life structures.

The Hoberman Arch is a prime example of how one individual pushed the technological envelope and created a new unbelievable structure. The Hoberman Arch is the world's largest unfolding structure to date at 36 feet high and 72 feet in diameter. The 30,000 pound arch is a semicircular aluminum curtain that towered over the Olympic Medals Plaza in the 2002 Winter Olympic Games in Salt Lake City, Utah. Every night during the games the 96 aluminum panels—each approximately 9 feet by 5 feet—spiraled outward and upward in a radial motion forming a ring to reveal the Olympic medals stage. The transforming motion of the structure was similar to the iris in your eye. Throughout the Olympics, 65 medals ceremonies which were seen by more than 3.5 billion people worldwide, watched the unbelievable unfolding aluminum structure transform its size and shape.

The arch, constructed of 16,000 pounds of aluminum, is named after Chuck Hoberman, the world-renowned inventor and toy designer whose best-known invention is the plastic ex-panding and contracting geometric ball known as the Hoberman Sphere. The Hoberman Sphere's unique link system is based on a mathematical principle that allows a structure to expand while keeping its shape. We bet you are wondering how Chuck Hoberman analyzed, designed, and built the Hoberman Arch. How did he take an idea he applied to children's toys and transform it into a 30,000-pound giant structure? The process you use to take an idea and make it a reality is similar whether you're building a skyscraper, creating an information system, or baking a cake. In the most general of terms you follow the same phases, which include plan, analysis, design, develop, test, implement and maintain. Following these phases is how Chuck Hoberman designed and built the Hoberman Arch and how information systems are developed.

It's easy to be impressed by a large structure built by a talented individual, but have you ever been impressed by a large information system? The answer to this question is probably no, because an information system is difficult to see with the human eye. Just imagine the type of talent and creativity it takes to develop an online banking system, a telecommunications billing system, or an airline reservation system.

If you're the least bit curious about how information systems are built, then we welcome you to the glorious and challenging world of systems development. We think you'll enjoy this chapter as it provides a high-level overview of how many wonderful and brilliant information systems are developed and brought to life by following the systems development life cycle.[1]

Introduction

Have you ever wondered why businesses build information systems or how a business knows when it's time to replace an old information system? Typically, new systems are created because knowledge workers request the systems in order to help them perform their work. For example, a marketing manager might request a system to produce product information and track customer sales information. A human resource manager might request a system to track employee vacation and sick days. Almost any position you take in a company today will require you to work with information systems because they are one of the most important parts of any business. Information systems supply the support structure for meeting the company's strategies and goals. It's even common to find that a company's competitive advantage relies heavily on its information systems.

There are many factors that must come together in order to develop a successful information system. This chapter focuses on the *systems development life cycle (SDLC),* a structured step-by-step approach for developing information systems (see Figure 6.1). Along with covering the SDLC, this chapter provides you with some of the primary activities you'll perform when building an information system. Many individuals make the mistake of assuming they won't benefit from learning about the SDLC because they're not planning on working in an IT department. These individuals are making a giant mistake. As a knowledge worker or a system end user, you and your work will definitely be affected by information systems, and you'll be involved in many of the activities performed during the systems development life cycle.

No matter what major you decide to pursue, whether it's accounting, marketing, or communications, you'll be involved in systems development. In fact, your involvement in developing systems is critical to the success of your company. Information systems that effectively meet your needs will help you be more productive and make better decisions. Systems that don't meet your needs may have a damaging effect on your productivity. Therefore, it's crucial you help your organization develop the best systems possible.

One way to ensure you develop successful information systems is to perform all seven phases in the systems development life cycle, or SDLC. As we move through the SDLC in this chapter, we'll focus on how the overall process works, key activities within each phase, and what roles you may play. We don't expect to make you into a systems development expert. Students majoring in IT or MIS often take as many as seven courses that deal with a different aspect of systems development. However, even if you're not majoring in IT or MIS, and don't plan to become an expert, you'll still have systems development roles and responsibilities throughout your career.

Figure 6.1
The Systems Development Life Cycle

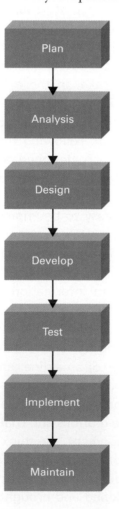

Seven Phases in the Systems Development Life Cycle

There are literally hundreds of different activities associated with each phase in the SDLC. Typical activities include determining budgets, gathering system requirements, modeling, and writing detailed user documentation. The activities you perform during each system development project will vary depending on the type of system you're building and the tools you use to build it. Since we can't possibly cover them all in this brief introduction, we chose a few of the more important SDLC activities detailed in Figure 6.2. These activities are typically performed on every systems development project, and chances are high you'll encounter them as a knowledge worker. Let's begin by taking a look at each phase in the SDLC and its associated activities.

PHASE 1: PLAN

The *planning phase* involves determining a solid plan for developing your information system. Planning is the first and most critical phase of any effort your organization undertakes. This is true regardless of whether you're developing a system that allows your customers to order products over the Internet, determining how to create the best logistical structure for warehouses around the world, or developing a strategic information alliance with another organization. If you don't carefully plan your activities (and determine why they are necessary), your system is doomed to failure. Let's discuss three of the most important activities involved in the planning phase.

SDLC Phase	Activities
1. Plan	• Define the system to be developed
	• Set the project scope
	• Develop the project plan including tasks, resources, and timeframes
2. Analysis	• Gather the business requirements for the system
3. Design	• Design the technical architecture required to support the system
	• Design system models
4. Develop	• Build the technical architecture
	• Build the database and programs
5. Test	• Write the test conditions
	• Perform the testing of the system
6. Implement	• Write detailed user documentation
	• Provide training for the system users
7. Maintain	• Build a help desk to support the system users
	• Provide an environment to support system changes

Figure 6.2

Important Activities in the Systems Development Life Cycle

IDENTIFY AND SELECT THE SYSTEM FOR DEVELOPMENT What systems are required to support the strategic goals of your organization? This is an excellent question, and if you can answer it correctly then you know which systems you must develop. Answering this question incorrectly will cost your organization a great deal of time and money since you'll be building the wrong systems.

Knowledge workers generate proposals to build new information systems when they are having a difficult time performing their jobs. For example, knowledge workers might have trouble gathering information, generating reports, or producing invoices. Hence, they would request a new information system in order to help solve their problems. Unfortunately, most organizations have limited resources and can't afford to develop all proposed information systems. So they look to critical success factors to help determine which systems to build.

A *critical success factor (CSF)* is a factor simply critical to your organization's success. In order to determine which system to develop, your organization tracks all of the proposed systems and prioritizes them by business impact or critical success factors. This allows the business to decide which problems require immediate attention and which problems can wait.

SET PROJECT SCOPE Once your organization defines the system to be developed, you must set the scope for the project. *Project scope* clearly defines the high-level system requirements. Scope is often referred to as the 10,000-foot view of the system or the most basic definition of the system. A *project scope document* is a written definition of the project scope and is usually no longer than a paragraph. Setting the project scope may seem like a simple and straightforward activity, but it's actually rather difficult. Can you imagine trying to define a project scope document, or a single paragraph, to summarize an entire telecommunications billing system including customers, products, charges, taxes, and the like? This is not an easy activity to perform, but it's critical as the project scope sets the boundaries on what will and will not be developed.

DEVELOP PROJECT PLAN Developing a project plan is one of the final activities you'll perform during the planning phase, and it's also one of the hardest and most important activities. The *project plan* defines the what, when, and who questions of system development including all activities to be performed, the individuals, or resources, who will perform the activities, and the time required to complete each activity. The project plan is the guiding force behind ensuring the on-time delivery of a complete and successful information system. It also logs and tracks every single activity that you perform during the project. If you miss one activity, or take longer to complete it than expected, you must adjust the project plan to reflect this change.

Project milestones represent key dates for which you need a certain group of activities performed. For example, completing the planning phase might be a project milestone. If you miss a project milestone then you know the project is experiencing major issues. A *project manager,* an individual who is an expert in project planning and management, defines and develops the project plan and tracks the plan to ensure all key project milestones are completed on time. The project plan is somewhat similar to the syllabus for your course. It tells you what things are due, when they are due, and who is expected to complete them.

To learn more about project planning and management, visit the Web site that supports this text at www.mhhe.com/haag.

THE TRUTH BEHIND BUSINESS REQUIREMENTS

The Standish Group, a research firm based in West Yarmouth, Massachusetts, reported that 31 percent of software projects are cancelled before they ever reach a customer's hands, and 53 percent ultimately cost 189 percent or more than the original budget. American corporations that do complete information system projects typically retain only about 42 percent of the features or business requirements that were originally proposed to the knowledge workers. Bad business requirements are one of the primary causes for so many system failures. Business requirements are the detailed set of knowledge worker requests that the system must meet in order to be successful. They can include anything from basic functions to a knowledge worker's wish list of extreme functions.

Gathering clear and accurate business requirements is essential to delivering a successful system that meets your knowledge worker's needs. Learning how to gather business requirements has become such an advantage to organizations that there are now several different training programs and certifications a knowledge worker can pursue to ensure success in this area. Microsoft Training and Certification center offers several classes on gathering and analyzing business requirements. A knowledge worker can even become Microsoft certified by passing the Analyzing Requirements and Defining Solution Architectures certification exam. The more knowledge workers know about gathering and analyzing business requirements, the greater their chances are for developing successful systems for their company.[2,3]

PHASE 2: ANALYSIS

Once your organization has decided which systems to develop you can move into the analysis phase. The *analysis phase* involves end users and IT specialists working together to gather, understand, and document the business requirements for the proposed system.

GATHER BUSINESS REQUIREMENTS *Business requirements* are the detailed set of knowledge worker requests that the system must meet in order to be successful. The key activity in this phase is gathering clearly defined business requirements. At this point, you're not concerned with any implementation or technical details. For example, you're not yet defining which types of technology you'll use to implement your solution such as an Oracle database or the Java programming language. You're simply focusing on gathering the true business requirements for the system. A sample business requirement might state, "The system must track all customer sales by product, region, and sales representative." This requirement states what the system must do from the business perspective, giving no details or information on how the system is going to meet this requirement.

Gathering business requirements is similar to performing an investigation. You must talk to everyone who has a claim in using the new system in order to find out what is required. An extremely useful way to gather system requirements is to perform a joint application development session. During a *joint application development (JAD)* session knowledge workers and IT specialists meet, sometimes for several days, to define or review the business requirements for the system.

Once you define all of the business requirements, you prioritize them in order of business importance and place them in a formal comprehensive document or the *requirements definition document.* The knowledge workers receive the requirements definition document for their sign-off. *Sign-off* is the knowledge workers' actual signatures indicating they approve all of the business requirements. One of the first major milestones on the project plan is the knowledge worker's sign-off on business requirements.

PHASE 3: DESIGN

The primary goal of the *design phase* is to build a technical blueprint of how the proposed system will work. During the analysis phase, end users and IT specialists work together to develop the business requirements for the proposed system from a *logical* point of view. That is, during analysis you document business requirements without respect to technology or the technical infrastructure that will support the system.

As you move into design, the project team turns its attention to the system from a physical or technical point of view. That is, you take the business requirements generated during the analysis phase and define the supporting technical architecture in the design phase.

DESIGN THE TECHNICAL ARCHITECTURE   The system you build must have a solid technical architecture or else the system will crash or malfunction. The *technical architecture* defines the hardware, software, and telecommunications equipment required to run the system. Most systems run on a computer network with each employee having a workstation and the application running on a server. During this phase, the IT specialists recommend what types of workstations and servers to buy, including memory and storage requirements. Along with the server hardware requirements, the IT specialists define the operating system software. The telecommunications requirements encompass access to the Internet and the ability for end users to dial-in remotely to the server. You typically explore several different technical architectures before choosing the final technical architecture.

The final architecture must meet your needs in terms of time, cost, technical feasibility, and flexibility. It's important to ensure that the final architecture not only meets your current system needs, but also your future system needs. For example, you want to ensure the database is large enough to hold the current volume of customers plus all the new customers you expect to gain over the next five years.

DESIGN SYSTEM MODELS   *Modeling* is the activity of drawing a graphical representation of a design. You model everything you build including screens, reports, software, and databases. There are many different types of modeling activities performed during the design phase including GUI screen design.

The *graphical user interface (GUI)* is the interface to an information system. *GUI screen design* is the ability to model the information system screens for an entire system. You must decide many things when modeling a GUI, including the placement of items on the screen and the number of items contained in a drop-down list. Figure 6.3 (on the opposite page) displays two different formats for an information system GUI design. Notice the menu items appear alphabetically in one design and categorically in the other. You base your decision on how and where to display menu items based on whatever is easiest for the knowledge workers to use. If the menu items are placed incorrectly on the GUI, knowledge workers could waste a significant amount of time just searching the GUI to find the correct item.

PHASE 4: DEVELOP

During the *development phase,* you take all of your detailed design documents from the design phase and transform them into an actual system. This phase marks the point where you go from physical designs to physical implementation. Activities during this phase include writing and coding the software, creating the databases, deploying the telecommunications equipment, and installing hardware and software.

GUI Design – Alphabetical order of buttons

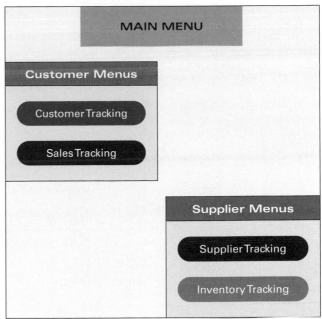

GUI Design – Categorical order of buttons

Figure 6.3

Graphical User Interface
(GUI) Screen Design

BUILD THE TECHNICAL ARCHITECTURE   In order for you to build your system, you must first build the platform on which the system is going to operate. In the design phase, you created a technical architecture blueprint displaying the design of the software, hardware, and telecommunications equipment. In the development phase, you purchase and implement equipment necessary to support the technical architecture.

Most new systems require new hardware and software. It may be as simple as assigning memory to workstations or as complex as setting up a wide area network across several states. Whatever the case, the IT specialists, for the most part, are responsible for buying and installing the software, hardware, and telecommunications equipment.

BUILD THE DATABASE AND SOFTWARE   Once the technical blueprint is built, you initiate and complete the creating of supporting databases and writing the software required for the system. These tasks are usually undertaken by IT specialists, and it may take months or even years to design and create the databases and write all the software.

You cannot take a passive role during development. For example, you are still responsible for ensuring that the databases contain the information that supports your business requirements. So, you need knowledge of databases and the database design process. If you haven't already, we would encourage you to read *Extended Learning Module C* for additional information on designing and building databases.

PHASE 5: TEST

You must perform testing before the knowledge workers begin using the system. The ***testing phase*** verifies that the system works and meets all of the business requirements defined in the analysis phase.

Test Number	Date Tested	Tester	Test Condition	Expected Result	Actual Result	Pass/ Fail
1	1/1/2004	Emily Hickman	Click on System Start button	Main Menu appears	Same as expected result	Pass
2	1/1/2004	Emily Hickman	Click on Logon button in Main Menu	Logon Screen appears asking for user name and password	Same as expected result	Pass
3	1/1/2004	Emily Hickman	Type Emily Hickman in the User Name field	Emily Hickman appears in the User Name field	Same as expected result	Pass
4	1/1/2004	Emily Hickman	Type Zahara123 in the Password field	Zahara123 appears in the Password field	Same as expected result	Pass
5	1/1/2004	Emily Hickman	Click on OK button	User logon request is sent to database and user name and password are verified	Same as expected result	Pass
6	1/1/2004	Emily Hickman	Click on Start	User name and password are accepted and the system Main Menu appears	Screen appeared stating logon failed and user name and password were incorrect	Fail

Figure 6.4

Test Conditions

TEST CONDITIONS: THE PRIMARY TOOL FOR TESTING SUCCESS   Testing is critical. You must have detailed test conditions in order to perform an exhaustive test. *Test conditions* are the detailed steps the system must perform along with the expected results of each step. Figure 6.4 displays several test conditions for testing user logon functionality in a system. The tester will execute each test condition and compare the expected results with the actual results in order to verify that the system functions correctly. Notice how each test condition is extremely detailed and states the result that should occur when executing each test condition. Each time the actual result is different from the expected result a "bug" is generated, and the system goes back to development for a "bug fix."

In Figure 6.4, test condition 6 displays a different actual result than the expected result because the system failed to allow the user to logon. Because this test condition fails, you can determine that the system is not functioning correctly, and it must be sent back to development for a bug fix.

A typical system development effort has hundreds or thousands of test conditions. You must execute and verify all of these test conditions, which ensures the entire system will function correctly. Writing all of the test conditions and performing the actual testing of the software takes a tremendous amount of time and energy and is critical to the successful development of any system. Try not to sacrifice testing time or your system may not work correctly all of the time.

PHASE 6: IMPLEMENT

The goal of phase 6—implementation—is to bring the proposed system to life by placing it in the organization. During the *implementation phase,* you distribute the system to all of the knowledge workers and they begin using the system to perform their everyday jobs.

USER DOCUMENTATION   When you install the system, you must also provide the knowledge workers with a set of *user documentation* that highlights how to use the system. Have you ever used a manual that accompanied a software program? This is the type of documentation that you provide along with the new system. Knowledge workers find it extremely frustrating to have a new system without documentation.

TRAINING   You must provide training for the knowledge workers who are going to use the new system. You can provide several different types of training, and two of the most popular are online training and workshop training.

Online training runs over the Internet or off a CD-ROM. Knowledge workers perform the training at any time, on their own computers, at their own pace. This type of training is convenient for knowledge workers because they can set their own schedule to perform the training. *Workshop training* is held in a classroom environment and led by an instructor. Workshop training is great for difficult systems where the knowledge workers need one-on-one time with an individual instructor.

PHASE 7: MAINTAIN

Maintaining the system is the final phase of any systems development effort. During the *maintenance phase,* you monitor and support the new system to ensure it continues to meet the business goals. Once a system is in place, it must change as your business changes. Constant monitoring and supporting the new system involves making minor changes (for example, new reports or information capturing) and reviewing the system to ensure that it continues to move your organization toward its strategic goals.

HELP DESK   To create the best support environment, you need to provide a way for knowledge workers to request changes. One of the best ways to support knowledge workers is to create a help desk.

A *help desk* is a group of people who respond to knowledge workers' questions. Typically, knowledge workers have a phone number for the help desk they call whenever they have issues or questions about the system. Have you ever found yourself in the situation where you couldn't figure out how to perform a function with a computer program? Imagine if you could simply call a help desk and the person answering is a system expert who will answer all of your questions. Providing a help desk that answers user questions is a terrific way to provide comprehensive support for knowledge workers using new systems.

SUPPORT CHANGES   As changes arise in the business environment, you must react to those changes by assessing their impact on the system. It might well be that the system needs to change to meet the ever-changing needs of the business environment. If so, you must modify the system in order to support the business environment. For example, imagine you work in the manufacturing department of a men's clothing company. You have a system that designs clothes by scanning in different patterns and displaying how

MARRIOTT INTERNATIONAL

The hospitality services industry is highly competitive and it's difficult for any one organization in the industry to achieve a competitive advantage. Marriott International, an international upscale hotel chain, set its strategic goals on becoming the world's leader in the hospitality services industry. Marriott took an ingenious idea and transformed it into an information system with the help from Accenture, one of the world's leading outsourcing companies.

Accenture and Marriott teamed to centralize all of Marriott's financial systems into a single service center. This service center provides Marriott with the ability to link all of its financial systems from around the world together into one single location. This service center allowed Marriott to leverage its operations to provide consistent, cost-effective services making the organization quicker and more flexible. This competitive advantage has quickly helped Marriott leap ahead as one of the top worldwide hospitality service providers.[4]

the patterns look on different outfits. What do you think happens to the system if you started to sell women's clothes? You must change the system to design different types of clothes, such as skirts and blouses.

Knowledge Workers and Their Roles in the Systems Development Life Cycle

Many people who have come before you, and undoubtedly many who will follow, say, "I'm not going to be an IT specialist—so why should I learn about the systems development process?" If you're asking that same question, congratulations, you're well on your way to becoming an information-literate knowledge worker. How so? Because you're asking, Why is this material important to me? What does it mean? How can I use it?

Your participation in the systems development process is vitally important because you are (or will be) a

1. Business process expert
2. Liaison to the customer
3. Quality control analyst
4. Manager of other people

First and foremost, in business you are the business process expert. You know and understand how the business works better than anyone else in the company. For example, if you're an administrator at a hospital and the development of a new nursing scheduling system is underway, who knows best how nursing scheduling should be done? That's right, you do. During systems development, knowledge workers know how things should work, what things should happen, how to handle exceptions, and so on. It would be ludicrous to tell a group of IT specialists to develop a new nursing scheduling system when they have no idea how to schedule nurses. You must tell them how the process currently works and how you currently schedule nurses based on certain criteria such as expertise, overload hours, and time of year. In business, you are a business process expert. Without your input, the new system will never meet your needs.

Second, your knowledge of and participation in the systems development process is vitally important because you're a liaison to the customer. That is, you know what a certain customer segment wants, and you can relay that information to the project development team. For example, if you work for a telephone company and manage a call center that fields billing questions, aren't you qualified to provide information pertaining to the appearance and content of new phone bills? Of course you are. In addition, if you want to make your customers happy, you have to act as a liaison between them and the project development team. The person who deals directly with the customers has the best insight into what the customers want and that person is you.

Third, your participation is important because you'll act as a quality control analyst during the systems development process. Once you help define the logical requirements of a new system, you can't simply walk away and expect a system that meets your needs. For example, you still need to help review alternative technical solutions, acting as a quality control analyst to assure that the chosen technical alternative meets your logical needs.

Finally, your participation in the systems development process is important because you have the ultimate responsibility for the work and productivity of others. In short, you will be a manager of other people, and it's your responsibility to see that new systems will improve the productivity of those you manage.

We have covered the general role knowledge workers play in systems development. Let's take a detailed look at each specific phase and the important role you must play.

PLAN

The most important activity knowledge workers undertake during the planning phase is defining which systems are to be developed. We can't stress the importance of this activity enough. Systems development focuses on either solving a problem or taking advantage of an opportunity. Your new system will be successful only if it solves the right problem or takes advantage of the right opportunity. You must also define the project scope along with the system to be developed. The project scope includes which requirements are in and out of scope for the project.

Developing the project plan is another critical activity in which you'll be directly involved. You must help the project manager define the activities for each phase of the systems development life cycle. The project manager is an expert in project management and you are the expert in the business operations; together the two of you will be able to develop a detailed project plan that meets everyone's needs.

Allocating individuals to work on the different activities is another area where your expertise is critical. There are certain tasks on the project plan that knowledge workers perform and there are certain tasks that IT specialists perform. There are also certain tasks that both knowledge workers and IT specialists perform. You're the expert in your area, and you'll be able to provide insight into which individuals have the skills required to perform certain activities. You'll also help define the project milestones, or important dates, by which certain activities must be performed.

ANALYSIS

You are the business process expert: That means you know how current processes and current systems work, and you know how things need to change. It's vitally important that you provide this information as the current system model will become the foundation for developing the new system model.

One of the primary activities you'll perform during the analysis phase is reviewing business requirements. One of the key things to think about when you are reviewing business requirements is the cost for the company to fix errors if the business requirements are unclear or inaccurate. Finding an error during the analysis and design phase is relatively inexpensive to fix; all you really have to do is change a word document. Finding an error during the testing or implementation phase, however, is incredibly expensive to fix because you have to change the actual system. Figure 6.5 displays how the cost to fix an error grows exponentially the later the error is found in the SDLC.

Imagine what happens if the following business requirement was supposed to have the word *green* instead of *red:* "System must have red GUIs to match colors in company logo." Finding this error during analysis or design is as simple as changing a Word document. But finding this error during testing or implementation requires the developers to rebuild all of the GUIs with the correct color. You must take your time and ensure that every business requirement is accurate and complete.

Figure 6.5

The Cost of Finding Errors

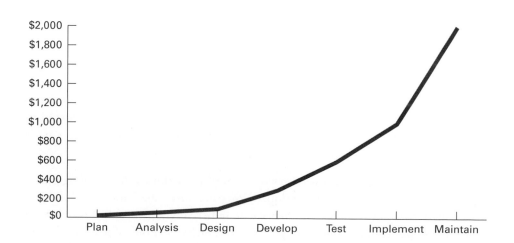

DESIGN

During design, your role decreases as a business process expert and increases as a quality control analyst. IT specialists perform most of the activities during the design phase, but quality assurance is a key role for you. The IT specialist will develop several alternative technical solutions. It's your job to analyze each and ensure that the recommended solution best meets your business requirements. Design walk-through meetings are a key activity during the design phase. You'll be asked to formally sign off on the detailed design documents indicating that you approve of the proposed technical solution.

DEVELOP

IT specialists complete many of the activities in the development phase. Your role during this phase is to confirm any changes to business requirements and track the progress of tasks on the project plan to ensure timely delivery of the system. Constantly reevaluating the project plan during this phase helps you to determine if you'll be able to meet the final system delivery due date.

TEST

IT specialists also perform many of the activities during the testing phase. Your involvement is still critical, as you are the quality assurance expert. You're directly involved with reviewing the test conditions to ensure the IT specialists have tested all of the system functionality and that every single test condition has passed.

You perform the **user acceptance testing (UAT)** to determine if the system satisfies the business requirements and enables the knowledge workers to perform their jobs correctly. UAT is usually the final test performed on the system, and if you decide that the system doesn't meet your expectations this is your last chance to stop the system implementation. You must sign off on the UAT as this gives your final approval to place the system into production.

IMPLEMENT

During implementation, you might attend training or help to perform the training. The system may have passed all of the tests but if the knowledge workers don't use the system properly, the system will fail. You must ensure that all of the knowledge workers have the required training in order to use the system correctly. For example, assume you built a system to calculate employee paychecks. The system is programmed to ask for two numbers, one indicating the amount of time the employee worked in hours, and the other indicating the employee's pay rate per hour. The system then calculates the employee's paycheck by multiplying the two numbers together. What would happen if the end user does not understand the system and he or she enters the amount in the time worked field in minutes instead of hours? The system would calculate incorrect paychecks. If the end user enters in a $10 pay rate per hour and 320 as the amount of time worked, the system would calculate a paycheck for $3,200. This is a serious error as the amount of time worked is supposed to be entered in hours. The employee's correct time is 8 hours instead of 320 minutes, and the paycheck should only be $800.

MAINTAIN

During maintenance, your primary role is to ensure all of the knowledge workers have the support they require in order to use the system. You might be responsible for setting up a help desk or for developing change request forms for your users to fill out if they

YOUR RESPONSIBILITIES DURING EACH PHASE OF THE SYSTEMS DEVELOPMENT LIFE CYCLE

As a knowledge worker, you're a business process expert, liaison to the customer, quality control analyst, and manager of other people. According to which phase of the SDLC you're in, your responsibilities may increase or decrease. In the table below, determine the extent to which you participate in each SDLC phase ac-

cording to your four responsibilities. For each row you should number the SDLC phases from 1 to 7, with 1 identifying the phase in which your responsibility is the greatest and 7 identifying the phase in which your responsibility is the least.

	Plan	Analysis	Design	Develop	Test	Implement	Maintain
Business Process Expert							
Liaison to the Customer							
Quality Control Analyst							
Manager of other people							

require a change to the system. Not only do you have to track the change requests, but also ensure any changes requested for the system are worth performing. Changes cost money, especially once a system has reached the maintenance phase. You must carefully weigh each requested change for merit and monetary worth.

IT SPECIALISTS AND KNOWLEDGE WORKERS WORKING TOGETHER

It's important to build systems with both the knowledge workers and IT specialists working together because the knowledge workers are the business process experts and quality control analysts, and the IT specialists are highly skilled in designing, implementing, and maintaining the systems. By having knowledge workers and IT specialists combine their unique skills when performing the activities during the SDLC you'll be sure to build a solid system that supports your organization's strategies and goals.

Why Systems Fail

Only 20 percent of systems built today are successful. That is correct, 80 percent of systems fail, or only 2 systems out of 10 will be successful. Are you wondering why so many systems development efforts fail? That is an excellent question and one difficult to answer as systems fail for so many different reasons. The following are five primary reasons why systems fail.

1. Unclear or missing requirements
2. Skipping SDLC phases
3. Failure to manage project scope
4. Failure to manage project plan
5. Changing technology

FAILED SYSTEMS CAN LEAD TO BIG LAWSUITS

There are so many reasons why systems fail that it's impossible to list them all. The bottom line is that systems do fail, costing some companies millions of dollars. One of the top outsourcing companies in the United States has had several lawsuits filed against it for failure to build and deliver information systems. The most recent lawsuit was for $350 million by a federal agency.

Elizabeth Ready, the auditor of accounts for the State of Vermont, said that significant problems cropping up in the state tax department's new automated system are causing her to consider investigating the $14 million system created by this company. Ready said she was aware of the $185 million settlement following the failed implementation of Mississippi's tax system,

and she has been following the developments in Ohio, where the same company has been named as a defendant in a class action lawsuit over the processing of child support payments. "Whenever you see the magnitude of problems we've had here in Vermont, you want to look at everything," Ready said. "It would not be right to blame the company for any of these problems at this point, but surely it would be appropriate to take a look."

Creating solid information systems that meet knowledge worker's needs is an incredibly difficult task. We can't promise that following the SDLC will automatically build a perfect system, but it's a great way to start and ensure you're on the path to success.[6]

UNCLEAR OR MISSING REQUIREMENTS

The most common reason why systems fail is because the business requirements are either missing or incorrectly gathered during the analysis phase. The business requirements drive the entire system, if they are not accurate or complete there is no way the system will be successful.

Let's look at an example of gathering an inaccurate requirement. Assume you're building a student registration system. What happens if you documented the business requirement as, "System must not allow students to add classes?" This requirement is incorrect and should be stated, "System must allow students to add classes." If you build a student registration system that doesn't allow students to add classes, the system will be a complete failure.

Let's take a look at an example of missing a requirement. What if you're in the development phase and suddenly realize that the system must also calculate a student's grade point average? This is a major requirement to miss and trying to add this functionality to the system at this late date would be extremely difficult and expensive.

SKIPPING SDLC PHASES

The first thing individuals tend to do when a project falls behind schedule is to start skipping phases in the SDLC. For example, a project is three weeks behind in the development phase so the project manager decides to reduce testing time from six weeks to three weeks. Obviously, you can't perform all of the testing in half of the time. But failing to test the system will lead to unfound errors, and chances are high that the system will fail. It's critical that you perform all phases in the SDLC during every project. Skipping any of the phases is sure to lead to system failure.

FAILURE TO MANAGE PROJECT SCOPE

As the project progresses, the project manager must track the status of each activity and adjust the project plan if an activity is added or is taking longer than expected. *Scope creep* occurs when the scope of the project increases. Let's return to the student registration system example. Imagine how the scope of the project would change if the knowledge worker suddenly requested that the system track instructor evaluations. This scope creep would cause the system development efforts to more than double in order to add in the extra request.

Feature creep occurs when developers add extra features that were not part of the initial requirements. An example of feature creep would be if the developer decided to add in an online Help feature for the students. Although this feature is a great idea, the knowledge workers had not requested it and it's not planned for in the budget or on the project plan. Building this feature would take time and money and jeopardize the project's success. Feature creep is difficult to manage and can easily put a project behind schedule.

FAILURE TO MANAGE PROJECT PLAN

Managing the project plan is one of the biggest challenges during systems development. Figure 6.6 provides a sample project plan. What is the first thing you notice about the project plan and the SDLC? The project plan outlines the SDLC as the primary phases performed during system development. Under each phase, you'll notice a sample activity that you'll complete during the phase. Beside each activity, you'll notice the estimated duration, or the time you have to complete the activity. Each activity also has a resource name indicating who must work on the activity. Notice that some activities have only one individual assigned and some activities have two individuals assigned. The project plan is the road map you follow during the development of the system. Developing the initial project plan is the easiest part of the project manager's job. Managing and revising the project plan is the hardest part.

There are many reasons why the project manager must continually review and revise the project plan. Imagine what happens to the plan if an individual is out sick or on vacation and can't complete his or her activities? What happens if you have to add some activities to the project plan? What happens if you have to delete some of the activities on the project plan? What happens if some of the activities take significantly longer to complete than expected? All of these questions answer why the project manager must continuously review and revise the project plan. For this reason, the project plan is a living document since it changes almost daily on any project. Failure to monitor, revise, and update the project plan is a primary reason why many projects fail.

Figure 6.6

Sample Project Plan

ID	Task Name	Duration	Resource Names	May 26, '02	Jun 2, '02	Jun 9, '02	Jun 16, '02	Jun 23, '02	Ju
1	**Plan**	**3 days**							
2	Set scope	3 days	Scott	Scott					
3	**Analysis**	**8 days**							
4	Gather Business Requirements	8 days	Anne, Martha		Anne, Martha				
5	**Design**	**3 days**							
6	Model GUI	3 days	David			David			
7	**Develop**	**2 days**							
8	Build Database	2 days	Logan			Logan			
9	**Test**	**3 days**							
10	Write Test Condition	3 days	Martha				Martha		
11	**Implement**	**1 day?**							
12	Install System	1 day?	Leigh				Leigh		
13	**Maintain**	**6 days**							
14	Setup Help Desk	6 days	Naomi						

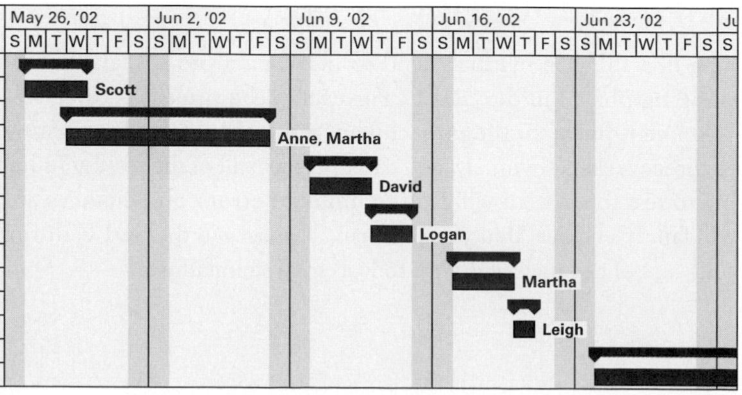

CHANGING TECHNOLOGY

Many of the system examples we discussed in this chapter are small and easy to implement, such as a student registration system. These projects are great for discussion and initial understanding, but they're not indicative of real-world projects. Many real-world projects have hundreds of business requirements, take years to complete, and cost millions of dollars.

Gordon Moore, cofounder of Intel Corporation, observed in 1965 that chip density doubles every 18 months. This observation, known as Moore's law, simply means that memory sizes, processor power, and so forth all follow the same pattern and roughly double in capacity every 18 months. As Moore's law states, technology changes at an incredibly fast pace. It's possible to have to revise your entire project plan in the middle of a project due to a change in technology. For example, imagine you're building a system that has a project time frame of three years to complete. What happens if one year into the project a new programming language is released that is far superior to the programming language you're currently using? If you decide to change to the new programming language you have to revise your entire project plan including rewriting any code that has already been written. Technology changes so fast that it's almost impossible to deliver an information system without feeling the pain of changing technology.

Now that you understand the SDLC and your roles within it, let's turn our attention to who is actually going to build the system. When approaching systems development as a knowledge worker, you have three choices for answering this question:

1. IT specialists within your organization—Insourcing
2. Knowledge workers such as yourself—Selfsourcing
3. Another organization—Outsourcing

Insourcing a project means that IT specialists within your organization will develop the system. If this is your decision, you're choosing to insource the development of a new system with internal employees. Internal employees are employees that work directly for the organization that is building the system. Insourcing is one of the most common methods for system development because it's typically the cheapest, as the company doesn't have to hire contractors. Insourcing is also popular because internal employees are already familiar with the operations of the company. In previous sections, we've introduced you to the SDLC and your roles within it when you choose to insource. So, you already understand the SDLC process through insourcing. Let's now turn our attention to selfsourcing and outsourcing.

Selfsourcing

What we want to look at now is how you, as a knowledge worker, can go about developing systems, which we call selfsourcing. *Selfsourcing* (also called *knowledge worker development* or *end-user development*) is the development and support of IT systems by knowledge workers with little or no help from IT specialists. Selfsourcing is becoming quite common in most organizations and is part of the overall concept of knowledge worker development or end-user computing.

It's important to understand that some selfsourcing projects still involve support from IT specialists. For example, Eaton Corporation, located in Minnesota, actively encourages the selfsourcing of systems development in Lotus Notes by providing training classes to knowledge workers. In these training classes knowledge workers learn how to set up a document database; use built-in templates to develop applications questions quickly; and create customized forms, views, and macros. And, when Eaton's knowledge workers actually begin creating their own systems, IT specialists are available to answer questions and handle more complicated technical issues, such as installing software on a client/server network or creating a local area network from scratch.[7]

THE SELFSOURCING PROCESS

You can probably create many of the small knowledge worker computing systems in a matter of hours, such as customizing reports, creating macros, and interfacing a letter in a word processing package with a customer database to create individualized mailings. More complicated systems, such as a student registration system or employee payroll system, require that you follow the formal SDLC process during development.

In Figure 6.7 we've illustrated the selfsourcing process and we've summarized the key tasks within some of the selfsourcing steps. As you can see, the selfsourcing process is similar to the phases in the SDLC. However, you should notice that the selfsourcing process includes prototyping (model building, which we'll discuss in detail in the next section). This is key—when you develop a system for yourself, you will most often go through the process of prototyping. As you consider the Key Tasks and Figure 6.7, we would alert you to several important issues.

Figure 6.7

The Selfsourcing Process and Key Tasks in Selfsourcing

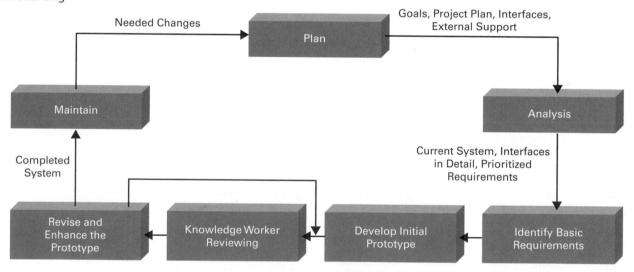

KEY TASKS IN SELFSOURCING

Plan
- Define system goals in light of organizational goals
- Create a project plan
- Identify any systems that require an interface
- Determine what type of external support you will require

Analysis
- Study and model the current system
- Understand the interfaces in detail
- Define and prioritize your requirements

Maintain
- Completely document the system
- Provide ongoing maintenance

HOW HAVE YOU SELFSOURCED?

You've probably performed the selfsourcing process many times. For example, if you've created a résumé, you probably prototyped it using a word processing package. And, if you've prepared a presentation for a class, you may have prototyped it using a presentation graphics software package.

Think about the many other instances when you've selfsourced and used personal productivity software.

For each, identify your goal, what personal productivity software you used, and how you performed the prototyping process. Do some types of personal productivity software packages lend themselves better to prototyping than others? What are they? What types of personal productivity software packages do not lend themselves well to prototyping? Why is this true?

ALIGNING YOUR SELFSOURCING EFFORTS WITH ORGANIZATIONAL GOALS
When you first begin planning a system you want to develop, you must consider it in light of your organization's goals. If you're considering developing a system for yourself that's counterintuitive to your organization's goals, then you should abandon it immediately. Obviously, you don't want to build a system that reduces sales or decreases the number of customers. You have to consider how you spend your time building systems carefully as you are busy and your time is extremely valuable. It's important to remember that developing a system through selfsourcing takes time—your time.

So, your first activity should always be to consider what you want to develop in conjunction with what your organization expects you to do.

DETERMINING WHAT EXTERNAL SUPPORT YOU WILL REQUIRE As we've already stated, some selfsourcing projects will involve support from IT specialists within your organization. Your in-house IT specialists are a valuable resource during the selfsourcing process. Don't forget about them and be sure to include them in the planning phase. The chances of building a successful system increase greatly when you have both knowledge workers and IT specialists working together.

DOCUMENTING THE SYSTEM ONCE COMPLETE Even if you're developing a system just for yourself, you still need to document how it works. When you get promoted, other people will come in behind you and probably use the system you developed and might even make changes to it. For this reason, you must document how your system works from a technical point of view as well as create an easy-to-use operation manual.

PROVIDING ONGOING SUPPORT When you develop a system through selfsourcing, you must be prepared to provide your own support and maintenance. Since you are the primary owner and developer of the system, you're solely responsible for ensuring the system continues to function properly and continues to meet all of the changing business requirements. You must also be prepared to support other knowledge workers who use your system, as they will be counting on you to help them learn and understand the system you developed. For example, if you develop a customer relationship database using Microsoft Office XP, you must be prepared to convert it to Microsoft Office 2004 when it becomes available and your organization adopts it. The systems development process doesn't end with implementation: It continues on a daily basis with support and maintenance.

THE ADVANTAGES OF SELFSOURCING

IMPROVES REQUIREMENTS DETERMINATION During insourcing, knowledge workers tell IT specialists what they want. In selfsourcing, knowledge workers essentially tell themselves what they want. This greatly improves the effectiveness of capturing requirements, which helps ensure the success of the new system.

INCREASES KNOWLEDGE WORKER PARTICIPATION AND SENSE OF OWNERSHIP No matter what you do, if you do it yourself, you always take more pride in the result. The same is true when developing an IT system through selfsourcing. If knowledge workers know that they own the system because they developed and now support it, they are more apt to participate actively in its development and have a greater sense of ownership.

INCREASES SPEED OF SYSTEMS DEVELOPMENT Many small systems do not lend themselves well to insourcing. These smaller systems may suffer from "analysis paralysis" because they don't require a structured step-by-step approach to their development. In fact, insourcing may be slower than selfsourcing for smaller projects.

POTENTIAL PITFALLS AND RISKS OF SELFSOURCING

INADEQUATE KNOWLEDGE WORKER EXPERTISE LEADS TO INADEQUATELY DEVELOPED SYSTEMS Many selfsourcing systems are never completed because knowledge workers lack the real expertise with IT tools to develop a complete and fully working system. It may seem like no big deal. The system couldn't have been that important if the people who needed it never finished developing it. But that's not true. If knowledge workers choose to develop their systems, they must spend time away from their primary duties within the organization. This diverted time may mean lost revenue.

LACK OF ORGANIZATIONAL FOCUS CREATES "PRIVATIZED" IT SYSTEMS Many selfsourcing projects are done outside the IT systems plan of an organization. This simply means that there may be many private IT systems that do not interface with other systems and possess uncontrolled and duplicated information. These types of systems serve no meaningful purpose in an organization and can lead only to more problems.

INSUFFICIENT ANALYSIS OF DESIGN ALTERNATIVES LEADS TO SUBPAR IT SYSTEMS Some knowledge workers jump to immediate conclusions about the hardware and software they should use without carefully analyzing all the possible alternatives. If this happens, knowledge workers may develop systems that are processing inefficiently.

LACK OF DOCUMENTATION AND EXTERNAL SUPPORT LEADS TO SHORT-LIVED SYSTEMS When knowledge workers develop systems, they often forgo documentation of how the system works and fail to realize that they can expect little or no support from IT specialists. All systems—no matter who develops them—must change over time. Knowledge workers must realize that those changes are their responsibility. They also need to realize that making those changes is easier if they document the system well.

Outsourcing

Your final choice is to outsource by choosing external employees from another organization, or contractors, to develop the system. Typically, large systems have both internal and external employees working on the development effort.

DEVELOPING STRATEGIC PARTNERSHIPS

The Outsourcing Research Council recently completed a study indicating that human resources (HR) is a top outsourcing area for many companies. Fifty percent of the companies surveyed said they were already outsourcing some or all of their payroll processing and another 38 percent said they were considering it.

Energizer, the world's largest manufacturer of batteries and flashlights, outsourced its HR operations to ADP, one of the top HR outsourcing companies. Energizer currently has more than 3,500 employees and 2,000 retired employees who all require multiple HR services. ADP provides Energizer with centralized call centers, transaction processing services, and Web-based employee self-service systems. Energizer's Vice President of Human Resources, Peter Conrad, stated, "ADP was clearly the most capable and offered the kind of one-stop shopping our company was looking for." For several of the systems provided by ADP employee usage has topped over 80 percent in the six months the systems have been active.[8]

Energizer's choice of using ADP to develop its human resource system is an example of outsourcing. **Outsourcing** is the delegation of specific work to a third party for a specified length of time, at a specified cost, and at a specified level of service. IT outsourcing today represents a significant opportunity for your organization to capitalize on the intellectual resources of other organizations by having them take over and perform certain business functions in which they have more expertise than the knowledge workers in your company. IT outsourcing for software development can take one of four forms (see Figure 6.8):

1. Purchasing existing software
2. Purchasing existing software and paying the publisher to make certain modifications

1. Purchase existing software.

2. Purchase existing software and pay publisher to make certain modifications.

YOUR ORGANIZATION

4. Outsource the development of an entirely new and unique system for which no software exists.

3. Purchase software and pay publisher for the right to make changes yourself.

Figure 6.8

Major Forms of Outsourcing Systems Development

HOW MANY OUTSOURCING COMPANIES ARE THERE?

Assume your company is looking to outsource its payroll activities including calculating the payroll and generating the paychecks each month. Try searching the Internet to find different companies that offer this outsourcing service. Fill in the following table comparing the advantages and disadvantages of the different companies you find. Discuss which one you would choose and why.

Company Name	Advantages	Disadvantages

3. Purchasing existing software and paying the publisher for the right to make modifications yourself

4. Outsourcing the development of an entirely new and unique system for which no software exists

In these instances, we're not talking about personal productivity software you can buy at a local computer store. We're talking about large software packages that may cost millions of dollars. For example, every organization has to track financial information, and there are several different systems they can purchase that help them perform this activity. Have you ever heard of Oracle Financials? This is a great system your organization can buy that tracks all of the organizational financial information. Building a financial system would be a waste of time and money since there are several systems already built that probably meet your organizational needs.

Another great example of purchasing a prebuilt system is a product called Arbor/BP. This product is a telecommunications billing system developed by a company called Kenan. Many telecommunications companies around the world have purchased Arbor/BP to track and bill customer phone calls and digital services. A company could choose to build its own telecommunications billing system; however, this would take a significant amount of time, money, and expertise. Most companies find it cheaper, faster, and easier to buy a prebuilt system and then customize it to the company's specific needs.

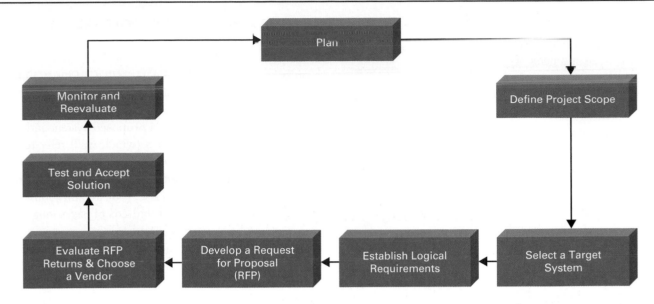

Figure 6.9
The Outsourcing Process

THE OUTSOURCING PROCESS

The outsourcing process is both similar to and quite different from the systems development life cycle. It's different in that you turn over much of the design, development, testing, implementation, and maintenance steps to another organization (see Figure 6.9). It's similar in that your organization begins with planning and defining the project scope. It's during one of these phases that your organization may come to understand that it needs a particular system but cannot develop it in-house. If so, that proposed system can be outsourced. Below, we briefly describe the remaining steps of the outsourcing process.

SELECT A TARGET SYSTEM   Once you've identified a potential system for outsourcing, you still have some important questions to answer. For example, will the proposed system manage strategic and sensitive information? If so, you probably wouldn't consider outsourcing it. That is, you don't want another organization seeing and having access to your most vital information. If you're building an ordering system you might not want people to view your product prices, as they may be a significant part of your strategic advantage.

You should also consider whether the system is small enough to be selfsourced. If so, let knowledge workers within your organization develop the system instead of outsourcing it. On the other hand, if the proposed system is fairly large and supports a routine, nonsensitive business function, then you should target it for outsourcing.

ESTABLISH LOGICAL REQUIREMENTS   Regardless of your choice of insourcing or outsourcing, you must still perform the analysis phase including the primary activity of gathering the business requirements for the proposed system. Remember that the business requirements drive the entire system; if they are not accurate or complete, there is no way the system will be successful. Regardless of your choice to insource or outsource, you must still gather accurate and complete business requirements. If you choose to outsource, part of gathering the business requirements becomes your request for proposal.

1. Organizational overview
2. Problem statement
3. Description of current system

   3.1 Underlying business processes
   3.2 Hardware
   3.3 Software (application and system)
   3.4 System processes
   3.5 Information
   3.6 System interfaces

4. Description of proposed system

   4.1 New processes
   4.2 New information

5. Request for new system design

   5.1 Hardware
   5.2 Software
   5.3 Underlying business processes
   5.4 System processes
   5.5 Information
   5.6 System interfaces

6. Request for implementation plan

   6.1 Training
   6.2 Conversion

7. Request for support plan

   7.1 Hardware
   7.2 Software

8. Request for development time frame
9. Request for statement of outsourcing costs
10. How RFP returns will be scored
11. Deadline for RFP returns
12. Primary contact person

Figure 6.10

Outline of a Request for Proposal (RFP)

DEVELOP A REQUEST FOR PROPOSAL   Outsourcing involves telling another organization what you want. What you want is essentially the logical requirements for a proposed system, and you convey that information by developing a request for proposal. A *request for proposal (RFP)* is a formal document that describes in detail your logical requirements for a proposed system and invites outsourcing organizations (which we'll refer to as "vendors") to submit bids for its development. An RFP is the most important document in the outsourcing process. For systems of great size, your organization may create an RFP that's literally hundreds of pages long and requires months of work to complete.

It's vitally important that you take all the time you need to create a complete and thorough RFP. Eventually, your RFP will become the foundation for a legal and binding contract into which your organization and the vendor will enter. At a minimum, your RFP should contain the elements listed in Figure 6.10. Notice that an RFP includes key information such as an overview of your organization, underlying business processes that the proposed system will support, a request for a development time frame, and a request for a statement of detailed outsourcing costs.

All this information is vitally important to both your organization and the vendors. For your organization, the ability to develop a complete and thorough RFP means that you completely understand what you have and what you want. For the vendors, a complete and thorough RFP makes it easier to propose a system that will meet most, if not all, your needs.

EVALUATE REQUEST FOR PROPOSAL RETURNS AND CHOOSE A VENDOR   Your next activity in outsourcing is to evaluate the RFP returns and choose a vendor. You perform this evaluation of the RFP returns according to the scoring method you identified in the RFP. This is not a simple process. No two vendors will ever provide RFP returns in the same format, and the RFP returns you receive are usually longer than the RFP itself.

Once you've thoroughly analyzed the RFP returns, it's time to rank them and determine which vendor to use. Most often, you rank RFP returns according to cost, time, and the scoring mechanism you identified. Again, ranking RFP returns is not simple. Although one vendor may be the cheapest, it may require the longest time to develop the new system. Another vendor may be able to provide a system quickly but without some of the features you have identified as critical.

Once you've chosen the vendor, a lengthy legal process follows. Outsourcing is serious business—and serious business between two organizations almost always requires a lot of negotiating and the use of lawyers. Eventually, your organization has to enter a legal and binding contract that very explicitly states the features of the proposed system, the exact costs, the time frame for development, acceptance criteria, and criteria for breaking the contract for nonperformance or noncompliance.

TEST AND ACCEPT SOLUTION   As with all systems, testing and accepting the solution is crucial. Once a vendor installs the new system, it's up to you and your organization to test the entire system before accepting it. You'll need to develop detailed test plans and test conditions that test the entire system. This alone may involve months of running and testing the new system while continuing to operate the old one (the parallel conversion method).

When you "accept" a solution, you're saying that the system performs to your expectations and that the vendor has met its contract obligations so far. Accepting a solution involves granting your sign-off on the system, which releases the vendor from any further development efforts or modifications to the system. Be careful when you do this because modifications to the system after sign-off can be extremely expensive. In 1996, Duke Power Company, a utility company based in Charlotte, North Carolina, continually tested but never accepted an outsourced system. Duke officially turned the lights out on a $23 million customer information system project after investing more than $12 million in its development. Duke Power outsourced the development of the customer information system and had no choice but to terminate the project when the vendor requested an additional two years to make necessary modifications.[9]

MONITOR AND REEVALUATE   Just like the systems you develop using the SDLC, systems you obtain through outsourcing need constant monitoring and reevaluation. You must continually evaluate and revise the project plan to ensure the system is going to meet its delivery schedule. In outsourcing, you also have to reassess your working relationship with the vendor. Is the vendor providing maintenance when you need it and according to the contract? Does the system really perform the stated functions? Do month-end and year-end processes work according to your desires? Does the vendor provide acceptable support if something goes wrong? These are all important questions that affect the success of your outsourcing efforts.

The most important question, though, is, Does the system still meet our needs and how much does it cost to update the system? In many outsourcing instances, if the system needs updating you must contract with the original vendor. This is potentially one of the greatest drawbacks to outsourcing. When you outsource a system, you create a heavy dependency on that vendor to provide updates to the system, and updates are not inexpensive.

THE ADVANTAGES AND DISADVANTAGES OF OUTSOURCING

Making the decision to outsource is critical to your organization's success. Throughout our discussions of outsourcing, we've directly or indirectly described many of the advantages and disadvantages of outsourcing. What follows is a summary of the major advantages and disadvantages of outsourcing the systems development process in order to help you make this important decision.

ADVANTAGES   Allows your organization to . . .

- *Focus on unique core competencies:* By outsourcing systems development efforts that support noncritical business functions, your organization can focus on developing systems that support important, unique core competencies.
- *Exploit the intellect of another organization:* Outsourcing allows your organization to obtain intellectual capital by purchasing it from another

organization. Often you won't be able to find individuals with all of the expertise required to develop a system. Outsourcing allows you to find those individuals with the expertise you need to get your system developed and implemented.

- *Better predict future costs:* When you outsource a function, whether systems development or some other business function, you know the exact costs. Zale Corporation, a discount jewelry store, outsourced some of its IT systems and tied payments to the vendor according to how well Zale's stores perform. After all, the new IT systems will affect a store's performance, so why not tie a vendor's payment to it?[10]

- *Acquire leading-edge technology:* Outsourcing allows your organization to acquire leading-edge technology without technical expertise and the inherent risks of choosing the wrong technology.

- *Reduce costs:* Outsourcing is often seen as a money saver for most organizations. And, indeed, reducing costs is one of the important reasons organizations outsource.

- *Improve performance accountability:* Outsourcing involves delegating work to another organization at a specified level of service. Your organization can use this specified level of service as leverage to guarantee that it gets exactly what it wants from the vendor.

DISADVANTAGES   Your organization may suffer from outsourcing because it . . .

- *Reduces technical know-how for future innovation:* Outsourcing is a way of exploiting the intellect of another organization. It can also mean that your organization will no longer possess that expertise internally. If you outsource because you don't have the necessary technical expertise today, you'll probably have to outsource for the same reason tomorrow.

- *Reduces degree of control:* Outsourcing means giving up control. No matter what you choose to outsource, you are in some way giving up control over that function.

- *Increases vulnerability of strategic information:* Outsourcing systems development involves telling another organization what information you use and how you use that information. In doing so, you could be giving away strategic information and secrets.

- *Increases dependency on other organizations:* As soon as you start outsourcing, you immediately begin depending on another organization to perform many of your business functions. For example, GE was set to introduce a new washing machine, but it didn't happen on time. It seems that GE outsourced some of its parts development and the vendor was late, resulting in a delayed product introduction that cost GE money.[11]

Now that you have a solid understanding of the selfsourcing, insourcing, and outsourcing processes, let's take a look at creating prototypes. Creating prototypes is another key decision you'll make during the design and development phases. When approaching systems development as a knowledge worker the decision to prototype has many significant advantages, which we'll discuss in detail in the next section.

A REQUEST FOR PROPOSAL AND THE SYSTEMS DEVELOPMENT LIFE CYCLE

If you review Figure 6.10 closely, you'll notice that an RFP looks very similar to the phases of the SDLC. In the table below, identify which phases of the SDLC correspond to each element of an RFP.

Elements of a Request for Proposal	Phase(s) of the SDLC
1. Organizational overview	
2. Problem statement	
3. Description of current system	
4. Description of proposed system	
5. Request for new system design	
6. Request for implementation plan	
7. Request for support plan	
8. Request for development time frame	
9. Request for statement of outsourcing costs	
10. How RFP returns will be scored	
11. Deadline for RFP returns	
12. Primary contact person	

Prototyping

Prototyping is the process of building a model that demonstrates the features of a proposed product, service, or system. A *prototype,* then, is simply a model of a proposed product, service, or system. If you think about it, people prototype all the time. Automobile manufacturers build prototypes of cars to demonstrate safety features, aerodynamics, and comfort. Building contractors construct models of homes and other structures to show layout and fire exits. Your instructor may give you sample test questions for an upcoming exam. These sample questions are a model of what you can expect on the exam.

Building a small prototype during the design phase allows you the opportunity to have other knowledge workers review the prototype and suggest changes, and further refine and enhance the prototype to include suggestions. Most notably, prototyping is a dynamic process that allows knowledge workers to see, work with, and evaluate a model and suggest changes to that model to increase the likelihood of success of the proposed system.

MICROSOFT UNVEILS LATEST MIRA PROTOTYPE

Imagine walking around your home with a computer monitor. This does not mean carrying around a laptop but just the computer monitor and yet you're still able to do everything the same as if you were carrying around an entire computer. You could rip the display off of your laptop and carry it around your home while browsing the Web, checking e-mail, looking at photos, and listening to music.

The Mira mobile monitor is the latest prototype developed by Microsoft. A new set of Windows-based technologies collectively called Mira enable wireless Webpad devices for your home. A wireless link between the Mira monitor and the computer keeps the connection alive. The full power of the computer is available along with access to all files and data stored on the computer. Bill Gates said the company is hoping to launch Mira-enabled devices at the end of 2002 and is looking at a price range of between $500 and $1,000 for first-generation Mira hardware.[12]

In systems development, prototyping can be a valuable tool to you. Prototyping is an iterative process in which you build a model from basic business requirements, have other knowledge workers review the prototype and suggest changes, and further refine and enhance the prototype to include suggestions. Most notably, prototyping is a dynamic process that allows knowledge workers to see, work with, and evaluate a model and suggest changes to that model to increase the likelihood of success of the proposed system.

You can use prototyping to perform a variety of functions in the systems development process. Some of these functions include:

- *Gathering requirements:* Prototyping is a great requirements gathering tool. You start by simply prototyping the basic systems requirements. Then you allow knowledge workers to add more requirements (information and processes) as you revise the prototype. Most people use prototyping for this purpose.

- *Helping determine requirements:* In many systems development processes, knowledge workers aren't sure what they really want: they simply know that the current system doesn't meet their needs. In this instance, you can use prototyping to help knowledge workers determine their exact requirements.

- *Proving that a system is technically feasible:* Let's face it, there are some things to which you cannot apply technology. And knowing whether you can is often unclear while defining the scope of the proposed system. If you're uncertain about whether something can be done, prototype it first. A prototype you use to prove the technical feasibility of a proposed system is a ***proof-of-concept prototype.***

- *Selling the idea of a proposed system:* Many people resist changes in IT. The current system seems to work fine, and they see no reason to go through the process of developing and learning to use a new system. In this case, you have to convince them that the proposed system will be better than the current one. Because prototyping is relatively fast, you won't have to invest a lot of time to develop a prototype that can convince people of the worth of the proposed system. A prototype you use to convince people of the worth of a proposed system is a ***selling prototype.***

THE PROTOTYPING PROCESS

Prototyping is an excellent tool in systems development. However, who uses prototyping and for what purpose determines how the prototyping process occurs. Most often, IT specialists use prototyping in the SDLC to form a technical system blueprint. In self-sourcing, however, you can often continue to refine the prototype until it becomes the final system. The prototyping process for either case is almost the same; only the result differs. Figure 6.11 illustrates the difference between insourcing and selfsourcing prototyping. Regardless of who does the prototyping, the prototyping process involves four steps:

1. *Identify basic requirements:* During the first step, you gather the basic requirements for a proposed system. These basic requirements include input and output information and, perhaps, some simple processes. At this point, however, you're typically unconcerned with editing rules, security issues, or end-of-period processing (for example, producing W-2s for a payroll system at the end of the year).

2. *Develop initial prototype:* Based on the basic requirements, you then set out to develop an initial prototype. Most often, your initial prototype will include only user interfaces, such as data entry screens and reports.

3. *Knowledge worker reviewing:* Step 3 starts the truly iterative process of prototyping. When knowledge workers first enter this step, they evaluate the prototype and suggest changes or additions. In subsequent returns to step 3

Figure 6.11

Prototyping Steps for Insourcing and Selfsourcing

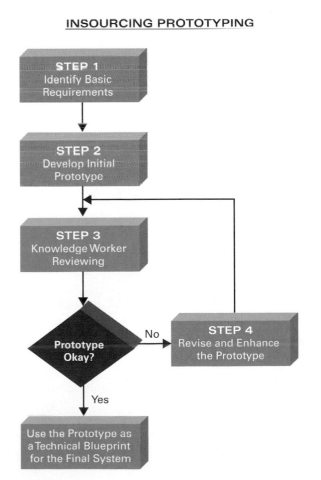

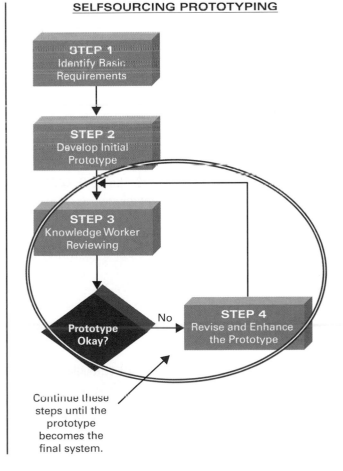

(after step 4), they evaluate new versions of the prototype. It's important to involve as many knowledge workers as possible during this step. This will help resolve any discrepancies in such areas as terminology and operational processes.

4. *Revise and enhance the prototype:* The final sequential step in the prototyping process is to revise and enhance the prototype according to any knowledge worker suggestions. In this step, you make changes to the current prototype and add any new requirements. Next, you return to step 3 and have the knowledge workers review the new prototype.

For either insourcing or selfsourcing, you continue the iterative processes of steps 3 and 4 until knowledge workers are happy with the prototype. What happens to the prototype after that, however, differs.

During selfsourcing, you're most likely to use the targeted application software package or application development tool to develop the prototype. This simply means that you can continually refine the prototype until it becomes the final working system. For example, if you choose to develop a customer service application using Lotus Notes, you can prototype many of the operational features using Lotus Notes development tools. Because you develop these prototypes using the targeted application development environment, your prototype can eventually become the final system.

That process is not necessarily the same when insourcing. Most often, IT specialists develop prototypes using special prototyping development tools. Many of these tools don't support the creation of a final system—you simply use them to build prototypes. Therefore, the finished prototype becomes a blueprint or technical design for the final system. In the appropriate stages of the SDLC, IT specialists will implement the prototypes in another application development environment better suited to the development of production systems.

THE ADVANTAGES OF PROTOTYPING

ENCOURAGES ACTIVE KNOWLEDGE WORKER PARTICIPATION First and foremost, prototyping encourages knowledge workers to actively participate in the development process. As opposed to interviewing and reviewing documentation, prototyping allows knowledge workers to see and work with working models of the proposed system.

HELPS RESOLVE DISCREPANCIES AMONG KNOWLEDGE WORKERS During the prototyping process, many knowledge workers participate in defining the requirements for and reviewing the prototype. The word *many* is key. If several knowledge workers participate in prototyping, you'll find it's much easier to resolve any discrepancies the knowledge workers may encounter.

GIVES KNOWLEDGE WORKERS A FEEL FOR THE FINAL SYSTEM Prototyping, especially for user interfaces, provides a feel for how the final system will look, feel, and work. When knowledge workers understand the look, feel, and working of the final system, they are more apt to determine its potential for success.

HELPS DETERMINE TECHNICAL FEASIBILITY Proof-of-concept prototypes are great for determining the technical feasibility of a proposed system.

HELPS SELL THE IDEA OF A PROPOSED SYSTEM Finally, selling prototypes can help break down resistance barriers. Many people don't want new systems because the

CUSTOMIZING YOUR PROTOTYPE FOR A GLOBAL MARKET

There are thousands of prototypes available for all different kinds of systems. System prototypes can be viewed on the Web, at conferences, or through individual meetings. One aspect you must consider when building a prototype is who is going to view it. If you place the prototype on the Web, anyone from anywhere in the world will be able to view your prototype. If you attend a conference, people from all over your country, and perhaps other countries, will be able to view your prototype. If you're going to a meeting, you'll know exactly who the individuals are that are going to view your prototype.

Knowing who is going to be able to view your prototype may cause you to make changes to the prototype. For example, if you build a calculator prototype for the Web you may want to have the ability to change the numbers on the prototype to the customer's language such as Chinese or Japanese. If you built a Web browser you might want the language to change depending on the customer's origin. If you build a billing system, you might want the currency to change depending on the customer's origin. Customizing your prototype for the correct audience is one way to ensure your customers will be happy with what you have to show them.

old one seems to work just fine, and they're afraid the new system won't meet their expectations and work properly. If you provide them with a working prototype that proves the new system will be successful, they will be more inclined to buy into it.

THE DISADVANTAGES OF PROTOTYPING

LEADS PEOPLE TO BELIEVE THE FINAL SYSTEM WILL FOLLOW SHORTLY When a prototype is complete, many people believe that the final system will follow shortly. After all, they've seen the system at work in the form of a prototype, how long can it take to bring the system into production? Unfortunately, it may take months or years. You need to be sure that people understand that the prototype is only a model, not the final system missing only a few simple bells and whistles.

GIVES NO INDICATION OF PERFORMANCE UNDER OPERATIONAL CONDITIONS Prototypes very seldom take all operational conditions into consideration. This problem surfaced for the Department of Motor Vehicles in a state on the East Coast. During prototyping, the system, which handled motor vehicle and driver registration for the entire state, worked fine for 20 workstations at two locations. When the system was finally installed for all locations (which included more than 1,200 workstations), the system spent all its time just managing communications traffic; it had absolutely no time to complete any transactions. This is potentially the most significant drawback to prototyping. You must prototype operational conditions as well as interfaces and processes.[13]

LEADS THE PROJECT TEAM TO FORGO PROPER TESTING AND DOCUMENTATION You must thoroughly test and document all new systems. Unfortunately, many people believe they can forgo testing and documentation when using prototyping. After all, they've tested the prototype; why not use the prototype as the documentation for the system? Don't make this mistake.

Prototyping is most probably a tool that you will use to develop many knowledge worker information systems. If you stick to the phases of the SLDC, have the correct resources, and learn how to make the most of your prototypes, you will be very successful in your career as a knowledge worker.

Summary: Student Learning Outcomes Revisited

1. **List the seven steps in the systems development life cycle (SDLC) and an associated activity for each step.** The *systems development life cycle (SDLC)* is a structured step-by-step approach for developing information systems. The seven steps and activities are as follows:

   1. Plan: Set project scope, develop project plan
   2. Analysis: Gather business requirements
   3. Design: Design technical architecture, design system models
   4. Develop: Build technical architecture, build database and programs
   5. Test: Write the test conditions, perform testing
   6. Implement: Perform user training, write user documentation
   7. Maintain: Provide a help desk, support system changes

2. **List four reasons why your participation during the systems development life cycle is critical.** Your participation during every step of the SDLC is critical because you are (or will be) a

   • business process expert: You know and understand how the business works better than anyone else does.

   • liaison to the customer: You know what a certain customer segment wants, and you can relay that information to the project team.

   • quality control analyst: You must review alternative solutions to assure that the chosen alternative meets your needs.

   • manager of other people: You have ultimate responsibility for the work and productivity of others.

3. **Describe three of the five reasons why projects fail.** Projects fail for many reasons and, throughout this chapter, we've discussed several of them. One of the primary reasons why projects fail is due to missing or unclear business

requirements. Since the entire project is based on the business requirements, if you fail to capture them correctly there is no way you will be able to build a successful system. Another common reason why projects fail is due to skipping phases in the systems development life cycle. It's critical that you perform all phases in the SDLC during every project. Skipping any of the phases is sure to lead to system failure. Another reason system failure occurs is because you fail to manage the project plan and project scope. Allowing *scope creep* or *feature creep* to occur will drastically increase the projects development effort. Finally, changing technology can be a big reason why projects fail. Technology changes so fast that it is almost impossible to deliver a system without having to deal with a change in technology, be it an operating system upgrade or the release of a new programming language.

4. **Define the three different ways you can staff a system development project.** Insourcing, selfsourcing, and outsourcing are the three different ways you can staff a system development project. *Insourcing* uses IT specialists within your organization, *selfsourcing* uses knowledge workers, and *outsourcing* uses another organization. It is important to note that most large projects typically use insourcing, selfsourcing, and outsourcing all at the same time.

5. **List two of the three advantages of selfsourcing.** When you selfsource a project you improve requirements determination, increase knowledge worker participation and sense of ownership, and increase the speed of systems development.

6. **Describe prototyping and profile an example of a prototype.** *Prototyping* is the process of building a model that demonstrates the features of a proposed product, service, or system.

A *prototype,* then, is simply a model of a proposed product, service, or system. If you think about it, people prototype all the time. Automobile manufacturers build prototypes of cars to demonstrate safety features, aerodynamics, and comfort. Building contractors construct models of homes and other structures to show layout and fire exits.

7. **Describe two of the five advantages of prototyping.** First, prototyping encourages active knowledge worker participation. Prototyping encourages knowledge workers to actively participate in the development process.

As opposed to interviewing and the reviewing of documentation, prototyping allows knowledge workers to see and work with working models of the proposed system. Second, prototyping helps resolve discrepancies among knowledge workers. During the prototyping process, many knowledge workers participate in defining the requirements for and reviewing the prototype. The word *many* is key. If several knowledge workers participate in prototyping, you'll find it's much easier to resolve any discrepancies the knowledge workers may encounter.

CLOSING CASE STUDY ONE

SOME PROTOTYPES HIT, SOME MISS, AND SOME WE ARE JUST NOT SURE ABOUT

Pick up any copy of a technology magazine and you'll see loads of new prototypes anxious to hit the consumer market. Would you like to buy a new mountain bike that is built without using any chains for only $5,593?

How about purchasing some Smart Trading Cards? This alternative to cardboard baseball cards comes with a CPU where you can review highlights and listen to important personal statistics such as the leading skateboarder's number of broken bones. Unfortunately, these Smart Cards don't come with a stick of chewing gum, which was the big perk with the traditional baseball trading cards. A stick of chewing gum can no longer compare to a CPU. Especially considering the price for traditional baseball cards was 10 cents and the Smart Cards sell for $8 plus $20 for the card reader. With those kind of prices, who cares about a stick of chewing gum?

How would you like a pair of snorkeling flippers that can change shape on the fly to help you adapt easily to your changing underworld environment. The list of new prototypes goes on and on ranging from wristwatches with a digital compass to Wave Boxes, the first portable hydraulic whirlpool perfect for those city-dwelling kayak fans.

But what do you think happens after you make a prototype? Chances are a prototype can take one of two paths. On the first path, the prototype is a big hit and the product goes into mass production and is found in every Wal-Mart and K-mart store in the country. On the second path, the prototype is unsuccessful and goes into storage for eternity. Let's take a look at a few of those prototypes that didn't make it to the mass consumer market.

Each year *Wired* magazine presents the Vaporware Awards, awarded to the top 10 most eagerly awaited technology products that never made it to consumers. As the technology industry continues to generate products that promise to revolutionize consumers' work and personal lives, *Wired News* follows them from planning to delivery. Thousands of products are nominated for this prestigious award each year, but only products that never reach the market can receive this award. The Vaporware winners for most overrated technologies of 2001 were

1. 3D Realm's Duke Nukem Forever—Taking top honors with its video game that's been four years in the making
2. Warcraft III—Blizzard Software's much anticipated next offering in its popular Warcraft series, making its second consecutive appearance on the Vaporware list
3. Photoshop for OS X—Adobe Photoshop is still not available for Apple's new operating system

4. Team Fortress—Groundbreaking multiplayer game promised to be released by Value Software for several years and counting

5. 3G Wireless Networks—Next-generation wireless service

6. Silicon Film's Electronic Film System—Digital film that is still vapor after a year of hype

7. Digiscents' iSmell—First consumer "personal scent synthesizer"

8. Artificial Intelligence—Talking, thinking, "living" computers

9. Peekabooty—"Anticensorship" Web-surfing tool promised early last year

10. Indrema—Purportedly groundbreaking open-source game console

Only about 10 percent of product prototypes make it to the consumer market. In Ithaca, New York, you can visit Robert McMath's failed product museum where he has been collecting failed consumer products for more than 30 years. Are you interested in purchasing edible deodorant, a nice can of aerosol toothpaste for kids, toaster eggs, or how about a garlic cake? The list of failed products is endless and for many of them you have to wonder what the inventor was thinking. If anyone can tell us when or why you would eat garlic cake we would be grateful.

Building prototypes is the only way to determine if your product is going to be a hit or a miss. Understanding the prototyping process and the advantages and disadvantages covered in this chapter is important to your career as a knowledge worker as you'll be working with information system prototypes and perhaps building some yourself.[14,15,16]

QUESTIONS

1. Some products hit, some products miss, and some we are still not sure what the inventor was thinking when he or she invented the product. Many products end up sitting on a self or in a failed products museum. Research the Web to find three examples of failed products that have never reached the consumer market. There are thousands of them out there, and some of these failed ideas are extremely entertaining.

2. Prototyping is an invaluable tool for systems development. Building a prototype allows knowledge workers to see, work with, and evaluate a model and suggest changes to the model. Refer back to the discussion of the cost of fixing errors and Figure 6.5. What do prototyping and this figure have in common? How can prototyping help you control your project budget and the cost to fix errors?

3. Prototyping can be used in the analysis phase to help you gather business requirements. Throughout this chapter we discussed the importance of gathering solid business requirements. How can building a prototype help you gather solid business requirements on an information systems development project?

4. We have discussed many examples of prototypes. Use your creativity and business knowledge to generate an idea for a new product. The product can be for a business, consumers, or a service that would help consumers perform their daily activities. Write a brief paragraph describing your idea along with a picture of the product.

5. Appearing on *Wired*'s Vaporware Winners List is not exactly a high spot for any company's or individual's career. What do you think is the driver behind some of these farfetched prototypes? What do you think would happen if companies and individuals stopped producing prototypes for the fear of being laughed at? What would have happened if garlic cake had been a hot item and consumers all over the world were anxious to buy it?

6. In this chapter we discussed several advantages and disadvantages to building prototypes. Please review these lists and define three advantages and disadvantages to building prototypes not mentioned in this chapter.

7. One of the disadvantages to building a prototype is that people will believe that the final system will follow shortly. Why do you think building a prototype will lead people to this inaccurate conclusion? If you were delivering a system prototype, how would you communicate to the system users that the real system would not be ready for another three years?

8. It is important to remember that communication is the primary key to deploying a successful prototype. When Planter's peanuts first started to market fresh roasted peanuts, the product was a complete failure. Consumers continuously confused the product with coffee and kept taking it home to grind it as they would fresh roasted coffee beans. The words *fresh roasted*

are probably what caused the product to initially fail. If you were in charge of this product, what could you do to change it in order to help consumers understand the product contained peanuts not coffee beans?

AL'S BARBEQUE RESTAURANT

Al's Barbeque Restaurant, located in Denver, Colorado, has successfully been in business for 20 years. Al's specializes in barbeque chicken and beef and includes scrumptious side dishes of potato salad, coleslaw, and baked beans. Customers come from all around for a good old-fashioned barbeque dinner. On a Friday night you can expect the line to be out the door and the wait close to an hour. It is estimated that Al serves more than 500 barbeque dinners every day.

The restaurant is filled with 20 picnic tables covered in red-and-white cloths. There are a total of 12 waitstaff workers, five of whom have been working at the restaurant since it opened. Al cooks and prepares all of the special barbeque sauce himself along with three other cooks. The restaurant runs today the same as it did 20 years ago. Al can call many of his customers by name. This is definitely part of the charm of the restaurant, but it is also one of the biggest problems with the restaurant. Everything in the restaurant is performed manually from taking orders to ordering inventory.

Al's daughter, Alana, has just graduated from college and has come home to help run the family-owned business. Alana is amazed at how long it takes to perform all of the manual processes required to run the business. Every night she must manually count all of the money in the cash register and compare it to the paper sales tickets that the waitstaff fills out representing the customer orders.

Alana also manually counts the inventory from cans of beans to slices of cheese. Deciding what to order each day is a complete mystery to Alana. Some days the restaurant sells tons of chicken dinners and other days the restaurant sells tons of beef dinners. There doesn't seem to be any pattern to which one is going to sell the best. She continually finds herself ordering too much of one item and not enough of the other. Each week she has to calculate the employee paychecks by reviewing each employee's cardboard handwritten time card. At the end of each month she calculates the sales tax reports. This is an incredibly difficult activity since the reports must match all of the monthly paper tickets, which total close to $45,000.

Alana quickly comes to the conclusion that the restaurant must be automated. Building an information system to support all of these manual processes will not only help the restaurant operate more efficiently but will also give Alana more time to spend talking and dealing with her customers. Alana and Al decide to visit a local restaurant trade show to see what types of information systems are available. The show displays all types of different restaurant systems. One system uses microwave frequencies that allow the waitstaff to carry around a type of PDA that automatically sends orders to a terminal in the kitchen. Some systems can track sales for up to 20 years and generate sales forecasts based on anything from the day of the week to the weather. All of the systems produce daily sales reports and monthly tax reports. This feature alone is a dream come true for Alana as this activity typically takes her from two to three hours a day.

Alana and Al are overwhelmed by the number of restaurant information systems available to purchase. Having no formal training with the SDLC or systems development, they are confused and frustrated with so many choices.

QUESTIONS

1. Al is not a believer in technology and he thinks the business works just fine the way it is. How would you convince Al that an information system will help his business become even more successful? How can you explain to Al that using the SDLC will help him successfully implement a new system?

2. Alana realizes that she does not have the expertise required to choose a restaurant

information system. Alana decides to ask you for help since you studied this type of information in college. How would you describe to Alana the phases in the SDLC and how she can use them to choose and implement a system?

3. At the beginning of the project you develop a project plan to help guide you through the systems development effort. Alana does not understand the plan or why you continually keep changing it. How can you explain to Alana the benefits of developing a project plan and why it must be continually revised and updated?

4. Al has hired you to help choose and implement the system for the restaurant. From the information you already know about the restaurant, write five of the business requirements. Remember, writing clear and accurate business requirements is critical to the success of the project.

5. Some members of the waitstaff have worked at the restaurant since it began. You're worried that they'll not be receptive to using an automated system. How would you convince the waitstaff that the new system will help them perform their jobs? Why is including them in the requirements gathering activity critical to the systems development effort?

6. Thanks to your help, Al has successfully implemented a new restaurant system. The system is up and running, and Al is extremely pleased with your work. You offer to spend an extra week writing user manuals and system documentation. Al declines your offer as he does not see any benefit in these tools. How would you convince Al that documentation is critical to the continued success of the system?

7. At the restaurant show Al and Alana saw many different restaurant information systems that they could purchase. Research the Web to find two restaurant information systems that might have been at the trade show. Of the systems you found, which one do you think you would choose and why?

Key Terms and Concepts

Analysis phase, 289
Business requirement, 289
Critical success factor (CSF), 288
Design phase, 290
Development phase, 290
Feature creep, 300
Graphical user interface (GUI), 290
GUI screen design, 290
Help desk, 293
Implementation phase, 293
Insourcing, 301
Joint application development (JAD), 289
Maintenance phase, 293
Modeling, 290
Online training, 293
Outsourcing, 305
Planning phase, 287
Project manager, 288
Project milestone, 288
Project plan, 288

Project scope, 288
Project scope document, 288
Proof-of-concept prototype, 312
Prototype, 311
Prototyping, 311
Request for proposal (RFP), 308
Requirements definition document, 289
Scope creep, 300
Selfsourcing (knowledge worker development, end-
   user development), 301
Selling prototype, 312
Sign-off, 289
Systems development life cycle (SDLC), 286
Technical architecture, 290
Test condition, 292
Testing phase, 291
User acceptance testing (UAT), 297
User documentation, 293
Workshop training, 293

Short-Answer Questions

1. What is the systems development life cycle (SDLC)?
2. What are the seven steps in the SDLC?
3. What is a critical success factor?
4. What is feature creep?
5. How does a project plan help the project manager do his or her job?
6. In what step in the SDLC do you define business requirements?
7. Why would a company outsource?
8. In what step in the SDLC do you build the technical architecture?
9. How do online training and workshop training differ?
10. Why must you provide sign-off on the business requirements?
11. Will a project be successful if you miss business requirements?
12. What is selfsourcing?
13. Why would you build a prototype?
14. What is a selling prototype?
15. What is an advantage of selfsourcing?
16. What is an advantage of prototyping?

Short-Question Answers

For each of the following answers, provide an appropriate question.

1. A factor simply critical to the organization's success.
2. Insourcing.
3. RFP.
4. Scope.
5. Group of people who respond to user's questions.
6. Continuously monitored, revised, and updated.
7. Using contractors to build the system.
8. Business requirement.
9. Technical architecture.
10. Changing technology.
11. Training performed at your own pace.
12. UAT.
13. Failure to manage scope.
14. Selfsourcing.
15. Lack of internal expertise.
16. Proof-of-concept prototype.

Assignments and Exercises

1. **SDLC AND THE REAL WORLD** Think of the seven steps in the SDLC and try to apply them to one of your daily activities. For example, getting dressed in the morning. First, you plan what you are going to wear. This will vary depending on what you are going to do that day and could include shorts, pants, jeans, and so forth. Second, you analyze what you have in your closet compared to what you planned to wear. Third, you design the outfit. Fourth, you get the clothes out of the closet and assemble them on your bed. Fifth, you test the outfit to ensure it matches. Sixth, you put on the outfit. Seventh, you wear the outfit throughout the day adjusting it as needed.

2. **HOW CREATIVE ARE YOU?** You've been appointed as the manager of the design team for Sneakers-R-Us. Your first activity is to design the GUI for the main system. The only requirements you are given is that the colors must be bold and the following buttons must appear in the screen.
   - Order Inventory
   - Enter Sales
   - Schedule Employees
   - Tax Reports
   - Sales Reports
   - Employee Vacation and Sick Time
   - Administrative Activities

Please create two different potential GUI screen designs for the main system. Provide a brief explanation of the advantages and disadvantages of each design.

3. **REQUEST FOR PROPOSAL** A request for proposal (RFP) is a formal document that describes in detail your logical requirements for a proposed system and invites outsourcing organizations (which we'll refer to as "vendors") to submit bids for its development. Research the Web and find three RFP examples. Please briefly explain in a one-page document what each RFP has in common and how each RFP is different.

4. **UNDERSTANDING INSOURCING** The advantages and disadvantages of selfsourcing and outsourcing are covered throughout this chapter. Compile a list of the different advantages and disadvantages of insourcing compared to selfsourcing and outsourcing.

5. **MANAGING THE PROJECT PLAN** You are in the middle of an interview for your first job. The manager performing the interview asks you to explain why managing a project plan is critical to a project's success? The manager also wants to know what scope creep and feature creep are and how you would manage them during a project. Please write a one-page document stating how you would answer these questions during the interview.

6. **WHY PROTOTYPE?** You are in the middle of the design phase for a new system. Your manager does not understand why it's important to develop a prototype of a proposed system before building the actual system. In a one-page document explain what potential problems would arise if you didn't develop a prototype and went straight to developing the system.

7. **BUSINESS REQUIREMENTS** Gathering accurate and complete business requirements is critical to the successful development of any system. Review the following requirements and explain any problems they might have.
   • The GUI must be red.
   • There should be three buttons labeled "Start" and "Stop."
   • Buttons 1 through 8 are required for the calculator function.
   • There should be a text field for the user name and a button for the user password.

8. **WHY PROJECTS FAIL** We've discussed five of the primary reasons why projects fail, but there are many more reasons why projects fail. In order to be prepared for your role as a knowledge worker, research the Web to find three additional reasons why projects fail. Prepare a document explaining the three additional reasons that projects fail and how you could prevent these issues from occurring.

9. **CONSTRUCTION AND THE SDLC** The systems development life cycle is often compared to the construction industry. Try to fill in the following chart listing some of the activities performed in building a house and how they relate to the different SDLC steps.

SDLC	Activities for Building a Home
Plan	
Analysis	
Design	
Develop	
Test	
Implement	
Maintain	

Discussion Questions _____

1. Why is it important to develop a logical model of a proposed system before generating a technical architecture? What potential problems would arise if you didn't develop a logical model and went straight to developing the technical design?

2. If you view systems development as a question-and-answer session, another question you could ask is, "Why do organizations develop IT systems?" Consider what you believe to be the five most important reasons organizations develop IT systems. How do these reasons relate to topics in the first five chapters of this book?

3. When deciding how to staff a systems development project, what are some of the primary questions you must be able to answer in order to determine if you will insource, selfsource, or outsource? What are some of the advantages and disadvantages of each.

4. Your company has just decided to implement a new financial system. Your company's financial needs are almost the same as all of the other companies in your industry. Would you recommend that your company purchase an existing system or build a custom system? Would you recommend your company insource, selfsource, or outsource the new system?

5. Why do you think system documentation is important? If you had to write system documentation for a word processing application what would be a few of the main sections? Do you think it would be useful to test the documentation to ensure it's accurate? What do you think happens if you provide system documentation that is inaccurate? What do you think happens if you implement a new system without documentation?

6. What would happen to an organization that refused to follow the systems development life cycle when building systems? If you worked for this organization what would you do to convince your manager to follow the systems development life cycle?

7. There are seven phases in the systems development life cycle. Which one do you think is the hardest? Which one do you think is the easiest? Which one do you think is the most important? Which one do you think is the least important? If you had to skip one of the phases which one would it be and why?

8. What would happen to a systems development effort that decided to skip the testing phase? If you were working on this project what would you do to convince your team members to perform the activities in the testing phase?

9. If you were working on a large systems development effort and after reviewing the business requirements you were positive several were missing would you still sign-off on the requirements? If you did what would happen?

10. You are talking with another student who is complaining about having to learn about the systems development life cycle because he is not going to work in an IT department. Would you agree with this student? What would you say to him to try to convince him that learning about the systems development life cycle is relative no matter where he works?

11. A company typically has many systems it wants to build, but unfortunately it doesn't usually have the resources to build all of the systems. How does a company decide which systems to build?

12. When you start working on a new system, one of your first activities is to define the project scope. Do you think this is an easy activity to perform? Why is the project scope so important? Do you think everyone on the project should know the project's scope? What could happen when people on the project are not familiar with the project scope?

13. People often think that a system is complete once it is implemented. Is this true? What happens after a system is implemented? What can you do to ensure the system continues to meet the knowledge workers' needs?

14. Imagine your friends are about to start their own business and they have asked you for planning and development advice with respect to IT systems, what would you tell them? What if their business idea was completely Internet-based? What if their business idea didn't include using the Internet at all? Would your answers differ? Why or why not?

Finding Freeware and Shareware on the Internet

When you buy your first computer, software seems a secondary decision since most computers come preloaded with software. But after a while you begin to feel a need for other software and that's when sticker shock sets in. Even upgrading to the latest version of your existing software can make a real dent in your pocketbook. And after installing new software, you may find it simply doesn't meet your needs. That's when you notice that you can't return opened software, you can only exchange it for a new copy. So if it doesn't meet your needs you're out of luck with commercial consumer software.

An alternative to commercial software that you might consider is shareware or freeware. Shareware is sometimes called "try before you buy" software because users are permitted to try the software on their own computer system (generally for a limited time) without any cost or obligation. Then you make a payment if you decide you want to keep using the software beyond the evaluation (trial) period. Freeware is software available at no charge to users for as long as they choose to use the software.

USING YOUR COMPUTER FOR MORE THAN WORK

By far the most popular freeware/shareware applications are games. The quality of these software titles is truly amazing for software that is free to download and begin playing immediately whenever you want. Shareware/freeware games are so numerous on the Internet that you'll often find games grouped by categories. Common categories are action/adventure, board, card, casino, educational, role-playing, simulation, sports, strategy and war, and word games.

When you're looking over the games available, remember that you should first ascertain whether the software is shareware or freeware. In some cases the Web site is not really clear on this issue. For example, some game descriptions make no mention of money, yet after you've downloaded the game it talks about registering your game for a price. At the other end of the spectrum you'll encounter traditional software that lists a price next to the description and requires a credit card to download and purchase, and often these games will describe themselves as shareware. Remember though, true shareware permits you to download the software and try it for free. So, in this case, the term *shareware* is a bit of a misnomer.

Connect to the Internet and several sites that offer freeware and shareware games. Pick at least two games and download them. For each, answer the following questions:

A. Is a description of the game provided?

B. Are system requirements listed?

C. Can you tell if the game is freeware or shareware without downloading it?

D. Are any of the games you selected really commercial software that requires a purchase before you download the game?

E. If the game is shareware, how long are you permitted to use it until registration is required?

F. If the game is shareware, does the game cease to function after the free period is over? How can you tell without waiting that long?

G. How long does it take to download the game? Is it worth it?

ANIMATING YOUR COMPUTER SCREEN

Wander through most any office or even your school computer lab and you'll see a variety of screen savers in action. Screen savers—the software that occupies your screen when the computer is unused for a period of time—are very common utilities. Sometimes the screen saver provides a beautiful scene with a recurring action. Others provide a different look every time they activate. Microsoft Windows includes several standard screen savers. In Windows 95 and beyond you'll also find *desktop themes* that do include a screen saver but go much further than that. In addition to providing software that activates when your computer is inactive, themes alter the look of the basic screen you see when you are working. Borders, standard application icons, and even the cursor are changed with desktop themes.

Connect to a couple of different sites that offer screen savers. Download at least two screen savers and answer the following questions:

A. Is a description of the screen saver provided?

B. Is the screen saver available for other operating systems?

C. Can you tell if the screen saver is freeware or shareware without downloading it?

D. Do any of the screen savers include desktop themes for Windows?

E. Are any other screen savers or desktop themes available at the site?

F. Does the screen saver work as advertised?

PROTECTING YOUR COMPUTER INVESTMENT

Have you ever been frantically typing away, desperately trying to make an assignment deadline, when all of a sudden something goes wrong with your computer? If you're lucky, the problem is something easy to identify, so you correct the problem and go on about your work. At other times the solution eludes you. Most of the time these problems have nice logical explanations such as hardware or software conflicts or failures of some kind. In a few rare instances, the problem may have been caused intentionally by a computer virus, a program that someone develops with malicious intent to harm an IT system.

So how does a computer virus get into your system? Anytime you download software, open a file attachment to an e-mail, or read a file off a diskette from another computer, you stand the chance of contracting a computer virus. And access to the Internet increases your opportunity to download files from many different sources. So on every computer it owns virtually every company installs anti-virus protection software that scans new files for known viruses and purges them from the system. The catch is that traditional anti-virus software can find only viruses that it knows about. As new viruses come along, anti-virus software must be updated. The deviant minds that develop viruses seem to find more and better ways to infiltrate your system every day.

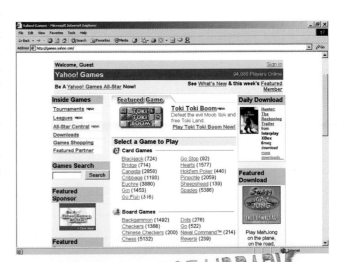

Connect to a site that allows you to download anti-virus software, download the software, and answer the following questions:

A. Is the anti-virus software shareware, freeware, or traditional retail software?

B. What viruses does the software detect?

C. Does the software remove the virus as well as detect it?

D. Are updates for the software available to detect new viruses? How often are they available? At what cost?

E. Does the software detect viruses not yet created? How does it do that?

F. Does the software site offer recommendations to reduce your chance of contracting a virus?

G. Does the site tell you what to do if you have already contracted a virus?

SEARCHING FOR SHAREWARE AND FREEWARE

So maybe the shareware/freeware software concept appeals to you. You'd like to be able to try the software before you buy. If you want software such as screen savers or anti-virus software you're in luck. But what if you want some shareware to help you compose music or to keep track of your soccer team's schedule? Well, then you'll have to go searching for that software. You could use a general-purpose search engine such as Yahoo! and type in shareware and music or soccer. If you do this you will find a few shareware software titles to download. But suppose those few titles don't meet your needs.

Finding shareware/freeware titles can be daunting for two reasons. First, currently there are over 1 million shareware and freeware titles available to you. Unless a search engine is designed specifically for this type of software, you'll probably miss many of these titles using a general-purpose search engine. Second, most shareware/freeware developers don't have their own Web sites. As many don't develop their software as a business, they can't justify the cost of supporting their own Web sites. To address both of these challenges, Web sites have been created that maintain databases of thousands of shareware/freeware software titles. Most also include a search engine to help you navigate through these thousand of titles.

Find a site that maintains a database of freeware and shareware software. As you peruse it, answer the following questions:

A. How does the site group the software?

B. Can you search by operating system or platform?

C. Does the site provide descriptions of the software?

D. Can you search by file size?

E. Are screen captures from the software provided?

F. Are reviews and/or ratings of the software provided?

G. When was the last update for the site?

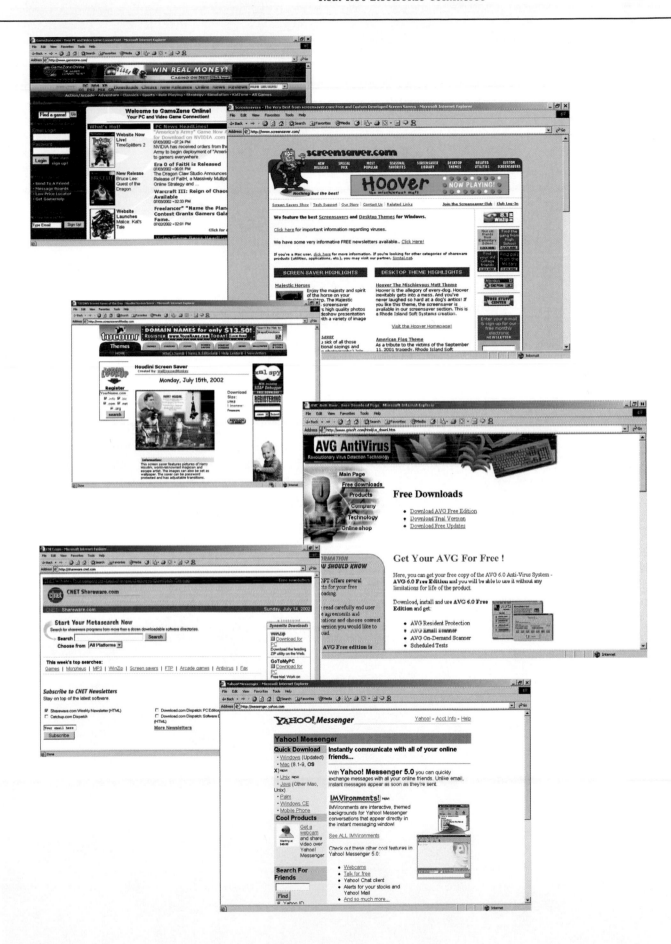

EXTENDED LEARNING MODULE F

BUILDING A WEB PAGE WITH HTML

Student Learning Outcomes

1. DEFINE AN HTML DOCUMENT AND DESCRIBE ITS RELATIONSHIP TO A WEB SITE.

2. DESCRIBE THE PURPOSE OF TAGS IN HYPERTEXT MARKUP LANGUAGE (HTML).

3. IDENTIFY THE TWO MAJOR SECTIONS IN AN HTML DOCUMENT AND DESCRIBE THE CONTENT WITHIN EACH.

4. DESCRIBE THE USE OF BASIC FORMATTING TAGS AND HEADING TAGS.

5. DESCRIBE HOW TO ADJUST TEXT COLOR AND SIZE WITHIN A WEB SITE.

6. DESCRIBE HOW TO CHANGE THE BACKGROUND OF A WEB SITE.

7. LIST THE THREE TYPES OF LINKS IN A WEB SITE AND DESCRIBE THEIR PURPOSES.

8. DESCRIBE HOW TO INSERT AND MANIPULATE IMAGES IN A WEB SITE.

9. DEMONSTRATE HOW TO INSERT LISTS IN A WEB SITE.

Taking Advantage of the CD

Creating a Web site . . . everyone seems to be doing it. Businesses create Web sites to sell products and services, provide support information, and conduct marketing activities. Individuals build Web sites for a variety of reasons. Some want a family Web site. Some want a Web site for their evening sports leagues. Your instructor has probably built a Web site to support your class. And we've created a Web site to support your use of this text.

Whatever the case, building a basic Web site is actually not that difficult. If you want a Web site that supports product ordering capabilities, then you'll need some specific expertise. But putting up a Web site with just content is simple and easy. In this extended learning module, we'll show you how. You'll find this extended learning module on the CD that accompanies this text. It's just like any other module in this text—it includes Team Work and On Your Own projects and great end-of-module Assignments and Exercises.

Before we begin, let's discuss several important issues. First, be careful what sort of private personal information you include on your Web site. We definitely recommend that you do not include your social security number, your address, or your telephone number. You always need to keep in mind that there are more than 1 billion people on the Internet. Do you really want them to know where you live?

You also need to consider your target audience and their ethics. Having a Web site with profanity and obscene images will offend many people. And, more than likely, your school won't allow you to build a Web site of questionable content. Even more basic than that, you need to consider your target audience and their viewing preferences. For example, if you're building a Web site for school-age children, you'll want to use a lot of bright colors such as red, blue, green, and yellow. If you're targeting college students to advertise concerts and other events, you'll want your Web site to be more edgy and include sharp contrasting colors (including black).

Just remember this: The most elegant solution is almost always the simplest. If you consider eBay, it uses a very simple and elegant presentation of information. The background is basic white. You'll see very little if any flashy movement. You'll hear very little sound. eBay is one of the most visited sites on the Web today. And it's making money with a very simple and elegant Web site.

We definitely believe it's worth your time and energy to pop in the CD and read this module. You'll learn many things including

- How to build and view a Web site on your own computer without connecting to the Web
- How to use a simple text editor to create a Web site
- How to size and position images in your Web site
- How to include e-mail links in your Web site
- How to change the background color or insert a textured background for your Web site
- How to change the color and size of text

If you're interested in learning more about what you can do with a Web site, we recommend that you connect to the Web site that supports this text at www.mhhe.com/haag (and select XLM/F). There, we've included more about building a Web site and useful resources on the Web.

CHAPTER SEVEN OUTLINE

STUDENT LEARNING OUTCOMES

1 Explain the relationship between the organization's roles and goals and the IT infrastructure.

2 List and describe four of the seven factors that help increase employee productivity.

3 Explain system integration and how it enhances decision making.

4 List and describe two different types of workflow systems.

5 List and describe two IT infrastructure components that create business partnerships and alliances.

6 List and describe two of the four IT infrastructure components that enable global reach.

WEB SUPPORT

www.mhhe.com/haag

- Online magazines
- Entertainment databases
- Cooking databases
- Highly useful miscellaneous Web sites
- Capacity Planning

CHAPTER SEVEN

IT Infrastructures
Business-Driven Technology

**OPENING CASE STUDY:
WHAT'S THE DIFFERENCE BETWEEN
NAPSTER AND GNUTELLA?**

Many of you have probably heard of Napster, software that allows people to share music over the Internet. Originally, all a person had to do to listen to music for free was download Napster from the Internet, check the Napster directory to see a list of available songs, download the songs in MP3 format, and play them using the Napster software. Unfortunately for Napster users, the Recording Industry Association of America (RIAA) filed a lawsuit against Napster claiming copyright infringement and tried to have Napster shut down.

Napster attempted to avoid the RIAA lawsuit by changing its IT infrastructure. MP3's were no longer saved on the company's servers. Instead, Napster kept a directory of MP3s stored on individuals' computers and users could share the MP3 files between each other. All Napster did was provide the software to play the MP3 files along with a list of places a user could find MP3 files. But Napster's attempt to avoid legal problems by changing its IT infrastructure didn't work and the company was shut down in December of 2001.

Today, there is a new product called Gnutella. How many of you have heard of Gnutella? Gnutella, like Napster, is a product that directly exchanges MP3 files between users. However, in a strange way there is no Gnutella. Gnutella doesn't have a Web site, doesn't have an address or office building, and doesn't have any employees. The Gnutella software is designed to allow a network to grow without any single person or particular company's involvement. Basically, once you install and launch Gnutella, your computer becomes both a client and a server in the network, called GnutellaNet, and you can now share files that other Gnutella users have made available. Each Gnutella user makes as many, or as few, of their files available for other users connected to the network to search through and download. The Gnutella network literally changes every time a user logs on and off. Do you think the RIAA should file a lawsuit against Gnutella for copyright infringement? If it did file a lawsuit, who would it sue?

This case study is a good demonstration of how a similar product using a different IT infrastructure can change significantly. Designing and building the correct IT infrastructure is critical to the success of any business. Do you think Napster would still be around today if it had implemented a different IT infrastructure?

The term *IT infrastructure* includes all the hardware, software, and telecommunications equipment that your organization employs to support its goals, processes, and strategies. An IT infrastructure can easily make or break a company. What do you think happens to a company that can't provide its knowledge workers with Internet access, or the access it does provide is extremely slow? A company must build a solid IT infrastructure that can handle all of the current and future IT needs which will play a major role in helping the company achieve its organizational goals.[1]

Introduction

IT infrastructure is a difficult term to define because it means different things to different organizations at different times. This makes it difficult for us to capture a definition of the term that will satisfy everyone and every possible meaning. For this reason, we have chosen the most basic and generic definition for this term. An ***IT infrastructure*** includes the hardware, software, and telecommunications equipment that, when combined, provide the underlying foundation to support the organization's goals.

Organizations today can choose from literally thousands of different components to build their IT infrastructure. IT infrastructure components can include anything ranging from software to strategic functions. Figure 7.1 provides a model of how the various components of an IT infrastructure support an organization's goals. Your organization's goals should drive everything, ranging from how the organization is structured to how it designs its IT infrastructure. For example, your organization can have a flat or hierarchical structure. A flat organizational structure has only a couple of managerial layers while a hierarchical organizational structure has many managerial layers. If your organization has a flat structure, it might be attempting to support the goal of information sharing. If your organization has a hierarchical structure, it might be attempting to support the goal of information privacy and security.

As a knowledge worker, you'll be continually faced with questions regarding how the IT infrastructure can best support your organizational goals. You'll be asked to make decisions regarding which type of IT infrastructure components you want to purchase, and how you want to implement them. Of the many technologies available, how will you choose the ones that best meet your organizational needs? And you'll face this type of question again and again as businesses and technologies continue to change.

This chapter discusses a few of the primary IT infrastructure components your organization can use to build a solid foundation that supports everything your organization does or plans to do. Enterprise application integration (EAI), customer relationship management (CRM), and enterprise resource planning (ERP) are just a few of the com-

Figure 7.1

The IT Infrastructure Supports the Organizational Goals

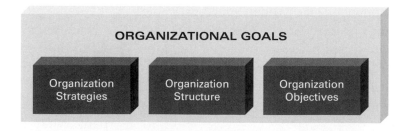

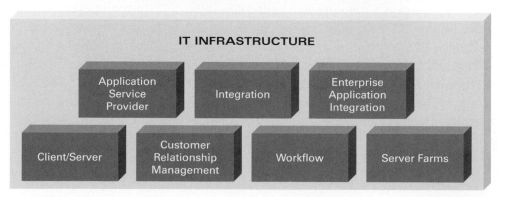

ponents we're going to discuss in the following pages. These components probably may not mean much to you now but, after reading this chapter, you'll have enough basic knowledge to understand how each one works.

Organizational Goals and Strategies

Organizations tend to spend a great deal of time determining primary goals, objectives, structures, and strategies. These critical components help your organization determine how it will operate in the marketplace, what its strategic directions or competitive advantages will be, and how it will achieve unlimited success. A good IT infrastructure will support all of your organization's business and information needs. An IT infrastructure that ignores your organization's business or information needs will cause certain failure.

Figure 7.2 lists the six primary roles and goals of information technology as we presented them in Chapter 1. The figure also provides a list of IT infrastructure

Figure 7.2

Roles and Goals of Information Technology and IT Infrastructure Components

Roles and Goals of IT	IT Infrastructure Components
Increase employee productivity	• Client/server network • Internet • Intranets and extranets • Backup/recovery • Disaster recovery plan
Enhance decision making	• Integration • Enterprise application integration (EAI) • Enterprise application integration middleware (EAI middleware) • Storage devices
Improve team collaboration	• Document management systems • Enterprise information portals (EIP) • Workflow systems
Create business partnerships and alliances	• Customer relationship management (CRM) systems • Sales force automation (SFA) systems • Electronic catalog • Supply chain management (SCM) systems
Enable global reach	• Internet service provider (ISP) • Application service provider (ASP) • Collocation facilities • Server farms
Facilitate organizational transformation	• Enterprise resource planning (ERP) and enterprise software • Data warehouse • Infrastructure documentation

components that support each of the six roles and goals. The remainder of this chapter walks you through each goal and its related IT infrastructure components.

Increase Employee Productivity

Employees are the heart and soul of any organization. Without employees there simply wouldn't be an organization. Building an IT infrastructure that supports employee needs should be one of the primary goals for any business. For example, every time a system crashes or fails, employees can't perform their jobs. Every time employees can't perform their jobs, the organization loses money. Employees are often sent home during system crashes since there is no reason for them to sit around for hours without being able to work. For this reason alone, millions of dollars are lost each year due to system failures.

Building a solid IT infrastructure will reduce system failures, which increases employee productivity. The following IT infrastructure components support increasing employee productivity:

- Client/server network
- Internet
- Intranets and extranets
- Backup/recovery
- Disaster recovery plan

CLIENT/SERVER NETWORK

Building a client/server network is one of the best ways to ensure that the IT infrastructure supports employee productivity. A ***client/server network*** is a network in which one or more computers are servers and provide services to the other computers, which are called clients. The server or servers have hardware, software, and/or information that the client computers can access. Figure 7.3 is an example of a client/server network. You can

Figure 7.3

A Typical Client/Server Network

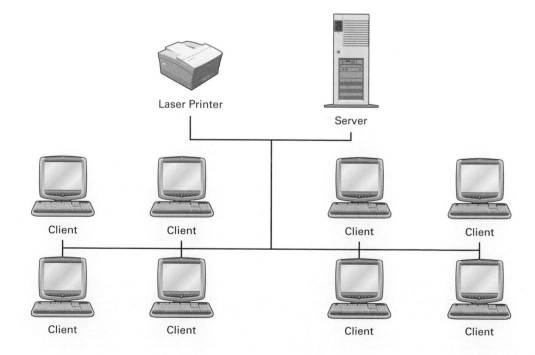

Laser Printer

Server

Client   Client   Client   Client

Client   Client   Client   Client

see that several clients access a single server and a single printer. Almost all of the computer processing is performed on the server, which allows your organization to purchase thin clients. A *thin client* is a workstation with a small amount of processing power and costs less than a full powered workstation. Purchasing thin clients can save your organization a tremendous amount of money when you consider every single knowledge worker in the company needs a client. A client/server network also allows your company to save money by purchasing a single printer that serves many individuals. Please review *Extended Learning Module E* for a detailed discussion of the many different types of client/server networks.

Prior to client/server networks, it was difficult for individuals to share information, applications, and hardware. For example, if a knowledge worker wanted to send a report out to several other knowledge workers, he or she had to either manually copy the report several times or create several floppy disks containing the report. Using a client/server network, knowledge workers can simply save the report on the server and other employees can directly access it, or they can distribute it by e-mail. A client/server network also allows employees to share applications such as personal productivity software and hardware such as printers.

INTERNET

It's impossible to count the many number of ways the Internet makes an organization successful. Today, in the information age, most employees require an Internet connection in order to perform their jobs. The Internet allows employees to send e-mail to customers, suppliers, and other employees all over the world for a fraction of the cost of a telephone call or surface mail. This advantage is referred to as *global reach*, the ability to extend a company's reach to customers anywhere there is an Internet connection, and at a much lower cost. Employees also receive the benefit of being able to search through volumes of information from organizations and libraries all over the world in a matter of minutes.

One thing to mention about the Internet is that it's not guaranteed to increase employee productivity. Sometimes it can actually decrease employee productivity. The Computer Security Institute/FBI recently reported that 78 percent of companies detected employee abuse of their Internet access privileges. The abuse included playing games, downloading movies, listening to music, gambling, trading stocks, e-mailing jokes, and even distributing critical company information. Employees also abuse the Internet by spending significant time sending personal e-mails to friends and family members. This sounds like a tiny problem, but studies indicate that the amount of time employees spend abusing the Internet directly affects employee productivity.[2]

One of the decisions you'll make regarding your IT infrastructure is how you're going to design your Internet access. Some companies implement full Internet access to all employees, while other companies provide full Internet access for only certain employees. Deciding which Internet infrastructure to develop will depend on employee needs and how much control the organization wants to have over how employees use the Internet.

INTRANETS AND EXTRANETS

An *intranet* is an internal organizational Internet that is guarded against outside access by a special security feature called a firewall (which can be software, hardware, or a combination of the two). The primary characteristic of an intranet is that people outside the organization can't access it. Employees must have a user name and password in order to logon to a company intranet.

EMPLOYEES' ABUSE OF THE INTERNET

The Internet doesn't always guarantee increased employee productivity; in fact, employee abuse of the Internet can significantly decrease employee productivity. Shawn Vidmar is the IT director of Vidmar Motor Company, a $40 million, 85 employee, automotive dealership in Pueblo, Colorado. Vidmar estimates that several employees were spending as many as six hours a day on the Internet playing games, gambling, buying stock, and sending personal e-mails. Vidmar stated, "Employees obviously weren't doing their jobs, and if they're trying to trade online and they're not doing their job, that's a problem. Productivity was being compromised and I was worried about corporate liability. If somebody gets offended by an e-mail, they could go after the company."

Vidmar has implemented new policies, employee education, and Internet monitoring software to help fix the problem. Vidmar decided to install Vericept Corporation's Vericept VIEW, a network abuse management system that tracks and analyzes network traffic. Vidmar stated, "Sending out an e-mail from here is like sending it out on Vidmar letterhead. I would hate to lose the business my grandfather started 60 years ago over a bad Internet joke."[3]

The intranet is an invaluable tool for supporting information dissemination throughout the organization. So, an intranet increases employee productivity by promoting information sharing and providing a central location where employees can go to look for information. An intranet hosts all kinds of company-related information such as benefits, schedules, strategic directions, and employee directories. At many companies, each department has its own Web page on the company intranet for departmental information sharing. The advantages an intranet gives an organization are tremendous and it should be a major piece of your IT infrastructure.

An *extranet* is an intranet that is restricted to an organization and certain outsiders, such as customers and suppliers. Many companies are building extranets as they begin to realize the tremendous benefit of offering individuals outside the organization access to intranet information.

When looking at the systems you're building be sure to ask yourself "What value can be added if employees, partners, vendors, and customers could access this system's information?" If giving access to system information helps your business, then you need to consider building an extranet. The benefits of finding new ways to disseminate and share information with external individuals is quickly becoming an extremely important form of organizational communication.

BACKUP/RECOVERY

How many times have you lost a document on your computer because your computer crashed and you hadn't saved or backed up the document? How many times have you accidentally deleted a file you needed? A *backup* is the process of making a copy of the information stored on a computer. *Recovery* is the process of reinstalling the backup information in the event the information was lost. There are many different media your organization can choose to back up information including tapes, disks, and even CD-ROMs. We can't stress the importance of making backups enough. Millions of dollars are lost every year because a system crashes and there isn't a backup of the lost information.

How many times do you think knowledge workers lose information because they didn't have a backup? How often do you think knowledge workers should back up their files? The answer to these questions varies depending on your organizational goals. For example, if your organization deals with large volumes of critical information, it might require daily backups. If your organization deals with small amounts of noncritical information, it might require only weekly backups. Deciding how often to back up computer information is a critical decision for any organization.

DISASTER RECOVERY PLAN

Unfortunately, disasters—such as power outages, floods, and even harmful hacking—occur all the time. Given that, your organization needs to develop a disaster recovery plan. A **disaster recovery plan** is a detailed process for recovering information or an IT system in the event of a catastrophic disaster such as a fire or flood.

A good disaster recovery plan takes into consideration the location of the backup information. Many organizations choose to store backup information in an off-site storage facility, or a place that is separately located from the company and often owned by another company. StorageTek is a company that specializes in providing off-site data storage and disaster recovery solutions.

A good disaster recovery plan also considers the actual facility where knowledge workers will work. A **hot site** is a separate and fully equipped facility where the company can move immediately after the disaster and resume business. A **cold site** is a separate facility that does not have any computer equipment but is a place where the knowledge workers can move after the disaster.

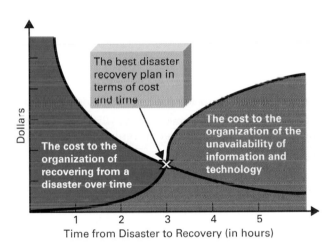

Figure 7.4

Deciding How Much to Spend on Disaster Recovery

A part of your disaster recovery plan should include a disaster recovery cost curve (see Figure 7.4). A **disaster recovery cost curve** charts (1) the cost to your organization of the unavailability of information and technology and (2) the cost to your organization of recovering from a disaster over time. Where the two intersect is, in fact, the best recovery plan in terms of cost and time. Being able to restore information and IT systems quickly in the event of a disaster is a great way to provide a support structure that helps to continually increase employee productivity.

FACTORS THAT INCREASE EMPLOYEE PRODUCTIVITY

AVAILABILITY   Do you think all knowledge workers in the United States work from 9 A.M. to 5 P.M.? If you said no, then you're absolutely correct. It's not uncommon for a knowledge worker to arrive at work early, stay late, or work on the weekend to meet a deadline. For this reason, it's crucial that the IT infrastructure supports the knowledge workers' varied schedules.

Availability is determining when your IT system will be available for knowledge workers to access. Some companies have IT systems available 24 x 7, or twenty-four hours a day, seven days a week. Can you think of any reason why an organization might offer system availability 24 x 7? What happens if your employees need to work late, or during the weekend, and they can't because the information systems are unavailable? This would certainly lead to a decrease in employee productivity.

Another reason a company might support 24 x 7 system availability is due to time zones. Imagine you work for a company based in Denver, Colorado, and the company also has an office in London, England. When the London employees are finishing work, the Colorado employees are just starting work. The same IT systems are worked on by both sets of employees so they must be available around the clock. What happens if the company had global customers? Supporting global customers mandates that a system be available 24 x 7 in order to support all of the customers in the different time zones.

ACCESSIBILITY   Accessibility is determining who has the right to access different types of IT systems and information. What do you think might happen if all employees have access to payroll information or bonus information? Payroll and bonus information is typically confidential, and at some companies you can be fired for having knowledge of or sharing this type of information.

Accessibility not only includes who can access the information, but also how they can access the information. "How" includes create, read, update, and delete, or what is often referred to as *CRUD* in the technology world. It's important that you define how each person can access information.

RELIABILITY   Reliability ensures your IT systems are functioning correctly and providing accurate information. We think you'll be surprised at how many times IT systems generate inaccurate or unreliable information. Inaccurate information occurs for many reasons, from the information being entered incorrectly to the information becoming corrupt. Whatever the reason, if employees can't receive reliable information, then they can't perform their jobs.

Ensuring information is reliable is a critical and difficult task for all organizations. *Data cleansing* is the term that describes the process of ensuring that all information is accurate. The more an organization can do to ensure its IT infrastructure promotes reliable information, the more money it will save by catching errors before they occur.

SCALABILITY   Estimating how much growth your organization is expected to experience over the next few years is an almost impossible task. *Scalability* refers to how well your system can adapt to increased demands. A number of factors can affect organizational growth including market, industry, and the economy. If your organization grows faster than anticipated, you might find your systems experiencing all types of issues including running out of disk space to a slowing in transaction performance speed. To keep employees working and productive, your organization must try to anticipate the expected growth and ensure the IT infrastructure supports it.

FLEXIBILITY   A single system can be designed in a number of different ways to perform exactly the same function. When you choose which design you want to implement, you must think about the system's flexibility, or the system's ability to change quickly. Building an inflexible system will cost your company money because it won't be able to handle market, business, or economic changes.

Let's walk through a quick example of an inflexible system design. Suppose you work for a company that sells fire hoses. The company decides to expand its business into different countries and must add new languages and currencies to its IT system. It will be a giant undertaking to modify the system to handle multiple languages and currencies. The significant amount of time it will take to make the system modifications will cause

IT COMPONENTS AND FACTORS

Supporting and increasing employee productivity is a primary goal for many organizations. In a group, review the list of IT infrastructure components and factors and rank them in order of their ability to increase employee productivity. Use a rating system of 1 to 12, where 1 indicates the biggest impact and 12 indicates the least impact.

IT Infrastructure Component/Factor	Ability to Increase Employee Productivity
Client/server network	
Internet	
Intranet and extranet	
Backup/recovery	
Disaster recovery	
Availability	
Accessibility	
Reliability	
Scalability	
Flexibility	
Performance	
Capacity planning	

the company to lose customers and sales. If the company had initially designed the system for this type of flexibility, it could have easily expanded the system to handle multiple languages and currencies.

PERFORMANCE　Have you ever tried to connect to a Web site and it seems to take forever for the page to return? After waiting for a minute or two, you probably gave up and headed for a different site. *Performance* measures how quickly an IT system performs a certain process. A *benchmark* is a set of conditions used to measure how well a product or system functions. Many factors affect the performance of an IT system ranging from the design of the system to the hardware that supports it, and performance directly affects knowledge worker productivity. If a system is slow, it will take knowledge workers twice as long to perform their jobs.

One of the most common performance issues you'll find occurs because of uncontrolled growth. For example, if business is booming and your company doubles the size of its order entry department, it must ensure the system functions exactly the same with twice as many users. If you had 50 order entry specialists and you now have 100 order entry specialists, your IT systems might not function correctly due to the increased number of users.

INCREASE STUDENT PRODUCTIVITY

You've been assigned the role as Student IT Infrastructure Lead. Your primary responsibility is to approve all designs for any new information system.

Your school is planning to build six new information systems next year. The primary reason your school is building the new information systems is to increase student productivity through the use of technology.

Your first assignment is to compile a list of three IT infrastructure components and factors that must be incorporated into every information system design. Along with the components and factors, provide a brief description of how each one will increase student productivity through the use of technology. You can choose only three IT infrastructure components for all six projects, so choose wisely.

CAPACITY PLANNING *Capacity planning* determines the future IT infrastructure requirements for new equipment and additional network capacity. It's cheaper for an organization to implement an IT infrastructure that considers capacity growth at the beginning of a system launch than to try to upgrade equipment and networks after the system has already been implemented. Not having enough capacity leads to performance issues and hinders the ability of knowledge workers to perform their jobs. For example, if you have 100 workers using the Internet to perform their jobs and you purchased modems that are too slow and the network capacity is too small, your workers will spend a great deal of time just waiting to get information from the Internet. Waiting for an Internet site to return information is not the most productive way for knowledge workers to spend their time.

To learn more about capacity planning, visit the Web site that supports this text at www.mhhe.com/haag.

Enhance Decision Making

Employees make decisions every day that affect the operations and ultimately the success of the business, as you read in Chapter 4. To make smart decisions, employees must be completely informed of everything that is happening in and around your business. This is an incredibly difficult task and becomes more and more difficult as your business and its information requirements grow. The following IT infrastructure components can help.

- Integration
- Enterprise application integration (EAI)
- Enterprise application integration middleware (EAI middleware)
- Storage devices

INTEGRATION

Typically, a business maintains separate systems for every department in the organization. For example, marketing might have its own pricing and market-forecasting systems, sales might have its own sales and customer tracking systems, and accounting might have its own financial systems. Some organizations have hundreds of different systems operating across all departments. What types of problems do you think occur when an organization has so many separate systems?

What do you think might happen if your professor assigned 50 different textbooks for this course and based each lecture on information from all 50 books? It would be almost impossible for you to read all 50 books each time you prepared for class. You might even run into the problem where the different textbooks contradicted each other on certain topics or key terms. This is exactly what happens to an organization that has separate systems. Employees have a hard time making informed decisions because the information they need is stored across several different systems and sometimes conflicts.

Let's take a look at a customer address change example to demonstrate the problems that arise from having separate systems. If a customer moves and sends a change of address form to your company, this information must be entered into every single system where the customer address information is stored. Chances are some of the systems will be missed, and the customer now has different address information in different systems, or conflicting addresses information. How would an employee know which address is correct when trying to send a letter to the customer?

To help alleviate this problem organizations build integrations. An *integration* allows separate systems to communicate directly with each other by automatically exporting data files from one system and importing them into another. Building integrations between systems helps your organization maintain better control of its information and helps quickly gather information across multiple systems.

Figure 7.5 provides an example of how your organization can integrate customer information systems. Each time new entries or changes occur, the information is integrated, or automatically passed, to all of the other systems that maintain customer information. This eliminates the problem of having to enter the same customer information into multiple systems.

Integrations enhance employees' decision making by ensuring they have accurate and timely information. However, integrations are extremely hard and expensive to build and maintain because you must find a way for systems that use different technologies to communicate. Integration issues also tend to increase exponentially as the number of systems in your company grows.

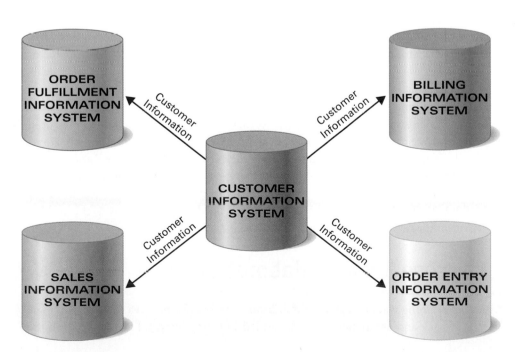

Figure 7.5

Integrating Customer Information into All Business Systems

ENTERPRISE APPLICATION INTEGRATION (EAI)

Enterprise application integration (EAI) is the process of developing an IT infrastructure that enables employees to quickly implement new or changing business processes. EAI is a way of increasing business value by integrating not only business information but also business processes. Companies are investing in EAI to streamline business processes while keeping all organizational information integrated. It's important to understand that EAI is not something you can buy like a product or a development tool—it's something organizations try to accomplish. Most businesses are successful at accomplishing certain types of EAI: database (sharing and copying information across databases) and system EAI (sharing information across multiple systems). The ultimate goal, a common virtual system EAI in which every business aspect connects together and appears as a single unified system, is something that almost every organization will attempt to achieve for many years to come. A few organizations will succeed, but most won't.[4]

ENTERPRISE APPLICATION INTEGRATION MIDDLEWARE

Enterprise application integration middleware (EAI middleware) allows organizations to develop different levels of integration from the information level to the business process level. EAI middleware simplifies integrations by eliminating the need for custom-built software. An organization can purchase an EAI package from a vendor that supplies a prebuilt connector that translates and transfers information from one system to another. An EAI package saves your organization time and money because system developers don't have to spend time custom building interfaces between systems.

ActiveWorks is one of the primary EAI middleware packages available today. Active software, founded in 1995, built ActiveWorks, an integration product that focuses on business process integration of front-office customer and back-end business systems.[5]

STORAGE DEVICES

Making informed decisions sometimes requires reviewing past information as well as current information. Viewing historical information, or archived information, allows a company to perform detailed analysis on sales trends, customer trends, product trends, employee trends, and so forth. There is a wealth of knowledge in historical information.

So, your IT infrastructure must define a storage architecture. A storage architecture takes into account the types and sizes of devices where information is stored. Typically, historical information is stored on the same server as the current information. After a certain amount of time, the information is archived or moved to a storage server. In order to view archived information, you must request that the archived information be restored.

You also have to determine an appropriate cut-off date to archive information. For example, if AT&T saved all billing information for every single customer throughout its history, it would need an incredible amount of space, and most of the information would be outdated. You have to determine a cut-off date that makes business sense. But if you make the cut-off date too soon, chances are you'll need frequent access to the archived information to answer questions and make decisions.

Improve Team Collaboration

Almost everything you do in your organization will be performed in a team environment. Very few tasks and assignments are performed individually in the working world. So,

1,900 GAP STORES COMMUNICATING

The Gap has 1,900 stores around the world, employing more than 3,000 people who generated $5.3 billion in revenue in 2001. The company's primary goal is to achieve and maintain a 20 percent growth rate each year. To maintain this goal, the Gap needed to keep all of the employees connected with immediate access to real-time information by sharing information between several different legacy systems and new applications. The Gap chose to implement CORBA middleware to build the integrations between the different systems.

CORBA stands for Common Object Request Broker Architecture and it allows programs at different locations developed by different vendors to communicate through integrations. Building an IT infrastructure based on CORBA integrations and the use of the Internet allowed the Gap to exchange real-time sales, inventory, and shipping information among all of its information systems and employees. The new infrastructure allowed the Gap to send information to and from any IT system in the world, which increased employee and company performance.[6,7]

improving team collaboration greatly increases your organization's productivity and should be a primary goal of your organization's IT infrastructure. Throughout the previous chapters, we've introduced you to a variety of IT tools that support team collaboration. Here we cover three more, including

- Document management systems
- Enterprise information portals (EIP)
- Workflow systems

DOCUMENT MANAGEMENT SYSTEMS

What do you think of when you hear the term *document?* We bet you all thought of different things, because the term *document* can mean many different things. A document can refer to any file that can be created and stored electronically including text, tables, forms, graphics, images, sound, or video.

It's not uncommon to find 15 or 20 knowledge workers editing the same document. Large companies produce thousands of documents every month and they need to be organized and categorized. A ***document management system*** manages a document through its life cycle. The following are the primary functions of a document management system:

- *Creation:* Allows knowledge workers to create different document types.
- *Modification:* Manages the integrity of a document as it's edited or modified by knowledge workers, otherwise known as version control.
- *Security:* Controls access to a document and allows only knowledge workers with appropriate access to view and edit the document.
- *Approval:* A document is sent to a particular knowledge worker for approval, similar to a workflow system discussed in detail below.
- *Distribution:* Knowledge workers distribute documents via e-mail or the Web.
- *Archiving:* Saving a document in a storage facility with the ability to extract the document in the future.

MANAGING MULTIPLE WEB SITES

Dow Corning Corporation develops and manufactures more than 7,000 products and services to customers all over the world. Every department in Dow Corning Corporation manages its own Web content, and the company had a concern that the rush to publish information to the Web could cause the overall look and feel of the Web sites to suffer from a lack of consistency. The company quickly realized it needed a document management system to ensure the consistency of its Web sites and company documentation while allowing experts in each department to contribute to the content. Dow Corning decided to implement Documentum 4i eBusiness Platform, an eBusiness document management solution for creating, publishing, and managing Web site documentation. With Documentum, Dow Corning increased customer satisfaction, raised employee productivity, and improved partner relationships.[8,9]

A typical document management system contains a relational database management system where the texts of all documents are stored and provides knowledge workers with the ability to perform full-text searches. Most systems allow businesses to capture data about paper documents, with one of the attributes being the documents location. If a knowledge worker requires a certain document to perform his or her job, they can simply search the document management system to find where the document is located.

ENTERPRISE INFORMATION PORTALS

Enterprise information portals (EIPs) allow knowledge workers to access company information via a Web interface. An EIP is similar to an Internet search engine such as Google, Yahoo, or Alta Vista, except the only information stored on an EIP is company information. Using an EIP a knowledge worker can find and view enterprisewide business information by performing a simple search.

Intranets are more of a corporate newsletter or static database of corporate information. An EIP is different from a corporate intranet because an EIP is dynamic and serves as an electronic workspace for knowledge workers. EIPs provide personalized access to key information and applications and real-time notification of important new information via e-mail. Critical information can also be presented in the form of graphics and charts that are continuously updated.

There are two primary categories of EIPs including collaborative processing EIP and decision processing EIP. A *collaborative processing enterprise information portal* provides knowledge workers with access to workgroup information such as e-mails, reports, meeting minutes, and memos. A *decision processing enterprise information portal* provides knowledge workers with corporate information for making key business decisions. EIPs are becoming increasingly popular in the workforce because of the amount of information sharing they provide for knowledge workers.

WORKFLOW SYSTEMS

Workflow defines all of the steps or business rules, from beginning to end, required for a process to run correctly. *Workflow systems* automate business processes. Workflow systems help manage the flow of information through the organization whenever a process is executed. As a process is executed, a workflow system tracks where the information is and what status it's in. Let's take a look at how you could use a workflow sys-

WORKING TOGETHER AS A TEAM

Document management systems, enterprise information portals, and workflow systems are all great infrastructure components for improving team collaboration. Assume you have been assigned to work on a group project with 10 other students. The project requires you to develop a detailed business plan for a business of your choice. How could you use a document management system to manage all of the documents required to create the business plan? Documentation might include market analysis, industry analysis, growth opportunities, Porter Five Forces model, financial forecasts, competitive advantage information, among other documents. How could you use the enterprise information portals to share and post information with group members? How could you use a workflow system to manage the tasks for the group members to perform?

tem to help you complete a group project. The following are four steps you usually take when completing a group project.

1. Find out what information and deliverables are required for the project and when they are due.
2. Divide up the work among the group members.
3. Determine due dates for the different pieces of work.
4. Compile all of the work together into a single project.

One of the hardest parts of a team project is getting information passed around among the various team members. Often one group member can't perform his or her work until another group member has finished. Group members waste a lot of time waiting to receive information from other group members. This same situation happens in the "real world." You'll find the actual work is sitting idle waiting for an employee to pick it up to either approve it or continue working on it. Workflow systems help to automate the process of passing work around the organization.

A workflow system can automatically pass documents around to different team members in the required order. There are two primary types of workflow systems: messaging-based and database-based. *Messaging-based workflow systems* send work assignments through an e-mail system. The workflow system automatically tracks the order for the work to be assigned and each time it's completed it automatically sends the work to the next individual in line. If you used this type of workflow system to complete your group project it would automatically distribute the work to each group member via e-mail. Each time you finished a part of the project that needed to be sent to another group member the system would take care of this for you.

Database-based workflow systems store the document in a central location and automatically ask the knowledge workers to access the document when it's their turn to edit the document. If you used this type of workflow system to perform your group project the project documentation would be stored in a central location and you would be notified by the system when it was your turn to log in and work on your portion of the project.

Either type of workflow system will help improve teamwork by providing automated process support allowing knowledge workers to communicate and collaborate within a unified environment.

Create Business Partnerships and Alliances

With the growing popularity of performing business over the Internet, your IT infrastructure must support electronic business partnerships or your organization will not survive long in today's e-centric world. Creating business partnerships and alliances is a key strategy for any company that intends to be a serious player in the information age. Four critical components to building a strong IT infrastructure to support these goals include

1. Customer relationship management (CRM) systems
2. Sales force automation (SFA) systems
3. Electronic catalog
4. Supply chain management (SCM) systems

CUSTOMER RELATIONSHIP MANAGEMENT SYSTEMS

What do you think is the primary driver for most organizations? If you said the customer, congratulations, you are correct. Without customers a business couldn't exist; in fact many businesses' primary goal is to increase customer satisfaction.

Keeping and retaining current and potential customers is one of the primary goals of any organization, and customer relationship management has become one of the hottest buzzwords in businesses today. *Customer relationship management (CRM) systems* use information about customers to gain insight into their needs, wants, and behaviors in order to serve them better. Customers interact with companies in many ways and each interaction or experience should be enjoyable, easy, and error free. Have you ever had an experience with a company that made you so angry you changed companies or returned the product? It's not uncommon for a customer to change companies after having a negative business experience. The goal of CRM is to limit these types of negative interactions and provide customers with positive business experiences.

It's important to note that CRM is not just software but also a business objective which encompasses many different aspects of a business including software, hardware, services, support, and strategic business goals. The IT infrastructure you create should support all of these aspects and must be designed to provide the organization with detailed customer information. Figure 7.6 is an example of a potential CRM system infrastructure. The *front office systems* are the primary interface to customers and sales channels, and send all of the customer information to the data warehouse. The *back office systems* are used to fulfill and support customer orders, and send all of the customer information to the data warehouse. The CRM system analyzes and distributes the customer information and provides the organization with a complete view of each customer's business experiences.

There are many systems available today a company can purchase that offer CRM functionality. Some of the big providers of these packages include Clarify, Oracle, SAP, and Siebel. Ensuring that your organization's IT infrastructure supports CRM is critical to the success of your business.

SALES FORCE AUTOMATION SYSTEMS

The sales process includes many factors such as contact management, sales lead tracking, sales forecasting, order management, and product knowledge. *Sales force automation (SFA) systems* automatically track all of the steps in the sales process. There are many SFA vendors including Clarify, Siebel, Vantive, and Salesforce. Some basic SFA systems per-

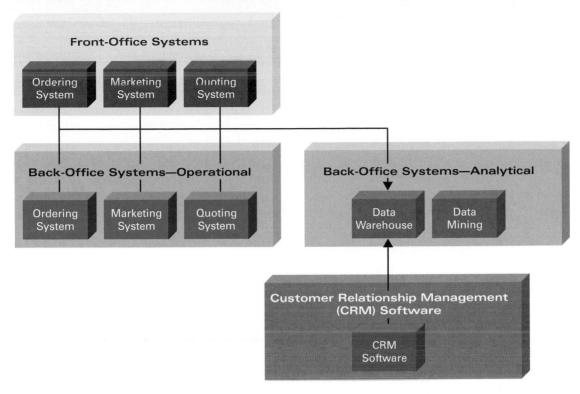

Figure /.6

A Sample Customer
Relationship
Management (CRM)
System Infrastructure

form sales lead tracking or listing potential customers for the sales team to contact. They
also perform contact management, which tracks all of the times a salesperson contacts a
potential customer, what they discussed, and the next steps. More sophisticated SFA systems perform detailed analysis on the market and on customers and even offer product
configuration tools where the customer can configure their own products.

One of the biggest problems organizations have when implementing SFA systems is
developing the integrations. Sales, marketing, customer service centers, and customer
billing are typically separate departments with separate systems. Often, these separate
departments have communication problems that can hurt customer relationships. For
example, a salesperson might talk to a customer and try to sell them a new product without realizing the customer has already been on the phone all day with another department in the company trying to resolve an issue with a current product. This is probably
not the best day for the salesperson to approach the customer and ask them to buy additional products.

Getting separate departments to talk to each other electronically is a big challenge. An
SFA system attempts to provide electronic communication between the sales systems al-
leviating such problems as previously mentioned. If the company had implemented an
SFA system, the salesperson in the above example would already know that the customer
had been talking to the company all day and would even know exactly what problem the
customer is experiencing. The salesperson could then approach the customer, help with
the current problem, and then try to sell the additional products. SFA is thereby an invaluable tool for increasing customer sales.

ELECTRONIC CATALOG

Providing an electronic catalog is a great way to enable business partnerships and alliances. An ***electronic catalog*** is designed to present products to customers or partners
all over the world via the Web. An electronic catalog provides much more detailed

FEDEX STREAMLINES SHIPPING

FedEx has become a master at supply chain management, using it to focus on building strong customer partnerships. FedEx had developed a tool, FedEx Ship Manager API, that can be downloaded for free from the Internet. FedEx Ship Manager API allows customers to connect into FedEx's information systems directly when placing shipping orders and scheduling pickups.

FedEx has created an incredible competitive advantage by allowing customers to directly connect to its information systems. Customers now have complete control over shipping preparation which helps to eliminate shipping errors since they enter the information directly. Customers can also monitor real-time shipping status right from their desk, which helps to increase employee productivity. FedEx has become a leader in the industry for its brilliant use of supply chain management.[10]

information about products than paper catalogs including real-time inventory status, photographs, product specifications, product instructions and safety procedures, video demonstrations, and so forth. Electronic catalogs even provide links to product reviews and industry information.

One of the biggest advantages of using an electronic catalog is the search functionality. A customer can search the catalog based on a key word, line item, inventory level, unit price, or other description. Giving a customer such powerful search capabilities makes it easier for a customer to find a product especially if they know exactly what they want. Sometimes, however, the search functionality can make finding a product more difficult.

Let's assume you need to order new wastebaskets for your office. You simply open up a supplier electronic catalog and type in the word *wastebasket*. Unfortunately, your search returns zero results. You then type in *trash bucket, waste bucket, trash bin, garbage bin,* and still nothing returns from your search results. You start to get a bit frustrated because you know this company sells office supplies and a wastebasket is an office supply. Finally you type in *garbage can* and several different types of wastebaskets appear.

This is one of the biggest issues with electronic catalogs—finding and associating all of the potential names for a given product. Everyone could potentially have a different name for a garbage can. If the company sells global products then it must also deal with offering the product in multiple languages. Trying to find all of the names and associating them with a given product is a critical and vital task to perform if the electronic catalog is going to be successful.

Electronic catalog software is available from many vendors including Actinic, Harbinger, Mercado, and Requisite Technology. The catalog software package already has the functionality to perform all of the catalog aspects and all a company that purchases this system must do is input its own unique product information. Implementing an electronic catalog is a huge advantage for any business and once again must be supported by the IT infrastructure.

SUPPLY CHAIN MANAGEMENT SYSTEM

Managing the supply chain is fundamental to the success of any business, and controlling inventory is one of the largest problems facing businesses today. **Supply chain management (SCM) systems** track inventory and information among business processes and across companies. The primary goal of SCM is to reduce the amount of

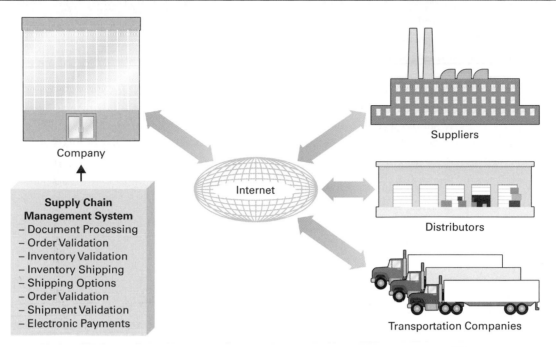

Figure 7.7

A Sample Supply Chain Management System (SCM) Infrastructure

inventory a company must keep on hand by providing the company with a complete view into its suppliers to understand inventory levels and production capacity. SCM helps a company improve its operations and inventory tracking.

The solution for a successful supply chain management system includes either purchasing sophisticated software with Web interfaces or hiring a third-party Web-based application service provider who promises to provide part or all of the SCM service. Figure 7.7 provides an overview of how an organization's IT infrastructure can support SCM. The knowledge workers query the SCM software for information for ordering of inventory. The SCM software connects to potential suppliers, distributors, and transporting companies to determine where to purchase the inventory and the best way to have the inventory delivered. The SCM system also performs such functions as order validation, message validation to potential suppliers and distributors, inventory routing and validation, and electronic payments.

The two largest vendors of SCM systems include i2 and Manugistics. Dell Computer Corporation, one of the largest computer system companies in the world, recently implemented an i2 supply chain solution. Dell is a leader and innovator in Web-based sales and operation and is continually looking to set the industry standards for customer service, sales, and distribution. Dell experiences enormous growth and decided to implement a SCM solution to help it manage its suppliers, distributors, transportation companies, and inventory. Dick Hunter, Vice President of Manufacturing Operations for Dell Computer Corporation, stated, "The supply chain solution from i2—and the processes we put around i2—is allowing us to move materials so fast around our supply chain that we're able to take advantage of lower-cost materials quicker and pass those lower-cost materials on to our suppliers. And that's allowing us to fuel our growth."[11]

Enable Global Reach

The world is becoming smaller and smaller. Not to say that the world is actually shrinking, but, with so many technological inventions that make it easier for businesses and individuals to communicate, the world seems like a smaller place. One hundred years ago the only way to get from America to Europe was to spend weeks traveling by boat. Today you can hold a videoconference whereby people in America and Europe can see and hear each other just as if they are in the same room.

The IT infrastructure of your organization must be able to support global employees, suppliers, distributors, and, most importantly, customers. The primary tool used to help all of these individuals communicate globally is the Internet. The following are four of the primary global IT infrastructure components your organization must consider:

1. Internet service provider (ISP)
2. Application service provider (ASP)
3. Collocation facilities
4. Server farms

INTERNET SERVICE PROVIDER

An ***Internet service provider (ISP)*** is a company that provides individuals, organizations, and businesses access to the Internet. Some of the larger ISPs include UUNet, MCI, and AT&T WorldNet. How many of you use an ISP to connect to the Internet from your home computer? There are hundreds of ISPs, and they all perform the same function of providing customers with Internet access.

APPLICATION SERVICE PROVIDER

Outsourcing is the delegation of specific work to a third party for a specified length of time, at a specified cost, and at a specified level of service (the guarantee of perfect delivery). An ***application service provider (ASP)*** is a company that provides an outsourcing service for business software applications. Hiring an ASP to manage your organization's software allows you to hand over the storage, operation, maintenance, and upgrade responsibilities for a system to an ASP.

Companies can outsource application and infrastructure services. Application services include business functions such as payroll, accounting, intranets, and e-mail. Infrastructure services include large systems such as customer relationship management systems, enterprise resource planning systems, and customer service call centers.

Figure 7.8 represents how your IT infrastructure might support using an ASP. Your company receives access to the software through the Internet. The company knowledge workers can log in to the software from their offices, laptops, and sometimes cellular equipment depending on how the software works. The ASP stores, maintains, and upgrades the software to ensure security and backups of the data.

One of the most important agreements between the customer and the ASP is the service level agreement. ***Service level agreements (SLAs)*** define the specific responsibilities of the service provider and set the customer expectations. SLAs include such items as availability, accessibility, performance, maintenance, backup/recovery, upgrades, equipment ownership, software ownership, security, and confidentiality. For example, an SLA might state that the ASP must have the software available and accessible from 7:00 A.M. to 7:00 P.M. Monday through Friday. It might also state that if the system is down for more than 60 minutes the charge for that day of service will be removed.

Most industry analysts agree that the ASP market is growing rapidly. International Data Corporation estimates the worldwide ASP market will grow from around $693.5 million in 2000 to $13.0 billion by 2005. The Aberdeen Group predicts the ASP market will grow to 16.1 billion in 2005. Zona Research (now the Sageza Group) reported in 2001 that 63 percent of the companies it surveyed are already using an ASP to access

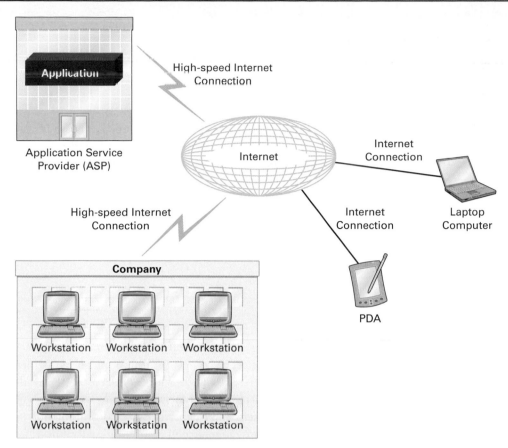

Figure 7.8

A Sample Application
Service Provider (ASP)
Infrastructure

an average of two to six applications. As a knowledge worker, you'll find yourself working with ASPs and outsourced applications. You might even find yourself in the position of having to make the decision to outsource one of your business applications.[12]

COLLOCATION FACILITIES

It's hard to believe but the correct spelling of the word *collocation* is yet to be defined. You could find collocation spelled co location, colocation, or collocation. Regardless of the way you choose to spell it, the word **collocation** simply means that a company rents space and telecommunications equipment from another company, or a collocation vendor. For example, if a company places a server that contains the company's Web site in a building owned by another company, the company has collocated its server with another company. Collocation facilities are typically large warehouse type buildings where hundreds of different companies can store computer hardware and software.

Can you guess why a company would want to use a collocation facility? It saves the company money because buying or renting an office is expensive. For example, if a company has a central office in Chicago and sales personnel in Chicago, Boston, and Toronto, the IT infrastructure must support all of the employees even if there is not a central office in the town where they work. By placing a server in a collocation facility in Boston and Toronto, the sales personnel in these places could dial in to the server and be connected to the Chicago office's intranet and information systems. This saves the company a lot of time and energy because the alternative to this configuration would be to have the employees dial a long distance number to the Chicago office or rent an office in each location to maintain the server. Renting space from a collocation facility is cheap and easy as compared to setting up an entire office.

EURORESINS'S UNIQUE STRATEGY

Euroresins is a leader in the European chemical products market and it decided to outsource its IT department to IBM Global Services. The company wanted to reduce their outsourcing costs and still be able to support the organization's IT infrastructure. The ASP model offered Euroresins a perfect solution, and the company chose to partner with Multrix, one of the first independent application service providers (ASPs) in the Netherlands. Multrix provides applications along with a complete range of other services such as management, maintenance, security, and support.

Since outsourcing with Multrix, Euroresins has experienced significantly lower costs, better and more sophisticated services, and greater flexibility for adding services in different locations, something that is critical when performing business globally. The overall service is far better than the company could have ever built themselves.[13]

SERVER FARM

A **server farm** is the name of a location that stores a group of servers in a single place. Server farms are also referred to as server clusters. A server farm, or cluster, provides centralized access and control to files, printers, and backups for each server. The advantage of having a server farm is that if a single server fails there are other servers that can perform the work, and the knowledge workers don't experience any downtime due to failed equipment or software. Server farms are often located in collocation facilities.

A **web farm** is either a Web site that has multiple servers, or an ISP that provides Web site outsourcing services using multiple servers. For the most part you can use a single server to handle user requests for files on a Web site. For large Web sites you might require multiple servers to handle user requests for files.

Facilitate Organizational Transformation

Change is inevitable. Everything changes, and your organization must be ready to change whenever the economy, industry, technology, or anything else changes. Being able to change quickly and easily is a huge advantage for an organization. The IT infrastructure has several critical components to help organizations change, including

- Enterprise resource planning (ERP) and enterprise software
- Data warehouse
- Infrastructure documentation

ENTERPRISE RESOURCE PLANNING AND ENTERPRISE SOFTWARE

Today, many organizations are taking a holistic view of their structure and processes as they develop the IT infrastructure and systems. That is, these organizations have come to realize that the development of a particular system without regard to the organization as a whole has serious disadvantages. To move toward a more holistic view, organizations are adopting the concept of enterprise resource planning (ERP) and using enterprise software to develop all systems in a coordinated fashion. We first introduced ERP systems in Chapter 4 and we'll delve deeper into the topic here.

Enterprise resource planning (ERP) is the method of getting and keeping an overview of every part of the business (a bird's eye view, so to speak), so that production, development, selling, and servicing of goods and services will all be coordinated to contribute to the company's goals and objectives. ERP may sound like a solid concept that all organizations should follow, but it just isn't that easy. In organizations of any size, seeing and understanding the whole corporate picture is difficult. Even more so, planning for all the required resources needed for any initiative is even more difficult.

Further complicating the problem is that processes and IT systems are already in place supporting a particular business function, but perhaps not the organization as a whole. So, just adopting ERP requires that most organizations undertake numerous reengineering efforts to ensure that the entire organization is operating as a single entity.

Enterprise software directly supports the concept of ERP. *Enterprise software* is a suite of software that includes (1) a set of common business applications, (2) tools for modeling how the entire organization works, and (3) development tools for building applications unique to your organization. Leading enterprise software vendors include SAP, Oracle, PeopleSoft, J. D. Edwards, Computer Associates, and Baan.

Figure 7.9 is an example of how an organization could implement enterprise software. Information from the different departments is sent to the enterprise software. The enterprise software maintains all of this data and provides a holistic view of the organization. Once you use enterprise software to develop a holistic view of your organization, you can use your enterprise software to make changes to your organizational model and processes.

To use enterprise software effectively in support of ERP, your organization must first model its existing structure, divisions and departments, and processes, such as inventory

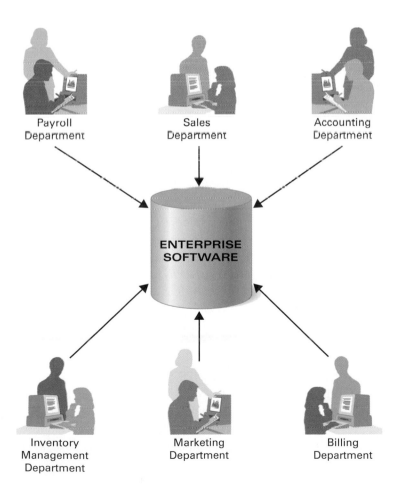

Figure 7.9

A Sample Enterprise Software Infrastructure

procurement, accounts receivable, customer service, and so on. In parallel, it must also develop a model of all IT systems, how they work together, and perhaps how they conflict with each other. Armed with that information, your organization can then undertake the process of ERP to determine how best to streamline processes and develop the appropriate underlying IT systems that will support those processes through decentralized computing and shared information.

In the future, it looks as if enterprise software suites will replace CASE tools. *Computer-aided software engineering (CASE)* tools are software suites that automate systems development. CASE tools were originally developed just to support systems development, which focuses only on the development of a single system. Later, planning capabilities were added to some CASE tools, but it seemed to be more an afterthought than a well-defined plan. So, CASE tools do not really require your organization to take a holistic view. For that reason, we see enterprise software suites replacing CASE tools in the future.

THE REALITY OF ENTERPRISE RESOURCE PLANNING AND ENTERPRISE SOFTWARE   Enterprise resource planning and enterprise software almost sound too good to be true. They are, however, a reality, and many organizations are exploiting them. In spite of their tremendous advantages, many organizations are either not using ERP and enterprise software or only partially implementing them. In the sections below, we list a few reasons why.

THE EXISTENCE OF LEGACY SYSTEMS   *Legacy systems* are IT systems previously built using older technologies such as mainframe computers and programming languages such as COBOL. Legacy systems may work well in isolation, but they tend to be very difficult to interface with when your organization develops new systems based on state-of-the-art technologies. Organizations have invested literally billions of dollars in developing and maintaining legacy systems, and they are not prepared to throw them away and switch to using an ERP system.

THE COST OF OWNERSHIP   Enterprise software is among the most expensive software your organization can purchase, costing millions of dollars for a complete system. After you purchase an enterprise software suite you have to customize it for your organization, which can easily cost millions of dollars more.

THE COST OF REENGINEERING   Fundamental to the concept of ERP is business process reengineering. Let's face it—organizations that have evolved over time have inefficient processes, redundant processes, and processes that do not work well together. To rectify this, your organization must undergo numerous business process reengineering efforts. *Business process reengineering (BPR)* is the reinventing of processes within a business. Many people today characterize BPR as a "knee-breaking" initiative in which you completely disregard what you're doing in favor of processes that are streamlined and completely integrated. This, again, represents a huge expense, which some organizations are not willing to undertake.

THE EXPERTISE NEEDED FOR ENTERPRISE SOFTWARE   Finally, to use enterprise software, your organization must provide extensive training for its IT staff. Developing IT systems within an enterprise software suite requires expertise unique to that particular suite. Enterprise software vendors such as SAP and J. D. Edwards provide months and even years of training to your organization if you choose to purchase one of their

HOW FLORIDA SAVED 10,000 HOURS A YEAR

The Orlando, Florida, city government drastically improved its performance by implementing enterprise software. The city government has been using the J. D. Edwards ERP system since 1998. Today, more than 400 Orlando government knowledge workers use the J. D. Edwards software.

Rob Garner, Comptroller, stated,

All managers can view their budgets, drill down through multiple levels of financial information to individual transactions, and extract information and format it into any kind of report right from their desktops. Before implementing J. D. Edwards software, we produced batch reports every month and shipped them to managers throughout city government. Now they don't have to rely on our IT department to generate financial information—they can get it themselves at any time, without having to ask anyone for it. We have redirected as much as 10,000 developer hours a year to supporting the needs of the user community.[14]

suites. This expertise is in such high demand that you can actually become a certified developer using different enterprise software suites. If you do, your career will be long and prosperous.

DATA WAREHOUSE

The promise of an ERP system is that one system could solve all of the information needs of the organization. ERP systems are great at capturing and storing data, but they lack the ability to understand and analyze the data. Knowledge workers find themselves frustrated with ERP systems because they can't get all the information they need from the system.

For this reason, many businesses have implemented data warehouses along with ERP systems. The data warehouse consolidates ERP information along with other sources of information in order to perform and support analysis. A data warehouse can help knowledge workers organize, understand, and analyze the information collected by the organization. This information is the true competitive advantage in the information age. For detailed information on data warehouses, review Chapter 3.

INFRASTRUCTURE DOCUMENTATION

One of the keys to building a solid IT infrastructure is to ensure every component is well documented and the documentation is available to all company employees. A major issue for organizations today is the lack of system documentation. For example, assume you are building a data warehouse that must integrate with all of the ERP systems in the organization, but there isn't any available documentation about how the ERP systems are designed and implemented. It'd be impossible for you to integrate two systems together successfully without having a complete knowledge of both systems.

IT Infrastructures and the Real World

Components of a solid IT infrastructure can include anything from documentation to business concepts to software and hardware. Throughout this chapter, we discussed many of these including flexibility, scalability, client/server networks, supply chain management, and enterprise resource planning. It may seem that we covered a great deal of

CHOOSING AN ERP VENDOR

Enterprise resource planning (ERP) is the coordinated planning of all an organization's resources involved in the production, development, selling, and servicing of goods and services. *Enterprise software* is a suite of software that includes (1) a set of common business applications, (2) tools for modeling how the entire organization works, and (3) development tools for building applications unique to your organization. Leading enterprise software vendors include SAP, Oracle, PeopleSoft, J. D. Edwards, Computer Associates, and Baan. Choose two of the leading enterprise software vendors and use the Internet to determine the primary differences between the two vendors' systems. Remember to think about the different IT infrastructure components mentioned in this chapter when you are performing your analysis.

material in this chapter, but there are actually thousands of additional components that'll be important to building a solid IT infrastructure. Deciding which pieces to implement and how to implement them is becoming an almost impossible task as new products are released daily and businesses are continually changing. An IT infrastructure that meets your organizational needs today may not meet those needs tomorrow. Building an IT infrastructure that is scalable, flexible, available, accessible, and reliable is key to your organization's success.

As a knowledge worker, you'll be responsible for approving the designs for the IT infrastructure for your systems. Remember to ask yourself the following questions before approving the IT infrastructure designs:

- How big is your department going to grow? Will the system be able to handle additional users?
- How are your customers going to grow? How much additional information do you expect to store each year?
- How long will you maintain information in the systems? How much history do you want to keep on each customer?
- When do the people in your department work? What are the hours you need the system to be available?
- How often do you need the information to be backed up?
- What will happen to your system if there is a disaster? What is the disaster recovery plan for your system?
- How easy is it to change the system? How flexible is the system?

Ensuring your system designs answer each of these questions will put you on the path toward building an IT infrastructure that will support your organization today and tomorrow.

Summary: Student Learning Outcomes Revisited

1. **Explain the relationship between the organization's roles and goals and the IT infrastructure.** An *IT infrastructure* includes the hardware, software, and telecommunications equipment that combined provides the underlying foundation supporting the organizational goals, processes, and strategies. Organizational goals drive everything the

organization does, ranging from how it's structured to how it designs its IT infrastructure. For example, an organization can have many structures including flat or hierarchical. A flat organizational structure has only a couple of managerial layers while a hierarchical organizational structure has many managerial layers. If an organization has a flat structure it might be attempting to support the goal of information dissemination. If an organization has a hierarchical structure it might be attempting to support the goal of information secrecy and security.

2. **List and describe four of the seven factors that help increase employee productivity.**

   - Availability is determining when your IT system will be available for knowledge workers to access.

   - Accessibility is determining who has the right to access different types of IT systems and information.

   - Reliability ensures your IT systems are functioning correctly and providing accurate information.

   - *Scalability* refers to how well your system can adapt to increased demands.

   - Flexibility ensures the system is designed with the ability to quickly change.

   - *Performance* measures how quickly an IT system performs a certain process.

   - *Capacity planning* determines the future IT infrastructure requirements for new equipment and additional network capacity.

3. **Explain system integration and how it enhances decision making.** Many times an organization will have a separate and distinct system for each department. Some organizations end up with hundreds of different systems that do not communicate with each other. In order to help alleviate the problem of so many separate systems containing separate information, some organizations build integrations. An *integration* allows separate systems to communicate directly with each other by automatically exporting data files from one system and importing them into another system. Building integrations between systems helps the organization to maintain better control of its information and helps quickly gather information across multiple systems.

4. **List and describe two different types of workflow systems.**

   - *Messaging-based workflow infrastructures* send work assignments through an e-mail system. The workflow system automatically tracks the order for the work to be assigned, and each time it's completed it automatically sends the work to the next individual in line.

   - A *database-based workflow* infrastructure stores the document in a central location and automatically asks the knowledge workers to access the document when it's their turn to edit the document.

5. **List and describe two of the four IT infrastructure components that create business partnerships and alliances.**

   - *Customer relationship management (CRM) systems* use information about customers to gain insights into their needs, wants, and behaviors in order to serve them better.

   - *Sales force automation (SFA)* is the process of automatically tracking all of the steps in the sales process.

   - *Electronic catalogs* are designed to present products to customers or partners all over the world via the Web.

   - *Supply chain management (SCM)* tracks inventory and information among business processes and across companies.

6. **List and describe two IT infrastructure components that enable global reach.**

   - An *Internet service provider (ISP)* is a company that provides individuals, organizations, and businesses with access to the Internet.

   - *Collocation* simply means that a company rents space and telecommunications equipment from another company, or a collocation vendor.

   - An *application service provider (ASP)* is a company that provides an outsourcing service for business software applications ranging from personal productivity programs to large enterprisewide systems that would otherwise be located on the company's computers in the company's office building.

   - A *server farm* is the name of a location that stores a group of servers in a single place.

UNIVERSITY INFRASTRUCTURES

The year is 1982. Universities around the country are filled with students who are pursuing business degrees in accounting, marketing, management, and finance. The life of a student in 1982 is drastically different from the life of a student in 2002. In 1982, only a couple of students had access to e-mail, none of the students had laptops, many of the students had never used a computer, and the idea of surfing the Internet was a concept students couldn't even understand. It's hard to believe that technology has come so far so fast.

Cheryl O'Connell graduated from university with a marketing degree in 1983. O'Connell stated, "I remember all of my papers were either handwritten or typed on a typewriter; nobody had a computer. There were about 15 computers in the business school for all 3,500 business students. The computers were in high demand and were primarily used for running statistical or spreadsheet programs, not word processing programs. I never dreamed that one day I would own a computer, the thought just never even crossed my mind."

In 1982, students didn't have access to e-mail, they weren't instant messaging their friends, they had to use a dictionary to check their spelling, and they had to go to the library to research a subject. If you had a conversation with these students and told them that in 20 years most students would own their own computers, could automatically spell check a 100-page paper in about 10 minutes, and could research libraries all over the world from their dorm rooms, they would have told you that you were crazy.

In 1982, Apple Computer offered the Lisa computer featuring a 5-MHz 68000 microprocessor, 1MB RAM, 2MB ROM, a 12-inch black-and-white monitor, dual 5.25-inch 860KB floppy drives, and a 5MB hard drive. Its initial price was $10,000. In the same year, IBM introduced the IBM PC-XT Model 370, with an 8088 CPU, 768K RAM, 360K drive, and 10 MB hard drive for $9,000. Can you even imagine a 10 MB hard drive? A hard drive this small wouldn't even be able to handle one software package today.

In the 20 years since 1982, everything has changed. More than 90 percent of freshman at Michigan University arrive on campus already owning a computer. Josh Michaels, a senior at the University of Illinois, controls all of the devices in his apartment from his laptop. He can sit in bed and turn on his coffee grinder, espresso machine, and stereo. He can even sit in bed and check to see if the pizza he ordered has arrived through his homemade security camera and monitor he set up on the desk across the room. Everything in his apartment is controlled by a wireless network he built.

Today, one of the biggest selling features of a university is its IT infrastructure. Offering Internet access to dorm rooms and supporting campuswide wireless networks is quickly becoming a requirement for universities to offer its students.

Charles Bartel at Carnegie Mellon University estimates that 30 percent of its network traffic is for e-mail, 40 percent is used to transfer files and downloads from the Internet, and 30 percent supports everything else including games, IM, and Web surfing. Carnegie Mellon offers a residential computing consultant (a school RA for the PC) for each dorm so that you have someone who can help you whenever you experience computer problems while you are in your dorm room.

The University of California at San Diego is passing out PDAs and encouraging students to send questions to their professor wirelessly to save the students from having to raise their hands in class.

A university's IT infrastructure is an important criterion students use when deciding which university they want to attend. For this reason alone it is critical that a university implement a solid IT infrastructure that meets the students' needs.[15,16]

QUESTIONS

1. Walking around your university you probably see all kinds of technological gadgets that didn't even exist 20 years ago including PDAs, cell phones, and wireless networks. How have these technological gadgets increased student productivity? How have these technological gadgets decreased student productivity?

2. Does your university have a client/server network? If so, where are the clients located? Where is the server located? What kind of access do you have to the Internet? What type

of activity do you think takes up the most capacity on the network? If your university does not have a client/server network, determine a design for the infrastructure to support one. Be sure to think about the factors that increase student productivity along with the IT infrastructure components. How big is your department going to grow? Will the system be able to handle additional users?

3. Imagine it's 2006 and your university has grown by 50 percent since 2002. How many students are now attending your university? Would the support departments such as accounting and human resources need to grow also as the number of students increases? What would happen to the university's IT infrastructure with the increased growth? What are some of the issues the university will encounter with its information systems due to this unexpected growth? What could your university have done to help prepare for this kind of unexpected growth?

4. There are many different departments that work at your university. Can you name the different departments, or are they listed on your school's Web site? What types of systems do the different departments use? Do you see any reason for these systems to be integrated?

5. Your university has decided to implement an electronic catalog for prospective students to view when considering attending your school. What types of information would be saved in the catalog? What would be three advantages of using an electronic catalog over a paper brochure? What would be one of the primary problems people would encounter with the electronic catalog?

6. Try to imagine what a university will be like 20 years from now. What types of new technological gadgets will drastically change the lives of students in the year 2022? How will student productivity be affected by the new gadgets? Use the Internet to see if you can find any articles on where universities are headed in the future.

CLOSING CASE STUDY TWO

DOCUMENT MANAGEMENT SOLUTIONS IN THE AUTOMOTIVE INDUSTRY

Ford Motor Company is one of the oldest and largest automobile manufacturers in the world with 114 manufacturing plants in over 40 countries. Ford has more than 350,000 employees worldwide. Steven Scheerhorn, manager of knowledge workplace infrastructure, stated, "At Ford, customer satisfaction is our number one goal. How and what we communicate internally and externally is inextricably linked to that goal. We believe that the Internet is one of our most important means of exchanging information between employees, customers, dealers, suppliers, and trading partners. Trusted content is at the heart of every such e-interaction. Effective enterprise content management is imperative in order to provide accurate, consistent, and up-to-date content via our hundreds of intranet Web sites, intranet business portals, and business-to-consumer and business-to-business sites."

Ford has to communicate with customers, suppliers, and distributors all over the world. In order to help disseminate information, Ford has implemented hundreds of internal and external Web sites. One of the problems that has developed from having so many internal and external Web sites is managing all of the information posted on all of these Web sites. All of the information needs to be current, accurate, consistent, accessible, and reliable. Imagine what a difficult task it is for Ford to try to manage all of this information. Not only are there thousands of documents posted on all of these Web sites, but they are also in multiple languages and currencies. How would you ensure that a document written in English is translated correctly into Spanish, French, Japanese, and Chinese? Ford also has the extra pressure of having to ensure its documentation is in compliance with all regulatory authorities.

In order to gain greater control of its information, Ford implemented Documentum 4iTM eBusiness Platform. Documentum provides enterprise documentation management solutions. Documentum is currently installed in 1,500 of the largest businesses in the world helping intelligently create and manage all types of documents.

Documentum helped Ford to automate its document life cycle processes while ensuring compliance with strict corporate records, management policies, and industry procedures. One example of Ford's success with Documentum is its implementation of an engineering system. Ford built the system using Documentum 4i that enables the engineering department to submit designs online that are automatically routed to marketing to be placed in product information documentation.

Ford is also going to integrate its new employee information portal with Documentum 4i producing a new search engine allowing any of Ford's employees with intranet access the ability to search all of the companies' and employees' documentation. Every department and process within Ford will have the ability to create and publish documents to the employee information portal. This new system will centralize document management and support the high-availability environment Ford requires.

It's also critical that Ford meet the legal automotive industry requirements and industry standards for automotive documentation. The new infrastructure also offers a workflow management system which has provided a way that Ford can ensure its documentation complies with all of the current laws. After a document is completed, it's automatically transferred to Ford's legal department for final approval before it is posted to the information portal.

The new systems also enable suppliers and dealers to access and add content to parts of the information portal. Creating part of the site that is available in the business-to-business environment provides Ford's business partners with the same information that the company maintains. Documentum ensures that the content received by the suppliers and dealers is consistent and can be trusted.

By implementing a document management system and employee information portal, Ford has helped to improve product quality and customer satisfaction by ensuring that content published by widely dispersed contributors to the hundreds of Ford internal and external Web sites is current and accurate. Ford has also improved its relationships with customers, suppliers, and partners by providing easy access to consistently accurate information.

The most important benefit of Ford's new infrastructure is that it has captured the company's intellectual capital and business processes to maximize reuse and encourage best practices. The system provides a common infrastructure, which complies with the company's legal and security requirements, for easier capture, searching, retrieving, and exchanging of information throughout the enterprise.[17]

QUESTIONS

1. Almost anything you do in an organization is performed in teams. Very few tasks and assignments are performed individually in the working world. Improving knowledge workers' ability to collaborate can be a huge benefit for companies. Do you think Ford would benefit from improving team collaboration? If so, how could it use Documentum to perform team or group tasks?

2. There are several alternatives to Documentum for document management systems. Do some research on the Internet to find a competitor to Documentum. What are the differences between the competitor and Documentum? If you had to choose one of the two document management systems to implement, which would you choose and why? Do you think Documentum was the best choice for Ford?

3. What is workflow? What is a workflow system? How has Ford used a workflow system to help improve its employee productivity and team collaboration?

4. What are the two primary types of workflow infrastructures? Explain the difference between the two primary types of workflow infrastructures including an example of how Ford might use each. Which type of workflow infrastructure has Ford implemented? What type of workflow infrastructure would you recommend Ford implement?

5. Enterprise information portals (EIPs) allow knowledge workers to access company information via a Web interface. How did Ford implement its EIP? Was the EIP successful? What was one of the major issues with Ford's EIP? How did Ford resolve the issue?

6. There are two primary types of EIPs including collaborative processing and decision processing.

Explain the primary difference between the two different types. Which type of EIP did Ford implement? Did Ford make the right decision implementing EIPs?

7. You've been hired as Ford's IT infrastructure expert. Ford would like you to explain how a solid IT infrastructure can help the company support its primary goals. Ford also wants to determine the best IT infrastructure components for increasing employee productivity and enhancing decision making. How would you respond?

Key Terms and Concepts

Application service provider (ASP), 350
Back office system, 346
Backup, 336
Benchmark, 339
Business process reengineering (BPR), 354
Capacity planning, 340
Client/server network, 334
Cold site, 337
Collaborative processing enterprise information portal, 344
Collocation, 351
Computer-aided software engineering (CASE), 354
Customer relationship management (CRM) system, 346
Data cleansing, 338
Database-based workflow system, 345
Decision processing enterprise information portal, 344
Disaster recovery cost curve, 337
Disaster recovery plan, 337
Document management system, 343
Electronic catalog, 347
Enterprise application integration (EAI), 342
Enterprise application integration middleware, 342
Enterprise information portal (EIP), 344

Enterprise resource planning (ERP), 353
Enterprise software, 353
Extranet, 336
Front office system, 346
Global reach, 335
Hot site, 337
Integration, 341
Internet service provider (ISP), 350
Intranet, 335
IT infrastructure, 332
Legacy system, 354
Messaging-based workflow system, 345
Performance, 339
Recovery, 336
Sales force automation (SFA) system, 346
Scalability, 338
Server farm, 352
Service level agreement (SLA), 350
Supply chain management (SCM) system, 348
Thin client, 335
Web farm, 352
Workflow, 344
Workflow system, 344

Short-Answer Questions

1. What is an IT infrastructure?
2. Why do you need a backup of information?
3. Why would you need to recover information?
4. What are two IT infrastructure components that increase employee productivity?
5. What is enterprise application integration middleware?
6. What are integrations and how are they used to enhance decision making?
7. Why does a business need a disaster recovery plan?
8. What is a customer relationship management system?
9. What is a sales force automation system?
10. What is one advantage of using an electronic catalog rather than a paper catalog?
11. How can you use supply chain management to create business partnerships and alliances?
12. Why would a company implement a document management system?
13. What is an ISP and how is it different from an ASP?
14. What is enterprise resource planning?
15. How can enterprise resource planning facilitate organizational transformation?

Short-Question Answers

For each of the following answers, provide an appropriate question.

1. CRM.
2. Capacity planning.
3. Disaster recovery plan.
4. ERP.
5. IT infrastructure.
6. SCM.
7. Server farm.
8. Performance.
9. Integration.
10. Disaster recovery cost curve.
11. EIP.
12. Workflow.
13. Workflow systems.
14. ASP.

Assignments and Exercises

1. **AN EIP FOR YOUR COURSE** Enterprise information portals (EIPs) allow knowledge workers to access company information via a Web interface. You have been asked to create an EIP for this course. Answer the following questions in order to determine how the EIP should be developed.
   - What type of information would be contained on the EIP?
   - Who would have access to the EIP?
   - How long would information remain on the EIP?
   - What is the difference between a collaborative processing EIP and a decision processing EIP?
   - Which type of EIP would you implement and why?

2. **SPONSOR OF THE IT INFRASTRUCTURE** In order to build a solid IT infrastructure you must have executive sponsorship. Your current boss doesn't understand the importance of building a solid IT infrastructure. In fact, your boss doesn't even understand the term IT infrastructure. First, explain to your boss what an IT infrastructure is and why it is critical for any organization. Second, you must explain each of the following organizational goals to your boss along with two related IT infrastructure components.
   - Increase employee productivity
   - Enhance decision making
   - Improve team collaboration
   - Create business partnerships and alliances
   - Enable global reach
   - Facilitate organizational transformation

3. **IT INFRASTRUCTURE COMPONENTS AND THE REAL WORLD** Throughout this chapter we discussed several IT infrastructure components including client/server, reliability, integrations, electronic catalogs, among others. Pick two of the components discussed in this chapter and try to find business examples of how companies are using these components in the real world. We also mentioned that there are thousands of additional components you can use to build an IT infrastructure. Try to research the Internet to see if you can find two additional IT infrastructure components that were not discussed in this chapter along with business examples of how businesses are using the components in the real world.

4. **CREATING THE IDEAL INFRASTRUCTURE** As a knowledge worker you'll be responsible for approving IT system designs which ultimately affect your company's IT infrastructure and its abilities to achieve its goals. This chapter focused on many different IT infrastructure components including ERP, SCM, client/server, integrations, and so on. Choose three of the different components discussed in this chapter and explain how you could use them to improve the IT infrastructure at your university. Be sure to think of current requirements as well as future requirements for the systems.

5. **THE COMPLETE IT INFRASTRUCTURE** A document management system manages a document through its life cycle. The following table on the opposite page lists the document

life cycle phases in the first column. Explain what tasks a document management system would perform during each phase. Explain how you could use a document management system to help you work on a group project.

6. **CREATING A CAMPUS IT INFRASTRUCTURE**
   Congratulations, you have been assigned the role as student infrastructure manager. Your first assignment is to approve the designs for the new on-campus Internet infrastructure. You're having a meeting at 9:00 AM tomorrow morning to review the designs with the student IT employees. In order to prepare for the meeting you must understand the student requirements and their current use of the Internet, along with future requirements. The following is a list of

questions you must answer before attending the meeting. Please provide your answer to each question.
   - Do you need to have a disaster recovery plan? If so what might it include?
   - Does the system require backup equipment?
   - When will the system need to be available to the students?
   - What types of access levels will the students need?
   - How will you ensure the system is reliable?
   - How will you build scalability into the system?
   - How will you build flexibility into the system?
   - What are the minimum performance requirements for the system?
   - How will the system handle future growth?

Document Lifecycle Phase	Tasks Performed	Group Project Tasks Performed
Creation		
Modification		
Security		
Approval		
Distribution		
Archiving		

Discussion Questions

1. IT infrastructures often mimic organizational hierarchies. Define two different types of organizational hierarchies and how the IT infrastructure would be built in order to support them.

2. IT infrastructure components can include anything ranging from software to strategic functions. After reading this chapter and learning about a few of the primary IT infrastructure components, explain why a company's IT infrastructure can include so many different components.

3. Organizations tend to spend a great deal of time determining their primary goals, objectives, structure, and strategies. Define your university's goals. Define your university's objectives, structure, and strategies that

support these goals. Explain how your university's IT infrastructure supports your university's goals.

4. Providing Internet access to employees is a great way to increase employee productivity. It's also a great way to decrease employee productivity if the employees abuse their Internet privileges. What does it mean to have employees abuse the Internet? What can you do as a manager to prevent your employees from abusing their Internet privileges? What would happen if all of the students in your university spent 10 hours a day surfing the Net? Use the Internet to find two different types of network monitoring software that you would recommend your university purchase in order to help deter Internet abuse.

5. Imagine you are working for a large cookie manufacturing company. The company is 75 years old and is just starting to implement technology to help improve operations. Your direct manager has asked you to put together a presentation discussing integrations. In your presentation you must include the definition of integration, EAI, and EAI middleware. You must also explain each concept in depth along with a "real-world" example of how the concept will help your company become more successful.

6. Customer relationship management (CRM) is the objective of managing the customer's relationship with the company thorough all of the different customer business experiences. Supply chain management (SCM) tracks inventory and information among business processes and across companies. What is the difference between these two IT infrastructure components? What do these two components have in common? Would a company implement both of these components? If they did, why would they want to implement both, and what would be the advantage of having both?

7. Your good friend, Lou Baker, has decided to open his own golf supply company. Lou has come to you for advice on supply chain management, ISPs, and ASPs. Lou has heard of these terms, but he is not sure what they are and how he can use them to help get his business started the right way. Explain each term to Lou along with an explanation of how Lou can use these components to help start his business.

8. A fellow student is trying to write a paper on third-party vendors for IT infrastructure components. Throughout this chapter we have discussed several different third-party vendors including ISPs, ASPs, collocation facilities, and server farms. Explain each one of these components to your fellow student along with a "real-world" example of each.

9. Enterprise resource planning (ERP) is the coordinated planning of all an organization's resources involved in the production, development, selling, and servicing of goods and services. Describe ERP and how an organization might benefit from implementing an ERP system.

10. IT infrastructures should support the creation of flexible and scalable IT systems that can quickly adapt to support new business requirements. What would be an example of an IT infrastructure that is inflexible and not scalable and a barrier to supporting a changing business? What is an example of an IT infrastructure that is flexible and scalable and supports expanding a business?

11. What is a client/server network? Does your university have a client/server network? How does your university's client/server network increase student productivity? How does your university's client/server network decrease student productivity?

12. What are the four major categories of EAI? Discuss each category along with an example of how the EAI could be used in your university. Also discuss two EAI middleware vendors. You can use the Internet to learn more detailed information about EAI middleware vendors.

13. Making informed decisions sometimes requires reviewing past information as well as current information. Research different types of storage devices and explain which type you would choose and why.

14. With the growing popularity of performing business over the Internet, creating business partnerships and alliances should become a primary goal for any organization's IT infrastructure. List two IT infrastructure components you could use to help a business create business partnerships and alliances.

Living Life on the Internet

The personal computer is quickly becoming a household necessity similar to a stove or a fridge. The primary reason the personal computer has become such an important part of our lives is the Internet. There are literally thousands of ways people use the Internet to perform tasks.

Do you have a personal computer with Internet connectivity in your home? How often do you use it and why? We bet you use it all the time to perform tasks ranging from sending e-mails to finding driving directions. Many great Web sites are available, and all of them can help you accomplish things such as finding movie times, cooking a delicious meal, or seeking medical advice.

In this section we'll provide you with a few key Web sites you can use to help you live your life, and you can find many more sites on the Web site that supports this text at www.mhhe.com/haag.

ONLINE MAGAZINES

Each year people spend an incredible amount of money buying magazines. Many of these magazines are received through the mail and are never read. These end up in a giant pile—a giant recycling pile. Do you receive magazines through the mail or buy them while doing your grocery shopping? How much are you paying for all of these magazines? Do you actually find the time to read them? Did you know that many magazines are available online for free? That's right, for free. Save yourself some money by using the Internet to get the latest news and fashion tips instead of buying those costly magazines. The following is a list of a few of the many hundreds of magazines available on the Internet:

- *National Geographic*—www.nationalgeographic.com
- *Rolling Stone*—www.rollingstone.com
- *Sports Illustrated*—sportsillustrated.cnn.com
- *Cosmopolitan*—http://magazines.ivillage.com/cosmopolitan
- *Newsweek*—www.newsweek.com
- *PC Magazine*—www.pcmagazine.com
- *TV Guide*—www.tvguide.com
- *Popular Mechanics*—www.popularmechanics.com

Connect to a few of these magazines and try answering the following questions.

A. Does the Web site contain the most recent magazine version?

B. Is it easy to view past issues or search for articles on a particular topic?

C. Can you find three additional magazines you enjoy that are not listed above?

D. Are there any additional features in the online version of the magazine that are not available in the paper version?

E. Do you enjoy reading the magazine online better than reading a paper magazine? Why?

ONLINE MOVIE LISTINGS AND REVIEWS

How often do you get to go to the movies? How many times do you head out to the movies without knowing the theater location, movie time, or movie rating. How often do you rent movies? Do you wander around the store unable to decide on which movie to rent? Your time is incredibly valuable and so is your money. Wasting time and money on a bad movie happens to us all, but there is a way to eliminate this problem, the Internet.

The Internet has a wealth of information regarding movies including theater locations, movie times, and movie ratings and reviews. Spending a few minutes on the Internet researching the movie you want to see or browsing movie lists will save you time and money. You can check out detailed movie reviews at the Movie Review Query Engine Web site, www.mrqe.com. If you want a quick overview of a movie from a wide variety of critics, visit Check the Grid, www.checkthegrid.com. If you are interested in what movies are coming out over the next few month, try the Coming Attractions Web site, corona.bc.ca/films/main.html. You can search for movie times at your local theaters by visiting the Moviefone Web site, www.moviefone.com. Lastly, you must visit the Internet Movie Database, www.imdb.com, for tons of information on any movie ever made.

A. Can you find the movies that are currently playing at a theater near you?

B. Try to research a classic movie such as *Grease* or *Animal House* to find out the movie's rating and the year it was released.

C. Try to locate three new movies that are coming out over the next year.

D. Log in to the Internet Movie Database and search for all of the movies made by your favorite actor or actress. Were any movies listed that you have not seen?

E. Log in to the Internet Movie Database and try to research the top 10 movies of all time.

COOKING FROM THE INTERNET

How many of you are great chefs? How many of you think making a box of Kraft Macaroni and Cheese categorizes you as an expert in the kitchen? Don't worry because help is only a few clicks away. There are hundreds of cooking Web sites that can provide you with recipes, detailed cooking instructions, and nutritional information. Let's review a few of the top Web sites in this area.

The first stop you should make is the Nutrition Analysis Tool (NAT) Web site, www.nat.uiuc.edu. NAT analyzes the foods you eat for various different nutrients and gives you recommendations on the types of food that are missing from your diet. Next, visit www.cooking.com for information on everything from cookbooks and cookware to recipes and cooking tips. For those of you interested in healthy meals try www.cookinglight.com, and those of you interested in gourmet cooking try www.goodcooking.com.

A. Try to find a recipe for barbequed chicken and mashed potatoes on one of the above Web sites.

B. Try logging into the Nutritional Analysis Tool and find out the nutritional value of your last meal.

C. Try to find a Web site that will help you plan a menu for a dinner party of six people.

D. Log in to the gourmet Web site and see how many different recipes you can find for your favorite food.

E. Log in to the cooking light Web site and find a few tips on how you can decrease cholesterol in your diet.

HIGHLY USEFUL MISCELLANEOUS SITES

There are so many helpful Web sites available that it's impossible to share them all with you. We did, however, want to point you in the direction of a few key sites that can help you as you make choices in your everyday life.

- Ever need to find out the exact time? Try the official U.S. time site at www.time.gov.
- If you need to find out the weather forecast quickly try weather.yahoo.com.
- You can also find the full text of more than 16,000 books online for free at digital.library.upenn.edu/books/.
- You can visit an online museum in Paris, France, at www.oir.ucf.edu/wm/.
- If you are sick and wondering if you should visit the doctor, try to seek advice at the world-famous Mayo Clinic, www.mayoclinic.com.
- A great site that can help you purchase or trade in a car is *Kelley's Blue Book* Web site, www.kbb.com.

A. Log in to the Mayo Clinic and research remedies for the common cold.

B. Log in to *Kelley's Blue Book* Web site and determine the current value of your car or a car you would like to purchase.

C. Log in to the online museum in Paris and view the most current art exhibit.

D. We have listed a few helpful Web sites for living your life on the Internet. Try to find three additional Web sites that you and your classmates will find useful.

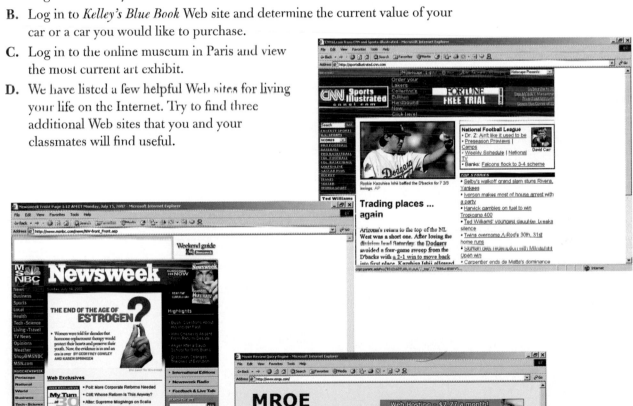

EXTENDED LEARNING MODULE G
OBJECT-ORIENTED TECHNOLOGIES

Student Learning Outcomes

1. EXPLAIN THE PRIMARY DIFFERENCE BETWEEN THE TRADITIONAL TECHNOLOGY APPROACH AND THE OBJECT-ORIENTED TECHNOLOGY APPROACH.

2. LIST AND DESCRIBE THE FIVE PRIMARY OBJECT-ORIENTED CONCEPTS.

3. EXPLAIN HOW CLASSES AND OBJECTS ARE RELATED.

4. DESCRIBE THE THREE FUNDAMENTAL PRINCIPLES OF OBJECT-ORIENTED TECHNOLOGIES.

5. LIST AND DESCRIBE TWO TYPES OF OBJECT-ORIENTED TECHNOLOGIES.

Taking Advantage of the CD

The explosion of object-oriented technologies is radically changing the way businesses view information and develop information systems. Object-oriented technologies are everywhere in the business world today. It's difficult to find a business or IT department that isn't using object-oriented concepts and technologies. Every single Fortune 500 company is using some type of object-oriented technology. System developers everywhere are quickly learning how to write software in object-oriented programming languages, create databases using object-oriented database management systems, and design new systems using object-oriented analysis and design techniques. The race to learn and understand object-oriented concepts began many years ago and is still going strong.

Extended Learning Module G, found on the CD that accompanies this text, provides an explanation of object-oriented technologies. This module is the same as the modules in your text—it includes Team Work and On Your Own projects and end-of-module Assignments and Exercises. The best part of this module is that it explains object-oriented concepts and terms in an easy and understandable way.

One of the primary goals of this module is to introduce you to the object-oriented approach for developing information systems. By taking a look at the traditional technology approach for developing systems you'll quickly understand the advantages you can gain by using an object-oriented approach. The ***object-oriented (OO) approach*** combines information and procedures into a single view. This statement probably seems a bit confusing but, after reading this module, it will become crystal clear. Just remember the key to understanding the object-oriented approach is to recognize that combining information and procedures is quite different from the traditional technology approach in which information is separated from procedures. Some of the other important object-oriented concepts you'll be introduced to include:

- The ***Traditional technology approach,*** which has two primary views of any system—information and procedures—and it keeps these two views separate and distinct at all times.
- The five primary concepts of object-oriented technologies including:
  1. Information as key characteristics stored within a system.
  2. A ***procedure*** that manipulates or changes information.
  3. A ***class*** that contains information and procedures and acts as a template to create objects (instances of a class).
  4. An ***object*** which is an instance of a class.
  5. ***Messages*** that allow objects to communicate with each other.
- The three fundamental principles of object-oriented technologies including inheritance, encapsulation, and polymorphism.
- Several real-world object-oriented examples.
- A detailed business case example, Ice Blue Snowboards, Inc., in which you can apply your object-oriented knowledge.
- Three types of object-oriented technologies including object-oriented programming languages, object-oriented databases, and object-oriented technologies and client/server environments.

Be sure to take advantage of this module on your CD. You'll be taking a giant leap towards understanding object-oriented concepts. You might already be familiar with a few of the key concepts related to object-oriented technologies—information, procedures, classes, objects, or messages. If you're unfamiliar with these concepts there's no need to worry, because you'll gain a solid understanding of each one of these important concepts in this module.

CHAPTER EIGHT OUTLINE

STUDENT LEARNING OUTCOMES

1   Define ethics and describe the two factors that affect how you make a decision concerning an ethical issue.

2   Define and describe intellectual property, copyright, Fair Use Doctrine, and pirated and counterfeit software.

3   Define privacy and describe the ways in which it can be threatened.

4   Describe the two ways that information is valuable to business.

5   Describe the ways in which information on your computer or network is vulnerable.

6   Define risk management and risk assessment and describe the seven security measures that companies can take to protect their information.

CHAPTER EIGHT

Protecting People and Information
Threats and Safeguards

OPENING CASE STUDY:
DIGITAL DESTRUCTION BEYOND ALL IMAGINATION

While it pales in comparison to the tragic loss of life, the extensive damage to computer and communications systems in New York on September 11th, 2001, was considerable. Although the whole event was unbelievable, the fact that most of the businesses that had been located in the World Trade Center (WTC) were back up and running within days is even more amazing.

Verizon Communications' main regional switching center was located next to WTC 7, which collapsed. The collapse of the towers sent a huge steel beam crashing through a bundle of optical fiber cables that had been buried 8 feet below ground level, severing more than 4 million high-speed access lines. Bursting water lines resulted in 10 million gallons of water flooding underground switching vaults. With primary power lost, backup power, running on diesel fuel generators, didn't last long. Lucent Technologies, one of Verizon's primary system providers, quickly sent a 100,000-line switch to the scene to replace the one that crashed through the window of the Verizon building. In addition to Verizon's damaged telecommunications system, at least 139 other fiber rings failed. In all, 1.5 million circuits serving the financial district went down.

Morgan Stanley estimates that about $500 million in computer equipment was lost when the Twin Towers collapsed. Other experts believe that it will cost up to $3.2 billion to replace the technology that was lost, including everything from servers to PCs and phone lines. And that's only the hardware. The most important part of a computer system is not the physical equipment, it's the information that's stored there. It's almost impossible to calculate the value of the paper records lost, or the value of the information on hard drives, servers, tape drives, and other storage media that was lost. Given the nature of the businesses located in the World Trade Center, including many financial and consulting organizations, a huge amount of information had been stored in that spot.

Even businesses not actually located in the WTC were strongly affected. For example, American Express of New York City had offices opposite the Twin Towers and had to evacuate indefinitely. Lufthansa lost phone service for several days when AT&T, its provider, lost equipment in the World Trade Center.

Despite all the mayhem, most financial institutions in or near the WTC were back in business within a few days. These companies were well prepared for disasters. Because of their foresight, fully 95 percent of the companies affected are expected to recover all of their applications and information. This recovery is quite spectacular given the results of one study, which found that only 6 percent of companies survive long term after a catastrophe.

One of the lessons learned from 9/11 is that with careful and thorough protection of important information, not even a calamity like the one that occurred in New York can put you out of business. Of course, most companies don't face such a severe test of their information protection systems, but smaller and less sensational attacks can do damage, too.[1,2,3,4,5]

Introduction

As you've already learned, the three components of an IT system are people, information, and information technology. Most of what you've seen in previous chapters has dealt with IT and how it stores and processes information. In this chapter we're going to concentrate on information—its use, ownership, role, and protection. The best environment for handling information is one that has stability without stagnation and change without chaos.

To handle information in a responsible way (see Figure 8.1) you must understand

- The importance of ethics in the ownership and use of information
- The importance to people of personal privacy and the ways in which it can be compromised
- The value of information to an organization
- Threats to information and how to protect against them (security)

The most important part of any IT system consists of the people who use it and are affected by it. How people treat each other has always been important, but in this information-based and digital age, with huge computing power at our fingertips, we can affect more people's lives in more ways than ever before. How we act toward each other, and this includes how we view and handle information, is largely determined by our ethics.

You don't have to look far to see examples of computer use that is questionable from an ethical viewpoint. For example,

- People copy, use, and distribute software they have no right to.
- Employees search organizational databases for information on celebrities and friends.
- Organizations collect, buy, and use information and don't check the validity or accuracy of that information.
- People create and spread viruses that cause trouble for those using and maintaining IT systems.
- Information system developers put systems on the market before they're completely tested. A few years ago, the developers of an incubator thermostat control program didn't test it fully, and two infants died as a result.[6]
- People break into computer systems and steal passwords, information, and proprietary information.
- Employees destroy or steal proprietary schematics, sketches, customer lists, and reports from their employers.
- People snoop on each other and read each other's e-mail and other private documents.

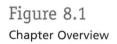

Figure 8.1

Chapter Overview

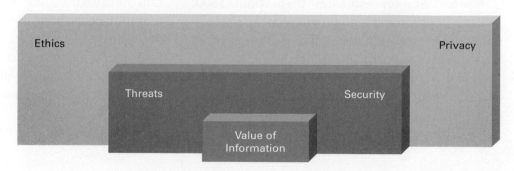

Ethics

Ethical people have integrity. They're people who are just as careful of the rights of others as they are of their own rights. They have a strong sense of what's fair and right and what isn't. But even the most ethical people sometimes face difficult choices.

Ethics are the principles and standards that guide our behavior toward other people. Acting ethically means behaving in a principled fashion and treating other people with respect and dignity. It's simple to say, but not so simple to do since some situations are complex or ambiguous. The important role of ethics in our lives has long been recognized. As far back as 44 B.C., Cicero said that ethics are indispensable to anyone who wants to have a good career. Having said that, Cicero, along with some of the greatest minds over the centuries, struggled with what the rules of ethics should be.

Our ethics are rooted in our history, culture, and religion, and our sense of ethics may shift over time. In this electronic age there's a new dimension in the ethics debate—the amount of personal information that we can collect and store, and the speed with which we can access and process that information.

TWO FACTORS THAT DETERMINE HOW YOU DECIDE ETHICAL ISSUES

How you collect, store, access, and use information depends to a large extent on your sense of ethics—what you perceive as right and wrong. Two factors affect how you make your decision when you're faced with an ethical dilemma (see Figure 8.2). The first is your basic ethical structure, which you developed as you grew up. The second is the set of practical circumstances involved in the decision that you're trying to make, that is, all the shades of gray in what are rarely black or white decisions.

Your ethical structure and the ethical challenges you'll face exist at several levels.[7] At the outside level are things that most people wouldn't consider bad, such as taking a couple of paper clips or sending an occasional personal e-mail on company time. Do these things really matter? At the middle level are more significant ethical challenges. One example might be accessing personnel records for personal reasons. Could there ever be a

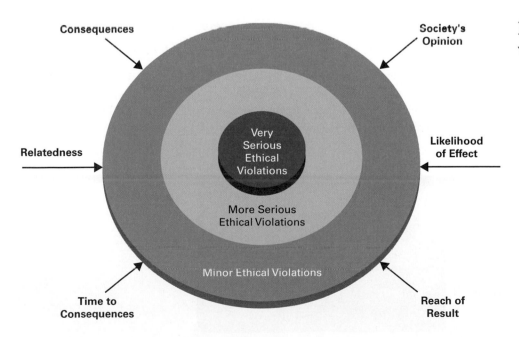

Figure 8.2
Your Ethical Structure

personal reason so compelling that you would not feel ethical discomfort doing this? Reading someone else's e-mail might be another middle-level example. At the innermost ethical level are ethical violations that you'd surely consider very serious, such as embezzling funds or selling company records to a competitor. And yet, over time, your ethical structure can change so that even such acts as these could seem more or less ethical. For example, if everyone around you is accessing confidential records for their own purposes, in time you might come to think such an act is no big deal. And this might spell big trouble for you.

It would be nice if every decision were crystal clear, and considerations such as these needn't be taken into account, but ethical decisions are seldom so easy. The practical circumstances surrounding your decision always influence you in an ethical dilemma.[8]

1. *Consequences.* How much or how little benefit or harm will come from a particular decision?
2. *Society's opinion.* What is your perception of what society really thinks of your intended action?
3. *Likelihood of effect.* What is the probability of the harm or benefit that will occur if you take the action?
4. *Time to consequences.* What length of time will it take for the benefit or harm to take effect?
5. *Relatedness.* How much do you identify with the person or persons who will receive the benefit or suffer the harm?
6. *Reach of result.* How many people will be affected by your action?

Hopefully, your basic sense of right and wrong will steer you in the right direction. But no matter what your sense of ethics is or how strong it is, practical aspects of the situation may affect you as you make your decision—perhaps unduly, perhaps quite justifiably. Ethical dilemmas usually arise, not out of simple situations, but from a clash between competing goals, responsibilities, and loyalties. Ethical decisions are complex judgments that balance rewards for yourself and others against responsibilities to yourself and others. Inevitably, your decision process is influenced by uncertainty about the magnitude of the outcome, by your estimate of the importance of the situation, sometimes by your perception of conflicting "right reactions," and more than one socially acceptable "correct" decision.

GUIDELINES FOR ETHICAL COMPUTER SYSTEM USE

It's sometimes difficult to decide what to do since there are few hard and fast rules. Knowing the law doesn't even help because what's legal is not always ethical and vice versa. In Figure 8.3 you see the four quadrants of ethical and legal behavior. You're pretty safe if you can manage to stay in quadrant I.

Figure 8.3

Acting Ethically and Legally Are Not Necessarily the Same Thing[9]

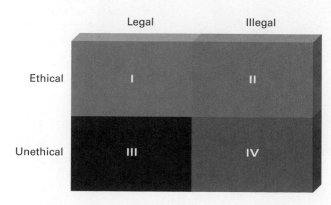

So, what do you do then if you're faced with a choice that is not perfectly ethically clear? If you think you are in an ethical quandary, you probably are. If you find you're giving the situation a whole lot of thought, the situation very likely deserves it. You may wish to talk to a friend, a teacher, a supervisor, or a mentor. Know that we're all faced with such dilemmas, they are real, and they do have consequences. And there *is* a line that you shouldn't cross, and most of us know where it is.

Let's look at an example. Say your organization is developing a decision support system (DSS) to help formulate treatments for an infectious disease. Other companies in the industry are working on similar projects. The first system on the market will most likely reap huge profits. You may know that your DSS doesn't yet work properly; it's good, but not yet totally reliable. But you're feeling extreme pressure from your boss to get the system onto the market immediately. You're worried about the harm that might come to a patient because of your DSS; but, on the other hand, it does work well most of the time. Is it up to you or not? You have a family to support and student loans to repay. And you like being employed. Can you hold out and get more information on the system's reliability? What do you do? Where can you get help?

You can certainly ask questions about what you're being asked to do—and you should. Sometimes legitimate actions look unethical, but if you find out more about the situation, you might find that it's perfectly all right. For instance, in the case mentioned, management may be planning to leave out the dubious part of the system or to warn customers of the problem. But, you must keep digging until you're very sure and comfortable with what you're being asked to do.

If you really believe that what you're expected to do is wrong, you'll have to say so to your boss and be prepared to quit if you have to. But first, explain what you think is so bad and couch it in terms of the company's future and reputation if at all possible.[10] Be sure to think also of your own future and reputation (many former Enron employees wish they had taken a firmer stand when they had the chance).

Your company may well have an office or person (sometimes called an ombudsman) whose job it is to give advice on work-related ethical dilemmas. Failing that, you could look up your company's code of ethics. If you can't find that or don't think it's taken seriously in your place of work, you can check your profession's ethical code. The ACM (Association for Computing Machinery), for example, has a code of ethics for IT employees. Or you can go to the Computer Ethics Institute Web site for its guidelines ("Ten Commandments") at www.cspr.org/program/ethics.htm.

INTELLECTUAL PROPERTY

An ethical issue you will almost certainly encounter is one related to the use or copying of proprietary software. Software is a type of intellectual property. ***Intellectual property*** is intangible creative work that is embodied in physical form.[11] Music, novels, paintings, and sculptures are all examples of intellectual property. So also are your company's product sketches and schematics and other proprietary documents. These documents along with music, novels, and so on are worth much more than the physical form in which they are delivered. For example, a single U2 song is worth far more than the CD on which it's purchased. The song is also an example of intellectual property that is covered by copyright law.

Copyright law protects the authorship of literary and dramatic works, musical and theatrical compositions, and works of art. ***Copyright*** is the legal protection afforded an expression of an idea, such as a song, video game, and some types of proprietary documents. Having a copyright means that no one can use your song or video game without your permission. As a form of intellectual property, software is usually protected by

INDUSTRY PERSPECTIVE

WHAT PRICE AN IDEA?

A patent is a form of intellectual property. A patent applies to the implementation of an idea, such as how to construct an ergonomic mouse. IBM, the computer industry's giant, has for nine years filed more patents with the U.S. Patent and Trademark Office than any other company. In 2001, IBM received 3,454 patents. That's almost 10 new patents *every day*. IBM has always been proud of its patent record, and it certainly gives stockholders and the public in general the impression that the company is working hard and is producing future technology. However, good press is not the only reason IBM files so many patent applications. There are many other reasons—1.5 billion of them, in fact. That's the amount of money that IBM got from licensing income in 2001 alone, money the company put back into research and development. Since it's very hard to tell which new technology will ultimately be successful, IBM patents everything, and then licenses out those ideas that other companies want to use.

IBM isn't the only technology company to take patents seriously. Also busy in the technology-patent-generating race are Hewlett-Packard, Lucent Technologies, NEC, and Microsoft. Many other industries are realizing great return on the licensing of patents, too. For example,

- Bayer AG, a German drug company, clears profits of 78 percent after expenses on its intellectual property licensing fees.
- Du Pont revenues from intellectual property were $100 million in 1996 and grew to $450 million in 2001.
- Eastman Kodak even created a separate company, Eastman Chemical's Global Technology Ventures (GTV) to extract value from the company's intellectual assets. Since 1999, the company has made 20 deals worth more than $50 million with a further $100 million in net present value of future earnings.[12,13]

copyright law, although sometimes it falls under patent law, which protects an idea, such as the design of a sewing machine or an industrial pump valve.

Copyright law doesn't forbid the use of intellectual property completely. It has some notable exceptions. For example, a TV program could show your video game without your permission. This would be an example of the use of copyrighted material for the creation of new material, i.e., the TV program. And that's legal; it falls under the Fair Use Doctrine. The *Fair Use Doctrine* says that you may use copyrighted material in certain situations, for example, in the creation of new work or, within certain limits, for teaching purposes. One of those limits is on the amount of the copyrighted material you may use.

Generally, the determining factor in legal decisions on copyright disputes is whether the copyright holder has been or is likely to be denied income because of the infringement. Courts will consider factors such as how much of the work was used and how, and when and on what basis the decision was made to use it.

Remember that copyright infringement is *illegal*. That means it's against the law, outside of a fair use situation, to simply copy a copyrighted picture, text, or anything else without permission, whether the copyrighted material is on the Internet or not. In particular, it's illegal to copy copyrighted software. But there's one exception to that rule: You may always make one copy of copyrighted software to keep for backup purposes. When you buy copyrighted software, what you're paying for is the right to use it—and that's all.

How many more copies you may make depends on the copyright agreement that comes with the software package. Some software companies say emphatically that you may not even put the software on a second computer, even if they're both yours and no

ARE YOU CAREFUL ABOUT YOUR POSTURE?

Health experts have developed guidelines for the safe use of computers. See below the upright, right-angled posture of a person using a computer correctly. You should look straight at, or a little down at the monitor. Choose three computers that you have access to, and answer the following questions for each.

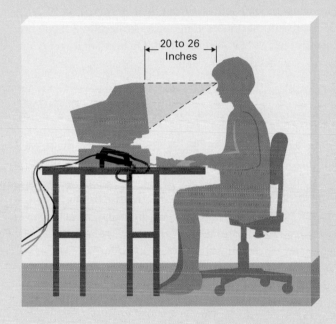

20 to 26 Inches

Question	Answer
1 Do you sit with your thighs parallel to the floor?	
2 Is your back straight when you type?	
3 How far is the monitor from your eyes?	
4 Do you feel discomfort when you work at a keyboard for an extended period? If so, where?	
5 Do you rest periodically, at least once an hour?	

one else uses either one. Other companies are a little less strict, and agree to let you put a copy of software on multiple machines—as long as only one person is using that software package at any given time. In this instance, the company considers software to be like a book in that you can have it in different places and you can loan it out, but only one person at a time may use it.

If you copy copyrighted software and give it to another person or persons, you're pirating the software. *Pirated software* is the unauthorized use, duplication, distribution, or sale of copyrighted software.[14] Software piracy costs businesses an estimated $12 billion a year in lost revenue. Microsoft gets more than 25,000 reports of software piracy every year, and the company reportedly follows up on all of them. Countries that experience the greatest losses are (in rank order) the United States, Japan, the United Kingdom, Germany, China, France, Canada, Italy, Brazil, and the Netherlands. One in four business applications in the United States is thought to be pirated.[15] In some parts of the world, more than 90 percent of business software is pirated. The Software and Information Industry Association (SIIA) and the Business Software Alliance (BSA) say that pirated software means lost jobs, wages, and tax revenues, and is a potential barrier to success for software start-ups around the globe.

With the crackdown by software manufacturers and the growing awareness of corporations, the amount of illegally copied software is actually declining in businesses. But a new threat is emerging in the form of counterfeit software. ***Counterfeit software*** is software that is manufactured to look like the real thing and sold as such. Counterfeit software is being sold by sophisticated crime organizations, and sometimes the counterfeit is so good that the software even includes a valid certificate of authenticity.[16] The results of counterfeit software are greater than just lost revenue, which in itself is considerable. Many resellers unwittingly buy counterfeit software from distributors and then find that they've sold buggy or infected software to their customers. The legitimate manufacturers have to deal with irate customers who believe that their software and its problems came directly from the software company. It's a public relations nightmare.

You should especially beware when buying software from the Internet. The BSA estimates that there are close to 950,000 Internet sites selling software illegally.[17] If you buy from a shady side, you might never receive your software at all. Or, you might get counterfeit software that has a virus. So, you need to be careful.

Privacy

Privacy is the right to be left alone when you want to be, to have control over your own personal possessions, and not to be observed without your consent. It's the right to be free of unwanted intrusion into your private life. Privacy has several dimensions. Psychologically, it's a need for personal space. All of us, to a greater or lesser extent, need to feel in control of our most personal possessions, and personal information belongs on that list. Legally, privacy is necessary for self-protection.[18] If you put the key to your house in a special hiding place in your yard, you want to keep that information private. This information could be abused and cause you grief. In this section, we'll examine some specific areas of privacy: individuals snooping on each other; employers' collection of information about employees; businesses' collection of information about consumers; government collection of personal information; and the issue of privacy in international trade.

PRIVACY AND OTHER INDIVIDUALS

Other individuals, like family members, associates, fellow employees, and hackers, could be electronically invading your privacy. Their motives might be simple curiosity, an attempt to get your password, or to access something they have no right to. Obviously, there are situations in which you're well within your rights, and would be well advised to see what's going on. Examples may be if you suspect that your child is in electronic contact with someone or something undesirable, or if you think that someone is using your computer without permission. Many Web sites are offering programs, collectively referred to as snoopware, to help people monitor what's happening on a computer.

For general snooping you can get key logger software and install it on the computer you want to monitor. ***Key logger***, or ***key trapper***, ***software***, is a program that, when installed on a computer, records every keystroke and mouse click. It records all e-mail (whether you're using Eudora or Microsoft Outlook), instant messages, chat room exchanges, Web sites you visit, applications you run, and passwords you type in on that computer. Spector Pro is an example of this type of monitoring software and is available from the same software company as eBlaster, which will actually e-mail you activity reports—every 30 minutes, if you'd like. If you go snooping be sure that you're not breaking the law. Of course, you'll have to decide the ethics of it for yourself. Family members

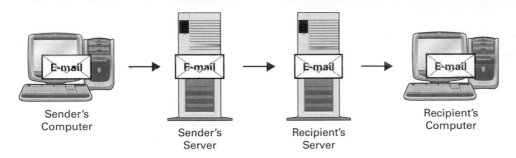

Figure 8.4
The E-Mail You Send Is
Stored on Many
Computers

(other than the parents of minor children who are supposed to keep track of their children's activities) and friends don't have unlimited rights to monitor each other.

If you're on the receiving end of snoopware and want to disable activity-monitoring programs like Spector Pro, you can get a free program from www.idcide.com called the Privacy Companion or one called Who's Watching Me from www.trapware.com.

Also available for monitoring computer use are screen capture programs that periodically record what's on the screen. (They get the information straight from the video card.) These programs don't trap every single screen, just whatever is on the screen when the capturing program activates. But they still give whoever is doing the monitoring a pretty good idea of what the computer user is up to. Other tools for monitoring include packet sniffers (that examine the information passing by) on switches, hubs, or routers (the devices on networks that connect computers to each other), and log analysis tools that keep track of logons, deletions, and so forth.

As you're probably already aware, e-mail is completely insecure. E-mail content might as well be written on a postcard for all the privacy it has. Not only that, but each e-mail you send results in at least three or four copies being stored on different computers (see Figure 8.4). It's stored first in the computer you're using. Second, it's stored by the e-mail server, the computer through which it gets onto the Internet. Third, it's stored on the recipient's computer, and may also be archived on the recipient's e-mail server.

For privacy's sake, some people like to encrypt their e-mail, and there are many products on the market that will do the job. ZixMail is an example. Others are CertifiedMail, PrivacyX, and SafeMessage. Disappearing Email gives you a slightly different type of e-mail protection. This software is free and sends a self-destructing message with the e-mail so that the e-mail deletes itself after the period of time you specify. However, you can defeat this feature by copying the text out of the e-mail and pasting it somewhere else so that you still have the text when the e-mail self-destructs.

PRIVACY AND EMPLOYEES

Companies need information about their employees and customers to be effective in the marketplace. But people often object to having so many details about their lives available to others. If you're applying for a job, you'll most likely fill out a job application, but that's not the only information a potential employer can get about you. For a small fee, employers, or anyone else, can find out about your credit standing, your telephone usage, your insurance coverage, and many other interesting things. An employer can also get information on what you said on the Internet from companies who collect and collate chat room exchanges. And an employer can ask a job applicant to take drug and psychological tests, the results of which are the property of the company.

After you're hired, your employer can monitor where you go, what you do, what you say, and what you write in e-mails—at least during working hours. The American Management Association says that in 2001, 63 percent of companies monitored employee

WHAT WOULD YOU DO?

Analyze the following situation. You have access to the sales and customer information in a flower shop. You discover that the boyfriend of a woman you know is sending roses to three other women on a regular basis. The woman you know is on the flower list, but she believes that she's the only woman in his romantic life. You really think you should tell the woman. Your dilemma is that you have a professional responsibility to keep the company's information private. However, you also believe that you have a responsibility to the woman. Do you tell her?

Are there factors that would change your decision? Each team member should individually consider the additional information below. Indicate whether any one or more of these factors would change your decision. Then form a consensus with your team.

Additional Facts	Yes	No	Why?
1. The woman is your sister.			
2. The man is your brother.			
3. The woman is about to give the man her life savings as a down payment on a house in the belief that they will soon be married.			
4. The woman is already married.			

Internet connections including about two-thirds of the 60 billion electronic messages sent by 40 million e-mail users.[19] One reason that companies monitor employees' e-mail is that they can be sued for what their employees send to each other and to people outside the company.

Chevron Corporation and Microsoft settled sexual harassment lawsuits for $2.2 million each because employees sent offensive e-mail to other employees and management didn't intervene. Other companies such as Dow Chemical Company, Xerox, the New York Times Company, and Edward Jones took preemptive action by firing people who sent or stored pornographic or violent e-mail messages.[20]

Another reason employers monitor their workers' use of IT resources is to avoid misuse of resources. Cyberslacking is a form of misuse of organizational resources, and includes visiting pornographic sites and news sites, chatting, gaming, stock trading, auction participation, shopping, checking sports scores, or anything else not related to your job. In May 2000, Victoria's Secret had an online fashion show at three o'clock in the afternoon on a weekday. About 2 million people watched the show, presumably many of them on their companies' computers. One employee watching the fashion show used as much bandwidth as it would take to download the entire *Encyclopedia Britannica*.[21] So, not only were the viewers wasting company time, but they were also slowing down the work of others.

About 70 percent of Web traffic occurs during work hours, and this is reason enough for companies to monitor what, and for how long, employees are surfing the Web. Again, various software packages are available to keep track of people's Web surfing. Some software actually blocks access to certain sites.

Businesses have good reasons for seeking and storing personal information on employees. They

- Want to hire the best people possible and to avoid being sued for failing to adequately investigate the backgrounds of employees.
- Want to ensure that staff members are conducting themselves appropriately and not wasting or misusing company resources. Financial institutions are even required by law to monitor all communications including e-mail and telephone conversations.
- Can be held liable for the actions of employees.

MONITORING TECHNOLOGY   Numerous vendors sell software products that scan e-mail, both incoming and outgoing. The software can look for specific words or phrases in the subject lines or in the body of the text. An e-mail-scanning program can sneak into your computer in Trojan-horse software. That is, it can hide in an innocent-looking e-mail or some other file or software.

Some companies use an approach less invasive than actually reading employees' e-mail. Their e-mail inspection programs just check for a certain level of e-mail to and from the same address. This indicates that there may be a problem, and the employee is informed of the situation and asked to remedy it. No intrusive supervisory snooping is necessary.[22]

An employer can track your keyboard and mouse activity with the type of key logger software that you read about in the previous section. An alternative that's sometimes harder to detect is a hardware key logger. A *hardware key logger* is a hardware device that captures keystrokes on their journey from the keyboard to the motherboard. These devices can be in the form of a connector (see Figure 8.5) on the system-unit end of the cable between the keyboard and the system unit. There's another type of hardware key logger that you can install into the keyboard. Both have enough memory to store about a year's worth of typing. These devices can't capture anything that's not typed, but they do capture every keystroke, including backspace, delete, insert, and all the others. To defeat them you'd have to copy the password (or whatever you want kept secret) and paste it into its new location. The key logger keeps a record of the keystrokes you use, if any, in your copy-and-paste operation, but not what you copied and pasted.[23]

There is little sympathy in the legal system for private-sector employees who are being monitored. Employers have the legal right to monitor the use of their resources and that includes the time they're paying you for. In contrast to your home, you have no expectation of privacy when using the company's resources.

The most recent federal bill that addressed electronic monitoring of employees is the Electronic Communications Privacy Act of 1986. Although, in general, it forbids the interception of wired or electronic communications, it has exceptions for both prior consent and business use.

Some state laws have addressed the issue of how far employers can go and what they can do to monitor employees. Connecticut has a law that took effect in 1999 that requires employers in the private sector to notify employees in writing of electronic monitoring. And Pennsylvania, a year earlier, permitted telephone marketers to listen in on calls for quality control purposes as long as at least one of the parties is aware of the action.[24]

Figure 8.5

A Key Logger Captures Everything You Type and Saves It for Later Scrutiny

PRIVACY AND CONSUMERS

Businesses face a dilemma.

- Customers want businesses to know who they are, but, at the same time, they want them to leave them alone.
- Customers want businesses to provide what they want, but, at the same time, they don't want businesses knowing too much about their habits and preferences.
- Customers want businesses to tell them about products and services they might like to have, but they don't want to be inundated with ads.

Like it or not, massive amounts of personal information are available to businesses from various sources. A relatively large Web site may get about 100 million hits per day, which means that the site gets about 200 bytes of information for each hit. That's about 20 gigabytes of information per day.[25] This level of information load has helped to make electronic customer relationship (eCRM) systems one of the fastest-growing areas of software development. Part of managing customer relationships is personalization. Web sites that greet you by name, and Amazon.com's famous recommendations that "People who bought this product also bought . . . " are examples of personalization, which is made possible by the Web site's knowledge about you.[26]

Apart from being able to collect its own information about you, a company can readily access consumer information elsewhere. Credit card companies sell information, as do the Census Bureau and mailing list companies. Web traffic tracking companies such as DoubleClick follow you (and other surfers) around the Web and then sell the information about where you went and for how long. DoubleClick can collect information about you over time and provide its customers with a highly refined profile on you. DoubleClick is also an intermediary for companies that want to advertise to Web surfers. When hired by a company wanting to sell something, DoubleClick identifies people who might be receptive and sends the ad to them as a banner or pop-up ad. Proponents of this practice claim that it's good for the surfers because they get targeted advertising and less unwanted advertising. You can judge for yourself how true this claim is. DoubleClick, at first, undertook to track consumers without attaching their identity to the information. Then, in 1999, DoubleClick changed its policy and announced that it would attach consumer names to personal information and e-mail addresses. However, in response to negative consumer reaction, DoubleClick withdrew its proposed change. Interestingly, DoubleClick didn't state it would never resume the abandoned policy, but agreed only to wait until standards for such activity are in place.[27]

COOKIES   The basic tool of consumer Web monitoring is the cookie. A *cookie* is a small file that contains information about you and your Web activities, which a Web site you visit places on your computer. A cookie has many uses. For example, it's used to keep ID and password information so that you don't have to go through the whole verification process every time you log onto a Web site. It's also used to store the contents of electronic shopping carts, so that the next time you log on, the Web site will be able to see your wish list (which is stored on your computer in a cookie).

A cookie can also be used to track your Web activity. It can monitor and record what sites you visit, how long you stay there, what Web pages you visited, what site you came from and the next site you went to. This type of cookie is called a *unique cookie.* Some cookies are temporary and some stay on your computer indefinitely.

Third-party or *common cookies* are the ones that have many privacy advocates disturbed. These are different from the unique cookies that a Web site you visit puts onto

THE JUDGE SAYS "GET PERSONAL" WITH CUSTOMERS

A ReplayTV system, made by SonicBlue, enables you to record TV shows, and even better, to skip over the commercials. Another feature is that ReplayTV allows you to send programs to other ReplayTV owners over the Internet. You can also ask the ReplayTV to find all the times and stations that a particular show is playing and get it to record them all—without commercials.

Several movie studios and television networks filed suit against the manufacturer, claiming that the commercial skipping and the sharing of programming violate copyright law. Before the court case was heard, there was a pretrial discovery process for each side to share information with the other party. The plaintiff wanted to know exactly how SonicBlue's customers were using ReplayTV. SonicBlue answered that the company didn't collect that information.

But the judge instructed SonicBlue to write software to monitor all shows that the customers watched, every skipped commercial, and all programs they sent over the Internet. The order was based on the published privacy policy of SonicBlue, which said that the company may collect audience data. SonicBlue said that although it originally planned to collect such information, it decided not to based on the negative reaction that Tivo, ReplayTV's competitor, encountered when it proposed the same idea.

So, SonicBlue found itself in the strange position of having to go to court to avoid collecting personal information on its customers. In effect, SonicBlue filed an appeal to protect the privacy of its customers, and the new judge overturned the previous ruling. However, the original ruling sent shock waves throughout the privacy advocate community.[28]

your hard disk. A common cookie is one that started out as a unique cookie, but the original site sold access to it to a third party, like DoubleClick, that can then change the cookie so that the third party can track the surfer's activity across many sites. The third party collects information about surfers without names or other identifiable personal information. What they usually collect is an IP address, which they then link to a random identifying ID so that the surfer can be identified at other sites. Surveys have shown that the vast majority of people (91 percent) don't like the idea of unknown companies gathering information about them that they have provided to sites with whom they chose to interact.[29]

You have two options if you want to block cookies. First, you can set your browser to accept or reject all cookies. Or you can get it to warn you when a site wants to put a cookie on your computer. Second, you can get cookie management software with additional options that are not available on your browser. For example, CookieCop 2, from *PC Magazine*, will let you accept or reject cookies on a per-site basis. It also allows you to replace banner ads with the image of your choice and to block ads for sites you find offensive. With this or other cookie-stopper software, you can disable pop-up windows, and stipulate that certain cookies can stay on your hard drive for the duration of one session only.

ADWARE AND SPYWARE   If you've downloaded a game or other software from the Web for free, you may have noticed that it came with banner ads. These ads are collectively known as adware. *Adware* is software to generate ads that installs itself on your computer when you download some other (usually free) program from the Web (see Figure 8.6). Adware is a type of *Trojan horse software,* meaning that it's software you don't want hidden inside software you do want. There's usually a disclaimer, buried somewhere in the multiple "I agree" screens, saying that the software includes this adware. At

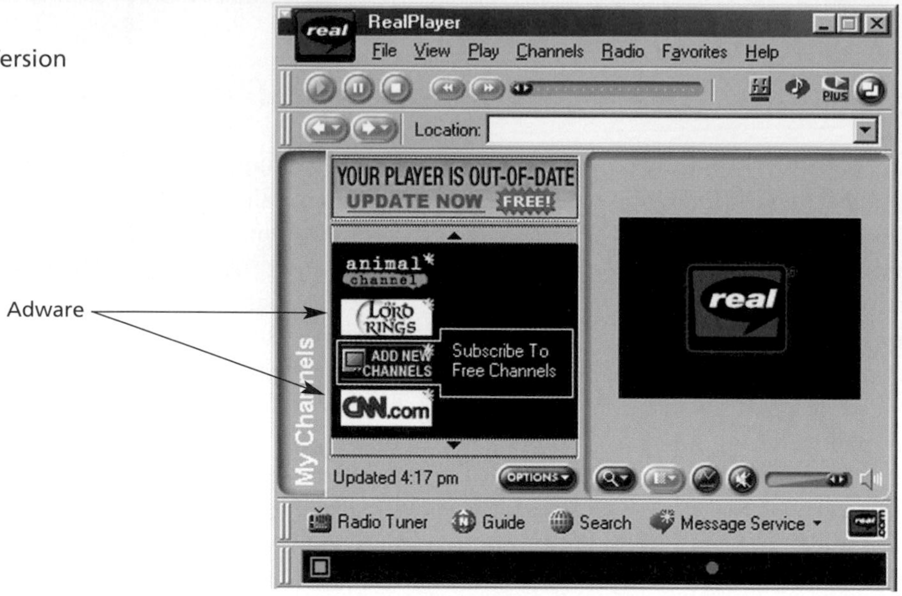

Figure 8.6

Adware in a Free Version
of RealPlayer

Adware

the bottom of several small-print screens you're asked to agree to the terms. Very few people read the whole agreement, and advertisers count on that. This sort of product is sometimes called *click-wrap* because it's like commercial software that has an agreement that you agree to by breaking the shrink-wrap.

Most people don't get upset about pure adware, since they feel it's worth having to view ads to get software for free. However, there's a more insidious extra that's often bundled with free downloadable software called spyware. ***Spyware*** (also called ***sneakware*** or ***stealthware***) is software that comes hidden in free downloadable software and tracks your online movements, mines the information stored on your computer, or uses your computer's CPU and storage for some task you know nothing about. The first release of Real-Networks' RealJukebox sent information back to the company about what CDs the people who downloaded the software were playing on that computer. This information collection was going on when the customer wasn't even on the Web.[30]

Spyware is fast becoming the hidden cost of free software. Software such as Kazaa Media Desktop and Audiogalaxy, the successors to Napster for sharing music and other files online, include spyware. If you download free software and it has banner ads, it's quite possible that it has spyware, too. There's usually something in the "I agree" screens telling you about spyware, but it can be hard to find.[31] Spyware can stay on your computer long after you've uninstalled the original software.

You can detect various kinds of Trojan horse software with The Cleaner from www.moosoft.com. Also check out www.wilders.org for Trojan First Aid Kit (TFAK). The best-known spyware detection programs, also called stealthware blockers, are Ad-Aware (free from www.lavasoftUSA.com) and PestPatrol. The software scans your whole computer, identifies spyware programs, and offers to delete them. If you want to check out free software for spyware before you download it, go online to www.spychecker.com, a site that will tell you if a particular free software includes adware or spyware.

Even without spyware, a Web site can tell a lot about its Web visitors from its Web log.[32] A ***Web log*** consists of one line of information for every visitor to a Web site and is usually stored on a Web server. At the very least, a Web log can provide a Web site company with a record of your clickstream.

YOU CAN BUY INSURANCE AGAINST IDENTITY THEFT

Insurance companies are beginning to cover one of the fastest growing white-color crimes—identity theft. Chubb Personal Insurance was one of the first to offer such coverage. Since 1999, Chubb has included $25,000 of coverage for expenses related to identity theft on all its homeowners' policies. American International Group (AIG) also offers this coverage. AIG's policy offers reimbursement of expenses and legal assistance with identity theft, the cost of virus damage, and physical damage to computers resulting from personal Internet or wireless use.

Identity theft was first reported in 1993, but it didn't even have a name at that time. By 1998, Congress had enacted the Identity Theft and Assumption Deterrence Act that made identity theft a federal crime. The Federal Trade Commission (FTC) was charged with receiving and processing complaints from victims. In 2000, the first full year of operation, the FTC fielded more than 40,000 inquiries, 69 percent of which were actual reports of identity theft, while the rest were requests for information. By 2001, the FTC was getting 2,000 complaints a week. The Justice Department says that there are over 500,000 identity-theft cases in the United States every year, and 42 percent of all consumer-fraud complaints in 2001 were for identity theft.[33]

A *clickstream* records information about you during a Web surfing session such as what Web sites you visited, how long you were there, what ads you looked at, and what you bought. If, as a consumer, you want to protect information about your surfing habits, you can use various software packages to do so. Apart from cookie management software you can avail yourself of *anonymous Web browsing (AWB)* services, which, in effect, hide your identity from the Web sites you visit. One way to do this is to use the Anonymizer at www.anonymizer.com. This site, and others like it, sends your Web browsing through its server and removes all identifying information. Some of the ABW services that are available include disabling pop-up promotions, defeating tracking programs, and erasing browsing history files. If you don't want to go through an outside server, you can download software to do the job. SurfSecret is a shareware antitracking package available from www.surfsecret.com.

As a final note on the subject, remember that even if a company promises, and fully intends, to keep its customer information protected, it may not be possible. When faced with a subpoena, the company will have to relinquish customer records. Furthermore, courts have ruled in bankruptcy cases that customer files are assets that may be sold to pay debts.

PRIVACY AND GOVERNMENT AGENCIES

Government agencies have about 2,000 databases containing personal information on individuals.[34] The various branches of government need information to administer entitlement programs, such as social security, welfare, student loans, law enforcement, and so on.

LAW ENFORCEMENT   You've often heard about someone being apprehended for a grievous crime after a routine traffic stop for something like a broken taillight. The arrest most likely ensued because the arresting officer ran a check on the license plate and driver's license. The officer probably checked the National Crime Information Center (NCIC) database and found the outstanding warrant there. This is how the culprits responsible for the Oklahoma City bombing were caught.

The NCIC database contains information on the criminal records of more than 20 million people. It also stores information on outstanding warrants, missing children, gang members, juvenile delinquents, stolen guns and cars, and so on. The NCIC has links to other government and private databases, and guardians of the law all over the country can access NCIC information. Sometimes they do so in response to something suspicious, and other times it's just routine. For example, Americans returning from outside the country are routinely checked through the NCIC when they come through customs.

Given the wealth of information and accessibility, it's not surprising that NCIC information has been abused. Several police departments have found that a significant number of employees illegally snooped for criminal records on people they knew or wanted to know.

The Federal Bureau of Investigation (FBI) has caused a stir lately because of its electronic surveillance methods. First there was Carnivore (a rather unfortunate name, which has since been changed to DCS-1000, which sounds much more innocuous). DCS-1000 connects hardware to an ISP to trap all e-mail sent to or received by the target of the investigation. It takes a court order to use DCS-1000, and, of course, the target is typically unaware of the surveillance. Intercepting communications is not new: The FBI put the first tap on a phone in 1885, just four years after the invention of the telephone.[35] DCS-1000, with a court order, traps all communications involving the individual named in the court order.

Because it can be hard to identify the data packets of one individual's e-mail amongst all the other Internet traffic, it's entirely possible that other people's e-mail might be scooped up in the net. And this is what happened in March 2000 when FBI agents were legally intercepting messages of a suspect, but someone else was caught in the trap. The information on the innocent party was obtained under the Freedom of Information Act. The FBI said the incident was an honest mistake and a result of miscommunication between it and the ISP.[36] But, this is the sort of mistake that scares people. Most people want law enforcement to be able to watch the bad guys—that's necessary for our collective safety. But the prospect of information being collected on law-abiding citizens who are minding their own business worries a lot of people.

In 2001, the FBI acknowledged an enhancement to DCS-1000 called Magic Lantern, which is key logger software. The FBI installs it by sending the target an innocent-looking Trojan-horse e-mail, which contains the key logger software. The hidden software then sends information back to the FBI periodically.[37]

Another federal agency, the National Security Agency (NSA), uses a system called Echelon that uses a global network of satellites and surveillance stations to trap phone, e-mail, and fax transmissions. The system then screens all this information looking for certain keywords and phrases and analyzes the messages that fit the search criteria.[38]

At the local level, the actions of the Tampa Police Department at the 2001 Super Bowl caused an outcry from privacy advocates. Police, with the agreement of the NFL, focused video cameras on the faces of tens of thousands of spectators as they entered the stadium. The images were sent to computers which, using facial recognition software, compared the images to a database of pictures of suspected criminals and terrorists. The police spokesperson said that the action was legal since it's permissible to take pictures of people in public places. That's true in so far as you have no expectation of privacy in a public place. Indeed surveillance of people has been going on for years without much protest in gambling casinos, Wal-Mart stores, and other businesses in the private sector. But the American Civil Liberties Union (ACLU) protested the surveillance of Super Bowl spectators on the grounds that it was surveillance by a government agency without court-ordered authorization.[39] The fact that the state was involved made it unacceptable to the ACLU.

WHAT ARE THE BIGGEST INTERNET SCAMS?

The U.S. Federal Trade Commission (FTC) is on the trail of Internet crime. On its Web site, the FTC has published a list of the top 10 online frauds. Below are two of these. Go to the FTC Web site at www.ftc.com and find the other eight along with the advice that the FTC gives to help you avoid such problems.

- *Online auction fraud:* In this case you get something less valuable than what you paid for, or you might even get nothing at all.
- *FTC says:* Always use a credit card or an escrow service.

- *Internet service provider (ISP) scams:* You get a check for a small amount ($3 or $4) in the mail and cash it. Then you find you're trapped into a long-term contract with an ISP that exacts a huge penalty if you cancel.
- *FTC says:* Read ALL the information about the check before you cash it and watch for unexpected charges.

OTHER FEDERAL AGENCIES   The Internal Revenue Service (IRS) gets income information from taxpayers. But the agency has access to other databases, too. For example, the IRS keeps track of vehicle registration information so that it can check up on people buying expensive cars and boats to make sure they're reporting an income level that corresponds to their purchases. The IRS can go to outside government databases as well. Verizon says that it gets 22,000 requests for phone records from the IRS, FBI, and other government agencies per year. It seldom informs the customer of the request.[40] America Online (AOL) has a special fax number reserved just for subpoenas.

The Census Bureau collects information on all the U.S. inhabitants it can find every 10 years. All citizens are requested to fill out a census form, and some people get a very long and detailed form requiring them to disclose a lot of personal information. The information that the Census Bureau collects is available to other government agencies and even to commercial enterprises. The bureau doesn't link the information to respondents' names but sells summarized information about geographic regions. Some of these regions are relatively small, however, consisting of fewer than 100 city blocks.

It's fairly safe to assume that anytime you have contact with any branch of government, information about you will be subsequently stored somewhere. For example, if you get a government-backed student loan, you provide personal information such as your name, address, income, parents' income, and so on. Some of the information nuggets attached to the loan would be the school you're attending, the bank dispersing the loan, your repayment schedule, and later, your repayment pattern.

PRIVACY AND INTERNATIONAL TRADE

If a customer in Europe buys books from Amazon.com's U.K. division, you'd probably be surprised to find out that Amazon, U.K., may not transfer the customer's credit card information to Amazon in the United States without being in compliance with "safe-harbor principles." *Safe-harbor principles* are a set of rules to which U.S. businesses that want to trade with the European Union (EU) must adhere. You probably wouldn't think twice about sending customer information, such as a name and address, via e-mail from one part of the company to another. But if you're in a subsidiary in an EU country and the recipient is in the United States you might have a problem.

ON YOUR OWN

WHAT'S YOUR OPINION?

A nationwide survey was conducted by the *Marketing Management* journal on consumer attitudes toward online privacy.[41] The survey wanted to know what impact privacy policies have on consumer purchasing behavior and what consumers considered to be acceptable levels of information gathering.

The questions and responses are listed below. State whether you agree or disagree with the answers and why.

Question	Survey Response	Your Response
1. Should a Web site be able to analyze Web traffic on an anonymous aggregate level?	Yes: 75%	
2. Is lack of control over who gets your personal information a strong privacy concern for you?	Yes: 39%	
3. Is spam a strong privacy concern for you?	Yes: 37%	
4. Is it very important to you to be able to access a site's information about you?	Yes: 22%	
5. Would it be acceptable to you if the site protected your privacy, but didn't let you see information about you?	Yes: 80%	

The EU has very stringent rules about the collection of personal information and in 1998 implemented a Directive on the Protection of Personal Data. This means that the EU set privacy goals and to comply, each member country had to make laws, based on its own culture and customs, to achieve these goals. There are still differences in privacy laws among European countries, but in general, the rights granted to EU citizens include the consumer's right to

- Know the marketer's source of information
- Check personal identifiable information for accuracy
- Correct any incorrect information
- Specify that information can't be transferred to a third party without the consumer's consent
- Know the purpose for which the information is being collected.

If information can be linked to you—either directly or indirectly—it's personal identifiable information. The list of identifying tags includes names, ID numbers, and unique physical characteristics.[42]

The United States and the European Union began negotiations on the heels of the EU directive to create safe-harbor principles for U.S.-based companies to be able to transfer personal information out of European countries. The safe-harbor rules cover every industry and almost all types of personal information. After extensive negotiations, in June 2000, the United States became the first country outside the EU to be recognized as meeting information privacy requirements of EU states.[43] Without this agreement, disruption of the $350 billion in trade between the United States and Europe would have been a distinct possibility.

So for your company to be able to transfer personal information out of EU countries, you'd have to first register with the U.S. Department of Commerce and agree to adhere to the safe-harbor principles. Although participation is theoretically voluntary, if you transfer personal information without having registered, you're risking punitive action from the U.S. Federal Trade Commission as well as from the European country from which you transferred the information.[44] See Closing Case Study Two for more information on the European Directive on the Protection of Personal Data and the Safe Harbor Agreement.

LAWS ON PRIVACY

The United States doesn't have a comprehensive or consistent set of laws governing the use of information. However, some laws are in place. See Figure 8.7 for a list of some well-established laws.

More recent legislation includes the Health Insurance Portability and Accountability Act (HIPAA) and the Financial Service Modernization Act. HIPAA, enacted in 1996, requires that the health care industry formulate and implement the first regulations to keep patient information confidential. The act seeks to

- Limit the release and use of your health information without your consent
- Give you the right to access your medical records and find out who else has accessed them
- Overhaul the circumstances under which researchers and others can review medical records
- Release health information on a need-to-know basis only
- Allow the disclosure of protected health information for business reasons as long as the recipient undertakes, in writing, to protect the information

The Financial Services Modernization Act requires that financial institutions protect personal customer information and that they have customer permission before sharing such information with other businesses. However, the act contains a clause that allows the sharing of information for "legitimate business purposes."

Figure 8.7

Well-Established Information-Related Laws

- The **Privacy Act** restricts what information the federal government can collect; allows people to access and correct information on themselves; requires procedures to protect the security of personal information; and forbids the disclosure of name-linked information without permission.
- The **Freedom of Information Act** says that citizens have the right to access the information that federal agencies have collected on them.
- The **Computer Matching and Privacy Protection Act** says that government agencies can't compare certain records trying to find a match. However, most records are not covered by this act.
- The **Bork Bill** (officially known as the **Video Privacy Protection Act**) prohibits the use of video rental information on customers for any purpose other than that of marketing goods and services directly to the customer.
- The **Communications Assistance for Law Enforcement Act** requires that telecommunications equipment be designed so that authorized government agents are able to intercept all wired and wireless communications being sent or received by any subscriber. The act also requires that subscriber call-identifying information be transmitted to a government when and if required.

Information

In this section we'll consider the dual roles of information in an organization. Nothing else is as universal or as versatile as information. What else can you sell or lease to someone else—and simultaneously retain for yourself? This unique resource called "information" has two functions in an organization: as raw material and capital (see Figure 8.8).

INFORMATION AS RAW MATERIAL

Raw materials are the components from which a product is made. For example, the raw materials for a chair might be wood, glue, and screws. But almost everything you buy has information as part of the product. If you doubt this, wander through a store and see how many products incorporate absolutely no information. Even bananas have stickers telling you something about them or their distributor. Of course, the amount of information varies. You get a lot more information if you buy a jet airplane than if you buy a cake mix. Sometimes it's the information that makes a product particularly valuable. Take the example of two identical pairs of sports shoes that were originally made by the same company but sold under different logos. It's very likely that the shoes with the more widely known or prestigious logo will sell for a higher price than those with the lesser logo. The more desirable logo doesn't increase the functional value of the shoes. They're the same shoes. But the information (in this case the logo) proclaims something to the world that the wearer wants to be associated with. For that statement, whatever it is, the customer is prepared to pay extra.

The most successful companies place the highest value on information. United Parcel Service (UPS) is an example. The company's IT budget is second only to its expenditures on aircraft. This is because UPS is selling not only a shipping service, but also information. You can connect to the UPS Web site and track your package. As UPS Chief Information Officer (CIO) Frank Ergbrick puts it, "A package without information has no value."[45]

General Motors doesn't just sell vehicles. Its Cadillac features an option called OnStar that combines a global positioning system (GPS), which identifies your position anywhere on earth, with networked sensors, a cell phone, and a link to customer support centers. With the OnStar system you can get directions to any destination and even receive advice on where to dine. OnStar also contributes to your safety. If the car's air bag inflates, the sensor sends a signal to the customer support center, which tries to contact you on the car phone. If there's no response, the support center uses the GPS component to locate your car, then alerts the emergency service nearest to you. The OnStar system can also help track your car if it's stolen. So a Cadillac is not just a car—it's an IT system on wheels.

INFORMATION AS CAPITAL

Capital is the asset you use to produce a product or service. Buildings, trucks, and machinery are examples of capital. For our chair manufacturer, the capital would be the factory building, the saw, the glue dispenser, screw

Figure 8.8

Information as Raw Material and Capital

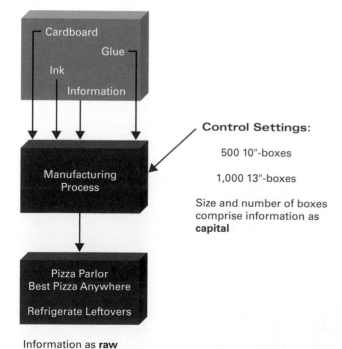

Control Settings:

500 10"-boxes

1,000 13"-boxes

Size and number of boxes comprise information as **capital**

Information as **raw material** becomes part of the product

drivers, and so on. These items are not part of the chair, but they're necessary to build it. You incur a cost in acquiring capital, and you expect a return on your investment. Additionally, you can sell or lease capital assets.

You can think of information as capital. It's used by companies to provide products and services. Organizations need information to provide what their target market wants. They need information in the form of manufacturing schedules, sales reports, marketing plans, accounting reports, and so on.

Information capital is one of the most important and universal types of capital in an organization. Not every company has a building or a truck, but every single one has information. We cannot state the case too strongly; an organization cannot exist without information any more than you can survive without oxygen.

Security

So, what can put your important information resource in jeopardy? Well, countless things. Hard disks can crash, computer parts can fail, hackers and crackers can gain access and do mischief, thieves engaged in industrial espionage can steal your information, and disgruntled employees or associates can cause damage. The FBI estimates that computer sabotage costs businesses somewhere close to $10 billion every year. Companies are increasing their spending on Internet security software, already having spent more than $4 billion in 2000; this figure is expected to double by 2003.[46]

SECURITY AND EMPLOYEES

Most of the press reports are about outside attacks on computer systems, but actually, companies are in far more danger of losing money from employee misconduct than they are from outsiders. It's a problem that's not restricted to computer misuse. A 300-restaurant chain with 30 employees in each location loses, on average, $218 per employee.

But white-collar crime is where the big bucks are lost (see Figure 8.9). White-collar crime in general, from Fortune 100 firms to video stores to construction companies, accounts for about $400 billion in losses every year—and information technology makes it much easier to accomplish and conceal. ($400 billion is $108 billion more than the whole federal defense budget.) Of all white collar fraud, the biggest losses are those incurred by management misconduct. Manager theft of various kinds is about four times that of other employees. Take embezzlement, for example. The average cost of a nonmanagerial employee's theft is $60,000, while that for managerial employees is $250,000. The most astonishing aspect of this is that most insider fraud (up to two-thirds) is never reported to the legal authorities, according to the Association of Certified Fraud Examiners (ACFE). A survey by Ernst & Young disclosed that two out of five businesses suffered more than five fraud losses, and fully one-quarter of those resulted in a loss of over $1 million. The reasons most often cited for lack of legal action was fear of damaging the company's reputation or brand name.[47]

Computer-aided fraud includes the old standby crimes like vendor fraud (sending payment to a nonexistent vendor or payment for goods not delivered), writing payroll

- White-collar crime costs an estimated $400 billion per year
- Average nonmanagerial embezzlement is $60,000
- Average managerial embezzlement is $250,000
- Two-thirds of insider fraud is not reported
- Of the known losses, one-quarter cost more than $1 million

Figure 8.9

Statistics on White-Collar Crime

checks to fictitious employees, claiming expense reimbursements for costs never incurred, and so on. In addition, there are newer crimes such as stealing security codes, credit card numbers, and proprietary files. Intellectual property is one of the favorite targets of theft by insiders. In fact, the companies that make surveillance software say that employers are buying and installing the software not so much to monitor employees as to track how intellectual property, like product design sketches, schematics, and so on, are moving around the network.[48]

Fraud examiners have a rule of thumb that in any group of employees, about 10 percent are completely honest, 10 percent will steal, and, for the remaining 80 percent, it will depend on circumstances. Most theft is committed by people who are strapped for cash, have access to funds that are poorly protected, and perceive a low risk of getting caught.

SECURITY AND COLLABORATION PARTNERS

Computer security was once considered to be an internal matter. It concerned only the company and those who actually used the computers. If you use collaboration systems, however, many representatives of other companies gain access to your computer systems. It's very important to be sure that the computer system of the company you're giving access to is at least as secure as yours, otherwise you'll create a backdoor into your own system. So now you need to be concerned about your partners', suppliers', and customers' computer security as well as your own.

Goodrich Corporation, an aerospace company that uses collaboration systems, has cut costs dramatically with its file-sharing capabilities allowing suppliers to view design drawings. A large portion of Goodrich's $4 billion in annual sales comes from the Department of Defense, so espionage is a real threat. Before a supplier can be part of the team, Goodrich checks out the newcomer's security measures. The Goodrich people examine firewalls and encryption, and even how physically secure the information on the system is. Then if everything meets its tough standards, the Goodrich team sets up a detailed procedure to be followed in case there's a security breach. The moral of the story is: If you want to do business with Goodrich, or many other companies, you'd better have a secure computer system.[49]

As Groove networks become more popular, the need for better security and trust will increase. Microsoft has invested $51 million in the Groove company and the two have agreed on a strategic alliance to offer peer-to-peer systems to businesses. The basic concept of Groove and other peer-to-peer systems is that computers are connected without a central server. This is the Napster concept, whereby computers are connected to each other as needed, to swap files. However, unlike Napster, participation in Groove networks is by invitation only and is not open to the general public. The Groove groupware tools allow people from different companies—partners, suppliers, distributors, and customers—to work together.[50]

GRID COMPUTING   A new kind of computer infrastructure is beginning to take hold of the business world. Grid computing creates a way to tap remote computing resources. *Grid computing* harnesses far-flung computers together by way of the Internet or a virtual private network to share CPU power, databases, and storage. The government is already engaged in grid computing as evidenced by the National Science Foundation's National Technology Grid and NASA's Information Power Grid. Grid computing software is in development by IBM, Sun Microsystems, and Hewlett-Packard. Grid computing includes peer-to-peer file sharing, but it's much more. The core of grid software is its common interface that allows any computer on the grid to tap into the CPU power or storage of other available computers. Companies as diverse as Pratt & Whitney, Bristol-Myers Squibb, and American Express are using grid computing. Analysts say

SETI

One of the first large-scale experiments in grid computing is a worldwide project that anyone can join. It's called the Project Phoenix and is an ongoing investigation into what's out there in space and whether it's trying to communicate with us. The project is part of the SETI Institute, an organization whose mission is "to explore, understand and explain the origin, nature, prevalence and distribution of life in the universe."

To investigate anything floating around that might be otherworldly, telescope data is constantly being collected. The amount of information defies the computational ability of one or even several computers, so the organizers enlisted the help of volunteers who let their computers work for SETI when they would otherwise be idle. If you'd like to be a part of this project, you can download a screensaver from www.seti-inst.edu, which makes your computer part of this huge worldwide grid of private computers. It works in a manner similar to a standard screensaver in that it pops up when your computer is inactive for a certain period (that you specify). But instead of showing pretty pictures or causing the screen to go black, the CPU helps out with data analysis.

that grid computing will turn computing power into a utility; the provider will simply send you as much or as little power or storage as you happen to need at that moment.[51]

The issues still to be resolved before grid computing becomes widespread are many and complex, but not least among them is security. Security issues involving computers from multiple locations span cultural and technical issues, ranging from rights of access to data sharing to legal and departmental policies.

SECURITY AND OUTSIDE THREATS

An FBI Computer Security Institute survey found that the computer systems of 85 percent of large companies and governmental agencies were broken into during 2001. Of those, 64 percent said they had suffered financial loss, but only 35 percent wanted to put a figure on the loss. Even so, the total of reported losses came to more than $375 million. "There's no Fortune 500 company that hasn't been hacked, I don't care what they tell you," says one hacker.[52] "Hacking" means unauthorized access to computers and computer information. 3Com gets "thousands of attacks a week. From kids to criminals to foreign governments," says David Starr, senior vice president.[53] Even Microsoft's computers have been hacked.

The threats from outside are many and varied. Competitors could try to get your customer lists or the prototype for your new project. Cyber vandals could be joyriding in cyberspace looking for something interesting to see, steal, or destroy. You could become the victim of a generalized attack from a virus or worm, or could suffer a targeted attack like a denial-of-service attack. If you have something worth stealing or manipulating on your system, there could be people after that, too. For example, the online gambling industry is plagued by attacks where hackers have illicitly gained access to the servers that control the gambling, corrupting games to win millions of dollars. Exploiting well-known system weaknesses accounts for 95 percent of hacker damage, while only 5 percent results from breaking into systems in new ways.[54,55]

The people who break into the computer systems of others are "hackers" (see Figure 8.10 on the next page). **Hackers** are generally very knowledgeable computer users who use their knowledge to invade other people's computers. They have varying motives. Some just do it for the fun of it. Others (called hacktivists) have a philosophical or political message they want to share, and still others (called crackers) are hired guns who

Figure 8.10

Hacker Types

- White-hat hackers find vulnerabilities in systems and plug the holes. They work at the request of the owners of the computer systems.
- Black-hat hackers break into other people's computer systems and may just look around, or they may steal credit card numbers or destroy information, or otherwise do damage.
- Hacktivists have philosophical and political reasons for breaking into systems. They often deface a Web site as a protest.
- Script kiddies, or script bunnies, find hacking code on the Internet and click-and-point their way into systems, to cause damage or spread viruses.
- Crackers are hackers for hire and are the hackers who engage in corporate espionage.
- Cyberterrorists are those who seek to cause harm to people or to destroy critical systems or information. They try to use the Internet as a weapon of mass destruction.

illegally break in, usually to steal information, for a fee. The latter can be a very lucrative undertaking. Some highly skilled crackers charge up to $1 million per job. There are also "good guys," called white-hat hackers, who test the vulnerability of systems so that protective measures may be taken.

TYPES OF CYBER CRIME   Cyber crimes range from electronically breaking and entering to cyberstalking and murder. In October 1999, a 21-year-old woman was shot and killed outside the building where she worked. Her killer had been electronically stalking her for two years. He became obsessed with the young lady and had even posted a Web site dedicated to her on which he announced his intention to kill her. He got her social security number online, found out where she worked, tracked her down, and shot her, after which he shot himself.

Most cyber crimes are not as bad as murder, but they can be serious nonetheless. Computer viruses and denial-of-service attacks are the two most common types of cyber crime against which companies need to protect themselves.

A *computer virus* (or simply a *virus*) is software that is written with malicious intent to cause annoyance or damage. A virus can be benign or malicious. The benign ones just display a message on the screen or slow the computer down, but don't do any damage. The malicious kind targets a specific application or set of file types and corrupts or destroys them.

Today, worms are the most prevalent type of virus (see Figure 8.11 for the genealogy of viruses). Worms are viruses that spread themselves; they don't need your help, just your carelessness.

A *worm* is a type of virus that spreads itself, not just from file to file, but from computer to computer via e-mail and other Internet traffic. It finds your e-mail address book

Figure 8.11

The Genealogy of Viruses

- 1980s: The first viruses in the 1980s were boot-sector viruses that attacked the operating system and spread when people traded floppy disks.
- 1990s: In the 1990s, macro viruses were all the rage. They spread when people traded disks or e-mail with attachments. The virus was part of the Word or Excel attachment and corrupted either the Word or Excel application respectively.
- 2000s: Polymorphic worms that change their form and are hard to detect started to appear. Also, viruses such as Klez that spoof the return address make it very difficult to track down the source of the virus.

and helps itself to the addresses and sends itself to your contacts, using your e-mail address as the return address. The Love Bug worm was one of the early worms that did a lot of damage and got major press coverage. It's estimated that the Love Bug and its variants affected 300,000 Internet host computers and millions of individual PC users causing file damage, lost time, and high-cost emergency repairs costing about $8.7 billion.[56,57] Ford Motor Company, H. J, Heinz, Merrill Lynch, AT&T, Capitol Hill, and the British Parliament all fell victim to the Love Bug worm. Newer versions of worms include Klez, a very rapidly spreading worm, Nimda, and Sircam.

A *denial-of-service attack (DoS)* floods a Web site with so many requests for service that it slows down or crashes. The objective is to prevent legitimate customers from accessing the target site. E*Trade, Yahoo!, and Amazon.com have all been victims of this type of attack. For more information about viruses and DoSs see *Extended Learning Module H*.

Code Red, first discovered in July 2001, was the first virus to combine the worm's ability to propagate with the denial-of-service attack's ability to bring down a Web site. Having infected a server, it used e-mail address lists to send itself to other servers. Then it lay dormant, ready for a signal. The idea was to send the signal to all of the infected servers (millions of them) and make them all try to access the White House Web site at the same time and bring it down. The White House Webmaster foiled the plot by changing the IP address of the site so that the attacks would go to a defunct address.

There are even virus hoaxes. This is e-mail sent to frighten people about a virus threat that is, in fact, bogus. People who get such an alert will usually tell others, who react in the same way. The virus is nonexistent, but the hoax causes people to get scared and lose time and productivity. The losses for a company can be very severe because computer professionals must spend precious time and effort looking for a nonexistent problem.

As well as knowing what viruses can do, you need to know what they can't do. Computer viruses can't

- Hurt your hardware, such as your monitor, or processor.
- Hurt any files they weren't designed to attack. A virus designed for Microsoft's Outlook, for example, generally doesn't infect Qualcomm's Eudora, or any other e-mail application.
- Infect files on write protected disks.

SECURITY PRECAUTIONS

It has been said that while in years past, managers had nightmares about takeover bids, they now have nightmares about teenagers with computers and Internet access. Lloyd's of London says that 70 percent of risk managers see the Internet and e-commerce as the biggest emerging risks in this new century.[58] Worldwide security software revenue is expected to grow from $6.3 billion in 2001 to $11.9 billion by 2004.[59]

The only really safe computer system is one that is never connected to any other computer and is locked away so that almost no one can get to it. In today's business world that's just not practical. Computers are like motor vehicles, they can be used to cause harm both unintentionally and maliciously, and just driving one puts you at risk, especially when you're on the road with other cars. However, we still use motor vehicles, although we build in safety features and take precautions to lessen the risk. So it is with computers. The big difference is that security threats in cyberspace are always changing.

Given the extraordinary importance of information in an organization, it's imperative that companies make their best efforts to protect that information; that is, they should practice risk management. *Risk management* consists of the identification of risks or threats, the implementation of security measures, and the monitoring of those measures for effectiveness. The first step in the process is establishing the extent of the potential threats and identifying the parts of the system that are vulnerable. That process is called risk assessment. ***Risk assessment*** is the process of evaluating IT assets, their importance to the organization, and their susceptibility to threats, to measure the risk exposure of these assets. In simple terms, risk assessment asks (1) What can go wrong? (2) How likely is it to go wrong? and (3) What are the possible consequences if it does go wrong?[60]

Implementing the correct amount and type of security is not an easy matter. Too much security can hamper employees' ability to do their jobs, resulting in decreased revenue. Too little security leaves your organization vulnerable. You need security strong enough to protect your IT systems but not so much that authorized people can't access the information they need in a timely fashion. Generally, security consists of a combination of measures such as backup procedures, anti-virus software, firewalls, access authentication, encryption, intrusion-detection software, and system auditing.

BACKUPS   As always, an ounce of prevention is worth a pound of cure. The easiest and most basic way to prevent loss of information is to make backups of all your information. A ***backup*** is the process of making a copy of the information stored on a computer. There's no action you can take that's more rudimentary or essential than making copies of important information methodically and regularly (at least once a week). Employee carelessness and ignorance cause about two-thirds of the financial cost of lost or damaged information.[61]

Take the example of one company whose accounting server went down the day that paychecks should have been distributed. The crisis arose during an administration transition. The people who had been temporarily running the system thought that backup occurred automatically. It didn't, so all payroll information was lost. To get the system up and running again, the company had to pay thousands of dollars to consultants to restore the network application, and had to pay four people for 300 hours of overtime to reenter information. In addition, it cost $48,000 for a disk-recovery company to retrieve the information from the damaged disk drive. And all this trouble and expense could have been avoided if backup procedures had been followed.

Make sure you back up *all* information. It's easy to forget about the information that's not stored in the main computer system or network, such as correspondence and customer information kept only by administrative assistants and receptionists, and private information not kept in the main organizational databases or data warehouses. Your backup schedule should include not only your information, but also your software. See Chapter 7 for more on backup and recovery.

ANTI-VIRUS SOFTWARE   Anti-virus software is an absolute must. ***Anti-virus software*** detects and removes or quarantines computer viruses. New viruses are created every day and each new generation is more deadly (or potentially deadly) than the previous one. When you're looking for virus protection, *PC World* magazine[62] has the following advice. Look for virus protection that finds

- Viruses on removable media like floppies, CDs, and Zip disks, as well as on the hard disk
- Trojan-horse viruses (viruses hiding inside good software) and backdoor programs (viruses that open a way into the network for future attacks)
- Polymorphic viruses and worms, which are sometimes hard for anti-virus programs to find because they change their form as they propagate
- Viruses in .zip or compressed files, and even .zip files inside other .zip files
- Viruses in e-mail attachments

Two final points: First, your anti-virus software should be able to get rid of the virus without destroying the software or information it came with. Second, you must update your anti-virus software frequently since new viruses come along every day. Some software sites will automatically send updates to your anti-virus software, if you set up the software to accept it.

FIREWALLS A *firewall* is hardware and/or software that protects a computer or network from intruders. The firewall examines each message as it seeks entrance to the network, like a border guard checking passports. Unless the message has the "right" markings, the firewall blocks the way and prevents it from entering. Any competent network administrator will have at least one firewall on the network to keep out unwelcome guests.

A firewall will also detect your computer communicating with the Internet without your approval, as spyware on your computer may be attempting to do. A very popular software firewall is ZoneAlarm from www.zonealarm.com. ZoneAlarm also offers protection from ads and cookies.

ACCESS AUTHENTICATION While firewalls keep outsiders out, they don't necessarily keep insiders out. In other words, unauthorized employees may try to access computers or files. One of the ways that companies try to protect computer systems is with authentication systems that check who you are before they let you have access.

There are three basic ways of proving your access rights: (1) what you know, like a password; (2) what you have, like an ATM card; (3) what you look like (or rather what your fingerprint or some other physical characteristic looks like).

Passwords are very popular and have been used since there were computers. You can password-protect the whole network, a single computer, a folder, or a file. But passwords are not by any means a perfect way to protect a computer system. People forget their passwords, so someone has to get them new passwords or find the old one. Banks spend $15 per call to help customers who forget their passwords. Then if a hacker breaks into the system and steals a password list, everyone has to get a new password. One bank had to change 5,000 passwords in the course of a single month at a cost of $12.50 each.[64]

Which brings us to biometrics, or what you look like. *Biometrics* is the use of physical characteristics—such as your fingerprint, the blood vessels in the retina of your eye, the sound of your voice, or perhaps even your breath—to provide identification.

CHASING THE BAD GUYS ALL OVER THE WORLD

In Chapter 4 you already saw how banks are using artificial intelligence systems to catch fraudulent credit card and check transactions. Worldwide, a problem just as big is sending large banks back to technology for solutions. Money laundering is always a concern when dealing with wealthy clients and large sums of foreign currency. The International Monetary Fund estimates that $590 billion from criminal and terrorist activities is sent through banks to be "cleaned." And a big bank can spend $15 million a year to meet legal requirements governing antilaundering activities. In the United States, the U.S. Bank Secrecy Act requires that financial companies file reports on any large financial transfers and any suspicious transactions. Other countries have similar laws.

Deutsche Bank, which is the largest banking group in Europe, has developed its own screening system to ferret out money-laundering schemes. The Deutsche Bank antilaundering system creates a risk score for people opening new accounts. This risk score is similar to those that banks assign people applying for loans and is based on past business transactions and other pertinent factors. The information that Deutsche Bank uses has been gathered on customers who have accounts in this 107-country banking system. Since implementing its system, Deutsche Bank needs only four full-time employees to monitor transactions looking for money laundering instead of the 50 people previously required.

The first antilaundering systems simply flagged deposits over a certain amount. But, the people doing the laundering figured it out and adjusted their bank transactions accordingly. The Bank Secrecy Act first obliged banks to report cash transaction of $10,000 or more, but during the 1990s, money-laundering crimes rose sharply and the U.S. Treasury was getting more reports than agents could read. So, the agency created the Financial Crimes Enforcement Network (FinCEN) to use technology to counter the increasingly complex transactions.

Internationally, FinCEN has joined forces with 28 other countries to share information and track money laundering worldwide. In fact, this coalition has threatened to impose sanctions on nations such as Egypt, Nigeria, the Philippines, and Russia for their banking practices.[65]

Roughly a dozen different types of biometric devices are available at the moment, with fingerprint readers being the most popular. About 44 percent of the biometric systems sold are fingerprint systems. It works just like the law enforcement system where your fingerprint is stored in the database, and when you come along, your finger is scanned, and the scan is compared to the entry in the database. If they match, you're in.

In Fresno, California, customers are buying lunch without producing any cash or credit cards. When they order, they press a finger on a fingerprint scanner and are asked what credit card they'd like to use. The McDonald's system then matches the fingerprint to a credit card number.[66]

Another promising type of biometric system is facial recognition. Chicago's O'Hare airport, the busiest in the world, has been using biometrics for years to authenticate employees' identity.[67] Many U.S. airport security officials are proposing biometric systems to check that passengers are who they say they are. Most envision the system as a voluntary recording of passengers' biological characteristics, so that frequent flyers could sign up, have their physical characteristic scanned, then in the future bypass the long manual clearing process.

In addition, there are also retinal scanners and iris scanners. Signature checkers activate as you sign your name and check the rhythm, pressure, speed, and acceleration of the signature and compare the scan with the stored pattern to see if they match. See Chapter 9 for more information on biometrics.

KEEPING TRACK OF SHOE SALES IS VERY IMPORTANT

Payless ShoeSource is North America's largest family footwear retailer. In 2001, Payless sold about $3 billion worth of shoes (with an average price per pair about $12) at its 4,900 stores in the United States, Canada, Puerto Rico, Central America, and Guam.

Shoes are shipped automatically to all stores. The entire system relies on a data center in Topeka, Kansas. All the data analysis, decision making, and control are based on the information that the Topeka data center collects and stores daily. Payless has a mainframe, several minicomputers, and thousands of PCs. The entire corporate network is controlled from the Topeka data center. Even if there is a network problem in Taiwan, the people in Topeka handle it. Since Kansas is located in "Tornado Alley," the data center is underground—all 16,000 square feet of it.

Every night, the data center polls all the stores, domestic and overseas, for information about their sales for that day. The company has a data warehouse with two years' worth of information on every shoe type and size sold in every store that's available for on-line analytical processing (OLAP). Since losing this information would be disastrous, Payless has lots of safeguards in place. Some of these safeguards include the following:

- In the case of a problem with AT&T, the phone system will automatically switch to Sprint.
- An array of 120 heavy-duty batteries takes over if the power goes down, then a backup generator kicks in. There's even a backup generator to the backup generator.
- The data center also has two backup air-conditioning systems in case the original one goes out.
- If fire breaks out, fire-fighting gas (FM 2000) is automatically sprayed from the ceiling to suffocate the flames within seconds. If that doesn't work, water sprinklers start up as a *last* resort (water isn't good for computer equipment).
- All information is backed up onto high-capacity cassette tapes. The company has about 30,000 of these. Each day the backup tapes are sent off site by truck.
- The company has an agreement for the use of a hot site in Philadelphia, where the entire data center can relocate and continue operations in case of a major disaster.
- Every year all the IT staff practice a disaster drill.

ENCRYPTION If you want to protect your messages and files and hide them from prying eyes, you can encrypt them. *Encryption* scrambles the contents of a file so that you can't read it without having the right decryption key. There are various ways of encrypting messages. You can switch the order of the characters, replace characters with other characters, or insert or remove characters. All of these methods alter the look of the message, but used alone, each one is fairly simple to figure out. So most encryption methods use a combination.

Companies that get sensitive information from customers, such as credit card numbers, need some way of allowing all their customers to use encryption to send the information. But they don't want everyone to be able to decrypt the message, so they might use public key encryption. *Public key encryption (PKE)* is an encryption system that uses two keys: a public key that everyone can have and a private key for only the recipient. So if you do online banking, the bank will give you the public key to encrypt the information you send them, but only the bank has the key to decrypt your information. It works rather like a wall safe, where anyone can lock it (just shut the door and twirl the knob), but only the person with the right combination can open it again.

INTRUSION-DETECTION AND SECURITY-AUDITING SOFTWARE   Two other types of security software are intrusion-detection and security-auditing software. *Intrusion-detection software* looks for people on the network who shouldn't be there or who are acting suspiciously. For example, someone might be trying lots of passwords trying to gain access. "Honey pots" are a type of intrusion-detection software that creates attractive, but nonexistent, targets for hackers. What actually happens is that hackers' keystrokes are recorded instead.

Security-auditing software checks out your computer or network for potential weaknesses. The idea is to find out where hackers could get in and to plug up the hole. Many third parties, such as accounting firms or computer security companies, also provide this service.

Summary: Student Learning Outcomes Revisited

1. **Define ethics and describe the two factors that affect how you make a decision concerning an ethical issue.** *Ethics* are the principles and standards that guide our behavior toward other people. How you decide ethical issues depends on your basic ethical structure and the practical circumstances surrounding your decision. Your basic ethical structure is your sense of ethics that you acquired growing up. The practical circumstances surrounding your decision include

   * *Consequences.* How much or how little benefit or harm will come from a particular decision?

   * *Society's opinion.* What is your perception of what society really thinks of your intended action?

   * *Likelihood of effect.* What is the probability of the harm or benefit that will occur if you take the action?

   * *Time to consequences.* What length of time will it take for the benefit or harm to take effect?

   * *Relatedness.* How much do you identify with the person or persons who will receive the benefit or suffer the harm?

   * *Reach of result.* How many people will be affected by your action?

2. **Define and describe intellectual property, copyright, Fair Use Doctrine, and pirated and counterfeit software.** *Intellectual property* is intangible creative work that is embodied in physical form. *Copyright* is the legal protection afforded an expression of an idea, such as a song or a video game and some types of proprietary

   documents. The *Fair Use Doctrine* says that you may use copyrighted material in certain situations. *Pirated software* is the unauthorized use, duplication, distribution or sale of copyrighted software. *Counterfeit software* is software that is manufactured to look like the real thing and sold as such.

3. **Define privacy and describe ways in which it can be threatened.** *Privacy* is the right to be left alone when you want to be, to have control over your own personal possessions, and not to be observed without your consent. Your privacy can be compromised by other individuals snooping on you; by employers monitoring your actions; by businesses who collect information on your needs, preferences, and surfing practices; and by the various government agencies that collect information on citizens.

4. **Describe the two ways that information is valuable to business.** Information is valuable as raw material, which uses information as part of the product and as capital, which is something that goes into the production of goods and services, but which is not actually part of the product.

5. **Describe the ways in which information on your computer or network is vulnerable.**

   * Employees can embezzle and perpetrate fraud of other types. Most of the financial losses due to computer fraud that is suffered by companies is caused by employees.

- You give access to your computer information to collaboration partners who could do damage.
- Grid computing will mean many computers working together with the potential for information to move between computers when it shouldn't.
- Hackers and crackers try to break into computers and steal, destroy, or compromise information.
- Hackers can spread **computer viruses** or launch **denial-of-service attacks (DoS)** that can cost millions in prevention and cleanup.

6. **Define risk management and risk assessment and describe the seven security measures that companies can take to protect their information.** **Risk management** consists of the identification of risks or threats, the implementation of security measures, and the monitoring of those measures for effectiveness. **Risk assessment** is the process of evaluating IT assets, their importance to the organization, and their susceptibility to threats, to measure the risk exposure of these assets. The seven security measures are

- **Backups.** Make sure there is more than one copy of everything, including files not on the main servers, like correspondence and other information stored on the computers of individual employees.
- **Anti-virus software** detects and removes or quarantines computer viruses. You can set your software to perform this task automatically. However, to be effective it must be updated regularly and often. Antivirus software should check *all* files that are introduced to your computer.
- A **firewall** is hardware and/or software that protects a computer or network from intruders.
- Access authorization makes sure that those who have access to information have the authorization to do so with password or biometrics. **Biometrics** is the use of physical characteristics—such as your fingerprint, the blood vessels in the retina of your eye, the sound of your voice, or perhaps even your breath to provide identification.
- **Encryption** scrambles the contents of a file so that you can't read it without having the right decryption key.
- **Intrusion-detection software** looks for people on the network who shouldn't be there or who are acting suspiciously.
- **Security-auditing software** checks out your computer or network for possible weaknesses.

CLOSING CASE STUDY ONE

PROTECTING MORE THAN HEALTH

When you go for medical care, do you assume that your information is safe and that it will be protected along with your health? Most of us do, and the Cleveland Clinic Health Systems, like every other organization today, faces threats to their computer system from outside and from inside. In a two-month period in 2001, the clinic detected eight security breaches. Six of these were caused by employees sending out e-mail that was infected with a virus, and the other two were scans that indicated that someone was trying to use the clinic's computer system to launch an attack on another organization's computer system.

A survey commissioned by the FBI and the Computer Security Institute discovered that while 70 percent of the attacks come from outside an organization, most of the financial loss comes from inside the organization through unauthorized access, misuse of resources, and other attacks. Health care institutions do their best to hire ethical people who will protect patients' personal information as well as their health, and who won't steal. But now and then employees act in a way that breaches the trust that was placed in them.

While many companies are concerned about their customers' privacy, the health industry will shortly be bound by law to protect their patients' personal information from unauthorized parties. The Health Insurance Portability and Accountability Act (HIPAA) demands that health care companies meet certain security standards by April 2003.

Even without laws, medical institutions operate in large part on trust and therefore must be particularly careful with personal information. To protect patient information from browsing or worse by staff members, many hospitals will soon be using biometrics to protect computer files. Biometrics involves using a personal characteristic such as a fingerprint or retinal scan to make sure that the person trying to access information has the right to do so. Biometrics is easier to use than passwords because staff members don't have to remember passwords. It's also safer since you can't give someone else your fingerprint and, in the end, is probably less costly since organizations often spend a lot of time and money replacing passwords that become compromised in some way.

Cleveland Clinic must also protect its computer system from viruses, worms, and other malicious software, which is software that is designed to cause trouble for computer users. The clinic also has to protect against intrusion by those who want to use its computers to launch attacks on other computers in denial-of-service attacks. Viruses are often spread by e-mail, although that's not the only propagation method, and can cause such trouble as destroying files, filling up memory so that the computer system crashes, and compromising applications like Word so that they don't work properly. Particularly malevolent viruses can even reformat a hard disk, making the files that were stored there hard to retrieve.

To prevent computer viruses from getting into their system, Cleveland Clinic installed software that scans all e-mail coming in and out. It has also installed firewalls on the network to prevent intruders, and intru-sion-detection software to catch those who get by the firewall.[68]

QUESTIONS

1. What steps could Cleveland Clinic take to ensure as much honesty as possible in its organization? Some studies show that the corporate culture that employees work in exerts a strong influence on their behavior. What management actions would encourage or discourage such a culture?

2. What could hospital staff steal that would be valuable? Describe three situations in which a hospital employee, who is an otherwise honest person, be motivated to do something unethical.

3. What sort of biometric system would work well in a hospital? What would be best—facial recognition, fingerprint checks, retinal scans, bone structure comparisons, or something else?

4. Apart from anti-virus and anti-intrusion software, what protective software could Cleveland Clinic install to protect the organization's information? Can you think of damage other than the theft of personal information that the hospital or its inhabitants could suffer if someone from the outside broke into a hospital's computer system?

5. Would it be practical for the hospital to keep all databases internal and not be connected to the Web or have any electronic paths to the outside world at all? What would the advantages of such a move be? What would the disadvantages be? Apart from a presence on the Web, which is almost required for any company in today's business world, with what other entities would a hospital need to be able to exchange information?

CLOSING CASE STUDY TWO

IS THE SAFE HARBOR SAFE FOR U.S. BUSINESSES?

European countries and Australia have passed laws protecting the privacy of name-linked consumer information. In Europe this law is the European Union Directive 95/46/EC, which was adopted in 1998, and in

Australia it's the Privacy Amendment Act of 2000. The Australian law says that personal information can be collected only with the consent of the person about whom it's being collected. The law goes further and forbids personal information being transferred to any other country that does not have privacy protection. The result of this is that U.S. companies with an Australian subsidiary cannot transfer personal information it collected back to the United States since this country has no privacy protection of this type.

In Europe, the 15 countries that belong to the European Union are supposed to have passed laws by now requiring that personal information can only be collected with the express and unambiguous consent of the person to whom the information applies. And this rule applies to invisible information collection such as the information collected in cookies and details on a person's Web surfing activities.

An individual's information can only be collected without consent under the following circumstances:

1. It's necessary to fulfill a contract
2. It's necessary to save a life, as when a procedure is necessary on an unconscious person
3. It's necessary for a greater good, such as tax collection
4. The processing of the information is required by a legal contract
5. The third party to the information has a lawful right to do so as in an arbitration situation

Even within these guidelines there is certain "sensitive information" that cannot be requested and cannot be processed without specific consent. This sensitive information includes a person's racial or ethnic origin, political and religious affiliations, trade union membership, and sexual preferences. This exception of sensitive information was deemed necessary in the light of hundreds of years of persecution in Europe of one ethnic or religious group by another.

The EU directive also says that people must be informed when information about them is to be used for direct mailings, and the rules apply anytime the information is being processed within the European Union, even if those who are providing the information are located elsewhere. So why does it matter to U.S. businesses what privacy laws the Europeans choose to have? It matters because it threatens the annual $350 billion in trade between the United States and the European Union, since European countries may refuse to allow the transfer of customer information. So, the U.S. Department of Commerce and the European Commission agreed on voluntary, so-called Safe Harbor provisions, which represented a compromise between the strict consumer privacy requirements of Europe and the more relaxed attitude of American law. At its incep-

tion, the Safe Harbor agreement was hailed as a great breakthrough and a guarantee that business would indeed continue to thrive.

However, the Safe Harbor agreement no longer seems to be quite as wonderful as it did at first. There are several reasons for this. First, it's a voluntary program and only about 75 U.S. companies had signed up for it by the middle of 2001. The problem for U.S. companies may be that, by signing up, they open themselves to scrutiny by the Federal Trade Commission (FTC), which is the agency that will investigate complaints. Second, not all European countries have actually passed laws yet to comply with the directive. (An EU directive is simply a statement of intent and each member country must enact its own laws to ensure the outcome of the directive.) France, Ireland and Luxembourg had not passed any such laws by the middle of 2001. Third, some European countries think that the Safe Harbor agreement is much too weak, and is not in keeping with the intent of the directive. The worry for U.S. companies is that countries like Sweden might refuse to allow information transfer to countries they deem to be deficient. Fourth, the Safe Harbor agreement may not be enforceable by law since the FTC doesn't have the authority to protect European consumers' rights within the United States. And finally, EU authorities have the power to intervene in cases of serious violations and suspend the transfer of information to that country until the matter has been resolved.

Many privacy advocates in the United States hope that companies in this country will be inclined to self-regulate in order to comply with the stricter laws of Europe and Australia. They argue that such compliance would be in the best interests of U.S. companies and would ensure their continued trade and good name. In fact, Microsoft, Intel, Hewlett-Packard, and Procter & Gamble have all promised to provide their customers outside the European Union with privacy protection as strong as the EU demands. This commitment might give these companies a competitive advantage even in the United States as consumers here become more privacy conscious.[69]

QUESTIONS

1. Imagine, for a moment, that a federal law, very similar to the EU directive were to take effect in the United States at the beginning of next year. What would the implications be for companies that collect huge amounts of personal information about their customers and clients?

2. Would you like to have stronger privacy laws in this country? If so, what form should they take? If not, do you have any reservations about your personal information being bought and sold like any other commodity? Should there be limits on who can buy what information and for what purposes? If so, what should they be? If not, provide some examples of the advantages of having all personal information available to anyone with the means to acquire it.

3. Strangely enough, the European Union is considering a law that appears to fly squarely in the face of the philosophy of the privacy directive. The proposal is to give border police access to e-mail and Internet use by citizens. The law would mean that police would be able to access any and all e-mail and Internet usage information from ISPs simply by requesting it. No court order would be needed. There would be no restrictions on the amount or type of information that the police could access on people's personal and business lives. What do you think of this law? What do the privacy directive and the proposed law imply about the European attitude toward access to personal information? Whom do the Europeans see as the abusers of personal information and who are the good guys? Is the attitude the same in the United States? How do the European and American philosophies differ?

4. Do you think that the United States should have stricter border laws? At airports the focus tends to be on luggage. Should there be more emphasis on who is traveling? For instance, should everyone, citizens included, be fingerprinted and checked out before they enter or leave the country? If so, would you be prepared to have a special ID card with your fingerprints or some other biometric feature on it to allow you to pass through the checkpoints at ports of entry faster?

5. Given that bankruptcy courts in the United States have ruled that customer information—even personal information—is an asset for the purposes of paying off debts, many privacy advocates question the safety of personal information even if a company promises privacy and fully intends to keep that promise. What do you think about this ruling? Would your opinion change if you were owed a lot of money by a company that just filed for bankruptcy protection?

Key Terms and Concepts

Adware, 383
Anonymous Web browsing (AWB), 385
Anti-virus software, 396
Backup, 396
Biometrics, 397
Clickstream, 385
Computer virus (virus), 394
Cookie, 382
Copyright, 375
Counterfeit software, 378
Denial-of-service attack (DoS), 395
Encryption, 399
Ethics, 373
Fair Use Doctrine, 376
Firewall, 397
Grid computing, 392

Hacker, 393
Hardware key logger, 381
Intellectual property, 375
Intrusion-detection software, 400
Key logger software (key trapper software), 378
Pirated software, 377
Privacy, 378
Public key encryption (PKE), 399
Risk assessment, 396
Risk management, 395
Safe-harbor principles, 387
Security-auditing software, 400
Spyware (sneakware or stealthware), 384
Trojan horse software, 383
Web log, 384
Worm, 394

Short-Answer Questions

1. What are ethics, and how do ethics apply to business?
2. What are the two factors that determine how you decide ethical issues?
3. Six practical circumstances affect how you decide ethical issues. What are they?
4. What situation would qualify as an exception to the copyright law?
5. What is privacy?
6. What is pirated software?
7. What is the difference between counterfeit software and pirated software?
8. What does a key logger do?
9. What is spyware?
10. What did the Bork Bill do?
11. What is grid computing?
12. What is a denial-of-service attack?

Short-Question Answers

For each of the following answers, provide an appropriate question.

1. Fair Use Doctrine.
2. Slows down or crashes a business Web site.
3. Cracker.
4. Risk assessment.
5. Hot site.
6. Anti-virus software.
7. Stealthware or sneakware.
8. Clickstream.
9. The FBI.
10. Safe-harbor principles.
11. Encryption.
12. Trojan horse software.

Assignments and Exercises

1. **HELPING A FRIEND** Suppose you fully intend to spend the evening working on an Excel assignment that's due the next day. Then a friend calls. Your friend is stranded miles from home and desperately needs your help. It will take most of the evening to pick up your friend, bring him home, and return to your studying. Not only that, but you're very tired when you get home and just fall into bed. The next day your friend, who completed his assignment earlier, suggests you just make a copy, put your own name on the cover, and hand it in as your own work. Should you do it? Isn't it only fair that since you helped your friend, the friend should do something about making sure you don't lose points because of your generosity? What if your friend promises not to hand in his or her own work so that you can't be accused of copying? Your friend wrote the assignment and gave it to you, so there's no question of copyright infringement.

2. **FIND ANTI-VIRUS SOFTWARE** You've read how important it is to have anti-virus software on your computer. Find out what choices are available and what their features and cost are at the following sites:

   - Norton Antivirus at www.symantec.com
   - McAfee at www.mcafee.com
   - PC-Cillin at www.pc-cillen.com
   - Dr. Solomon Antivirus Toolkit at www.drsolomon.com
   - Kaspersky Lab Antivirus at www.kaspersky.com
   - Panda Antivirus at www.pandasoftware.com

3. **FIND OUT WHAT HAPPENED** In December 2001, British Telecom (BT) filed a lawsuit against Prodigy in New York federal court, claiming it owns the hyperlinking process. If BT wins this lawsuit then the company will be able to collect licensing revenue from the 100 billion or so links on the Web. BT has a patent that it says amounts to ownership of the hyperlinking process.

Prodigy (and everyone else in the world) stores Web pages with a displayed part, which the browser shows, and a hidden part that the viewer doesn't see, and which contains hidden information including the addresses that are used by the displayed portion. This, BT said, is the essence of its U.S. patent No. 4,873,662. In reference to this case, answer the following questions:

A. Has a ruling been handed down on this matter yet? If so, what was the result?

B. If any kind of hyperlinking is, in fact, the essence of the patent held by BT, what about library card catalogs; are they infringements, too? Why or why not? What else could be?

4. **INVESTIGATE MONITORING SYSTEMS** The text listed several monitoring systems, other systems that defeat them, and an e-mail encryption program. Find two more of the following:

A. Programs that monitor keyboard activity

B. Programs that find keyboard monitoring programs

C. E-mail encryption programs

5. **CHECK OUT THE COMPUTER ETHICS INSTITUTE'S ADVICE** The Computer Ethics Institute's Web site at www.cspr.org/program/ethics.htm offers the "Ten Commandments of Computer Ethics" to guide you in the general direction of ethical computer use. The first two are

- *Thou shalt not use a computer to harm other people.* This one is the bedrock for all the others.
- *Thou shalt not interfere with other people's computer work.* This one includes small sins like sending frivolous e-mail, big ones like spreading viruses, and the really big ones like electronic stalking.

Look up the other eight and give at least two examples of acts that would be in violation of these guidelines.

Discussion Questions

1. When selling antiques, you can usually obtain a higher price for those that have a provenance, which is information detailing the origin and history of the object. For example, property owned by Jacqueline Kennedy Onassis and Princess Diana sold for much more than face value. What kinds of products have value over and above a comparable product because of such information? What kind of information makes products valuable? Consider both tangible (resale value) and intangible value (sentimental appeal).

2. Personal checks that you use to buy merchandise have a standard format. Checks have very few different sizes, and almost no variation in format. Consider what would happen if everyone could create his or her own size, shape, and layout of personal check. What would the costs and benefits be to business and the consumer in terms of buying checks, exchanging them for merchandise, and bank check processing?

3. Consider society as a business that takes steps to protect itself from the harm of illegal acts. Discuss the mechanisms and costs that are involved. Examine ways in which our society would be different if no one ever broke a law. Are there ever benefits to our society when people break the law, for example, when they claim that the law itself is unethical or unjust?

4. Can you access all the IT systems at your college or university? What about payroll or grade information on yourself or others? What kinds of controls has your college or university implemented to prevent the misuse of information?

5. You know that you generally can't use a PC to access the information stored on a Macintosh-formatted disk. What other instances of the lack of difficulty in accessing information have you experienced personally or heard of? For example, have you used different versions of MS PowerPoint or MS Access that won't work on all the PCs that you have access to?

6. Have you, or someone you know, experienced computer problems caused by a virus? What did the virus do? Where do you think you got it? How did you fix the problem? What was the cost to you in time, trouble, and stress?

7. What laws do you think the United States should pass to protect personal information? None? Laws such as the European Union has? Stricter laws than the EU? Why? Should some personal information be more protected than other information? Why or why not?

8. The issue of pirated software is one that the software industry fights on a daily basis. The major centers of software piracy are in places like Russia and China where salaries and disposable income are comparatively low. Given that people in developing and economically depressed countries will fall behind the industrialized world technologically if they can't afford access to new generations of software, is it reasonable to blame someone for using pirated software when it costs two months' salary to buy a legal copy of MS Office? If you answered no, specify at what income level it's okay to make or buy illegal copies of software. What approach could software companies use to combat the problem apart from punitive measure, like pressuring the government to impose sanctions on transgressors?

Making Travel Arrangements on the Internet

It's very likely that in the course of business you'll be expected to travel either within the United States or abroad. You can use the Internet to check out all aspects of your journey, from mode of travel to the shopping opportunities that are available. The Internet can also give you pointers and direction about aspects of the trip you might not even have thought about.

In this section, we've included a number of Web sites related to making travel arrangements on the Internet. On the Web site that supports this text (www.mhhe.com/haag), click on "Electronic Commerce Support," select "REAL HOT Electronic Commerce Project Support," and then select "Making Travel Arrangements on the Internet." We've provided direct links to all these Web sites as well as many, many more. This is a great starting point for completing this REAL HOT section. We would also encourage you to search the Internet for other sites.

TRANSPORTATION

If you're not taking your own transportation—your private jet, or your car—you'll have to find flights, buses, trains, and/or rental cars to suit your needs. Let's look at sites where you can get this kind of information.

AIR TRAVEL

Some people are happy to travel with whatever airline provides the flight that fits into their schedule. Others insist on certain airlines or won't travel on particular airlines. No matter how you feel, the Internet can help you find a flight. On the Internet, you can even get maps of the airports you'll be using. Many airports have sites on the Internet, such as Dallas/Ft. Worth International Airport at www.dfwairport.com. These sites can help you with provisions that the airport has for disabled people, and other available services.

The Federal Aviation Authority site (www.faa.com) has a comprehensive list of airlines in this country and all over the world. Find five appropriate Web sites and answer the following questions:

A. Can you make a flight reservation online at this site?

B. If you can book flights, does the site ask you to type in your departure and destination cities, or can you choose from a menu?

C. Again, if you can book flights at this site, on a scale of 1 to 10, rate how difficult it is to get to the flight schedule. That is, how many questions do you have to answer, how many clicks does it take, how much do you have to type in?

D. Is there information on when the lowest fares apply (for example, three-week advance booking, staying over Saturday night, other restrictions)?

E. Does the site offer to send you information on special deals via e-mail?

F. Does the site offer information on frequent-flier mileage? Can you check your frequent-flier account online?

G. Does the site offer you a map of the airports you will be using?

TRAINS AND BUSES

If you want to travel by rail or long distance bus, you can find many helpful sites. Here is a sample of what's available:

- Monterey Salinas Transit System at www.mst.org has information on bus travel in the United States.
- Amtrak at www.amtrak.com has a site that lets you look up train travel times and fares and buy tickets online for train travel in the United States.
- RailEurope at www.raileurope.com offers comprehensive coverage of all modes of travel in Europe, including, of course, rail travel.
- The Orient Express site at www.orient-expresstrains.com is a great help if you're interested in traveling by rail in Asia or Australia.

Look at two of these sites and see whether you can book tickets online. Do you need a password to see schedules? Incidentally, when you're looking up sites outside the United States, remember that the date is often expressed with the day first, then the month, then the year, so that August 10, 2003, would be 10.8.03 or 10-8-03. Also, most of Europe uses 24-hour time, so that 2:15 P.M. would be 14:15.

RENTAL CARS

When you arrive at your destination, you may need a car. Some sites such as Rental Car Info's site at www.bnm.com have information on multiple companies, and all the large car rental companies have sites on the Internet. Find six Web sites that rent cars and answer the following questions:

- **A.** Can you reserve a car at the Web site?
- **B.** Can you search by city?
- **C.** Is there a cancellation penalty? If so, how much?
- **D.** Can you get a list of car types? Does this company rent sports utility vehicles?
- **E.** Are there special weekend rates?
- **F.** What does the site say about collision insurance purchased from that company in addition to your own insurance?
- **G.** Can you get maps from the site?
- **H.** Are special corporate rates specified on the site?

ROAD CONDITIONS AND MAPS

You can generate maps online at several sites. MapQuest at www.mapquest.com is one of the most popular. Its TripQuest section has city-to-city and turn-by-turn directions, and its Map Shortcuts module gives you a list of cities and countries for which you can get maps. Examine three map sites and answer the following questions:

- **A.** Do these sites all give turn-by-turn driving directions?
- **B.** Will they provide a map of an area without start and end points?
- **C.** Do they have zoom in and zoom out capabilities?
- **D.** Can you customize the map, perhaps by inserting a landmark or circling an area?
- **E.** Are hotels, restaurants, or other facilities marked on the map?
- **F.** If the site offers driving directions, can you specify whether you want the scenic route or the main highways?

G. Are the maps restricted to the United States? If not, what other countries are included?

LODGING

Hotels, especially the larger chains, usually have Web sites. Here you have access to a wealth of information about rates, amenities, and sometimes even information about the hotel's surroundings. The National Hotel Directory at www.evmedia.com has lists of a variety of hotels and also trade shows. The Hotel Guide site at www.hotelguide.com has information on 60,000 hotels all over the world, and the Trip.com (www.thetrip.com) has hotel reviews and promises discounted prices for certain hotels. Choose four Web sites and answer the questions below:

A. Can you search for a particular city?

B. Can you book a room online?

C. Are there properties belonging to this hotel chain outside the United States?

D. Can you see a picture of the room on the Internet?

E. Does the site tell you about special deals or promotions?

F. Is there information about perks you can get by staying there frequently?

G. Do you get a discount for booking online?

ONE-STOP TRAVEL SITES

Some travel sites on the Internet allow you to book your entire trip from start to finish, offering a combination of airline, hotel, and other helpful information. Two of the most widely used are Microsoft's Expedia at expedia.msn.com and Travelocity at www.travelocity.com. Choose five Web sites and answer the following questions:

A. How many different booking services are offered from this site (airlines, hotels, rental cars, rail travel, or others)?

B. If the site offers flight booking, how many flight alternatives does it offer? 3? 10? 20? 30? More than 30?

C. Does the site have information on low-cost specials for airlines, hotels, and/or rental cars?

D. Is there a travelers' assistance section?

E. Will the site answer your specific questions?

F. Can you search by destination or company for flights and lodging?

DESTINATION INFORMATION

You might like to know before you get to your destination what restaurants, museums, shows, shopping, and special attractions are available. Many of the sites previously mentioned have this kind of information. MapQuest (www.mapquest.com) is an excellent example of such a site, as are many of the one-stop travel sites.

No matter what your interest or hobby, the Internet has a site for you. You can find sites dedicated to bird watching, bungee jumping, golf, or anything else that takes your fancy. Many others cater to entertainment events such as concerts. You can find destination information sites on the Web at the following sites:

- Excite's Travel site (city.net), which has destination information from Fodor's Travel.

- The Trip at www.thetrip.com includes restaurant reviews among its services.

- Restaurant Row (www.restaurantrow.com) has a list of 100,000 restaurants in 25 countries. You can search by country, city, and cuisine.
- The Open World site at www.openworld.co.uk/cityguides has information on 100 of the most popular cities to visit.

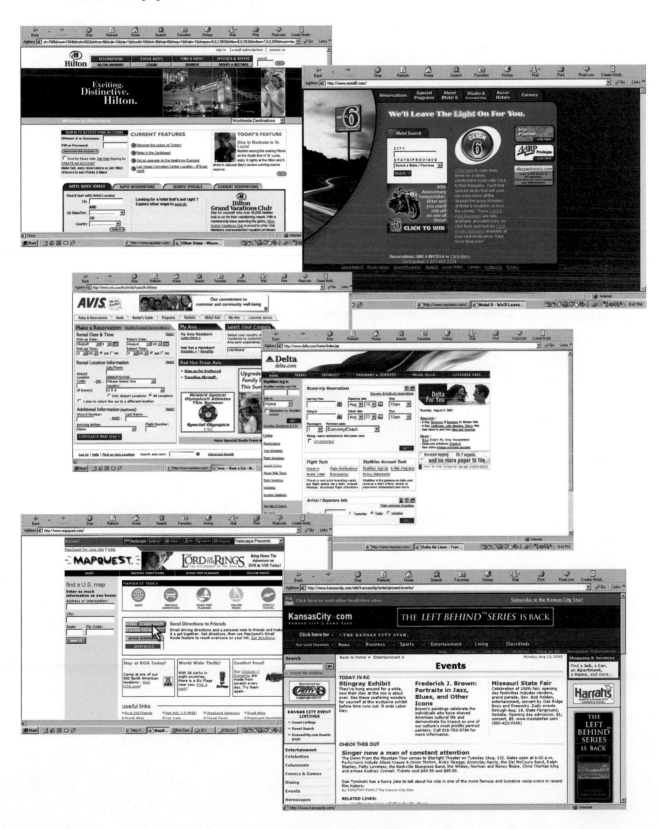

EXTENDED LEARNING MODULE H
COMPUTER CRIME AND FORENSICS

Student Learning Outcomes

1. DEFINE COMPUTER CRIME AND LIST THREE TYPES OF COMPUTER CRIME THAT CAN BE PERPETRATED FROM INSIDE AND THREE FROM OUTSIDE THE ORGANIZATION.

2. IDENTIFY THE SEVEN TYPES OF HACKERS AND EXPLAIN WHAT MOTIVATES EACH GROUP.

3. DEFINE COMPUTER FORENSICS AND DESCRIBE THE TWO PHASES OF A FORENSIC INVESTIGATION.

4. IDENTIFY AND DESCRIBE THREE PLACES ON A STORAGE MEDIUM WHERE YOU CAN FIND STRAY INFORMATION.

5. IDENTIFY AND DESCRIBE SEVEN WAYS OF HIDING INFORMATION.

Introduction

Computers play a big part in crime: they're used to commit and to solve crimes. This should be no surprise since they're such a big part of almost every other part of our lives. Computers are primarily used two ways in the commission of a crime or misdeed: as targets and as weapons. A computer is a target when someone wants to bring it down or make it malfunction, as in a denial-of-service attack or a computer virus infection. Crimes that use a computer as a weapon would include acts such as changing computer records to commit embezzlement, breaking into a computer system to damage information, and stealing customer lists. See Figure H.1 for examples of computer-related offenses that use computers as weapons and targets.

Some crimes are clearly what we'd call computer crimes, like Web defacing, denial-of-service attacks, and so on. But, as is the case in so many parts of our modern lives, computers are so integrated into crime that it's sometimes hard to separate them out. Here's an example from the case files of Walt Manning, an expert in computer forensic investigation.

A member of a crime syndicate was sprayed with drive-by gunfire and was severely wounded. Believing that his services were no longer wanted by his crime gang, he switched sides, agreeing to become a witness for the state. The police secured an isolated intensive care unit room for him and guarded it heavily, only allowing access to medical staff and those on a very short list of visitors. Because the man was so badly wounded, there was a distinct danger of infection, and since he was allergic to penicillin, the doctor prescribed a synthetic alternative.

One evening, a nurse wheeling a medicine cart went through the police cordon and into the man's room. He injected the patient with penicillin, and the patient died shortly thereafter. An investigation started immediately and the nurse was potentially in big trouble. He insisted that when he looked at the patient's chart on the computer, there was an order there for penicillin. Subsequent examination of the computer records showed no such order. Eventually, it occurred to someone that perhaps a computer forensics expert should look at the computer angle more closely. Having retrieved the backup tapes (nightly backups are standard operating procedure in most places), the expert found evidence that exonerated the nurse. The patient chart had been changed in the computer to indicate penicillin and later changed back to its original form. Examination further revealed the point and time of access, and indicated that the medical record was changed by someone outside the hospital. A hacker had electronically slipped into the hospital's network unnoticed, made the change, and slipped out again—twice.

Inside the Organization | Outside the Organization

Computers as Weapons

Inside the Organization:
- Intellectual property theft
- Accessing information on others for personal reasons
- Spite or revenge
- Extortion
- Reading the e-mail of others

Outside the Organization:
- Murder
- Theft of information
- Embezzlement
- Harassment
- Extortion
- Credit card theft
- Cargo theft by diverting shipments

Computers as Targets

Inside the Organization:
- Information destruction
- Planting destructive code
- Stealing customer information
- Altering information

Outside the Organization:
- Virus attacks
- Denial-of-service attacks
- Web defacing
- Rerouting network traffic
- Crashing servers

Figure H.1

Examples of Computer Crimes that Organizations Need to Defend Against

Most crimes involving a computer are not as lethal as murder, but that doesn't mean they're insignificant. Organizations want to make sure their networks' defenses are strong and can prevent their computers from being used for unlawful or unethical acts. That's why so much time, money, and effort goes into security. We discussed that in Chapter 8.

This module focuses on the sort of threats that computer systems are susceptible to and the examination of electronic evidence. The latter is called computer forensics.

Computer Crime

For our purposes, a **computer crime** is a crime in which a computer, or computers, play a significant part. See Figure H.2 for a list of crimes in which computers, although perhaps not essential, usually play a large part.

In this section we'll focus on crime from the organization's viewpoint. First, we'll examine some of the more high-profile types of computer crime committed against organizations that are perpetrated from the outside. Then we'll discuss the varying motivations of people who commit these acts. Lastly, we'll briefly discuss computer crime within the organization.

OUTSIDE THE ORGANIZATION

Businesses are very concerned about the threat of people breaking into their computers and causing damage. In 2001, 90 percent of U.S. companies discovered online security breaches, according to the Computer Security Institute, and only 34 percent of those companies reported the attack. The cost to business was $455 million, compared to $377 million in 2000. The losses that are reported, and experts say that most are not, average about $1.8 billion per year.[1] Ninety-four percent of companies detected computer viruses in 2001 and that figure is up from 85 percent in 2000. To combat these and other attacks, businesses spent about $7.5 billion in 2000 on security software.[2] That market is expected to triple to $21 billion by 2005.

VIRUSES

The term *computer virus* is a generic term for lots of different types of destructive software. A **computer virus** (or **virus**) is software that was written with malicious intent to

Figure H.2

Crimes in Which Computers Usually Play a Part

- Illegal gambling
- Forgery
- Money laundering
- Child pornography
- Hate message propagation
- Electronic stalking
- Racketeering
- Fencing stolen goods
- Loan sharking
- Drug trafficking
- Union infiltration

cause annoyance or damage. Two hundred new ones are developed every day.[3] There are two categories of viruses. The first category comprises benign viruses that display a message or slow down the computer but don't destroy any information.

Malignant viruses belong in the second category. These viruses do damage to your computer system. Some will scramble or delete your files. Others will shut your computer down, or make your Word software malfunction, or damage flash memory in your digital camera so that it won't store pictures anymore. Obviously, these are the viruses that cause IT staff (and everyone else) the most headaches.

The macro virus is one very common type of malignant computer virus. ***Macro viruses*** spread by binding themselves to software such as Word or Excel. When they infect a computer, they make copies of themselves (replicate) and spread from file to file destroying or changing the file in some way.

This type of virus needs human help to move to another computer. If you have a macro virus on your system and you e-mail an infected document as an attachment, the person who gets the e-mail gets the virus as soon as the infected attachment is opened. When you click on the attachment, Word (or the appropriate program) also loads, thereby setting the executable statements in motion.

Worms are the most prevalent type of malignant virus. A ***worm*** is a computer virus that replicates and spreads itself, not only from file to file, but from computer to computer via e-mail and other Internet traffic. Worms don't need your help to spread. They find your e-mail address book and help themselves to the addresses, sending themselves to your contacts. The first worm to attract the attention of the popular press was the Love Bug worm, and permutations of it are still out there.

Released on an unsuspecting world in 2000, the Love Bug worm caused the Massachusetts state government to shut down its e-mail, affecting 20,000 workers. It also caused problems on Capitol Hill and shut down e-mail in the British Parliament building. Companies as diverse as Ford Motor Company, H. J. Heinz, Merrill Lynch & Company, and AT&T were infected.[4] All in all, the Love Bug and its variants affected 300,000 Internet host computers and millions of individual PC users causing file damage, lost time, and high-cost emergency repairs totaling about $8.7 billion.[5,6]

A closer look at the Love Bug worm will give you a general idea of what worms do. The Love Bug arrives in your e-mail as an attachment to an e-mail message. The subject of the e-mail is "I LOVE YOU"—a very alluring message to be sure. The text says to open the attached love letter, the name of which is, appropriately, LOVE LETTER. However, what's attached is anything but love. It's a mean piece of software that is set loose in your computer system as soon as you open the attachment.

The Love Bug has three objectives: to spread itself as far and as fast as it can, to destroy your files, and to gather passwords and other information (see Figure H.3 on the next page). First, it spreads itself by mailing itself to everyone in your Outlook address book. (A previous worm of the same type named Melissa sent itself only to the first 50 people listed in Outlook's address book.) And, as if that weren't enough, it also uses your Internet chat software to spread itself to chat rooms.

Second, the Love Bug locates files on your computer that have certain extensions, .MP3 music files, .jpg picture files, .doc Word files, .xls Excel files, .wav sound files, .html browser files, and many others. Having found these files it wipes them out and puts itself in their place, appending .vbs to the end of the filename. For example, if you had a file called MySong.wav on your hard disk drive, the Love Bug virus would change the name to MySong.wav.vbs after it had done its dirty work.

Before it's done, the Love Bug worm changes your Internet Explorer start page and downloads a program that looks for passwords and network information, sending this information off by e-mail to the virus originator.[7]

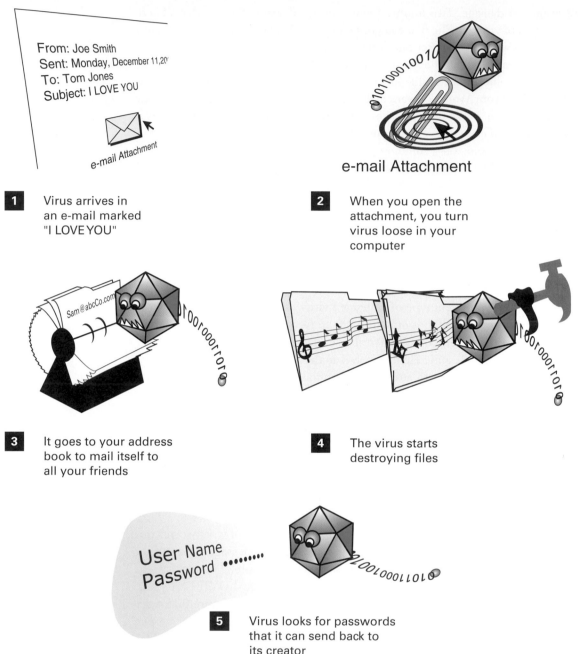

From: Joe Smith
Sent: Monday, December 11, 20'
To: Tom Jones
Subject: I LOVE YOU

e-mail Attachment

1 Virus arrives in an e-mail marked "I LOVE YOU"

e-mail Attachment

2 When you open the attachment, you turn virus loose in your computer

Sam@abcCo.com

3 It goes to your address book to mail itself to all your friends

4 The virus starts destroying files

User Name Password

5 Virus looks for passwords that it can send back to its creator

Figure H.3

The Love Bug Worm

There are at least 29 versions of the Love Bug virus. After people were warned not to open the LOVE LETTER attachment, the originators of the virus changed the name of it to something else. For example, one version is MOTHER'S DAY, and the body of the text says that the receiver has been charged hundreds of dollars for a Mother's Day "diamond special." You have to open the attachment to print the invoice, and then the virus goes into action.

The moral of the story is that you should be very careful about opening an attachment if you're not sure what it is and where it came from. That won't necessarily save you from all virus attacks, but it will certainly help.

If you buy new shrink-wrapped software, you may feel secure thinking that it can't have a virus if it came from the manufacturer. However, the counterfeit software business is growing rapidly (see Chapter 8), and although the store might think that it bought software for resale from a reliable source, it might be counterfeit and carry a virus. So, as a precautionary measure, always check new software with a virus checker before you install it.

DENIAL-OF-SERVICE ATTACKS

Many organizations have been hit with denial-of-service attacks. *Denial-of-service (DoS) attacks* flood a Web site with so many requests for service that it slows down or crashes. The objective is to prevent legitimate customers from getting into the site to do business. There are several types of DoS attacks. A DoS attack can come from a lone computer that tries continuously to access the target computer, or from many, perhaps even thousands, of computers simultaneously. The latter is called a distributed denial-of-service attack and is considerably more devastating.

DISTRIBUTED DENIAL-OF-SERVICE ATTACKS

Distributed denial-of-service (DDos) attacks are attacks from multiple computers that flood a Web site with so many requests for service that it slows down or crashes. A common type is the Ping of Death, in which thousands of computers try to access a Web site at the same time, overloading it and shutting it down. A ping attack can also bring down the firewall server (the computer that protects the network), giving free access to the intruders. E*Trade, Amazon.com, and Yahoo!, among others, have been victims of this nasty little game. The process is actually very simple (see Figure H.4 on the next page).

The plan starts with the hackers planting a program in network servers that aren't protected well enough. Then, on a signal sent to the servers from the attackers, the program activates and each server "pings" every computer. A ping is a standard operation that networks use to check that all computers are functioning properly. It's a sort of roll call for the network computers. The server asks, "Are you there?" and each computer in turn answers, "Yes, I'm here." But the hacker ping is different in that the return address of the are-you-there? message is not the originating server, but the intended victim's server. So on a signal from the hackers, thousands of computers try to access E*Trade or Amazon.com, to say "Yes, I'm here." The flood of calls overloads the online companies' computers and they can't conduct business.

For many companies, a forced shutdown is embarrassing and costly but for others it's much more than that. For an online stockbroker, for example, denial-of-service attacks can be disastrous. It may make a huge difference whether you buy shares of stock today or tomorrow. And since stockbrokers need a high level of trust from customers to do business, the effect of having been seen to be so vulnerable is very bad for business.

COMBINATION WORM/DOS

Code Red, discovered in 2001, was the first virus that combined a worm and DoS attack. Code Red attacked servers running a specific type of system software. It used e-mail address books to send itself to lots of computers, and it was very efficient, with the ability to infect as many as 500,000 new servers per day. Its first action was to deface the Web site it infected. Then it went about finding other servers to infect. The last part of the plan was for all the infected servers to attack the White House Web site and shut it down. Having been warned of the impending attack, the White House changed the IP address of its Web site. Before it was all over, Code Red cost an estimated $2.4 billion in prevention, detection, and cleanup even though it didn't destroy files or otherwise do much damage. However, this type of attack power is potentially very dangerous.

VIRUS HOAXES

There are even virus hoaxes. This is e-mail sent intending to frighten people about a virus threat that is, in fact, bogus. People who get such an alert will usually tell others, who react in the same way. The virus is nonexistent, but the hoax causes people to get

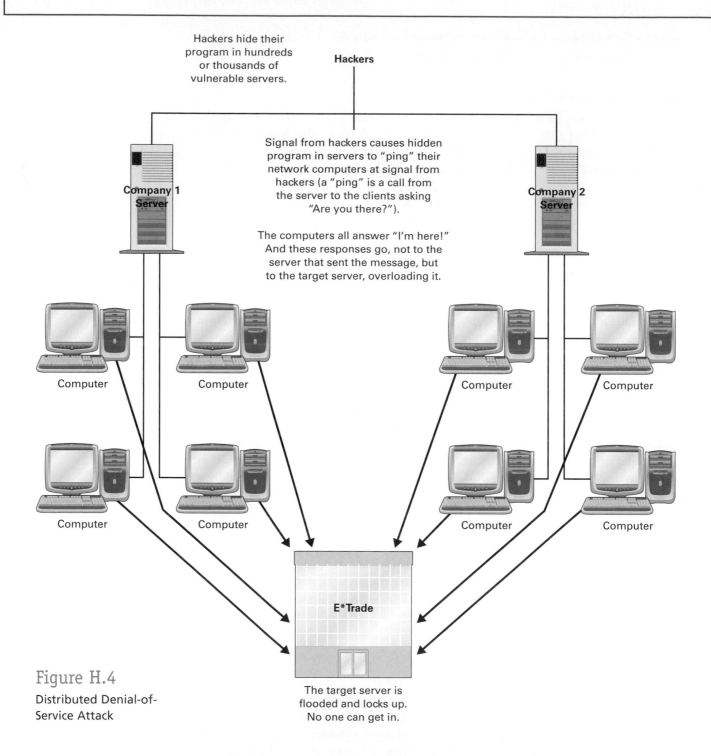

Hackers hide their program in hundreds or thousands of vulnerable servers.

Hackers

Signal from hackers causes hidden program in servers to "ping" their network computers at signal from hackers (a "ping" is a call from the server to the clients asking "Are you there?").

The computers all answer "I'm here!" And these responses go, not to the server that sent the message, but to the target server, overloading it.

Company 1 Server

Company 2 Server

Computer Computer Computer Computer

Computer Computer Computer Computer

E*Trade

The target server is flooded and locks up. No one can get in.

Figure H.4

Distributed Denial-of-Service Attack

scared and lose time and productivity. Within companies the losses can be very severe since computer professionals must spend precious time and effort looking for a nonexistent problem.

Following are some general guidelines for identifying a virus hoax.[8] The e-mail

- Says to forward it to everyone you know, immediately
- Describes the awful consequences of not acting immediately
- Quotes a well-known authority in the computer industry

WHAT POLYMORPHIC VIRUSES ARE FLOATING AROUND CYBERSPACE?

In the wake of the Love Bug worm, a new and potentially deadly worm called NewLove popped up. This worm had two new features: First, it disguised its destructive logic in a way that makes it much harder to find. NewLove disables Windows and makes other files unusable. Second, it changes its code every time it succeeds in infecting a computer, adding some code randomly and growing with each infection. It didn't spread very far, but it caused a stir within the IT community because of its ability to change its code. It was a new kind of virus called a polymorphic virus. A polymorphic virus changes itself to evade detection. Essentially it encrypts itself to evade detection by antivirus software, but changes the way it does it each time.

Visit the Web and look up five currently active polymorphic viruses. For each one find out

1. The name of the virus
2. What it does
3. The name of antivirus software that finds it
4. The symptoms of infection

These are signs that the e-mail is not meant to help but to cause harm. If you get an e-mail like this, delete it immediately.

STAND-ALONE VIRUSES

In any given month, between 200 and 300 viruses are traveling from system to system around the world, seeking a way in to spread mayhem.[9] And they're getting more deadly. Whereas the Love Bug worm was Visual Basic script virus (i.e., it needed Visual Basic to run), the latest worms can stand alone and run on any computer that can run Win32 programs (Windows 98 or later versions). Examples are SirCam, Nimda, and Klez. Nimda adds JavaScript to every home page on the server it infects, then passes it on to visitors to the site. Viruses of this independent type are very numerous.

The Klez virus is actually a family of worms that introduced a new kind of confusion into the virus business. They spoof e-mail addresses. *Spoofing* is the forging of the return address on an e-mail so that the e-mail message appears to come from someone other than the actual sender. Previous worms went to the recipient from the infected sender's computer and contained the infected person's return e-mail address. The worm found recipient addresses in the infected computer's address book.

Klez goes a step further and uses the address book to randomly find a return address as well as recipient addresses. The result is that people who are not infected with the virus get e-mail from the irate recipients and spend time looking for a virus they may not have. Even worse, some of virus-laden e-mails look as though they came from a technical support person, leading an unsuspecting victim to open them, believing them to be safe.

TROJAN HORSE VIRUSES

A type of virus that doesn't replicate is a Trojan-horse virus. A *Trojan horse virus* hides inside other software, usually an attachment or download. The principle of any Trojan horse software is that there's software you don't want hidden inside software you do want. For example, Trojan horse software can carry the ping-of-death program that hides in a server until the originators are ready to launch a DoS attack.

Key-logger software is usually available in Trojan horse form, so that you can hide it in e-mail or other Internet traffic. ***Key logger,*** or ***key trapper, software*** is a program that, when installed on a computer, records every keystroke and mouse click. Key logger software is used to snoop on people to find out what they're doing on a particular computer. You can find out more in Chapter 8.

WEB DEFACING

Web defacing is a favorite sport of some of the people who break into computer systems. They replace the site with a substitute that's neither attractive nor complimentary (see Figure H.5). Or perhaps they convert the Web site to a mostly blank screen with an abusive or obscene message, or the message may just read "So-and-so was here." In essence, Web site defacing is electronic graffiti, where a computer keyboard takes the place of a paint spray can.

In 2000, during a flair-up in tensions between Israel and Palestine, Israelis defaced the Web sites of Hezbollah and Hamas. In retaliation, Palestinians brought down Israeli government sites and then turned their attention to Web sites of pro-Israeli groups in the United States.

Figure H.5

The Defacing of the Department of Justice's Web Site

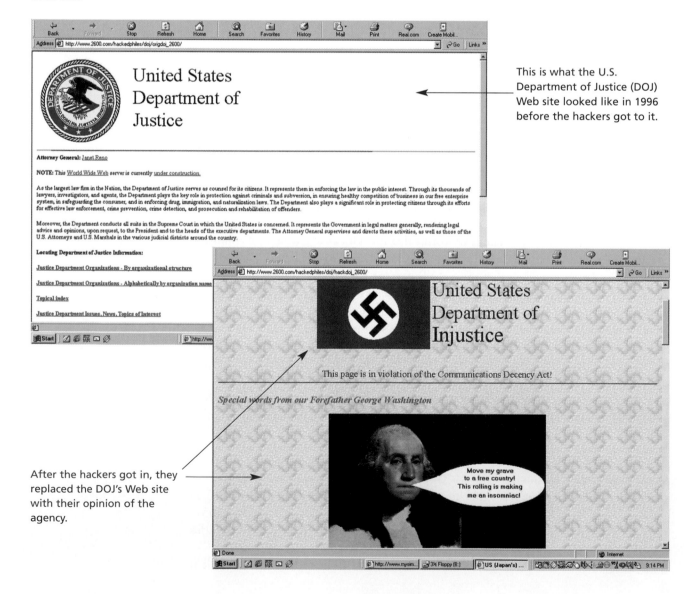

This is what the U.S. Department of Justice (DOJ) Web site looked like in 1996 before the hackers got to it.

After the hackers got in, they replaced the DOJ's Web site with their opinion of the agency.

Web site defacing is becoming increasingly popular, and sites that are accessed by many people worldwide are particular favorites. The USAToday.com site was attacked in July 2002, causing the newspaper to shut down the whole site for three hours to fix the problem. The hackers replaced several news stories on the site with bogus stories that were full of spelling errors. One story said that the Pope had called Christianity "a sham." The phony stories were only on the site for 15 minutes before they were spotted and the site was taken offline.[10]

THE PLAYERS

Who's spreading all this havoc? The answer is hackers. This is the popular name for people who break into computer systems. *Hackers* are knowledgeable computer users who use their knowledge to invade other people's computers. There are several categories of hackers, and their labels change over time. The important thing to note in the following discussion is that the motivation and reasons for hacking are as many and varied as the people who engage in it.

THRILL-SEEKER HACKERS

Thrill-seeker hackers break into computer systems for entertainment. Sometimes, they consider themselves to be the "good guys" since they expose vulnerabilities and some even follow a "hackers' code." Although they break into computers they have no right to access, they may report the security leaks to the victims. Their thrill is in being able to get into someone else's computer. Their reward is usually the admiration of their fellow hackers. There's plenty of information on the Web for those who want to know how to hack into a system—about 2,000 sites offer free hacking tools, according to security experts.[11]

WHITE-HAT HACKERS

The thrill-seeker hackers used to be called white hat hackers. But lately, the term *white-hat* is being increasingly used to describe the hackers who legitimately, with the knowledge of the owners of the IT system, try to break in to find and fix vulnerable areas of the system. These *white-hat hackers,* or *ethical hackers* are computer security professionals who are hired by a company to break into a computer system. These hackers are also called counter hackers, or penetration testers.

BLACK-HAT HACKERS

Black-hat hackers are cyber vandals. They exploit or destroy the information they find, steal passwords, or otherwise cause harm. They deliberately cause trouble for people just for the fun of it. They create viruses, bring down computer systems, and steal or destroy information.

A 16-year-old black-hat hacker was sentenced to detention for six months after he hacked into military and NASA networks. He caused the systems to shut down for three weeks. He intercepted more than 3,000 e-mails and stole the names and passwords of 19 defense agency employees. He also downloaded temperature and humidity control software worth $1.7 billion that helps control the environment in the international space station's living quarters.[12]

CRACKERS

Crackers are hackers for hire and are the people who engage in electronic corporate espionage. This can be a pretty lucrative undertaking, paying up to $1 million per gig. Typically an espionage job will take about three weeks and may involve unpleasant tasks like dumpster diving to find passwords and other useful information and "social engineering." *Social engineering* is conning your way into acquiring information that you have

MAKE UP A GOOD PASSWORD

One way to protect files, folders, entry into stock trading, banking, and other sites is to have a good password. That's the theory anyway. The problem is that most people choose passwords that are easy to remember, and consequently they're easy for others, who perhaps have malevolent intentions, to crack. Others write passwords down, which makes them very accessible to anyone who comes near your desk. Often hackers can get access to a server by way of a legitimate user's ID and password.

Another problem that companies face is that people seem to be unaware of how important it is to keep passwords secret. In a London underground (subway) station, an experiment was conducted in which commuters were offered a cheap pen if they would disclose the password to their company's system. A very large number of people took the deal. Of course, there's no way to know whether they actually gave their real passwords or not, but based on other studies, it's not unlikely that they did.

ZDNet offers some good advice on picking pass-words. You should never pick a password that has a word from any dictionary, or one that is a pet's name or a person's. Instead, you should pick a phrase and use the first letter of each word. Then capitalize some letters and substitute punctuations and digits for others.

For example, the saying "just hang loose, just have fun, you only live once" would become JhL?H6+oLo. If you can remember the mnemonic and your substitutions, you'll certainly have a password that will be hard to break.

To find out about breaking passwords, look on the Web for information about "Jack the Ripper," which is a well-known password-cracking problem. Find three more password-cracking programs and note whether they're public domain, freeware, shareware, or whether you have to pay for them. At www.elcomsoft.com you'll find all sorts of password crackers for Microsoft and other popular products. The stated purpose of this site is to help you recover lost corporate files. What other "helpful" products does this and other similar sites have and what do they do?

no right to. Social engineering methods include calling someone in a company and pretending to be a technical support person and getting that person to type in a login and password, sweet talking an employee to get information, and for difficult jobs, perhaps even setting up a fake office and identity. Often when crackers have accumulated about $500 million, they retire to some country that doesn't have an extradition agreement with this country.[13]

HACKTIVISTS

Hacktivists are politically motivated hackers who use the Internet to send a political message of some kind. The message can be a call to end world hunger, or it can involve an alteration of a political party's Web site so that it touts another party's candidate. It can be a slogan for a particular cause or some sort of diatribe inserted into a Web site to mock a particular religious or national group.

Hacktivism, in the form of Web defacing, is becoming a common response to disagreements between nations. When the U.S. military plane made an emergency landing in China and a dispute arose about the return of the crew and plane, U.S. hackers started to attack Chinese Web sites, and Chinese hackers returned the favor, targeting government-related sites.

CYBERTERRORISTS

Since September 11th, officials have become increasingly worried about the threat of cyberterrorists. This group of hackers, like the hacktivists, is politically motivated, but its agenda is more sinister. A *cyberterrorist* is one who seeks to cause harm to people or de-

DIGITAL SIGNATURES AND CERTIFICATES

Digital signatures are a way of protecting electronic messages, like e-mails, on their journey through cyberspace. They are antitampering devices. The basis of a digital signature is that a set of characters in the message is used in arithmetic operations to generate a unique "key" for that message. When the message arrives, the recipient repeats the operations in the exact order. The result should be the original key. If it's not, then the message has been tampered with.

Digital signatures are often used in conjunction with digital certificates. What are digital certificates? Do some research and write a one-page report on digital certificates and how they're used.

stroy critical systems or information. Possible targets of violent attacks would be air traffic control systems and nuclear power plants, and anything else that could harm the infrastructure of a nation. At a less lethal level, cyberterrorist acts would include shutting down e-mail or even part of the Internet itself, or destroying government records, say on social security benefits or criminal records.

However, the FBI and other government agencies are very much aware of the threats they face from computer-based attacks, and have taken steps to protect the infrastructure that supports cyberspace. They can enjoy a reasonable expectation of success since a computer system is a lot easier to protect than public structures like buildings and bridges.

SCRIPT KIDDIES

Script kiddies or *script bunnies* are people who would like to be hackers but don't have much technical expertise. They download click-and-point software that automatically does the hacking for them. An example of this was the young man in Holland who found a virus toolkit on the Web and started the Kournikova worm. It was very similar to the Love Bug worm in that it sent itself to all the people in the Outlook address book. Tens of millions of people got the virus after opening the attachment hoping to see a picture of Anna Kournikova.[14]

The concern about script kiddies, according to the experts, apart from the fact that they can unleash viruses and denial-of-service attacks, is that they can be used by more sinister hackers. These people manipulate the script kiddies, egging them on in chat rooms, encouraging and helping them to be more destructive.

INSIDE THE COMPANY

There are plenty of attacks visited on an organization's computer system from outside the organization but insider fraud and embezzlement are where the big bucks are lost. You can find more information on insider crime in Chapter 8.

Along with the traditional crimes of fraud and other types of theft managers sometimes have to deal with harassment of one employee by another. Chevron Corporation and Microsoft settled sexual harassment lawsuits for $2.2 million each because employees sent offensive e-mail to other employees and management didn't intervene. Other companies such as Dow Chemical Company, Xerox, the New York Times Company, and Edward Jones took preemptive action by firing people who sent or stored pornographic or violent e-mail messages.

But companies have learned to be careful when investigating harassment complaints, as the following example from Walt's case file shows. One company had a complaint from a woman who claimed a male colleague was sending her offensive e-mail. The colleague denied it, but when his computer was checked, the pornographic pictures that the woman claimed she had received from him in e-mails, were found. This could have meant his dismissal. But, fortunately for the man, a computer forensics expert was called in. The expert looked beyond the pictures and discovered that the times and dates the e-mails were downloaded and sent corresponded with times the man was out of town. Later, the woman admitted that she had downloaded the pictures and e-mailed them to herself from the man's computer. If the company hadn't been as thorough in its investigation, it could have escaped a harassment lawsuit only to find itself facing a wrongful termination lawsuit. So what exactly did the computer forensics expert do? We'll discuss that in the next two sections.

Computer Forensics

We're used to the idea of computers being used in the analysis of crime scene evidence for matching DNA, tracing credit card purchases, and so on. We see examples of this all the time in mystery novels, on TV shows like *CSI* and *Law and Order,* and, of course, in real life. But computers themselves are often where the clues and evidence are. So, instead of just helping to solve crimes, computers are sometimes the actual crime scene.

Many computer forensic investigations involve intellectual property cases, where a company believes that an employee is secretly copying, and perhaps selling, proprietary information like schematics, customer lists, financial statements, product designs, or notes on private meetings. Other investigations involve child exploitation, domestic disputes, labor relations, and employee misconduct cases. In all such cases, computer forensics is usually the appropriate response strategy.

Computer forensics is the collection, authentication, preservation, and examination of electronic information for presentation in court. Electronic evidence can be found on any type of computer media, such as hard disks, floppy disks, or CDs and also on digital cameras, PDAs, cell phones, and pagers. Computer forensic experts are trained in finding and interpreting electronic evidence to discover or reconstruct computer-related activities.

There are basically two motivations for engaging in computer forensics. The first is to gather and preserve evidence to present in court. The second is to establish what activities have occurred on a computer, often for the purposes of dispute settlement. You probably know that if you're going to court, you must meet different evidentiary standards for criminal and civil cases. In criminal cases, the standard is "beyond a reasonable doubt." In civil cases, it's the "preponderance of evidence." If you don't have to, and don't want to, involve the legal system, your standard can be lower, perhaps just enough to release someone from employment while reducing the risk of being caught in a wrongful termination lawsuit.

Walt Manning is a computer forensic expert who worked for the Dallas police force for 20 years and now conducts computer forensic investigations to aid in civil and criminal litigation. He also investigates internal cases for companies that suspect funny business. His advice to those undertaking a computer forensic investigation is to always conduct the investigation as though it will end up in criminal court, since there's often a chance that it will—you don't really know what you'll find until you start looking. If you've contaminated the evidence, it won't be of any use in the courtroom.

In a well-conducted computer forensics investigation, there are two major phases: (1) collecting, authenticating, and preserving electronic evidence; and (2) analyzing the findings.

THE COLLECTION PHASE

Step one of the collection phase is to get physical access to the computer and related items. Thus, the computer forensic team collects computers, disks, printouts, post-it notes, and so on. This process is similar to what police do when investigating crime in the physical world, collecting hair, clothing fibers, bloodstained articles, papers, and anything else that they think might be useful. The crime investigators usually take these potential clue carriers with them and secure them under lock and key, where only authorized personnel may have access, and even they must sign in and out.

Computer forensic experts use the same kind of protocol. To conduct a thorough investigation, they look in all the places that information might be stored. The hard disk is an obvious place to look, but computer forensic investigators also collect *all* floppy disks, CDs, Zip disks, and backup tape. If they can't take a clue source with them, they secure it and create an exact copy of the contents of the original media.

As well as electronic media, investigators collect any other potentially helpful items, especially passwords, for use in case any of the files they come across are encrypted or are otherwise difficult to access. Apparently, a favorite hiding place for passwords that people write down (which you should *not* do) is under the keyboard, so that's the first place that investigators look. Then they look in desk drawers and anywhere else that passwords might be, perhaps on post-it notes or slips of paper. Other helpful items might be printouts and business cards of associates or contacts of the person being investigated.

Step two of the collection process is to make a forensic image copy of all the information. A *forensic image copy* is an exact copy or snapshot of the contents of an electronic medium. It is sometimes referred to as a bit-stream image copy. To get a forensic image copy, specialized forensic software copies every fragment of information, bit-by-bit, on every storage medium—every hard disk (if there's more than one), every floppy disk, every CD, every Zip disk. That's usually a lot of stuff. Remember that a CD holds about a half a gigabyte of information, and you can build a hard disk array (several hard disks tied together into one unit) that holds a terabyte (one trillion bytes) or more. It can take a long, long time to copy it all. And the investigator must be able to swear in court that he or she supervised the entire copying process, and that no one and nothing interfered with the evidence. This could mean sitting in the lab literally for days just copying files. Also, many experts advise that the investigator make two copies of everything in case there's a problem later with the first copy.

THE AUTHENTICATION AND PRESERVATION PROCESS

To get a forensic image copy of hard disk and other media contents, investigators physically remove the hard disk from the computer. They never turn the suspect computer on, because when the PC is turned on, Windows performs more than 400 changes to files. Access dates change, and so do temporary files, and so on. So, once turned on, the hard drive is no longer exactly the same as it was when it was shut down.[15] Thus, opposing counsel could argue that this is not the same hard disk that the suspect used.

Having removed the hard disk, investigators connect it to a special forensic computer that can read files but can't write or rewrite any medium. Then they use forensic software like EnCase to extract a forensic image copy of the original medium without changing the files in any way.

How do we know that nothing changed on any disk during the entire investigation, from the time the computer was seized up to the present time? That's the question that opposing counsel will ask the computer forensic expert on the witness stand. So, during the collection phase and later, the analysis phase, the investigators have to make absolutely sure that evidence to be used in a trial could not have been planted, eliminated, contaminated, or altered in any way. This is a basic evidentiary rule for all court proceedings. They have to be able to document a chain of custody and be able to account for the whereabouts and protection of evidence.

In a computer forensic investigation, investigators use an authentication process so that they can show sometime in the future—perhaps in two years' time—that nothing changed on the hard drive or other storage medium since seizure. They can do this with an MD5 hash value. An ***MD5 hash value*** is a mathematically generated string of 32 letters and digits that is unique for an individual storage medium at a specific point in time. The MD5 hash value is based on the contents of that medium. Any change in the content changes the MD5 hash value.

A hash value is a seemingly meaningless set of characters. An example of a hash value would be the sum of the ISBNs and the number of pages in all the books on a bookstore shelf. The result, which would be a mixture of ISBN codes and quantities of pages, would be meaningless for anything except identification. If a book, or even a page, were added to or removed from the shelf, the hash total would change, so the contents of the shelf could be shown not to be the same as they were when the hash value was originally computed. Similarly, adding so much as one space in one tiny Word document on a disk will change the MD5 hash value. See Figure H.6 for an example of an MD5 hash value generated by EnCase forensic software.

Figure H.6

MD5 Hash Value

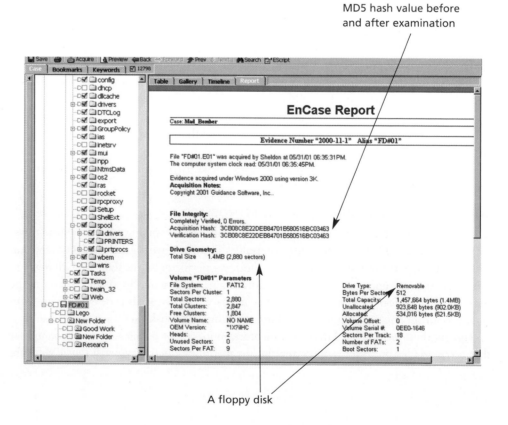

MD5 hash value before and after examination

A floppy disk

MD5 hash values are considered very reliable and have become an industry standard accepted by the FBI, the U.S. Marshall Service, and most other law enforcement authorities, as well as private professional firms, as a way of uniquely authenticating a set of contents on a particular storage medium. This confidence in MD5 hash values is based on the fact that the probability of two hard disks with different contents having the same MD5 hash value is 1 in 10 to the 38th power: that's 1 with 38 zeros behind it. This makes the MD5 hash value a sort of DNA or fingerprint for computer media contents. Actually, it's more reliable than those physiological identifiers, since the probability of two sets of hard disk contents resulting in the same MD5 hash value are less than the odds of two individuals' DNA and fingerprints being identical. As an example of this probability, consider that you would have better odds of winning the Powerball lottery 39 times in your lifetime than you would of finding two hard disks with different contents that have matching MD5 hash values.

FORENSIC HARDWARE AND SOFTWARE TOOLS

As we've already mentioned, computer forensic experts use special hardware and software to conduct investigations. Usually the computer system has more power than the standard computer on a desktop and much more RAM, as well as much more hard disk capacity. This is to speed up the copying and analysis process. Computer forensic experts are also very careful not to let static electricity cause any damages or changes to magnetic media (like hard disks, Zips, and floppies). Therefore they use nonconductive mats under all computer parts, and wear wristbands that connect by wire to the ground of an electrical outlet. And just in case they need a tool, such as a screwdriver, they have a special non-magnetic set of tools nearby, too.

There are many kinds of software, in addition to forensic software, that can help in computer forensic investigations. Quick View Plus, used by many forensic experts, is an example. This is software that will load Word, Excel, image, and many other file formats. If it comes across a file with an .xls extension, which is actually an image and not a spreadsheet file, Quick View will show the file as an image regardless of its extension. That saves the investigator having to try it in multiple programs after loading fails in Excel.

For investigations that might be headed toward litigation, computer forensic experts often use EnCase, since it's widely accepted as robust and reliable. EnCase has repeatedly been judged acceptable by the courts in meeting the legal standard for producing reliable evidence.

THE ANALYSIS PHASE

The second phase of the investigation is the analysis phase when the investigator follows the trail of clues and builds the evidence into a crime story. This is the phase that really tests the skill and experience of the investigators. The analysis phase consists of the recovery and interpretation of the information that's been collected and authenticated. If all the necessary files were there in plain sight with names and extensions indicating their contents, life would be much easier for the forensic investigator, but that's seldom the case. Usually, particularly if those being investigated know that they're doing something wrong, the incriminating files will have been deleted or hidden.

Investigators can recover all of a deleted file pretty easily as long as no new information has been written to the space where the file was. But, they can also recover fragments—perhaps rather large fragments—of files in parts of a disk where new files have been written, but have not completely filled the space where the old file was. With the

Figure H.7

Some of the Files
Recoverable from
Storage Media

E-Mail Files

- E-mail messages
- Deleted e-mail messages

Program Files and Data Files

- Word (.doc) and backup (.wbk) files
- Excel files
- Deleted files of all kinds
- Files hidden in image and music files
- Encrypted files
- Compressed files

Web Activity Files

- Web history
- Cache files
- Cookies

Network Server Files

- Backup e-mail files
- Other backup and archived files
- System history files
- Web log files

appropriate software they can recover files or fragments of files from virtually any part of any storage medium (see Figure H.7).

Computer forensic programs can pinpoint a file's location on the disk, its creator, the date it was created, the date of last access, and sometimes the date it was deleted, as well as file formatting, and notes embedded or hidden in a document (see Figure H.8).

Figure H.8

History of File Activity

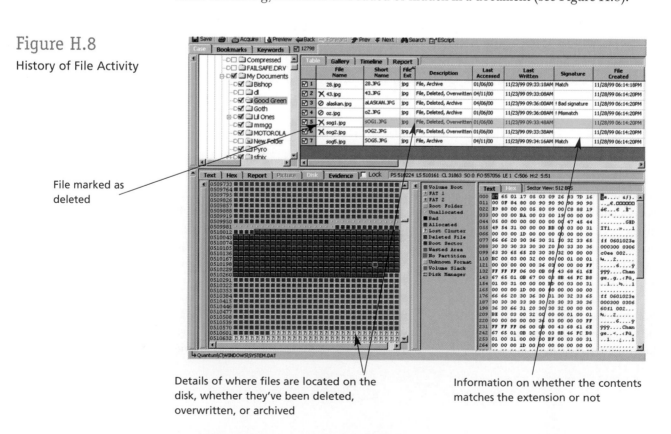

File marked as deleted

Details of where files are located on the disk, whether they've been deleted, overwritten, or archived

Information on whether the contents matches the extension or not

Also stored on the hard disk is information about where the computer user went on the Web. For example, every graphic image you view on the Internet is copied to your hard disk, usually without your knowledge. In addition, Web servers have information on which computer connected to the Web and when. The same server can also tell you the sites visited by the user of that computer, the date and time of the visits, and the actions of the user at the site. These attributes are useful if the suspect claims to have reached an inappropriate site by accident, since delving deeper into the site implies a deliberate action. And, of course, if a password was required to reach the material in question, you can rest your case.

Recovery and Interpretation

As with all evidence, the analysis of the electronic clues and the assembling of the pieces into a credible and likely scenario of what happened are very important. Much of the information may come from recovered deleted files, currently unused disk space, and deliberately hidden information or files. Some of the people whose e-mail was recovered to their extreme embarrassment (or worse) were the arresting officer in the Rodney King case, Monica Lewinsky, and believe it or not, Bill Gates of Microsoft (see Figure H.9).

Figure H.9

Recovered E-mail Messages

From the arresting officer in the Rodney King beating

"oops I haven't beaten anyone so bad in a long time...."

From Monica Lewinsky to Linda Tripp

From:	Lewinsky, Monica, OSD/PA	833-DC-00009446
To:	Tripp, Linda, , OSD/PA	
Subject:	I'm back!	
Date:	Wednesday, February 19, 1997 8:09AM	
Priority:	High	

LRT— Hi, I missed you!!!! I hope you enjoyed your few days of sanity with me gone because I'm back and NOT in good spirits.

1. I have a small present for you. Everything was SOOOOO expensive so I'm sorry it's small.

2. Nice that the Big Creep didn't even try to call me on V-day and he didn't know for sure that I was going back to London.

3. He could have called last night and didn't. He was out of town.

4. Finally, the ????? went away and it was the same night he was gone. ██ me!!!!

HHHEEELLPPP!!!!

Maybe we can have lunch or meet sometime today cuz I want to give you your present.

Bye...msl

From Bill Gates in an intraoffice e-mail about a competitor in the Microsoft antitrust action

"...do we have a clear plan on what we want Apple to do to undermine Sun...?"

Following is a discussion, not necessarily exhaustive, of places from which computer forensic experts can recover information.

PLACES TO LOOK FOR STRAY INFORMATION

Information is written all over a disk, not only when you save a file, but also when you create folders, print documents, repartition the disk, and so on. System and application software alike continually create temporary files resulting in space and file locations being rearranged. Leftover information stays on the disk until another file writes over it, and is often recoverable with forensic software. Next, we'll examine three places where files or file remnants could be: slack space, unallocated disk space, and unused disk space.

DELETED FILES AND SLACK SPACE

It's actually not very easy to get rid of electronically stored information completely. A surprising number of people think that if they delete a file it's gone. It's not—at least not immediately, and perhaps never. When you delete a file, all you're actually doing is marking it as deleted in the disk's directory. The actual file contents are not affected *at all* by a delete action.

If you delete a file from a hard disk you usually get a message asking you if you want it in the *Recycle Bin* and then you can recover it simply by using the *Undelete* option. On a removable medium, like a Zip or floppy disk, it's a little harder, but not much. The message you get asks whether you're sure you want to delete the file because it may not be recoverable. Actually that message should read "not as easily recoverable as files in the recycle bin," since you can get it back with utility programs such as Norton Utilities, and of course, forensic software.

When you mark a file as deleted, the space is freed up for use by some other file. So, another file may shortly be written to that space. However, it's not quite that straightforward. The operating system divides storage space into sectors of bytes or characters. The sectors are grouped into clusters. A file is assigned a whole number of clusters for storage, whether it completely fills the last cluster or not. This storage allocation method usually leaves unused portions of clusters. This is analogous to writing a three and one-half page report. You'd have to use the top half of the fourth page and leave the rest of the page blank. So, the fourth page is allocated to the report but not completely used. If the previously stored file (the deleted one) was bigger and used that last part of the space, then the remnants of the deleted file remain and can be recovered using the appropriate software. The space left over from the end of the file to the end of the cluster is called ***slack space,*** and information left there from previous files can be recovered by forensic software (see Figure H.10).

Can you never completely erase information from a storage medium, then? Yes, you can, but you have to know what you're doing. You can get disk-wiping programs that erase information from a disk drive by writing nonsense information over all the previous contents. Utilities like Norton have this feature. However, erasing a disk takes a lot of time. A 10-gigabyte hard disk (not that big) would take several hours to clean. Even then you're not necessarily safe, for two reasons. First, a single overwrite may not get everything. The Department of Justice and other government agencies write over old information seven (*seven!*) times to be sure it's gone completely. Second, some programs keep track of what was deleted when and by whom, and that record is viewable if you know how to find it.

UNALLOCATED DISK SPACE

If your hard disk gets a lot of use, it's probable that each sector has had information put into it many times. The operating system is always moving files around, and if you

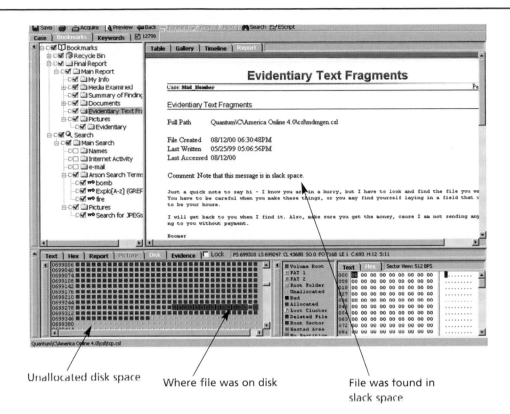

changed a Word file and resaved it, the previous version is marked as deleted and the space becomes unallocated. ***Unallocated space*** is the set of clusters that has been marked as available to store information, but has not yet received a file, or still contains some or all of a file marked as deleted. Until the new information takes up residence, the old information remains. The bigger the hard disk, the longer it usually takes for old space to be used.

UNUSED DISK SPACE

Unused space results from rearranging disk space. For example, when a hard drive is repartitioned, the new partitioning may not use all the space on the hard disk. So, again, those unused portions are not overwritten. The partition table and other operating system information are stored on their own tracks and are not visible under normal circumstances, but may have once stored a Word document. To be able to see the fragments of files tucked away in these tracks the user needs forensic software.

WAYS OF HIDING INFORMATION

There are many ways of deliberately hiding information (other than deleting the file) and some are easy to defeat and others are not so easy. Following is a sampling of methods that people use to try to hide files.

RENAME THE FILE

The simplest, and most easily detected, way of deliberately hiding a file in Windows is to change the extension of the file. Say you had an Excel file that had calculations you didn't want anyone to know about, you could name the file Space Needle.jpg. Then it would appear in Explorer in the list of files as a .jpeg image file, with the name implying that it's just a vacation photo or something else innocuous.

However, if you try to click on that file, Windows will try to load it with the default .jpg viewer. And, of course, it won't load. What computer forensic experts usually do is load the file into a program that accommodates many file formats. This way, you save a lot of time trying to load the renamed file into lots of different types of software. Even more helpful is a forensic tool like EnCase that actually flags files with extensions that don't match the contents and also show files in their true formats.

MAKE THE INFORMATION INVISIBLE

They always say that the best hiding place is in plain sight. A very simple way to hide information inside a file, say a Word document, is to make the information the same color as the background. This works in Excel and other types of files, too. So if you suspect that something interesting is hidden this way, you could check the size of the file to see if it looks consistent with the contents. Also, software like EnCase is not affected by formatting. So, even white-on-white text will be easily searchable and readable by the forensic investigator.

USE WINDOWS TO HIDE FILES

Windows has a utility to hide files of a specific type. You simply open up that drive or folder, choose *View,* then *Options,* and hide the files by indicating what extensions you want hidden. If you go through this process, you'll probably see that there's a list of hidden files already on your computer. These are files that have to do with the correct functioning of your computer and to list them would just clutter up Windows Explorer and risk their being changed or deleted by accident. Again, forensic software takes special note of hidden files and flags them for further investigation.

PROTECT THE FILE WITH A PASSWORD

Word lets you password protect files so that when someone tries to open the file a pop-up window asks for the password. Unless you know the password, you won't be able to read the file. Forensic software can view the contents of many file types without opening the file, eliminating the effectiveness of many types of password protection.

ENCRYPT THE FILE

Encryption scrambles the contents of a file so that you can't read it without the right decryption key. Often investigators can find the decryption key in a password file or on a bit of paper somewhere around the keyboard. There are also password-cracking programs that will find many passwords very easily (alarmingly easily, in fact). They have dictionaries of words from multiple languages, so whole words from any language are not hard to crack. Some people put a digit or two on the front or back of a word. That doesn't fool password-cracking programs at all.

Sometimes investigators can figure out passwords from knowing something about the person. That's why birthdays, anniversaries, children's or pet's names are not good passwords. Also, since you usually need passwords for lots of reasons and it's hard to remember lots of different random ones, many people use just two or three different passwords. So if investigators find one password, they can try that in multiple places. Also, having one password often offers a clue as to what the other passwords might be. For example, if one password an investigator discovers is a fragment of a nursery rhyme, then the others might be, too.

USE STEGANOGRAPHY

Steganography is the hiding of information inside other information. Paper money is a good example of steganography. If you hold a dollar bill up to the light you'll see a watermark. The watermark image is hidden inside the other markings on the bill, but can be viewed if you know what to do to see it.

Figure H.11
Steganography Hides a
File in an Image

You can't see the parts of the picture that were changed to encode the hidden message. You'll only be able to access the hidden file when you put the right password into a pop-up window.

You can electronically hide information using this method. For example, if you want to hide a text file inside an image file, you can use a program called Staganos that does the work for you. Steganos takes nonessential parts of the image and replaces them with the hidden file. "Nonessential" means that these are parts of the picture that you can't see anyway, so changing those to the hidden message makes the message invisible (see Figure H.11). Steganography is a process is similar to file compression, where nonessential information is removed to save space, rather than to hide it.

The FBI and other law enforcement agencies believe that worldwide terrorist networks communicate using steganography. They set up a Web site and find pictures in which they can hide messages. When the message is hidden, the innocent-looking picture goes back up on the Web site. Fellow terrorists can download the picture, and open it with special software. With the correct password, the hidden message appears. Forensic investigators look for clues about steganography by searching for the names of steg programs.

COMPRESS THE FILE

Compressing a file makes it invisible to keyword searches. To find out what's in it you'll have to decompress it with the right software. This may be on the hard disk or on another disk somewhere around the suspect's desk. That's why investigators take all media for examination.

A DAY IN THE LIFE OF COMPUTER FORENSIC EXPERTS

Being a computer forensic expert is a profession that's very demanding. You have to know a lot about computers, and you have to keep learning because things change fast in the computer world. You have to be infinitely careful and patient. You also have to be good at explaining to juries how computers work and must be cool under pressure, since some of the situations you face will be quite adversarial. Angela Morelock and Lanny Morrow have these qualities—and share an interesting job.

Angela and Lanny are computer forensic experts with the Forensics and Dispute Consulting division of BKD, LLP, one of the largest accounting firms in the United States. Organizations, both for-profit and not-for-profit, as well as legal firms, who need some detective work done inside computers, hire BKD's computer forensic services called Data Probe.

Angela and Lanny's cases are many and varied. Their lives are certainly not boring. Some cases take a long time, and some are resolved pretty fast like the divorce case where the wife believed that her husband was hiding assets and that the records were on their home computer. No one (wife, lawyers, friends) could find anything incriminating on the hard drive or on any floppies or Zip disks. But the wife was adamant that the records were there. Lanny was called in. His first step as always was to open up the computer and have a look inside to see if anything in there looked unusual. And there it was—a second hard drive that wasn't plugged in, and was just sitting inside the system unit. When the husband wanted to do his secret accounting, he just opened up the box and swapped hard disk connections, reversing the process when he was done.

A more complex case involved an employee the employer suspected of viewing child pornography using company computers. The employee argued that anything found on company computers could have been put there by any one of many other people since the computers were available to lots of people.

Lanny established dates and times, some of which turned out to be weekends, when the Web activity was taking place. He also assessed the duration and intent of the activity by inspecting entries that showed the amount of time spent on each Web site. He demonstrated that downloads couldn't have been made by accident since there were warnings in pop-up boxes between Web pages about the nature of the material and, to continue, the surfer would have had to click okay multiple times.

Next, he talked to a custodian who saw this employee working on that computer at times during weekends and holidays when the two of them were the only ones in the building. In the face of the mounting evidence, the employee admitted his wrongdoing.

Some cases are solved in a manner similar to the way a knitted sweater unravels, by pulling on one stray strand. One instance of stolen design drawings was investigated like that. A supervisor suspected that an employee who was leaving for a more prestigious position with a competing company had bought his way in by stealing schematics for that company. The IT staff at the company couldn't find any smoking gun. And the job was handed off to Angela and Lanny.

While collecting the computer and other items, they picked up a floppy disk and were told that it had been checked in Windows Explorer and had been found to be blank. They took it with them anyway. Later, they examined the disk with EnCase and found a deleted file called "Sales Quotes.txt," but when they tried to open it in Notepad, it wouldn't load, indicating that, despite its extension, it wasn't a text file. Next they tried Quick View Plus, which opens many different formats, and found that the file contained a schematic. Further investigation revealed that this file had originated on the hard drive and had been renamed to hide its true contents. Not only that, but the file had been copied to the hard disk from the company's intranet. Interesting!

But could Angela and Lanny prove that the employee had done anything more than download a company file to his computer? They went looking for a list of the employee's contacts to see if anything turned up. The name and e-mail address of an officer of the competing company in a business contact database was found—and this record had been deleted.

They then used the keyword search feature of EnCase to search all storage media for the competitor company's name. And an outgoing e-mail was revealed addressed to this competitor officer from the suspect employee, complete with an attachment called "Sales Quotes.txt." After that, it was just a matter of tying up loose ends. Lanny documented the sequence of events using the time and date stamps on all the files involved, and criminal proceedings were initiated against the ex-employee. Civil litigation is ongoing against the competitor that accepted the stolen goods.

Summary: Student Learning Outcomes Revisited

1. **Define computer crime and list three types of computer crime that can be perpetrated from inside and three from outside the organization.** *Computer crime* is a crime in which a computer, or computers, played a significant part in its commission. Crimes perpetrated outside the organization include
   - *Computer viruses*
   - *Denial-of-service (DoS) attacks*
   - Web defacing
   - *Trojan-horse virus*

   Crimes perpetrated inside the organization include
   - Fraud
   - Embezzlement
   - Harassment

2. **Identify the seven types of hackers and explain what motivates each group.** *Hackers* are knowledgeable computer users who use their knowledge to invade other people's computers. The seven types are
   - *Thrill-seeker hackers,* who are motivated by the entertainment value of breaking into computers
   - *White-hat hackers,* who are hired by a company to find the vulnerabilities in its network
   - *Black-hat hackers,* who are cyber vandals and cause damage for fun
   - *Crackers,* who are hackers for hire and are the people who engage in electronic corporate espionage
   - *Hacktivists,* who are politically motivated hackers who use the Internet to send a political message of some kind

   - *Cyberterrorists,* who seek to cause harm to people or destroy critical systems or information for political reasons
   - *Script kiddies* or *script bunnies,* who would like to be hackers but don't have much technical expertise

3. **Define computer forensics and describe the two phases of a forensic investigation.** *Computer forensics* is the collection, authentication, preservation, and examination of electronic information for presentation in court. Electronic evidence can be found on any type of computer storage medium. A computer forensic investigation has two phases: (1) collecting, authenticating, and preserving electronic evidence; and (2) analyzing the findings. The collection phase consists of
   - Getting physical access to the computer and any other items that might be helpful
   - Creating a *forensic image copy* of all storage media
   - Authenticating the forensic image copy by generating an *MD5 hash value,* that, when recalculated at a later date will be the exact same number, as long as nothing at all on the storage medium has changed in any way
   - Using forensic hardware that can read storage media but cannot write to them
   - Using forensic software that can find deleted, hidden, and otherwise hard-to-access information

   The analysis phase consists of
   - Finding all the information and figuring out what it means
   - Assembling a crime story that fits the information that has been discovered

4. **Identify and describe three places on a storage medium where you can find stray information.** The three places are
   - *Slack space* which is the space left over from the end of the file to the end of the cluster
   - *Unallocated space,* which is the set of clusters that has been marked as available to store information
   - Unused space that results from actions like repartitioning a disk

5. **Identify and describe seven ways of hiding information.** The seven ways of hiding information are
   - Rename the file to make it look like a different type of file
   - Make information invisible by making it the same color as the background
   - Use the Windows operating system's hide utility to hide files
   - Protect the file with a password, so that the person who wants to see file must provide the password
   - *Encrypt* the file, scrambling the contents of the file and you have to have the key to unscramble it again
   - Use *steganography* to hide a file inside another file
   - Compress the file so that a keyword search can't find it

Key Terms and Concepts

Black-hat hacker, 421
Computer crime, 414
Computer forensics, 424
Computer virus (virus), 414
Cracker, 421
Cyberterrorist, 422
Denial-of-service (Dos) attack, 417
Distributed denial-of-service (DDoS) attack, 417
Encryption, 432
Ethical hacker, 421
Forensic image copy, 425
Hacker, 421
Hacktivist, 422
Key logger (key trapper) software, 420

Macro virus, 415
MD5 hash value, 426
Script bunny (script kiddie), 423
Script kiddie (script bunny), 423
Slack space, 430
Social engineering, 421
Spoofing, 419
Steganography, 432
Thrill-seeker hacker, 421
Trojan horse virus, 419
Unallocated space, 431
White-hat hacker (ethical hacker), 421
Worm, 415

Short-Answer Questions

1. In what two ways are computers used in the commission of crimes or misdeeds?
2. What constitutes a computer crime?
3. What kind of software is a computer virus?
4. What differentiates a worm from a macro virus?
5. How does a denial of service attack work?
6. What is the effect of a virus hoax?
7. What is the difference between the Klez family of viruses and previous worms?
8. What is a white-hat hacker?
9. What do crackers do?
10. Is there a difference between a cyberterrorist and a hacktivist? If so, what is it?
11. What is computer forensics?
12. What are the two phases of a computer forensic investigation?

Short-Question Answers

For each of the following answers, provide an appropriate question.

1. Macro virus.
2. Distributed denial-of-service attack.
3. Code Red.
4. Spoofing.
5. Web defacing.
6. Hackers.
7. Social engineering.

8. Hacktivist.
9. Computer forensic experts.
10. Collecting and authenticating electronic evidence.
11. MD5 hash value.
12. Forensic image copy.

Assignments and Exercises

1. **FIND COMPUTER FORENSICS SOFTWARE** On the Web there are many sites that offer computer forensic software. Find five such software packages and for each one answer the following questions:

   • What does the software do? List five features it advertises.
   • Is the software free? If not, how much does it cost?
   • Is there any indication of the software's target market? If so, what market is it (law enforcement, home use, or something else)?

2. **IS YOUR FINANCIAL IDENTITY AT RISK FOR THEFT?** The FBI says that identity theft is one of the fastest growing crimes. It uses a computer as a weapon to steal the financial identity of someone with good credit. The thief runs up a huge credit card debt, takes out loans, writes bad checks, travels to exotic destinations, all the while pretending to be you, financially speaking. After that, your financial reputation is ruined. You can't cash a check, your credit cards are refused, and you can't get a bank loan. You probably won't have to cover the bad debts, but that doesn't mean you're not seriously affected. You'll have to create a new financial identity, getting new bank accounts, credit cards, a new social security number and driver's license. That's not easy since the latter two were intended to stay with you for life. How can you avoid becoming a victim of identity theft? Do some research and find out. The following sites can help.

   • The Federal Trade Commission Consumer Information on ID theft at www.consumer.gov/idtheft

   • The Office of the Comptroller of the Currency at www.occ.treas.gov/chcktfd.idassume.htm
   • The Office of the Inspector General at www.ssa.gov/oig/when.htm
   • U.S. Department of Justice at www.usdoj.gov/criminal/fraud/idtheft.html

3. **THE INTERNATIONAL ANTI-CYBERCRIME TREATY** Find out what the provisions of the international anti-cybercrime treaty are and how they will affect the United States. One of the concerns that will have to be addressed is the issue of whether laws of one country should apply to all. For example, if certain sites are illegal in Saudi Arabia, should they be illegal for all surfers? Or if Germany has a law about hate language, should a German or a U.S. citizen be extradited to stand trial for building a neo-Nazi Web site? What do you think?

4. **DOES THE FOURTH AMENDMENT APPLY TO COMPUTER SEARCH AND SEIZURE?** The U.S. Department of Justice's Computer Crime and Intellectual Property Section has an online manual to guide computer forensics experts through the legal requirements of the search and seizure of electronic information. It's available at www.cybercrime.gov/searchmanual.htm and has a section on "Reasonable Expectation of Privacy." There are four subsections: General principles, reasonable expectation of privacy in computers as storage devices, reasonable expectation of privacy and third-party possession, and private searches. Read and summarize these four subsections.

CHAPTER NINE OUTLINE

STUDENT LEARNING OUTCOMES

1   Describe why information filtering is becoming important and list and define the two trends that will support information filtering.

2   Describe the movement toward intellectual computing including automatic speech understanding and the role of people in decision making.

3   Define biometrics, automatic speech recognition, virtual reality, and CAVEs as they relate to changes in physiological interaction.

4   Describe the various technology innovations and trends that will increase portability and mobility.

5   Discuss the challenges of and technological innovations for the coming digital frontier.

6   Describe the broadening of e-government and the coming C2C explosion as they relate to the rebirth of e-commerce.

WEB SUPPORT

www.mhhe.com/haag

- MBA programs
- Specialized MBA programs
- Graduate school information and tips
- Tele-education (distance learning)
- Speech recognition systems (ASR)

CHAPTER NINE

Emerging Trends and Technologies
Business, People, and Technology Tomorrow

OPENING CASE STUDY: WOULD YOU USE AN INTERNET-ENABLED TOILET?

Does the question in the title sound too strange or far-fetched? Matsushita recently announced its plan to make Internet-enabled toilets widely available to the public. The toilets are electronic and can be connected to the Internet.

Sensors within the toilet take readings of your biological output. That information can be sent to your doctor's computer for immediate analysis. Your doctor's office could then notify you, for example, that your blood sugar is low or that you have the beginning symptoms of the flu. The toilet seat may even be able to take your pulse, which would provide more information for your doctor to use.

Aside from personal use in your home, many assisted-care living facilities are already planning to install Internet-enabled toilets. This will enable the nursing staff to monitor the health of its patients constantly. Many people in assisted-care living facilities need around-the-clock attention, especially with respect to the early diagnosis of seemingly simple health problems such as a cold or the flu.

Internet-enabled toilets are an example of the coming future of technology and how technological innovations will forever change your life. These types of toilets are also an example of how your physiological interactions with technology will change. In the case of these types of toilets, a computer will essentially measure your biometrics and use that information for some purpose (e.g., checking your health status). Biometrics is certainly growing in importance, and we'll discuss it within this chapter.

Internet-enabled toilets also illustrate the growing care with which you should evaluate each technological innovation within the context of ethics and privacy. For example, what if your employer began using Internet-enabled toilets for random drug testing? Is that an invasion of your privacy? It depends on how you look at it. What if you used an Internet-enabled toilet at your house to test a nanny for drug and alcohol use? Is that an invasion of the nanny's privacy? Considering that you're trusting a nanny to keep your children safe and treat them well, do you have the right to test a nanny for drug and alcohol use? Again, it depends on how you look at it.

As we move into this exciting future, all eyes will be on numerous technological innovations such as the Internet-enabled toilet. You should watch for them as well. But we would encourage you to think beyond each innovation and determine how it will impact your life. Even more important, you need to consider how it will impact your privacy. Most new technological innovations will, in fact, affect your privacy. Those innovations will allow organizations and other people to gather and use vast amounts of information about you. It's your responsibility—to yourself and to society at large—to ensure that any new technological innovation is used in the best possible way while minimizing any negative impact it may have on individual privacy.

Introduction

Technology is changing every day. But even more important than simply staying up with the changes in technology, you need to think about how those changes will affect your life. It's often "fun" to read and learn about leading- and bleeding-edge technologies. It is something that we would encourage you to do. However, the consequences of those technology changes have a more far reaching impact than you may imagine.

In this final chapter, we want to take a look at several leading- and bleeding-edge technologies, including speech recognition, implant chips, and digital cash. And even more important is how those new technologies can and will impact your personal and business life. Technology for the sake of technology is never a good thing. Using technology to enhance your personal life and to move your organization toward its strategic initiatives are, on the other hand, both good things.

To say the least, this has been both an exciting and challenging chapter to write. The excitement is in the opportunity to talk with you about some emerging technological innovations. The challenge has been not to spotlight the discussions of those technologies too much, but rather to focus on how those technologies can and will impact your life.

So, as you read this chapter, don't get caught up too much in the technology advances on the horizon. Instead, try to envision how those new technologies will change the things that you do, both from a personal and organizational perspective.

To introduce you to just a few of the many new technologies on the horizon, we've chosen those that we believe will have the greatest impact. We present those emerging technologies within the context of six important trends, including (see Figure 9.1):

1. The need for information filtering
2. The movement toward intellectual computing
3. The changing of physiological interaction

Figure 9.1

Emerging Trends and Technologies

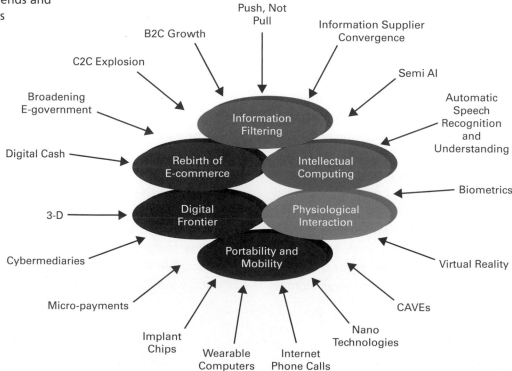

4. Increasing portability and mobility
5. The digital frontier
6. The rebirth of e-commerce

We sincerely hope you enjoy reading this chapter.

The Need for Information Filtering

In the information age, "information" is certainly not at a premium. Quite the opposite, we seem to have an abundance of it. And too much of a good thing is not a good thing. Every day, you probably receive unsolicited e-mail (spam). Much of it probably comes from viral marketing, in which one of your friends or a family member has provided your information to a Web site. You may receive other spam just because you've visited a Web site.

In business, people are constantly provided with access to vast amounts of information. The real problem lies in sifting through it and deciding what is and is not important. Decision makers can suffer from "analysis paralysis" because they simply have too much information to consider. That's why many people use intelligent agents, called data-mining agents (refer back to Chapters 3 and 4) to find important relationships among information stored in a data warehouse.

Information filtering, then, is a must. We see two advances here: (1) push, not pull; and (2) information supplier convergence.

PUSH, NOT PULL TECHNOLOGIES

Right now, we live in a pull technology environment. That is, you go to request and find what you want. On the Internet for example, you visit a specific site and request information, services, and products. So, you're literally "pulling" what you want. Future emphasis will be on push technologies. In a ***push technology*** environment, businesses and organizations come to you with information, services, and product offerings based on your profile (see Figure 9.2). This isn't spam or mass e-mailings.

Pull Technology

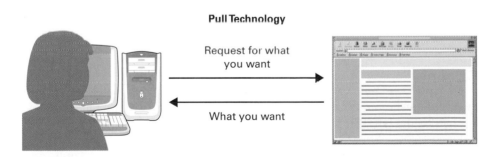

Request for what
you want

What you want

Figure 9.2

Pull versus Push
Technology

Push Technology

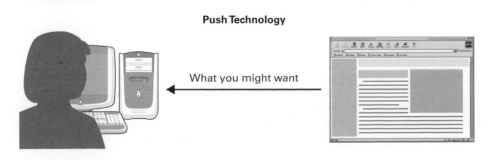

What you might want

THE INTERNET APPLIANCE FUTURE

Internet appliances are those devices that provide you with Internet access and e-mailing capabilities and little (or nothing) more. Essentially, they're stripped down versions of traditional desktop computers complete with a monitor, mouse, and keyboard. However, they contain only a small storage device such as a hard disk and they contain only enough RAM for you to run e-mail software and enjoy surfing the Web.

These types of devices may certainly enable information filtering on a broad scale because of their affordability. You can buy many Internet appliances for as little as $99. Of course, you still have to pay a monthly fee for Internet access. Because they are so affordable, many homes are opting for Internet appliances instead of full-scale desktop or notebook computers. And, as more homes have Internet access, more businesses will be better able to determine the wants and needs of people. Those same businesses can then push information, products, and services to homes that would otherwise not have the technology in place.

The growth of Internet appliance purchases is certainly staggering. According to IDC, 18.5 million Internet appliances were to be shipped to U.S. households in 2001, compared with only 15.7 million traditional desktops and notebooks. And, by the end of 2002, the Internet appliance market is expected to reach $15.3 billion. We are certainly seeing explosive growth in this area. Only time will tell if Internet appliances are a standard product of the future or just a fad.

If you're interested in learning more about popular Internet appliances, we recommend that you search the Web for the following products[1]:

- Palm VII
- iOpener
- iPhone
- WebTV
- Mailbug
- NeoPoint 1000

For example, in some parts of the country you can subscribe to a cell service that pushes information to you in the form of video rental information. Whenever you pass near a video store, your cell phone (which is GPS-enabled) triggers a computer within the video store that evaluates your purchasing history to see if any new videos have arrived that you might be interested in viewing. If so, the video store computer will call your cell phone with a message concerning a new release. It will also give you street-by-street directions to the video store and hold the video for you. If the video store doesn't have any new releases that might interest you, you won't receive a phone call.

You might also someday receive a personalized pizza delivery message on your television as you start to watch a ball game. The message may say, "We'll deliver your favorite sausage and mushroom pizza to your doorstep before the game begins. On your remote control, press the ORDER NOW button."

Of course, situations such as these rely on IT's ability to store vast amounts of information about you. Technologies such as databases and data warehouses will definitely play an important role in the development of push technologies that do more than just push spam and mass e-mail. In the instance of the pizza delivery message on your television, a local pizza store would have determined that you like sausage and mushroom pizza and that you order it most often while watching a ball game.

INFORMATION SUPPLIER CONVERGENCE

You'll notice a greater ability to filter information when you start to enjoy the convergence of information suppliers. Information suppliers include businesses that provide you with magazines, newspapers, Internet access, telephone service, cable TV, books, and the like. Right now, you probably receive many of these information-based products and services from numerous suppliers. In that case, it's difficult for any single organization to filter information for you because it's coming from so many sources.

In the future, for example, you could receive your newspaper from the same organization that provides you with Internet access. In doing so, that organization could determine your preferences and provide you with an electronic newspaper tailored to what you want. That same organization could own and operate a worldwide news source arm that would search international news and provide it to you, if its content meets with your interests.

You may already be seeing this happen. Perhaps your cable TV provider is also your telephone service provider. Perhaps you use an information service on the Web that delivers daily articles to you based on your reading preferences. That information service is probably gathering daily information from numerous other news services, filtering it, and providing only what you want.

The Movement toward Intellectual Computing

The key term in artificial intelligence (AI) is most certainly *artificial.* Of the many AI tools you studied in Chapter 4, including expert systems, neural networks, and genetic algorithms, they are designed to mimic human thinking, but they still must be programmed concerning what to do. Expert systems, for example, must be supplied with specific rules and outcomes for each rule. The expert system then follows those rules exactly. It is not capable of changing its own rules or adding new rules with new outcomes.

There is much debate surrounding whether or not we'll ever be able to create truly intelligent software. And there's just as much debate concerning whether or not we *should,* even if we have the capability. We'll not take a side on those arguments here. But, if we can and do create intelligent software, we see two important future impacts: automatic speech understanding and the realization that people will still make the decisions.

AUTOMATIC SPEECH UNDERSTANDING

Automatic speech recognition (which we'll discuss in more detail in the next section) has come a long way in the past several years. But it still has a ways to go with simple tasks such as determining your words when you have a cold, determining the words of another person using your system, and even distinguishing between content and commands. We do, however, expect speech recognition to become standard.

If we someday create intelligent software, then speech recognition will become speech understanding. Consider the sentence, "The glory that was Greece." In written form, you know exactly what it means. In spoken form, however, a computer may determine that your spoken word *Greece* is actually the word *grease.* If the computer understood that you were dictating a term paper on Greek and Roman mythical figures, it would then know that the appropriate word was Greece. However, speech recognition systems can't do that. You must have an intelligent system that is capable of understanding what you're saying. Who knows—if this happens, your computer may become your friend. Food for thought.

PEOPLE WILL STILL MAKE THE DECISIONS

Regardless of how intelligent a computer system may become, it will never completely replace people in all aspects of decision making. This is important for you to keep in

WHERE SHOULD THE DECISION REST?

The degree to which you allow a computer to take over a decision-making task is often a function of the decision being made. For example, most inventory management systems are very good at determining what quantities of a given product line to reorder. If the system orders too many, no real harm is done because excess inventory just sits on the shelf. If not enough is ordered, the business will simply experience a stock-out for a given period of time.

On the other hand, you should never let a computer system tell you how much dosage of a given medicine to give a patient without first verifying the recommendation. The wrong dosage—either too much or too little—can have catastrophic and detrimental effects on the patient, potentially leading to serious illness and even death.

Your task is to list three decisions in the business world that can be largely left to a computer and list three decisions in the business world that should definitely not be left to a computer. You cannot use the examples given in this chapter.

mind. Some systems may make good solid recommendations on courses of actions based on certain conditions, but we must always hold to the fact people need to have the final say-so, not a computer.

Why? Because no matter what happens, computers will never be able to grasp and use true human intuition, insight, and feeling. Most decisions do not have an absolute right or wrong answer. Even if they did, you might come across a set of circumstances that would change your mind even when you know the "right" answer. People, as a whole, are unique because they possess intuition, insight, and feelings. That uniqueness gives us the ability to live and work together, and often make decisions that are not necessarily in the best interest of bottom-line profits, but rather the best interests of society. A computer will never be able to do that.

The Changing of Physiological Interaction

Right now, your primary physical interfaces to your computer include a keyboard, mouse, monitor, and printer. These are physical interfaces, not physiological. Physiological interfaces capture and utilize your real body characteristics, such as your breath, your voice, your height and weight, and even the retina in your eye. These all fall within the realm of biometrics. **Biometrics** is the use of your physical characteristics—such as your fingerprint, the blood vessels in the retina of your eye, the sound of your voice, or perhaps even your breath—to provide identification. That's the strict definition of biometrics, but it is beginning to encompass more than just identification.

Technological advances are appearing that allow you to interact physiologically with a computer system. In the strictest definition of biometrics for the purpose of identification, high-security environments require fingerprints or palm prints for entry into restricted areas. The military uses biometrics extensively in this way. Many banks now use a retina scan to determine your identification for using an ATM machine. Essentially, you have no ATM card, you allow the ATM to scan the retina of your eye.

When biometrics is broadened beyond using your physiological characteristics for only identification, we will see a whole new generation of computing applications. Technologies to watch in this area include automatic speech recognition, virtual reality, and CAVEs.

GETTING SMALL WITH NANOTECHNOLOGIES

One of the single greatest drawbacks to technological advances is size. The best chip manufacturers can do is to make circuit elements with a width of 130 nanometers. A nanometer is one-hundred-thousandth the width of a human hair. That may seem very, very small, but current manufacturing technologies are beginning to limit the size of computer chips, and thus their speed and capacity.

Nanotechnologies aim to change all that. In nanotechnology, everything is simply atoms. Nanotechnology researchers are attempting to move atoms and encourage them to "self-assemble" into new forms. Consider this:

Change the molecular structure of the materials used to make computer chips, for instance, and electronics could become as cheap and plentiful as bar codes on packaging. Lightweight vests enmeshed with sensors could measure a person's vital signs. Analysis of a patient's DNA could be done so quickly and precisely that designer drugs would be fabricated on the fly. A computer the size of your library card could store everything you ever saw or read.

Nanotechnology—It's a bleeding-edge technology worth watching. The changes it will bring about will be unbelievable.[2]

AUTOMATIC SPEECH RECOGNITION

The most common and well-known example of the broader consideration of biometrics is automatic speech recognition. An *automatic speech recognition (ASR)* system not only captures spoken words but also distinguishes word groupings to form sentences. To perform this, an ASR system follows three steps.

1. *Feature analysis*—The system captures your words as you speak into a microphone, eliminates any background noise, and converts the digital signals of your speech into phonemes (syllables).

2. *Pattern classification*—The system matches your spoken phonemes to a phoneme sequence stored in an acoustic model database. For example, if your phoneme was "dü," the system would match it to the words *do* and *due*.

3. *Language processing*—The system attempts to make sense of what you're saying by comparing the word phonemes generated in step 2 with a language model database. For example, if you were asking a question and started with the phoneme "dü," the system would determine that the appropriate word is *do* and not *due*.

ASR is certainly now taking its place in computing environments. For example, Microsoft's Office XP and Office 11 include easy-to-use speech recognition capabilities for both content and commands. The important point is that ASR allows you to speak in a normal voice instead of using a "clunky" mouse and keyboard. Visit the Web site that supports this text (www.mhhe.com/haag) to learn more about ASR systems.

VIRTUAL REALITY

On the horizon (and in some instances here today) is a new technology that will virtually place you in any experience you desire. That new technology is *virtual reality*, a three-dimensional computer simulation in which you actively and physically participate. In a virtual reality system, you make use of special input and output devices that capture

FINDING APPLICATIONS OF VIRTUAL REALITY

Virtual reality is quickly taking its place in the technology world. In our discussion of it, we listed several well-known applications of virtual reality.

Your task is twofold in this project. First, search the Web for more applications of virtual reality. Find at least three and provide a brief description of each. Only one of these applications can be in the area of entertainment. That is, you cannot use more than one game-oriented application of virtual reality.

Second, identify five potential applications for virtual reality. For each application, describe how virtual reality would be used and why it would be beneficial. Each of these potential applications must relate to the use of virtual reality by an organization. As you describe each of the potential applications, list the type of organization or industry that would use it.

your physiological movements and send physiological responses back to you. These devices include a

- **Glove**—An input device that captures and records the shape and movement of your hand and fingers and the strength of your hand and finger movements
- **Headset**—A combined input and output device that (1) captures and records the movement of your head, and (2) contains a screen that covers your entire field of vision and displays various views of an environment based on your movements
- **Walker**—An input device that captures and records the movement of your feet as you walk or turn in different directions

APPLICATIONS OF VIRTUAL REALITY Virtual reality applications are popping up everywhere, sometimes in odd places. The most common applications are found in the entertainment industry. There are a number of virtual reality games on the market, including downhill Olympic skiing, race-car driving, golfing, air combat, and marksmanship. Other applications include

- *Matsushita Electric Works*—You design your kitchen in virtual reality and then choose the appliances you want and even request color changes
- *Volvo*—For demonstrating the safety features of its cars
- *Airlines*—To train pilots how to handle adverse weather conditions
- *Motorola*—To train assembly-line workers in the steps of manufacturing a new product[3]
- *Health care*—To train doctors how to perform surgery on virtual cadavers[4]

Let's consider the potential ramifications of virtual reality and how you might someday interact with your computer. New virtual reality systems include aroma-producing devices and devices that secrete fluid through a mouthpiece that you have in your mouth. So, you could virtually experience a Hawaiian luau. The aroma-producing device would generate various smells and the mouthpiece would secrete a fluid that tastes like pineapple or roasted pig. If you were using virtual reality to surf big waves, the mouthpiece would secrete a fluid that tastes like salt water.

Those examples are the "fun" uses of virtual reality. In business, building contractors would use virtual reality to show a new building and the location of fire exits. Managers may be able to experience how a proposed "downsizing" effort would affect productivity. The possibilities are virtually limitless.

CAVE AUTOMATIC VIRTUAL ENVIRONMENT

A ***CAVE (cave automatic virtual environment)*** is a special 3-D virtual reality room that can display images of other people and objects located in other CAVEs all over the world. CAVEs are ***holographic devices,*** devices that create, capture, and/or display images in true three-dimensional form. If you watch any of the *Star Trek* movies, you'll see an example of a holographic device called the *holodeck.*

In working form, you would enter a CAVE room. At the same time, someone else would enter another CAVE room in another location (see Figure 9.3). Numerous digital video cameras would capture the likenesses of both participants and re-create and send those images to the other CAVEs. Then, you and the other person could see and carry on a normal conversation with each other, and you would feel as if that other person were in the same room with you.

Current CAVE research is also working on the challenges of having other physical objects in the room. For example, if you sat on a couch in your CAVE, the couch would capture the indentation you made in it and pass it to the couch in the other CAVE. That couch would respond by constricting a mesh of rubber inside it so that your indentation would also appear there. And what about playing catch? Which person would have the virtual ball and which person would have the real ball? The answer is that both would have a virtual ball. When throwing it, the CAVE would capture your arm movement to determine the speed, arc, and direction of the ball. That information would be transmitted to the other CAVE, and it would use that information to make the virtual ball fly through the air accordingly.

Unlike virtual reality, you don't need any special gear in a CAVE. Let your imagination run wild and think about the potential applications of CAVEs. An unhappy customer could call a business to complain. Within seconds, a customer service representative would not answer the phone but rather appear in the room with the unhappy customer. That's an example of great customer service. Your teacher may never attend your class. Instead he or she would enter a CAVE and have his or her image broadcast into the classroom. Of course, you may not really be in class either but rather a holographic likeness of you.

Are CAVEs a realistic possibility? The answer is definitely yes. We believe that CAVEs are the successor to virtual reality. So, virtual reality may not be a long-term technological innovation but rather a stepping-stone to the more advanced CAVE. Whatever the case, CAVEs will not only significantly alter how you interact with your computer (can you imagine the thrill of video games in a CAVE?), they will even more significantly alter how you interact with other people. With CAVE technologies, you can visit your

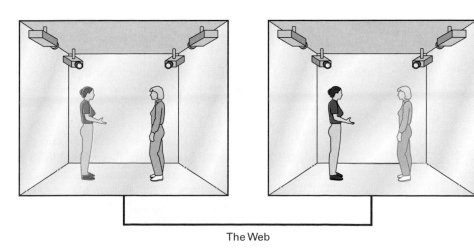

Figure 9.3

CAVEs (Cave Automatic Virtual Environments)

The Web

friends and relatives on a daily basis no matter where they live. You may even have television shows and movies piped into your home CAVE.

Increasing Portability and Mobility

Portability and mobility go hand-in-hand. Portability, in this instance, refers to how easy it is for you to carry around your technology. Mobility is much broader and encompasses what you have the ability to do with your technology while carrying it around. For example, PDAs are very portable; they weigh less than a pound and easily fit in your pocket or purse. However, your mobility may be limited with a PDA. That is, while you can manage your schedule, take some notes, and even use e-mail with a PDA, you certainly can't generate spreadsheets with elaborate graphs. You want technology that is no more intrusive than your wallet or purse. Ideally, your watch would really be a powerful computer system with speech and holographic capabilities (it may happen someday). And, if your watch is a powerful computer system, then it maximizes your mobility.

It goes without saying that, to achieve maximum portability and mobility, we'll need completely wireless communications. This is a vast and dynamically changing field. We won't delve into it here, but we will need it for portability and mobility.

People today, and especially tomorrow, need portable technologies that maximize their mobility. You shouldn't have to sit at a desk to generate a spreadsheet with elaborate graphs. You shouldn't have to find your credit card every time you want to make a purchase on the Internet. Literally no one should know you're carrying and working on your computer as you walk down the street. Within that context, let's discuss free Internet phone calls, micropayments and financial cybermediaries, wearable computers, and implant chips.

Figure 9.4

Making an Internet Phone Call

The Basics

A Computer with a Sound Card, Microphone, and Set of Speakers

Getting Started

Software to Make an Internet Phone Call

Registration and One-Time Fee

PhoneFree's Web Site

Making The Call

PhoneFree's Web Site

FREE INTERNET PHONE CALLS

The Internet offers worldwide communication. Today, that already includes making phone calls through your computer while you're connected to the Internet. Many services offer this type of long-distance phone calling capability for just a few pennies per minute (limited to the continental United States). Others, such as PhoneFree, offer this service completely free if you're using your computer to call another person using his or her computer. Standard computers today include speakers and microphones, so you really have all the technology you need to make the call.

To use PhoneFree, you connect first to its Web site (www.phonefree.com) and download and install some simple software (see Figure 9.4). You also pick a user name and password. Later, when you connect to the Internet again, you go to PhoneFree's Web site and place yourself on an active contact list. You'll be able to see everyone else on the Internet who also has PhoneFree service. To place a call, you select someone to call and click on a few buttons. You then use your computer's microphone and speakers as if they were an actual telephone.

Internet phone calling will certainly increase your mobility, not to mention reduce your phone bill. And, as we discussed in Chapter 5, this type of Internet telephony will increase customer service on the Internet by providing integrated call centers with Web sites.

MICRO-PAYMENTS AND FINANCIAL CYBERMEDIARIES

In Chapter 5, we also discussed micro-payments and cybermediaries. Micro-payments are techniques to facilitate the exchange of small amounts of money for an Internet transaction. *Micro-payments* enable you to make purchases for very small amounts (say, $0.25) on the Internet. You certainly can't do that with a credit card. *Financial cybermediaries* are Internet-based companies that make it easy for one person to pay another person over the Internet. Think of a financial cybermediary as a "Western Union in cyberspace" that allows you to wire money to another person.

Micro-payments and financial cybermediaries will enhance your mobility. That is, they will allow you to make payments, wire money, and even pay your utility bills no matter where you are. Of course, you'll need your technology to perform such transactions, so portability is a necessity for your use of micro-payments and financial cybermediaries.

WEARABLE COMPUTERS

Focusing on portability now, let's turn our attention to wearable computers. A *wearable computer* is a fully-equipped computer that you wear as a piece of clothing or attached to a piece of clothing similar to the way you would carry your cell phone on your belt. Wearable computers are not some far-off bleeding-edge technology. Today, Levi Strauss, Charmed Technology, and Xybernaut are already manufacturing and selling wearable computers (see Figure 9.5). Levi Strauss makes a jacket that contains a fully functional computer in it, with various parts located in the lapel, pockets, and waistband.

Figure 9.5

Wearable Computers

Xybernaut's wearable Poma clips onto your belt and includes a small screen that covers one of your eyes.

Levi Strauss's wearable computer comes in the form of a jacket.

Charmed Technology offers a belt with a buckle that contains a CPU and RAM.

Xybernaut makes a computer that you wear like a cell phone by attaching it to your clothing. At the time we wrote this text, Xybernaut's Poma wearable computer retailed for about $1,500. It included a 128MHz processor, 32MB RAM, an optical pointing device, and a 640 × 480 VGA full-color headset. Its software primarily supported e-mail, Internet access, music, and games. So, you can't use it for word processing and spreadsheet applications, but new releases will undoubtedly include those features. You can purchase a Poma directly from Xybernaut on its Web site at www.xybernaut.com.

Again, the focus of wearable computers is portability first and mobility second. Right now, wearable computers are very nonintrusive (portability). But they do have limited processing capabilities, so your mobility is limited. You can certainly expect that to change very soon. As technology increases in capability and decreases in price and size, wearable computers will offer you as much processing capability (mobility) as a standard desktop or notebook computer.

Let your imagination run wild again. Imagine carrying and using your wearable computer as if it were a cell phone. You would have high-speed wireless access to the Internet. You could use one eye to view your headset and work on a spreadsheet application while using your other eye to watch a baseball game. No matter where you were or what you were doing, you could still use your wearable computer to write term papers, send and receive e-mail, buy products on the Internet (m-commerce using micro-payments or digital cash, which we'll discuss in a moment), or just having fun surfing the Web.

IMPLANT CHIPS

Finally, in the areas of portability and mobility, let's discuss a widely debated use of technology: implant chips. An ***implant chip*** is a technology-enabled microchip implanted into the human body. Implant chips serve two functions. First, they contain memory that stores important information about you: your identification, medical history, medications to which you're allergic, contact information in case of an emergency, and so on. Second, many of these chips are GPS-enabled. The ***global positioning system (GPS)*** is a collection of 24 earth-orbiting satellites that continuously transmit radio signals to determine your current longitude, latitude, speed, and direction of movement.

If you consider the advantages of the first function, you could be vacationing in Florida and have some sort of waterskiing accident. The hospital could quickly scan your implant chip to view your medical history and determine what medications you might be allergic to. Many people are in favor of implant chips that serve this purpose. However, the tracking function of implant chips has raised heated debates.

If your implant chip is GPS-enabled, then the government could conceivably track your every move. Many people are not in favor of that use. But think a little more. What about the case of lost or kidnapped children? The police could find a missing child via a GPS-enabled implant chip. So, there are advantages to the technology.

Already in parts of Europe, people are using implant chips. As in many cases, certain countries in Europe tend to more easily accept leading-edge uses of technology than U.S. residents. But, it was recently reported that a family of four in Florida was the first U.S. family to receive implant chips. And those implant chips are GPS-enabled. There is other evidence that implant chips are becoming more acceptable. Most zoos implant chips into rare animals to track them if they are ever stolen. Many veterinarians now recommend that chips be implanted into household pets. In the Iditarod race, the famed dogsled race across Alaska, implants chips are inserted into the dogs. When the race is complete, the race organizers can scan the dogs to ensure that they are the same ones who started the race.

GPS is not used exclusively with implant chips. You can buy a GPS system for a couple of hundred dollars that comes complete with city and road maps. Airline pilots and fishermen commonly use a GPS system to fly around no-fly zones and return to places in an ocean or sea where the fishing was particularly good the day before. GPS is an invaluable technology in many instances. You may not agree with its use in implant chips for tracking people, but it does provide other benefits.

So, what's your take on GPS-enabled implant chips? Do you want Big Brother looking over your shoulder as you shop on the weekend? Should parents be able to use GPS-enabled implant chips to find their children if they're late coming home for dinner? If children receive GPS-enabled implant chips at birth, at what age should they have the right to have them removed? Should the implant chips ever be removed? Think long and hard about these types of questions. You'll have to answer them in your lifetime.

The Digital Frontier

In Chapter 1, we alluded to the coming *digital economy,* marked by the electronic movement of all types of information, not limited to numbers, words, graphs, and photos but including physiological information such as voice recognition and synthesization, biometrics (your retina scan and breath for example), and 3-D holograms. And in this chapter, we've already introduced you to a variety of leading- and bleeding-edge technologies that will enable the arrival of the digital economy.

Are we there yet? Absolutely not. The full-fledged digital economy will not arrive for about 10 or more years. In many parts of the world, the digital economy may not be realized for as many as 50 years. What seems to be the most major challenges: the technology or the willingness of people to embrace these new technologies? The answer is both. People are certainly resistant to change, no matter how good it may be. And, in spite of major strides and innovations in technology, it cannot yet fully support a digital economy.

You may have noticed this while working at home on the Internet. Your connection is really fast at school or work but seems to slow to a crawl while at home. If so, you're experiencing the problem called the last-mile bottleneck. The *last-mile bottleneck problem* occurs when information is traveling on the Internet over a very fast line for a

FACIAL RECOGNITION SOFTWARE AT THE AIRPORT

Airport security is now a must. And most airports and airlines are no longer relying on government-issued forms of identification for determining who should and who should not be allowed on plane. Instead, they're relying on facial recognition software such as FaceIt, a joint-venture product of ARINC and Visionics Corporation. FaceIt creates a digital map of a person's face and compares it to a database that contains the facial images of unwanted fliers and known terrorists.

Facial recognition software plays an important role in the use of biometrics for providing and authenticating identification. FaceIt's ARGUS system can handle an unlimited number of video cameras capturing facial images and comparing them to a database that is also unlimited in size. To learn more about FaceIt, visit ARINC at www.arinc.com and Visionics at www.visionics.com.[5]

certain distance and then comes near your home where it must travel over a slower line. For example, if you're using a 56Kbps modem to dial into the Internet, the information you request moves much slower from your telephone company to your home than it does from a Web site to your telephone company. Even if CAVEs, virtual reality, and other information-intensive applications were cheap and widespread, you probably still couldn't use them because of the last-mile bottleneck problem.

Again, just about everything we've introduced you to in this chapter—speech recognition, virtual reality, biometrics, CAVEs, Internet phone calls, micro-payments, and GPS-enabled implant chips—centers around enabling the upcoming digital economy. Let's now look specifically at two more technology innovations that will support a digital economy and the digital frontier—3-D and digital cash.

THREE-DIMENSIONAL TECHNOLOGY

Real *three-dimensional (3-D)* technology presentations of information give you the illusion that the object you're viewing is actually in the room with you. You can see the depth of the image, turn it to reflect different angles to see its various perspectives, and in some ways understand the density of the object. Real 3-D is a fundamental technology for other technologies such as virtual reality and CAVEs. In fact, 3-D is essential for them. However, widespread use of 3-D is not here yet. For example, most spreadsheet software offers you pseudo-3-D graphs by incorporating shades and shadows to simulate depth and angles. But you're not seeing those graphs in true 3-D form.

The only real obstacle to widespread 3-D use is speed. It takes a lot of computing horsepower to manipulate and display images in 3-D form. And it takes significant throughput across the Internet to pipe 3-D Web sites into your home. But, the widespread use of 3-D is just a matter of time—perhaps a couple of years.

DIGITAL CASH

When the digital economy arrives, so must digital money. Coins and folding cash have no real value, they are simply surrogate representations of value. They have become the standard on which the worldwide economy works because it's much easier to pay for products and services with them than it is to use gold and silver. It makes sense then that, in a digital economy, money will also be digital. In Chapter 5 and previously in this chapter, we've discussed micro-payments, a technique for making a purchase for a small

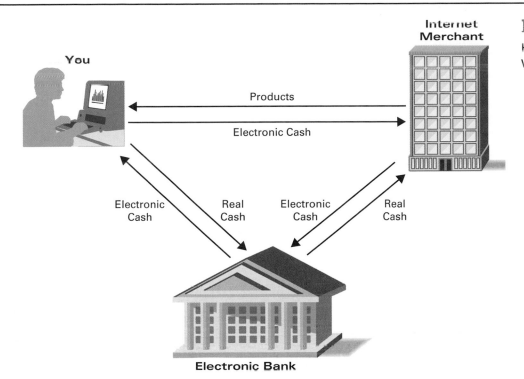

Figure 9.6

How Digital Cash Will
Work on the Internet

amount of money over the Internet. Micro-payments are a small (no pun intended) part of the much larger picture called digital cash. **Digital cash** (also called **electronic cash** or **e-cash**) is an electronic representation of cash.

To use digital cash, you must first purchase it from an electronic bank (see Figure 9.6). You can do this by sending real cash in the mail, using a debit or credit card, or by actually opening an account with the electronic bank and requesting that an amount of digital cash be deducted from your balance and sent to you. Whatever the case, the electronic bank will electronically send you your digital cash files. For example, you could request $100 in digital cash in $20 increments. What you would end up with is five digital cash files, each representing $20 on your hard disk.

Of course, in the case of micro-payments, you may have hundreds of digital cash files, with each ranging in value from $0.05 to $0.50. Now all you have to do is find a product or service on the Internet you want to buy. You would send the merchant the appropriate number of digital cash files to equal the purchase amount. The merchant could then use those digital cash files to buy other merchandise or return it to the electronic bank for real money.

The concept is actually quite simple when you think about it. The implementation, however, has turned out to be extremely difficult for many reasons including the following:

- If your system crashes and your digital cash files are wiped clean, you've lost your money. It's rather like losing your wallet. The electronic bank will not replace the files.

- There is no standard for how digital cash should look. So, a digital cash file from one electronic bank may not look like digital cash from another electronic bank. That makes many merchants very hesitant to accept digital cash.

- Digital cash makes money laundering easy. Because none of your personal information travels with the digital cash when you use it to make a purchase, it's extremely difficult to tell from where it came. So, illegally obtained cash can be easily exchanged for digital cash.

- Digital cash travels across the vast Internet and is susceptible to being stolen. Digital information (which includes digital cash) is easy to steal and hard to trace. This may be the single biggest obstacle to the widespread use of digital cash.

In spite of the above challenges and many others, digital cash is destined to take its place as a standard technology. The real question is how soon.

The Rebirth of E-Commerce

In the late twentieth century and the early part of the twenty-first century (which seems almost odd to say), e-commerce was highly touted as the next big business frontier. Venture capitalists and individuals alike poured literally trillions of dollars into dot-com businesses. Most of those dot-coms had no idea what they were doing and could very seldom show a clear and reasonable path to profitability (P2P). Of course, the e-commerce balloon popped in the middle of the year 2000. As a result, many "millionaires on paper" became "paupers on paper" overnight.

But e-commerce as a business principle survived; the dot-coms who failed to implement it correctly did not and became dot-bombs. We will over the next 10 years or so see a strong resurgence in the e-commerce area, this time by companies backed by sound business principles and clear paths to profitability. As you witness this, you'll see some interesting trends, including the broadening of e-government and the explosion of consumer-to-consumer (C2C) e-commerce.

BROADENING OF E-GOVERNMENT

In Chapter 5, we briefly introduced you to the role of government in e-commerce, known as e-government. Within the e-government arena, there are four primary focuses (see Figure 9.7).

1. *Government-to-Government (G2G)*—This is limited to performing electronic commerce activities within a single nation's government focusing on vertical integration (local, city, state, and federal) and horizontal integration (within or among the various branches and agencies)

2. *Government-to-Business (G2B)*—The electronic commerce activities performed between a government and its business partners for such purposes as purchasing direct and indirect materials, soliciting bids for work, and accepting bids for work

Figure 9.7

The Primary Focuses of E-Government

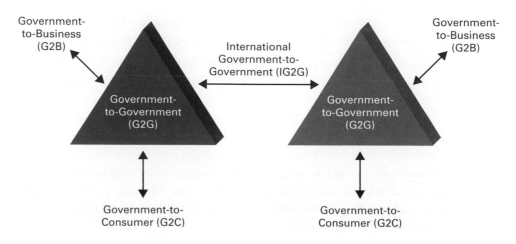

BUYING SODA WITH A CELL PHONE

In many countries in Europe, especially in Scandinavian countries, you can't find a slot on a vending machine to insert money to buy a soda. No, it's not because the sodas are free or because there's an extremely high criminal and vandalism rate. You have to buy the soda with your cell phone.

On the soda machine is a telephone number you call. When you do, the telephone call automatically triggers the soda machine so you can make a selection. The best part is that the cost of the soda is charged to your cell phone bill. No more trying to find the right change when the "CORRECT CHANGE" message is blinking. No more trying to get the creases out of a dollar bill. You simply charge the cost of the soda to your cell phone. Of course, at the end of every month you still have to pay for it, but it is indeed convenient.

This is an example of how B2C (business-to-consumer) e-commerce is beginning to incorporate nontraditional computing technologies. Within the context of C2C (consumer-to-consumer) e-commerce, it should help you expand your mind and think of endless and wild possibilities for selling products and services to other consumers.

Can you set up some sort of product-selling business that requires consumers to use a cell phone to charge the cost of the product to their cell phone bill? If you answered no, then our next question to you is, Have you actually contacted an ISP and cell phone service provider to determine that you can't do it? How would you answer that question?

C2C e-commerce will require that everyone "think outside the box" or "beyond your ears" as we like to put it. Don't rule out any idea, no matter how strange or far-fetched. Thomas Watson, CEO and Chairman of IBM in 1943, stated, "I think there is a world market for maybe five computers." He was definitely wrong and, to some extent, narrow-minded in his futuristic views. Don't make the same mistake.

3. **Government-to-Consumer (G2C)**—The electronic commerce activities performed between a government and its citizens or consumers including paying taxes, registering vehicles, and providing information and services

4. **International Government-to-Government (IG2G)**—The electronic commerce activities performed between two or more governments including providing foreign aid

We offer you this insight into e-government for two reasons. First, many e-government applications will have a direct impact on your personal and business life. In the not-too-distant future, the IRS will no longer accept paper-based income tax returns. That is, you'll be using G2C to submit your tax forms electronically. Many governmental agencies are also using G2B to send out and accept bids for work. Those government agencies simply refuse to work with businesses that cannot perform this electronic commerce activity. If your organization can't, don't rely on getting any government contracts.

Most important, there are substantial career opportunities in the e-government arena. Governments of all types desperately need motivated knowledge workers skilled in the creation and execution of all types of e-commerce initiatives. It's a business segment worth looking into.

EXPLOSION OF C2C E-COMMERCE

Of all the types of private-sector e-commerce activities—B2B, B2C, C2C, and C2B—the least amount of revenue dollars right now is in the C2C (consumer-to-consumer) space. But we expect that to change rather dramatically in the next several years. EBay is a good example. It's really just a cyber-market in which consumers buy and sell products from and to each other. EBay doesn't guarantee the quality or authenticity of any products or services sold in its auction format. It simply provides a convenient mechanism for allowing consumers to gather and buy and sell products and services.

But consider the impacts of push technologies, m-commerce, digital cash and micropayments, wearable computers, and even GPS-enabled implant chips. You could, for example, drive around your neighborhood in search of garage sales. As you neared one, your GPS-enabled implant chip would trigger someone's personal computer that would call you on your cell phone and notify you what they have for sale and even provide you with driving directions. Once you arrive at the garage sale and find something to buy, you could make a digital cash or micro-payment transfer.

Of course, garage sales aren't the only possibility. You may someday be able to create and store a C2C Web site on a personal digital assistant (PDA). People would access your PDA, view the products you have to sell, and then make digital cash payments. Throughout the day, your PDA would constantly update your inventory records and notify you instantly of any stockouts. At the end of the day, your PDA would display to whom you need to send what products and the address of where to send those products.

These are not far-fetched ideas. Right now, we think in terms of setting up e-commerce Web sites and hosting them on Web server computers. That will change someday, and your home computer, wearable computer, or even PDA will become a server computer that hosts your Web site and includes all the necessary e-commerce software. When that happens, expect C2C e-commerce to explode.

The Most Important Considerations

Throughout this chapter, we've been discussing some key emerging trends and technologies. They certainly are exciting and hold great promise that the future will be dynamic and changing to say the least.

As we close this chapter and potentially your studies in this course, let's take a close look at five key topics. Each is a culmination in some way of the material you've learned in this course. Each is inescapable in that they will happen and you must deal with them. Finally, each is vitally important and reaches far beyond the technologies that either necessitate or support them. For you, these last few pages are a chance to reflect on what you've learned and place that knowledge within the bigger picture.

THE NECESSITY OF TECHNOLOGY

Like it or not, technology is a necessity today. It's hard to imagine a world without it. Just as we need electricity to function on an everyday basis, we need technology as well.

Of course, that doesn't mean you should adopt technology for the sake of the technology. Rather, you need to carefully evaluate each technology and determine if it will help you become more productive, enhance your personal life, enrich your learning, or move your organization in the direction of its strategic goals and initiatives.

Technology is not a panacea. If you throw technology at a business process that doesn't work correctly, the result is that you'll perform that process incorrectly millions of times faster per second. At the same time, you can ill afford to ignore technology when it will help you and your organization become more efficient, effective, and innovative.

CLOSING THE GREAT DIGITAL DIVIDE

We must, as a human race, completely eliminate the great digital divide. The power of technology needs to be realized on a worldwide scale. We cannot afford to have any

CREATING A WIRELESS INTELLIGENT HOME

Zensys, a Danish/U.S. high-tech and really bleeding-edge technology developer, recently announced its plan to create a wireless digital control system, called Z-Wave, for the typical home owner. As Michael Dodge, Zensys's vice president of marketing, explained it, "Z-Wave will truly make the 'intelligent home' available to everyone, by allowing the average consumer to effectively control his lighting, appliances, heating, air-conditioning, and other home systems at a reasonable cost."

Z-Wave will allow a home owner to connect each home appliance device to a central device such as a computer or even a PDA. The home owner then uses the latter device to control all of the other devices. This could even include turning on the water sprinklers, setting a freezer to defrost, and starting the recording of the VCR, all while perhaps driving down the road several hundred miles away. Your home of the future may be more than you can ever imagine.[6]

technology-challenged nation or culture (within reason). If you live and work in a technology-rich country, don't keep it to yourself. When possible, take it to other countries by creating international business partnerships and strategic alliances. The world will benefit greatly from your efforts.

TECHNOLOGY FOR THE BETTERMENT OF PEOPLE AND SOCIETY

The business world isn't just about making money. As you approach the development and use of technological innovations (or even standard technologies), think in terms of the betterment of people and society in general.

Medical research is performing marvelous work in the use of technology to treat ailments and cure diseases. But, if they are only profit-driven, we may never realize them. For example, people are using virtual reality to teach autistic people to cope with increasingly-complex situations. We know for a fact that this use of technology isn't making anyone any money. But it isn't always about making money. It's about helping people who face daily challenges far greater than ours. You're fortunate to be in an environment of learning. Give back when you have the chance.

EXCHANGING PRIVACY FOR CONVENIENCE

On a personal level, you need to consider how much of your personal privacy you're giving up in exchange for convenience. The extreme example is GPS-enabled implant chips. The convenience is knowing where you are and being able to get directions to your destination. But you're obviously giving up some privacy. And convenience takes on many forms. When you use a discount card at a grocery store to take advantage of sales, that grocery store then tracks your purchasing history in great detail. You can bet that grocery store will use that information to sell you more tailored products.

It really is a trade-off. In today's technology-based world, you give up privacy when you register for sweepstakes on certain Web sites. You give up privacy just surfing the Web because tracking software monitors your activities. Even when you click on a banner ad, the Web site you go to knows from where you came. Although such trade-offs may seem insignificant, small trade-offs add up to a big trade-off over time.

NECESSITY, CONVENIENCE, AND PRIVACY

As you consider your own use of technology, it's important that you consider that use within the context of necessity, convenience, and your own privacy. You really have two questions to answer. They are

1. *Necessity*—If you truly need technology to perform a personal task, how much of your personal privacy are you willing to forgo?

2. *Convenience*—If you can use technology to make your life more convenient (but your use of it isn't an absolute necessity), how much of your personal privacy are you willing to forgo?

Regarding question 1, provide your answer on a scale of 1 to 5. A 1 represents the fact that you would relinquish all your privacy to use technology that is a necessity. A 5 represents the fact that you would not relinquish any privacy even if it meant not being able to use a technology that was a necessity.

Regarding question 2, provide your answer on a scale of 1 to 5. A 1 represents the fact that you would relinquish all your privacy in exchange for using technologies that would make your life more convenient. A 5 represents the fact that you would not relinquish any of your privacy even if it meant not being able to use a technology that made your life more convenient.

Compare your answers with those of several classmates. How do your answers compare to everyone else's?

Because you are very much a part of this, it's often hard to see the big picture and understand that every day you're giving up just a little more privacy in exchange for a little more convenience. Don't ever think that organizations won't use the information they're capturing about you. They're capturing it so they can use it. Of course, much of it will be used to better serve you as a customer, but some of it may not.

ETHICS, ETHICS, ETHICS

And, as our final note to you, we cannot stress enough the importance of ethics. Ethics guide your behavior that affects other people. And the ethics of others guide their behavior that affects you. We realize that business is business and that businesses need to make money to survive. But they shouldn't do it to the detriment of people. It's quite possible to be very ethical and very successful. That's our challenge to you.

Summary: Student Learning Outcomes Revisited

1. **Describe why information filtering is becoming important and list and define the two trends that will support information filtering.** Information filtering is becoming important because the information age has literally created a gluttony of information. Two trends that will support information filtering include

   - *Push technology*—An environment in which businesses and organizations come to you with

   information, services, and product offerings based on your profile

   - *Information supplier convergence*—A merging of all types of organizations that provide information and access to information

2. **Describe the movement toward intellectual computing including automatic speech understanding and the role of people in decision making.** Right now, the key term in

artificial intelligence is *artificial.* But much research is underway to create truly intelligent computer systems. If these systems are created, then you'll be able to carry on a normal conversation with your computer through automatic speech understanding. Everyone must realize, however, that computers—no matter how smart they may be—will never be able to grasp and use human intuition, insight, and feeling. So, the final decision must always rest with a person, not a computer.

3. **Define biometrics, automatic speech recognition, virtual reality, and CAVEs as they relate to changes in physiological interaction.** Most people use a keyboard, mouse, and monitor to work with a computer on a physical level. This is rapidly changing to an environment that will include purely physiological interactions. Key technologies here include:

- *Biometrics* The use of your physical characteristics—such as your fingerprint, the blood vessels in the retina of your eye, the sound of your voice, or perhaps even your breath—to provide identification

- *Automatic speech recognition (ASR)*—A system which not only captures spoken words but also distinguishes word groupings to form sentences

- *Virtual reality*—A three-dimensional computer simulation in which you actively and physically participate

- *CAVEs (cave automatic virtual environments)*—Special 3-D virtual reality rooms that can display images of other people and objects located in other CAVEs all over the world

4. **Describe the various technology innovations and trends that will increase portability and mobility.** To further increase portability (the ability to easily carry around technology) and mobility (what you can do with your technology as you carry it around), you can look toward the following technologies:

- Free Internet phone calls—Using your computer and the Internet to make free long-distance phone calls

- *Micro-payments*—Techniques to facilitate the exchange of small amounts of money for an Internet transaction

- *Financial cybermediaries*—Internet-based companies that make it easy for one person to pay another person over the Internet

- *Wearable computers*—Fully equipped computers that you wear as a piece of clothing similar to the way you would carry your cell phone on your belt

- *Implant chips*—Technology-enabled microchips implanted into the human body

- *Global positioning system (GPS)*—A collection of 24 earth-orbiting satellites that continuously transmit radio signals to determine your current longitude, latitude, speed, and direction of movement

5. **Discuss the challenges of and technological innovations for the coming digital frontier.** The coming digital frontier, also called the *digital economy,* will be marked by the electronic movement of all types of information. One challenge of the digital frontier is to overcome the *last-mile bottleneck problem.* It occurs when information is traveling over the Internet over a very fast line for a certain distance and then comes near your home where it must travel over a slower line. Technological innovations for the digital frontier include:

- *3-D*—Technology presentations of information that give you the illusion that the object you're viewing is actually in the room with you

- *Digital cash*—Electronic representations of cash

6. **Describe the broadening of e-government and the coming C2C explosion as they relate to the rebirth of e-commerce.** The broadening of e-government will come in four forms:

- *Government-to-government (G2G)*—Within a country's government focusing on vertical and horizontal integration

- *Government-to-business (G2B)*—Between government and its business partners

- *Government-to-consumer (G2C)*—Between government and its citizens or consumers

- *International government-to-government (IG2G)*—Between two or more governments

You can also expect to see an explosion of C2C (consumer-to-consumer) e-commerce as part of the rebirth of e-commerce. This will enable individuals to easily buy and sell products from and to each other.

AIRTEXTING: WAVE YOUR CELL PHONE MESSAGE IN THE AIR

U.S. manufacturers of cell phones and providers of cell phone service are heavily targeting one select group of customers—teenagers. In the United States, only about 38 percent of all teenagers have cell phones, compared to over 80 percent in most European countries and some Asian countries. Cell phone providers and manufacturers know that there is plenty of room to grow in the teenage market, not only because 62 percent don't currently have cell phones but also because teenagers are very quick to embrace and use new technologies. Those same companies know that teenagers aren't as frugal with money and tend to spend much more time talking on a cell phone than adults.

Of course, cell phones aren't really new technologies, but what you can do with them is. Motorola, for example, manufacturers a cell phone with FM radio capability (XM radio may not be far behind). Samsung offers a cell phone service that includes AOL Instant Messenger (with audio and limited video). Sony Ericsson offers cell phones with cameras and multimedia messaging.

One of the future leaders in this dynamic and changing industry is Wildseed. It regularly holds cell phone focus groups just for teenagers. Wildseed has determined that teenagers have three cell phone concerns:

1. *Visual appeal*—A cell phone should make a fashion statement. Teenagers also believe that cell phones should be a statement of individuality ("I want a cell phone that doesn't look like anyone else's").
2. *Functionality*—A cell phone should do more than just support phone-calling capabilities.
3. *Price*—Long-term calling plans are not the way to go.

VISUAL APPEAL

Wildseed has tested numerous cell phone designs on teenagers. One cell phone holder was designed to be worn like a garter belt, and it flopped in a big way. According to one young man in the focus group, "Is a guy supposed to wear that?" And a young girl in the focus group commented, "It looks like something for a pros-

titute." But Wildseed did hit upon a good idea. It now manufactures "smart skins," cell phone covers that have an embedded computer chip. According to what the teenager is wearing, he or she can quickly change the design of the cell phone face plate. While skateboarding one day, for example, a young man could change his cell phone face plate to a splashy rendition of hard colors such as red, yellow, and green.

FUNCTIONALITY

Cell phones are certainly no longer devices just for talking. Most cell phones have e-mail capabilities and support surfing the Web. Those are no longer a competitive advantage for any cell phone manufacturer. Wildseed tried a couple of new ideas on teenage focus groups: the first failed and the second met with great success. The first additional functionality was a cell phone that supported Morse code. No one liked that because no one knew how to send and interpret Morse code. Additionally, teenage girls stated they would have problem sending Morse code because their long fingernails made it difficult to type. The second function was "airtexting." Using an airtexting-enabled cell phone, you type in a brief message (e.g., "Call me") and then wave your cell phone back and forth in the air. Blinking red lights on the cell phone are synchronized to display the message in the air. That way, someone across the room can receive your message without having to use a cell phone. You may have seen airtexting clocks that have an arm that moves back and forth through the air and seems to suspend the time and day in the air. As one young lady put it, "That's tight."

PRICE

Price is a major drawback for most teenagers, not necessarily the per-minute charge but rather the long-term contract that must be signed. In the United States, as opposed to most other countries, you must typically sign a six-month or one-year contract for cell phone service. That prohibits many teenagers from getting a cell phone because they have to get their parents to co-sign on the contract. Unfortunately, Wildseed is a man-ufacturer of cell phones and not a cell phone service provider.[7]

QUESTIONS

1. The role and purpose of cell phones have certainly changed over the past few years. Not too long ago, business professionals were the only ones to use cell phones. Now, over one in every three teenagers have a cell phone and about 99 percent of them don't use them for business. Are cell phones becoming a technology of convenience and not of necessity? If people use them just for the convenience of communicating anywhere at anytime, are they really a necessity? On the other hand, if you use a cell phone as your primary mode of communications, is it no longer just a convenience?

2. Airtexting sounds like a good idea. From across a room, you'll be able to easily send someone a short message without using your minutes or having the other person's cell phone ring. But you are giving up some privacy. If you airtext your message, everyone in the room will be able to see it. Are you willing to give up some amount of privacy to use an airtexting feature? Why or why not? What about while sitting in a classroom? Should you be able to airtext a message in the middle of class? Does your school have a policy requiring you to turn off your cell phone when entering a classroom? If so, should this policy apply to airtexting? Why or why not?

3. Functionality is very important for cell phones. What types of functionality does your cell phone support beyond making and receiving phone calls? If you could design the "perfect" cell phone, what additional functionality would you include?

4. Do you foresee a day when cell phones will be the standard phone and we'll simply do away with land-based phone lines? It's probably going to happen. How easy will it then be to move? If you have a cell phone, will you need to change your phone number? Your area code? If cell phones do become the standard, how will you access the Internet from home?

CLOSING CASE STUDY TWO

STADIUMS OF THE FUTURE

There are several industries that always seem to be the leaders in using technological innovations. The movie industry, for example, quickly embraced the use of 3-D technologies and animation to create such movies as *Shrek, Terminator,* and *The Matrix,* all blockbusters in part because of their use of technological innova-tions. The movie industry is even exploring how to cre-ate and use virtual actors and actresses. Real people may no longer be used in movies; instead, likenesses of them will be computer-generated and controlled.

Another related industry always on the forefront of the use of new technologies is professional sports. It may not be an industry that immediately popped into your mind, but that industry must strive daily to at-tract and retain large audiences (just check out the salaries many professional athletes make and you'll un-derstand why). The professional sports industry wants your business in one of two ways: either by having you watch a sporting event on television or by attending a sporting event. For the latter, sports franchises are building some unbelievable arenas and stadiums that make use of technological innovations. Consider these technology-based activities that you'll be able to per-form in the stadium of the future.

ORDER AND PAY FOR FOOD AND BEVERAGES AT YOUR SEAT

In future stadiums, you won't have to catch the atten-tion of a stadium vendor selling popcorn, beverages, and hot dogs. Instead, you'll use a small keypad at your seat to view a menu and order exactly what you want. You'll use the same keypad to pay for your order by swiping your credit card. Your order will be transmitted to a kitchen where it's made and then given to a runner who will deliver it to you.

WATCH REPLAYS ON A PRIVATE SCREEN

Your seat will also have a private screen that folds down and within your arm rest. At any point during the game, you can unfold the screen and view replays. You'll be able to choose from among a variety of camera angles from which to see the replay, and you'll be able to use a zooming function to see the entire field or just a portion of it.

VIEW HOLOGRAPHIC REPLAYS SUSPENDED IN THE AIR

Ideally, you'll be able to watch replays not on a flat two-dimensional screen but rather suspended in the air in front of you as a holographic image. These holographic images will be completely three-dimensional, allowing you to turn them at different angles to view the replay from different perspectives. Many people believe that much of the audience will opt to watch an entire game in this fashion as opposed to through binoculars.

PARTICIPATE IN REAL-TIME INTERVIEWS WITH PLAYERS

Almost all player interviews occur after the game is over and are primarily viewed by people watching a game on television. In a future stadium, you'll be able to request and participate in a real-time interview with a player during the game. For example, after a player makes a great catch in a baseball game to end the inning, you'll be able to interview that player and ask him or her how the catch was made.

VIEW STATISTICS ON ANY PLAYER

You'll also be able to use your screen and keypad to pull up any statistics you might want to view. These could include career statistics for a specific player, season statistics for a specific team, current game statistics for a specific player, and even records within a particular sport. You'll even be able to request that this type of information be presented in graphical form perhaps accompanied by an audio analysis provided by a sport or statistics expert.

VIEW SCORES AND HIGHLIGHTS OF OTHER GAMES

And you certainly won't have to wait for a stadium to display scores and highlights of other games on a hanging big-screen monitor. You'll be able to view scores and highlights of other games at the press of a button. You'll even be able to attend one game and watch another completely on your screen.

SEND MESSAGES TO PEOPLE IN THE STADIUM

If you buy tickets the day before a sporting event, it's often difficult to get a grouping of tickets all in the same area. If you can't get tickets all together, then you'll miss out on some of the fun associated with attending a sporting event with friends. That won't be a problem in future stadiums. You'll soon be able to use videoconferencing software to communicate with any other person in the stadium.

QUESTIONS

1. Will this type of stadium of the future further widen the digital divide? It makes sense that people who don't have enough money to buy personal technologies will also not have enough money to attend sporting events. Will that group of people fall further behind because they can't take advantage of technological innovations in the stadium of the future? Or is this use of technology one of convenience and not of necessity?

2. How do you think players will react to being interviewed during the middle of a game? Can you think of some professional athletes who would not want to do this? Can you think of some professional athletes who would want to do this? Many governing bodies of professional sports such as the NBA and NFL require that athletes be available before and after the game for interviews. Should those same governing bodies require that athletes be available during games for interviews? Why or why not?

3. Do you believe that stadiums of the future will encourage more people to attend sporting events? Why or why not? Right now, you can sit at home, watch picture-in-picture to see multiple games, and change channels to see yet other games. And let's not forget that these stadiums of the future will be extremely expensive to build and maintain, so you can expect ticket prices to go up as well.

4. In this chapter, we introduced you to several leading-edge and bleeding-edge technologies. Which of those, that we didn't highlight in this

case study, do you believe could be used to enhance the experience of attending a sporting event? How would you use them? Would the use of those technologies further encourage you to attend a sporting event? Why or why not?

Key Terms and Concepts

Automatic speech recognition (ASR), 445
Biometrics, 444
CAVE (cave automatic virtual environment), 447
Digital cash (electronic cash, e-cash), 453
Digital economy, 451
Feature analysis, 445
Financial cybermediary, 449
Global positioning system (GPS), 450
Glove, 446
Government-to-business (G2B), 454
Government-to-consumer (G2C), 455
Government-to-government (G2G), 454
Headset, 446

Holographic device, 447
Implant chip, 450
International government-to-government (IG2G), 455
Language processing, 445
Last-mile bottleneck problem, 451
Micro-payment, 449
Pattern classification, 445
Push technology, 441
Three-dimensional (3-D), 452
Virtual reality, 445
Walker, 446
Wearable computer, 449

Short-Answer Questions

1. Why is it becoming important to filter information?
2. How will push technologies work?
3. How does automatic speech understanding differ from automatic speech recognition?
4. Why are currently popular input and output technologies such as keyboards, mice, and monitors physical interfaces and not physiological interfaces?
5. What are the three types of input and output devices commonly used in virtual reality?
6. How is a CAVE a form of a holographic device?
7. How can you make a free long-distance phone call using the Internet?
8. Why are micro-payments important for increasing portability and mobility?
9. What two purposes do implant chips serve?
10. What is the digital economy?
11. What is the last-mile bottleneck problem?
12. What are the four forms of e-government?
13. In what ways will C2C e-commerce explode?

Short-Question Answers

For each of the following answers, provide an appropriate question.

1. Pull technology.
2. Information supplier convergence.
3. Always with people.
4. Fingerprints, the blood vessels in the retina of your eye, the sound of your voice, and your breath.
5. Pattern classification.
6. A phoneme.
7. Glove.
8. Portability.
9. Mobility.
10. Financial cybermediary.
11. Implant chip.
12. GPS.
13. 3-D.
14. Digital cash.
15. Ethics.

Assignments and Exercises

1. **RESEARCHING WEARABLE COMPUTERS** One of the leading-edge manufacturers of wearable computers is Xybernaut. Connect to its Web site at www.xybernaut.com and research its Poma wearable computer. What is its CPU speed? How much RAM does it include? What functions can you perform with a Poma? What sort of technology devices can you add to a Poma? Is the Poma advanced enough and cheap enough that you would consider buying one? Why or why not?

2. **INFORMATION SUPPLIER CONVERGENCE IN YOUR AREA** Do a little research of the various organizations in your area that either provide information to you (such as a cable TV company) or provide you with access to information (such as an ISP). Which of those organizations can provide you with more than one type of information? Which of those organizations can provide you with information and also access to information?

3. **FINDING A GOOD AUTOMATIC SPEECH RECOGNITION SYSTEM** Research the Web for automatic speech recognition (ASR) systems. Make a list of the ones you find. What are the prices of each? Are they speaker-independent or speaker-dependent? Do they support continuous speech recognition or discrete speech recognition? What sort of add-on vocabularies can you purchase? How comfortable would you feel speaking the contents of a term paper as opposed to typing it? Would you have to be more or less organized to use speech recognition as opposed to typing? Why?

4. **UNDERSTANDING THE RELATIONSHIPS BETWEEN TRENDS AND TECHNOLOGICAL INNOVATIONS** In this chapter, we presented you with numerous key technologies and how they relate to six important trends. (See Figure 9.1 on page 440 for the list of technologies and trends.) For each trend, identify all the technologies presented in this chapter that can have an impact. For each technology that you do identify, provide a short discussion of how it might have an impact.

5. **MAKING A PHONE CALL ON THE INTERNET** Visit the Internet and find a Web site that provides free long-distance phone calling. PhoneFree is one such Web site, but there are many others. Download and install the necessary software and subscribe as a user. Now, make a phone call to someone you know. What was your overall experience? What was the quality of the call? How did you go about scheduling the call with the other person? Did you ever notice a "crackle" in the communications? Should organizations be using these types of Web sites for long-distance phone calls to cut down on their expenses?

6. **LEARNING ABOUT FINANCIAL CYBERMEDIARIES** Visit PayPal, the most well-known financial cybermediary, at www.paypal.com. As you peruse its site, answer the following questions. What is the process of signing up with PayPal? What information do you have to provide? What is the sign-up fee? What sort of fee do you pay each time you make a payment through PayPal? Can you have an account with PayPal that has money in it? How can you use your credit card to pay someone through PayPal? How has PayPal developed a business partnership with eBay, the leading online auction house?

7. **RESEARCHING INTELLIGENT HOME APPLIANCES** Visit a local appliance store in your area and find three home appliances that contain some sort of intelligence. For each appliance, prepare a short report that includes the following information:

   - A description and price for the intelligent home appliance
   - The "intelligent" features of the appliance
   - How those features make the appliance better than the nonintelligent version

8. **RESEARCHING E-GOVERNMENT SERVICES** Visit the Web sites for your local, city, and state governments. As you do, find electronic services that you would commonly use. What are they? Can you really sign up for these services electronically or can you simply download forms that you must fill out and send via regular mail? Why is it so important that various government agencies get into the "e" game?

Discussion Questions _____

1. There is currently much legislation pending right now in many states that would make it illegal for people to use a cell phone while driving a car. The reason is that society has already noticed a significant increase in the number of traffic accidents in which one of the drivers involved in the accident was using a cell phone. Think beyond that for a moment and include wearable computers. As this new technology becomes more widely available, isn't it possible for someone to be driving a car while using a computer? Should the government enact legislation to prevent it? Why or why not?

2. In a push technology environment, businesses and organizations will come to you with information, services, and product offerings based on your profile. How is a push technology environment different from mass mailings and spam? Is it an invasion of your privacy to have organizations calling you on your cell phone every time you come near a store? Why or why not? Should you be able to "opt in" or "opt out" of these offerings? Is this really any different from someone leaving a flyer at your house or on your car while it's parked in a parking lot?

3. There are three steps in automatic speech recognition (ASR): feature analysis, pattern classification, and language processing. Which of those three steps is the most challenging for a computer to perform? Why? Which of those three steps is the least challenging for a computer to perform? Why? If ASR systems are to become automatic speech understanding systems, which step must undergo the greatest improvement in its capabilities? Why?

4. Using a service such as PhoneFree, you can in fact make free long-distance phones calls on the Internet within the continental United States. Will this eventually spell the demise and eventual bankruptcy of traditional long-distance telephone providers such as AT&T and MCI? How can these traditional long-distance telephone providers overcome such a challenge? Is the entire world destined to have free long-distance calling just by having access to the Internet? Why or why not?

5. Micro-payments, financial cybermediaries, and digital cash are destined to greatly impact the use of coins and folding cash. What sort of future do you foresee if we do away completely with traditional forms of currency and just use electronic forms? Will this help eliminate the digital divide or will the digital divide provide a barrier to the widespread use of electronic forms of payment? Justify your answer.

6. What's your opinion of GPS-enabled implant chips? Should we all have them? Why or why not? Some states are now releasing criminals on parole and making them wear GPS-enabled bracelets so their every movement can be tracked. In your view, is this appropriate? Why or why not? Are there any groups of people that should be required to wear some type of GPS-enabled tracking technology? If not, why not? If so, what are those groups of people and why should they have to wear such devices?

7. What are the ethical dilemmas associated with using facial recognition software? Is the use of this type of software really any different from a store asking to see your driver's license when you use your credit card? Why or why not? Should the government be able to place digital video cameras on every street corner and use facial recognition software to monitor your movements? Why or why not?

8. When (and if) CAVEs become a common reality, you'll be able to visit your family and friends anytime you want no matter where they live. What sort of impact will this have on the travel industry? If you can see your relatives in a CAVE as often as you want, will you be more or less inclined to buy a plane ticket and visit them in person? Why or why not?

Continuing Your Education through the Internet

For many of you, this course may mark the end of your endeavors in higher education. Indeed, you may be preparing right now to enter the business world by sending out résumés, participating in job interviews, and building an e-portfolio (see *Extended Learning Module I*). If so, we certainly hope you're letting the Internet help (see the REAL HOT Electronic Commerce section in Chapter 1, "Using the Internet as a Tool to Find a Job"). For others of you, you may still have another year or two before completing your education. Whatever the case, you need to consider the current landscape of the business world and what it's going to take for you to compete now and in the future.

To be perfectly honest, it's a dog-eat-dog world out there. The competitive landscape of business is more intense than it ever has been. And that competitiveness spills into your personal life. Many of you are in school right now to get an education to better compete in the job market. But many knowledge workers are finding out that an undergraduate degree is simply not enough to compete in the business world.

So, many people are turning once again to higher education to obtain a master's degree, professional certification such as a CPA or CFP (certified financial planner), or perhaps even a Ph.D. in business. You may also be considering the same, either immediately upon graduation or sometime in the near future.

And, just like businesses, graduate schools (and all schools in general) are using the Internet as a way to communicate information to you. Many of these schools are even offering online courses you can complete through the Internet to further your education.

On the Web site that supports this text (www.mhhe.com/haag), we've provided many links related to continuing your education through the Internet. These are a great starting point for completing this REAL HOT section.

MBA PROGRAMS

Many of you will undoubtedly choose to continue your education by obtaining an MBA. And you probably should. The market for the best business positions is extremely competitive, with hiring organizations seeking individuals who can speak more than one language, have job experience, and have extended their educational endeavors beyond just getting an undergraduate degree. Indeed, there are more than 400,000 people in the United States seeking an MBA right now (that's an all-time high), and you must compete against some of those people in the job market.

Each year, the *U.S. News & World Report* ranks the top business schools in the nation. On the Web site that supports this text, you'll find a list of the Web sites for the top 50 business schools in the nation.

Choose a couple of different business schools from the list of 50, visit their Web sites, and answer the following questions for each:

A. What business school did you choose?

B. Does that school offer a graduate program in your area of interest?

C. Does the graduate program Web site contain biographical sketches of faculty?

D. Can you apply online?

E. Is there a major benefactor for the business school? If so, who is it?

F. Does the site list tuition and fee costs?

G. Does the site contain a list of the graduate courses offered in your area of interest?

As you prepare to enter the workforce and perhaps think about pursuing a master's in business, we would encourage you to return to the Web site that supports this text and visit the list of the top 50 business schools. On a yearly basis, we will update that list to include any new schools among the most elite to offer graduate programs in business.

SPECIALIZED MBA PROGRAMS

In the previous section, you explored a few of the top 50 business schools in the nation. Those schools were ranked irrespective of any specialization, focusing rather on overall academic reputation. *U.S. News & World Report* also compiles an annual list of the best business schools in 10 specializations: accounting, entrepreneurship, finance, health services administration, management information systems, international business, general business, marketing, nonprofit organizations, and production/operations. And if you're interested in a specialized MBA, you should consider viewing schools in these lists. On the Web site that supports this text, you'll find the complete lists of the top 10 business schools in each area.

Choose at least three schools that offer a specialization in your area of interest and visit their Web sites. Based on what you find, rank those three schools according to your first, second, and third choices. What factors did you consider? Was cost an overriding concern? Before you began your analysis, did you already have a preconceived notion of the best school? Did you change your mind once you visited the schools' sites?

GRADUATE SCHOOL INFORMATION AND TIPS

Before you begin your decision-making process concerning which graduate school to attend, you should gather a variety of material. For example, obtaining a directory of universities (both domestic and international) would be helpful. Perhaps even more important, you should ask yourself several questions. Are you ready for graduate school? Why are you considering going to graduate school? How do you determine which school is best for you based on such issues as price, location, and area of specialization?

Many of these questions are very personal to you. For example, we can't help you determine if you're really ready for graduate school or answer why you're considering going to graduate school. But what we can do is point you toward some valuable resources on the Internet to help you answer some of your questions and find a wealth of information relating to universities. On the Web site that supports this text, we've included many links to those types of sites.

At your leisure, we recommend that you connect to several of these sites and see what they have to offer. Some simply provide a list of universities, whereas others may be particularly useful as you make that all-important decision.

TELE-EDUCATION (DISTANCE LEARNING)

Throughout this text, you've explored the concept of 24 x 7 connectivity through information technology. Using IT (part of which is the Internet), organizations today are sending out telecommuting employees, and medical and health facilities are establishing telemedicine practices. Your school may be doing the same using IT to develop the environment of tele-education.

Tele-education, which goes by a number of terms including e-education, distance learning, distributed learning, and online learning, enables you to get an education without "going" to school. Quite literally, you can enroll in a school on the East Coast and live in Denver, enjoying great winter skiing. Using various forms of IT (videoconferencing, e-mail, chat rooms, and the Internet), you can take courses from schools all over the world. Some of those schools even offer complete degree programs via IT.

And these schools definitely include graduate programs in business. For example, the Massachusetts Institute of Technology and Duke University have graduate programs that combine traditional classroom instruction courses and computer-delivered courses. In 1997, Ohio University (Athens) introduced MBA without Boundaries, an MBA program that is completely online except for a required six-week orientation session.

As well, many for-profit organizations offer courses on the Internet that range from preparing for the CPA exam to IT-focused courses such as Windows NT and COBOL programming. You should definitely connect to the Web site that supports this text and view the list of sites related to tele-education. And if you're interested in taking online courses from a specific school, we recommend you connect to its Web site to determine if it offers courses over the Internet.

Connect to at least five of these sites and explore the possibilities of tele-education. As you do, consider the issues below.

    A. Can you just take courses or enroll in a complete degree program?

    B. What is the cost of tele-education?

    C. What process do you go through to enroll in a tele-education program?

    D. How would you feel about staying at home instead of going to class?

    E. How do tele-education programs foster interactivity between students and teachers?

    F. How much do you think you would learn in a tele-education program compared to a traditional in-class program?

    G. For what type of individual is a tele-education program best suited?

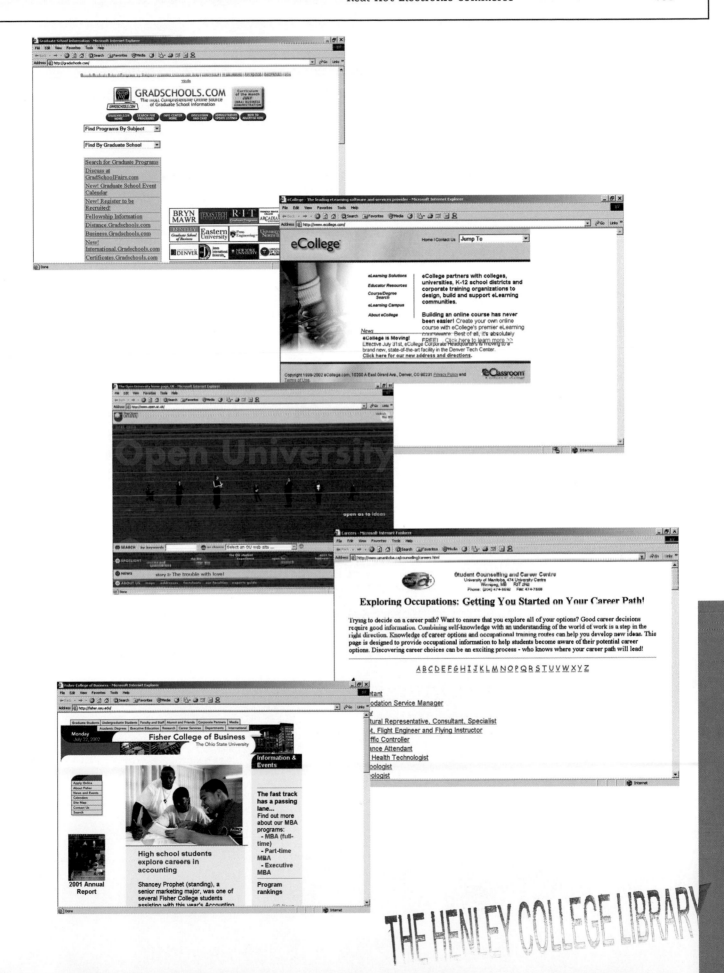

EXTENDED LEARNING MODULE I

BUILDING AN E-PORTFOLIO

Student Learning Outcomes

1. DESCRIBE THE TYPES OF ELECTRONIC RÉSUMÉS AND WHEN EACH IS APPROPRIATE.

2. DISCUSS NETWORKING STRATEGIES YOU CAN USE DURING A JOB SEARCH.

3. EXPLAIN HOW SELF-ASSESSMENT IS VALUABLE TO RÉSUMÉ WRITING.

4. USE THE INTERNET TO RESEARCH CAREER OPPORTUNITIES AND POTENTIAL EMPLOYERS.

5. DEVELOP POWERFUL JOB SEARCH E-PORTFOLIO CONTENT.

6. DOCUMENT EFFECTIVE WEB SITE STRUCTURE AND DESIGN COMPONENTS.

7. CREATE A JOB SEARCH E-PORTFOLIO WEB SITE AND PLACE IT ON AN INTERNET SERVER.

Introduction

The Internet is an accepted part of our daily life at work, school, and play. It should be no surprise that businesses are turning to the Internet to recruit and retain employees. Although there are many forms of electronic recruitment, this module will concentrate on electronic documents that you as a potential employee need to have prepared in order to compete effectively in the electronic job market. The final product is an electronic portfolio designed to help you successfully promote your skills in the electronic job market.

In this module, we assume that you're familiar with the Internet, research tools, and have at least a little knowledge of HTML. For a review of the Internet, see *Extended Learning Module B*. For a review of HTML, see *Extended Learning Module F*.

The Electronic Job Market

The ***electronic job market*** makes use of Internet technologies to recruit employees and is growing by leaps and bounds. The *Industry Standard* (www.thestandard.com), a leading magazine on the Internet economy reports that the average cost of online recruiting is $152 per hire while the cost of more traditional methods is $1,381.[1] Additionally, a much broader worldwide selection of candidates can be screened, significantly increasing the likelihood of finding a good match for the hiring organization. As more and more hiring employers turn to the Internet to recruit employees, it's critical that you learn to capitalize on the technologies that help organizations locate and evaluate potential employees. Although the basic parts of your résumé stay the same and the purpose of your résumé is still to present your skills and qualifications, how you do so must change dramatically in the electronic job market.

The Internet provides 24x7 access to information for both the employer and you as a potential employee. During your electronic job search, your effective use of Internet tools is critical to a successful job hunt. Since meeting the needs of employers is the basis for getting hired, your pre-résumé tasks must center on gathering intelligence about who is hiring, what skills are in demand, how much those skills are worth, and what you need to do to be considered for the available jobs. With this information in hand, you're prepared to create the electronic documents that will place you in a position to be considered for the job of your dreams (see Figure I.1 on the next page).

Preparations Before You Write

In the always-available job market created by the Internet, organizations post and remove jobs on a continuous and instantaneous basis. Businesses have many options for where and how to list positions. Most Internet-savvy organizations have recruiting pages on their Web sites. Others use job database Web sites such as www.monster.com that reach a worldwide audience. You learned about various job database Web sites while completing the REAL HOT Electronic Commerce project at the end of Chapter 1. Some organizations even use their intranets to recruit from within.

Even in this all-encompassing electronic job market, some jobs are never posted. Collectively, unposted positions are referred to as the ***hidden job market.*** It is important to prepare yourself to search for jobs in the traditional (newspaper and magazine), electronic, and hidden job markets to maximize your job opportunities.

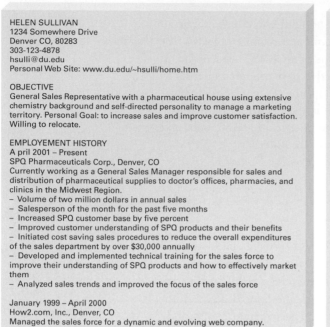

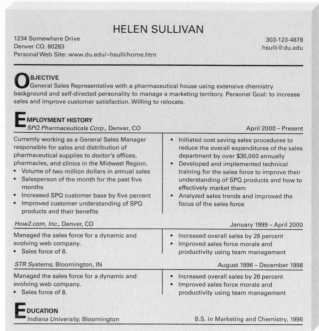

Figure I.1

Sample Electronic Job
Search Documents

START TO NETWORK

If you read the want ads, send out résumés, and wait for employers to discover you, the odds of finding a satisfying job are not very good. According to JobStar (www.jobstar.org), a job board and collection of job search information offered in association with the *Wall Street Journal* (www.CareerJournal.com), "80 percent of all positions are filled *without* employer advertising. These positions are filled by—or created for—candidates who come to an employer's attention through employee recommendations, referrals from trusted associates, recruiters, or direct contact with the candidate."[2] This means that networking and preparing résumé content targeted to a specific job and industry are critical to your success.

Networking involves creating relationships with people who are in a position to further your career search. Networks take time and energy to develop, so it's never too early to begin. Start by making a list of everyone that you call on the phone, e-mail, electronically chat with, or have even had passing conversations with. This list should be quite long. Include even the people that you see and speak to infrequently. The goal here is to get a list of potential contacts. Do not rule anyone out. Unlikely people can often put you in contact with someone else. Remember that each of these people know people who also know people. A third-tier contact may be just the person you need to talk to.

Before contacting anyone on your list, develop a 30-second commercial. This is a short description of who you are, what job you're looking for, and the skills that make you suited for the job. Having a short script makes it easier to contact people and avoids wasting their time.

Face-to-face and phone networking are critical to a successful job search, but you should also employ electronic means. No matter how you're contacting people, use the script and include personal information. For example, when contacting Bob Smith who was referred to you by Jim Jones, include how you know Jim Jones and why he thought Bob Smith could be helpful. And always thank people for their time.

Avoid sending bulk e-mails to everyone in your address book. You're asking people to take time out of their busy schedules to help you, so the personal touch of sending in-

BUILD YOUR COMMERCIAL

Building a quality 30-second commercial can be tougher than it sounds. The goal is to be able to contact a stranger and let them know who you are, what your skills are, and why you are approaching them.

1. Narrow your focus by selecting one job type (a job type can encompass several job titles but the skills are the same) and one industry. Write your job description. For example,

   - *Online researcher* for a major law firm specializing in corporate contracts and patents

   - *Java and C++ programmer* in the Texas oil and gas industry

2. Start a list of job title synonyms. For example, a Java and C++ programmer could also be called a Web Applet developer or simply a programmer/analyst. This list will help you research and write your résumé.

3. Create a list of words describing your skills and interests. Begin broadly and then narrow your list to skills related to your current job search (see Figure I.2 on page 474).

4. Put together your script. Include who you are, how you came in contact with this person, your top three skills, and what you would like from this contact. For example,

   Hello my name is _____. I am working on an Information Technology degree at the University of Denver. You are registered as a mentor in the Career Placement Center and your job title is listed as Java Developer. I am very analytical, have enjoyed all of my programming courses, and am particularly interested in Java programming. Can you give me some advice on how to secure a job?

5. Practice your script before attending face-to-face networking functions. Edit your script as appropriate before using it in electronic communications.

6. Create a list of follow-up questions to use when your contact responds. For example,

   - How did you get your first job in this area?

   - Do you know of any open positions that I should apply for?

dividual e-mail is more likely to obtain results. Set a goal to contact a specific number of people each week, keep track of who you've contacted and the responses you've received, and finally don't be afraid to follow up.

In addition to e-mail, join as many relevant mailing lists as you can keep up with. *Mailing lists* are discussion groups organized by area of interest. By subscribing to such a list, you can send and receive member's e-mail. Mailing lists allow you to gain industry information and make contacts that would not otherwise be available. On occasion, job announcements are also circulated through these lists. You can find mailing lists by topic at www.topica.com, www.tile.net/listserv, or groups.google.com.

PERFORM SELF-ASSESSMENT

Remember that the paper and electronic documents you create are your personal marketing tools. Most people want to jump right in and write a résumé, but you must get *employer focused* first. Employers typically process résumés looking for things that exclude candidates by sorting applicants into three groups: Definitely, Maybe, and No. Ideally, you would like to be in the Definitely group, but the Maybe group can result in a position if you've done your homework and stringently documented what you offer an employer.

Contrary to popular belief and traditional résumé-writing styles, employers are not really interested in what you've already done; they want to know what you will do for

Figure I.2

Sample Self-assessment Tool

Transferable Skills

Transferable skills are those that can be applied to any job or work situation. Everyone has them. Each transferable skill has keywords that can be used to describe your strengths. Select each skill below that applies to you and then write how you effectively exhibit that skill.

General Keywords			
___ critical thinking	___ self-discipline	___ general knowledge	___ self-confidence
___ research techniques	___ insight	___ cultural perspective	___ imagination
___ perseverance	___ writing	___ teaching ability	___ leadership

Research Keywords			
___ initiating	___ attaining	___ achieving	___ reviewing
___ updating	___ interpreting	___ analyzing	___ synthesizing
___ communicating	___ planning	___ designing	
___ performing	___ estimating	___ implementing	

Teaching Keywords			
___ organizing	___ assessing	___ public speaking	___ reporting
___ counseling	___ assessing	___ coordinating	___ administering
___ motivating	___ problem solving		

Personality Keywords			
___ dynamic	___ sensitive	___ responsible	___ creative
___ imaginative	___ accurate	___ easygoing	___ adept
___ innovative	___ expert	___ successful	___ efficient
___ perceptive	___ astute	___ humanistic	___ honest
___ outstanding	___ calm	___ outgoing	___ self-starting
___ reliable	___ unique	___ experienced	___ talented
___ vigorous	___ versatile	___ diplomatic	

Object Keywords			
___ data	___ systems	___ relations	___ theories
___ recommendations	___ programs	___ events	___ outputs
___ facts	___ conclusions	___ goals	___ surveys
___ procedures	___ methods	___ statistics	___ strategy
___ feelings	___ designs	___ tools	___ journals
___ techniques	___ communications	___ charts	___ presentations
___ reports	___ research projects	___ information	___ human resources

them and to have documented evidence of those skills. In order to effectively communicate your skills and how they will benefit a potential employer, you must know what those skills are and that means spending some time evaluating yourself. While it's nice to be a "people person," that doesn't tell an employer that you work well under stress, mediate, negotiate contracts, and follow procedures. Being a "people person" will not get you a job, but detailing your skills in that area may.

There are many good tools for self-assessment. Personality profiles, checklists (see Figure I.2), strength identification, achievement lists, and any number of writing and projection exercises. You can even ask people what your strengths are. Believe it or not, others are often better at articulating your strengths than you. Most colleges and universities have an array of assessment tools available to their students. There are also many organizations offering testing from the Web. Some are free, for example, www.jobstar.org, and others charge a fee, for example, www.careermaze.com. Use the methods that are available and suit your needs, but don't shortchange this step. Time spent here will pay off when you do begin to write.

The goal of this exercise is to develop a list of evocative words that you can use to describe your objective and experience in a manner that employers can understand. Typically these words are nouns and adjectives called *skill words* that stress your capabilities, and you should definitely weave them into the text of your résumé.

RESEARCH CAREERS, INDUSTRIES, AND COMPANIES

The Web is an incredible resource for researching topics such as résumé writing, career forecasts, job availability, skills required to be hirable, industry trends, and virtual communities. Although there are other approaches, most Web users find that search tools significantly improve the quality of the material located when browsing.

SEARCH TOOLS

Most of you have probably used Web search engines with varying degrees of success. There are two main types of search engines: directory search engines and true search engines.

A *directory search engine* organizes listings of Web sites into hierarchical lists. Yahoo! is the most popular and well-known of these. If you want to find information using a directory search engine, you start by selecting a specific category and continually choose subcategories until you arrive at a list of Web sites with the information you want. Because you continually narrow down your selection by choosing subcategories, directory search engines are hierarchical.

A *true search engine* uses software agent technologies to search the Internet for key words and then places them into indexes. In doing so, true search engines allow you to ask questions as opposed to continually choosing subcategories to arrive at a list of Web sites. Ask Jeeves is the most popular and well-known true search engine (see Figure I.3).

All search engines match words or phrases entered in the search box against information in their databases. Most search engines have tips or help that provide instructions on how to create the most effective search for that engine. Once matching values from the database have been located, they're organized by relevance and presented to you. Understanding how relevance is determined will help you reduce your search time. Some of the many methods used to determine ranking include

- The number of times the search terms appear in the site
- Site design ranking (easy to use, frames, . . .)
- Link popularity
- Partnerships and subscriptions

Figure I.3

Ask Jeeves Home Page

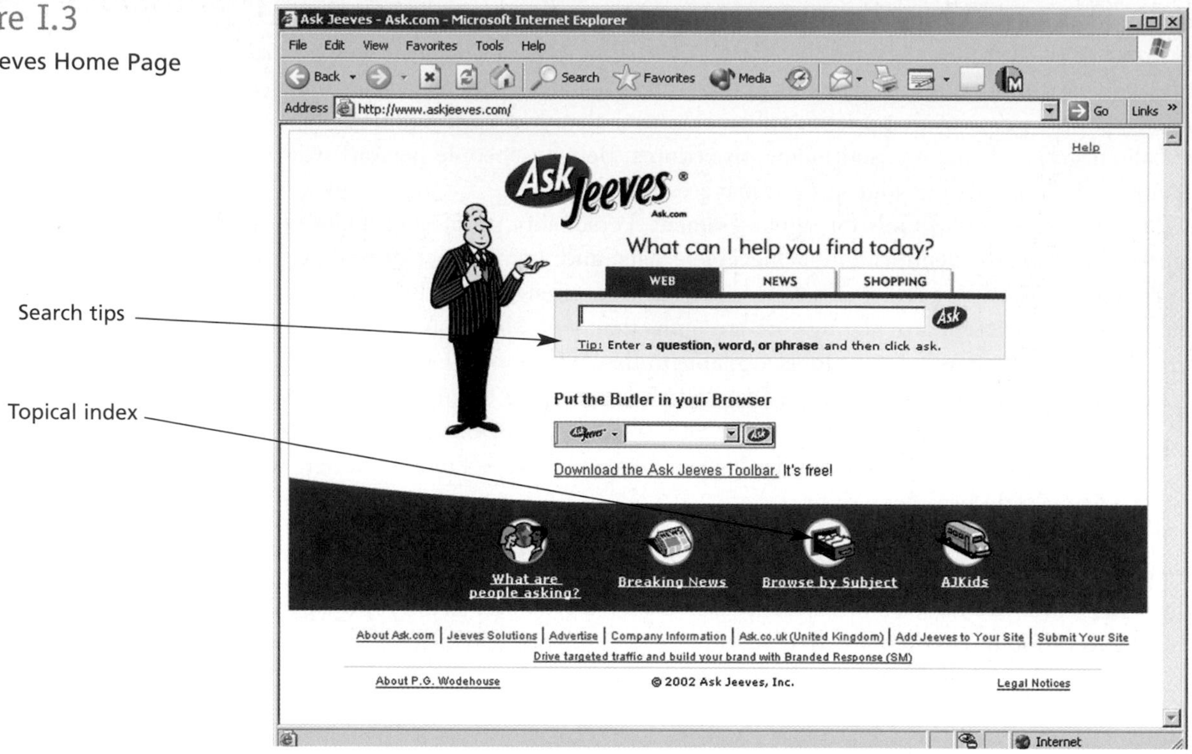

Search tips

Topical index

SUCCESSFUL WEB RESEARCH

Many job seekers underestimate the role of research in creating effective documents such as a résumé. A résumé is not simply a history of your education and work, but should be a document targeted to one position and industry. You can achieve this well-defined targeting by carefully selecting your relevant life experiences and presenting them in a fashion that highlights the qualifications employers want to see. Successful targeting results from understanding the benefits that organizations expect to obtain from employees in your field. It isn't enough to document your skills and wait for people reviewing your résumé to determine the services you could provide; you must tell them exactly what you can do and how you would benefit their organization.

Research is the key to creating powerful employer-centered résumé content directed to a specific industry. There is so much information available to help you develop powerful résumé content that the task of sifting through it is daunting. There are two approaches that work to narrow the search process. Determining where you are in your preparation for the job market will help you select the best approach.

When looking for careers requiring you to complete education or training to gain the skills needed to succeed, search for industries, career paths, schools, and job titles in your area of interest. To target your writing based on existing skills, search using your skills to find jobs, industries, and organizations matching your qualifications. Either way you should visit an array of general Web resources, government sites, job database Web sites, and business sites before you write.

To make the most of the available information, develop a list of search terms based on your goals and then visit media sites, job database Web sites, search engines, government sites, and business Web pages. You should be able to find information on planning your career, the education or training needed to be successful, expected earnings by geographic location, the work environment, attire, normal career path, projected number of openings, and current job postings. Additionally you should find specific organizations, contacts, and communities that will help you fine-tune your target.

START YOUR RESEARCH

Research is time-consuming and the sheer volume of information available on the Web is daunting. Target your research and stay focused. When you come upon items of interest that will not further your current goal, copy and paste their URLs into an open word processing document and then proceed with the your research.

In a second open word processing document, track career-related data and their sources gathered from your search. Refine your search words as necessary. Remember that you should be gathering as much data as you can about your chosen career, but it may be helpful to search for each type of information separately. For example, salary information may not be available from the sources discussing the projected number of jobs over the next five years or the normal work week in an industry. Use the following list of Web resources as a starting point.

Search Engines

- www.google.com—The largest Web index
- www.search.com—Search using several search engines at once
- www.searchengineguide.com—Listing of search engines by topic
- www.job-search-engine.com—A meta job search engine dedicated to employment

Media

- www.enews.com—Online magazines on any topic with online forums

- www.careerpath.com—Online classifieds
- www.classifieds2000.com—Online classifieds

Government

- www.bls.gov—Bureau of Labor Statistics. Excellent source for work environment, job forecast, and regional data. Try the kids' pages.
- To locate government jobs, use www.google.com. Click the Advanced Search link and enter .gov as the domain to search

Job Boards

- www.monster.com—Largest job board consistently listed in the top five sites
- www.hotjobs.com—Job postings by location, industry, or company. International postings and salary wizard.
- www.collegegrad.com—Excellent resource for entry-level job seekers. Offers job search, résumé, and networking strategies.

Other Resources

- www.careers.org—Job search and career resource directory organized by topic and region
- Don't forget to visit the Web sites of some businesses in your chosen industry.

Writing Targeted Résumé Content

Through beginning to network, assessing your skills, and researching, you'll gain the knowledge critical for creating targeted résumé content. Use the job titles, skills, and jargon from one industry to describe yourself and your experience. If you're job seeking in multiple industries or in a variety of position titles, you may need to develop a separate résumé for each.

When you begin writing, concentrate on creating solid content that is targeted, is grammatically correct, and convincingly outlines your skills. And don't worry about formatting your content right now; you'll do that later. Since we're concentrating on electronic documents, old rules governing the writing style, length, and content of paper résumés do not apply. For example, creating a résumé that will print on one page (or two at most) is not relevant in this arena.

POWERFUL OBJECTIVE STATEMENTS

A well-developed objective statement is a potent tool for getting employers to look more deeply into your potential. Although some résumé styles omit this statement, it can be a critical résumé component when it provides an executive summary of your qualifications. Typical objective statements are short—between one and three sentences and appear below the contact information.

For first-time job seekers or those changing careers, an objective should include a job title, an industry, the top three to five skills that qualify you for the job, and the benefit you will bring to the hiring organization. This is a tall order, but using a decisive writing style lets employers know that you understand their business and helps them better determine that your skills can benefit their organization.

Experienced job seekers can break this content into two sections, a single-line objective with a job title and industry followed by a summary of qualifications section. The summary of qualifications should highlight your skills and accomplishments that benefited previous employers. We recommend that you present this content in the form of a bulleted list (see Figure I.4).

In addition to basic job skills, it is important to let potential employers know about your cultural, language, and communication talents. While being multilingual may not be a requirement for a position, it is certainly a nice bonus that will get you noticed. Being willing to relocate may allow you to be considered for a wider range of jobs in an organization. Be decisive about what you want to do and showcase your skills whether they have been gained in the classroom, through life experiences, travel, or on the job.

Regardless of whether you're writing a stand-alone objective statement or including a summary of qualifications, write for your audience, or, in other words, write from the hiring organization's perspective. Remember to state what you can do for the organization that hires you using the industry jargon and skills keywords uncovered through networking, self-assessment, and research to describe yourself and what you offer an organization. Do not use words that indicate that you are not competent at a skill. Examples of such words are entry level or beginner.

Avoid statements that appear self-centered or self-serving. For instance, don't mention money or promotions. Instead state that you're willing to accept increasing levels of responsibility. Money and promotions benefit you, while increasing your responsibility

Figure I.4

Objective and Summary Examples

Entry-level Objective Statement	
Objective	Public accounting auditor position in the Midwest capitalizing on internal and external audit experience gained in a four-month PricewaterhouseCoopers internship. Familiar with payroll, tax, and general ledger processing. Multilingual and willing to travel.
Entry-level Objective Statement with Summary	
Objective Summary	Public accounting auditor position in the Midwest. Accounting coursework and internships • PricewaterhouseCoopers auditor internship with four months of experience in both internal and external general ledger audit techniques • Bookkeeping and coursework experience with payroll, cost, and tax accounting • Spanish fluency gained through extensive travel in Mexico and South America • Willing to travel and relocate

WRITE YOUR OBJECTIVE

Strong objective statements clearly state the position and industry of interest along with your strongest skills. Do not use "I," "me," or "my." Focus on the benefit to the employer.

- Pharmaceutical sales representative capitalizing on extensive chemistry background and self-directed personality to manage a marketing territory.

- Researcher in investment and analysis. Interests and skills include securities analysis, financial planning, and portfolio management. Long-range goal: to become a chartered financial analyst. Willing to travel and relocate.

1. Identify the position, industry, skill words, and jargon in the sample objectives.

2. Rewrite the following weak objective statement:
   A position in marketing with a progressive firm

3. Create a strong objective statement for your planned career. Start with "I would like a job where I can use my ability to _____ which will result in _____." Rewrite the statement to be employer centered, contain industry jargon, and use skills keywords.

benefits the organization. Don't include statements with "I," "my," or "me," since these personal pronouns focus on you rather than on the organization.

Stay away from canned or hyped phrases normally associated with résumé writing. For example, a "position with a progressive company" and "opportunity for advancement" are commonly seen in résumés but don't communicate anything important about the applicant. Write honestly about your abilities and skills in a way that demonstrates your value to employers.

Most people reviewing résumés visually scan the objectives and summary of qualifications to determine whether or not to review the remaining résumé content. If you do not have enough skills to create competitive objective and summary statements, create a plan to acquire them, but do not include even small untruths in your résumé. "White lies" may get you considered for more jobs, but eventually your lack of skill will become apparent and cost you your credibility and maybe even your career.

IMPORTANT CONTACT INFORMATION

After building your objective statement, you should dedicate the first section of your résumé to your name and how you can be contacted. Although this seems obvious, there are a couple of important contact issues to mention. Contact information must be complete, correct, and permanent. Depending on the policies of the company receiving your résumé, it could remain on file for months or even years. If your résumé is pulled for consideration six months from now, the contact information should still be valid.

Since we're focusing on electronic documents, it's important to note that privacy is a concern. While paper documents are typically routed to a person or department within an organization who has the responsibility of protecting your privacy, electronic documents can be generally distributed with no party directly responsible for privacy. Especially for documents posted to the Internet, it may be preferable to omit your address and phone numbers; instead use an e-mail account devoted to job hunting. If you elect to use an e-mail address, be sure to check your e-mail regularly and then provide the remaining contact information to legitimate organizations who contact you.

FEEDBACK, FEEDBACK, FEEDBACK!

As you probably learned in your composition courses, it is important to proofread and obtain feedback before submitting written work. This is even more essential for projects as important as your job search e-portfolio. Either formally or informally, create a group of two to three people who will provide constructive feedback throughout the remainder of your e-portfolio development.

1. Begin by each discussing your overall career goals and your work to date on this module.

2. Test your 30-second commercial on the group and solicit feedback.

3. Test your objective on the group and solicit feedback.

4. Discuss the other sections needed for your résumé and how to make your content employer centered.

5. Repeat steps 2 through 4 for the other group members.

OTHER VALUABLE RÉSUMÉ SECTIONS

The other sections included in your résumé are determined by what you need to communicate. Ideally all other content would directly support your objectives and skills. This does not mean that work experience and education in other fields should never be mentioned. Remember that general skills such as critical thinking, analysis, writing, communication, and so on are relevant to almost any position. Include jobs and education that demonstrate these skills. It's also important in many instances to show increasing job responsibility even though the positions are not directly relevant to your current job search.

Most résumés should include sections outlining your education and work experience. Place the section most important to your marketable skills first. Within each section organize the information to best present your skills. In general, hiring organizations prefer chronological presentations because they are traditional and easy to follow, but other styles can be effective as long as it does not appear that you're trying to hide or omit anything.

Use the same writing techniques outlined for creating a powerful objective statement to describe and demonstrate your relevant coursework and job skills. It isn't enough to list course and job titles. Include descriptions documenting relevant skills and their organizational benefit using jargon relevant to your position and industry. For example, "responsible for coding and testing Visual Basic applications" is an adequate job description for a programmer but "coded Visual Basic applications consisting of thousands of executable lines to solve complex business problems, manage system throughput, and improve end-user satisfaction" demonstrates both the level of skill being offered and how the organization benefited from them.

On most résumés, the last section should present information on references. Commonly this section contains a single statement, "References available upon request." There are several reasons not to include actual references in this section. First, references are not needed until you're actually being considered for a position. Second, going through the interview process and learning more about the organization will help you to select more effective references. Third, it saves space. Finally, especially in the electronic arena, your references should not have to worry about their personal contact information being distributed without their permission.

Other sections to consider include Awards, Publications, Personal Information, and anything specific to the particular job being applied for. For example, a "Statement of Belief" could be important when applying for a job with a religious organization but probably shouldn't be included otherwise. Personal information can be troublesome. When applying for a position with a formal organization, too much personal information can make you look informal. However, the same information can make you look like a good fit in a less formal institution. Use your research to determine what to include and omit.

Developing e-Portfolio Content

An *electronic portfolio (e-portfolio)* is a collection of Web documents used to support a stated purpose such as demonstrating writing or photography skills. You should design your job search e-portfolios to provide everything that a prospective employer needs to evaluate your employment potential. That means that it should include several résumé formats, permanent contact information, and a gallery designed to demonstrate your skills.

ELECTRONIC FILE FORMATS

To be effective in every situation, you should prepare your résumés in a variety of electronic file formats, but this isn't necessarily a time-consuming task. Each format should be incorporated into your e-portfolio. Begin by building an unformatted résumé with solid content and then add formatting to create the other required formats.

SCANNABLE RÉSUMÉS

Scannable résumés (also called *ASCII résumés* or *plain-text résumés*) are designed to be evaluated by skills-extraction software and typically contain all résumé content without any formatting (see Figure I.5).

Figure I.5

Partial Scannable Résumé

Double space before headings

All caps for section headings

Use separate lines for dates, titles, and locations

For bulleted list

HELEN SULLIVAN
1234 Somewhere Drive
Denver CO, 80283
303-123-4878
hsulli@du.edu
Personal Web Site: www.du.edu/~hsulli/home.htm

OBJECTIVE
General Sales Representative with a pharmaceutical house using extensive chemistry background and self-directed personality to manage a marketing territory. Personal Goal: to increase sales and improve customer satisfaction. Willing to relocate.

EMPLOYEMENT HISTORY
April 2001 – Present
SPQ Pharmaceuticals Corp., Denver, CO
Currently working as a General Sales Manager responsible for sales and distribution of pharmaceutical supplies to doctor's offices, pharmacies, and clinics in the Midwest Region.
– Volume of two million dollars in annual sales
– Salesperson of the month for the past five months
– Increased SPQ customer base by five percent
– Improved customer understanding of SPQ products and their benefits
– Initiated cost saving sales procedures to reduce the overall expenditures of the sales department by over $30,000 annually
– Developed and implemented technical training for the sales force to improve their understanding of SPQ products and how to effectively market them
– Analyzed sales trends and improved the focus of the sales force

January 1999 – April 2000
How2.com, Inc., Denver, CO
Managed the sales force for a dynamic and evolving web company.

Scannable résumés can be delivered for evaluation in an electronic format (file) or can be printed. When potential employers receive printed scannable résumés, they use optical character recognition (OCR) software to create a file. To improve OCR performance, submit original copies printed on white bond paper using a high-quality printer. When printed, scannable résumés should not be folded, stapled, or paper clipped since the quality of the document can significantly impact scan accuracy.

Skills-extraction software is designed to create an applicant profile from the electronic version of your résumé. Your résumé file is submitted to an *extraction engine,* smart software with a vocabulary of job-related skills that allows it to recognize and catalog recognized terms in your résumé. The engine's vocabulary can be updated with industry-specific jargon and emerging skills. Terms and phrases are associated with a context to improve the recognition of synonyms and antonyms. Context recognition also allows the software to differentiate between an ADA programmer, a member of ADA (American Dental Association), and someone who works on ADA (Americans with Disabilities ACT) issues. Additionally, the software understands the typical résumé sections such as Education and Work History, allowing it to create a complete profile. The profile is then classified by broad vocational category (accounting, marketing, engineering, and so on). The result of extracting skills from all résumés submitted to an organization is a hierarchical index of job applicants based on vocational category.

When a position for a new employee opens in an organization that has implemented skills extraction, a list of specific job skills is developed that is then matched to the database profiles extracted from applicant's ASCII résumés. This process is similar to the techniques you use to search for Web sites with words and phrases. A list of applicants with the desired skills is returned. Reviewers have access to the applicant profiles as well as the full résumé text.

To serve you well in this mechanized environment, your résumé must follow fairly standard section naming conventions, and contain the skill words most likely to be used by prospective employers. You should have uncovered these skill words during your research and woven them into your text as you created your résumé.

General guidelines for creating scannable résumés include

- Create a text-only file.
  In Microsoft Word select **File** from the menu, click **Save As,** and then set the **Save As Type** to Plain Text (*.txt) or use Notepad to create your document.
- Use only Courier or Times New Roman 10 or 12 point font.
- Do not include character formatting such as bold, underline, italics, or text color.
- Do not center or tab indent text (every line should be left justified).
- Press Enter at the end of each line. Line length should be between 65 and 70 characters for optimal skills extraction.
- Do not include tables or graphics.
- Leave two blank lines between sections.
- Capitalize all letters in section headings.
- Use asterisks (*), dashes (-), or another standard keyboard character for bullets (do not use automated bulleted or numbered lists).

A properly created scannable résumé should be visually *unappealing* and long. This format is designed for machines, but do not skimp on content quality because a person is likely to try to read it at some point. The ASCII plain text format should be used for most electronically submitted résumés. Use this format to copy and paste résumé content for job database Web sites and Internet-based résumé builders and to deliver your résumé in the body of an e-mail message.

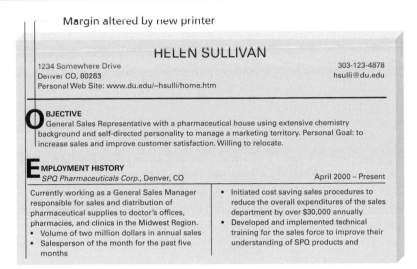

Figure I.6
Undesirable Presentation
Résumé Print

PRESENTATION RÉSUMÉS

A *presentation résumé* is the nicely formatted paper résumé that most people are familiar with. This type of résumé is designed for visual impact, should be well laid out on the page, and is most often between one and two printed pages. Presentation résumés are sent to potential employers who do not use skills-extraction software, and these are carried with you to any face-to-face interviews. Although ASCII résumé content can be edited to create this presentation format, be careful not to make significant changes since the same people are likely to review both a scannable and presentation copy of your résumé.

Microsoft Word and other word processing applications contain templates that will help you with presentation résumé formatting. Typically removing the Enter commands (hard returns) from your ASCII résumé and then copying and pasting selected text into the template is effective. Additional templates and formatting suggestions are widely available on the Internet. You should also have someone from your school's career resource center review your presentation résumé.

We don't advise that you electronically submit a heavily formatted presentation résumé. The page layout is typically specific to your printer and your computer on which you created the document. When formatted documents are printed on another printer, the results are haphazard at best. For example, information can be dropped from a table, text can be misaligned, and page breaks can be altered (see Figure I.6).

PDF RÉSUMÉS

Portable document format (PDF) is the standard electronic distribution file format. The benefit of PDF is that documents created in any application can be shared across platforms and still look exactly as designed. All fonts, indentions, graphics, links, tables, and alignment are retained. This format is widely used to distribute books and forms electronically. For example, most U.S. tax forms are available as PDF downloads from a Web site. You can download Adobe Acrobat Reader from www.adobe.com at no cost to view PDF documents.

Once you convert your presentation résumé to a PFD format, anyone can view and print it exactly as you designed it. You can easily distribute your PDF résumé as an e-mail attachment or a Web download. The process of creating a PDF file is simple but requires access to Adobe Acrobat software, which is available in several versions. Currently, a **Create Adobe PDF Online** link is available from www.adobe.com that will allow you to subscribe and create up to five free PDF files.

HTML

As you create and deliver Web content, you create files with either .htm or .html as the extension. Within these files (called HTML documents), you use hypertext markup language (HTML) tags to provide document formatting instructions to Web browsers such as Microsoft Internet Explorer or Netscape Communicator.

A good e-portfolio Web site should include a home page that acts as a site overview and menu, all of your résumé text, and additional supporting materials using HTML tags to format attractive pages. Résumés and supporting content already formatted for other delivery modes (.txt, .pdf, .doc, .ppt, .xls, and so on) for other purposes are usually not converted to HTML. You can refer back to *Extended Learning Module F* for using HTML to create a Web site and provide links to downloadable files. In the remainder of this module, we'll specifically address designing and building the pages of your e-portfolio.

GALLERY

Besides the ability to deliver your résumé in multiple formats, an e-portfolio provides you with the opportunity to demonstrate your skills through a gallery of works (see Figure I.7). Because the Web allows viewers to click on links to view materials that are of interest to them, there is no absolute limit to the number of supporting pages that you can develop.

The simplest way to compose a gallery is to make use of materials that you already have in hand. Remember that the gallery should display your skills, so consider including the following:

- Writing samples
- Spreadsheets or other applications of business tools
- Demonstrations of analytical, tracking, planning, or management skills
- Presentations that you've developed

Existing documents may need to be edited to remove confidential materials or to shorten the content. For example, you might include the introduction, problem analysis, and summary sections of a 30-page report since it's unlikely that anyone would read the entire report; they would thereby miss those sections that sufficiently demonstrate your talent. Don't include proprietary employer information or group projects without giving appropriate credit and obtaining permission.

Figure I.7

Sample Job Search
e-Portfolio Gallery

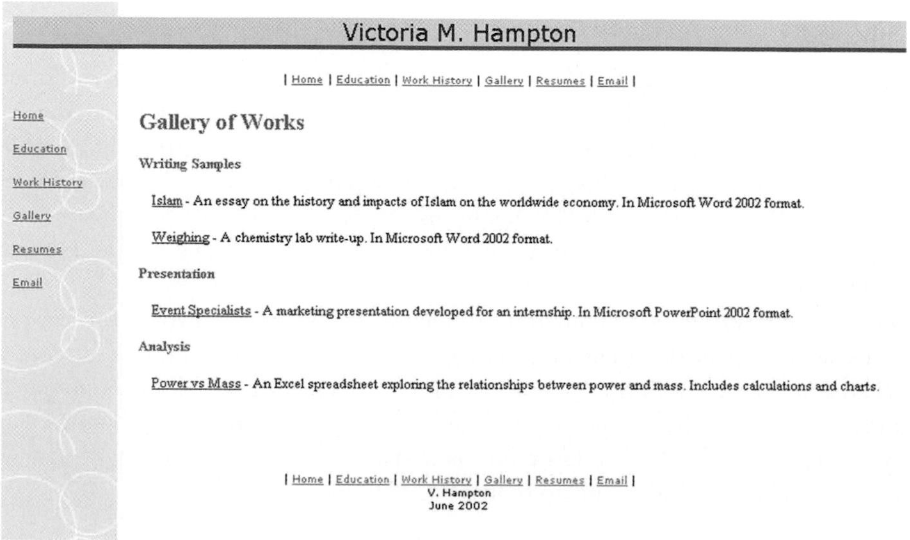

Victoria M. Hampton

| Home | Education | Work History | Gallery | Resumes | Email |

Home
Education
Work History
Gallery
Resumes
Email

Gallery of Works

Writing Samples

Islam - An essay on the history and impacts of Islam on the worldwide economy. In Microsoft Word 2002 format.

Weighing - A chemistry lab write-up. In Microsoft Word 2002 format.

Presentation

Event Specialists - A marketing presentation developed for an internship. In Microsoft PowerPoint 2002 format.

Analysis

Power vs Mass - An Excel spreadsheet exploring the relationships between power and mass. Includes calculations and charts.

| Home | Education | Work History | Gallery | Resumes | Email |
V. Hampton
June 2002

If you don't have existing documents that sufficiently demonstrate your job skills, create them from scratch. This can be time-consuming, but they create a much stronger statement about your talent and dedication than just saying you can do the job. Start small and spend the time to do an excellent job. One of the biggest benefits of a Web-based gallery is that you can add and remove components at any time.

There are no hard-and-fast rules about what to include in your gallery, but remember to keep it focused on your goal of obtaining a job. Label and organize your gallery content so that viewers can click on only what they want to see. For example, provide links from your job and education descriptions to documents demonstrating related skills. Alternatively, a gallery link can lead to a page outlining your skills with links to specific documents.

Web Design Considerations

Web design is a complex art requiring technical knowledge, research, skill, and an understanding of your audience. The good news is that you don't have to become a Web designer to have an effective e-portfolio. The sections that follow outline a few basic rules that will help you organize your content.

BASIC WEB DESIGN PRINCIPLES

If you search the Web for Web design principles, you'll find many lists of suggestions that have only a few elements in common. Every Web design expert has an opinion about what makes a good site and so does everyone browsing the Web. Can they all be right? Probably yes, depending on the context. Here, we'll cover effective Web design principles for creating a job search e-portfolio, which is definitely different than creating a B2C Web site.

DEFINE THE SITE AUDIENCE AND PURPOSE

You create and use a job search e-portfolio to market yourself for a job or ranges of related jobs to the hiring organizations of a particular industry. To make this clear, add the industry and job title(s) to your job search e-portfolio. In doing so, you've defined both your audience and your purpose. The key to developing a Web site that will appeal to your audience is to build what they like, not what you like. Again, your research should pay off. Think about the industry and business sites that you visited while researching your chosen career.

Some of the questions you can ask yourself to help gain insight into your target audience are

- What is the average age of managers (the people who do the hiring)? Employees (the people you would work with)?
- How conservative is this industry?
- Are employees expected to be artistic?
- How do employees dress?
- What do the backgrounds, colors, graphics, and navigation of business sites in the industry look like?
- How does this industry promote itself?

There are no absolutes in e-portfolio design. A site that works well for an artist, while beautiful, would probably be inappropriate for an accountant. Remember that this is not a personal site. It should demonstrate your business personality without being too personal.

WEB LAYOUT

The difference between content designed for printed viewing and content designed for electronic viewing on the Web is dramatic to say the least. You should keep in mind that good printed layout does not translate effectively to the Web. There are many reasons for this; the primary reasons include:

- Printed pages are designed to be read, while Web pages are designed to be browsed.
- All printed pages are the same size, while Web pages are not. The viewable area of a Web page is also much smaller than a printed page.
- Printed pages stay visually the same, while Web page layout varies depending on the Web browser, screen resolution, operating system, and monitor being used.

Even with the improved resolution of today's monitors, it's more difficult to read from a computer screen than it is from a printed document. Few readers will actually read long passages online; they most often print it or skip it altogether. Consider breaking long text (three or more screens) up so that the user is presented with an overview and can then link to the details. If you need to present long text as a single unit, be sure that it's printer friendly by using the dimensions outlined in Figure I.8.

Web content must be concise, well labeled, and formatted for browsing. Every page needs to contain information about who, what, when, and where, so that a person who just pops into that page has a point of reference. Although Web pages look very different when graphics and colors are applied, most Web designers employ a common zone-based layout. The top of each page contains a header that holds the organization's name, logo, and other identifying information. Many sites also include navigational links in the header. The bottom of each page contains a footer outlining the origin (author and institution), contact point, and age of the page. Many sites also include navigation in the

Figure I.8

Printer Friendly Web
Page Dimensions

Safe dimensions for Web page graphics

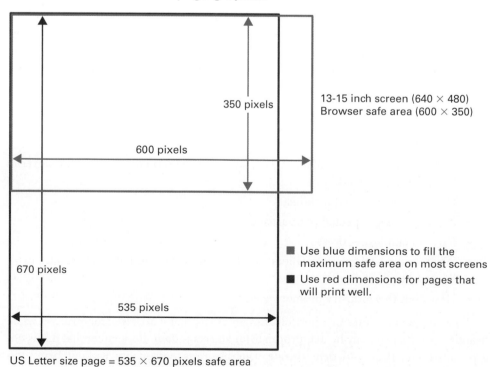

350 pixels

13-15 inch screen (640 × 480)
Browser safe area (600 × 350)

600 pixels

670 pixels

■ Use blue dimensions to fill the maximum safe area on most screens
■ Use red dimensions for pages that will print well.

535 pixels

US Letter size page = 535 × 670 pixels safe area

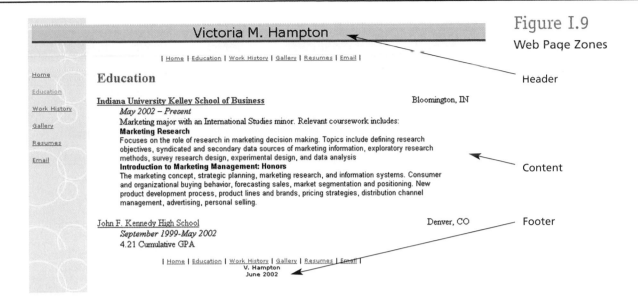

Figure I.9
Web Page Zones

footer. The middle of each page contains the content which should be displayed in a manner that helps viewers find topics of interest (see Figure I.9).

Often the left-hand side of the content zone contains a menu of links. This is particularly important in large sites with long pages. Whether or not you add a menu column to the left of your content, white space to the left and right of your text will make it easier to read. Also, make sure to leave white space between headings and other page elements to avoid a cluttered look.

SITE STRUCTURE

The structure of a Web site is how the various pages of the site are linked together. There are two main schools of thought when it comes to Web page length: scrolling or clicking. Long pages of content require the viewer to scroll to see everything while short pages contain clickable links that provide the full content. Overall, Web users prefer small fast-loading pages that allow them to click directly to the desired content. In other words, most people prefer to click rather than scroll. It isn't possible to avoid scrolling altogether, but try *not* to annoy your users by having them scroll too much.

To create a site of linked pages, you must segment or break your content into usable units. Each segment becomes a separate Web page in your site. Try to think of screens of text rather than pages of text. At 800 × 600 screen resolution, the average Web browser screen displays about one-half page of text when there is nothing else on the screen. The page title, navigation, and footer information can cut that to one-third of a page for text. So, to view one printed page of text, the person reading your e-portfolio would have to scroll down at least two screens. More than three screens of scrolling is beyond the tolerance of the average user unless the text is very interesting or must logically be presented as a unit.

Once you've determined your Web site segments, your next step is to determine how pages will be linked together. The home page is the preferred entry point to your site and should start the navigation. Users should also be able to move from topic to topic in your site without returning to the home page. Web sites can contain linear, hierarchical, grid, and Web navigation. Linear sites are the simplest to build and navigate but are appropriate only for sequential information such as a book. Grid structures are appropriate for sites with multiple topics or entry points (see Figure I.10 on the next page).

Because an e-portfolio has a structured entry point (the home page), we recommend using some combination of the hierarchical and Web structures. Simple sites can use a

Figure I.10

Documenting Web Site
Structure

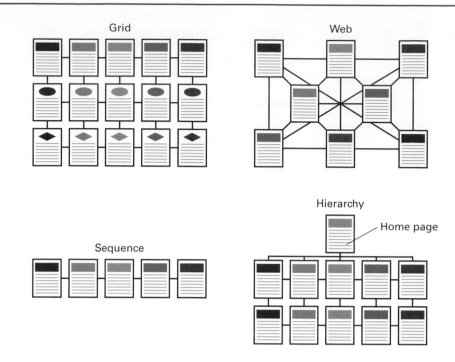

basic hierarchy with just two levels. The home page would comprise the first level and all second level HTML pages would be linked back to the home page. More complex sites will need three hierarchical levels with the level under the home page representing site topics. At least some of the third-level pages should link back to both the second and third levels creating a Web hierarchy navigational structure. We don't recommend that your job search e-portfolio include more than three levels.

Regardless of how you structure your site, it is important for the navigation to be well marked and intuitive. Make sure to descriptively label your links and to group content that logically belongs together. With few exceptions, each HTML page of a site should contain links to the home page and other site topics. Non-HTML pages such as Word or Excel documents don't usually contain links. It's important to create a Web site navigation chart to have a checklist of pages and links to build and test.

DESIGN YOUR HOME PAGE

When designing a group of Web pages that are structured to work together, such as an e-portfolio site, it's critical that each page contain common color, font, navigation, and layout design elements. It should be obvious to a user who has clicked on a link to another site page that he or she is still in your e-portfolio site. Similarly, someone who has clicked from another site into a subpage of your site should be able to easily navigate to content matching their interests. Design your opening or home page and then apply those navigation, layout, font, and color elements throughout the remaining site pages.

COLOR

Color impacts the look and feel of your site. We speak of colors as being warm, cool, muted, light, dark, and garish. Decide what type of color description is appropriate for your audience and then select colors within that description. For example, mocha is a warm color while cyan is a cool color.

There are four colors to select for your Web site: one each for text, link, visited link, and background. These colors interact to create the canvas for site content. It's impor-

BUILD YOUR RÉSUMÉS AND VISIT E-PORTFOLIO SITES

Although documents created in Microsoft Windows have filenames that are not case sensitive and handle spaces well (My Résumé.doc), more than likely your e-portfolio will be posted on a UNIX server. UNIX is the most common operating system for Web servers. Make your files UNIX friendly by using consistent capitalization and no spaces in the filenames (MyRésumé.doc). Open a Notepad or Microsoft Word document to create an ASCII résumé. Enter all of your résumé content without any formatting. Be sure to follow the guidelines outlined in the module text. If you use Microsoft Word, be sure to change the **Save As Type** to Plain Text (*.txt).

To create a presentation résumé, open your ASCII résumé in Microsoft Word and save it with a **Save As Type** of Word document (*.doc). Remove all of the extra hard returns (where you pressed Enter) in the document and then select **Theme** from the Format menu. Click the Style Gallery button and select one of the résumé templates. Update the text and formatting to create a résumé that can be printed in one or two pages.

Visit www.adobe.com and register to create free PDF files. Use this service to create a PDF version of your presentation résumé. Create a folder for your Web site development and place copies of all of your résumés there.

To enhance your understanding of job search e-portfolio content, segmenting, navigation, layout, and design, visit www.mhhe.com/haag and select the XLM/I link. Look through the available portfolios paying attention to the content, use of color, fonts, navigation, page layout, and graphics.

1. How important was color in your initial assessment of a site?

2. What attributes made it easy to move through a site?

3. What was your favorite site? Why? Evaluate the way that site content was segmented. Sketch out the navigation structure of this site.

4. What was your least favorite site? Why?

---

tant that the colors match your audience preferences and work well together. The default link color is blue while links that have already been visited are usually purple or red.

Both visited and unvisited links should be easily seen on your selected background and effortlessly distinguished from each other. High contrast between background and foreground colors improves readability. Typically, light backgrounds and dark text work best. Pick a site that you want to emulate, and use the **View** menu to take a look at the color settings in the HTML code.

In Web page design, browser-safe colors are important. *Browser-safe colors* are 216 different colors that can be displayed by a computer using an eight-bit representation scheme. When a Web browser encounters a color that it cannot interpret, it substitutes a color that it knows, resulting in unpredictable Web page displays. For that reason, we recommend that you use browser-safe colors that can be displayed by all monitors and Web browsers. You can easily find a chart of browser-safe colors by searching the Web.

Current Web design, however, is moving away from browser-safe colors. Statistics from April 2002 indicate that more than 90 percent of Web users are using 16-, 24-, or 32-bit color settings.[3] These settings make eight-bit browser-safe colors obsolete.

But it's still wise to be cautious with color because there is a significant variation in how the same color displays from monitor to monitor and Web browser to Web browser. Test your color selections on as many systems as possible. Visit professionally designed Web sites and study their uses of color to improve your understanding.

BACKGROUND COLOR

A page background can be set to a color or to an image (what we called a textured background in *Extended Learning Module F*). Inappropriate background images can slow

Titling Images

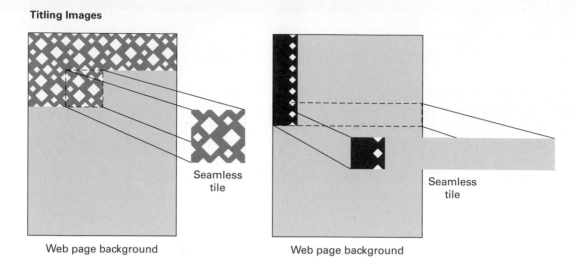

Web page background   Web page background

Titles for Web Pages

Initial Caps Cause Pointless Bumps

Start cap with bold omits pointless bumps

Figure I.11

Backgrounds and Titles

download time and decrease the readability of your text. Images must be in either .jpg or .gif format, but compressed .jpg files often provide a higher quality graphic look for your site.

Figure I.11 shows the two styles of tiling backgrounds. The square tile repeats to fill the Web browser window, which provides a seamless background. The wide rectangular tile also repeats, but, if it is sufficiently wide, only tiles downward. The image in the example could be used to provide a graphic differentiation for a menu that appears down the left-hand side of the browser window.

FONTS AND FORMATTING

The Web is a widely used marketing forum, and it's important to remember that you're using it to market your skills. Fonts and formatting applied to your Web site usually can't match your presentation résumé, but should take full advantage of Web formatting without succumbing to overkill. For example, scrolling text and cute animations rarely have a place in an e-portfolio.

Using different fonts for headings and the body of your document can provide a more professional image, but remember that all computers will not have the same fonts loaded, so your font tags should list alternative fonts. For example, Arial, Helvetica, and Sans Serif fonts are roughly equivalent. Specialty fonts such as Chiller do not have readily accessible alternatives on all computers and should be avoided.

As we've already mentioned, reading is more difficult on a computer monitor than on paper. To simplify reading, headings should be easily identified and use sentence case, not title case as they would in a written document. Title case causes unnecessary bumps in a line of text as we show in Figure I.11.

Use tables, bulleted lists, and ** ** to control the layout of your pages. Tables can provide white space, make columns, and control the placement of graphic elements. For both print and screen reading, three-inch lines of text provide the best readability, so columns are an effective design tool. Bulleted lists make items under a heading easy to identify. The ** ** instruction adds a space to your page and is the most effective way to indent a first line of text. Use the **<BLOCKQUOTE>** tag to indent the left (and on some browsers the right) margin of a block of text. Make sure that all of the design elements that you select work well to create the desired visual impact.

HOME PAGE CONTENT

As we mentioned previously, the content for your Web site needs to be segmented into logical units that will become the pages of your Web site. The opening or home page is the entrance to your Web site and deserves special attention. If at all possible, this page should all display in one screen at 800×600 screen resolution. The goal is to load fast and provide the viewer with enough information to assess the site and navigate to pages of interest. Remember that each site page should include who, what, when, and where.

Recall that each page of your site should contain the same footer. This is the easiest content to develop. At a minimum, your footer should include your name, institution, e-mail address, and the last update date for the site. It's often a good idea to include links to the other pages of your site above this information.

Each page of your site should also contain a header. The header needs to include your name and contact information. Organizations typically include a logo in the header. If you have a business logo or graphic relevant to your job search, you can incorporate it in your header. Although it's uncommon to include a photograph in a printed résumé, many people include a high-quality business attire photo in their e-portfolio Web site. However, don't include your photo in the header that will appear on every page of the site, since that would appear egotistical. Again, it's a good idea to include links to the other pages of your site in the heading.

Page content is displayed between the header and footer, often with a menu bar down the left-hand side. Since you're developing an e-portfolio site, your objective statement, a description of your dream job, or a summary of skills can be effective home page content. Avoid uninformative text such as "Welcome to my e-Portfolio." Overall, your home page should be both inviting and informative (see Figure I.12).

DOCUMENT THE SITE DESIGN

After designing your home page, you should have a good idea of how to segment and link (organize) your remaining e-portfolio content. Ideally, you should create logical groupings of content so that you have no more than eight links on your home page. For example, you could create a résumé page that, in turn, links to your presentation, PDF, and ASCII résumés. Similarly, you might provide a gallery page with links to your work.

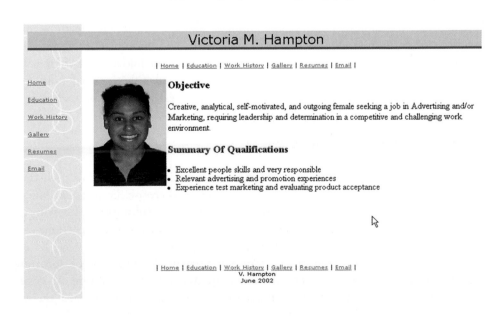

Figure I.12

A Sample e-Portfolio Home Page

Figure I.13

Sample e-Portfolio
Navigation Chart

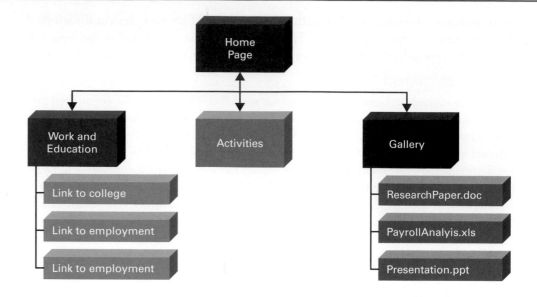

Be sure that your Web site segments account for all of your gallery content and all résumé file formats (including HTML) before developing a navigational or hierarchy chart. The navigational chart will document the content of each page and how it's linked to the other pages of the site. You'll use it to determine the content and links to place on each page during development and then to test each link once you build the site.

The various résumé formats (PDF, presentation, and ASCII) that you've already developed should be placed on the Web as is so that potential employers have access to all formats. The navigation chart makes this distinction by including the file extension (.txt, .doc, and so on) that identifies the file format. You can also place much of the content of your gallery in their native formats since your goal is to demonstrate your skills.

Links using the anchor **<A HREF="filename">** tag can link to all of these file formats. We don't recommend that you provide links from these documents back to your e-portfolio site since your site viewers will most likely save them. The navigation chart shows a link to these non-HTML files, but provides no return link (see Figure I.13).

Preparing Web Content

Use the navigation chart first to develop and link each page of your site. Begin by placing your existing résumé and gallery files in a site folder and then create an abbreviated HTML document for each HTML Web site page in the same folder. Each abbreviated HTML page should contain a word or two that describes what the page will hold once you fully develop it. You'll use these "dummy" pages to test your links on each page as you finish developing them.

HTML VERSUS GENERATED CODE

You can develop the HTML for your e-portfolio Web pages with a simple text editor such as Notepad or with Web authoring software such as Microsoft FrontPage or Macromedia Dreamweaver. The biggest advantage of Web authoring software is that it will generally provide a WYSIWYG (what you see is what you get) interface and speed the coding process.

Although Web authoring software can simplify many tasks, there may be a learning curve to become efficient in their use. Additionally, Web authoring software can generate unnecessary code, making it more difficult for you to make manual modifications and slowing page load time. Sometimes the Web site management portion of this software can introduce errors in Web page links through the default settings and assumptions. In general, we believe it's a good idea to get comfortable with some basic HTML before using Web authoring software so that you're familiar enough with the code to read it and apply simple changes manually.

FILE TRANSFER PROTOCOL (FTP)

After you've constructed and tested your site, you'll need to move the files to your Web space on a Web server so that they will be available to anyone on the Internet. The software used to move files between computers is called an FTP (File Transfer Protocol) client. If you do not already have FTP software, you'll need to download and install it. You can download WS_FTP LE (Learning Edition) from www.download.com at no charge for educational use.

In order to FTP the files for your site, you'll need an account on the Web server. Your account information is used to set up the FTP client so that it will connect to the Web server (see Figure I.14). Most FTP clients require

- *Profile Name.* A name you select to identify this connection.
- *Host Name/Address.* The name of the server that will host your site. For example, agora.cair.du.edu.
- *Host Type.* Use whatever your Web host indicates. If you don't know, Auto Detect almost always works.
- *User ID.* This is your user name. In most cases this is the name you use to log in to your normal Web host account to check e-mail and surf the Web.
- *Password.* This is usually the same password you use to access the Internet.

When you've successfully connected to your server, you'll be able to transfer files between your local drive (C: usually) and the server's drive. WS_FTP and similar products have a Windows-like environment. The left window contains the files on your local

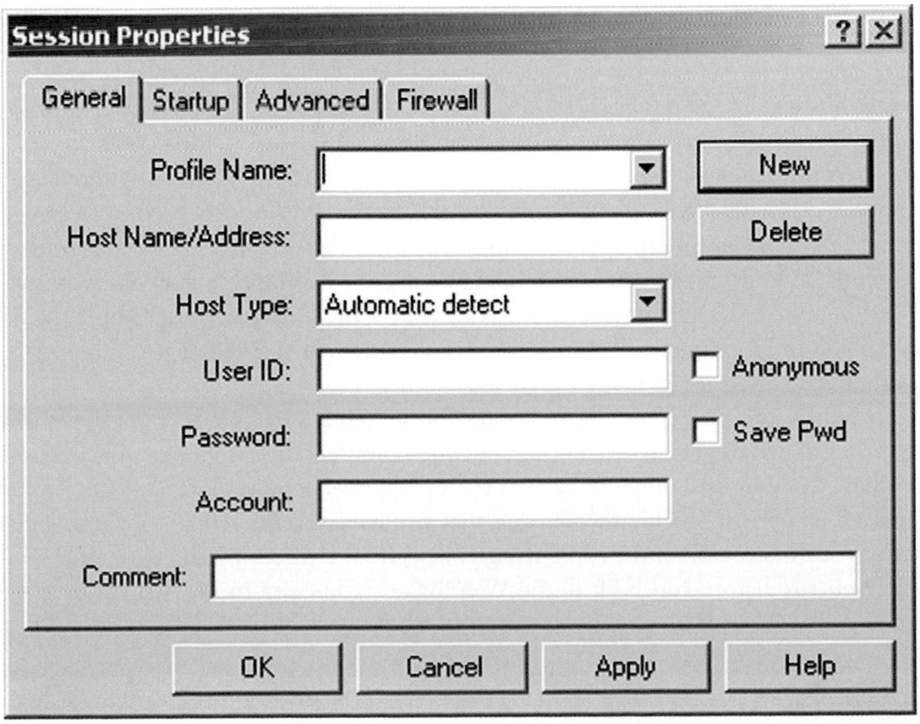

Figure I.14
WS_FTP Setup

computer. You can click to navigate to the folder containing the files to be transferred. The right window displays folders and files in your account on the server.

File transfers can be accomplished in ASCII or binary. If your FTP client has an Auto setting, use it; otherwise, select ASCII for text files such as your HTML pages and ASCII résumé and binary for graphics and Zip files. Most Web server accounts will contain a folder named public_html. All files that will be publicly available from the Internet must be placed in this folder. Open public_html and then drag and drop files as you would to copy from drive to drive in Microsoft Windows.

After you've placed all of your e-portfolio files on the Web server, connect to the Internet and test each link. The URL (uniform resource locator or address) of your site is usually the host address/~accountname/file, for example, www.du.edu/~mewells/My-Page.htm. Remember that naming your opening page index.htm allows you to omit the filename in the URL. Also remember that Web filenames are usually case sensitive.

Most schools now provide Web space for their students. If this is the case at your school, we recommend that you contact your school's technology support department to learn more about your Web space, more about file naming conventions, and how to perform the FTP process.

THINGS TO WATCH FOR

A word of caution: it's critical that you test your Web site many times and from multiple platforms. Statistics gathered in April 2002 indicate that 82 percent of people browsing the Web use Microsoft Internet Explorer (www.w3shcools.com).[4] That being the case, 18 percent of your audience is using another Web browser. In addition, about 5 percent of Internet users have a Macintosh. At a minimum, view your site in multiple versions of Internet Explorer and Netscape Communicator to get a feel for how most people will see it.

It's also best to develop your site in its own folder to make it easier to move. The folder should contain all gallery files, HTML pages, and graphics (including backgrounds) from your site.

Move your site (all files, pages, and graphics) to another computer and test it again. Often links that work on your development computer may not work when pages are moved. These are called broken links and you should definitely repair them before placing your site on a Web server. Testing on multiple computers will also let you see color and resolution variances that your viewers will experience.

Finally, when you place your site on a Web server, test it again. Most Web servers use the UNIX operating system. UNIX is case sensitive and prefers filenames without spaces or special characters (!@#$%^&*,. and so on). Microsoft Windows is not case sensitive and accepts filenames with spaces. This is an important difference because Web sites that work on your local computer running a version of Windows may not work when placed in a UNIX environment. The usual cause is the filename. For example, in Windows a link to Page2.htm will work when the file is actually named page2.htm; in UNIX it will not (case sensitivity being the issue).

That ends our module of how to build a job search e-portfolio. If you've been working through the projects in this module and you complete the assignments and exercises to follow, you'll be well on your way to developing an effective e-portfolio.

As a final note, we highly recommend that you have several people—including classmates, your instructor, and people from your school's career placement center—view your Web site before you FTP to the Web for everyone else to see. An effectively designed and well-worded e-portfolio can in fact help you find a really great job. On the other hand, an ineffectively designed and poorly worded e-portfolio can be disastrous. Take some extra time to have other people review your e-portfolio before placing it on the Web for potentially millions of people to see and scrutinize.

Summary: Student Learning Outcomes Revisited

1. **Describe the types of electronic résumés and when each is appropriate.** The four types of electronic résumés presented are *scannable* (also called ASCII or plain text), *presentation, portable document format (PDF),* and HTML. A scannable résumé can be submitted in print or electronically to organizations using skills extraction software. A presentation résumé is created using a word processor to design a pretty one- to two-page summary of your qualifications. This résumé can be mailed to organizations not using *extraction engines* or can be personally handed to an interviewer. A PDF résumé is a version of your presentation résumé that can be delivered electronically (via e-mail or a Web page link) without impacting your formatting. A job search *e-portfolio* contains HTML résumé content and a gallery supporting your skills designed for Web delivery.

2. **Discuss networking strategies you can use during a job search.** Because up to 80 percent of jobs are in the *hidden job market,* networking is critical to a successful job search. Networking involves contacting people and asking them to help you to uncover hidden jobs. Both electronic and face-to-face contacts are necessary to optimize your job opportunities. Strategies involve creating a contact list, developing a 30-second commercial, setting a weekly contact goal, joining *mailing lists,* tracking responses, and following up.

3. **Explain how self-assessment is valuable to résumé writing.** Employers want to hire employees who are focused. Employees want a job that not only produces an income but is satisfying. A good self-assessment will clarify the skills you have to offer an employer, the work environment that best suits you, and employment qualities that lead to your satisfaction.

4. **Use the Internet to research career opportunities and potential employers.** The World Wide Web offers a wide array of tools that can help you research your chosen career. Effective career research should make use of area-specific search engines, *directory search engines, true search engines,* job boards, newsgroups, media sites, government statistics, and employer sites. By combining the information provided by these resources, you should be able to get a complete picture of the employment market you wish to enter and the *skill words* that should be included in your résumé.

5. **Develop powerful job search e-portfolio content.** Powerful job search e-portfolio content is employer centered and documents the skills that will make you an attractive employee. Quality research and self-assessment are critical to developing content centered on the skills employers want and the benefits these skills provide in an easy-to-use Web site. All traditional résumé content should be developed with these requirements in mind in a manner that does not appear self-centered. Additional e-portfolio content to demonstrate your skills is included as a gallery for potential employees to peruse.

6. **Document effective Web site structure and design components.** Documenting effective Web site structure involves segmenting Web site content and outlining what will be presented on each site page. A navigation chart is developed showing how the various pages of the site will be linked together. Each page of the site should use the same design components outlining the who, what, when, and where of the site. Select a *browser-safe color* scheme for effective viewing by the widest possible audience and use standard content in the header and footer of each page to create a site identity.

7. **Create a job search e-portfolio Web site and place it on an Internet server.** A job search e-portfolio consists of anything that will help a potential employer evaluate your worth as an employee. Use the site navigation chart to develop HTML pages displaying traditional résumé content and linking to your ASCII résumé, PDF résumé, and a gallery of works that demonstrate your skills to allow the evaluator to see how effective you could be in their organization. Once all of your content (HTML pages, supporting documents, résumés, and graphics) has been stored in a folder and tested locally, it can be moved to a Web server using FTP client software. The site should be tested again from the Web.

Key Terms and Concepts

Browser-safe colors, 489
Directory search engine, 475
Electronic job market, 471
Electronic portfolio (e-portfolio), 481
Extraction engine, 482
Hidden job market, 471
Mailing list, 473

Portable document format (PDF), 483
Presentation résumé, 483
Scannable résumé (ASCII résumé, plain-text résumé), 481
Skill words, 475
True search engine, 475

Short-Answer Questions

1. What is the main purpose of a scannable résumé?
2. How is designing a Web page different from designing a print document?
3. Why should multiple résumé formats be included in a job search e-portfolio?
4. What elements of a Web site home page should be carried throughout the rest of the site pages? Why?
5. Why is the gallery of a job search e-portfolio as important as a well-written and researched résumé?
6. What factors do you believe contribute to 80 percent of available jobs never being publicized?
7. Why is it important to include job and industry-specific skill words in the content of your résumé?
8. What important audience preferences should you consider when designing a job search e-portfolio?
9. Why should a Web site that works on your computer be retested after it is placed on a Web server?
10. How do you know what skill words to include in your résumé? Where do you put these skill words?
11. How do you determine how much content to put on a single Web page?
12. Why is it important to view a newly developed Web site on multiple computers using a variety of browsers?
13. Discuss the significance of the PDF file format in the Internet and World Wide Web community.
14. Why should you consider using browser-safe colors on your e-portfolio site?
15. How does the hidden job market complicate the job search?
16. Visit the job board www.monster.com and review the site content. Is this a site that you would recommend for first-time job hunters? Why or why not?

Short-Question Answers

For each of the following answers, provide an appropriate question.

1. Visit an array of government, industry, and job databases as well as using search engines.
2. 216.
3. Web site home page.
4. Available upon request.
5. Web page header.
6. A short script that can be used when networking.
7. Web site navigation chart.
8. Because changing printers can produce unexpected results with a heavily formatted word processing document.
9. Three or fewer levels.
10. Background image.
11. FTP.
12. Mailing list.

Assignments and Exercises

1. **DESCRIBE YOUR CAREER** Using the research methods we've outlined in the module, locate information about your career. Document your findings in a paper being sure to include job title synonyms, educational standards, work environment, job forecast statistics, normal work week, and any other pertinent information. Cite your sources.

2. **VISIT INDUSTRY WEB SITES** Using the research methods we've outlined in the module, locate and visit at least three business Web sites in the industry you've selected. For each site document the page layout, the colors, and the formality of the site. Did you find press and news releases? If so, what did they tell you about the company? Did you find recruitment pages? If so, what types of positions are available? What skill words did you find on these sites that should be included in your résumé?

3. **ENTRY-LEVEL JOB POSTINGS** Visit www.collegegrad.com and search for entry-level job postings in your area of interest. How many postings did you find? Are you qualified, or will you be qualified for the available positions when you complete your current educational goals? Are the listings for a geographic location that you would consider? What skill words should you include in your résumés to be considered for these positions?

4. **FINALIZE YOUR RÉSUMÉS** If you compiled your résumés as you completed the module, review them for presentation effectiveness and content. If you didn't build your résumés as you went through the module, do so now. Start by building all of the content in an unformatted document and then create ASCII, presentation, and PDF versions. Unless you have sufficient business experience to use a Summary of Qualifications section, use an Objective statement that includes the job title, industry, your best skill words, and the benefit you could provide to the hiring organization. In addition to the Objective statement, include Work, Education, and References sections. Other sections can be included to suit your background and career. Solicit feedback from at least one classmate.

5. **SELECT CONTENT FOR YOUR E-PORTFOLIO GALLERY** Look through the files on your computer for work that represents your current skills and could be of interest to a potential employer. Create a list of at least three files that would be appropriate for a job search e-portfolio along with a short description of the skills the files exhibit. What other skills should you develop documents to demonstrate? What types of documents would best showcase these skills?

6. **SEARCH THE WORLD WIDE WEB** Use search tools to locate e-portfolios that have already been posted on the Web. How many e-portfolios did you locate? How many of these e-portfolios were designed for a job search? Pick the best e-portfolio you located and critique its content and design.

7. **BUILD YOUR E-PORTFOLIO SITE** Use either a text editor or Web authoring software to build the HTML pages of your job search e-portfolio Web site. Do not use office productivity software such as a word processor. Include a minimum of three HTML pages, your ASCII résumé, your PDF résumé, and three gallery pages using another document format such as Word or PowerPoint.

EXTENDED LEARNING MODULE J

IMPLEMENTING A DATABASE
WITH MICROSOFT ACCESS

Taking Advantage of the CD

In Chapter 3 we discussed the important role that databases play in an organization. We followed that with *Extended Learning Module C*, in which you learned how to design the correct structure of a relational database. That module includes four primary steps. They are

1. Defining entity classes and primary keys
2. Defining relationships among entity classes
3. Defining information (fields) for each relation (the term relation is often used to refer to a file while designing a database)
4. Using a data definition language to create your database

In *Extended Learning Module C,* you followed the process through the first three steps above. In this module, we'll take you through the fourth step—using a data definition language to create your database—by exploring the use of Microsoft Access, today's most popular personal database management system package (it comes as a standard part of Microsoft Office).

You'll find this extended learning module on the CD that accompanies this text. This module, however, is a little different. We refer to it as a bonus module because we've had a few, but not many, instructors ask for it. So, it doesn't include the typical projects within the text or the end-of-module Assignments and Exercises. Nonetheless, as you follow along, you can easily implement our example database and learn to use Microsoft Access.

Not only that, we've included coverage of

- Creating a simple query using one relation
- Creating a conditional query using one relation
- Creating an advanced query using more than one relation
- Creating a conditional query using more than one relation
- Generating a report

We believe this material is vitally important. As the business world increasingly moves toward empowering employees with technology tools, you'll be better prepared for the job market if you know how to design, implement, and access a database. Module C covered how to design a database, and this module covers how to implement and access a database using Microsoft Access.

If you need proof of the growing importance of databases, just connect to any job database Web site and enter "Microsoft Access" as a search term. We did that at Monster.com (www.monster.com) and found over 550 job listings requiring expertise in Microsoft Access. Some of the job titles included

- Financial Analysis Manager
- Education Administrator
- Logistics Engineer
- Military Intelligence
- Corporate Trust Administrator
- Market Research Analyst
- Medical Finance Coordinator

- Guest Satisfaction Agent
- Training Coordinator
- Data Consumption Analyst
- Project Manager
- Retail Support Analyst
- Quality Engineer
- Reinsurance Accountant

If you look carefully at the above list, not a single job title is IT-specific. Rather, they represent job openings in such areas as finance, hospitality, logistics, retail sales, medicine, and insurance.

We applaud you for popping in the CD and reading this module.

CASE 1:
ASSESSING THE VALUE OF INFORMATION

TREVOR TOY AUTO MECHANICS

Trevor Toy Auto Mechanics is an automobile repair shop in Phoenix, Arizona. Over the past few years, Trevor has seen his business grow from a two-bay car repair shop with only one other employee to a 15-bay car repair shop with 21 employees.

Up to now, Trevor has always advertised that he will perform any work on any vehicle. But that's becoming problematic as cars are becoming increasingly more complex. Trevor has decided he wants to create a more focused repair shop, and is asking for your help. He has provided you with a spreadsheet file that contains a list of all the repairs his shop has completed over the past year. The spreadsheet file contains the fields provided in the table below.

Column	Name	Description
A	MECHANIC #	A unique number assigned to the mechanic who completed the work
B	CAR TYPE	The type of car on which the work was completed
C	WORK COMPLETED	The type of repair that was performed on the car
D	NUM HOURS	The number of hours it took to complete the work
E	COST OF PARTS	The cost of the parts associated with completing the repair
F	TOTAL CHARGE	The amount charged to the customer for the repair

Trevor is open to any suggestions you might have. So, your analysis could include any combination of (1) keeping only certain mechanics; (2) repairing only certain types of cars; and/or (3) performing only certain types of repairs.

It is your responsibility to analyze the list and make a recommendation to Trevor concerning how he should focus his business.

SOME PARTICULARS YOU SHOULD KNOW

1. As you consider the information provided to you, think in terms of what information is important. You might need to use the existing information to create new information.

2. All mechanics are paid the same hourly wage.

3. Disregard any considerations associated with downsizing such as overhead; simply focus on the information provided to you.

4. Disregard any considerations for potential competition located near Trevor.

5. Upon completing your analysis, please provide concise yet detailed and thorough documentation (in narrative, numeric, and graphic forms) that justifies your recommendations.

6. File: TREVOR.xls (Excel file).

CASE 2:
ASSESSING THE VALUE OF INFORMATION

AFFORDABLE HOMES REAL ESTATE

In late 1995, a national study announced that Eau Claire, Wisconsin, was the safest place to live. Since then, housing development projects have been springing up all around Eau Claire. Six housing development projects are currently dominating the Eau Claire market: Woodland Hills, Granite Mound, Creek Side Huntington, East River Community, Forest Green, and Eau Claire South. These six projects each started with 100 homes, have sold all of them, and are currently developing phase 2.

As one of the three partners and real estate agents of Affordable Homes Real Estate, it is your responsibility to analyze the information concerning the past 600 home sales and choose which development project to focus on for selling homes in phase 2. Because your real estate firm is so small, you and your partners have decided that the firm should focus on selling homes in only one of the development projects.

From the Wisconsin Real Estate Association you have obtained a spreadsheet file that contains information concerning each of the sales for the first 600 homes. It contains the following fields:

Column	Name	Description
A	LOT #	The number assigned to a specific home within each project
B	PROJECT #	A unique number assigned to each of the six housing development projects (see table to follow)
C	ASK PRICE	The initial posted asking price for the home
D	SELL PRICE	The actual price for which the home was sold
E	LIST DATE	The date the home was listed for sale
F	SALE DATE	The date on which the final contract closed and the home was sold
G	SQ. FT.	The total square footage for the home
H	# BATH.	The number of bathrooms in the home
I	# BDRMS	The number of bedrooms in the home

The following numbers have been assigned to each of the housing development projects:

Project Number	Project Name
23	Woodland Hills
47	Granite Mound
61	Creek Side Huntington
78	East River Community
92	Forest Green
97	Eau Claire South

It is your responsibility to analyze the sales list and prepare a report that details which housing development project your real estate firm should focus on. Your analysis should cover as many angles as possible.

SOME PARTICULARS YOU SHOULD KNOW

1. You don't know how many other real estate firms will also be competing for sales in each of the housing development projects.

2. Phase 2 for each housing development project will develop homes similar in style, price, and square footage to their respective first phases.

3. As you consider the information provided to you, think in terms of what information is important and what information is not important. Be prepared to justify how you approached your analysis.

4. Upon completing your analysis, please provide concise, yet detailed and thorough, documentation (in narrative, numeric, and graphic forms) that justifies your decision.

5. File: REALEST.xls (Excel file).

CASE 3:
EXECUTIVE INFORMATION SYSTEM REPORTING

POLITICAL CAMPAIGN FINANCE CONSULTANTS

When it comes to campaign finance, Americans want a system that minimizes the influence of "fat cats" and organized money, which keeps campaign spending at sensible levels, that fosters healthy electoral competition, that doesn't take advantage of wealthy candidates, and that doesn't require candidates to spend all of their waking hours raising money.

Indeed, the much maligned congressional campaign finance system we have now is itself a product of well-intended reform efforts, passed by Congress in 1974 to achieve these ideals. Moreover, dozens of new reform plans have emerged during the 1990s that also reach for these goals. Yet, no reform scheme, however well intended, is likely to produce a perfect congressional campaign finance system.

The city of Highlands Ranch, Colorado wishes to organize its campaign contributions records in a more linear format. The city council people are considering various executive information system packages that can show them overall information views of the contribution information as well as give them the ability to access more detailed information. You have been hired to make recommendations about what reports should be available through the soon-to-be-purchased executive information system.

The table below is a list of the information that will be the foundation for the reports in the proposed executive information system. To help you develop realistic reports, the city has provided you with a spreadsheet file that contains specific contributions over the last six months.

Column	Name	Description
A	DATE	The actual date that the contribution was made
B	CONTRIBUTOR	The name of the person or organization that made the contribution
C	DISTRICT	The district number that the councilperson belongs to
D	AMOUNT	The amount of the contribution
E	TYPE	The description type of where the contribution amount was given
F	COUNCILPERSON	The councilperson's name
G	PARTY	The councilperson's political party

What the city council people are most interested in is viewing several overall reports and then being able to request more detailed reports. So, as a consultant, your goal is to develop different sets of reports that illustrate the concept of drilling down through information. For example, you should develop a report that shows overall campaign contributions by district (each of the eight different districts) and then also develop more detailed reports that show contribution by political party and contribution by type.

SOME PARTICULARS YOU SHOULD KNOW

1. The council people would much rather see information graphically than numerically. So, as you develop your reports, do so in terms of graphs that illustrate the desired relationships.

2. As you consider the information provided to you, think in terms of overall views first and then detailed views second. This will help you develop a logical series of reports.

3. If you wish, you can explore a variety of software tools to help you create the reports. When complete, prepare your presentation using a presentation graphics package that lets you create a really great presentation of your recommendations.

4. Again, your goal is not to create reports that point toward a particular problem or opportunity. Rather, you are to design sets of logical series of reports that illustrate the concept of drilling down.

5. File: CONTRIBUTE.xls (Excel file).

CASE 4:
BUILDING VALUE CHAINS

STARLIGHT'S CUSTOMERS DEFINE VALUE

StarLight is a Denver-based retailer of high-quality apparel, shoes, and accessories. In 1915, with money earned in the Colorado gold mines, Anne Logan invested in a small downtown Denver shoe store. A few years later, Anne expanded her business by adding fine apparel. Today, StarLight has 97 retail stores and discount outlets throughout the United States. Since the beginning, StarLight's business philosophy has reflected its founder's beliefs in exceptional service, value, selection, and quality. To maintain the level of service StarLight's customers have come to expect, the company empowers its employees to meet any customer demand, no matter how unreasonable it may seem. With so many stores, it's difficult for Cody Sherrod, StarLight's Vice President for Business Information and Planning, to know the level of service customers receive, what customers value, and what they don't. These are important questions for a retailer striving to provide the finest customer experience and products while keeping costs to a minimum.

Cody decided a value chain analysis would be helpful in answering these questions. So, customer surveys were designed, distributed, completed, collected, and compiled into a database. Customers were asked to value their experience with various processes in the StarLight value chain. Specifically, for each value chain process, customers were asked whether this area added value to their experience or reduced the value of their experience. Customers were asked to quantify how much each process added or reduced the value of the services they received. Using a total of 100 points for the value chain, each customer distributed those points among StarLight's processes. The survey results in the database consist of the fields shown in the accompanying table on the next page.

Field Name	Description
Survey ID	An ID number uniquely identifying the survey
VA/VR	A field that identifies whether the current row of information reflects a value-added response or a value-reducing response
Date	Survey response date
Mgmt/Acctg/Finance/Legal	Customer value experience, if any, with management, accounting finance, and the legal departments
HR Mgmt	Customer value of the attitude and general personnel environment
R&D/Tech Dev	Customer perceived value of the quality of research and technology support
Purchasing	Customer value placed on the quality and range of product selection
Receive and Greet Customers	Customer value placed on initial contact with employees
Provide Direction/Advice/Info	Customer value placed on initial information provided by employees
Store Location/Channel Availability & Convenience	Customer value placed on location, availability, and convenience
Product Display/Site or Catalog Layout	Customer value placed on aesthetic appeal of merchandise display and layout
Sales Service	Customer value placed on quality of service provided by sales associates
Marketing	Customer value placed on the effectiveness of marketing material
Customer Follow-up	Customer value placed on postsales service and follow-up

Cody has asked you to gather the raw survey material into two value chains, the value-added chain and the value-reducing chain. You'll create chains that summarize the survey information and size the process areas proportionately as described in Chapter 2. Specifically, your job is to perform the following:

1. Create queries or reports in the provided database to summarize the value-added amounts and the value-reducing amounts for each process.
2. Draw two value chains using that summary information to size the depicted area for each process. Use the value chains in Chapter 2 as reference.
3. Compare the value-added and value-reducing process percentages. Do they correlate in any way? If so, why do you think that is? If not, why not?
4. In the table description provided, a dashed line is drawn between the "purchasing" process and the "receive and greet customers" process. Processes above the line are considered support processes, while processes below are considered primary processes. Create a database query to compare how customers value the total of support processes versus primary processes. Do this for both value-added and value-reducing processes. Do the results make sense or are they surprising? Explain your answer.

SOME PARTICULARS YOU SHOULD KNOW

1. Remember that the total value-added/value-reducing amount for each process must equal 100 percent.
2. The survey values in the database are not percentages although the sum of all responses for a given survey equals 100.
3. File: STARLIGHT.mdb (Access file).

CASE 5:
USING RELATIONAL TECHNOLOGY TO TRACK PROJECTS

PHILLIPS CONSTRUCTION

Phillips Construction Company is a Denver-based construction company that specializes in subcontracting the development of single family homes. In business since 1993, Phillips Construction Company has maintained a talented pool of certified staff and independent consultants allowing the flexibility and combined experience required to meet the needs of its nearly 300 completed projects in the Denver metropolitan area. The field of operation methods that Phillips Construction is responsible for as it relates to building include: structural development, heating and cooling, plumbing, and electricity.

The company charges its clients by billing the hours spent on each contract. The hourly billing rate is dependent on the employee's position according to the field of operations (as noted above).

Figure RHGP.1 shows a basic report that Phillips Construction managers would like to see every week concerning what projects are being assigned. Phillips Construction organizes its

Figure
RHGP.1

Phillips
Construction
Project Detail

PHILLIPS CONSTRUCTION PROJECT DETAIL

PROJECT NAME	ASSIGN DATE	EMP LAST NAME	EMP FIRST NAME	JOB DESCRIPTION	ASSIGN HOUR	CHARGE/HOUR
Chatfield						
	Monday, June 10, 2002	Jones	Anne	Heating and Ventilation	3.4	$84.50
	Monday, June 10, 2002	Sullivan	David	Electrical	1.8	$105.00
	Tuesday, June 11, 2002	Frommer	Matt	Plumbing	4.1	$96.75
	Wednesday, June 12, 2002	Newman	John	Electrical	1.7	$105.00
	Wednesday, June 12, 2002	Bawangi	Terry	Plumbing	4.1	$96.75
Summary of Assignment Hours and Charges					15.10	$1,448.15
Evergreen						
	Monday, June 10, 2002	Smithfield	William	Structure	3.0	$35.75
	Monday, June 10, 2002	Newman	John	Electrical	2.3	$105.00
	Monday, June 10, 2002	Nenior	David	Plumbing	3.3	$96.75
	Tuesday, June 11, 2002	Marbough	Mike	Heating and Ventilation	2.6	$84.50
	Wednesday, June 12, 2002	Johnson	Peter	Electrical	2.0	$105.00
	Wednesday, June 12, 2002	Newman	John	Electrical	3.6	$105.00
	Wednesday, June 12, 2002	Olenkoski	Glenn	Structure	1.9	$35.75
Summary of Assignment Hours and Charges					18.70	$1,543.65
Roxborough						
	Monday, June 10, 2002	Washberg	Jeff	Plumbing	3.9	$96.75
	Monday, June 10, 2002	Ramora	Anne	Plumbing	2.6	$96.75

Wednesday, June 26, 2002

Page 1 of 2

internal structure in four different operations: Structure (500), Plumbing (501), Electrical (502), and Heating and Ventilation (503). Each of these operational departments can and should have many subcontractors who specialize in that area.

Because of the boom in home sales over the last several years, Phillips Construction has decided to implement a relational database model to track project details according to project name, hours assigned, and charges per hour for each job description. Originally, Phillips Construction decided to let one of its employees handle the construction of the database. However, that employee has not had the time to completely implement the project. Phillips Construction has asked you to take over and complete the development of the database.

The entity classes and primary keys for the database have been identified as the following:

Entity	Primary Key
Project	Project Number
Employee	Employee Number
Job	Job Number
Assign	Assign Number

The following business rules have also been identified:

1. A job can have many employees assigned but must have at least one.
2. An employee must be assigned to one and only one job code.
3. An employee can be assigned to work on one or more projects.
4. A project can be assigned to only one employee but need not be assigned to any employee.

Your job is to be completed in the following phases:

1. Develop and describe the entity-relationship diagram.
2. Use normalization to assure the correctness of the tables (relations).
3. Create the database using a personal DBMS package (preferably Microsoft Access).
4. Use the DBMS package to create the basic report in Figure RHGP.1.

SOME PARTICULARS YOU SHOULD KNOW

1. You may not be able to develop a report that looks exactly like the one in Figure RHGP.1. However, your report should include the same information.
2. Complete personnel information is tracked by another database. For this application, include only the minimum employee number, last name, and first name.
3. Information concerning all projects, employees, and jobs is not readily available. You should, however, create information for several fictitious systems to include in your database.
4. File: Not applicable.

CASE 6:
BUILDING A DECISION SUPPORT SYSTEM

CREATING AN INVESTMENT PORTFOLIO

Most experts recommend that if you're devising a long-term investment strategy you should make the stock market part of your plan. You can use a DSS to help you decide on what stocks to put into your portfolio. You can use a spreadsheet to do the job. The information you need on 10 stocks is contained in a Word file called STOCKS.doc. This information consists of

1. Two years of weekly price data on 10 different stocks.
2. Stock market indices from
   - The Dow Jones Industrial Average
   - NASDAQ Composite
3. Dividends and cash flow per share over the last 10 years (Source: Yahoo Finance).

Using this information, build a DSS to perform stock analysis consisting of the following tasks:

1. Examine Diversification Benefits
   A. Calculate the average return and standard deviation(s) of each of the 10 stocks.
   B. Form six different portfolios: two with two stocks each; two with three stocks each; two with five stocks each.

Answer the following questions using your DSS:

- How does the standard deviation of each portfolio compare to the (average) standard deviation of each stock in the portfolio?
- How does the average return of the portfolio compare to the average return of each stock in the portfolio?
- Do the benefits of diversification seem to increase or diminish as the number of stocks in the portfolio gets larger?
- In the two-stock and five-stock portfolios what happens if you group your stocks toward similar industries?

2. Value Each of the Stocks
   A. Estimate the dividend growth rate based on past dividends.
   B. Estimate next year's dividend using this year's dividend and the estimated growth rate.
   C. Generate two graphs, one for past dividends and one for estimated dividends for the next five years.

SOME PARTICULARS YOU SHOULD KNOW

1. When performing your calculations, use the weekly returns. That is, use the change in the price each week rather than the prices themselves. This gives you a better basis for calculation because the prices themselves don't usually change very much.
2. File: STOCKS.doc (Word file).

CASE 7:
ADVERTISING WITH BANNER ADS

HIGHWAYSANDBYWAYS.COM

Business is booming at HighwaysAndByways, a dot-com firm focusing on selling accessories for car enthusiasts (e.g., floor mats, grill guards, air fresheners, stereos, and so on). Throughout the past year, HighwaysAndByways has had Web site management software tracking what customers buy, the Web sites from which customers came, and the Web sites customers went to after visiting HighwaysAndByways. That information is stored in a spreadsheet file and contains the fields in the accompanying table on the next page. Each record in the spreadsheet file represents an individual visit by a customer that resulted in a purchase.

Column	Name	Description
A	CUSTOMER ID	A unique identifier for a customer who made a purchase
B	TOTAL PURCHASE	The total amount of a purchase
C	PREVIOUS WEB SITE	The Web site from which the customer came to visit HighwaysAndByways
D	NEXT WEB SITE	The Web site the customer went to after making a purchase at HighwaysAndByways
E	TIME SPENT	The amount of time that the customer spent at the site.

HighwaysAndByways is interested in determining three items and has employed you as a consultant to help. First, HighwaysAndByways wants to know on which Web sites it should purchase banner ad space. Second, HighwaysAndByways wants to know which Web sites it should contact to determine if those Web sites would like to purchase banner ad space on the HighwaysAndByways Web site. Finally, HighwaysAndByways would like to know which Web sites it should develop reciprocal banner ad relationships with; that is, HighwaysAndByways would like a list of Web sites on which it would obtain banner ad space while providing banner ad space on its Web site for those Web sites.

SOME PARTICULARS YOU SHOULD KNOW

1. As you consider the information provided to you, think about the levels of information literacy. In other words, don't jump to conclusions before carefully evaluating the provided information.

2. You don't know if your customers made purchases at the Web site they visited upon leaving HighwaysAndByways.

3. Upon completing your analysis, please provide concise yet detailed and thorough documentation (in narrative, numeric, and graphic forms) that justifies your recommendations.

4. File: CLICKSTREAMS.xls (Excel file).

CASE 8:
OUTSOURCING INFORMATION TECHNOLOGY
CREATING FORECASTS

Founded in 1992, A&A Software provides innovative search software, Web site accessibility testing/repair software, and usability testing/repair software. All serve as part of its desktop and enterprise content management solutions for government, corporate, educational, and consumer markets. The company's solutions are used by Web site publishers, digital media publishers, content managers, document managers, business users, consumers, software companies, and consulting services companies. A&A Software solutions help organizations develop long-term strategies to achieve Web content accessibility, enhance usability, and comply with U.S. and international accessibility and search standards.

You manage the customer service group for the A&A Software development group. You have just received an e-mail from the A&A Software CIO, Sue Downs, that the number of phone calls from customers having problems with one of your newer applications is on the increase. This company has a 10-year history of approximately 1 percent in turnover a year and its focus had always been on customer service. With the informal motto of "Grow big, but stay small," it took pride in 100 percent callbacks in customer care, knowing that its personal service was one thing that made it outstanding.

The rapid growth to six times its original customer-base size has forced A&A Software to deal with difficult questions for the first time, such as, How do we serve this many customers? How do we keep our SOUL—that part of us that honestly cares very much about our customers? How will we know that someone else will care as much and do as good a job as we have done?

In determining what to do, A&A Software reviewed a similar scenario of a major e-BANK company that was considering outsourcing its customer service in order to handle a large projected number of customers through several customer interaction channels. Although e-BANK had excellent people, it felt that its competencies were primarily in finance, rather than in customer service, and that it needed to have the expertise that a customer-service-focused company could offer. E-BANK also discovered that it would be cost-effective to outsource its customer service center.

Additionally, the outsourcing approach would be relatively hassle-free, since e-BANK would not have to set up its own CIC (customer interaction center/call center).

SOME PARTICULARS YOU SHOULD KNOW

1. Create a weekly analysis from the data provided in FORECAST.xls.

2. The price of the products, the actual product type, and any warrantee information is irrelevant.

3. Develop a growth, trend, and forecast analysis. You should use a three-day moving average: a shorter moving average might not display the trend well and a much longer moving average would shorten the trend too much.

4. Upon completing your analysis, please provide concise yet detailed and thorough documentation (in narrative, numeric, and graphic forms) that justifies your recommendations.

5. File: FORECAST.xls (Excel file).

CASE 9:
DEMONSTRATING HOW TO BUILD WEB SITES
WITH HTML

Building a good Web site is simple in some respects and difficult in others. It's relatively easy to learn to write HTML code. Building an effective and eye-catching Web site is a horse of a different color. That is to say, there is a stretch between just using the technology and using the technology to your best advantage.

Your task in this project is to build a presentation (using presentation graphics software such as Microsoft PowerPoint) that achieves two goals. First, your presentation should show your audience how to write simple HTML code to create a Web site. Your presentation should include the HTML code for

- Text formatting (bold, italic, and the like)
- Font families and sizing
- Font colors
- Background colors and images
- Links
- Images
- Numbered and bulleted lists

Next, your presentation should provide the audience with a list of guidelines for creating an effective Web site. For this, you should definitely embed links into your presentation that go to Web sites that illustrate good Web site design, displaying examples of both effective and ineffective designs.

SOME PARTICULARS YOU SHOULD KNOW

1. In a file called HTML.doc, we've provided many links to Web sites that teach you how to write HTML code.
2. In a file called DESIGN.doc, we've provided many links to Web sites that teach you how to design Web sites effectively.
3. Files: HTML.doc and DESIGN.doc (Word files).

CASE 10:
MAKING THE CASE WITH PRESENTATION SOFTWARE

INFORMATION TECHNOLOGY ETHICS

Management at your company is concerned about the high cost of computer crime, from lawsuits over e-mail received to denial-of-service attacks and crackers breaking into the corporate network to steal information. You've been asked to make a presentation to inform your colleagues. Develop a presentation using a presentation package such as Microsoft's PowerPoint.

You can choose your presentation's emphasis from the following topics:

- Ethics as it relates to IT systems
- Types of crime aimed at IT systems (such as viruses)
- Types of crime that uses IT systems as weapons (such as electronic theft of funds from one account to another)
- Security measures, how good they are, what they cost, how expensive they are to implement
- Electronic monitoring of employees (from employer and employee standpoints)
- Collection and use of personal information on consumers

SOURCES OF INFORMATION

- In the file ETHICS.doc, you'll find sources for the topics listed above.
- The Web is a great place to find lots of information.
- Most business publications, such as *Business Week, InformationWeek, Fortune,* and the *Wall Street Journal,* frequently have good articles on ethics, cybercrime, and security. You can get some of these articles on the Web.
- General news publications such as *Newsweek* and *USA Today* print articles on these topics.

Your task is to weave the information you find into a coherent presentation using graphs and art where appropriate.

SOME PARTICULARS YOU SHOULD KNOW

1. Content Principles
   - Each slide should have a headline
   - Each slide should express one idea
   - Ideas should follow logically

2. Design Principles
   - Follow the "Rule of 7," which is no more than 7 lines per slide and 7 words per line
   - Keep it simple
   - Keep it organized
   - Create a path for the eye
   - Divide space in an interesting way
   - Use at least 30-point type
   - Use color and graphics carefully, consistently, and for a specific purpose
   - Use high-contrast colors (black/white, deep blue/white, etc.)
3. File: ETHICS.doc (Word file)

CASE 11:
E-CLASSIFIED@GABBYGAZETTEER.COM

A WEB-BASED CLASSIFIED SYSTEM

With the emergence of the Internet as a worldwide standard for communicating information, *Gabby's Gazetteer,* a medium-size community newspaper in central Colorado is looking to enter into the electronic commerce market.

In the listing of classified ads, advertisers place a small ad that lists items that they wish to sell and provide a means (e.g., telephone number) by which prospective buyers can contact them.

The nature of a sale via a newspaper classified system goes as follows:

- During the course of the sale, the information flows in different directions at different stages.
- First, there is a downstream flow of information (from seller to buyer)—the listing in print on the newspaper. (Thus, the classified ad listing is just a way of bringing a buyer and seller together.)
- When a potential purchaser's interest has been raised, then that interest must be relayed upstream, usually by telephone or in person.
- Finally, a meeting should result that uses face-to-face negotiation to finalize the sale if the sale can be agreed.

By placing the entire system on the Internet, the upstream and downstream communications are accomplished using a Web browser. The sale becomes more of an auction, because many potential buyers, all with equal status, can bid for the same item. So it's fairer for all purchasers and gets a better deal for the seller.

Any user who is trying to buy an item can

- View items for sale
- Bid on an item they wish to purchase

Any user who is trying to sell an item can

- Place a new item for sale
- Browse a list of the items that he or she is trying to sell, and examine the bids that have been made on each of those items
- Accept a bid on an item that he or she is selling

This system should also allow users to do some very basic administrative tasks, such as

- Browse the listings to see what is for sale
- Register with the system (users can browse without registering; but they must register if they want to sell an item or bid for an item)

Figure RHGP.2

Gabby's Gazetteer Classified Registration System

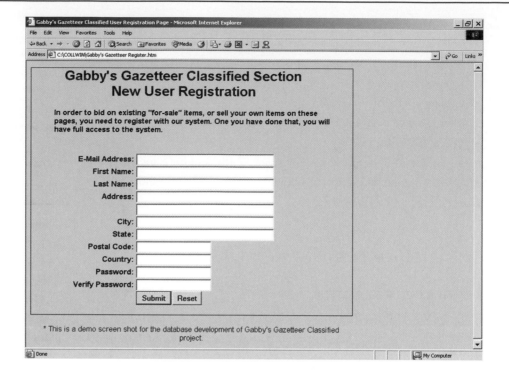

- Log on to the system
- Change their registration details

Your job will be to complete the following:

1. Develop and describe the entity-relationship diagram for the database that will support the above activities.
2. Use normalization to ensure the correctness of the tables.
3. Create the database using a personal DBMS package.

SOME PARTICULARS YOU SHOULD KNOW

1. Use Figure RHGP.2 as a baseline for your database design.
2. File: Not applicable.

CASE 12:
SHOULD I BUY OR SHOULD I LEASE?

DECISION SUPPORT SYSTEMS

A leading supplier of grapes to the wine-producing industry in California, On the Vine Grapes, wants to expand its delivery services and expand its reach to market by increasing its current fleet of delivery trucks. Some of the older vehicles were acquired through closed-end leases with required down payments, mileage restrictions, and hefty early termination penalties. Other vehicles were purchased using traditional purchase-to-own loans, which often resulted in high depreciation costs and large maintenance fees. All vehicles were acquired one at a time through local dealers.

On the Vine Grapes has asked you to assist in developing a lease/buy cost analysis work sheet in order to make the most cost-effective decision. Currently the director of operations, Bill Smith, has identified a 2002 Ford F-550 4x2 SD Super Cab 161.8 in. WB DRW HD XLT as the truck of choice for the business. This vehicle has a retail price of $34,997.00 or a lease price for $600/month through Ford Motor Credit Company.

Here are some basic fees and costs that you need to factor in:

1. **Lease Costs**

Refundable security deposit	$500
First month's payment at inception	$500
Other initial costs	$125
Monthly lease payment for remaining term	$600
Last month payment in advance	No
Allowable annual mileage	15,000
Estimated annual miles to be driven	20,000
Per mile charge for excess miles	0.10

2. **Purchase Costs**

Retail price including sales taxes, title	$34,997
Down payment	$4,000
Loan interest rate	8.75%
Will interest be deductible business or home equity interest	Yes
Is the gross loaded wait of the vehicle over 6,000 lbs?	Yes

3. **Common Costs and Assumptions**

Total lease/loan term	36
Discount percent	8.75
Tax bracket—combined federal and state	33%
Business use percentage	100%

SOME PARTICULARS YOU SHOULD KNOW

1. In the file BUYORLEASE.xls is a template you can use to enter the information above. There is also a sheet that has been developed to assist you with the annual depreciation for an automobile.
2. Create a detailed summary sheet of the lease/buy option for On the Vine Grapes.
3. File: BUYORLEASE.xls (Excel file).

CASE 13:
HIGHER EDUCATION PLANNING AND DATA PROCESSING

ERP

The State Annual Report on Enterprise Resource Planning and Management was developed to provide a comprehensive view of the management and use of technology by the Higher Educational System of Colorado. This report shows the statewide issues surrounding information technology, priorities for the ensuing two years, initiatives and projects, performance management, and the information technology resources utilized to support the business processes of Higher Education during fiscal year 2000–2001. A comparison report is also generated to produce a percentage change in funds from fiscal year 1999–2000 and fiscal year 2000–2001.

Chief information officer (CIO) for the Department of Higher Education, David Paul, was required to report the estimated expenditures for technology across five appropriation categories: Employee Salaries/Benefits, Other Personal Services (OPS—noncareer service employees with no permanent status), Expenses (all hardware purchases under $1,000, travel, training, and general office expenses), Operating Capital Outlay (OCO), and Data Processing Services. Most of these performance management initiatives have been measured using manual processes. Several reporting units documented the need for automated measurement tools in the future to take advantage of the full opportunities for improvement. David Paul has asked you to assist him in organizing this information and calculating some of the requirements established by the State Board of Education. Along with the appropriation categories mentioned above, each institution is categorized according to status (2 Year, 4 Year Public, or 4 Year Private). This will aid in the overall analysis for current and future resource planning.

SOME PARTICULARS YOU SHOULD KNOW

1. You need to create a detailed report on:
   a. Summary of overall change from 1999–2000 fiscal year (FY) and 2000–2001 FY
   b. Percentage of budget allocated to data processing services
   c. Percentage of 2 year, 4 year public, and 4 year private institutions allocating resources to data processing services
2. Develop a graphical representation of the percentage of 2 year, 4 year public, and 4 year private institutions allocating resources to data processing services
3. File: COLORADOHIGHERED.xls (Excel file)

CASE 14:
ASSESSING A WIRELESS FUTURE

EMERGING TRENDS AND TECHNOLOGY

"Intelligent wireless handheld devices are going to explode, absolutely explode over the next several years."—Steve Ballmer, CEO, Microsoft.

Wireless, mobility, small form factor, pervasive computing, the anytime network—whatever name you choose—it's here. The price of easy-to-handle devices which provide access to a variety of applications and information is rapidly falling while the efficiencies of such devices are increasing. More and more, the business user is looking to use mobile devices to perform tasks that previously could be handled only by the desktop PC. End user adoption is skyrocketing. The next 18 months will demonstrate a true growing period for mobile computing as the world changes to one characterized by the mobile user.

As this market sector grows, software and information companies are beginning to evolve their products and services. Wireless mobility and associated functionality provide new market opportunities for both established companies and new entrants to increase efficiency and take advantage of new revenue possibilities. The services to Internet-enabled mobile devices create a vast array of new business opportunities for companies as they develop products and services that utilize location, time, and immediate access to information in new and innovative ways.

Some of the lower profile topics that are currently being developed at this time include:

- Hard drives for wireless devices
- Global-roaming movement
- Mobile power supplies that run on next-generation fuel cells.

All three could bring about significant changes in the wireless space.

You have been asked to prepare a presentation using a presentation package such as Microsoft's PowerPoint. Using the list of wireless solution providers and manufacturers provided in WIRELESS.htm, select at least two developers and create a presentation that will emphasize the following topics:

1. What are the current products or services under development?
2. What is the target market for that product or service?
3. What are the key features that product or service will bring to the wireless industry?
4. Which provider/manufacturer/developer seems to be the first to market with their product?
5. How is the wireless product or service content being delivered?
6. Are the products or services able to deploy interactive multimedia applications to any digital wireless device, on any carrier, or across any type of network?
7. Are there any new privacy concerns that are being discussed in relation to the new products or services? (These can include concerns from being able to track users' preferences, purchasing history or browsing preferences, or the capability to track a user's physical location while using a wireless device.)
8. How does this product or solution affect the global marketplace?
9. What is the current retail price for the wireless products or solutions?
10. Is current bandwidth available to the wireless industry a concern?

Your task is to weave the information you find into a coherent presentation using graphs and art where appropriate.

SOME PARTICULARS YOU SHOULD KNOW

1. Content Principles
   - Each slide should have a headline
   - Each slide should express one idea
   - Ideas should follow logically
2. Design Principles
   - Follow the "Rule of 7" — no more than 7 lines per slide and 7 words per line
   - Keep it simple
   - Keep it organized
   - Create a path for the eye
   - Divide space in an interesting way
   - Use at least 30-point type
   - Use color and graphics carefully, consistently, and for a specific purpose
   - Use high-contrast colors (black/white, deep blue/white, etc.)
3. File: WIRELESS.htm (html file)

CASE 15:
THE NEXT GENERATION: DOT-COM ASPS

E-COMMERCE

E-commerce is creating a new set of challenges for dot-com startups to well-established brick-and-mortar companies. Driven by the need to capture increasing shares of business online, IT managers take the first step by deciding on a commerce application. Then they face the most important decision; whether to assign implementation, deployment, and application hosting to internal IT resources or to contract for these services with an ASP.

Twelve to 18 months ago, no one had even heard the term *application service provider (ASP)*. Now the ASP market is a certified phenomenon. In the short space of a year and a half, the concept of leasing applications to businesses has grown to an interesting but unproven proposition in an ever-expanding industry.

You have been hired by Front Range Car Rental, a major car rental company in Colorado, to research ways in using technology to leverage more business. The company needs a Web Service written which transacts reservations on its back-end mainframe system. This Web Service will need to be made available to airline partners to integrate the travel booking process. When consumers book a flight, they are also given the option to reserve a car from the airline site. The rental details will need to be captured and transported to the car rental company's Web Service, which processes the reservation. This new capability will help the car rental company to drive more bookings and achieve a competitive advantage in a highly commoditized market.

The major task that the Front Range Car Rental needs you to research is what the cost benefits would be for in-house implementation and an ASP deployment. You have been given an analysis spreadsheet, DOTCOMASP.xls, with all the detailed information; however, you will need to use the Internet in order to find current price information. Another file, DOTCOMASP_SEARCH.htm, has been developed for you with a list of search engines that will provide you with a focal point for your research.

SOME PARTICULARS YOU SHOULD KNOW

1. All ASPs are not created equal. Here are some questions to help you identify their strengths, weaknesses, capabilities and core competencies.
   - Does the ASP offer full life-cycle services, including proof-of-concept, installation, operations, training, support, and proactive evolution services?
   - What is the ASP's depth and breadth of technical expertise? What are the company's specialties?
   - Where and how did key technical staff obtain their expertise?
   - Does the ASP have actual customers online and if so, what results have they achieved?
   - Does the ASP offer service-level agreements and what are the penalties for SLA violations?
   - Specifically, how does the ASP's infrastructure deliver:
     - High availability (uptime)?
     - Assured data integrity?
     - Scalability?
     - Reliability?
     - High performance?
     - Security and access control?
   - Does the ASP offer 24 × 7 technical support to end users? Escalation procedures? High-priority problem resolution? Dedicated account managers?
   - Can the ASP provide development expertise to customize the applications?
   - How does the ASP handle updates? Adding product modules?
   - Is the ASP capable of assisting with add-on projects such as bringing a new factory online or adding a new supplier?
   - Can the ASP provide a comprehensive suite of integrated applications (versus a single application)?
2. File: DOTCOMASP.xls (Excel File) and DOTCOMASP_SEARCH.htm (html file)

CASE 16:
PONY ESPRESSO: ANALYZING OPERATING LEVERAGE

STRATEGIC AND COMPETITIVE ADVANTAGE

Pony Espresso is a small business that sells specialty coffee drinks at office buildings. Each morning and afternoon, trucks arrive at offices' front entrances, and the office employees purchase various beverages with names such as Java du Jour and Café de Colombia. The business is profitable. But Pony Espresso offices are located to the north of town, where lease rates are less expensive, and the principal sales area is south of town. This means that the trucks must drive cross-town four times each day.

The cost of transportation to and from the sales area, plus the power demands of the truck's coffee brewing equipment, is a significant portion of the variable costs. Pony Espresso could reduce the amount of driving—and, therefore, the variable costs—if it moves the offices much closer to the sales area.

Pony Espresso presently has fixed costs of $10,000 per month. The lease of a new office, closer to the sales area, would cost an additional $2,200 per month. This would increase the fixed costs to $12,200 per month.

Although the lease of new offices would increase the fixed costs, a careful estimate of the potential savings in gasoline and vehicle maintenance indicates that Pony Espresso could reduce the variable costs from $0.60 per unit to $0.35 per unit. Total sales are unlikely to increase as a result of the move, but the savings in variable costs should increase the annual profit.

You have been hired by Pony Espresso to assist in the cost analysis and new lease options to determine a growth in profit margin. You will also need to calculate a degree of operating leverage to better understand the company's profitability. Degree of operating leverage (DOL) will give the CEO of Pony Espresso, Darian Presley, a great deal of information for setting operating targets and planning profitability.

SOME PARTICULARS YOU SHOULD KNOW

1. Consider the information provided, especially look at the change in the variability of the profit from month to month. From November through January, when it is much more difficult to lure office workers out into the cold to purchase coffee, Pony Espresso barely breaks even. In fact, in December of 2002, the business lost money.

2. First, develop the cost analysis on the existing lease information using the monthly sales figures provided to you in the file PONYESPRESSO.xls. Second, develop the cost analysis from the new lease information provided above.

3. You need to calculate the variability that is reflected in the month-to-month standard deviation of earnings for the current cost structure and the projected cost structure.

4. Do not consider any association with downsizing such as overhead; simply focus on the information provided to you.

5. You will need to calculate the EBIT—earnings before interest and taxes.

6. Would the DOL and business risk increase or decrease if Pony Espresso moved its office? *Note:* Variability in profit levels, whether measured as EBIT, operating income, or net income, does not necessarily increase the level of business risk as the DOL increases.

7. File: PONYESPRESSO.xls (Excel file).

GLOSSARY

A

Adaptive filter asks you to rate products or situations and also monitors your actions over time to find out what you like and dislike.

Adaptivity the ability of intelligent agents to discover, learn, and take action independently.

Adware software to generate ads that installs itself on your computer when you download some other (usually free) program from the Web.

Affiliate programs arrangements made between e-commerce sites that direct users from one site to the other and by which, if a sale is made as a result, the originating site receives a commission.

Alliance partner a company you do business with on a regular business in a cooperative fashion, usually facilitated by IT systems.

Analysis phase involves end users and IT specialists working together to gather, understand, and document the business requirements for the proposed system.

Anonymous Web browsing (AWB) services hide your identity from the Web sites you visit.

Anti-virus software detects and removes or quarantines computer viruses.

Application architects information technology professionals who can design creative technology-based business solutions.

Application generation subsystem contains facilities to help you develop transaction-intensive applications.

Application service provider (ASP) provides an outsourcing service for business software applications.

Application software software that enables you to solve specific problems or perform specific tasks.

Arithmetic/logic unit (A/L unit) performs all arithmetic operations (for example, addition and subtraction) and all logic operations (such as sorting and comparing numbers).

Artificial intelligence (AI) the science of making machines imitate human thinking and behavior.

Artificial neural network (ANN) also called a **neural network,** an artificial intelligence system that is capable of finding and differentiating patterns.

ASCII (American Standard Code for Information Interchange) the coding system that most personal computers use to represent, process, and store information.

AutoFilter function filters a list and allows you to hide all the rows in a list except those that match criteria you specify.

Automatic speech recognition (ASR) a system that not only captures spoken words but also distinguishes word groupings to form sentences.

Autonomy the ability of an intelligent agent to act without your telling it every step to take.

B

B2B marketplace an Internet-based service which brings together many buyers and sellers.

Back office system used to fulfill and support customer orders.

Back-propagation neural network a neural network trained by someone.

Backup the process of making a copy of the information stored on a computer.

Bandwidth or capacity of the communications medium, refers to the amount of information that a communications medium can transfer in a given amount of time.

Banner ad a small ad on one Web site that advertises the products and services of another business, usually another dot-com business.

Bar code reader captures information that exists in the form of vertical bars whose width and distance apart determine a number.

Basic formatting tag HTML tag that allows you to specify formatting for text.

Benchmark a set of conditions used to measure how well a product or system functions.

Binary digit (bit) the smallest unit of information that your computer can process.

Biometrics the use of your physical characteristics—such as your fingerprint, the blood vessels in the retina of your eye, the sound of your voice, or perhaps even your breath—to provide identification.

Black-hat hackers cyber vandals.

Bluetooth technology that provides entirely wireless connections for all kinds of communication devices.

Broadband high-capacity telecommunications pipeline capable of providing high-speed Internet service.

Browser-safe colors 216 colors that can be represented using 8 bits and are visible in all browsers.

Business intelligence knowledge about your customers, your competitors, your partners, your competitive environment, and your own internal operations. Business intelligence comes from information.

Business process a standardized set of activities that accomplishes a specific task, such as processing a customer's order.

Business process reengineering (BPR) the reinventing of processes within a business.

Business requirement a detailed knowledge worker request that the system must meet in order to be successful.

Business to business (B2B) companies whose customers are primarily other businesses.

Business to consumer (B2C) companies whose customers are primarily individuals.

Buyer agent or **shopping bot** an intelligent agent on a Web site that helps you, the customer, find the products and services you want.

Buyer power high when buyers have many choices of whom to buy from, and low when their choices are few.

Byte a group of eight bits that represents one natural language character.

C

Cable modem a device that uses your TV cable to deliver an Internet connection.

Capacity planning determines the future IT infrastructure requirements for new equipment and additional network capacity.

Cat 5 (or **Category 5**) a better-constructed version of the phone twisted-pair cable.

CAVE (cave automatic virtual environment) a special 3-D virtual reality room that can display images of other people and objects located in other CAVEs all over the world.

CD-R (compact disc-recordable) optical or laser disc that offers one-time writing capability with about 800MB of storage capacity.

CD-ROM optical or laser disc that offers no updating capabilities with about 800MB of storage capacity. Most software today comes on CD-ROM.

CD-RW (compact disc-rewritable) offers unlimited writing and updating capabilities on the CD.

Central processing unit (CPU) the actual hardware that interprets and executes the software instructions and coordinates how all the other hardware devices work together.

Chief information officer (CIO) responsible for overseeing an organization's information resource.

Choice the third step in the decision-making process where you decide on a plan to address the problem or opportunity.

Class contains information and procedures and acts as a template to create objects.

Clicks-and-mortar a retailer, like Nordstrom, which has both an Internet presence and one or more physical stores.

Clickstream is a stored record about your Web surfing session, such as what Web sites you visited, how long you were there, what ads you looked at, and what you bought.

Click-throughs a count of the number of people who visit one site and click on an ad, and are taken to the site of the advertiser.

Client/server network a network in which one or more computers are servers and provide services to the other computers which are called clients.

Coaxial cable (coax) one central wire surrounded by insulation, a metallic shield, and a final case of insulating material.

Cold site a separate facility that does not have any computer equipment but is a place where the knowledge workers can move after the disaster.

Collaboration system a system that is designed specifically to improve the performance of teams by supporting the sharing and flow of information.

Collaborative filtering a method of placing you in an affinity group of people with the same characteristics.

Collaborative planning, forecasting, and replenishment (CPFR) a concept that encourages and facilitates collaborative processes between members of a supply chain.

Collaborative processing enterprise information portal provides knowledge workers with access to workgroup information such as e-mails, reports, meeting minutes, and memos.

Collocation a vendor that rents space and telecommunications equipment to other companies.

Communications medium the path, or physical channel, in a network over which information travels.

Communications protocol (protocol) a set of rules that every computer follows to transfer information.

Communications satellite a microwave repeater in space.

Communications service provider third party who furnishes the conduit for information.

Communications software helps you communicate with other people.

Competitive advantage providing a product or service in a way that customers value more than what the competition is able to do.

Complementor provides products and services that complement the offerings of the enterprise and thereby extends its value-adding capabilities to its customers.

Composite primary key the primary key fields from two intersecting relations.

Computer-aided software engineering (CASE) software suites that automate system development.

Computer crime a crime in which a computer, or computers, plays a significant part.

Computer forensics the collection, authentication, preservation, and examination of electronic information for presentation in court.

Computer network (or network) two or more computers connected so that they can communicate with each other and share information, software, peripheral devices, and/or processing power.

Computer virus (or simply a virus) software that is written with malicious intent to cause annoyance or damage.

Conditional formatting highlights the information in a cell that meets some criteria you specify.

Connectivity software enables you to use your computer to "dial up" or connect to another computer.

Control unit interprets software instructions and literally tells the other hardware devices what to do, based on the software instructions.

Conversion rate the percentage of customers who visit a site who actually buy something.

Cookie a small record deposited on your hard disk by a Web site containing information about you and your Web activities.

Copyright the legal protection afforded to an expression of an idea, such as a song, video game, and some types of proprietary documents.

Counterfeit software software that is manufactured to look like the real thing and sold as such.

Cracker a hacker for hire; a person who engages in electronic corporate espionage.

Crash-proof software utility software that helps you save information if your system crashes and you're forced to turn it off and then back on again.

Creative design one that solves the business problem in a new and highly effective way rather than the same way others have done it.

Critical success factor (CSF) a factor simply critical to your organization's success.

Crossover the process within a genetic algorithm where portions of good outcomes are combined in the hope of creating an even better outcome.

CRT a monitor that looks like a television set.

CRUD (*C*reate, *R*ead, *U*pdate, *D*elete) the four primary procedures, or ways, a system can manipulate information.

Culture the collective personality of a nation or society, encompassing language, traditions, currency, religion, history, music, and acceptable behavior, among other things.

Custom AutoFilter function allows you to hide all the rows in a list except those that match criteria, besides "is equal to," you specify.

Customer-integrated system (CIS) an extension of a TPS that places technology in the hands of an organization's customers and allows them to process their own transactions.

Customer relationship management (CRM) system uses information about customers to gain insights into their needs, wants, and behaviors in order to serve them better.

Cyberterrorist one who seeks to cause harm to people or destroy critical systems or information.

D

Data raw facts that describe a particular phenomenon.

Data administration the function in an organization that plans for, oversees the development of, and monitors the information resource.

Data administration subsystem helps you manage the overall database environment by providing facilities for backup and recovery, security management, query optimization, concurrency control, and change management.

Database a collection of information that you organize and access according to the logical structure of that information.

Database-based workflow system stores the document in a central location and automatically asks the knowledge workers to access the document when it's their turn to edit the document.

Database administration the function in an organization that is responsible for the more technical and operational aspects of managing the information contained in organizational databases (which can include data warehouses and data marts).

Database management system (DBMS) helps you specify the logical organization for a database and access and use the information within the database.

Data cleansing ensures all information is accurate.

Data definition subsystem helps you create and maintain the data dictionary and define the structure of the files in a database.

Data dictionary contains the logical structure for the information.

Data management component of DSS that performs the function of storing and maintaining the information that you want your DSS to use.

Data manipulation subsystem helps you add, change, and delete information in a database and mine it for valuable information.

Data mart subset of a data warehouse in which only a focused portion of the data warehouse information is kept.

Data-mining agent an intelligent agent that operates in a data warehouse discovering information.

Data-mining tool software tool you use to query information in a data warehouse.

Data warehouse a logical collection of information—gathered from many different operational databases—used to create business intelligence that supports business analysis activities and decision-making tasks.

DBMS engine accepts logical requests from the various other DBMS subsystems, converts them into their physical equivalent, and actually accesses the database and data dictionary as they exist on a storage device.

Decentralized computing an environment in which an organization splits computing power and locates it in functional business areas as well as on the desktops of knowledge workers.

Decision processing enterprise information portal provides knowledge workers with corporate information for making key business decisions.

Decision support system (DSS) a highly flexible and interactive IT system that is designed to support decision making when the problem is not structured.

Demand aggregation combines purchase requests from multiple buyers into a single large order which justifies a discount from the business.

Denial-of-service (DoS) attack floods a Web site with so many requests for service that it slows down or crashes.

Design where you consider possible ways of solving the problem, filling the need, or taking advantage of the opportunity.

Design phase the stage of system planning where the planner builds a technical blueprint of how the proposed system will work.

Desktop computer the most popular choice for personal computing needs.

Desktop publishing software extends word processing software by including design and formatting techniques to enhance the layout and appearance of a document.

Development phase takes all of your detailed design documents from the design phase and transforms them into an actual system.

Digital cash (also called electronic cash or e-cash) an electronic representation of cash.

Digital divide the fact that different peoples, cultures, and areas of the world or within a nation do not have the same access to information and telecommunications technologies.

Digital economy marked by the electronic movement of all types of information, not limited to numbers, words, graphs, and photos but including physiological information such as voice recognition and synthesization, biometrics (your retina scan and breath for example), and 3-D holograms.

Digital Subscriber Line (DSL) a high-speed Internet connection using phone lines, which allows you to use your phone for voice communications at the same time.

Direct material material that is used in production in a manufacturing company or is placed on the shelf for sale in a retail environment.

Directory search engine organizes listings of Web sites into hierarchical lists.

Disaster recovery cost curve charts (1) the cost to your organization of the unavailability of information and technology, and (2) the cost to your organization of recovering from a disaster over time.

Disaster recovery plan a detailed process for recovering information or an IT system in the event of a catastrophic disaster such as a fire or flood.

Disintermediation the use of the Internet as a delivery vehicle, whereby intermediate players in a distribution channel can be bypassed.

Disk optimization software utility software that organizes your information on your hard disk in the most efficient way.

Distributed denial-of-service (DDos) attack attack from multiple computers that flood a Web site with so many requests for service that it slows down or crashes.

Distribution chain the path followed from the originator of a product or service to the end consumer.

Document management system manages a document through its life cycle.

Domain expert the person who provides the domain expertise in the form of problem-solving strategies.

Domain expertise the set of problem-solving steps; it's the reasoning process that will solve the problem.

Domain name identifies a specific computer on the Web and the main page of the entire site.

Dot pitch the distance between the centers of a pair of like-colored pixels.

DVD-R optical or laser disc that offers one-time writing capability with upward of 17GB of storage capacity.

DVD-ROM optical or laser disc that offers no updating capabilities with upward of 17GB of storage capacity. The trend is now for movie rentals to be on DVD.

DVD-RW, DVD-RAM, or DVD+RW (all different names by different manufacturers) optical or laser disc that offers unlimited writing and updating capabilities on the DVD.

E

ebXML a set of technical specifications for business documents built around XML designed to permit enterprises of any size and in any geographical location to conduct business over the Internet.

E-government the application of e-commerce technologies in governmental agencies.

Electronic Bill Presentment and Payment (EBPP) a system that sends us our bills over the Internet and gives us an easy way to pay them if the amount looks correct.

Electronic catalog designed to present products to customers or partners all over the world via the Web.

Electronic commerce commerce, but it is commerce accelerated and enhanced by information technology, in particular, the Internet.

Electronic data interchange (EDI) the direct computer-to-computer transfer of transaction information contained in standard business documents, such as invoices and purchase orders, in a standard format.

Electronic job market consists of employers using Internet technologies to advertise and screen potential employees.

Electronic portfolio (e-portfolio) collection of Web documents used to support a stated purpose such as demonstrating writing, photography, or job skills.

E-mail software (electronic mail software) enables you to electronically communicate with other people by sending and receiving e-mail.

Encapsulation information hiding

Encryption scrambles the contents of a file so that you can't read it without the right decryption key.

Enterprise application integration (EAI) the process of developing an IT infrastructure that enables employees to quickly implement new or changing business processes.

Enterprise application integration middleware (EAI middleware) allows organizations to develop different levels of integration from the information level to the business-process level.

Enterprise information portal (EIP) allows knowledge workers to access company information via a Web interface.

Enterprise resource planning (ERP) the method of getting and keeping an overview of every part of the business (a bird's eye view, so to speak), so that production, development, selling, and servicing of goods and services will all be coordinated to contribute to the company's goals and objectives.

Enterprise software a suite of software that includes (1) a set of common business applications; (2) tools for modeling how the entire organization works; and (3) development tools for building applications unique to your organization.

Entity class a concept—typically people, places, or things—about which you wish to store information and that you can identify with a unique key (called the primary key).

Entity-relationship (E-R) diagram a graphic method of representing entity classes and their relationships.

Entry barrier a product or service feature that customers have come to expect from companies in a particular industry.

E-tailer an Internet retail site.

Ethernet card the most common type of network interface card.

Ethical (or white-hat) hacker a computer security professional who is hired by a company to break into its computer system.

Ethics the principles and standards that guide our behavior toward other people.

Executive information system (EIS) a highly interactive IT system that allows you to first view highly summarized information and then choose how you would like to see greater detail, which may alert you to potential problems or opportunities.

Expandability refers to how easy it is to add features and functions to a system.

Expansion bus moves information from your CPU and RAM to all of your other hardware devices such as your microphone and printer.

Expansion card a circuit board that you insert into an expansion slot.

Expansion slot a long skinny socket on the motherboard into which you insert an expansion card.

Expert system (also called a **knowledge-based system**) an artificial intelligence system that applies reasoning capabilities to reach a conclusion.

Explanation module the part of an expert system where the "why" information, supplied by the domain expert, is stored to be accessed by knowledge workers who want to know why the expert systems asked a question or reached a conclusion.

External information describes the environment surrounding the organization.

Extraction engine smart software with a vocabulary of job-related skills that allows it to recognize and catalog terms in your scannable résumé.

Extranet an intranet that is restricted to an organization and certain outsiders, such as customers and suppliers.

F

Fair Use Doctrine allows you to use copyrighted material in certain situations.

Feature analysis the step of ASR in which the system captures your words as you speak into a microphone, eliminates any background noise, and converts the digital signals of your speech into phonemes (syllables).

Feature creep occurs when developers add extra features that were not part of the initial requirements.

File transfer protocol (ftp) the communications protocol that allows you to transfer files of information from one computer to another.

Financial cybermediaries Internet-based companies that make it easy for one person to pay another person over the Internet.

Financial EDI (FEDI) the use of EDI for payments.

Firewall hardware and/or software that protects a computer or network from intruders.

First mover the company first to market with a new IT-based product or service.

Five forces model a model developed to determine the relative attractiveness of an industry.

Flat-panel display thin, lightweight monitor that takes up much less space than a CRT.

Floppy disk storage device that is great for portability of information and ease of updating but holds only 1.44MB of information.

Foreign key a primary key of one file (relation) that appears in another file (relation).

Forensic image copy an exact copy or snapshot of the contents of an electronic medium.

Front office system the primary interface to customers and sales channels.

FTP (file transfer protocol) server maintains a collection of files that you can download.

G

Genetic algorithm an artificial intelligence system that mimics the evolutionary, survival-of-the-fittest process to generate increasingly better solutions to a problem.

Geographic information system (GIS) a decision support system designed specifically to work with spatial information.

Gigabyte (GB or **Gig)** roughly 1 billion characters.

Gigahertz (GHz) the number of billions of CPU cycles per second.

Global digital divide the term used specifically to describe differences in IT access and capabilities between different countries or regions of the world.

Global economy one in which customers, businesses, suppliers, distributors, and manufacturers all operate without regard to physical and geographical boundaries.

Global positioning system (GPS) a collection of 24 earth-orbiting satellites that continuously transmit radio signals to determine your current longitude, latitude, speed, and direction of movement.

Global reach the ability to extend a company's reach to customers anywhere there is an Internet connection, and at a much lower cost.

Glove an input device that captures and records the shape and movement of your hand and fingers and the strength of your hand and finger movements.

Government-to-business (G2B) the electronic commerce activities performed between a government and its business partners for such purposes as purchasing direct and indirect materials, soliciting bids for work, and accepting bids for work.

Government-to-consumer (G2C) the electronic commerce activities performed between a government and its citizens or consumers including paying taxes, registering vehicles, and providing information and services.

Government-to-government (G2G) the electric commerce activities limited to a single nation's government focusing on vertical integration (local, city, state, and federal) and horizontal integration (within the various branches and agencies).

Graphical user interface (GUI) the interface to an information system.

Graphics software helps you create and edit photos and art.

Grid computing harnesses far-flung computers together by way of the Internet or a virtual private network to share CPU power, databases, and storage.

Group document database a powerful storage facility for organizing and managing all documents related to specific teams.

Groupware the popular term for the software component that supports the collaborative efforts of a team.

GUI screen design the ability to model the information system screens for an entire system.

H

Hacker a very knowledgeable computer user who uses his or her knowledge to invade other people's computers.

Hacktivist a politically motivated hacker who uses the Internet to send a political message of some kind.

Handspring a type of PDA that runs on the Palm Operating System (Palm OS).

Hard disk storage device that rests within your system box and offers both ease of updating and great storage capacity.

Hardware the physical devices that make up a computer (often referred to as a computer system).

Hardware key logger a hardware device that captures keystrokes on their journey from the keyboard to the motherboard.

Heading tag HTML tag that makes certain information, such as titles, stand out on your Web site.

Headset a combined input and output device that (1) captures and records the movement of your head, and (2) contains a screen that covers your entire field of vision and displays various views of an environment based on your movements.

Help desk responds to knowledge workers' questions.

Hidden job market the collective term used to describe jobs that are not advertised. Up to 80 percent of new jobs fall into this category.

High-capacity floppy disk storage device that is great for portability and ease of updating and holds between 100MB and 250MB of information. Superdisks and Zip disks are examples.

Holographic device a device that creates, captures, and/or displays images in true three-dimensional form.

Home PNA (Home Phoneline Networking Alliance) allows you to network your home computers using telephone wiring.

Horizontal market software application software that is general enough to be suitable for use in a variety of industries.

Hot site a separate and fully equipped facility where the company can move immediately after the disaster and resume business.

HTML document a file that contains your Web site content and HTML formatting instructions.

HTML tag specifies the formatting and presentation of information on a Web site.

Hypertext markup language (HTML) the language you use to create a Web site.

Hypertext transfer protocol (HTTP) the communications protocol that supports the movement of information over the Web, essentially from a Web server to you.

I

Implant chip a technology-enabled microchip implanted into the human body.

Implementation the final step in the decision-making process where you put your plan into action.

Implementation phase distributes the system to all of the knowledge workers and they begin using the system to perform their everyday jobs.

Indirect material (commonly called MRO materials) material that is necessary for running a modern corporation, but does not relate to the company's primary business activities.

Inference engine the processing component of the expert system. It takes your problem facts and searches the knowledge base for rules that fit your problem facts.

Information data that have a particular meaning within a specific context.

Information age a time when knowledge is power.

Information decomposition breaking down the information and procedures for ease of use and understandability.

Information granularity the extent of detail within the information.

Information-literate knowledge workers can define what information they need, know how and were to obtain that information, understand the information once they receive it, and act appropriately based on the information to help the organization achieve the greatest advantage.

Information partnership two or more companies that cooperate by integrating their IT systems, thereby providing customers with the best of what each can offer.

Information technology (IT) any computer-based tool that people use to work with information and support the information and information-processing needs of an organization.

Information view includes all of the information stored within a system.

Infrared a wireless communications medium that uses light waves to transmit signals or information.

Inheritance the ability to define superclass and subclass relationships among classes.

Inkjet printer makes images by forcing ink droplets through nozzles.

Input device a tool you use to capture information and commands.

Insourcing means that IT specialists within your organization will develop the system.

Instance an occurrence of an entity class that can be uniquely described.

Integration allows separate systems to communicate directly with each other by automatically exporting data files from one system and importing them into another.

Integrity constraints   rules that help ensure the quality of the information.

Intellectual property   intangible creative work that is embodied in physical form.

Intelligence   the first step in the decision-making process where you find or recognize a problem, need, or opportunity (also called the diagnostic phase of decision-making).

Intelligent agent   software that assists you, or acts on your behalf, in performing repetitive computer-related tasks.

Interactive chat   lets you engage in real-time typed exchange of information between you and one or more other individuals over the Internet.

Interface   any device that calls procedures and can include such things as a keyboard, mouse, and touch screen.

Intermediary   a specialist company that provides services better than its client companies can themselves.

Internal information   information that describes specific operational aspects of the organization.

International government-to-government (IG2G)   the electronic commerce activities performed between two or more governments, including providing foreign aid.

International virtual private network (international VPN)   virtual private networks that depend on services offered by phone companies of various nationalities.

Internet   a vast network of computers that connects millions of people all over the world.

Internet backbone   the major set of connections for computers on the Internet.

Internet server computer   computer that provides information and services on the Internet.

Internet service provider (ISP)   a company that provides individuals, organizations, and businesses access to the Internet.

Internet telephony   a combination of hardware and software that uses the Internet as the medium for transmission of telephone calls in place of traditional telephone networks.

Interorganizational system (IOS)   automates the flow of information between organizations to support the planning, design, development, production, and delivery of products and services.

Intersection relation (sometimes called a **composite relation**)   a relation you create to eliminate a many-to-many relationship.

Intranet   an internal organizational Internet that is guarded against outside access by a special security feature called a firewall (which can be software, hardware, or a combination of the two).

Intrusion-detection software   looks for people on the network who shouldn't be there or who are acting suspiciously.

IRC (Internet relay chat) server   supports your use of discussion groups and chat rooms.

IrDA (infrared data association) port   for wireless devices that work in essentially the same way as the remote control on your TV.

IT infrastructure   the hardware, software, and telecommunications equipment, that when combined, provides the underlying foundation to support the organization's goals.

J

Joint application development (JAD)   occurs when knowledge workers and IT specialists meet, sometimes for several days, to define or review the business requirements for the system.

Just-in-time (JIT)   an approach that produces or delivers a product or service just at the time the customer wants it.

K

Keyboard   today's most popular input technology.

Key logger (or key trapper) software   a program that, when installed on a computer, records every keystroke and mouse click.

Knowledge acquisition   the component of the expert system that the knowledge engineer uses to enter the rules.

Knowledge base   stores the rules of the expert system.

Knowledge-based system   also known as an **expert system,** an artificial intelligence system that applies reasoning capabilities to reach a conclusion.

Knowledge engineer   the person who formulates the domain expertise into an expert system.

Knowledge worker   works with and produces information as a product.

L

Language processing   the step of ASR in which the system attempts to make sense of what you're saying by comparing the word phonemes generated in step 2 with a language model database.

Laser printer   forms images using an electrostatic process, the same way a photocopier works.

Last-mile bottleneck problem   occurs when information is traveling on the Internet over a very fast line for a certain distance and then comes near your home where it must travel over a slower line.

Legacy system   a previously built system using older technologies such as mainframe computers and programming languages such as COBOL.

Link (the technical name is **hyperlink**)   clickable text or an image that takes you to another site or page on the Web.

Linux   an open-source operating system that provides a rich operating environment for high-end workstations and network servers.

List   a collection of information arranged in columns and rows in which each column displays one particular type of information.

List definition table   a description of a list by column.

Local area network (LAN)   a network that covers a limited geographic distance, such as an office, a building, or a group of buildings in close proximity to each other.

Logical view   focuses on how you as a knowledge worker need to arrange and access information to meet your particular business needs.

M

Mac OS the operating system for today's Apple computers.

Macro virus spreads by binding itself to software such as Word or Excel.

Mailing list discussion groups organized by area of interest.

Mail server provides e-mail services and accounts.

Mainframe computer (sometimes just called a **mainframe**) a computer designed to meet the computing needs of hundreds of people in a large business environment.

Maintenance phase monitors and supports the new system to ensure it continues to meet the business goals.

Management information systems (MIS) deals with the planning for, development, management, and use of information technology tools to help people perform all tasks related to information processing and management.

Marketing mix the set of marketing tools that a firm uses to pursue its marketing objectives in the target market.

Mass customization when a business gives its customers the opportunity to tailor its product or service to the customer's specifications.

M-commerce the term used to describe electronic commerce conducted over a wireless device such as a cell phone or personal digital assistant.

MD5 hash value a mathematically generated string of 32 letters and digits that is unique for an individual storage medium at a specific point in time.

Megabyte (MB or M or Meg) roughly 1 million bytes.

Megahertz (MHz) the number of millions of CPU cycles per second.

Message how objects communicate with each other.

Messaging-based workflow system sends work assignments through an e-mail system.

Meta tag a part of a Web site text not displayed to users but accessible to browsers and search engines for finding and categorizing Web sites.

Micro-payment a technique to facilitate the exchange of small amounts of money for an Internet transaction.

Microphone for capturing live sounds such as a dog barking or your voice (for automatic speech recognition).

Microsoft Windows 2000 Millennium (Windows 2000 Me) an operating system for a home computer user with utilities for setting up a home network and performing video, photo, and music editing and cataloging.

Microsoft Windows 2000 Professional (Windows 2000 Pro) an operating system for people who have a personal computer connected to a network of other computers at work or at school.

Microsoft Windows XP Home Microsoft's latest upgrade to Windows 2000 Me, with enhanced features for allowing multiple people to use the same computer.

Microsoft Windows XP Professional (Windows XP Pro) Microsoft's latest upgrade to Windows 2000 Pro.

Microwave a type of radio transmission used to transmit information.

Minicomputer (sometimes called a **mid-range computer**) designed to meet the computing needs of several people simultaneously in a small to medium-size business environment.

Modeling the activity of drawing a graphical representation of a design.

Model management component of a DSS that consists of the DSS models and the DSS model management system.

Monitoring-and-surveillance agents (or **predictive agents**) intelligent agents that observe and report on equipment.

Mouse today's most popular "pointing" input device.

Multidimensional analysis (MDA) tools slice-and-dice techniques that allow you to view multidimensional information from different perspectives.

Multifunction printer scans, copies, and faxes, as well as prints.

Multitasking allows you to work with more than one piece of software at a time.

Municipal area network (MAN) a network that covers a metropolitan area.

Mutation the process within a genetic algorithm of randomly trying combinations and evaluating the success (or failure) of the outcome.

N

Network two or more computers connected so that they can communicate with each other and possibly share information, software, peripheral devices, and/or processing power.

Network access point (NAP) a point on the Internet where several connections converge.

Network hub a device that connects multiple computers into a network.

Network interface card (NIC) an expansion card or a PC Card (for a notebook computer) that connects your computer to a network and provides the doorway for information to flow in and out.

Network service provider (NSP) such as MCI or AT&T, owns and maintains routing computers at NAPs and even the lines that connect the NAPs to each other.

Neural network (often called an **artificial neural network** or **ANN**) an artificial intelligence system that is capable of finding and differentiating patterns.

Nonrecurring, or ad hoc, decision one that you make infrequently (perhaps only once) and you may even have different criteria for determining the best solution each time.

Nonstructured decision a decision for which there may be several "right" answers and there is no precise way to get a right answer.

Normalization a process of assuring that a relational database structure can be implemented as a series of two-dimensional relations.

Notebook computer a fully functional computer designed for you to carry around and run on battery power.

O

Object   an instance of a class.

Objective information   quantifiably describes something that is known.

Object-oriented (OO) approach   combines information and procedures into a single view.

Object-oriented database   works with traditional database information and also complex data types such as diagrams, schematic drawings, videos, and sound and text documents.

Object-oriented programming language   a programming language used to develop object-oriented systems.

Online analytical processing (OLAP)   the manipulation of information to support decision making.

Online training   runs over the Internet or off a CD-ROM.

Online transaction processing (OLTP)   the gathering of input information, processing that information, and updating existing information to reflect the gathered and processed information.

Operating system software   system software that controls your application software and manages how your hardware devices work together.

Operational database   a database that supports OLTP.

Operational management   manages and directs the day-to-day operations and implementations of the goals and strategies.

Optical fiber   a telecommunications medium that uses a very thin glass or plastic fiber through which pulses of light travel.

Optical mark recognition (OMR)   detects the presence or absence of a mark in a predetermined place (popular for multiple choice exams).

Output device   a tool you use to see, hear, or otherwise accept the results of your information-processing requests.

Outsourcing   the delegation of specific work to a third party for a specified length of time, at a specified cost, and at a specified level of service.

P

Palm   a type of PDA that runs on the Palm Operating System (Palm OS).

Palm Operating System (Palm OS)   the operating system for Palm and Handspring PDAs.

Parallel connector   has 25 pins, which fit into the corresponding holes in the port. Most printers use parallel connectors.

Pattern classification   the step of ASR in which the system matches your spoken phonemes to a phoneme sequence stored in an acoustic model database.

Peer-to-peer network   a network in which a small number of computers share hardware (such as a printer), software, and/or information.

Performance   measures how quickly an IT system performs a certain process.

Permission marketing   when you have given a merchant your permission to send you special offers.

Personal agent (or user agent)   an intelligent agent that takes action on your behalf.

Personal digital assistant (PDA)   a small hand-held computer that helps you surf the Web and perform simple tasks such as note taking, calendaring, appointment scheduling, and maintaining an address book.

Personal finance software   helps you maintain your checkbook, prepare a budget, track investments, monitor your credit card balances, and pay bills electronically.

Personal information management (PIM) software   helps you create and maintain (1) to-do lists, (2) appointments and calendars, and (3) points of contact.

Personalization   when a Web site can know enough about your likes and dislikes that it can fashion offers that are more likely to appeal to you.

Personal productivity software   helps you perform personal tasks—such as writing a memo, creating a graph, and creating a slide presentation—that you can usually do even if you don't own a computer.

Physical view   deals with how information is physically arranged, stored, and accessed on some type of storage device such as a hard disk.

Pirated software   is the unauthorized use, duplication, distribution or sale of copyrighted software.

Pivot table   enables you to group and summarize information.

Planning phase   involves determining a solid plan for developing your information system.

PNA adapter card   an expansion card that you put into your computer to act as a doorway for information flowing in and out.

PocketPC   a type of PDA that runs on Pocket PC OS that used to be called Windows CE.

Pocket PC OS (or Windows CE)   the operating system for the PocketPC PDA.

Pointing stick   small rubberlike pointing device that causes the pointer to move on the screen as you apply directional pressure (popular on notebooks).

Point-of-sale (POS)   for capturing information at the point of a transaction, typically in a retail environment.

Polymorphism   to have many forms.

Port   the plug-in found on the outside of your system box (usually in the back) into which you plug a connector.

Portable document format (PDF)   the standard electronic distribution file format for heavily formatted documents such as a presentation résumé because it retains the original document formatting.

Presentation résumé   a format-sensitive document created in a word processor to outline your job qualifications in one to two printed pages.

Presentation software   helps you create and edit information that will appear in electronic slides.

Primary key   a field (or group of fields in some cases) that uniquely describes each record.

Privacy   the right to be left alone when you want to be, to have control over your own personal possessions, and not to be observed without your consent.

Private network   the communications media that your organization owns or exclusively leases to connect networks or network components.

Procedure   manipulates or changes information

Procedure view   contains all of the procedures within a system.

Profile filtering   requires that you choose terms or enter keywords to provide a more personal picture of you and your preferences.

Program   a set of instructions that, when executed, causes a computer to behave in a specific manner.

Programming language   the tool developers use to write a program.

Project manager   an individual who is an expert in project planning and management, defines and develops the project plan and tracks the plan to ensure all key project milestones are completed on time.

Project milestone   represents a key date for which you need a certain group of activities performed.

Project plan   defines the what, when, and who questions of system development including all activities to be performed, the individuals, or resources, who will perform the activities, and the time required to complete each activity.

Project scope   clearly defines the high-level system requirements.

Project scope document   a written definition of the project scope and is usually no longer than a paragraph.

Project team   a team designed to accomplish specific one-time goals, which is disbanded once the project is complete.

Proof-of-concept prototype   a prototype you use to prove the technical feasibility of a proposed system.

Prototype   a model of a proposed product, service, or system.

Prototyping   the process of building a model that demonstrates the features of a proposed product, service, or system.

Psychographic filtering   anticipates your preferences based on the answers you give to a questionnaire.

Public key encryption (PKE)   an encryption system that uses two keys: a public key that everyone can have and a private key for only the recipient.

Public network   a network on which your organization competes for time with others.

Pure play   an Internet retailer such as Amazon.com that has no physical stores.

Push technology   an environment in which businesses and organizations come to you with information, services, and product offerings based on your profile.

Q

Query-and-reporting tools   similar to QBE tools, SQL, and report generators in the typical database environment.

Query-by-example (QBE) tool   helps you graphically design the answer to a question.

R

RAM (random access memory)   temporary storage that holds the information you're working with, the application software you're using, and the operating system software you're using.

Recovery   the process of reinstalling the backup information in the event the information was lost.

Recurring decision   a decision that you have to make repeatedly and often periodically, whether weekly, monthly, quarterly, or yearly.

Relation   describes each two-dimensional table or file in the relational model (hence its name *relational* database model).

Relational database   uses a series of logically related two-dimensional tables or files to store information in the form of a database.

Repeater   a device that receives a radio signal, strengthens it, and sends it on.

Report generator   helps you quickly define formats of reports and what information you want to see in a report.

Request for proposal (RFP)   a formal document that describes in detail your logical requirements for a proposed system and invites outsourcing organizations (which we'll refer to as "vendors") to submit bids for its development.

Requirement definition document   defines all of the business requirements and prioritizes them in order of business importance and places them in a formal comprehensive document.

Resolution of a printer   the number of dots per inch (dpi) a printer produces, which is the same principle as the resolution in monitors.

Resolution of a screen   the number of pixels a screen has. Pixels (picture elements) are the dots that make up an image on your screen.

Reverse auction   the process in which a buyer posts its interest in buying a certain quantity of items, and sellers compete for the business by submitting successively lower bids until there is only one seller left.

Risk assessment   the process of evaluating IT assets, their importance to the organization, and their susceptibility to threats, to measure the risk exposure of these assets.

Risk management   consists of the identification of risks or threats, the implementation of security measures, and the monitoring of those measures for effectiveness.

Rivalry among existing competitors   makes an industry less attractive to enter when high and more attractive to enter when low.

Robot   a mechanical device equipped with simulated human senses and the capability of taking action on its own.

Router   a device that acts as a smart hub connecting computers into a network, and it also separates your network from any other network it's connected to.

Rule-based expert system   the type of expert system that expresses the problem-solving process as rules.

S

Safe-harbor principles   the set of rules to which U.S. businesses that want to trade with the European Union (EU) must adhere.

Sales force automation (SFA) system   automatically tracks all of the steps in the sales process.

Satellite modem   a modem that allows you to get Internet access from a satellite dish.

Scalability   refers to how well your system can adapt to increased demands.

Scannable résumé (ASCII résumé, plain-text résumé) designed to be evaluated by skills-extraction software and typically contain all résumé content without any formatting.

Scanner   captures images, photos, and artwork that already exist on paper.

Scope creep   occurs when the scope of the project increases.

Script bunny (or script kiddie)   someone who would like to be a hacker but doesn't have much technical expertise.

Script kiddie (or script bunny)   someone who would like to be a hacker but doesn't have much technical expertise.

Search engine   a facility on the Web that helps you find sites with the information and/or services you want.

Security auditing software   checks out your computer or network for potential weaknesses.

Selection   the process within a genetic algorithm that gives preference to better outcomes.

Self-organizing neural network   a network that finds patterns and relationships in vast amounts of data by itself.

Selfsourcing (also called knowledge worker development or end-user development)   the development and support of IT systems by knowledge workers with little or no help from IT specialists.

Selling prototype   a prototype you use to convince people of the worth of a proposed system.

Serial connector   usually has 9 holes but may have 25, which fit into the corresponding number of pins in the port. Serial connectors are often most used for monitors and certain types of modems.

Server farm   a location that stores a group of servers in a single place.

Service Level Agreement (SLA)   defines the specific responsibilities of the service provider and sets the customer expectations.

Shared information   an environment in which an organization's information is organized in one central location, allowing anyone to access and use it as he or she needs to.

Sign-off   the knowledge workers' actual signatures indicating they approve all of the business requirements.

Skill words   nouns and adjectives used by organizations to describe job skills which should be woven into the text of applicants' résumés.

Slack space   the space left over from the end of the file to the end of the cluster.

Smart cards   plastic cards the size of a credit card that contain an embedded chip on which digital information can be stored.

Sociability   the ability of intelligent agents to confer with each other.

Social engineering   conning your way into acquiring information that you have no right to.

Software   the set of instructions that your hardware executes to carry out a specific task for you.

Software suite   bundled software that comes from the same publisher and costs less than buying all the software pieces individually.

Spam   unsolicited e-mail.

Spoofing   the forging of the return address on an e-mail so that the e-mail message appears to come from someone other than the actual sender.

Spreadsheet software   helps you work primarily with numbers, including performing calculations and creating graphs.

Spyware (also called sneakware or stealthware)   software that comes hidden in free downloadable software and tracks your online movements, mines the information stored on your computer, or uses your computer's CPU and storage for some task you know nothing about.

Steganography   the hiding of information inside other information.

Storage device   a tool you use to store information for use at a later time.

Strategic management   provides an organization with overall direction and guidance.

Structured decision   a decision where processing a certain kind of information in a specified way ensures you will always get the right answer.

Structured query language (SQL)   a standardized fourth-generation query language found in most DBMSs.

Structure tag   HTML tag that sets up the necessary sections and specifies that the document is indeed an HTML document.

Subjective information   attempts to describe something that is unknown.

Supercomputer   the fastest, most powerful, and most expensive type of computer.

Supplier power   high when buyers have few choices of whom to buy from, and low when there are many choices.

Supply chain   the paths reaching out to all of a company's suppliers of parts and services.

Supply chain management (SCM) system   tracks inventory and information among business processes and across companies.

Switch   a device that connects multiple computers into a network in which multiple communications links can be in operation simultaneously.

Switching costs   costs that can make customers reluctant to switch to another product or service.

System bus the electronic pathways that move information between basic components on the motherboard, including between your CPU and RAM.

System development life cycle (SDLC) a structured step by step approach for developing information systems.

System software handles tasks specific to technology management and coordinates the interaction of all technology devices.

T

Tactical management develops the goals and strategies outlined by strategic management.

TCP/IP (transport control protocol/Internet protocol) the primary protocol for transmitting information over the Internet.

Technical architecture defines the hardware, software, and telecommunications equipment required to run the system.

Technology-literate knowledge worker a person who knows how and when to apply technology.

Telecommunications device a tool you use to send information to and receive it from another person or location.

Telecommuting the use of communications technologies (such as the Internet) to work in a place other than a central location.

Telephone modem (or modem) a device that connects your computer to your phone line so that you can access another computer or network.

Temporary advantage an advantage that, sooner or later, the competition duplicates or even leap-frogs you with a better system.

Terabyte (TB) roughly 1 trillion bytes.

Test condition a detailed step the system must perform along with the expected result of the step.

Testing phase verifies that the system works and meets all of the business requirements defined in the analysis phase.

Thin client a workstation with a small amount of processing power and costs less than a full-powered workstation.

Threat of new entrants high when it is easy for competitors to enter the market and low when it's difficult for competitors to enter the market.

Threat of substitute products or services alternatives to using a product or service.

Three-dimensional (3-D) technology presentations of information give you the illusion that the object you're viewing is actually in the room with you.

Three generic strategies cost leadership, differentiation, or a focused strategy.

Thrill-seeker hacker a hacker who breaks into computer systems for entertainment.

Top-level domain three-letter extension of a Web site address that identifies its type.

Touch pad another form of a stationary mouse on which you move your finger to cause the pointer on the screen to move (popular on notebooks).

Touch screen special screen that lets you use your finger to point at and touch a particular function you want to perform.

Trackball an upside-down, stationary mouse in which you move the ball instead of the device (mainly for notebooks).

Traditional technology approach has two primary views of any system—information and procedures—and it keeps these two views separate and distinct at all times.

Transaction processing system (TPS) a system that processes transactions that occur within an organization.

Transnational firm firm that produces and sells products and services in countries all over the world.

Trojan horse software software you don't want hidden inside software you do want.

Trojan horse virus hides inside other software, usually an attachment or download.

True search engine uses software agent technologies to search the Internet for key words and then places them into indexes.

U

Unallocated space the set of clusters that has been marked as available to store information but have not yet received a file, or still contain some or all of a file marked as deleted.

Uninstaller software utility software that you can use to remove software from your hard disk that you no longer want.

URL (uniform resource locator) an address for a specific Web page or document within a Web site.

USB (universal serial bus) becoming the most popular means of connecting devices to a computer. Most standard desktops today have at least two USB ports, and most standard notebooks have at least one.

User acceptance testing (UAT) determines if the system satisfies the business requirements and enables the knowledge workers to perform their jobs correctly.

User agent (or personal agent) an intelligent agent that takes action on your behalf.

User documentation highlights how to use the system.

User interface management the component of the expert system that you use to run a consultation.

Utility software software that provides additional functionality to your operating system.

V

Value-added network (VAN) a semipublic network that provides services beyond the movement of information from one place to another.

Value chain a tool that views the organization as a chain—or series—of processes, each of which adds value to the product or service for the customer.

Value network all of the resources behind the click on a Web page that the customer doesn't see, but that together create the customer relationship-service, order fulfillment, shipping, financing, information brokering, and access to other products and offers.

Vertical market software application software that is unique to a particular industry.

View allows you to see the contents of a database file, make whatever changes you want, perform simple sorting, and query to find the location of specific information.

Viral marketing encourages users of a product or service supplied by a B2C company to ask friends to join in as well.

Virtual private network (VPN) uses software to establish a secure channel on the Internet for transmitting data.

Virtual reality a three-dimensional computer simulation in which you actively and physically participate.

Virtual workplace a technology-enabled workplace. No walls. No boundaries. Work anytime, anyplace, linked to other people and information you need, wherever they are.

Virus (or computer virus) software that is written with malicious intent to cause annoyance or damage.

W

Walker an input device that captures and records the movement of your feet as you walk or turn in different directions.

Wearable computer a fully-equipped computer that you wear as a piece of clothing or attached to a piece of clothing similar to the way you would carry your cell phone on your belt.

Web authoring software helps you design and develop Web sites and pages that you publish on the Web.

Web browser software enables you to surf the Web.

Web farm either a Web site that has multiple servers, or an ISP that provides Web site outsourcing services using multiple servers.

Web log consists of one line of information for every visitor to a Web site and is usually stored on a Web server.

Web page a specific portion of a Web site that deals with a certain topic.

Web portal a site that provides a wide range of services, including search engines, free e-mail, chat rooms, discussion boards, and links to hundreds of different sites.

Web server provides information and services to Web surfers.

Web Services software applications that talk to other software applications over the Internet using XML as a key enabling technology.

Web site a specific location on the Web where you visit, gather information, and perhaps even order products.

Web site address a unique name that identifies a specific site on the Web.

Web space a storage area where you keep your Web site.

White-hat (or ethical) hacker a computer security professional who is hired by a company to break into its computer system.

Wide area network (WAN) a network that covers large geographic distances, such as a state, a country, or even the entire world.

WiFi stands for **wireless fidelity** (also known as **IEEE 802.11b**) a way of transmitting information in wave form that is reasonably fast and is often used for notebooks.

Wired communications media that transmit information over a closed, connected path

Wireless communications media that transmit information through the air.

Wireless Internet service provider (wireless ISP) a company that provides the same service as a standard Internet service provider except that the user doesn't need a wired connection for access.

Wireless network access point or **wireless access point** a device that allows computers to access a network using radio waves.

Word processing software helps you create papers, letters, memos, and other basic documents.

Workflow defines all of the steps or business rules, from beginning to end, required for a process to run correctly.

Workflow system automates business processes.

Workshop training held in a classroom environment and led by an instructor.

World Wide Web, or Web a multimedia-based collection of information, services, and Web sites supported by the Internet.

Worm a type of virus that spreads itself, not just from file to file, but from computer to computer via e-mail and other Internet traffic.

X

XML (eXtensible Markup Language) a coding language for the Web that lets computers interpret the *meaning* of information in Web documents.

CHAPTER 1

1. Seibert, Trent, "Photo-Radar Idea Shields Adulterers," *The Denver Post,* April 2, 2002, pp. 1A, 10A.

2. Zuckerman, Mortimer, "America's Silent Revolution," *U.S. News & World Report,* July 18, 1994, p. 90.

3. Keohan, Martin, "The Virtual Office: Impact and Implementation," *Business Week,* September 11, 1995, pp. 95–98.

4. Baig, Edward, "Welcome to the Officeless Office," *Business Week,* June 26, 1995, pp. 104–106.

5. *Fortune*: August 1975; August 11, 1980; August 19, 1985; July 30, 1995; August 7, 2000.

6. Sprout, Alison, "The Internet Inside Your Company," *Fortune,* November 27, 1999, pp. 161–168.

7. http://www.systransoft.com/ Corporate/Enterprise.html.

8. Dumaine, Brian, "What Michael Dell Knows That You Don't," *Fortune Small Business,* June 3, 2002.

9. Stewart, Thomas, "Intellectual Capital: Ten Years Later, How Far We've Come," *Fortune,* May 28, 2001, pp. 192–193.

10. Kallman, Ernest; and John Grillo, *Ethical Decision Making and Information Technology.* San Francisco: McGraw-Hill, 1993.

11. Peyser, Marc; and Steve Rhodes, "When E-Mail Is Oooops Mail," *Newsweek,* October 16, 1995, p. 82.

12. Kirkpatrick, David, "GROOVE: Software's Humble Wizard Does It Again," *Fortune,* February 19, 2001.

13. Holstein, William, "Samsung's Golden Touch," *Fortune,* April 1, 2002.

14. http://www.nokia.com/aboutnokia/ inbrief/history.html.

15. Orr, Alicia, "Clothing Retailer Uses Database to Serve Executive Clientele," *Target Marketing,* July 2000, p. 68.

16. http://www.acxiom.com.

CHAPTER 2

1. Business 2.0, May 2002, www.business2.com/articles/mag/ print/0,1643,39407,FF.html.

2. http://www.gomez.com/ benchmarks/scorecard.asp.

3. www.dell.com/us/en/gen/ corporate/vision_directmodel.htm.

4. Fingar, Peter; and Ronald Aronica, *The Death of e and the Birth of the Real New Economy.* Tampa Bay: Meghan-Kiffer Press, 2000, p. 25.

5. www.cisco.com/commarch/html/ eprocurement/ariba/punchout. html.

6. Porter, Michael E., "Strategy and the Internet," *Harvard Business Review,* March 2001, pp. 62–78.

7. Applegate, Lynda M., F. Warren McFarlan; and James L. McKenney, *Corporate Information Systems Management: Text and Cases,* fifth edition. New York: Irwin/McGraw-Hill, 1999, p. 64.

8. "EMC, CISCO and ORACLE Unveil New Ecostructure Blueprint for Accelerated Information Access," ECOStructure press release, May 22, 2001, www.eecostructure.com/ 052201.html.

9. http://www.sedb.com/edbcorp/ index.jsp.

10. Business 2.0, December 2001, http://www.business2.com/articles/ mag/print/0,1643,35201,00.html.

11. Edwards, Owen, "Bow Tech: ASAP Case Study," *Forbes ASAP,* June 3, 1996, pp. 54–58.

12. www.cpfr.org.

13. *Business Week* Online, May 13, 2002, http://www.businessweek. com:/print/premium/content/ 02_19/b3782131.htm?mainwindow.

14. www.egghead.com.

15. http://www.eink.com/technology/ index.html.

16. McFarlan, F. Warren; and Duncan G. Copeland, "Note on Airline Reservation Systems" (Revised), Part II, Harvard Business School Product Number 189099, 10/31/88.

17. Johnson, Michael, "Think Channel Collaboration, Not Conflict," Digitrends.net, July 12, 2001, www.digitrends.net/ebiz/13643_144 71.html.

18. Computerworld, February 5, 2001, http://www.computerworld.com/ securitytopics/security/story/0,10801, 57280,00.html.

19. www.onstar.com.

20. www.speedpass.com.

CHAPTER 3

1. George, Tischelle, "Battling Truancy with Wireless Devices," *InformationWeek,* April 3, 2002, www.informationweek.com/story/ IWK20020403S0001.

2. Zulman, Shelley, "Dressing Up Data," *Oracle Magazine,* January–February 1995, pp. 46–49.

3. "The Chain Store Age 100," *Chain Store Age,* August 1996, p. 3A.

4. Cash, James, "Gaining Customer Loyalty," *InformationWeek,* April 10, 1995, p. 88.

5. Greenemeier, Larry, "Web Services Help MetLife Get Closer to Its Customers," *InformationWeek,* May 27, 2002, www.informationweek. com/story/IWK20020524S0005.

6. Lais, Sami, "Satellite Ho!" *Computerworld,* May 29, 2000, pp. 70–71.

7. www.royalcaribbean.com.

8. Anthes, Gary, "Car Dealer Takes the Personal Out of PCs," *Computerworld,* August, 14, 1995, p. 48.

9. Brown, Eryn, "Slow Road to Fast Data," *Fortune,* March 18, 2002, pp. 170–172.

10. Watterson, Karen, "A Data Miner's Tools," *BYTE,* October 1995, pp. 91–96.

11. Maselli, Jennifer, "Insurers Look to CRM for Profits," *InformationWeek,* May 6, 2002, www.informationweek.com/story/ IWK20020502S0007.

12. Kling, Julia, "OLAP Gains Fans among Data-Hungry Firms," *Computerworld*, January 8, 1996, pp. 43, 48.

13. Hutheesing, Nikhil, "Surfing with Sega," *Forbes*, November 4, 1996, pp. 350–351.

14. LaPlante, Alice, "Big Things Come in Smaller Packages," *Computerworld*, June 24, 1996, pp. DW/6–7.

15. Cafasso, Rosemary, "OLAP: Who Needs It?," *Computerworld*, February 2, 1995, p. 12.

16. George, Tischelle, "Big Bucks Dry Up," *InformationWeek*, April 29, 2002, www.informationweek. com/story/IWK/20020426S0005.

17. Phillips, Ben, "Ice Service's Data Warehouse Goes with the Flow," *PC Week*, January 22, 1996, pp. 45–46.

18. Whiting, Rick, "Analysis Gap," *InformationWeek*, April 22, 2002, www.informationweek.com/story/IWK20020418S0007.

19. "Mining the Data of Dining," *Nation's Restaurant News*, May 22, 2000, pp. S22-S24.

20. Brown, Erika, "Analyze This," *Forbes*, April 1, 2002, pp. 96–98.

CHAPTER 4

1. "When Intelligence Rules, the Manager's Job Changes," *Management Review*, July 1994, pp. 33–35.

2. Krause, Kristin, "Airlines Feel Your Pain," *Traffic World*, April 30, 2001, pp. 28–30.

3. Gambon, Jill, "A Database that 'Ads' Up," *InformationWeek*, August 7, 1995, pp. 68–69.

4. Maynard, Roberta, "Leading the Way to Effective Marketing," *Nation's Business*, October 1996, pp. 10–11.

5. McCartney, Scott, "Airlines Catch Technology Tailwind: Computers Discover Ways to Cut Costs to Offset Higher Fuel, Labor Expenses," *Star Tribune* (Minneapolis, MN), p. 1d.

6. Simon, Herbert, *The New Science of Management Decisions*, rev. ed., Englewood Cliffs, NJ: Prentice Hall, 1977.

7. Kauderer, Steven; and Amy Kuehl, "Adding Value with Technology," *Best's Review*, October 2001, p. 130.

8. "M/W Planning: It's All in the Data," *Railway Age*, January 2001, pp. 60–61.

9. Marlin, Steven; Cristina McEachern; and Anthony O'Donnell, "Cross Selling Starts with CRM System," *Wall Street & Technology*, December 2001, pp. A8–A10.

10. Korzeniowski, Paul, "New Ways to Stay Connected," *Utility Business*, January 2000, pp. 58–60.

11. Fingar, Peter, "Don't Just Transact—Collaborate," *CIO*, June 1, 2001.

12. McGee, Marianne Kolbasuk; and Chris Murphy, "Collaboration Is More about Squeezing Out Supply-Chain Costs," *InformationWeek*, December 10, 2001.

13. McGee, loc. cit.

14. McGee, Marianne Kolbasuk, "Diagnostic Tools Take Aim at Terrorism," *InformationWeek*, February 4, 2002, pp. 31–32.

15. McGee and Murphy, loc.cit.

16. www.groove.net/solutions/scenarios.

17. McGee and Murphy, loc. cit.

18. Smelcer, J. B.; and E. Carmel, "The Effectiveness of Difference Representations for Managerial Problem Solving: Comparing Tables and Maps," *Decision Sciences*, 1997, pp. 391–420.

19. Brewin, Bob, "IT Helps Waste Hauler Handle Anthrax Safely," *Computerworld*, November 12, 2001, p. 8.

20. Johnson, Robert, "AM/FM/GIS Moves to the Web," *Transmission & Distribution World*, October 2001, pp. 52–57.

21. Dunkin, Amy, "The Quants May Have Your Numbers," *Business Week*, September 25, 1995, pp. 146–147.

22. Port, Otis, "Computers that Think Are Almost Here," *Business Week*, July 17, 1995, pp. 68–71.

23. Williams, Fred, "Artificial Intelligence Has Small But Loyal Following," *Pensions & Investments*, May 14, 2001, pp. 4, 124.

24. Stuart, Ann, "A Dose of Accuracy," *CIO*, May 15, 1996, pp. 22–24.

25. Hitzik, Michael, "A.I. Robots," *Technology Review*, March 2002, pp. 46–55.

26. Hutchinson, Harry; Jean Sharke Thilmany; and Paul Easton, "The Healing Hand," *Mechanical Engineering*, November 2001, pp. 68–72.

27. Grimes, Rob, "Consumer Acceptance of Robots Could Signal Future Use by Foodservice," *Nation's Restaurant News*, August 20, 2001, p. 59.

28. Overholt, Alison, "True or False: You're Hiring the Right People," *Fast Company*, February 2002, pp. 110–114.

29. Kay, Alexx, "Artificial Neural Networks," *Computerworld*, February 12, 2001, p. 60.

30. Kay, loc. cit.

31. Perry, William, "What Is Neural Network Software?" *Journal of Systems Management*, September 1994, pp. 12–15.

32. Port, Otis, "Diagnoses That Cast a Wider Net," *Business Week*, May 22, 1995, p. 130.

33. Baxt, William G.; and Joyce Skora, "Prospective Validation of Artificial Neural Network Trained to Identify Acute Myocardial Infarction," *The Lancet*, January 6, 1997, pp. 12–15.

34. McCartney, Laton, "Technology for a Better Bottom Line," *InformationWeek*, February 26, 1996, p. 40.

35. Michlig, Greg, "To Catch a Thief," *Credit Union Management*, January 2001, pp. 48–50.

36. Punch, Linda; and Jason Fargo, "The Downside of Convenience Checks," *Credit Card Management*, November 2000, pp. 78–82.

37. Whiting, Rick, "Companies Boost Sales Efforts With Predictive Analysis," *InformationWeek*, February 25, 2002.

38. Whiting, loc. cit.

39. Punch, Linda, "Battling Credit Card Fraud," *Bank Management,* March 1993, pp. 10–22.

40. "Cigna, IBM Tech Tool Targets Health Care Fraud," *National Underwriter Property & Casualty-Risk & Benefits,* October 1994, p. 5.

41. Anthes, Gary H., "Picking Winners and Losers," *Computerworld,* February 18, 2002, p. 34.

42. Moody, Patricia E., "What's Next after Lean Manufacturing?" *Sloan Management Review,* Winter 2001, pp. 12–13.

43. Johnson, Colin, "Breeding Programs," *Financial Management,* February 2001, pp. 18–20.

44. Ruggiero, Murray, "Enhancing Trading with Technology," *Futures,* June 2000, pp. 56–59.

45. Patrick, C. I. Hui; S. F. Frency; Keith Ng; and C. C. Chan, "A Study of the Roll Planning of Fabric Spreading Using Genetic Algorithms," *International Journal of Clothing Science & Technology,* 2000, pp. 50–62.

46. Begley, S., "Software au Naturel," *Newsweek,* May 8, 1995, pp. 70–71.

47. Goldbert, David E., "Genetic and Evolutionary Algorithms Come of Age," *Communications of the ACM,* March 1994, pp. 113–119.

48. Baumohl, Bernard, "Can You Really Trust Those Bots?" *Time,* December 11, 2000, p. 80.

49. Swartz, Nikki, "App Intelligence," *Wireless Review,* September 1, 2001, pp. 8A–10A.

50. O'Brien, Mike, "Virtually Helpful," *Telephony,* February 11, 2002, p. 56.

51. Dobbs, Sarah Boehle Kevin; Donna Gordon Goldwasser; and Jack Stamps, "The Return of Artificial Intelligence," *Training,* November 2000, p. 26.

52. Whiting, Rick, "Companies Boost Sales Efforts with Predictive Analysis," *InformationWeek,* February 25, 2002.

53. Totty, Patrick, "Pinpoint Members with New Data-Mining Tools," *Credit Union Magazine,* April 2002, pp. 32–34.

54. Wolinsky, Howard, "Advisa Helps Companies Get More from Their Data: Helps Managers to Understand Market," *Chicago Sun-Times,* December 20, 2000, p. 81.

55. Allen, Maryellen Mott, "The Myth of Intelligent Agents," *Online,* November/December 2000, pp. 45–51.

56. "Weblining," *Business Week Online,* April 3, 2000, issue at www.BusinessWeek.com.

57. Woodward, Pamela R., "Measuring Patient Reported Data and Outcomes," *Health Management Technology,* September 9, 2001, pp. 28–32.

58. Catrini, Vincent, "No Catch-22 Here," *Health Management Technology,* March 2002, pp. 24–33.

CHAPTER 5

1. Neuborne, Ellen, "Pepsi's Aim Is True: The Cola Giant's Web Strategy Finds the New Generation of Customers," *BusinessWeek Online,* January 21, 2001.

2. Rayport, Jeffrey F.; and Bernard J. Jaworski, *e-Commerce.* New York: McGraw-Hill/Irwin MarketspaceU, 2001, p. 4.

3. http://cyberatlas.internet.com /big_picture/geographics/article/ 0,1323,5911_151151,00.html, March 21, 2002.

4. Jupiter Research, "Over a Third of B2B Online by 2006," September 27, 2001, www.nua.com/surveys/ ?f=VS&art_id=905357238&rel=true.

5. www.nua.com/surveys/ how_many_online/index.html, February 2002.

6. ElectricNews, "B2B ecommerce sales set to increase," May 9, 2002, www.nua.com/surveys/ ?f=VS&art_id=905357936&rel=true.

7. TechNews.com, "B2B spending to exceed USD1 trillion in 2004," April 26, 2002, www.nua.com/surveys/ ?f=VS&art_id=905357891&rel=true.

8. Kelley, Joanne, "The Right Tool: Ace Hardware's Online Community Makes Dealers Far More Productive," *Context Magazine,* December 2000/January 2001, www.contextmag.com.

9. Keen, Peter G. W.; and Ron Mackintosh, *The Freedom Economy: Gaining the mCommerce Edge in the Era of the Wireless Internet.* Berkeley, CA: Osborne McGraw-Hill, 2001, p. 5.

10. Wylie, Ian, "Who Runs This Team, Anyway?" *Fast Company,* Issue 57, April 2002, p. 32, www. fastcompany.com/online/57/finland. html.

11. Sheats, James R., "Information Technology, Sustainable Development, and Developing Nations," *Greener Management International,* Winter 2001, Issue 32, p. 33, 9 pp. Taken from abstract posted on http://www. green-ecommerce.com/news.html.

12. Toni Will-Harris, www.efuse.com/ Design/top_10_do_s_and_don_ts. html.

13. www.pressroom.ups.com/ pressreleases/0,1602,666,00.html, February 20, 2002.

14. Kotler, Philip, *Marketing Management: Analysis, Planning, Implementation, and Control,* ninth edition. Upper Saddle River, NJ: Prentice Hall, 1997, p. 92.

15. http://www.iab.net/main/ measuringvol1no4.pdf.

16. Schoenberger, Chana, "Web? What Web?" *Forbes,* June 10, 2002, p. 132.

17. Keen, Peter; and Mark McDonald, *The eProcess Edge.* Berkeley, CA: Osborne, McGraw-Hill, 2000, p. 96.

18. www.motive.com/newsevents/ pressreleases/pr.asp?id=382.

19. www.unece.org/cefact/.

20. http://www.oasis-open.org/who/.

21. Knorr, Eric, "Make Way for Web Services. They're Inevitable. Just Ask the Big Guys," *CIO Magazine,* October 15, 2001, http://www.cio. com/archive/101501/et_article.html.

22. Cope, James, "Dairy Industry Gets Set for B2B Exchange: Dairy.com to Use Spot Market Model for Perishables," January 21, 2001, www.computerworld.com/ managementtopics/ebusiness/story/ 0,10801,56627,00.html.

23. www.cio.com/research/intranet/extranet_sites.html.

24. www.ebags.com/info/aboutebags/index.cfm?Fuseaction=press.

25. www.informationweek.com/story/IWK2002032950043.

CHAPTER 6

1. Scanlon, Jessie, "Olympic Metal," *Wired*, February 2002, www.wired.com.

2. Abbott, Bruce, "Requirements Set the Mark," *Infoworld*, March 2, 2001, www.inforworld.com.

3. www.microsoft.com.

4. Prescott Carter, Anne, "Marriott Redefines the Shared Service Model," www.accenture.com.

5. Patrizio, Andy, "Consumer Electronics Loves PC," *Wired*, January 11, 2002, www.wired.com.

6. Wait, Patience, "Federal Lawsuit Adds to AMS Woes," *Washington Technology*, July 30, 2001, Vol. 16, No. 9.

7. Fryer, Bronwyn, "When Users Take Notes," *Computerworld*, August 8, 1994, p. 82.

8. www.adp.com.

9. Hoffman, Thomas; and Julia Kling, "Utility Unplugs Object Project," *Computerworld*, February 26, 1996, pp. 1, 125.

10. Caldwell, "The New Outsourcing Partnership," loc. cit.

11. Byrne, John, "Has Outsourcing Gone Too Far?" *Business Week*, April 1, 1996, pp. 26–28.

12. Patrizio, Andy, "Consumer Electronics Loves PC," *Wired*, January 11, 2002, www.wired.com.

13. Haag, Stephen; and Peter Keen, *Information Technology: Tomorrow's Advantage Today.* New York: McGraw-Hill, 1996.

14. Patrizio, Andy, "Consumer Electronics Loves PC," *Wired*, January 11, 2002, www.wired.com.

15. Manjoo, Farhad, "Vaporware 2001: Empty Promises," *Wired*, January 2002, www.wired.com.

16. Jerome, Carole, "Failed Products," *Marketplace*, February 1, 2000, www.cbcnews.com.

CHAPTER 7

1. Barr, Joe, "Opinion: Napster, Gnutella, and Internet Guerillas," *CNN.com*, May 15, 2000, www.cnn.com.

2. Gaudin, Sharon, "Employee's Abuse of Internet Rampant," *Internetnews.com*, April 24, 2002, www.Internetnews.com.

3. Gaudin, loc. cit.

4. www.webopedia.com.

5. Sweat, Jeff, "The Integrated Enterprise," *Information Week Online*, April 26, 1999, www.informationweek.com.

6. "The Gap Inc.," September 17, 2001, www.corba.org/industries/retail/gap.html.

7. www.corba.org.

8. "Forging Stronger Relationships with Customers and Partners through Content Management," www.documentum.com/products/customer/dow_corning.htm.

9. www.documentum.com.

10. www.fedex.com.

11. www.i2.com.

12. www.aspindustry.org.

13. Dragstra, Lindy, "Multrix Winds ASPire Award for Management and Operations," January 15, 2002, www.multrix.com.

14. "City of Orlando Gives Managers Immediate Access to Budget-Critical Financial Information," www.jdedwards.com/content/enUS/Customer-Customers/orlando.pdf.

15. www.obsoletecomputermuseum.org.

16. Brown, Eryn, "33 Days 8 Campuses 127 Kids and an Infinity of Gizmos," *Fortune*, June 24, 2002, pp. 126–138.

17. "Improving Customer Satisfaction through Global Content Management," www.documentum.com/products/customer/ford.htm.

CHAPTER 8

1. Garvey, Martin, "Disaster Recovery Isn't Just for Big Business," *InformationWeek*, April 1, 2002, p. 44.

2. Verton, Dan, "Digital Destruction Was Worst Imaginable," *Computerworld*, March 4, 2002, p. 8.

3. Savitz, Eric, "Read This, Then Go Back Up Your Data," *Time Incorporated*, Winter 2002, pp. 28–29.

4. Grotticelli, Michael, "Planning for the Worst," *Broadcast Engineering*, April 2002, pp. 82–86.

5. Gruenwald, Juliana, "Communications That Won't Quit," *Fortune*, Winter 2002, pp. 88–92

6. Pliagas, Linda, "Learning IT Right from Wrong," *InfoWorld Publications*, October 2, 2000, pp. 39–40.

7. Fogliasso, Christine; and Donald Baack, "The Personal Impact of Ethical Decisions: A Social Penetration Theory Model," Second Annual Conference on Business Ethics Sponsored by the Vincentian Universities in the United States, New York, 1995.

8. Jones, T. M., "Ethical Decision-Making by Individuals in Organizations: An Issue-Contingent Model," *Academy of Management Review*, 1991, pp. 366–395.

9. Kallman, Ernest; and John Grillo, *Ethical Decision-Making and Information Technology.* San Francisco: McGraw-Hill, 1993.

10. Zhivago, Kristin, "Et Tu Enron?" *AdWeek Magazines' Technology Marketing*, April 2002, p. 33.

11. Baase, Sara, *The Gift of Fire: Social, Legal and Ethical Issues in Computing.* Upper Saddle River, NJ: Prentice Hall, 1997.

12. Moores, Trevor, "Software Piracy: A View from Hong Kong," *Communications of the ACM*, December 2000, pp. 88–93.

13. www.siaa.net/sharedcontent/press/.2000/5-24-00.html.

14. James, Geoffrey, "Organized Crime and the Software Biz," *MC Technology Marketing Intelligence,* January 2000, pp. 40–44.

15. James, loc. cit.

16. Jonietz, Erika, "Economic Bust Patent Boom," *Technology Review,* May 2002, pp. 71–72.

17. Stevens, Tim, "Cashing in on Knowledge," *Industry Week,* May 2002, pp. 39–43.

18. Rittenhouse, David, "Privacy and Security on Your PC," *ExtremeTech,* May 28, 2002, www.extremetech. com.

19. Adams, Hall III, "E-Mail Monitoring in the Workplace: The Good, the Bad and the Ugly," *Defense Counsel Journal,* January 2000, pp. 32–46.

20. Corbin, Dana, "Keeping a Virtual Eye on Employees," *Occupational Health & Safety,* November 2000, pp. 24–28.

21. Corbin, loc. cit.

22. Pliagas, loc. cit.

23. Glass, Brett, "Are You Being Watched?" *PC Magazine,* April 23, 2002.

24. Vaught, Bobby; Raymond Taylor; and Vaught Steven, "The Attitudes of Managers Regarding the Electronic Monitoring of Employee Behavior: Procedural and Ethical Considerations," *American Business Review,* January 2000, pp. 107–114.

25. Medford, Cassimir, "Know Who I Am," *PC Magazine,* February 7, 2000, pp. 58–64.

26. Medford, loc. cit.

27. Charters, Darren, "Electronic Monitoring and Privacy Issues in Business-Marketing: The Ethics of the DoubleClick Experience," *Journal of Business Ethics,* February 2002, pp. 243–254.

28. Hayes, Frank, "Assault on Privacy," *Computerworld,* May 13, 2002, p. 74.

29. Naples, Mark, "Privacy and Cookies," *Target Marketing,* April 2002, pp. 28–30.

30. Graven, Matthew P., "Leave Me Alone," *PC Magazine,* January 16, 2001, pp. 151–152.

31. Konrad, Racheal; and John Vorland, "Guess What's in Your Hard Drive?" *ZDNet News,* April 18, 2002, at zdnet.com.com/2100-1104-885792. html.

32. Mirsky, Dara, "Tap Your Web Site's Log Files to Improve CRM," *Customer Inter@action Solutions,* May 2001, pp. 42–43.

33. Panko, Ron, "Identity Indemnity," *A.M. Best Company,* March 2002, pp. 54–59.

34. Baase, loc. cit.

35. Rittenhouse, loc. cit.

36. Soat, John, "IT Confidential," *InformationWeek,* June 3, 2002, p. 98.

37. Salkever, Alex, "A Dark Side to the FBI's Magic Lantern," *BusinessWeek Online,* November 27, 2001, at www.businessweek.com.

38. Rittenhouse, loc. cit.

39. Carey, Jack, "ACLU Decries Super Bowl Surveillance," *USA Today,* February 2, 2001, p. 1C.

40. Baase, loc. cit.

41. Shimanek, Anna, "Do You Want Milk with Those Cookies?: Complying with the Safe Harbor Privacy Principles," *Journal of Corporation Law,* Winter 2001, pp. 455–477.

42. Han, Peter; and Maclaurin, Angus, "Do Consumers Really Care about Online Privacy?" *Marketing Management,* January/February, 2002, pp. 35–38.

43. De Bony, Elizabeth, "EU Overwhelmingly Approves U.S. Data-Privacy Regulations," *Computerworld,* June 5, 2000, p. 28.

44. Banham, Russ, "Share Data At Your Own Risk," *World Trade,* November 2000, pp. 60–63.

45. Caldwell, Bruce, "We Are the Business," *InformationWeek,* October 28, 1996, pp. 36–50.

46. Mogelefsky, Don, "Security Turns Inward," *Incentive,* May 2000, p. 16.

47. Conley, John, "Knocking the Starch Out of White Collar Crime," *Risk Management,* November 2000, pp. 14–22.

48. Bannen, Karen, "Watching You, Watching Me," *PC Magazine,* July 2002, pp. 100–104.

49. Hulme, George, "In Lockstep on Security," *InformationWeek,* March 18, 2002, pp. 38–52.

50. Chudnow, Christine, "Grid Computing," *Computer Technology Review,* April 2002, pp. 35–36.

51. Neel, Dan, "Plug-and-Pay Computing," *InfoWorld,* April 15, 2002, pp. 1, 38a.

52. Radcliff, Deborah, "Hackers, Terrorists, and Spies," *Software Magazine,* October 1997, pp. 36–47.

53. Hulme, George V.; and Bob Wallace, "Beware Cyberattacks," *InformationWeek,* November 13, 2000, pp. 22–24.

54. "Europe Plans to Jail Hackers," zdnet.com.com/2100-11105-889332. html, April 23, 2002.

55. Meyer, Lisa, "Security You Can Live With," *Fortune,* Winter 2002, pp. 94–99.

56. "Fast Times," *Fortune,* Summer 2000, pp. 35–36.

57. Zemke, Ron, "Tech-Savvy and People-Stupid," *Training,* July 2000, pp. 16–18.

58. Spencer, Vikki, "Risk Management: Danger of the Cyber Deep," *Canadian Underwriter,* September 2000, pp. 10–14.

59. Meyer, loc. cit.

60. Paul, Brooke, "How Much Risk Is Too Much?" *InformationWeek,* November 6, 2000, pp. 116–124.

61. Eastwood, Alison, "End-Users: The Enemy Within?" *Computing Canada,* January 4, 1996, p. 41.

62. Luhn, Robert, "Eliminate Viruses," *PC World,* July 2002, pp. 94–95.

63. Radcliff, Deborah, "Beyond Passwords," *Computerworld,* January 21, 2002, pp. 52–53.

64. Ammenheuser, Maura, "The Business Case for Biometrics," *Bank Systems & Technology,* February 2002, p. 42.

65. Wagley, John, "Tech Detectives," *Institutional Investor,* August 2001, pp. 18–20.

66. Clark, Ken, "Pointing to the Future," *Chain Store Age,* May 2002, p. 170.

67. "Turn Time into Money in the Blink of an Eye," *InformationWeek,* March 4, 2002, p. 53.

68. Simpson, Roy, "2002 Guide to New Technology—Information Technology: 'Techno-Marvels' Just around the Corner," *Nursing Management,* December 2001, pp. 50–53.

69. Fjetland, Michael, "Global Commerce and the Privacy Clash," *Information Management Journal,* January/February 2002, pp. 54–58.

EXTENDED LEARNING MODULE H

1. Bradner, Scott, "Your Confession Is Good for Us," *Network World,* April 15, 2002, p. 30.

2. Savage, Marcia, "The White Hats: Security Consultants," *Computer Reseller News,* November 13, 2000, pp. 137–138.

3. Pack, Thomas, "Virus Protection," *Link-Up,* January/February 2002, p. 25.

4. Meserve, Jason, "People around the World Bitten by 'Love Bug,'" *Network World,* May 8, 2000, pp. 14, 28.

5. Zemke, Ron, "Tech-Savvy and People-Stupid," *Training,* July 2000, pp. 16–18.

6. York, Thomas, "Invasion of Privacy? E-Mail Monitoring Is on the Rise," *InformationWeek,* February 21, 2000, pp. 142–146.

7. Meserve, loc. cit.

8. Landolt, Sara Cox, "Why the Sky Isn't Falling," *Credit Union Management,* October 2000, pp. 52–54.

9. Luhn, Robert, "Eliminate Viruses," *PC World,* July 2002, p. 94.

10. "Hackers Attack *USA Today* Web Site," *Morning Sun,* July 13, 2002, p. 6.

11. Mogelefsky, loc. cit.

12. Hulme, George, "Vulnerabilities Beckon Some with a License to Hack," *InformationWeek,* October 23, 2000, pp. 186–192.

13. Bischoff, Glenn, "Fear of a Black Hat," *Telephony,* September 3, 2001, pp. 24–29.

14. Kornblum, Janet, "Kournikova Virus Maker: No Harm Meant," *USA Today,* February 14, 2001, p. 3D.

15. Kruse, Warren G.; and Jay G. Heiser, *Computer Forensics: Incident Response Essentials.* New York: Addison-Wesley, 2002.

CHAPTER 9

1. www.idc.com.

2. Corcoran, Elizabeth, "The Next Small Thing," *Forbes,* July 23, 2001, pp. 96–106.

3. Adams, Nina, "Lessons from the Virtual World," *Training,* June 1995, pp. 45–47.

4. Flynn, Laurie, "VR and Virtual Spaces Find a Niche in Real Medicine," *New York Times,* June 5, 1995, p. C3.

5. www.businesswire.com/webbox/bw.050201/211220321.htm.

6. www.businesswire.com/webbox/bw.050201/211220321.htm.

7. www.nytimes.com/2002/05/30/technology/circuits/30TEEN.html.

EXTENDED LEARNING MODULE I

1. McCool, Joseph, "Adventures in Online Recruiting," *Industry Standard,* June 12, 2000, www.thestandard.com.

2. Ask Electra, "The Hidden Job Market," *The Career Journal,* no date available, www.jobstar.org.

3. Refsnes Data, "Monitor Stats," www.w3schools.com, copyright 1999–2002 by Refsnes Data.

4. Refsnes Data, "Browser Stats," www.w3schools.com, copyright 1999–2002 by Refsnes Data.

PHOTO CREDITS

CHAPTER 1

Fig. 1.9a, p. 22, © Michael Newman/Photo Edit
Fig. 1.9b, p. 22, © David Young-Wolf/Photo Edit

MODULE A

Fig. A.2a, p. 42, © Hewlett-Packard
Fig. A.2b, p. 42, © Spencer Grant/Photo Edit
Fig. A.2c, p. 42, Courtesy of International Business Machines Corporation. Unauthorized use not permitted.
Fig. A.2d, p. 42, © Corbis
Fig. A.2e, p. 42, Photo courtesy of Intel Corporation
Fig. A.2f, p. 42, http://www.rage3d.com—The largest ATI fansite on the net.
Fig. A.4a, p. 45, © Hewlett-Packard
Fig. A.4b, p. 45, © Hewlett-Packard
Fig. A.4c, p. 45, © Jason Reed/Ryan McVay Photo Disc
Fig. A.5a, p. 46, © Steve Chenn/Corbis
Fig. A.5b, p. 46, © Roger Russmeyer/Corbis
Fig. A.5c, p. 46, © Hewlett-Packard
Fig. A.9a, p. 54, © Hewlett-Packard
Fig. A.9b, p. 54, Photo courtesy of Kinesis Corporation
Fig. A.9c, p. 54, © Walt & Co.
Fig. A.9d, p. 54, Courtesy of International Business Machines Corporation. Unauthorized use not permitted.
Fig. A.9f, p. 54, © Spencer Grant/Photo Edit
Fig. A.9g, p. 54, © Hewlett-Packard
Fig. A.9h, p. 54, Courtesy of International Business Machines Corporation. Unauthorized use not permitted.
Fig. A.10a, p. 55, Courtesy of International Business Machines Corporation. Unauthorized use not permitted.
Fig. A.10b, p. 55, Courtesy of International Business Machines Corporation. Unauthorized use not permitted.

Fig. A.11a, p. 56, © Hewlett-Packard
Fig. A.11b, p. 56, Photo courtesy of Minolta-QMS
Fig. A.11c, p. 56, Photo courtesy of Cannon
Fig. A.13a, p. 59, Photo courtesy of Iomega Corporation
Fig. A.13b, p. 59, Courtesy of International Business Machines Corporation. Unauthorized use not permitted.
Fig. A.13c, p. 59, © Nance Trueworthy
Fig. A.18a, p. 63, © Daisuke Morita/Photo Disc
Fig. A.18b, p. 63, © Nance Trueworthy
Fig. A.18c, p. 63, Photo courtesy of Belkin Components
Fig. A.18d, p. 63, Photo courtesy of Belkin Components.

CHAPTER 2

Fig. 2.3a, p. 76, © Bob Daemmrich/The Image Works
Fig. 2.3b, p. 76, © Davis Barber/Photo Edit
Fig. 2.3c, p. 76, © Michael Newman/Photo Edit
Fig. 2.3d, p. 76, © Spencer Grant/Photo Edit
Fig. 2.3e, p. 76, © Ryan McVay/Photo Disc
Fig. 2.3f, p. 76, © Leslye Borden/Photo Edit

MODULE C

Fig. C.1, p. 165, © Microsoft

CHAPTER 8

Fig. 8.5, p. 381, Photo courtesy of Amecisco Inc.

CHAPTER 9

Fig. 9.5a, p. 449, Photo courtesy of Xybernaut Corporation
Fig. 9.5b, p. 449, Photo courtesy of Levi Strauss Co.
Fig. 9.5c, p. 449, Photo courtesy of Charmed Technology